Suspended God

Suspended God

Music and a Theology of Doubt

Maeve Louise Heaney

LONDON • NEW YORK • OXFORD • NEW DELHI • SYDNEY

T&T CLARK

Bloomsbury Publishing Plc

50 Bedford Square, London, WC1B 3DP, UK
1385 Broadway, New York, NY 10018, USA
29 Earlsfort Terrace, Dublin 2, Ireland

BLOOMSBURY, T&T CLARK and the T&T Clark logo are trademarks of Bloomsbury Publishing Plc

First published in Great Britain 2022

Copyright © Maeve Louise Heaney VDMF, 2022

Maeve Louise Heaney has asserted her right under the Copyright, Designs and Patents Act, 1988, to be identified as Author of this work.

For legal purposes the Acknowledgements on p. xvii constitute an extension of this copyright page.

Cover design: Terry Woodley
Sky image courtesy of Vai Da/Unsplash

All rights reserved. No part of this publication may be reproduced or transmitted in any form or by any means, electronic or mechanical, including photocopying, recording, or any information storage or retrieval system, without prior permission in writing from the publishers.

Bloomsbury Publishing Plc does not have any control over, or responsibility for, any third-party websites referred to or in this book. All internet addresses given in this book were correct at the time of going to press. The author and publisher regret any inconvenience caused if addresses have changed or sites have ceased to exist, but can accept no responsibility for any such changes.

A catalogue record for this book is available from the British Library.

Library of Congress Cataloging-in-Publication Data
Names: Heaney, Maeve Louise, 1967- author.
Title: Suspended God: music and a theology of doubt / Maeve Louise Heaney.
Description: London; New York: T&T Clark, 2022. |
Includes bibliographical references and index. | Identifiers: LCCN 2021041847 (print) |
LCCN 2021041848 (ebook) | ISBN 9780567695604 (pb) | ISBN 9780567695611 (hb) |
ISBN 9780567695628 (epdf) | ISBN 9780567695635 (epub)
Subjects: LCSH: Theology. | Faith. | Thought and thinking–Religious aspects–Christianity. | Music, Influence of.
Classification: LCC BR118 .H42215 2022 (print) | LCC BR118 (ebook) |
DDC 230–dc23
LC record available at https://lccn.loc.gov/2021041847
LC ebook record available at https://lccn.loc.gov/2021041848

ISBN: HB: 978-0-5676-9561-1
PB: 978-0-5676-9560-4
ePDF: 978-0-5676-9562-8
ePUB: 978-0-5676-9563-5

Typeset by Deanta Global Publishing Services, Chennai, India

To find out more about our authors and books visit www.bloomsbury.com and sign up for our newsletters.

To

Peter, Kate, Claire, Olivia, Emily, Georgia, Anna Valori, Lily, James, Sam, Sean, Dara and Harriet

The next generation.

This is for you.

And to the strangers on planes and trains whose questions gave me the impetus to start writing.

CONTENTS

List of figures xiii
Foreword xiv
Acknowledgements xvii

Introduction: An apologetics of theological thinking 1
    Theology for the twenty-first century 1
    The role of doubt in a theology of faith 3
    Theology as multimodal: Meaning in musical form 6
    Who is the book for? 8

PART I The theological dimension of Christian songwriting 13

1   Truth matters and living in the incomplete 15
    It is the theologian who does theology 15
    A brief history of truth and doubt 19
    In defence of doubt in a theology of faith 24
    Broken bridges: Theological aesthetics, beauty and the arts 30
    The embodied, open form of music 37

2   The hidden story of music in theology 39
    Music and musicking: Defining our terms 39
    Unwritten scores: Behind the scenes of theological creativity 43
    The discord of epistemological dissonance 53
    A syncopated story: Key figures 56

3 Unsung sources: Theology in the public square of music-making 65

   Unsung sources 65

   In the beginning was sound 67

   From faith-shaped musicking to God-sized ventriloquism 69

   Musical figures of theology performed 76

   The counter-reform of music: Postmodern and post-tonal musical movements 82

   A coda: Theological endings? 91

4 From theory to interiority: When is song-writing theological? 95

   A theological method with space for the arts 96

   A theological method defined by questions 100

   Accessing Foundations: The sense music makes of faith 109

   Patterns of consciousness in theological self-appropriation and authenticity 112

   Caveats and consequences: Foundations, doctrines and the community of faith 115

PART II Musicking theology: A theopoetical weaving of Christian thinkers through music 119

Introduction to Part II 119

5 Can the arts contribute to our knowledge of truth? 123

   What place do music and the arts have in human life and knowledge? 123

   Bernard Lonergan, SJ: An 'orthodox who thinks a lot!' 127

   Look, sense, breathe: Stretching human experience so God can break in 135

   Come Alive 140

6 Is Scripture a world for women? 144

   The issue of women and Scripture: A foundational problem 144

   Sandra Marie Schneiders: 'Some woman for one woman!' 153

Colliding worlds: From claimless to powerful 159
Nameless 164

7 Is beauty superfluous to human life and Christian faith? 168

When did we lose sight of God's beauty and power of attraction? 168

Hans Urs von Balthasar: Theology on our knees 171

Eyes closed to see: Beauty, glory and the crucified Christ 182

Every Moving Light 187

8 How to believe in God in such an unjust world? 190

Poverty and faith in God: A different reading 190

Jon Sobrino SJ: When suffering wakes up knowledge 196

Between you and I: No salvation without the poor 201

Jerusalem: Salvation in the Poor 205

9 Is original sin an outdated doctrine? 209

When new life is so heartbreakingly beautiful, why do Christians talk about sin? 209

Sebastian Moore: Taking human experience seriously 212

We all change names: The original blessing of (God's and our) goodness 218

Song Unfolding (for Julian) 225

10 Who's going to go to Heaven? 229

What will happen to those we love who are not Christians? 229

Karl Rahner, SJ: Our 'last' systematic theologian? 233

Standing in the gap as theology becomes Church teaching 241

Meet My Friend 247

11 What is it with Christianity and martyrdom? 251

What can one life achieve in such a messed-up world? 251

Dietrich Bonhoeffer: When thought costs a life 254

One Life: Faith in the public square of the Body of Christ 265

Strange Life 269

12 Is celibacy ever a good idea? 274

Why would Christianity bless an option to *not* love? 274

Teresa of Avila: From friend of God to doctor of the Church 280

You complete me: When love demands the consecration of one's whole being 288

I Think I Might 291

13 Where on earth is God? 296

Where on earth can God be found? 296

Denis Edwards: A natural theologian 300

Where are you and where am I? Finding God *in* the world 306

Meet You in the Middle of the Air 314

14 Is how we name God important? 320

Between past, present and future: 'What is your name'? 320

Elizabeth A. Johnson, CSJ: On a quest for the living God 323

She who is 330

God by Any Other Name 335

15 How can we know if God is trustworthy? 339

How do the 'reasons of the heart' fit into faith seeking understanding? 339

Pierangelo Sequeri: Theologizing 'from the centre of the soul to one's fingertips' 343

Show me your face: God as utterly trustworthy 349

Lament: In the Pouring Rain 354

16 What role does sexuality have in Christian faith? 358

Does Christian faith frustrate or empower romance and human sexuality? 358

Rosemary Luling Haughton: A fully lived life (1927–) 361

Come move in me: God is passionate 371

Can I Have This Dance? 378

Coda: An invitation to autoethnography: Being an Irish
    theologian 383
  Down Under 386

Bibliography 389
Name Index 417
Subject Index 425

FIGURES

3.1　Four bars of Wagner's *Tannhäuser*　70

3.2　An image of the four-line stave created by Guido d'Arezzo　70

3.3　Four-line stave in Cistercian Antiphonary for day hours　71

3.4　'Cantate Domino'　72

3.5　'Organum' by Magister Perotinus　72

3.6　Joaquin Des Prez's three evangelic motets　72

FOREWORD

There is an anecdote told of Ludwig Beethoven. This particular day he had composed a piano sonata. Come evening, he was sharing a meal at his house with friends. After the meal, he played them his new piano sonata. When he had finished, one of his friends asked: 'Ludwig, tell us, what does it mean?' And the story goes that Beethoven, without a word, went back to the piano and began to play the sonata right through again, from beginning to end. When the last note faded away, he turned to his friend and said: 'That's what it means!'

Maeve Heaney's *Suspended God* comes with a soundtrack; it is as much a musical as a book. Heaney takes us on a mystery tour, drawing us into the mystery of God, the mystery of faith and the mystery of how we human beings give expression to faith. In that quest for expression, words are often not enough. Certainly, words alone can't capture it all. Aesthetic experience is perhaps the closest analogue we have to the experience of faith. In their various ways, the arts can capture depths to the mystery of life beyond words. And, according to the German poet Heinrich Heine (whose poems came to be put to music by composers such as Schumann and Schubert): 'Where words leave off, music begins.'

Much that Heaney perceives is grounded in perhaps *the* fundamental shift undertaken by the Second Vatican Council, as presented above all in its Dogmatic Constitution on Divine Revelation, *Dei Verbum*. Here, especially in its first chapter, revelation is presented in terms of a personal and interactive relationship between God and human beings – not primarily as a collection of truths put into words as doctrine. Divine revelation is primarily God's loving proposal to humanity, desirous of a loving response. Faith is the human reception of that divine revelation. Accordingly, faith is seen to be not primarily some passive assent to authoritative words *about* God but *a knowing of God* personally through an active loving relationship. Expressing the wondrous mystery of that relationship can come in multiple forms. So often, theologies of faith have focused on the relationship of faith and reason (and the need for logical clarity in verbal expression); this was the emphasis of the neo-scholastic theology so dominant on the eve of Vatican II. But Vatican II recognized that this was one-dimensional. The council was certainly not wanting to reject the importance of words, or doctrine, or of getting the words right about God. Rather it was wanting to say that this is not all that Christian faith is. There are deeper dimensions that words alone can't capture.

But even words have their levels of meaning. Importantly, *Dei Verbum*, after chapter one, goes on to highlight how the Bible uses a variety of genres to express the human experience of faith, including stories, poems, and indeed songs, as in the Psalms (but, unfortunately, the Bible doesn't come with a soundtrack, as Heaney's book does). Rarely does the Bible use apodictic statements of beliefs; much of the time, it uses imaginative language. In the second half of the 1980s, I had the opportunity of studying at the Gregorian University in Rome, and I did some courses at the Pontifical Biblical Institute close by, across the square. One of those courses was with an old Spanish scripture scholar called Alonso Schökel; with his long grey beard, he seemed to be what I imagined an Old Testament prophet would look like. Often in those lectures, he would speak about the 'hermeneutics' (the art of interpretation) that biblical genres such as the poems and songs, and indeed narratives, of the Bible require of the contemporary receiver. He would say: 'What was written with imagination must be read with imagination.'

Maeve Heaney's book and her accompanying songs invite us to ponder the mystery of faith and its various dimensions – not only reason (with its penchant for words and logic) but also *the heart* (with its focus on loving relationship), *the will* (with its focus on decision and action), *the imagination* (with its focus on endless possibilities of human meaning, expressible or inexpressible). One could list other dimensions. But it is the 'imagination' at work in the arts, and music in particular, that we find highlighted so finely in this book. Faith has an imaginative capacity for making meaning of one's unique relationship with God and its implications for living in the world. This imaginative capacity of *fides* (faith) is sometimes referred to as a *sensus fidei* (a sense or organ for making sense of one's faith relationship with God). Vatican II's dogmatic constitution on the church, *Lumen Gentium*, puts great store in this capacity. It even states that it guarantees faithful reception by the whole church of divine revelation across the centuries (*Lumen Gentium*, 12). One of many ways the church's *sensus fidei* finds expression, the imaginative art of music-making is a particularly powerful way in which 'the faith' is passed down through the ages. In *Suspended God*, the reader-listener is invited to enter into this dimension of the mystery of faith and to ponder its meanings through the medium of song.

Questions are the engine of human learning. They arise out of a quest for meaning and ignite a desire for understanding. So too, theology is generated by questions; faith quests for answers. But those answers will not necessarily be found in apodictic statements. Song can invite us into the contemplation of mystery that opens up the heart to an answer that is satisfying but perhaps incomplete. The quest is always ongoing. The subtitle of *Suspended God* includes the word 'doubt'. The second and longest part of the book is structured around a series of questions that theologians have long pondered. Here the book broadens out to explore the wide vista of human religious wondering. Doubt and the search for answers is presented almost as a divinely given condition of the divine–human relationship. Each chapter poses a question. A particular theologian is explored, someone for whom that question was important in their own theological quest. These twelve theologians include the greats of the last hundred years. We are invited to meditate not only on their questions but on a broad range of methodologies employed in the search. Such diversity is an example that theology itself is an art with a diversity of renditions.

Each of these chapters ends with an invitation to engage with one of Maeve's songs. Invitation was the predominant style of Jesus' teaching. He would challenge with an aphorism, a wisdom saying ('You cannot get grapes from a bramble bush'), and invite his hearers to ponder the meaning for themselves in their own lives. He would tell a parable and invite the hearers to enter into the world of the story, in order to choose whom they would identify with – and then imagine how they would react and act in those circumstances. Jesus engaged the imagination of his hearers. May the readers-hearers of this book-musical find the imaginative engagement a transforming experience.

Ormond Rush,
Australian Catholic University

ACKNOWLEDGEMENTS

I consider the theologians and thinkers whose life and thought are interwoven in these pages to be companions and mentors on a shared journey, and I am deeply grateful for their lives and their courage. Alongside them, there are many people who have played a part in this book. Even the somewhat solitary task of writing a book is accompanied by many. At the risk of leaving someone out, I need to name a few people, but I will premise it with the obvious truth that everyone I care for and who forms a part of my life is in these pages, in one way or another. First, thank you to my own religious community and family: *Verbum Dei* is young, enthusiastic and in many ways, still finding its way. Their support for this theological pathway I am trying to open *for us all* is essential, especially the 'cheering from the sidelines' of the founding generation of Mallorquin women. To them, ¡*gracias*!

Many friends have accompanied and supported this intuition of the importance of music *as* theology over the years, but I want to thank in a special way Willem Marie Speelman, whose musical semiotics informs much of my ongoing exploration and understanding of music. Since I have arrived in Australia, colleagues and friends at Australian Catholic University (ACU) and The Australian Catholic Theological Association have provided space, encouragement and feedback, as well as a semester's sabbatical to bring this project to fruition. I am grateful for the grace of having colleagues one can call friends. In terms of the background research of this book, I need to thank Kathleen Williams RSM of Yarra Theological College and the late James Maher MSC, for kick-starting my thoughts on music-making as an act of Foundations in Lonergan's theological method. Also, a heartfelt thank you to Neil Ormerod, for many moments of thoughtful conversation about what I was trying to formulate; and Ormond Rush, for his friendship, encouragement and the understated way he makes the life of a theologian look attractive. Similar friendship, witness and support come from the women I am honoured to call friends who have paved a way for myself and many others: in a very particular and real way, thank you, Mary L. Coloe and Sandra M. Schneiders, for your support, wisdom and incorrigible sense of fun.

A book takes a long time to write, and space for thought is essential, so I am grateful to the Lonergan Institute at Boston College for welcoming me as a research fellow in 2019, especially its Director Pat Byrne, Fred and Sue Lawrence, the scholars of the Lonergan Research Fellowship Group, and the practical support of Susan Leggere, Mary Elliot and Kerry Cronin. Those months of uninterrupted study and thought made all the difference. The community at Holy Spirit Provincial Seminary, Queensland have also enabled me to carve out time and space for the book, by assuming what I could not, and celebrating with me as I emerged from the tunnel of sleepover write-ins! Thanks are due as well to seminarians William Brennan and Sean Woods for taking up the offer of a reading group on these themes, and whose perspective from the student side of theologizing has been really helpful.

The book brings words and music together and would not have been possible without the generous and insightful help of Monica O'Brien from Willow Publishing, who has supported my music since I arrived in Australia in 2013. I am also deeply grateful to Addie, Barb and Josh Hannan at The SongStore in Victoria, for making me sound so good, first and foremost! But also for hospitality and friendship shared over food and wine. Thanks need to go to Jonathan Sage at Boston College as well, for his support and mastering expertise.

Finally, in the months leading up to its submission, I have counted on a team of theological accomplices and friends who have spent time and energy to bring their thoughts, creative insights and eagle-eyed editing skills to bear on the manuscript: Danielle A. Lynch, Lori King, Mary L. Coloe, Gunter Prüller-Jagenteufel, Julie Trinidad, Ren Perkins and David Kirchhoffer. The title *Suspended God* was also David's brainchild – ever the creative ethicist! The support of ACU's exceptional library team, especially Freya Bruce and Kelly Dann, needs also to be named.

The book is dedicated to my nieces and nephews, the next generation of my family. I write from Australia during month seventeen of a national border lockdown – and counting. Despite the distance, my family know that they are ever the human centre holding together my love for life, God and any thought worth expressing. This book on how theology needs to work in the future is for them.

---

*A link to the archive of all the songs mentioned in this book can be found here: bloomsbury.pub/suspended-god

Introduction

An apologetics of theological thinking

Theology for the twenty-first century

This book is an invitation to theological thinking for the twenty-first century. Some might object that theology is the same yesterday, today and tomorrow, but that is not, in fact, true. We name 'God' as the one eternal and ever-changing reality we can imagine or discover,[1] but our apprehension and understanding of that one God develop and grow over time. Even Jesus, the clearest point of connection between God and humanity, lived *in a historical time and place* we need make an effort to access, understand, and interpret if faith is to flourish and inform our lives. So theological investigation is a contextual quest for understanding that needs to develop and adapt over time to the shifts in culture, human understanding and the expanding plurality of traditions within which it emerges, or it will not serve its purpose.

And theology *has* a purpose, and it is one which we are ever more in need of. That awareness is at the heart of this book. The time is over – if there ever really was one – in which Christians could afford to stay at a basic or immature understanding of their faith. The nature of life in all its facets moves towards growth and development: a child's quest to learn is simply the first delightful expression of all humanity's wonder and heuristic desire to grasp the world we live in and achieve our potential therein. When we are not held back by the shadow side of life, every human experience is followed by a 'what was that?' moment in which we reach to know more. Faith provokes

---

[1] For centuries our understanding of eternal has been linked to notions of an unchanging or static reality, but revelation and current scientific explorations of the world we live in converge in inviting us to think of, and to imagine, the real and the divine in more dynamic terms.

that same dynamic, and always has, since the very first group of followers that Jesus drew to himself, who all struggled to understand who He was and the significance of what had happened to Him *and them*. Over time, this led to the gradual development and shaping of what we call today the 'discipline of theology'.

There are two convictions underlying this book: first, that while theology is an academic discipline like any other, with methods and standards, dedicated scholars and experts, we need to broaden the quality of theological formation in the church from the ground up. People need to understand their faith! The flourishing of internet theological-opinion sites – verified or otherwise – witnesses to that need. The effect of the lack of, or bad, theology on our personal decisions, sociopolitical positions and witness is obvious – and at times excruciating. Good theological thinking has never been more important. Thinking intelligently about our faith is not an extra, added and optional, to said faith but a condition of possibility for its quality and any service it may give birth to. The second conviction is that doing theology implies exploring *how* to theologize in each time and place in history, which may necessitate exploring new forms. Questions define methods,[2] by which theological methodology needs to be informed by the experience and questions of each generation as well as how they deal with them. The title of this book names both. First, a God on hold, unconvincing more than rejected, an exclusion less certain, more tentative, than generations past: suspended faith in God until further notice. Second, the suggestion that music has a role to play in the way forward. Or rather that in this space, music can work theologically.[3]

Music in theology as a field is becoming sexy. When my field of research comes up in conversation – in the many spaces and walks of life it can and does – the reaction is usually some version of a heartfelt 'how interesting!'. Music in and as theology, at the very least, sounds like an innovative way of balancing two aspects of life, work and play, one a bit dull, the other more entertaining. But it is both less and much more than this. To start with, theology is anything but boring, but also because bringing music, a symbolic form whose meaning is notoriously difficult to tie down conceptually, into the heart of a discipline defined by and worked out in and through words, is no easy task. But it is essential. Why? Not to challenge the importance of discipline-specific precision in theological investigation! Words are important in theology: it has been forged for years in and through careful use of verbal

---

[2]Cf. Hans Georg Gadamer, *Truth and Method*, trans. Joel Weinsheimer and Donald G. Marshall, Second Revised ed. (New York and London: Continuum, 2004); in particular 362–7 on the priority of the question in human knowledge.

[3]For readers who are unfamiliar with musical terminology, 'suspended notes', such as a suspended 2nd or 4th, are a particular type of harmonic used in music that are usually held briefly before resolving into what sounds like a more complete chord.

and conceptual discourse, and therefore it needs equally careful integration of communicative variations. So why bother with music? Because of the task theology has to accomplish.

There are many definitions of theology, the broadest and perhaps most inclusive being John Macquarrie's 'God-talk'.[4] Others include eleventh-century St Anselm's classic and unaged 'faith seeking understanding',[5] Congar's 'a reasoned account of God'[6] or the broader 'study of the nature of God and religious belief' defined by the *Oxford Dictionary*. These all describe *what theology does*, but theology is best understood when we also grasp its aim and intent, when *what* it does is guided by *why and to what end*! What is the purpose of theology? In the words of Canadian theologian Bernard Lonergan, theology is reflection on religion[7] which, in every context in which it finds itself, *seeks to mediate between that cultural matrix (or matrices) and the significance and role of a given religion in that matrix.*[8] In other words, and because we are all culturally situated beings, theology seeks to bridge the experience of faith and its expression in lived religion to the cultures that surround it; and let us not forget that the first cultures needing explanation are the ones inside ourselves, as we seek to assimilate and integrate the encounter with God that our enculturated selves have welcomed. Theology is about meaning: making sense of God in our personal, social and global histories. We can't allow such an essential and universal means of human meaning-making that is music remain marginal to the discipline whose very task hinges on the interpretation of human faith and life.

That being said, however, and as we shall see, the book is not solely about music but about the importance of theology and theologians to open a space for the uncertainties of life – in the trust that there are answers to be found – through words and music.

The role of doubt in a theology of faith

The entry point and axis of the book's approach to theology is that of our questions, even those that shake our faith. 'Ten thousand difficulties do not

---

[4]John Macquarrie, *God-Talk: An Examination of the Language and Logic of Theology* (New York: Seabury Press, 1979).
[5]Cf. Anselm, *St. Anselm's Proslogion with a Reply on Behalf of the Fool*, ed. Anselm, M. J. Charlesworth, and Gaunilo (Notre Dame IN: University of Notre Dame Press, 1979), which was originally titled '*Fides quaerens intellectum*' ('Faith Seeking Understanding').
[6]Yves Congar, *A History of Theology*, ed. H. Guthrie (New York: Doubleday, 1968), 25. He goes on to define it as 'a body of knowledge which rationally interprets, elaborates and ordains the truths of religion'.
[7]Bernard J. F. Lonergan, *Method in Theology* (New York: The Seabury Press, 1972), 267, 355.
[8]Cf. Lonergan, *Method in Theology*, xi; emphasis mine.

make one doubt',[9] according to John Henry Newman, but *pace* Newman, it is our understanding of those words and where they meet that needs to be clarified. The mandate Christians of past generations were given in the name of faith to excise questioning and doubt from their minds caused unspoken damage, and not only when it conflated trust in God with trust in the voices claiming to speak in God's name. On a more fundamental level, it confused the distinction between what we believe about God and divine teaching, with trust *in God*, born of surrendering to the gift of God's love, which grows (or fades) as can every other dimension of human knowing and believing. There is a place in faith for doubt and a need for questions in theological knowledge. In fact, censuring them not only stifles faith but also overlooks the historicity of our grasp of truth and the development of doctrine, which grows as we outgrow historically and culturally conditioned expressions of the truth that cannot be fully contained in them.

We need to question! In fact, the central thesis of this whole book is that knowledge comes through questions and theology only advances where people are willing to face the limits of their certainties and certitude to explore further. Real questions don't emerge out of nowhere but imply prior knowledge and the sense that something is out of place, that something doesn't quite fit. 'You know more than you think' is the gut feeling I often have on planes and trains, in conversations with people who don't really identify with the ecclesial worlds Christian theologies represent, but who dare to think something, or ask something, that challenges me. What they often do not realize is that their questions are usually born not of ignorance but of the awareness of a gap, something that does not quite ring true or consonant with the rest of their certainties. Similarly with students who make the whole class pause while they work through something I had not thought to explain or perhaps even ask. We learn better at the edge of our knowledge. The world's most important insights have come from people trusting those intuitions, facing problems and pulling the threads of their underlying convictions that won't conform to given answers.

So, this is an apologetics of Christian theology based less on what theology knows than on its capacity to make space for the knowledge it does not yet have, and is not scared to name. As an approach to Christian understanding, it is grounded on the Second Vatican Council's teaching on revelation and faith. In *Dei Verbum*, the Dogmatic Constitution on Divine Revelation, and building on Vatican I's magisterial integration of faith and reason, the council bishops move from presenting divine revelation as the manifestation of divine truths which would otherwise not be known to revelation as primarily the self-disclosure of God. It is a shift from 'emphasizing "knowing about God" to "knowing God" personally'.[10] The

---

[9]John Henry Newman, *Newman's Apologia Pro Vita Sua* (London: H. Frowde, 1913), 239.
[10]Gerald O'Collins, *The Second Vatican Council: Message and Meaning* (Collegeville, MN: Liturgical Press, 2014), 157.

two are not separate, and growth in one will enhance and pull the other forward, but this awareness opens spaces for us to better understand *how our faith works*. It is a necessary development. The richness of the Second Vatican Council's presentation on divine revelation in *Dei Verbum* is not matched by its one number on faith describing it as an obedient response to the God who reveals and the truth revealed (cf. *Dei Verbum* 5). Spaces for reflection,[11] Church teaching[12] and theological investigation have emerged to do just that over recent years, and as part of that process, the issue of how to understand our questioning, and when and how to integrate doubt as an intrinsic part of a living faith, is an increasingly frequent theme.[13]

The courage to question and to make space for doubt is the lens through which we shall look at the lives and thought of a number of key theologians who can teach us how to stand in faith while holding firm to the issues that challenge us and need to be faced. And there are many! Christians belong to a long tradition of exceptional thinkers who have paved the way for our own understanding and belonging. They have lived out their faith, grappled with their questions, faced the challenges of the historical and cultural moment they lived in, and thought through what it means to be believers in ways that have directly and profoundly informed our faith now. The problem is they are often not known, because thinking is a mainly hidden action. What is vaguely remembered are some of the conclusions they came to without appreciating the cost whence such insights emerge. This may be normal but does not teach us much. Thought changes the world, albeit slowly and from within – more effective than fads or personalities and more enduring than the powers of selfishness and populism – despite all evidence to the contrary! – because truth has its own power. But we need to want truthful thinking, because as we shall see in the pages that follow, access to that path is costly, attained only by sustained and shared collaborative seeking.

---

[11] For example, the year of faith proposed by Pope Benedict XVI to commemorate the fiftieth anniversary of the Second Vatican Council, from 11 October 2012 to 24 November 2013. Cf. http://w2.vatican.va/content/benedict-xvi/en/motu_proprio/documents/hf_ben-xvi_motu-proprio_20111011_porta-fidei.html (accessed 6 October 2019).

[12] For example, Francis, *Lumen Fidei: Encyclical Letter of the Supreme Pontiff Francis to the Bishops, Priests, and Deacons, Consecrated Persons, and the Lay Faithful on Faith* (Image, 2013).

[13] For example, Anthony C. Thiselton explores the biblical and historical emergence of our understanding of faith, doubt and certainty in Anthony C. Thiselton, *Doubt, Faith, and Certainty* (Grand Rapids, IN: William B. Eerdmans, 2017). For a comprehensive, theological analysis of the issue of doubt as a creative dimension in a theology of faith and the life of a Christian, see Frank D. Rees, *Wrestling with Doubt: Theological Reflections on the Journey of Faith* (Collegeville, MN: Liturgical Press, 2001). See also chapter two, 'Doubt: Virtue of Doubt?', of Christian D. Kettler, *The God Who Believes: Faith, Doubt and the Victorious Humanity of Christ* (Eugene, OR: Cascade Books, 2005), 36–57. I explore this area more fully in chapter one.

The theologians who have paved a way forward – and this book could only select a few – are exceptional mentors. But to appreciate this, we need to take some time, and read afresh what they said and why they said it: What were the issues they faced? What challenges questioned their sense of God or belonging to the church? Was it difficult? Has it affected how *we* understand our faith? And perhaps more importantly, what questions remain unanswered or even unasked?

Theology as multimodal: Meaning in musical form

In this book, I propose we do this through words and music. Why? Because the Word of God can never be fully contained in words: revelation is God's personal entry into our human world of meaning,[14] and how we make sense of life and faith involves much more than words. One important element of human meaning-making *and* faith seeking an understanding of itself is that of listening to and making music, although where and how that intersects with and informs theology is an ongoing quest. Some would object that there is a difference between drawing on music as a source and calling music-making a form of theological interpretation. I would agree only in part, because music is more than a source and has been an intrinsic element of the development of thought for centuries. But this is a forgotten story.

There is a hidden presence of music in the history of Christian meaning and theology which needs to be recovered. However we interpret the shifting sands of premodern, modern and postmodern cultural awareness and modes of learning, at its core is the changing way in which people understand the worlds they live in and how words relate to those worlds. It is George Steiner's *epi-logos*, 'time of the afterword'[15] in which forms of theologizing that draw on the lived experiences of people of faith beyond, or rather, to inform the theoretical are needed. Howard Gardner's groundbreaking work on the various forms of human intelligence has hardly made a dent in the universe of theological research, despite its influence in education and religious education.[16] While Gardner's thesis begs development and

---

[14]Cf. Bernard J. F. Lonergan, 'Theology in Its New Context', in *A Second Collection. Papers by Bernard J. F. Lonergan S. J.*, ed. F. J. Ryan and B. J. Tyrell, 55–68 (62) (London: Darton, Longman and Todd, 1974).
[15]George Steiner, *Real Presences: Is There Anything in What We Say?* (London: Faber, 1991).
[16]Howard Gardner, *Frames of Mind: The Theory of Multiple Intelligences* (New York: Basic Books, 1983) and his follow-up work on mapping these intelligences in major figures of Western culture, in Howard Gardner, *Creating Minds: An Anatomy of Creativity Seen through the Lives of Freud, Einstein, Picasso, Stravinsky, Eliot, Graham, and Gandhi* (New York: Basic-Books, 1993). For examples of his influence in the field of religious education and catechesis, see Carl J. Pfeifer and Janann Manternach, 'The Processes of Catechesis', in *Empowering*

revision, the basic intuition that people interact with and make meaning in diverse ways is no longer a novelty. Furthermore, the implications of theology's gap in this area are not innocent. There is power in knowledge and in the hands of its gatekeepers. Theology needs to make room for and interact with other forms of exploring Christian truth. Bringing music into theological investigation does not seek to blur boundaries and lower academic standards, but rather to uncover blind spots and step up to the challenges facing theology in the current moment *so that it can do what, as a discipline, is required of it.* The place for different methods in theological investigation is already commonplace. To this I add space for multimodal expressive forms. Furthermore, the proposal is that music is a *useful* symbolic form to help make space for questions and challenges, precisely because of how it works in human understanding. The work in this book builds on carefully laid foundations in exploring musical meaning from the perspective of musicology, musical semiotics, musical hermeneutics and various paradigms of theological method.[17] Repeating past work is unnecessary but the newness of this theme in theological writings might make summarizing key points helpful. The way in which the symbolic form that is music works in human intelligence emphasizes embodiment, shared spaces and a form of interaction with the world around us, others and the present moment (space and time) which finds its best theological grounding in ascension theology; that is to say: how Christians inhabit and experience the risen, ascended and glorified body of Jesus of Nazareth, the Christ.[18] Its application to theology implies a thorough, multifaceted and hermeneutical approach to the experience of making and listening to music.[19] Above all, the way in which music interacts with scriptural and theological classic texts can be a tremendously rich form of critical, second naïveté, transformative interpretation of foundational theological insights.[20] The place of the

---

Catechetical Leaders, ed. T. H. Groome and M. J. Corso (Washington, DC: National Catholic Educational Association, 1999); Ronald James Nuzzi, *Gifts of the Spirit: Multiple Intelligences in Religious Education* (Washington, DC: National Catholic Educational Association, 1996).

[17] By way of example, see Willem Marie Speelman, *The Generation of Meaning in Liturgical Songs* (Kampen: Kok Pharos Publishing House, 1995); Jean-Jacques Nattiez, *Music and Discourse. Toward a Semiology of Music* (Princeton, NJ: Princeton University Press, 1990); Jean-Jacques Nattiez, 'Musical Semiology: Beyond Structuralism, after Postmodernism', in *The Battle of Chronos and Orpheus: Essays in Applied Musical Semiology* (Oxford: Oxford University Press, 2004), 3–53.

[18] Maeve Louise Heaney, *Music as Theology: What Music Has to Say about the Word* (Eugene, OR: Pickwick Publications Wipf and Stock, 2012).

[19] Maeve Louise Heaney, 'Can Music "Mirror" God? A Theological-Hermeneutical Exploration of Music in the Light of Arvo Part's Spiegel Im Spiegel', *Religions* 5, no. 2 (2014): 361–84; Maeve Louise Heaney, 'Music and Theological Method: A Lonerganian Approach', *Theological Studies* 77, no. 3 (2016): 678–703; Maeve Louise Heaney and Roger Hillman, 'Music's Multilayered Subversion of the Word', *Literature and Theology* 31, no. 2 (2017): 200–14.

[20] Maeve Louise Heaney, 'A Hermeneutical Exploration of the Revelatory Text of John 4:1–42, in a Performative Key', *Theological studies (Baltimore)* 81, no. 2 (2020): 278–302.

aesthetic in hermeneutical approaches to truth and method has been intrinsic to its insights since the seminal work of Gadamer and Ricoeur on historical consciousness.[21] Musical interpretation can be a coherent form of critical existential interpretation of classic texts that voices the questions raised in ways that academic theology does not. Music is not a 'transcendent language' above critical reasoning, and gone is the notion of the individual genius composer whose creation sits forever above all its performances. We are all interpreting, in one way or another; and musical interpretation has a lot to offer theological thought, including the time it takes to make and to listen to, properly. Music stretches our attentiveness and suspends our conclusions, at the very least until the piece is heard. It can open spaces for us to pause and listen for questions beneath the surface and answers that don't come immediately, or possible alternative viewpoints for the academy and the church to hear and discern, accept, reject or complement. My hope is that it might help people listen for and hear how God surprises human worlds. If revelation is God interrupting history,[22] perhaps music can interrupt theology and enrich it in the process.

Who is the book for?

The primary group of people I'd like to benefit from this book are future theologians, so it is written with them in mind as well as the professors who mark the rhythm of their teaching, the conductors of the theological symphony, if you will, who accept or exclude the voices to be heard. However, it is also written for pastors and ministers who seek to guide, feed and accompany the ongoing intellectual formation of their communities, within which there are many who are hungry for learning – searchers grappling with the issues facing our worlds. A third oft-forgotten group I want to benefit from the book are the Christian artists in our midst. It is no easy calling to hold together the gift of musical creativity (composing, performing or producing) with the Christian vocation. They are two callings that complement, stretch and at times can pull against one another, about which theology has written little, to date. To paraphrase one of the authors in this book, it is not the same to be a good artist who is also a Christian as a good Christian artist.[23] My aim is to help close that gap, so

---

[21]See, for example, Gadamer, *Truth and Method*; H. G. Gadamer, 'Artworks in Word and Image: 'So True, So Full of Being!' (Goethe) (1992)', *Theory, Culture and Society* 23, no. 1 (2006): 57–83; Paul Ricoeur, *Essays on Biblical Interpretation*, ed. L. S. Mudge (Philadelphia: Fortress Press, 1980).

[22]Lieven Boeve, *God Interrupts History: Theology in a Time of Upheaval* (New York: Continuum, 2007).

[23]Cf. Rosemary Haughton, *The Passionate God* (London: Darton Longman and Todd, 1982), 51.

I hope the existence of this book will encourage musicians to understand better their gifts, and others to work with them so those gifts can bear fruit. Finally, this book is written with the people who keep me real in mind: those who have interrogated my life and demanded of me more honesty and coherence of thought. I write for the doubters and seekers who don't conform to easy answers and who keep theology real because they force us to engage with questions and doubts *as* they emerge and *how* they show up. Though they may never know it, without them, the Church will ever continue to arrive on the scene, in the words of one theologian this book draws from, 'a little late and out of breath',[24] unprepared for the task at hand.

Can a book serve all of these audiences? It is a challenge to write, and different sections will interest different people, but I think there is value, from time to time, in having everything in one place for all those with a stake in its outcome. The many classes, seminars and workshops interwoven in its writing have taught me that while opinions on and knowledge about music and theology vary enormously, the theme always draws a crowd of all levels of experience and expertise, in both areas. And very few have no opinion on the matter: music's role in life and faith cuts too close to the bone for all of us to allow for indifference towards music's role in theology. To facilitate these groups' reading, a clearer idea of the structure is important:

- Part I of the book is more academic and presents quite a comprehensive overview of the issues involved and their history in theological investigation. The intent is to make a case for music as a theological act for peers and colleagues who are interested in agreeing or disagreeing with me! The first chapter sets the tone for the book, by exploring the role of our questions, doubts and certainties in relation to truth, and presenting convergences with emerging strands of theology such as theological aesthetics and theopoetics. Chapter two defines our terms in relation to music and music-making (*musicking*) and explores the little noted history of music's presence in and influence on the sources of Christian faith and on theologians of the past. Chapter three continues that exploration of history, this time through the lens of music, presenting the theological sources of our oft deemed 'secular' musical heritage. Finally, chapter four takes a step forward, developing our case for the place of music in theological method now *as a theological act*. The foundation is laid through these chapters for the contribution of Christian composers and

---

[24]Cf. 'The Quotable Lonergan', in *Time*, April 1970, 59.

musicians to theological discourse, and why, in the words of Rahner: 'we have need of them'.[25]

- Part II of the book implements this thesis by presenting the thought of a series of exceptional theologians and influencers from the history of the Christian tradition, each through the lens of *a question or conundrum they dedicated their life to unravelling* and an original piece of music. It is an apologetics of good thinking that seeks to provoke further creative thought, through words and music: two different symbolic forms and interpretations interwoven in seeking an understanding of faith and knowledge of God. The words explain each theologian's background, questions and theological insights; the music opens a space to explore the resonance of their insights. These chapters are written in a way that seeks to be accessible to a wider readership and to make sense without reading Part I, so that students or those less familiar with the language of theological discourse can start here, if they prefer. This means that at times, there is a slight overlap, when a point needs to be made which emerged in Part I. But I do not think it is excessive and can aid a broader reception of the theologians under discussion and the points being made.

In both Part I and Part II, I footnote source references and comments for clarification and academic rigour. I also provide a reading list for exploration pertaining to the theme or theologian being explored at the end of each chapter.

The issue of addressing various 'audiences' perhaps also depends upon where you situate yourself. I self-identify as a Catholic Christian theologian, for whom the certitude of faith and belonging to my Church is essential, but even that identity is a liminal space, daily, between the God I know and my incapacity to understand Her better; between a Church whose Eucharistic lifeblood I cannot live without and those I love who will no longer darken its doorstep; a woman in a male-led Church between those who welcome her work and those who deep down wish she would disappear or at least *think* less; an artistic academic planted between the vehement gatekeepers of the already-known in theological discourse and those who come behind who *need* to think differently, for a world and Church for whom the writing is on the wall. The line between faith and doubt is not really external but runs right through us. There is a world of reasons to question and doubt, and there is also the given reality of a trustworthy God with whom to wrestle, that our faith might be full, and true, and worth something for those who need our certitude.

---

[25]Karl Rahner, 'Prayer for Creative Thinkers', *Theological Investigations* VIII (London: Darton, Longman and Todd, 1971), 130–1.

Selected further reading

Boeve, Lieven. *God Interrupts History: Theology in a Time of Upheaval*. New York: Continuum, 2007.

Congar, Yves. *A History of Theology*. Edited by Hunter Guthrie. New York: Doubleday, 1968.

Gardner, Howard. *Frames of Mind: The Theory of Multiple Intelligences*. New York: Basic Books, 1983.

Heaney, Maeve Louise. *Music as Theology: What Music Has to Say about the Word*. Eugene, OR: Pickwick Publications Wipf and Stock, 2012.

Lonergan, Bernard J. F. *Method in Theology*. New York: The Seabury Press, 1972.

Lonergan, Bernard J. F. 'Theology in Its New Context'. In *A Second Collection. Papers by Bernard J. F. Lonergan S. J.*, edited by F. J. Ryan and B. J. Tyrell, 55–68. London: Darton, Longman and Todd, 1974.

Thiselton, Anthony C. *Doubt, Faith, and Certainty*. Grand Rapids, IN: William B. Eerdmans, 2017.

PART I

The theological dimension of Christian songwriting

1

Truth matters and living in the incomplete

Among the greatest insights that Plato's account of Socrates affords us is that, contrary to the general opinion, it is more difficult to ask questions than to answer them.

HANS GEORG GADAMER[1]

It is the theologian who does theology

Over the past few years, I have noticed that the style of the presentations I am hearing in theological conferences is changing: there is more music, more dialogical interactions, more performance and creative expression. I also notice that these variations are often introduced by younger theologians of various backgrounds, race and gender. 'It is the theologian who does theology.' These words, spoken to me by my first postgraduate studies professor, have come to mind time and time again over the years, the single most helpful interpretative key for the work I try to do. Why? Because they voice the crux of all theological investigation across the world and over the ages: thought is personal. It is born of the life, experiences, context, church affiliation, questions and insights of each individual, notwithstanding the social and communitarian nature of all human understanding; for good and bad, as meaning received can be truth-filled or biased. No one can think for us. We can try to surrender that privilege to others we consider more intelligent, wiser or better informed, and in the English language the expression exists to 'let others think for you', but it is a misnomer. Others *cannot* think for

---

[1]Hans Georg Gadamer, *Truth and Method*, trans. Joel Weinsheimer and Donald G. Marshall, Second Revised ed. (New York and London: Continuum, 2004), 356.

us. What happens when we abrogate our responsibility and let others do the work of perceiving, assessing, discerning and deciding – in the personal, political or religious sphere – is that we drift (or rather become drifters)[2] and the shape of the world around us is configured by others. More importantly, we are less than who we could be and are called to be. Life is gift and task, although how difficult it can be to take ownership of the fact that 'one has to find out for oneself that one has to decide for oneself what one is to make of oneself'![3]

On the plus side, this means that *who each person is* colours and gives depth and density to the things they think and write. Theological thought is the fruit of the experiences, challenges, wounds (undoubtedly) and insights born of real lives. Academics tend to write their persons out of the research they present – all the more true if 'objective' and unpolluted by the author behind the scenes – but a hidden subject is a subject nonetheless. Thought is not naked but *always* embedded in the lived, embodied, reality whence it emerges. Even beyond the achievement of liberation and contextual theologies in reminding us that unclaimed context is suspect, the humanities are reaching for ways to bring authors back into their writings.[4] And theology is seeking other ways of doing the same.[5] For those beginning their theological journey this is of particular importance. We step into a field that has a history and a style, even if ever in the process of diversifying, but how it will look and what themes it will address in the future are in the hands

---

[2]Cf. Bernard J. F. Lonergan, 'Existenz and Aggiornamento', in *Collection. Papers by Bernard Lonergan S.J.*, ed. F. E. Crowe and R. M. Doran (New York: Herder and Herder, 1967), 224.

[3]Bernard J. F. Lonergan, *Method in Theology* (New York: The Seabury Press, 1972), 121.

[4]Of interest here is the move in the social sciences towards autoethnography as a valid mode of gaining honest access to one dimension of a text's origin. Cf. Tony E. Adams, Arthur P. Bochner, and Carolyn Ellis, 'Autoethnography: An Overview', *Forum: Qualitative Social Research* 12, no. 10 (2011); Arthur P. Bochner, Carolyn Ellis, *Ethnographically Speaking: Autoethnography, Literature, and Aesthetics* (Walnut Creek, CA: AltaMira Press, 2002); Arthur P. Bochner, 'Criteria against Ourselves', *Qualitative Inquiry* 6, no. 2 (2000); James Buzard, 'On Auto-Ethnographic Authority', *The Yale Journal of Criticism* 16, no. 1 (2003); Carolyn Ellis and Brydie-Leigh Bartleet, *Music Autoethnographies: Making Autoethnography Sing/Making Music Personal* (Bowen Hills, QLD: Australian Academic Press, 2010).

[5]By way of example, Vergilius Ferm (ed.), *Contemporary American Theology: Theological Autobiographies*, 2 vols. (New York: Round Table Press, 1932–3) shows how early this theme began to emerge and the insight already present of its usefulness to the advancement of theological investigation. Other more recent contributions include Gesa Elisbeth Thiessen and Declan Marmion, *Theology in the Making: Biography, Contexts, Methods* (Dublin, Ireland: Veritas, 2005); Ted Peters, Joshua M. Moritz, and Derek R. Nelson, *Theologians in Their Own Words* (Minneapolis: Fortress Press, 2013); James Wm McClendon, Jr., *Biography as Theology: How Life Stories Can Remake Today's Theology* (Nashville: Abingdon Press, 1974). McClendon's position equates autobiography with self-deception, but while we need the perspectives of others to know ourselves, this is surely too blanket a statement to be fully truthful. We have some sense of ourselves and seeking access to that, as well as allowing others in, if and when possible and appropriate, is part of the spectrum that allows us think honestly about truth.

of those who take up that task. This is one reason why Part II of this book dedicates a section in each chapter to the life, context and questions of each theologian: to learn from their lives as well as from their conclusions. The invitation is to ownership of the theological task, critical reflection on the biographical nature of this vocation and willingness to learn to live at peace in the incomplete, ever-questioning nature of theological investigation. Knowledge is heuristic. We advance in understanding by listening to the questions that stretch us, pulling the threads of the certitudes underlying those questions. These open us to new spaces of awareness. There are gems to be found underground, below the surface of a theoretical discourse in theology that emphasizes clarity over conundrums. But it takes courage to name and tackle them, not only because we might bring to the fore areas that those around us, near and far, might not like to hear but also because we ourselves might not like to face them!

The point is emphasized by recent interest in the notion of theological 'formation'.[6] The term is a contested one, as it begs reflection about who forms whom and for what purposes? – that is to say, the power of knowledge and the constitution of the theological subject. But even if we find a more appropriate term the notion will not go away, for it expresses the fact that good theology implies more than discipline expertise and intellectual prowess. There is a personal, ethical, integrated dimension to the intellectual life of a Christian that cannot be reduced to correct knowledge and is clearly expressed in documents guiding the training of leaders. Seminary formation, for example, rests upon the explicit thesis that the primary person responsible for formation is the seminarian themselves and implies the integration of the human, spiritual, intellectual and pastoral dimensions of the person.[7]

---

[6]There is growing interest in theological formation for ministry across various Christian denominations. For example, the establishment of a national centre for theological formation in Australia as a result of requests for theological formation across the educational, health and ecclesial spheres: https://www.acu.edu.au/about-acu/faculties-directorates-and-staff/faculty-of-theology-and-philosophy/professional-learning-and-consulting; the Templeton Foundations' investment in research into theological formation and analytic theology: http://analytictheology.fuller.edu/theological-formation/; and the United Church of Christ: https://www.ucc.org/news_shaping_theological_formation_from_the_ground_up_11142017. In the educational sphere, individual conferences and research projects also seek to explore theological formation: for example, the theological exploration of Catholic education as developed in Leuven's *Enhancing Catholic School Identity* (ETSI) project and its application around the world, and other localized conferences focussed more on higher education, such as 'Mapping the Terrain': https://www.bc.edu/content/bc-web/academics/sites/ila/events/Formative-Edu.html. Also of interest is the theological dimension being developed by a variety of health care organizations worldwide, such as Ascension: cf. https://www.ascension.org/Our-Mission/Spiritual-and-Theological-Formation.

[7]John Paul II, *Pastores Dabo Vobis: Post-Synodal Exhortation on the Formation of Priests in the Circumstances of the Present Day* (Vatican City: Libreria Editrice Vaticana, 25 March 1992), 79. Congregation for the Clergy, *The Gift of the Priestly Vocation. Ratio Fundamentalis Institutionis Sacerdotalis* (Vatican City: Osservatore Romano, 8 December 2016), 89–92.

Furthermore, the presumption that theological education in non-ecclesial contexts does *not* have a formative dimension is untrue and, as a claim, not innocent. Education is always framed by the culture and values of those facilitating it. These might be worthy responses to the needs and signs of the times or more ambiguously driven by economics or ideological powers, but either way they have to be named, making the cultivation of a personal awareness and ownership of theology's present and future by those learning the trade, essential. Why are you doing theology – to what end? Under whose authority are you working and where, ultimately, does authority lie for a theologian? Where do faith and understanding, or contemplation and theological speculation, intersect and overlap? And when these are clear, there are other blind spots to check for: who are you reading, and in this time of diversified knowledge, who will you work with? What theological strands are you exposed to and which questions and challenges you are allowed to explore? These are essential, and often unnamed, issues. It is the theologian who does theology, and the quality of theological thought depends upon the quality of the questions asked and the challenges faced.

This chapter's title asks a question: 'is our knowledge of truth and God incomplete?' Surely reason *can* access true knowledge of Jesus Christ as the embodiment and plenitude of God's revelation? The notion of certitude in knowing God and proof of the existence of God is a long-standing tenet of Christian, and especially Catholic, theology. 'The first Vatican Council declares it to be a matter of *faith* that reason can know God.'[8] With Paul, 'we know in whom we have placed our trust' (cf. 2 Tim. 1.12), but that does not mean our knowledge is complete! God is infinitely greater than our apprehension and understanding. When theology is understood as 'faith seeking understanding' within and across historical consciousness and cultural diversity, it is a matter of intellectual honesty to recognize that between who God is and how we experience that God, between revealed truth and our ongoing grasp of said truths, there are gaps. So we receive, welcome and trust in the revelation of God at the same time as we acknowledge the incompleteness of every human understanding, even as we strive for truth. This is a tension we can never overcome, and it is not new. It is an essential part of the history of our faith and theological tradition, which the felt insecurity of religious faith when attacked tends to reject or hide from. However, an exploration of the history of thought on scepticism and doubt and a nuanced differentiation of the elements of a theology of faith

---

While it is clear that the current strength and richness of theology worldwide are in large part due to the diversification of those involved – women, men, religious and new communities – it is also true that reflections on formation found in documents on priesthood and religious life are serving as a basis for their application well beyond those spheres.

[8] Denys Turner, *Faith, Reason, and the Existence of God* (Cambridge, UK: Cambridge University Press, 2004), xvi.

can soften these defence-mechanisms. To that end, this chapter addresses four areas: the complex and wounded history of Western philosophical and theological epistemology – that is to say, our battle with truth and its effect on how we think about theology (and think theologically); elements of a more integrated theological approach to faith that help address this dilemma; the appearance and contribution of theological aesthetics and theopoetics to our understanding of the arts in theology; and the resonance of music in and as theology with this approach to faith and knowledge.

A brief history of truth and doubt

Two overlapping historical perspectives are needed to understand the place of doubt and questioning in theology: on the one hand, the more recent cultural shifts of the Western world in the mega-phenomenon we call 'modernity' (or more precisely, the transition from a premodern paradigm of thought, through modernity, to our current world view, however we interpret the word 'post-modern') and its effect on Christian faith practice and theology; on the other, a big-picture view of the history of human knowledge, religious faith and doubt, which situates the current challenges in that larger framework and allows us to read more accurately the challenges and opportunities of the current situation, and better define our terms. The former recognizes the origins and heritage of first Jewish and then Greek thought on Christian theology and doctrine, which, although the Church's centre of gravity in the world is currently shifting south, have conditioned the development of Christian doctrine for two centuries and therefore need at least to be understood, if not frozen in time. The second focusses on the broader and more specific dynamic of human subjectivity in its coming to know. History is a good teacher, and conversely, ignorance of history leaves us dangerously vulnerable to short-sightedness, manipulation and repetition of errors.

In terms of the more recent history of Western philosophy and theology, perhaps a good starting point is to try and imagine the medieval world in Europe when Christian faith was the norm. The writings of St Anselm in the twelfth century which gave us the definition of theology as 'faith seeking understanding' were framed as a sort of philosophical defence of the existence of God for the 'one fool who says in his [sic] heart, God does not exist' (Pss. 14.1 and 55.1).[9] In Anselm's words:

> *Suppose someone did not know* – either because he had not heard or because he did not believe – that there is one nature, the highest of all

---

[9]Anselm, *Proslogion with a Reply on Behalf of the Fool*, chapter II.

things that are, who is alone sufficient for himself in his eternal happiness, and who through his omnipotent goodness grants and brings about that all other things are something and that they are in some way well, and the many other things that we believe to be necessarily the case about God and his creation: I think that, to a great extent, if he were modestly intelligent, he could persuade himself of them by reason alone.[10]

Anselm's starting point implies an exercise in imagination: to 'suppose' there may be 'someone who did not know' in all certainty of the existence of one God, the implication being that such a person was the exception to the rule. Furthermore, Anselm presumes that the only barrier between this person's acceptance of the existence of God is that he (or she) be 'modestly intelligent' and that reason's proof provides an access point to faith.

The historical events that changed that world view slowly but surely to the one, or rather ones, we have now are legion, passing through the birth of the age of printing and ensuing shift from oral to written culture, the reformation, the counter-reformation, the renaissance, the expansion of the 'known world' beyond Europe and the age of colonialism, the enlightenment, the French Revolution and its ripple effects on our understanding of self and state around the world, the industrial revolutions of the eighteenth century onwards, to name but a few of the main events. These are all part of the second millennium of Christianity, a time in which *many of the contemporary issues of theology and philosophy were framed*. It is hard to overemphasize how important it is to grasp the historical backdrop to today's problems. Why? Because alongside, or rather within and as an intrinsic cause and effect of these changes, how people understood the world, themselves and God, was changing in ways that we are still catching up with. From an enchanted world in which myth, magic and religious faith made sense of life and God, we moved to a world in which first reason, then science (in all its evolving forms) and now a virtually uncontrollable world of communications, at once real and false, have gradually reframed all our bearings in relation to truth and the world around us. In Lonergan's words, 'Classical culture has given way to modern culture, and, I would submit, the crisis of our age is in no small measure due to the fact that modern culture has not yet reached its maturity.'[11]

At the heart of these seismic changes, the West performs its epistemological drama. It is worth naming some of the key players, who often interweave philosophy and theology before their separation as we know it. The passion of Martin Luther (1483–1684) for a trust-based faith free of ecclesial control and corruption. The genius of René Descartes (1596–1650) and his quest

---

[10]Anselm, *Monologion*, chapter I. I chose not to correct the anachronic use of solely male pronouns for God *and* the paradigmatic thinking subject. At times, it is useful to read the past *as it was written*.
[11]Lonergan, 'Dimensions of Meaning', 259.

for a certainty in the humanities analogue to mathematics that led him to seek self-evident principles of knowledge in need of no proof or external opinion. Based on a method of systematic doubt, his 'I think, therefore I am' (*cogito, ergo sum*) gave Western philosophy and culture its first formulation of the division between subjective consciousness and the 'objective' world around us in our quest for truth. He was convinced his position was 'so firm and assured that all the most extravagant suppositions of the sceptics were unable to shake it'.[12] And yet many would situate in him a well-intentioned beginning of the West's battle over knowledge: if and how human beings can know anything at all, including God. Immanuel Kant (1724–1804) will forever be at the centre of Christianity's deistic turn. Framed by a quest to understand the human person *within* the limits of reason and *without* those of authority beyond the reasoning self, Kant held that if God is known at all, it is through a universal moral law within human understanding,[13] which (when weak!) can look to the example of Jesus for a model. From a theological perspective, Søren Kierkegaard (1815–55) shared with Kant his suspicion of organized religion and also sought to redefine the focus of Christian faith within the parameters of human consciousness, but for him it is reason that holds no hope of giving us access to the knowledge of truth. Faith is defined as an 'existential' he called 'subjectivity' in dialectical opposition to what is objective and certain. This meant that to remain in faith one must 'constantly be intent upon holding fast to the absolute paradox of "objective uncertainty", in which faith is preserved'.[14] A different approach is sought by the originality of Friedrich Schleiermacher (1768–1834), who drew attention to the affective side of religious thought as the powerful feeling of dependence on something greater than ourselves and the need to pay attention to it.[15]

And so, the history of Western thought pulls us between an idealism that denies our capacity to know anything and an empiricism that affirms the priority of the real over and above our knowing minds, which in some sense leads us to the same conclusion, for what do we know at all, if the 'out there and real' is more itself without us? Rational idealism claims victory over religious deference, leading fideists to believe and defend what they wish – since nothing can be proven anyway! – deists to spill copious amounts of ink defending the provability of God, romanticists to seek out other ways of

---

[12]René Descartes, *Discourse on Method*, trans. Laurence J. Lafleur (New York: Liberal Arts Press, 1970), 21.
[13]Cf. Immanuel Kant, *Religion within the Limits of Reason Alone* (New York: Harper, 1960). Frank D. Rees, *Wrestling with Doubt: Theological Reflections on the Journey of Faith* (Collegeville, MN: Liturgical Press, 2001), 8–9.
[14]Cf. Søren Kierkegaard, *Kierkegaard's Concluding Unscientific Postscript*, trans. David F. Swenson (Princeton: Princeton University Press, 1941).
[15]Cf. Friedrich Schleiermacher, *On Religion: Speeches to Its Cultured Despisers*, trans. Richard Crouter (Cambridge: Cambridge University Press, 1996); Friedrich Schleiermacher, *The Christian Faith*, ed. H. R. Mackintosh and J. S. Stewart (Edinburgh: T&T Clark, 1976).

rediscovering the subject and some sense of the sublime in the midst of this reign of reason and phenomenologists to try and bridge the gap by calling us to read reality *as it presents itself* and is experienced. This story of Western thinking's approach to truth and knowledge could, therefore, also be called a 'history of doubt'. Postmodernity came to birth in a world unsure of itself and how the human and divine interact, if at all.

However, while doubt is of particular concern to the contemporary moment, it is not new; and here we step back to take in the big-picture view of doubt in human history. We can trace the first explicit signs of scepticism in human philosophizing to the sixth century BC[16] that saw people denying our capacity to know the gods, ourselves or things around us. In fact, there is a way of reading history that would recognize the issue of doubt as the underlying, ever-present human reality! Such is the approach of Jennifer Michael Hecht in a fascinating study on religious doubt across the world's histories of thought and religions.[17] She identifies two schisms underpinning human life and meaning-making as the ground for human uncertainty and existential questioning. The first is between human beings and the non-human universe, which is *other* than us and which we try to make sense of, in one way or another; the second, between who we are and who we feel we are meant to be – the wonder of life and its internal contradiction – in her words: 'the fact that the human heart so often disagrees with and disobeys the human brain'.[18] From this starting point she reads, categorizes and maps out the patterns of doubt that have defined the great religious and thought traditions and how they interweave, identifying seven. Two of these are scientific: materialism and rationalism; a third is the genre of nontheistic transcendence programmes (religion without god); the fourth is cosmopolitan relativism (in the face of discovery of diversity); the fifth, moral rejection of injustice and the quest to separate religion and state; and the sixth is philosophical relativism. The last she names as the doubt of the ardent believer.[19] She traces the ongoing emergence and interweaving of these seven types across the eras and countries she studies. As a history, she says, 'it looks different than other histories, because it highlights what goes on between periods of certainty. It's like seeing a map upside down – it takes time for the new contours to take shape. The history of being awake to certain contradictions of our condition as the negative image of the history

---

[16]In the writing of Xenophanes of Colophon. Cf. Anthony C. Thiselton, *Doubt, Faith, and Certainty* (Grand Rapids, IN: William B. Eerdmans, 2017), 19–21.
[17]Jennifer Michael Hecht, *Doubt: A History: The Great Doubters and Their Legacy of Innovation, From Socrates and Jesus to Thomas Jefferson and Emily Dickinson* (San Francisco: Harper, 2003). The parameters of Hecht's study cover mainly Asia, Europe and some of the Americas but seem sufficiently comprehensive to invite similar reflections on other histories not covered.
[18]Hecht, *Doubt: A History*, xvi.
[19]Hecht, *Doubt: A History*, xx.

of certainty'.[20] It is an insightful provocation to appreciate the intrinsic value of doubt and questions as a perspective on human knowledge!

The twentieth century's recognition of the historicity of human knowledge brings with it an unavoidable challenge to the validity and permanence of all truth claims.[21] Openness to experience itself has the structure of a question because 'all questioning and desire to know *presuppose a knowledge that one does not know*; so much so, indeed, that a particular lack of knowledge leads to a particular question'.[22] This has always been the case, even if our awareness of that fact and the articulation of historical consciousness are more recent. Furthermore, the separation between faith and science is a false one: first because scientific knowledge, just like every other field of expertise, builds on (read trusts) the achievements of others until proven false; but more importantly, because it has discovered movement, change and uncertainty at the core of the universe in which we live.[23] So probability is the language of scientific hypotheses, statistical estimates, business planning and marketing, and embracing uncertainty the key to psychological health.[24]

In this context we can understand the current explosion of writings on doubt in theology and spirituality.[25] They are echoing – and at times

---

[20]Hecht, *Doubt: A History*, 2.
[21]Cf. Gadamer, *Truth and Method*; Paul Ricoeur, *Essays on Biblical Interpretation*, ed. Lewis Seymour Mudge (Philadelphia: Fortress Press, 1980); Paul Ricoeur, *Figuring the Sacred: Religion, Narrative, and Imagination*, ed. Mark I. Wallace (Minneapolis: Fortress Press, 1995); and from the perspective of historical theology: John W. O'Malley, *Catholic History for Today's Church: How Our Past Illuminates Our Present* (Lanham, MA: Rowman & Littlefield, 2015).
[22]Cf. Gadamer, *Truth and Method*, 356–9; emphasis mine.
[23]Cf. Mark Schaefer, *The Certainty of Uncertainty: The Way of Inescapable Doubt and Its Virtue* (Eugene, OR: Wipf & Stock, 2018). Schaefer offers a brief and accessible study of the history of uncertainty in recent science, although I would not accept his identification of all religion as metaphorical and would further nuance the role of certitude in faith.
[24]For example, Paul Buerkner, 'Embracing Uncertainty', no. 18, November 2019.
[25]Alongside Rees' book, which presents an intellectually consistent theological take on the theme of doubt, an examination of the biblical dimensions of faith and doubt is found in Thiselton, *Doubt, Faith, and Certainty*, and Robert Davidson, *The Courage to Doubt: Exploring an Old Testament Theme* (London: SCM Press, 1983). Madhuri M. Yadlapati, in *Against Dogmatism: Dwelling in Faith and Doubt* (Urbana, Chicago and Springfield: University of Illinois Press, 2013) takes a non-confessional approach to explore a middle way between certitude and scepticism in various religions and thought-systems; Roger Lundin, in *Believing Again: Doubt and Faith in a Secular Age* (Grand Rapids, MI: William B. Eerdmans, 2009) explores the emergence and normalization of the modern mindset, while Guy Collins, in *Faithful Doubt: The Wisdom of Uncertainty* (Eugene, OR: Cascade Books, 2014), explores the contribution of intelligent questioning, doubt and atheism to theology through the lens of contemporary philosophy and fiction. See also Val Webb, *In Defense of Doubt: An Invitation to Adventure* (St. Louis, MO: Chalice Press, 1995). John D. Suk, in *Not Sure: A Pastor's Journey from Faith to Doubt* (Grand Rapids, MI: William B. Eerdmans, 2011), traces a personal journey into uncertainty with intellectual humility and theological wisdom; Lesslie Newbigin, in *Proper Confidence: Faith, Doubt, and Certainty in Christian Discipleship* (Grand Rapids, MI: William B. Eerdmans, 1995) offers a perspective from the United Reformed Church. A Christological perspective on Jesus' identity and mission can be found in Christian D. Kettler,

following – insights from every other area of human knowledge and expertise, which a theology of faith needs to make sense of, in the awareness that it is not a new problem but the unveiling of an underlying feature of human life and meaning.[26] Of the seven types of doubt identified by Hecht and found at every stage of human history, one is the doubt of the ardent believer, epitomized in the figure of Job! Our current problem is the way we were taught to believe and to understand faith; and this as a direct result of the more recent history of Christian theology and how it has sought to deal with the tides of modernity. In the quest for a better understanding of what it means to believe, the next section traces those developments.

In defence of doubt in a theology of faith

Lessons from the past

We need a renewed theology of faith. In Christian terms, faith is understood as a response to the revealing God (*Dei Verbum 1–5*), however we may understand the interaction of grace, trust and reason in its birth and growth. Christian faith is not separate from the human capacity to believe: trust is essential to human life and who or what we recognize as worthy of our faith and trust constitutes what we invest our lives in. However, to understand where doubt, questioning, critical reflection and inquiry fit into Christian faith and theology, the starting point has to be an awareness of how the God we are responding to manifests Godself. Or history will repeat itself – and the history of apologetics has a very clear lesson to teach.

Contrary to a superficial reading of (and reaction to) the emergence of modern thought and, with it, atheism, most of the thinkers influential in its development were actually committed Christians intent on finding ways to defend faith for (and against) a world seeking to understand itself without God. In this quest to defend God, theologians learnt to talk of God and defend themselves with the tools offered to them from the philosophical apparatus of the time. In a comprehensive study on the topic, Michael Buckley

---

The God Who Believes: Faith, Doubt and the Victorious Humanity of Christ (Eugene, OR: Cascade Books, 2005). The world outside Christianity is also exploring the reality of faith and believing in human life. From an anthropological and evolutionary perspective, Augustín Fuentes explores believing as an intrinsic element of human life and development, within and beyond the realm of religious belief: cf. Augustín Fuentes, *Why We Believe Evolution and the Human Way of Being* (New Haven: Yale University Press, 2019). From the perspective of philosophy and psychoanalysis, see Anne Dufourmantelle, *In Praise of Risk* (New York: Fordham University Press, 2019).

[26] For an interesting defence of doubt in the life of an atheist, see William Irwin, *God Is a Question, Not an Answer: Finding Common Ground in Our Uncertainty* (Lanham: Rowman & Littlefield, 2019).

analyses at length the fact that Christian defenders of faith forgot the role of revelation, religious experience and the centrality of Jesus as God's witness in their endeavours, or did not dare to use it in the face of the attacks received, and in doing so actually laid the foundations for atheism to thrive.[27] That is to say, philosophers and theologians accepted a narrow understanding of reason as the sole access point to acceptable knowledge and sought to defend Christian faith with those tools allotted to them by the culture they inhabited. From a Catholic perspective, this is not completely unfounded: reason is welcomed as a *capax dei a priori* for the plus of revelation's contribution. But at the time, it unfolded as an acceptance, so to speak, of 'the enemy's' terms of battle. The result was that theology defended a God with precious little content of the Christian God of Revelation, a tragedy in which 'theologians allowed themselves to be hijacked unto alien grounds'.[28] The problem was not only the defence of a false image of God ('God became incredible because God became small.'[29]) but epistemological: the assumption without discernment of the tools of knowledge for the comprehension and defence of Christian faith. 'If religion has no intrinsic justification, it cannot be justified from outside.'[30] The corresponding effect on our theology of faith is that it became trapped between two positions that left the believing subject internally divided: on the one hand, faith was understood as an intellectual assent to doctrinal propositions reason could access, and on the other, faith's assent involved blind acceptance of (supernatural) propositions beyond reason's grasp. There was no integrated articulation of their point of connection! The dilemma affected the internal dynamics of faith and the foundations of theology, with momentous consequences.

This backdrop allows us to understand how deeply doubt constituted modernity's mutation into postmodernity. In his comprehensive work on a theological understanding of doubt,[31] Frank D. Rees proposes that the modern period can be characterized in terms of four theological categories of doubt: doubt of God's mercy (represented especially by Luther and the human struggle to trust in God); doubt about God's justice and governance of the world born of experiences of suffering and the precarity of the universe; pragmatic doubt, by which concern for truth is trumped by an

---

[27]Buckley's first book explored the origins of modern atheism. The second continued that exploration into the ongoing development of Western thought, reiterating his position that religious experience, life and consciousness cannot be bracketed and excluded in reasoning about God without contributing to world view devoid of God. Cf. Michael J. Buckley, *At the Origins of Modern Atheism* (New Haven: Yale University Press, 1987); Michael J. Buckley, *Denying and Disclosing God: The Ambiguous Progress of Modern Atheism* (New Haven, CT: Yale University Press, 2004).
[28]Cf. Michael Paul Gallagher, *What Are They Saying about Unbelief?* (New York: Paulist Press, 1995), 49.
[29]Gallagher, *What Are They Saying about Unbelief?*, 41.
[30]Cf. Buckley, *At the Origins of Modern Atheism*, 360.
[31]Rees, *Wrestling with Doubt*.

idea's adequacy or usefulness in the social situation; and epistemological doubt, which concerns the character and even possibility of all religious knowledge.[32] While epistemological doubt is the one that most characterizes modernity, it is fair to say that all four dimensions play into the contemporary struggle with Christian faith in a loving God. We live in a time in which doubt is at the heart of our certainty and certitude, and this is a consequence of cultural movements that have little to do with the strength or lack thereof of an individual's faith. We can fight against this historical heritage, attempt to turn a blind eye to it, or embrace it to find what it might teach us about faith for the world today. This latter position is the one Richard Niebuhr takes, by identifying the internalization of self-doubt as an unavoidable fruit of the individual's empathy and porosity to the world around:

> The believer brings this doubting on himself. Like Christian in Bunyan's allegory, *Pilgrims' Progress,* he must traverse the vicinity of the Doubting Castle for it is in part the geography of his own soul. . . . Curiously, or perversely, we are enriched by such uncertainty. Therefore, doubting is not simply a sign of weakness. It is, rather, one of the threads in the ever more complex web binding the individual into his generation.[33]

Modernity's confidence about all things human shattered into postmodernity's comfortable familiarity with an unsure sense of the meaning of their past, present and future but this does not necessarily imply the death of hope.[34] Doubt, questioning as well as the need to find and verify a way forward in knowing and believing is at the very core of the theological quest in the twenty-first century. And we can welcome and think through what this implies for the present and future of theological thinking, especially in how we understand and develop a theology of faith, one of the core *loci* of current theological investigation.

The shape of faith in a trustworthy God

So how can we articulate the place of questions and doubt in a theology of faith? Scripture witnesses to a conversationalist God who reaches out to people and individuals,[35] who interrupts human plans,[36] who asks for us and

---

[32]Cf. Rees, *Wrestling with Doubt*, 4–6.
[33]Richard R. Niebuhr, *Experiential Religion*, 1st ed. (New York: Harper & Row, 1972), 10, 13. See also 70–6 on 'Believing and Doubting'.
[34]David Newheiser, *Hope in a Secular Age: Deconstruction, Negative Theology, and the Future of Faith* (Cambridge: Cambridge University Press, 2019).
[35]Rees, *Wrestling with Doubt*, 228.
[36]Cf. Lieven Boeve, *God Interrupts History: Theology in a Time of Upheaval* (New York: Continuum, 2007).

of us: 'where are you?' (Gen. 3.8); 'what do you see?' (Jer. 1.10); 'who do you say I am?' (Mt. 16.15); 'What do you want me to do for you?' (Lk. 18.41); 'do you love me?' (Jn 21.15-17): a Godself who often provokes questions and doubts about life and the image of God held by those who listen. Jesus' conversations with the Pharisees and teachers of the law are an example – ever questioning the status quo in the name of the God they represented. God interrupts and disrupts – an invasive God, one could say, or at the very least problematic and problematizing. The life, death, resurrection and ascension of Jesus places an embodied God at the heart of human life. Ever present in and through the sacramental and mystical body of Christ, God is nearly too close for comfort, a relational God entwined with humanity and characterized by utter commitment to loving human brokenness back to life. This is the God our faith reveals to us, a passionate, unbelievable God, really, who performs and expects an obedience comprehensible only in terms of surrender and love.

From that perspective, what is faith, and where do questioning, inquiry and doubt fit in? In fact, what are the distinctions between them? During the nineteenth and twentieth centuries, there have been noteworthy contributions to the theme. In John Henry Newman's (1801–90) theology, faith came as a result of a complex convergence of factors gathered by what he called a person's illative sense – the capacity to draw together layers of reasoning that could lead to the assent of faith – and for him, doubt had no place in the certitude of faith after this apprehension of and surrender to the revealed God.[37] For Kierkegaard, faith was 'believing against understanding' and therefore always accompanied by doubt, not least because it has to be sustained moment by moment. Paul Tillich (1886–1965) integrated doubt into the very heart of Christian believing, by which doubt could be the expression of a person's seriousness about faith and their search for authenticity in believing.[38] It led him to develop his well-known 'correlational method', bringing questions from and about the world and faith into mutual critical collaboration. Karl Barth (1886–1968), on the other hand, refused to draw his understanding of Christian faith from human knowing and believing but instead gave priority to the Word of revelation which awakens faith and knowledge of God in the believer, above, before and beyond human capacity.[39] Although doubt features little in his understanding of faith, the humility of thought to recognize and name what one does not know was something he defended vigorously. Towards the end of his life,

---

[37]John Henry Newman, *An Essay in Aid of a Grammar of Assent* (London: Burns & Oates, 1881).
[38]Cf. Paul Tillich, *The Shaking of the Foundations* (New York: C. Scribner's Sons, 1948); Paul Tillich, *Dynamics of Faith* (New York: Harper & Row, 1957).
[39]Cf. Karl Barth, *Church Dogmatics, Vol. 1 'The Doctrine of the Word of God: Prolegomena to Church Dogmatics'*, trans. G. W. Bromiley, 1st American ed. (Edinburgh: T&T Clark, 1975). Of particular note for our theme are Barth's later writings on doubt in the life of a theologian.

Barth dealt explicitly and eloquently with the issue of inquiry and doubt in the life and faith of the theologian.[40] He was very aware of the limitations of any doctrinal position and often responded to questions with a resounding 'I don't know'.[41]

Theology has long distinguished between the content of our faith and the faith by which we adhere to God, *fides quae* and *fides qua* respectively. Following this distinction, *certainty* tends to be used to describe convictions about what we believe and *certitude* as the subjective, inner trust of the person who has welcomed and surrendered to the reality of a personal God. It is clear that one can hold together the certitude that God is good with questions and doubts about certain aspects of what we think God has revealed or wants of us. In fact, a relational quality of faith would demand stages of growth in faith on a journey as disciples of Christ.[42] The temptation to build a wall out of our certainties to hide insecure or immature commitment is at the heart of most fundamentalist and dogmatist positions.[43] A contributing factor to this defensive approach is an incomplete understanding of faith's assent prevalent during the second millennium of our Christian tradition, focused mainly on reason. More recently, it is the practical, symbolic and affective dimensions of faith at work in our trust and surrender to God that has caught the attention and inspired theological minds to better understand how things work.[44] Developing a Thomistic perspective, for example, Louis Roy differentiates three dimensions operative in the faith process: 'affective craving, quest for meaning and aspiration for truth'.[45] In his view, they respond to the questions about '*why* do I believe?' (love of God to which I surrender), '*what* do I believe', as I make sense of faith, and '*whom* do I believe?' and obey.

---

[40] Karl Barth, *Evangelical Theology: An Introduction* (Grand Rapids, MI: Eerdmans, 1979), particularly parts three and four.

[41] Cf. Karl Barth, *Karl Barth's Table Talk*, ed. John D Godsey (Edinburgh: Oliver and Boyd, 1963), 24; 46-7.

[42] Cf. James W. Fowler, *Stages of Faith: The Psychology of Human Development and the Quest for Meaning* (New York: HarperOne a division of HarperCollins Publishers, 1995); Richard W. Kropf, *Faith, Security and Risk: The Dynamics of Spiritual Growth* (New York: Paulist Press, 1990); Webb, *In Defense of Doubt*.

[43] For an exploration of the dynamic and effects of this idolization of certainty, see Gregory A. Boyd, *Benefit of the Doubt: Breaking the Idol of Certainty* (Grand Rapids, MI: Baker Books, 2013).

[44] Areas of continental Europe stand out in this approach to a theology of faith. For example, the Settentrionale Faculty of Theology in Milan has done significant work on this theme: cf. Convegno Pontificia Facoltà teologica dell'Italia settentrionale, Angelini, Giuseppe, *Una Fede per Tutti?: Forma Cristiana e Forma Secolare, Disputatio* (Milano: Glossa, 2014). It has also been the focus of the work of Italian theologian Pierangelo Sequeri, whose work exploring the spiritual quality of human life and Christian faith we explore in chapter fifteen. For example, Pierangelo Sequeri, *L'idea della Fede: Trattato di Teologia Fondamentale* (Milano: Glossa, 2002).

[45] Louis Roy, *The Three Dynamisms of Faith: Searching for Meaning, Fulfillment, and Truth* (Washington, DC: Catholic University of America Press, 2017), 158-60.

But what about doubt? We are not helped by the limitations of the English language in that for two nouns to speak of 'faith' and 'trust', with different nuances, doubt is used as the opposite to both. So attempts are being made to stretch our understanding of faith. Westerhoff, for example, suggests we use 'faithing' as a verb for the entire activity of faith, of which believing is but one part.[46] Drawing on a type of phenomenology of doubt as experienced in Christian life, Webb argues that doubt is not the antonym of either faith or belief but the awareness of difficulties or questions about the content of belief or the meaning of faith – a discrepancy between 'faith' and 'belief'. The opposite of faith, she asserts, is to be without the experience of faith, while unbelief is the opposite of belief.[47] But when does questioning pass over into the lack of trust or doubt that Jesus seems (at times unreasonably?) to challenge?

This is a difficult question to answer. From a Scriptural perspective, the polymorphic nature of doubt, faith and certainty seems to leave a place for doubt![48] Jesus' human life witnesses to a growth in understanding of the will of God, including clearly challenging experiences of distance and difficulty. However we interpret the inner faith of Jesus of Nazareth, that he prayed a psalm of lament to God from the cross sets him 'right at the heart of the stream of doubting responses seen throughout the Bible'.[49] Jürgen Moltmann notes that in Gethsemane, for the first time in Jesus' life he does not wish to be alone with his Father, asking the disciples to stay awake with him because it is terrifying to face this call of God: 'The Gethsemane story (Mk. 14.32-42) reflects the frightening eclipse of God in which Jesus died, but which places despair and felt absence at the heart of the faithful one's life.'[50] A helpful distinction might be where the line between doubt and scepticism is drawn. Tillich recognizes doubt and scepticism as powerful forces in unmasking false gods, a fundamental tenet in Protestant theology known as the Protestant principle.[51] But for Rees, the issue is also about motivation: the doubting person operates out of concern or engagement. It is only when doubt or scepticism turns to pessimism, cynicism and apathy that hope is abandoned.[52] He speaks of faithful doubt and names three types found in Scripture: the questioning and protest of the psalms, the inconsolable lament

---

[46]John H. Westerhoff, *Will Our Children Have Faith?* (Harrisburg, PA: Morehouse Pub., 2012), 99–103; Rees, *Wrestling with Doubt*, 143.
[47]Webb, *In Defense of Doubt*, 4; Rees, *Wrestling with Doubt*, 132–3.
[48]This is the position of Thiselton in *Doubt, Faith, and Certainty*.
[49]Rees, *Wrestling with Doubt*, 203.
[50]Cf. Rees, *Wrestling with Doubt*, 203; Jürgen Moltmann, *The Way of Jesus Christ: Christology in Messianic Dimensions* (London: SCM Press, 1990), 166.
[51]Cf. Rebecca Kuiken, 'The Living Edge of Faith: Doubt and Scepticism in the Formation of Pastor-Theologians', in *The Power to Comprehend with All the Saints: The Formation and Practice of a Pastor-Theologian* (Grand Rapids, MI: William B. Eerdmans, 2009), 121.
[52]Rees, *Wrestling with Doubt*, 169.

of Rachel, and Job's broken silence.[53] Doubt, protest and a humble quest for new ways of responding to God are appropriate expressions of a living faith that is not complacent but allows the mystery of an unfathomable God, intent on reaching a broken world, to shake us up. In conclusion, there is intellectual responsibility to the life of faith, and as Newman defended in recognizing the importance of conscience in the 'grammar' of believing, error can be morally culpable.[54] Intellectual honesty demands attention to the edges of our knowledge and the questions this present to our faith. Two strands of theological reflection emerging in recent decades enrich this quest for matters of truth: theological aesthetics and theopoetics.

Broken bridges: Theological aesthetics, beauty and the arts

When the artists left the room

Around the same time as twentieth-century theologians were getting their heads around historical consciousness and its effect on doctrinal development and theological language, another movement broke through: the retrieval of God as beauty and aesthetics as a marginalized dimension of human knowledge and Christian faith. The former was fruit, in the main, of the work of Swiss theologian Hans Urs von Balthasar, one of the authors explored more at depth later in the book. He reminded theologians that there was a dimension of God which the modern world had forgotten, or sidelined, in the embattled field of Christianity's fight with the modern world: the glory or beauty of God.

His starting point was philosophy and theology's understanding of the nature of being and God, which included four essential and intrinsic characteristics, or attributes, known as 'transcendentals'[55] and identified as one, true, good and beautiful.[56] The point Balthasar makes in a seven-volume work called *The Glory of the Lord* is that 'the transcendentals are inseparable . . . neglecting one can only have devastating effect on

---

[53]Rees, *Wrestling with Doubt*, 175–9.
[54]Newman, *An Essay in Aid of a Grammar of Assent*; Cf. W. Jay Wood, *Epistemology: Becoming Intellectually Virtuous* (Downers Grove, IL: InterVarsity Press, 1998).
[55]For the history of the meaning of this word as applied here, see John D. Dadosky, *The Eclipse and Recovery of Beauty: A Lonergan Approach* (Toronto: University of Toronto Press, 2014), 29–54.
[56]While I am aware of the minor differences in how beauty is treated in relation to the other three, it is sufficiently accepted and integrated into theology now to be taken as an essential dimension of being, whether that is understood as a fourth distinct transcendental alongside the others or resulting from the combination of the three and their effect on human desire to know and love.

the others';[57] and that this is precisely what modern theology had done – not only to separate them but to completely sideline the supreme beauty and attractiveness of the God revealed in and through Christ. So theology over the centuries continued to understand God as *truth*, explaining and developing doctrines; and the *goodness* of God was explored and defended through considered attention to the ethical and moral dimensions of life, but the concept of *beauty* was left on the margins of thought from Aquinas to the last century, to the detriment of faith *and* life.[58] 'In a world without beauty . . . in a world which is perhaps not wholly without beauty, but which can no longer see it or reckon with it: in such a world the good also loses its attractiveness, the self-evidence of why it must be carried out.'[59] Once again, we find ourselves facing a foundational question and starting point: what underlying image of God conditions our investigations? Scripture may not use the term 'beauty' much, but its equivalent can be found in the words describing God's glory – *tob, kalos, kabod* – words applied as much to the God perceived in the created world as the crucified Christ who draws all things to Himself. The beauty of the revealed God is not superficial but manifested in the very death of God made human – Paul would say sin (2 Cor. 5:21) – for us. If our understanding of faith does not integrate truth, good and beauty, our sense of God is incomplete, truncated.

Interestingly and not coincidently, during the same period in which theology forgot about beauty, the artists also left the building. The reasons for this are complex and also linked, I believe, to the intrinsic connection between art and freedom, and the impossibility of containing artistic creativity under the surveillance adopted by the Church in its historically documented defensive reaction to modernism. That shrinking box of thought could simply not contain what art is meant to do! This is not to say that for artists anything goes but to recognize that there is a tension to be maintained between belonging and creative thought that is inescapable for Christian thought to flourish. Strangely, Balthasar wrote about the incompatibility of the artistic and religious callings,[60] but I would affirm the direct opposite: the maturity of a people (defined by religion *or* state) can be seen in how it manages, dialogues with and supports its artists. There is a reason why they are the first to disappear in dictatorial regimes!

---

[57]Hans Urs von Balthasar, *The Glory of the Lord: A Theological Aesthetics. Vol. 1, Seeing the Form*, (Edinburgh: T&T Clark, 1982), 9.
[58]Cf. Rino Fisichella, 'Beauty', in *Dictionary of Fundamental Theology* (New York: Crossroad, 1994), 78.
[59]Balthasar, *The Glory of the Lord I*, 19.
[60]See Pierangelo Sequeri, *Anti-Prometeo. Il Musicale Nell'estetica Teologica di Hans Urs von Balthasar* (Milano: Glossa, 1995). I have explored his position in depth in Maeve Louise Heaney, 'Musical Space: Living in-between the Artistic and Christian Callings', in *Secular Music and Sacred Theology*, ed. Tom Beaudoin, 16–31. (Collegeville, MN: Liturgical Press, 2013).

Artists tend to think ahead, read afresh or even anticipate what is around the corner of intellectual awareness – potentially a dynamic meeting point of experience, freedom, discipline and craft. Something of this dynamic is recorded in a little-known encounter between Paul VI and artists in the Sistine Chapel on Ascension Thursday of 1964. A later letter and message to artists by John Paul II[61] and Benedict XVI,[62] respectively, are well known, but it is this homily given nearly twenty years earlier which captures best, in my opinion, the underlying tensions and missteps that cost both Church and culture dearly. Paul VI recognizes a rift, caused by both sides, in what reads like a public confession that is clear in its content and moving in its tone. It is worth quoting at length, because although the homiletic language is dated, its honesty and depth transcend that barrier:

> The topic is this: it is necessary to re-establish the friendship between the Church and artists. In truth, it is not that the friendship was ever broken. . . . However, as occurs between relations, as occurs between friends, it has become a little spoiled. We have not broken but we have upset our friendship. Will you allow Us a frank word? You have abandoned Us a little, you have gone far away to drink from other fountains in the still legitimate search to express other things; but no longer ours.
>
> But to be sincere and daring . . . we recognise that we, also, have made you suffer a little. We have made you suffer because we have imposed imitation as the first rule upon you, on you who are creators, always full of life, gushing with a thousand ideas and a thousand new things. We – it was said – have this manner, we must adapt to it; we have this tradition and we must be faithful to it; we have these masters and we must follow them; we have these canons and there is no way out. Sometimes we put a cloak of lead on you, we can say. Forgive us! And then we also had abandoned you. We did not explain our things to you. We did not bring you into the secret cell where God's mysteries make man's heart jump for joy, out of hope, of gladness, of exhilaration. We did not keep you as pupils, friends, in dialogue. For this reason you did not recognise us . . .
>
> And – we will perform a complete *Confiteor* this morning, at least here – we treated you even worse. We turned to surrogates, to 'oleography', to works of art of little worth and little value, even though, in our defence, we did not have the means to accomplish great things, beautiful things, new things, things worthy to be admired; and so even we were sidetracked down paths where art and beauty and – which is the worst for us – the worship of God were poorly served.

---

[61]John Paul II, *Letter of His Holiness Pope John Paul II to Artists* (Vatican City, 1999).
[62]Benedict XVI, *Meeting with Artists: Address of Pope Benedict XVI* (Vatican City: Libreria Editrice Vaticana, 2009).

Shall we make peace again? Today? Here? Do we want to be friends again? Shall the Pope become once again the friend of artists?[63]

A compelling witness to a tragic rift between Church and culture, and the felt urgency of bridging the gap! It has been followed by other meetings and messages, and the ongoing creation of various forums to open and continue a dialogue inclusive of artistic creativity.[64] One wonders why theology struggles so hard to follow suit. Of course, there are forums of interested academics,[65] research that broadens and applies Balthasar's initial work in theological aesthetics[66] and individuals who are pulling the threads of various art forms, but a consistent, focussed, interdisciplinary dialogue and the work necessary to place the particular gift of artistic craft and creative freedom at the service of faith's understanding and theology in spaces that can inform future artwork, are still weak. The thought and work of Sequeri, in this regard, stand out. Concerned by the impoverished spiritual quality of contemporary culture, he identifies the link between theology, spirituality and art. Drawing on Balthasar, he recognizes that the beautiful will return to theological discourse only when our understanding of revelation, beauty and creativity comes together.[67] And for that to happen, he calls for an unprejudiced new opening to the universe of artistic creation and the development by 'convinced believers of passionate faith and real talent and formation', to be allowed to work and draw with them the interest of a culture.[68] That kind of intersection between the ecclesial nourishing of faith and calling, an artist's dedication to their craft and the theological formation needed to bear fruit is what this book is seeking to help provoke. Of course, things may become unruly!

---

[63]Paul VI, *Homily*, *'Artists' Mass' in the Sistine Chapel* (Thursday, 7 May 1964). Pope Paul VI installed a new wing in the Vatican museums for contemporary art.
[64]For example, John Paul II founded the Pontifical Council of Culture on 20 May 1982 with the aim of establishing dialogue between the Church and the cultures of our time, including the world of the arts.
[65]For example, the *Institute for Theology, Imagination and the Arts*, at St Andrews, in Scotland, https://itia.wp.st-andrews.ac.uk/; the *International Network for Music Theology*, in Durham, https://www.dur.ac.uk/musictheology/; and *Art, Religion, Culture* (ARC): *A Creative Collaborative for Theopoetics*. Cf. https://artsreligionculture.org/.
[66]For example, Oleg V. Bychkov and James Fodor, *Theological Aesthetics after von Balthasar* (Aldershot, England: Ashgate, 2008), and a special issue of *Modern Theology* in 2018 on the theme of *Naming God Today: Contemporary Approaches to the Divine Attributes* 34, no. 3: 313–491. It should be noted, however, that Balthasar's focus was on a theology of revelation framed by the beauty of Christ, *not* a more aesthetic or artistic approach to beauty.
[67]Pierangelo Sequeri, *L'estro di Dio: Saggi di Estetica* (Milano: Glossa, 2000), 102.
[68]Pierangelo Sequeri, 'Coscienza Cristiana, Ethos della Fede e Canone Pubblico', in *A Misura di Vangelo: Fede, Dottrina, Chiesa*, ed. M. Vergottini and Associazione Teologica Italiana (Cinisello Balsamo: San Paolo, 2003), 29.

Theopoetics and the importance of uncertainty

One of the most significant spaces in which questioning and multiform modes of accessing, expressing and performing theological meaning find their voice is the field of theopoetics.[69] A comprehensive description of this emerging field in which a plurality of perspectives on truth or *polyphilia* (love of multiplicity)[70] seems to be essential, is still difficult, but some identifying characteristics are possible to name. From the combination of the Greek *thea* with *poiein*, meaning 'to make or shape', etymologically theopoetics is described as 'a means of making God, of shaping experience of the divine, and the study of ways in which people come to know the Spirit'.[71] For those who identify with this field, this does not mean inventing or reinventing God but paying due attention to the fact that *how* theology is shaped and expressed does as much (or more?) to inform our image and understanding of the divine than the doctrinal content written or taught.

Theopoetics has known intermittent waves of writings since the 1960s, usually coinciding with moments of crisis in faith. The term was first coined by Stanley Hopper as *theopoisis* in a 1971 talk on *The Literary Imagination and the Doing of Theology*,[72] and its first authors challenged theological discourse to a 'depth of thought' which recognizes that we live more out of myth, dream, metaphor, archetype and so on than rational thought,[73] and that words can cage our understanding of things even as they give us access to their meaning.[74] Since then, in the 1980s and again more recently in the early years of the twenty-first century, momentum has gathered around the term and its multiple forms of practice, fed by the quest to explore how the context within which thought on God is expressed and its medium

---

[69]Even the explanations theopoetics gives of itself are found in videos, performances and poetry, as well as texts. For example, see Callid Keefe-Perry and Silas Krabbe on what theopoetics is: https://www.youtube.com/watch?v=nHuHn3vxePg and https://www.youtube.com/watch?v=1xTePvgsE1U.

[70]L. Callid Keefe-Perry, 'Theopoetics: Process and Perspective', *Christianity & Literature* 58 (2009): 579–601, at 596.

[71]L. Callid Keefe-Perry, 'Theopoetics: Process and Perspective', *Literature and Christianity* 58, no. 4 (2009): 579–80.

[72]Cf. Stanley Romaine Hopper, 'The Literary Imagination and the Doing of Theology', in *The Way of Transfiguration: Religious Imagination as Theopoiesis*, ed. Melvin Keiser and Tony Stoneburner (Louisville: Westminster/John Knox, 1992), 207–29.

[73]See Amos Niven Wilder, *Theopoetic: Theology and the Religious Imagination* (Philadelphia: Fortress, 1976), 81.

[74] Foundational writers include Hopper, 'The Literary Imagination and the Doing of Theology', in *Theopoetic: Theology and the Religious Imagination*, ed. Amos Niven Wilder (Philadelphia: Fortress, 1976); Rubem A. Alves, *The Poet, the Warrior, the Prophet* (Philadelphia: Trinity Press International, 1990); Rubem A. Alves, 'Theopoetics: Longing and Liberation', in *Struggles for Solidarity: Liberation Theologies in Tension* (Minneapolis: Fortress Press, 1992); Walter Brueggemann, *Finally Comes the Poet: Daring Speech for Proclamation* (Minneapolis: Fortress Press, 1989).

have much more influence than has been recognized in the development of academic theology.[75]

The range of authors either referring to theopoetics or identified as part of the same style of thinking is broad, including philosophers addressing postmodern theology and the 'death of God', process theologians, biblical scholars and liberation theologians invested in naming power plays and hearing the voices of those on the margin.[76] The intent is much more than a theology in poetic form, but an embodied attempt to say something, experienced and accessible, about the God we can host but not control, a conversation opener towards further truth, so that 'whether theology is inscribed in the genre of poetry, in the form of narrative, or in a thicker, theoretical style of prose, it remains a *poiesis*: an inventive, imaginative act of composition performed by authors'.[77] Theology implies radical engagement with the lived human experience of embodiment in all its dimensions. In Latin '"knowledge" and "taste" come from the same root ... to know something is to feel its taste',[78] implying that kinaesthetic, embodied knowing has a trustworthy role to play in making sense of the faith we believe.[79] For theopoetics, the knowledge of God born of embodied knowing is nothing more than the consequence of taking the Incarnation seriously: 'The challenge is to think of the difference of "God" and "world" with a radicality that actually deepens their interdependence. Or put differently, we will want to complicate the boundaries by which these two terms are

---

[75] Their recent history has been facilitated and led by the work of Callid Keefe-Perry, which began with a website called Theopoetics.net set up in 2009 to serve as a base to gather and communicate writings around the theme for educational purposes. Interest led to the creation of the Association for Theopoetics Research and Exploration (ATRE), which met annually, in turn leading to the creation of the online journal *Theopoetics* in 2013. In 2015 ATRE hosted its own inaugural conference and in 2017 would merge with its main sponsor, The Society for Arts, Religion, and Contemporary Culture (SARCC) taking on the name *Art, Religion, Culture* (ARC): *A Creative Collaborative for Theopoetics*. Cf. https://artsreligionculture.org/.

[76] By way of example, Richard Kearney, *Anatheism: Returning to God after God* (New York: Columbia University Press, 2011); Catherine Keller, 'The Flesh of God', in *Theology That Matters: Ecology, Economy, and God*, ed. Kathleen Ray Darby (Minneapolis: Fortress Press, 2006); Roland Faber, ed., *Theopoetic Folds Philosophizing Multifariousness, Perspectives in Continental Philosophy* (Bronx: Fordham University Press, 2013); John Caputo and Catherine Keller, 'Theopoetic/Theopolitic', *CrossCurrents* 56 (2007); Melanie A. May, *A Body Knows: A Theopoetics of Death and Resurrection* (New York: Continuum, 1995); Scott Holland, 'The Poet, Theopoetics, and Theopolitics', *CrossCurrents* 64, no. 4 (2014); Scott Holland, 'Theopoetics is the Rage', *The Conrad Grebel Review* 31, no. 2 (2013); Gabriel Vahanian, *Theopoetics of the Word: A New Beginning of Word and World* (New York: Palgrave Macmillan, 2014).

[77] Scott Holland, *How Do Stories Save Us? An Essay on the Question with the Theological Hermeneutics of David Tracy in View* (Grand Rapids, MI: William B. Eerdmans, 2006), 109.

[78] Alves, *The Poet, the Warrior, the Prophet*, 85.

[79] For an overview of its origin, progress and representative writers, see Callid Keefe-Perry, *Way to Water: A Theopoetics Primer* (Eugene, OR: Cascade Books, 2014); Silas C. Krabbe, *A Beautiful Bricolage: Theopoetics as God-Talk for Our Time* (Eugene, OR: Wipf and Stock, 2016); Keefe-Perry, 'Theopoetics: Process and Perspective', 579–601.

opposed, while releasing mystery into the first term and creativity into every level of the second.'[80] While more textual in its origins, the field is currently pushing towards other forms of art and areas of thought such as film, theatre, music, hip hop and studies on trauma.[81] The intent is to face what 'the twilight of the church and the twilight of conventional theologies'[82] demand of us: 'finding fresh words and forms of speaking about God that honour the deep traditions of Christianity while managing to capture a sense of the *experience* of the divine'.[83]

Their significance for this chapter is the comprehensive way in which they approach the intersection between theology and the arts, and the courageous engagement with the issues of real life *as they show up*. For theopoetics, questions and aims are as important as the answers found, since knowledge is always incomplete,[84] and faith is to be understood more as a 'wager on God' based on life and trust than certainty of concepts. Its most eloquent definition, to my mind, is the one that runs right through Keefe-Perry's 2014 theopoetics primer, *Way to Water*. Theopoetics is

> An acceptance of cognitive uncertainty regarding the Divine, an unwillingness to attempt to unduly banish that uncertainty, and an emphasis on action and creative articulation regardless. It also suggests that when the dust has settled after things have been said and done in the name of God, the reflection and interpretation to be done ought to be grounded in dialogue and enacted with a hermeneutic of hospitality and humility, an acceptance of cognitive uncertainty...

And around we go. Theological formulation is ever incomplete, but theopoetics holds together the necessary tension of standing for faith while avoiding the idol of the finished picture, by *whoever* is claiming ownership. And *who* is claiming ownership is important, as theopoetics often sits on,

---

[80]Keller, 'The Flesh of God', 94.
[81]A 'State of the Conversation' collection can be found in a recent online Symposium at Syndicate: https://syndicate.network/symposia/theology/theopoetics/. Some of the more recent authors and writings are Mayra Rivera, *Poetics of the Flesh* (Durham: Duke University Press, 2015); Ashley Theuring, 'Holding Hope and Doubt: An Interreligious Theopoetic Response to Public Tragedies', *CrossCurrents* (2014); Ashley Theuring, *Toward a Catholic Feminist Practical Theology of Hope after Domestic Violence* (Boston University, 2018); Shelly Rambo, *Spirit and Trauma: A Theology of Remaining* (Louisville, KY: Westminster John Knox Press, 2010).
[82]Holland, 'Theopoetics Is the Rage', 122.
[83]L. B. C. Keefe-Perry, 'Theopoetics: Process and Perspective', *Christianity & Literature* 58, no. 4 (2009): 583.
[84]Krabbe, *A Beautiful Bricolage*, 33–8, 89–108. Krabbe names six questions theopoets ask: 'How do we move forward? Who am I (in this moving world)? Can humans communicate with the divine? How are human beings participants in communication (the nature of human knowing – what is it to know)? What do humans need to be freed from? How do we engage power?', with an explicit reference to the symbolic meaning of the number six as incomplete.

dialogues with, and theologizes from the margins and the edges. The task before us is not to resort to scepticism or disbelief but to 'keep always in mind how humanly constructed are the models whereby we know anything at all'.[85] According to Wilder, theopoetics has two detractors: those who may be seeking spirituality but who believe that the whole project of Christian theology should be abandoned as no longer viable, and the rationalists and religious dogmatists for both of whom experience lacks its deeper creative registers.[86]

The embodied, open form of music

Throughout this chapter, the refusal to question and its connection to a lack of depth emerges as one of the more troubling aspects of the whole issue of questions and doubt in faith. Drive tension or conflict underground and you deaden yourself;[87] if you silence the voices that need to know more and better, then life and faith are less than they could be. Music has only slowly begun to find expression and a place in both theological aesthetics and theopoetics, but their expressed convictions resonate with what music brings to the theological table and evoke dimensions already connected with music's specific way of working. The embodied nature of the musical symbolic form and its emotional resonance and connection to the human experience of temporality differentiate it from conceptual abstraction, and situate it as a potentially fruitful tool for the poietic exploration of the human experience of the divine. It resonates with invitations of theopoetic writings to shift from the quest to 'see God' to 'seeing as God sees',[88] so as to find a way of thinking God in the world and connected to it without conflating the human and divine realities. Theological writings on how music as a symbolic form works identify its potential to do just this.[89] But this is not completely new. The history of music's place in theology and vice versa, as explored in Chapters 2 and 3, reshapes the dimensions and importance of our intent.

---

[85]Keller, 'The Flesh of God', 103.
[86]Wilder, *Theopoetic: Theology and the Religious Imagination*, 101–2.
[87]Cf. H. A. Williams, *Tensions: Necessary Conflicts in Life and Love* (Springfield: Templegate, 1977), 16.
[88]David Miller, 'Introduction', in *Why Persimmons? and Other Poems: Transformations of Theology in Poetry*, ed. Stanley R. Hopper (Atlanta: Scholars, 1987), 8. See also Keefe-Perry, 'Theopeotics, Process and Perspectives', 586.
[89]For some background exploration of research into this area, see chapters three and four of Maeve Louise Heaney, *Music as Theology: What Music Has to Say about the Word* (Eugene, OR: Pickwick Publications Wipf and Stock, 2012).

Selected further reading

Brueggemann, Walter. *Finally Comes the Poet: Daring Speech for Proclamation*. Minneapolis: Fortress Press, 1989.

Collins, Guy. *Faithful Doubt: The Wisdom of Uncertainty*. Eugene, OR: Cascade Books, 2014.

Gallagher, Michael Paul. *What Are They Saying about Unbelief?* New York: Paulist Press, 1995.

Hecht, Jennifer Michael. *Doubt: A History; the Great Doubters and Their Legacy of Innovation, from Socrates and Jesus to Thomas Jefferson and Emily Dickinson*. San Francisco. HarperSanFrancisco, 2003.

Irwin, William. *God Is a Question, Not an Answer: Finding Common Ground in Our Uncertainty*. Lanham: Rowman & Littlefield, 2019.

Keefe-Perry, Callid. *Way to Water: A Theopoetics Primer*. Eugene, OR: Cascade Books, 2014.

Lundin, Roger. *Believing Again: Doubt and Faith in a Secular Age*. Grand Rapids, MI: William B. Eerdmans, 2009.

Newheiser, David. *Hope in a Secular Age: Deconstruction, Negative Theology, and the Future of Faith*. Cambridge: Cambridge University Press, 2019.

Paul VI. *Homily, 'Artists' Mass' in the Sistine Chapel*. Thursday, 7 May 1964.

Rivera, Mayra. *Poetics of the Flesh*. Durham, NC: Duke University Press, 2015.

2

The hidden story of music in theology

You don't have to sing it right; who could call you wrong?
You put your emptiness to melody; your awful heart
to song . . .
At best, you find a little remedy; at worst the world will
sing along.

HOZIER[1]

Music and musicking: Defining our terms

What is music? Or rather, what comes to our minds when we think of music? In many ways the answer depends on our sociocultural context and experience, both personal and communal. We may think of our favourite groups, composers and the assorted playlists we turn to according to need. The question evokes images of CDs, vinyls or notated music and the kinds of spaces we visit or create to listen to them: concerts, park runs, pub nights or family singsongs. Those who self-identify as musicians will also be drawn to action-based images – the practices and relationships that go into music-making: solitary quests for inspiration and/or creative collaboration in discovering the right sounds at the right time. For some cultures, music is so intrinsic to their identity and way of life that it can be hard to separate clearly in a definition: music is everywhere and part of everything. There are languages in which music does not even exist as a

---

[1] Hozier 'To Noise Making' in *Wasteland Baby* 2019. Sony/ATV Music Publishing (UK) Ltd and Evolving Music (Ireland). All Rights Reserved. Used with permission.

noun. What constitutes the essence of music, or of musical activity, has been an ever-present question in academic discussions on music of theorists, musicologists, ethnomusicologists and philosophers of music.[2] This book takes the position that music is best grasped not as a noun but as a verb, an activity and one that is not only personal but relational and socially embedded. The 'embodied practices'[3] related to *music-making* and *music-hearing* are best described with Christopher Small's notion of 'musicking', rather than music.

As this stance colours the whole book, the position and writings of Christopher Small merit attention. They also give expression to a much broader shift in music studies to a critical re-evaluation of assumed canons on music. The keyword 'musicking', present participle or gerund form of a non-existent verb 'to music', was coined by Small in a book on the contribution of Afro-American music to the world written in 1987[4] and developed more fully in a later book entitled *Musicking: The Meanings of Performing and Listening*.[5] Fulfilling his expressed desire that it become a proper English-language verb, musicking *has* found its way into non-specialist dictionaries and influenced a number of contextually sensitive studies on music since then.[6] However, the radicality of his thought (in the etymological sense of rethinking things 'from their root') is helpful for theological reflection as it implies reimagining the very nature of how music works, and its role in shaping our lives and performing our relationships and social structures.

According to Small, music is not an object, whose general and universal meaning we will one day be able to pin down (and control). 'What does music mean?' is, therefore, a non-question. Music is not the sum total of

---

[2] Of the many definitions, Blacking's 'humanly organized sound' or 'temporally organized patterns of pitched sounds' stands out, together with Jean-Jacques Nattiez's hermeneutical approach: 'The "musical" (as there is not a music, but many musics) is any sonorous fact constructed, organized, or thought by a culture.' Cf. John Blacking, *How Musical Is Man?* (London: Faber, 1976), 89; Jean-Jacques Nattiez, *Music and Discourse: Toward a Semiology of Music* (Princeton, NJ: Princeton University Press, 1990), 67.
[3] Jeremy Begbie and Steven R. Guthrie, *Resonant Witness: Conversations between Music and Theology* (Grand Rapids, MI: William B. Eerdmans, 2011), 5.
[4] Christopher Small, *Music of the Common Tongue: Survival and Celebration in African American Music* (Hanover, NH: University Press of New England, 1987), 13.
[5] Christopher Small, *Musicking: The Meanings of Performing and Listening* (Hanover, NH: University Press of New England, 1998), especially the introduction, 1–18.
[6] Cf. Matthew Rahaim, *Musicking Bodies: Gesture and Voice in Hindustani Music* (Middletown, CN: Wesleyan Press, 2012); Swee Hong Lim, 'Forming Christians through Musicking in China', *Religions* 8, no. 4 (2017): 1–10; Michael Golden, 'Musicking as Education for Social and Ecological Peace: A New Synthesis', *Journal of Peace Education: Music and Peace Education* 13, no. 3 (2016): 266–82; Roberta R. King, 'Performing Witness: Loving Our Religious Neighbors through Musicking', in *Arts as Witness in Multifaith Contexts*, ed. R. R. King and W. A. Dryness, 39–66 (Downers Grove, IL, 2019). A two-day symposium was organized by Queens University, Belfast, on 'Musicking for Peacebuilding. Sounding Conflict: From Resistance to Reconciliation' in 2019: https://mrulster.com/2019/12/02/musicking-for-peacebuilding/.

musical productions that someone decides merits the name (according to the shifting if predictable guardians of the music world/s). Rather, the musical act is a human social activity, whose proper function is 'the establishment of real relationships, and exploration of values or of identity'.[7] And it is a function we are all involved in. '*To music is to take part, in any capacity, in a musical performance, whether by performing, by listening, by rehearsing or practicing, by providing material for performance (what is called composing), or by dancing.*'[8] It may be live or recorded, regardless of its perceived quality or lack thereof. 'To music' is a *descriptive*, not prescriptive, definition which does not permit of evaluation. And everyone musics! It is an essential part of the human way of inhabiting the world. Adding his voice to those challenging the hegemony of Western classical music as the ultimate paradigm of musical prowess and expertise, Small chooses the term 'vernacular' rather than 'folk' or 'popular' to refer to music that does not come under the rubric 'classical'.[9] The analogy is clear: in the same way everyone converses in their own language, everyone musics – in one way or another – and any consideration of what the activity might mean, in musicology and every other discipline, needs to take this into account if it is to be taken seriously.

On one level the notion is simple: everyone involved in any form in the preparation and delivery of musical experience is 'musicking'. On another, it constitutes a fundamental shift in perspective that upends (and upsets) the cart of historical studies on music, inviting us to re-examine each one in the broader context of who was involved in their production and in what way. Small continuously confronts the question about what kind of social relationships any given style of musicking enacts, including the underlying image and place of the transcendent, or God. It is not surprising that Susan McClary saw in his approach, more than in any other, a 'model for the future of music studies'.[10] By defining musical activity in this way, Small is challenging various assumptions of the world of music theorists, musicologists and aestheticians (the hermeneutical trio of music analysis): first and foremost, the assumed priority of the musical work over its performance; second, the non-identity (or non-entity!) of the performer in terms of added value to the meaning of music; third, a passive, non-contributory understanding of the listener as mere 'receiver'; and finally, the

---

[7]Cf. Small, *Music of the Common Tongue*, 476.
[8]Small, *Musicking*, 9. Emphasis in original.
[9]Small, *Music of the Common Tongue*, 8. The term 'classical' here refers less to the 'classical period' musical specialists use to refer to music of a certain style emerging in the eighteenth century than its widely accepted use for mainly European and American classical music, although as with every demarcation of music style, the ground and borders are always shifting, making it notoriously difficult to pin down genres for any length of time.
[10]Quoted in his obituary in the *Guardian* on 20 September 2011, written by Dave Laing: https://www.theguardian.com/music/2011/sep/19/christopher-small-obituary

autonomy of the work from its cultural context and any political, religious or social intentionality underlying its origin. Each of these challenges has implications in terms of making sense of music in life and thought, but they share a fundamental, common denominator: performance. In Small's approach and that of this book, the musical work, written or recorded, is but *one element* of this broader picture of music's enactment in *any* particular moment for any person or group of persons. 'For *performance does not exist in order to present musical works, but rather, musical works exist in order to give performers something to perform.*'[11] And every performance presents, actualizes and shapes a series of relationships that give, or consolidate, identity and meaning: personal, communal, sociopolitical and/or religious.

Small is not a lone voice in challenging engrained assumptions about the composition, reception and status of the 'musical work'. Hermeneutical approaches to musical meaning demand that attention be paid to the worlds behind, within and in front of every musical text *and* its performance.[12] A growing awareness of the ignored history of women in music[13] and feminist critiques of musical understanding[14] stand out as both an achievement and ongoing challenge of this focus. Cultural studies into musical genres the world over, with a cross-fertilization of styles and modes of making music since the twentieth century, also challenge assumptions in practical ways, carrying the reality of music and thought into broader fields without asking permission (as art rarely does). Some music genres and practices (such as jazz or rap) consciously subvert standard music-making's delineation between composition and performance, but the majority of practising and performing musicians in the world do not limit 'true composing' to the written score that one person creates and appreciate viscerally the role of their fellow musicians *and* audiences in the event of music-making. Audiences, in turn, appreciate the performing artist as much (or more?) than the songwriter/composer, and current trends involving electronic elements in music place the 'behind the scenes' artistic producer centre stage in terms of recognition and fame.

Music happens and is celebrated, bought, consumed and revisited without much thought to its philosophical status or even the economic factors influencing what music reaches our ears. But in the context of a book on

---

[11] Small, *Musicking*, 8. Emphasis in original.
[12] Cf. Jean-Jacques Nattiez, *Fondements d'une Semiologique de la Musique* (Paris: Unions Générale d'Editions, 1975).
[13] Cf. Karin Pendle, *Women & Music: A History* (Indiana: Indiana University Press, 2001); Jane M. Bowers and Judith Tick, *Women Making Music: The Western Art Tradition, 1150-1950* (Illinois: University of Illinois Press, 1987); Ellen Koskoff, *Women and Music in Cross-Cultural Perspective*, vol. 79 (Illinois: University of Illinois Press, 1987); Mina Carson, Tisa Lewis, and Susan M. Shaw, *Girls Rock!: Fifty Years of Women Making Music* (University Press of Kentucky, 2014).
[14] Cf. Susan McClary, *Feminine Endings: Music, Gender, and Sexuality* (Minneapolis: University of Minnesota Press, 2002); Heidi Epstein, *Melting the Venusberg: A Feminist Theology of Music* (New York: Continuum, 2004).

thought and theologizing about music, this is an essential point of reflection, because the 'canon' that defined musical works in the past is parallel (in time and style) to the one that shaped theological thinking, for good *and* bad. In calling out classical European-American music's limited understanding of itself and placing it into a broader framework of musicking as a form of meaning-making and identity-creation, the invitation is to reimagine the role of music in every sphere of life, including and in this case, especially, the theological. The intent not only helps theology reshape how it understands music's contribution to theological reflection[15] but also invites, or rather requires, that we reimagine theology. From noun to verb, more performance than product.[16] This does not undermine academic theology as it has developed over history, nor its service to church and society. In fact, one of the concerns of the book is the underestimation of theology's importance and the need to theologize in a way that safeguards its role. The point, rather, is to open our eyes to blind spots developed over time, recover lost dimensions of human thinking and advance spaces for music *within* current theological investigation as a dimension that complements and enriches the whole, even as it opens it out to other worlds of meaning. When did theology forget that music is an intrinsic part of making sense of life and faith? Is the exclusion of one of humanity's most essential life-spaces one (more) sign of theology's marginalization from mainstream society's worldview?[17] And why are these not essential theological questions?

Unwritten scores: Behind the scenes of theological creativity

The unwritten history of music as theology is not completely unknown. There are a few writings where theologians name a musical influence sustaining their life's work, and biographies are starting to emerge that record the musical influences on philosophers or theologians of the past, decades after their demise. But these facts and stories still sit at the edge of theology proper, interesting trivia or at best metadata for conference titbits

---

[15]The work of Bruce Ellis Benson here is foundational: Bruce Ellis Benson, *The Improvisation of Musical Dialogue: A Phenomenology of Music* (Cambridge: Cambridge University Press, 2003); Bruce Ellis Benson, 'Improvising Texts, Improvising Communities: Jazz, Interpretation, Heterophony, and the Ekklesia', in *Resonant Witness: Conversations between Music and Theology*, ed. J. Begbie and S. R. Guthrie, 295–319 (Grand Rapids, MI: William B. Eerdmans, 2011).
[16]Philip Edward Stoltzfus, *Theology as Performance: Music, Aesthetics, and God in Western Thought* (New York: T&T Clark International, 2006).
[17]Notwithstanding the possibility that Christianity functions best as a minority belief system and that it is reasonable to view the secular age as one that emerges out of, rather than as a reaction against, modernity. Cf. Charles Taylor, *A Secular Age* (Cambridge, MA: Belknap Press of Harvard University Press, 2007).

or historical archives. The aim here is not to make them more important than they are – forcing an anachronic theological content or method when it was not there – but rather to build a truer picture of music's place in the history of theological thought by bringing together disperse experiences and insights into their connection. To do so in a way that is consistent with the approach outlined earlier, recognizing not just composers and works but the place of music in the social ordering contemporary to these theologians means that there are two strands to the story of music in theology: the place of music in the very development of a Christian worldview and the history of thought, and the influence of music on the work and thought of key figures in the history of theology. In this section of the chapter I trace both.[18] As these narratives are mapped, the invitation is to an exercise in *imagination* into what other times might have looked or even *felt* like. It is hard enough to step outside our own culture to comprehend another contemporary to ours, harder still to comprehend times past! But in a discipline for which the past is foundational and tradition essential to its self-understanding, a felt historical awareness of how things have developed over time is a non-negotiable element of our commitment to truth, in all its complexity.

Music in a Scriptural worldview

Scripture, an expression of the Judaeo-Christian worldview and the soul of Christian theology (*Dei Verbum* 24), is a natural starting point. What kind of musicking do we find there? And how has it carried forth into the development of theological thinking? Within the world of the Jewish Scriptures, there are two traditions of music: temple worship with musicians and cantors, and less structured, vocal chant-like praying. Of the two, vocal music is by far the stronger. Instrumental music is not to be trusted, according to some of the prophets, due to its association with music in pagan worship.[19] Accordingly, temple worship with instruments is a later development and never replaced or overtook the centrality of vocal worship in Jewish gatherings, a preference reflected in Paul's references to songs. 'The result is that throughout much of its history Christianity shared with Judaism a belief in the superiority of vocal over instrumental music.'[20] So it begs the question: Did Jesus and his disciples sing?[21] That is to say: How

---

[18]It would be impossible – and perhaps unnecessary – to explain at depth any one position or thinker, as there are plenty of individual resources that do just that. An overview which tells this hidden story is the intent here.
[19]For example: Isa. 5.11-12.
[20]Stephen H. Webb, *The Divine Voice: Christian Proclamation and the Theology of Sound* (Grand Rapids, MI: Brazos Press, 2004), 227.
[21]The question is raised and developed by Michael O'Connor, 'The Singing of Jesus', in *Resonant Witness: Conversations between Music and Theology*, ed. J. Begbie and S. R. Guthrie (Grand Rapids, MI: William B. Eerdmans, 2011).

did the foundational culture of Christian faith within which Jesus lived and prayed his Jewish faith '*musick*'? And because imagination grounds thought, how have we imagined that reality over the history of theological thought? More fundamentally, do we imagine Jesus as singing? And if not, why? Although the gospels only explicitly mention it once (at the end of the Last Supper with his disciples),[22] 'Jesus would have experienced singing and chanting in the home and at play. And like any other faithful Jew, he would have experienced singing in public worship'.[23]

This fact has not played a major part in Christian imagination over history, and the exceptions focus more on the role of the risen Christ as head of the worshipping body that is the Church than on his historical existence. For example, Clement of Alexandria (150–215) imagined a heavenly music with Christ the leader of its performance.[24] In Augustine (354–430) we find joyful exclamations about the interweaving voices of the one Christ, head and members: 'He prays for us as our priest, prays in us as our head, and is prayed to by us as our God. Let as therefore acknowledge our voice in him and his voice in us.'[25] Reformation theologian John Calvin (1509–64) and later Methodist founder John Wesley (1703–91) take up the singing of Christ as part of the body of Christ, leading our worship; and the lesser known Lutheran composer and music theorist Johann Mattheson (1681–1764) explores the continuity between the music of Christ and the angels at the 'beginning of creation and the music led by Christ in the world to come'.[26]

If the singing of Jesus is a minor theme in the history of Christian theology, there are other aspects of the Scriptural worldview that have not only coloured but founded the history of Western music in essential and long-lasting ways, such as the primacy of the word over music; the biblical understanding of time, as both a history of salvation which cuts through contemporary cyclical notions of human history to point to final resolution (read salvation) and the *chronos* versus *kairos* understanding of how God interrupts time with eternity-life presence (Aquinas' '*nunc*'); and the incarnated, anti-gnostic nature of Scripture's understanding of both God and human life.[27] This last one – Scriptures' witness to an incarnate God

---

[22]'When they had sung the hymn (*hymnesantes*), they went out to the Mount of Olives.' Cf. Mk 14.26; Mt. 26.30.
[23]O'Connor, 'The Singing of Jesus', 435–6.
[24]Cf. O'Connor, 'The Singing of Jesus', 449–51.
[25]Augustine, *Enarrationes in Psalmos*, 85, I (PL37).
[26]Cf. O'Connor, 'The Singing of Jesus', 441, referring to Johann Mattheson, *Behauptung der Himmlischecn Musik aus den Grüden der Vernunft, Kirchen-Lehre und Heiliger Schrift* (Hamburg, 1747).
[27]Cf. Pierangelo Sequeri, *Musica e Mistica: Percorsi nella Storia Occidentale delle Pratiche Estetiche e Religiose* (Città del Vaticano: Libreria Editrice Vaticana, 2005). Sequeri's study exploring the spaces and ways in which music and mysticism are intertwined over the history of Western music is exceptional, and perhaps unsurpassed. In fact, as we shall see in chapter

communing with the incarnated spirit made in the image and likeness of the divine – will be an ongoing battlefield at the very centre of theology's quest to make sense of music. But as we shall see, theology's best thinkers rarely surrender the flesh to the spirit, even when the tools at their disposal are inadequate to the task at hand.

A musical cosmos

The other worldview that guides Christian thought on music emerged in sixth century BC's Pythagoras (570–495 BC), a Greek philosopher whose thought influenced Plato, Aristotle and through them much of Western thought. It is Pythagoras who is credited with discovering that when musical consonances are produced by vibrating strings, the length of the strings relate to one another by small integer ratios,[28] initiating music's connection with mathematics. Its most significant presentation is found in Boethius (c. 477–524), a fifth-century Roman senator and philosopher, considered one of the most important intermediaries between ancient philosophy and the Latin Middle Ages, who captured the place of music in and for the medieval worldview in a book called *De institutione musica*. Boethius distinguished between 'cosmic' music (*musica mundana*), 'human' music (*musica humana*) and 'instrumental' music (*musica instrumentalis*) to paint a picture of how essential music is to our understanding of the world. Of these, only the third category refers to music as we understand it! 'Cosmic' music is the music of the spheres resulting from celestial movement, also present in interrelationships between the seasons and the four elements; 'human' music represents the orderly interrelationship of body and soul and the coalescence of sense and reason; and 'instrumental' music is the human production of actually sounding music, whether produced by instrument or by voice.[29] This metaphysical worldview explains why music was included as one of the four subjects of the quadrivium of liberal arts education and, alongside arithmetic, as foundational to astronomy and geometry.

It is hard to exaggerate the centrality of music born of this understanding and its influence on Christian thought. Music was ontologically significant,

---

fifteen, Sequeri's thought on music and Christian theology is of the most nuanced I have found. Regrettably, little of his writing has been translated, as yet, into English.

[28]Cf. John Paul Ito, 'On Music, Mathematics and Theology: Pythagoras, the Mind and Human Agency', in *Resonant Witness: Conversations between Music and Theology*, ed. J. Begbie and S. R. Guthrie, 109–34 (110) (Grand Rapids, MI: William B. Eerdmans, 2011).

[29]Cf. Ito, 'On Music, Mathematics and Theology', 109–34 (111); Férdia J. Stone-Davis, *Musical Beauty: Negotiating the Boundary between Subject and Object* (Eugene, OR: Cascade Books, 2011), 1–25.

helped human understanding of the world and was a force for its harmonic working. This was a fundamentally theological worldview:

> a Christian world bursting with theological symbols but it was equally a Neo-Platonic world and an occultic one – indeed, in practice, the three were often interchangeable. What held this magical universe together was music. The ancient cosmos was literally en*chant*ed – it sang. The music of the spheres ordered the universe with its inaudible harmonies. It was truly an absolute music.[30]

This line of thought led Plato and Aristotle, in different ways, to take position on the importance and risk of music. For the former, music was not only a 'tool to form man's character' but an instrument 'for the right ordering of society's legal structure'.[31] However, not every kind of music! Plato warned against the unsettling effect of musical innovation, as lawlessness in art could lead to anarchy in society. Too much music would make a man 'effeminate', and in the ideal Republic he limited acceptable musical modes (Phrygian and Dorian), according to their effect on human character. For Aristotle, melodies and rhythms affect ethos, as music can imitate life and therefore affect character and behaviour.[32] Therefore, certain styles of music were appropriate for the training of leaders, and others not. While less nervous about musical styles than Plato, he reacted against the multiplication and complexity of musical styles and advised against too much professional training in music. In various ways, versions of these theories of music had an impact on Western education and music well into the seventeenth century through the influential astrologer and mathematical theorist Johannes Kepler's (1571–1630) laws of planetary motion in elliptic orbits around the sun,[33] colouring the beginnings of the first scientific revolution. As we shall see, this worldview only began to break down with Descartes.

Foundational figures

Of the Fathers and Mothers of the Church we know to be relevant to this theme, three stand out: the first is Clement of Alexandria (150–215),

---

[30]Daniel K. L. Chua, 'Music as the Mouthpiece of Theology', in *Resonant Witness: Conversations between Music and Theology*, ed. J. Begbie and S. R. Guthrie, 137–61 (139–40) (Grand Rapids, MI: William B. Eerdmans, 2011).
[31]Cf. Josef Pieper, *Only the Lover Sings: Art and Contemplation* (San Francisco: Ignatius Press, 1990), 17, referring to *The Republic*.
[32]Cf. Aristotle, *Politics* 8.5, quoted in Barbara Russano Hanning, *Concise History of Western Music*, ed. D. J. Grout, 3rd ed. (New York: W.W. Norton, 2006), 6–7.
[33] Cf. Johannes Kepler, *The Harmony of the World*, trans. E. J. Aiton, A. M. Duncan, and J. V. Field (Philadelphia, PA: American Philosophical Society, 1997); Bruce Stephenson, *The Music of the Heavens: Kepler's Harmonic Astronomy* (Princeton: Princeton University Press, 2014).

whose consideration of Jesus as the true Orpheus provided a Christian response to the prevailing musical cults and myths of enchanting deities in the milieu of ancient Egypt. Christ is the resurrection and the life, and therefore the New Song in person.[34] The second, from the Syriac tradition, is St Ephrem (c. 306–373), acknowledged as a great Syriac poet, preacher, rhetor and an excellent biblical commentator.[35] His contribution to the Church in the area of hymnody and women's role in a liturgical context is of particular interest.[36] The third, of course, is Augustine. Against the backdrop presented earlier, is it comprehensible that 'musicking' would have been suspect for him, linked as it was to pagan cult and theatres. Therefore, Augustine separated the practice of music from its study as an element of liberal education in the ordering of the cosmos and a reflection of Godself. His essay dedicated to music[37] has this latter focus (and only addresses rhythm, as Augustine never completed his planned treatise on harmony). For Augustine, 'God *is* music: he [*sic*] is the supreme measure, number, relation, harmony, unity and equality.'[38] Music is the very form and order given to creation, and as such, for Augustine, is at the very heart of life. As with every other aspect of his teaching, Augustine is aware of the fallen nature of humanity and the danger of being enslaved by a wrong use of anything good, rather than living in and through creation towards the Creator. From here, we can understand his well-known wariness of the enjoyment implicit in music, lest it distract and hold the creature's attention away from God. That being said, his discernment is actually quite pastoral, favouring music's use for the benefits afforded in bringing the affect towards God, as this quotation from his *Confessions* exemplifies: 'Thus I vacillate between the danger of sensuality and the undeniable benefits. Without pretending to a definitive opinion I am more inclined to approve the custom of singing in church, to the end that through the pleasures of the ear a weaker mind may rise up

---

[34]Cf. O'Connor, 'The Singing of Jesus', 449–51.
[35]Cf. Mor Polycarpus A. Aydin, 'A Wedding Feast of Song': St. Ephrem and the Singing Ministry of Women in the Church', in *Geschichte, Theologie, Liturgie und Gegenwartslage der Syrischen Kirchen. Beiträge zum sechsten Deutschen Syrologen-Symposium in Konstanz*, ed. D. Weltecke, 59–64 (1) (Wiesbaden: Harrassowitz Verlag, 2012).
[36]Cf. Aydin, 'A Wedding Feast of Song': St. Ephrem and the Singing Ministry of Women in the Church', 59–64. Mor Polycarpus A. Aydin, 'From the Pauline Admonition to Remain Silent to St. Ephrem's Creation of Women's Choirs in the Liturgy', in *Churches and Moral Discernment: Learning from History*, ed. M. Wijlens, V. Shmaliy, and S. Sinn, 221–32, Faith and Order Paper No. 229 (Oikoumene World Council of Churches Publications, 2021).
[37]Augustine, *De Musica*, ed. M. Jacobsson and L. J. Dorfbauer (Berlin: Walter de Gruyter, 2017).
[38]Carol Harrison, 'Augustine and the Art of Music', in *Resonant Witness: Conversations between Music and Theology*, ed. J. Begbie and S. R. Guthrie, 27–45 (31) (Grand Rapids, MI: William B. Eerdmans, 2011).

to loving devotion.'[39] Despite his language, which emphasizes reason over sense and calls for the use of music rather than its enjoyment, we cannot underestimate music's importance for Augustine. Music was the *first* theme he chose to write on after his conversion, and remained a means of transformation of the soul in its ascent 'through music', to God: 'The keyword for Augustine here is "through" (*per*): it is not by rejecting and dismissing music that he moves towards God, but in and "through" it.'[40] Another important if oft-overlooked element of Augustine's thought is how he identifies perfect music, *not* with that of the angels or immaterial neoplatonic notions of spiritual music without bodies, but rather as that of the resurrected bodies. In a passionate defence of the embodied nature of our lives now *and* in the eschaton, Augustine proclaims the 'happy alleluia' we shall sing when we are delivered of our anxious and worried state: 'how carefree, how safe from all opposition, where nobody will be an enemy, no one cease to be a friend!'[41] In this *jubilus* (or jubilation) of the resurrected bodies, Augustine enshrines his most important gift to a theology of music: 'perfect music is neither that of the vibrant bodies, nor that of the thinking minds, it is what will accompany the pure infinite spiritual vitality of our resurrected bodies.'[42]

Music as ministry in a medieval world

The twelfth and thirteenth centuries saw the infusion of the Western world with the thought of Aristotle and the intense intellectual dynamism invested in understanding and appropriating it. Still within an ordered worldview that included music, as theology advanced, music often functioned as a 'ministry discipline' that helped exemplify theological concepts to the people of the time, a 'paradigm for the abstract' for those who mind needed aid to grasp them. French theologian Phillip the Chancellor (1160–1236) typifies this use of music by not only using but possibly also composing music to enable people to grasp Christian faith in creation.[43] Musical style served theological purpose. For example, what later became known as 'polyphony' illustrated the theological principle of the pre-existent material from which

---

[39]Augustine, *Confessions*, ed. D. V. Meconi, trans. M. Boulding (San Francisco: Ignatius Press, 2007), 10.33.50.
[40]Harrison, 'Augustine and the Art of Music', 27–45 (43).
[41]Augustine, 'Sermon 356', in *The Works of Saint Augustine: A Translation for the 21st Century*, ed. J. E. Rotelle, 167–71 (170). (Brooklyn, NY: New City Press, 1990).
[42]Pierangelo Sequeri, 'Music and Resurrection', *Toronto Journal of Theology* 29, no. 2 (2013): 417–24 (420).
[43]Cf. Hans Tischler, *The Earliest Motets (to Circa 1270): A Complete Comparative Edition* (New Haven: Yale University Press, 1982), vol. I, 109–11; vol. III, 4, 59–60.

God created the world and a composer fashioned a multilayered piece of music.[44]

> Rather than simply connecting the arts and theology, Western music at crucial phases in its history drew its most significant stylistic principles from its clear ministry to make theological concepts comprehensible to the mind through the rationality of temporal time-lapse, to the eyes through musical notation, to the ears through the unseen substance of sound, and thus to the soul.[45]

The standout figure of the medieval world in relation to the intersection of theology and music, however, is Hildegard of Bingen (1098–1179), despite the fact that she is only mentioned in histories of music since the 1990s. Abbess of the Benedictine convent of Rupertsberg, her synthesis of thought and creativity manifests itself in an integrated vision of the cosmos, creation, redemption and lived faith expressed through words, music and praxis of life. Current fascination with this figure is not surprising,[46] and yet, even now, music is often left as a side note to the visions and writings of this exceptional woman who founded and governed monasteries, and advised bishops, popes and kings. Not so in her own understanding, however! Music is at the centre of her life, reflecting (and sustaining?) her prophetic insights. Her compositions include more than seventy hymns, sequences, antiphons, versicles and responsaries.[47] Her music played with range, rhythm and imagery in new ways, resembling the plainsong of her time but breaking the norms of that genre by jumping fourths and fifths (when chant did not usually exceed a third) and at times spanning two and half octaves (a much wider range than normal at that time). The influence of contemporary folk music is also tangible, and she used the popular genre of a sung verse play in Latin to create the earliest extant morality play we have record of: the

---

[44]Cf. Nancy Van Deusen, 'Material: Phillip the Chancellor and the Reception of Aristotle's Physics', in *Resonant Witness: Conversations between Music and Theology*, ed. J. Begbie and S. R. Guthrie, 46–64 (63–4) (Grand Rapids, MI: William B. Eerdmans, 2011).
[45]Deusen, 'Material: Phillip the Chancellor and the Reception of Aristotle's Physics', 46–64 (63).
[46]For example, Helen J. John, *Hildegard of Bingen: A New Twelfth-Century Woman Philosopher?* (JSTOR, 1992); Sabina Flanagan, *Hildegard of Bingen, 1098-1179: A Visionary Life*, 2nd ed. (London and New York: Routledge, 1998); Anne H. King-Lenzmeier, *Hildegard of Bingen: An Integrated Vision* (Collegeville, MN: Liturgical Press, 2001); Mary T. Malone, *Four Women Doctors of the Church. Hildegard of Bingen, Catherine of Siena, Teresa of Ávila, Thérèse of Lisieux* (Dublin: Veritas, 2015); John D. Dadosky, 'The Original Green Campaign: Dr. Hildegard of Bingen's Viriditas as Complement to Laudato Si', *Toronto Journal of Theology* 34, no. 1 (2018): 79–95.
[47]Cf. Tim Dowley, *Christian Music: A Global History* (Minneapolis, MN: Fortress Press, 2011), 62–3.

Ordo Virtutum.⁴⁸ Hildegard is known for her mystical writings⁴⁹ but she claimed that her songs, like her prose, were divinely inspired.⁵⁰ The radical understanding of human life as called to praise God, with the angels, through which the cosmos achieves its end, inseparably links her thought and music. She rereads the history of salvation and music in tandem: prophets not only sang inspired psalms but created musical instruments in humanity's quest to re-capture Paradise. While music notation followed the tradition of Augustine and Boethius in the quest for orderly and cogent argument, 'Hildegard ... used poetry and music to express a visionary "symphony of the harmonies of heavenly relations" ... Hildegard's is a lyricism of mystical immediacy'.⁵¹

The centrality of music in Hildegard's theological and doctrinal understanding is best exemplified in her response to a punishment imposed by the local bishop for allegedly having buried an excommunicated noble in the monastery grounds: the nuns were denied the sacraments of confession, the Eucharist and permission to worship through song.⁵² It is this last prohibition that draws forth her strongest words.

> She openly declares the irresponsible excess of a punishment that imposes on the nuns, without proportionate cause, to fail to obey divine law which commands the practice of the sacraments and the musical praxis of praise ... the *practice* of vocal and instrumental music, is a symbolic act which acts efficaciously on the human soul conforming it to the condition of a creature formed by God and destined to live with God, by the vibration of that original experience of praise that Adam once enjoyed ... [This punishment was] forcing the nuns to sin.⁵³

---

⁴⁸*The Virtues* (estimated 1151) is a non-liturgical allegoric play in which every character sings except the devil – a sign of his separation from God. Cf. Hildegard of Bingen, 'Ordo Virtutum: The Play of the Virtues by Hildegard of Bingen', in *Nine Medieval Latin Plays*, ed. P. Dronke, 147–84 (Cambridge: Cambridge University Press, 1994). This edition includes an introduction by the editor, Peter Dronke. Interestingly and without any sign of knowing Hildegard's work, C. S. Lewis extends this tradition in his profoundly theological children's book series, which portray Aslan (Jesus) as singing creation into existence while evil covers her ears as she cannot stand its beauty. Cf. Clive Staples Lewis, *The Chronicles of Narnia* (New York: Harper Collins, 2001).
⁴⁹Hildegard, *Hildegard of Bingen's Book of Divine Works: With Letters and Songs* (Santa Fe, NM: Bear & Co., 1987).
⁵⁰Hanning, *Concise History of Western Music*, 44.
⁵¹Richard Taruskin, *Retheorizing Music* (New York: Oxford University Press), 90–1. Hildegard's main work in which she gathered her music is called *Symphonia armonie celestium revelationum* (*Symphony of the Harmony of Heavenly Revelations*).
⁵²Hildegard, *Epi 1*, Lett XXIII, 61
⁵³Cf. Sequeri, *Musica e Mistica: Percorsi nella Storia Occidentale delle Pratiche Estetiche E Religiose*, 137–8. Translation mine.

In her words: 'Those who, without legitimate cause, force silence on those churches that usually sing to the honour of God, will not deserve to hear the admirable symphony of angels who will sing God's praise in heaven.'[54]

Thomas Aquinas (1224–74) wrote no treatise specifically on music, but his position can be gathered from comments in various writings. He shared the worldview of his time in which music was defined as the discipline that deals with numbers in their relationship to sounds. However, he rejected the Platonic–Pythagorean notion of music as connecting spheres and souls, considering music more of a skill than a fine art, studied within mathematics in the quadrivium. Aquinas maintained (as did his age) that the sounds of instruments are modelled on the human voice (*libros de anima*, ii, lesson 18) and focussed on the harmonic potential of music *consonantia sonorum* (in *libros de anima*, i, lesson 9) as an analogia for the ultimate harmony of God as three in perfect unity.[55] It is fair to note that although Aquinas valued music in worship for its capacity to turn humanity's affection to God,[56] and was, in fact, the author of a number of influential hymns on the Eucharist which are still sung today, the visual resonances of his influential understanding and description of beauty (integrity/unity, proportion/harmony and clarity) have marked the history of theological aesthetics until today.

Reformation theologies of music

Three central figures of the Reformation period took quite different positions on music's role in faith, human life and worship: Martin Luther (1483–1546), John Calvin (1509–64) and Huldrych Zwingli (1484–1531).[57] Despite the different conclusions they came to, for each of them music was an essential theme for consideration. They were all much more open to the aural symbolic representation of the Word than the visual, although Luther's dedication to music stands out. He regarded it as 'the greatest gift of God which has often induced and inspired me to preach' and which 'next to the Word of God . . . deserves the highest praise'.[58] His love of music was second only to theology, and in at least one instance he recognized music's potential

---

[54]Quoted in Sequeri, *Musica e Mistica: Percorsi nella Storia Occidentale delle Pratiche Estetiche E Religiose*, 138, note 14; translation mine.
[55]Cf. Edward Booth and S. Gallagher, 'Thomas Aquinas', *The New Grove Dictionary of Music and Musicians* (1980), 512.
[56]Aquinas, in *psalmos Davidis*, xxxii, 2.
[57]For a clear and nuanced presentation of the theological convergences and differences between these three figures, see chapter six of Jeremy Begbie, *Resounding Truth: Christian Wisdom in the World of Music* (London: SPCK, 2008).
[58]Richard J. Platinga, 'The Integration of Music and Theology in the Vocal Composition of J. S. Bach', in *Resonant Witness: Conversations between Music and Theology*, ed. J. Begbie and S. R. Guthrie, 215–39 (222), quoting Robin A. Leaver, 'Music and Lutheranism', in *The Cambridge Companion to Bach*, ed. J. Butt, 35–45 (40–1) (Cambridge University Press, 1997).

for preaching, challenging the age-old suspicion of music's appeal to the senses and effect on the Word.[59] It is unsurprising that this love of music gave Lutheran theology of music a distinct impulse and even clarity, although his position was understood in different ways and a Lutheran theology of music was only worked out over time, especially during the seventeenth-century debate between Lutherans and Calvinists.[60] During the sixteenth and seventeenth centuries, as the modal system gave way to the major–minor one with ensuing reflections on theological significance of triadic harmony, theology navigated its way through new themes in relation to music, such as music's power over emotion, affect and devotion; music's likeness to rhetoric and capacity to transmit faith; and (with the emergence of the Lutheran Pietism), a greater attention to the personal spirituality of composer, performer and listener than ever before. At the doorway of the West's shift of balance from church music to other forms of music, these theologians defend its importance for human life and Christian faith.

The discord of epistemological dissonance

Enter Descartes! Most theologians and theology students are aware of the epistemological challenges of the history of Western thought. What is less known is how this affected theology's understanding of music. The epistemological shifts initiated by Descartes' 'I think, therefore I am' built a Cartesian wall between interior and exterior worlds,[61] complicating for centuries the relationship between mind and world, reason and feeling, matter and the spirit, music and thought. This played out primarily in the dichotomy between vocal and instrumental music:

> From this dualistic perspective, instrumental music was relegated to the body because it had no concept for the mind to grasp; it was explained, instead, by Newtonian physics and was experienced as physiological vibrations. That could quite literally slacken one's moral fibers. Vocal music, on the other hand, emanated from the inner sanctum of the human being; the alignment of word and tone provided clear and distinct

---

[59]Cf. Joyce L. Irwin, '"So Faith Comes from What Is Heard": The Relationship between Music and God's Word in the First Two Centuries of German Lutheranism', in *Resonant Witness: Conversations between Music and Theology*, ed. J. Begbie and S. R. Guthrie, 65–82 (65), referring to Martin Luther, *Works*, ed. J. J. Pelikan and H. T. Lehmann, (Saint Louis: Concordia Pub. House, 1955), 54:129.
[60]Joyce L. Irwin, *Neither Voice for Heart Alone: German Lutheran Theology of Music in the Age of the Baroque* (New York: Peter Lang, 1993), chapter one.
[61]Cf. Ito, 'On Music, Mathematics and Theology', 109–34 (114).

concepts that signified the presence of the thinking 'I am' that was the moral identity of the Cartesian self.[62]

At times, the history of thought and music weaves so closely together that it is impossible to differentiate or to identify in which direction the influence is stronger. Such is the case in the shift from the medieval world to the modern one: the metamorphosis from a mythical world in which the universe (literally, not figuratively) sang its order according to divine creation[63] to one in which that centre-point shifts to humanity's much debated 'soul' is perhaps only best reflected in the desperation of Friedrich Nietzsche's madman.[64] But it is a musical story as much as a rational one, in which musical theorists and sociocultural thinkers (often overlapping roles in the one person)[65] pave the way for or echo philosophy's core tenets. Because music was so literally understood in the premodern divinely created world, held together in harmony and tuned by God's harmonic hand, as the modern world began to define itself without (and against) God, one would expect music's demise to follow. Instead, in a myriad of ways, music became theology's surrogate in expressing the transcendent and giving access to the divine. And this not only in some vague, nostalgic reinterpretation of musical taste but in verifiable steps of modernity's self-understanding.

In brief, its key players: it was Galileo's father, Vincenzo Galilei (1520–91), who first 'broke the Pythagorean monochord' theory of the universe held together through music, through a series of experiments that landed music solidly in the acoustic nature of the external world. This led to an attempt to move the study of music from the scientific space of the quadrivium to the humanities' trivium, but more importantly, it inaugurated a split in the nature of sound, with music as an external factor of nature and scientific study, on one hand, and music as the inner expression of moral will, on the other. 'This epistemic division is the source of a historical dialectic in music history, pitting tone against word, voice against instrument, and harmony against melody.'[66] Herein lies philosophy's fascination with language, its origin and translation during the eighteenth and nineteenth centuries. And so, the history of thought played out with the quest for the uprooted soul (and its eventual abandonment).

---

[62]Chua, 'Music as the Mouthpiece of Theology', 137–61 (146).
[63]'When music moved, the earth moved with it.' Chua, 'Music as the Mouthpiece of Theology', 137–61 (140).
[64]For the notion of the universe's disenchantment as the interpretative key of modernity, see German sociologist Max Weber, 'Science as a Vocation', in *From Max Weber Essays in Sociology*, ed. H. H. Gerth, C. W. Mills, and B. S. Turner, 129–56 (Milton Park, Abingdon, Oxon: Routledge, 2009).
[65]For an exceptional overview and analysis of key moments and thinkers in this shift, see Chua, 'Music as the Mouthpiece of Theology', 137–61.
[66]Chua, 'Music as the Mouthpiece of Theology', 137–61 (143).

These polar positions are well framed in the figures of Jean-Philippe Rameau (1683–1764) and Jean-Jacques Rousseau (1712–1878). Rameau, composer and music theorist, echoes the experimental physiology of his age by presenting the body as a '*corps sonore*', a kind of harmonic resonator for the particles of nature. He constructs a theory of musical harmony that grounds the place of instrumental music in Western music for centuries. Rousseau, mostly known for his contributions to political philosophy, also an active composer and music theorist, defends melody – against harmony – as the voice of the soul, leading him to explore the nature of language itself, a focus of study at the time. For him, vocal music was a weapon against the materialism that was eroding humanity's moral fibre.[67] This polemic affects philosophy and theology alike. Immanuel Kant (1724–1804) solidifies the epistemological divide, laying the foundations for the Age of Enlightenment's shift from the en*chant*ed cosmos to reasonable hu*man*ity as the centre of the universe, with its commitment to inductive thinking as the sole authoritative voice. Rousseau's influence on Kant is widely recognized.[68] Within Kant's quest for how fine art contributes to knowledge, his stance on music is unclear and even inconsistent, but ultimately negative:

> Those who have recommended the singing of spiritual songs as part of the domestic rites of worship have not considered that means of such a noisy (and precisely for that reason usually Pharisaical) form of worship they have imposed a great inconvenience on the public, for they have forced the neighbourhood to join in their singing or to give up their own train of thought.[69]

> The dominant attitude of the *Critique of Judgment* is that music intrudes upon thought. It equates music primarily with sound rather than with tonal organization, thus classifies it as mere sensation, and denies its contribution to cognition. . . . By denying that music is anything but sensory Kant denies its involvement with reflection, disallows its connection with pure aesthetic judgment and thereby cognition in general, and precludes its inclusion amongst the fine arts. It is for this reason that Kant even refers to music, as noise, distracting the mind from thought.[70]

---

[67]For a summary of the conflict between them and its effect on the unfolding of modernity's self-understanding, see Daniel K. L. Chua, *Absolute Music and the Construction of Meaning* (Cambridge, UK: Cambridge University Press, 1999); Chua, 'Music as the Mouthpiece of Theology', 137–61 (146–59).
[68]Chua, 'Music as the Mouthpiece of Theology', 137–61 (153, note 51).
[69]Immanuel Kant, *Critique of the Power of Judgment*, vol. 53, 5:330, n. 1 (Cambridge: Cambridge University Press, 2000), 207.
[70]Stone-Davis, *Musical Beauty*, 79. For Stone-Davis' thorough exploration and critique of Kant's position, see pages 79–157.

While Kant is not usually cited as significant in relation to music's link with theology, he had a marked influence on the history of Western thought on music. His definition of *Geist* (soul) as 'self-maintaining' and of the creative genius as one who 'prescribes the law to himself' finds a sonic reflection in the early Romantics' definition of instrumental music's autonomy as 'independent and free . . . it prescribes its own laws to itself'.[71] By separating and subordinating the aesthetic to the rational, the door opened for Romanticism's (and opera's) pushback by raising the importance of affect, emotion and music, leading to the nineteenth-century enthronement of absolute music as a substitute for divine revelation. It is the beginning of a chasm that Christian philosophy and theology is still struggling to overcome. This dialectic between romantic and idealistic aesthetics interweaves the history of thought and music for the next few centuries. From Rousseau we can trace influences on Wilhelm Heinrich Wackenroder (1773–98), Friedrich Schleiermacher and expressionist understandings of music. Building on (and reacting against) Rameau's harmonic theories we find Eduard Hanslick's *On the Musically Beautiful,* Schopenhauer, Nietzsche, Karl Barth and Richard Wagner. Both strands of thought lead to modern music's counter-reaction and the twentieth-century overturning of the tonal system.

A syncopated story: Key figures

I shall pick up the threads of the West's music–theological story in chapter three, but against this backdrop, the influence of music on some key Christian thinkers of the past two centuries is worthy of mention. In choosing these figures, my intent is double: to show the presence and importance of music in their lives, in line with the strands of reflection just outlined, and as a consequence of this, on their thought.[72] A comprehensive overview is impossible, but Schleiermacher, Schopenhauer and Kierkegaard from the nineteenth century, and Barth, Balthasar and Bonhoeffer from the twentieth century give a pretty clear overview of just how central music has been to theology's development as we know it.

Friedrich Schleiermacher (1768–1834) is considered the most outstanding theologian of the nineteenth century[73] and the father of

---

[71]Cf. Chua, 'Music as the Mouthpiece of Theology', 137–61 (155).
[72]Philip Stoltzfus' exceptional work is a reference point here. By exploring the musical-aesthetic approaches and connections between music and theological performance in three key thinkers of the twentieth century, he uncovers how they acknowledge, 'in startlingly blunt fashion, the impact of music not only upon their lived experience, but also upon their methodological outlook and writing style'. Stoltzfus, *Theology as Performance*, 2. The authors Stoltzfus focusses on are Friedrich Schleiermacher, Karl Barth and Ludwig Wittgenstein.
[73]David Ford, *The Modern Theologians: An Introduction to Christian Theology in the Twentieth Century, Volume 2* (Blackwell, 1989), 973. Stanley J. Grenz and Roger E. Olson, in *20th Cen-*

modern theology,[74] for his response to contemporary reductive opinions or outright rejections of Christianity and his attempts to craft an accessible and more truthful understanding of Christian faith. Based on his view of religion as neither primarily a system of beliefs nor moral standards but rather as *Gefühl* – 'an immediate self-consciousness or feeling of absolute dependence on God'[75] – he inaugurated an essential rethinking of Christian faith and Christology in relational terms rather than rational ones.[76] He pioneered modern hermeneutics[77] and reformulated the place of religion and theology in university education. Where and how did music fit into and/or condition his thought? Steeped in the experience of music's educational influence, both as a listener and as a performer, his formative years were nurtured and shaped by Moravian piety, a deeply musical spirituality with a strong emphasis on song as the best expression of truth and hymn-singing by heart as an expression of Christian feeling.[78] Schleiermacher delighted in the music of Mozart and Beethoven, frequently losing himself 'sunken in the notes', and he explicitly attributes the inspiration of his writing on a *Christmas Eve Celebration* to a recital attended in Halle by the blind flautist Friedrich Dulon on 2 December 1805.[79] Not surprisingly, this charming classic – the only place Schleiermacher explicitly writes about music – holds the key to Schleiermacher's understanding of music's place in Christian knowledge and believing. Music is the art that can best express the religious dimension of the human person: 'every fine feeling comes completely to the fore only when we have found the right musical expression for it . . . it is precisely to religious feeling that music is most closely related.'[80] Both music and religion facilitate a direct, or rather pre-descriptive, awareness of self.[81] From a theoretical perspective,

---

tury *Theology: God & the World in a Transitional Age*, Twentieth-Century Theology (Downers Grove, IL: InterVarsity Press, 1992), 39 refer to Schleiermacher as being 'to Christian theology what Newton is to physics, what Freud is to psychology, and what Darwin is to biology.'
[74]Jeremy Begbie, 'Three Musical Theologians', *Resounding Truth: Christian Wisdom in the World of Music*, 141–62 (141–2 referring to London: SPCK, 2008).
[75]David Ford, *The Modern Theologians: An Introduction to Christian Theology in the Twentieth Century*, 3rd ed. (Oxford and New York, NY: Blackwell, 2013), 994–5.
[76]His main work in this regard is Friedrich Schleiermacher, *Christian Faith: A New Translation and Critical Edition*, ed. T. N. Tice (Louisville, KY: Westminster John Knox Press, 2016).
[77]Cf. Friedrich Schleiermacher, *Hermeneutics: The Handwritten Manuscripts*, ed. H. Kimmerle (Atlanta, Georgia: Scholars Press, 1977); Friedrich Schleiermacher, *Hermeneutics and Criticism and Other Writings*, ed. A. Bowie (Cambridge, UK and New York: Cambridge University Press, 1998).
[78]Cf. Stoltzfus, *Theology as Performance*, 52.
[79]See Tice's introductory note to this classic writing on Christmas for the significance of the presence of music in the scene and the character most representative of Schleiermacher himself: Josef Friedrich Schleiermacher, *Christmas Eve Celebration: A Dialogue*, trans. T. N. Tice (Eugene, OR: Cascade Books, 2010), ix–xxv.
[80]Schleiermacher, *Christmas Eve Celebration: A Dialogue*, 29.
[81]Albert L. Blackwell, 'The Role of Music in Schleiermacher's Writings', in *Internationaler Schleiermacher-Kongress Berlin 1984*, ed. Kurt-Victor Selge, 439–48 (443) (Berlin: de Gruyter, 1985).

he consciously opted for expressionist approaches to music against formalist options current at the time. His understanding of faith shows its dependence on the writing of Romanticism's Wackenroder:[82] while never conflating music with language about God, Schleiermacher drew on musical analogies to address the issue of theological expression of the divine. He held up music as the ideal paradigm for understanding the character of the linguistic act, 'a public, communicative activity, which nevertheless has the unique character of corresponding to the interior of life – its tonic, notes, modulations, sequences, phrases, and so consciousness itself is structured along the lines of musical affectivity'.[83] His thought on faith is inseparable from his experience of and comprehension of music, and his influence on contemporary understanding of both is hard to overestimate. It is only surprising that so many writings on this foundational thinker in Western theology ignore this connection.

From a very different theological backdrop, Arthur Schopenhauer (1788–1860) proposed that music expresses metaphysical truth more directly than traditional philosophy does. Writing in the era of German romanticism and *against* philosophy's rationalist idealism, he defends the fundamental irrationality of the world and the priority of moral and aesthetic perception as access points to the essence of reality. He separates music from the other arts as the highest art form, a non-representational and non-propositional art, situated on the side of the subject rather than as a neoplatonic mirror of reality, expressing the inner nature of the Will itself and allowing us access to the inner essence of reality.[84] Apart from his influence on the literary and theological world, Schopenhauer influenced composers such as Johannes Brahms, Antonín Dvorák, Gustav Mahler, Hans Pfitzner, Arnold Schönberg and Richard Wagner.

Søren Kierkegaard's (1813–55) position on music is the most paradigmatic in holding together spirit and matter: music expresses sensuality in its immediacy. 'In elemental sensuous-erotic originality, music has its absolute theme. This, of course, does not mean that music cannot express anything else, but nevertheless this is its theme proper.'[85] His position is based on an analysis of Mozart's opera *Don Giovanni*,[86] a parable of erotic beguilement

---

[82]Cf. Wilhelm Heinrich Wackenroder, *Confessions and Fantasies* (University Park, PN: Penn State University Press, 1971).
[83]Stoltzfus, *Theology as Performance*, 71.
[84]His thought on music runs through both volumes of Arthur Schopenhauer, *The World as Will and Representation*, trans. E. F. J. Payne (New York: Dover Publications, 1969). For an accessible presentation of this thought, see chapter VII of Anthony Storr, *Music and the Mind* (New York: Ballantine Books, 1997), 128–49.
[85]Søren Kierkegaard, 'The Immediate Erotic Stages or the Musical-Erotic', in *Kierkegaard's Writing, III, Part I*, ed. H. V. Hong and E. H. Hong, 45–136 (65), *Either/Or* (Princeton University Press, 1987).
[86]There is considerable debate about Kierkegaard's position on music. A case can be made that the position of his Pseudonym A in *Either/Or* is a deliberate misinterpretation of the religious

in which the form (music) perfectly expresses the opera's content (seduction for seduction's sake). This stance is founded on Kierkegaard's understanding of how language works: when something is defined, that which is excluded in the naming of a fact is also, by way of a reverse kind of logic, defined. In this way, sensuality is defined by Christianity: it existed before, of course, but its place as 'outside' the Spirit is defined by the Christian logos and understanding.[87] Music expresses the sensuous immediacy which language cannot express.[88] This explains, in his view, why the development of music is linked to Christianity and why it is such an object of suspicion for religious practitioners: 'the more rigorous the religiousness, the more music is given up and words are emphasized.'[89] It also relates to the fact that music does not exist except in time, 'it actually exists only when it is being performed. . . . It is indeed a demonstration that it is a higher, a more spiritual art'.[90] Kierkegaard was the first of many to discuss the theological significance of Mozart's music (a lead Barth, Küng and Balthasar would follow), threatening to 'stir up the entire church from custodian to consistory' to get them to recognize that among all the great men, Mozart was the greatest. Failing that, he would 'take his leave? Sever relations with "their communion," and found a sect which would not only exalt Mozart but honor only him'.[91] On a more serious and perhaps more sinister note, Kierkegaard leads the way in conflating music and woman in the opposition of matter versus spirit. Even avoiding anachronic bias, it is hard to deny that 'while Kierkegaard's successors will laud Mozart's powers of harmonizing opposites, [his own text] reinforces a different yet parallel strain within the tradition – music's dangerous, gendered, engendering powers . . . the erotic sensuality oozing from Don Giovanni validates the predictions of church authorities across history – listening to sensual music leaves one soft, weak, womanish'.[92]

Finally, there are some twentieth-century theological giants whose attention to music is both significant and underestimated. Karl Barth's (1886–1968) love of Mozart is well documented.[93] He left written testimony

---

undertones of the Opera in order to suggest that passion can be a proper theme of music. Cf. Shao Kai Tseng, 'Kierkegaard and Music in Paradox? Bringing Mozart's Don Giovanni to Terms with Kierkegaard's Religious Life-View', *Literature and Theology* 28, no. 4 (2014): 411–24 (422).
[87] Kierkegaard, 'The Immediate Erotic Stages or the Musical-Erotic', 45–136 (67).
[88] Kierkegaard, 'The Immediate Erotic Stages or the Musical-Erotic', 45–136 (71).
[89] Kierkegaard, 'The Immediate Erotic Stages or the Musical-Erotic', 45–136 (72).
[90] Kierkegaard, 'The Immediate Erotic Stages or the Musical-Erotic', 45–136 (68–9).
[91] Quoted in Karl Barth, *Wolfgang Amadeus Mozart*, trans. C. K. Pott (Grand Rapids, MI: William B. Eerdmans, 1986), 27.
[92] Epstein, *Melting the Venusberg*, 45–6.
[93] Cf. Theodore A. Gill, 'Barth and Mozart', *Theology Today* 43, no. 3 (1986): 403–11 (403); Philip Edward Stoltzfus, 'Barth on Music as Timelessly Valid Form', in *Theology as Performance: Music, and God in Western Thought*, 113–18 (New York: T&T Clark International, 2006).

to Mozart's effect on both his spirituality and theology.[94] Barth named two mystical experiences related to Mozart: one at the age of five or six upon hearing Mozart played by his father on the piano; the other, in a concert towards the end of his life, an apparition of some sort that brought him to tears.[95] Barth also explored *what is was* about Mozart's music that made it so special and where it converged with his theological vision: Mozart was neither intent on personal self-expression (like Beethoven) nor trying to communicate a message or doctrine in musical form (like Bach).[96] He simply made music and in fact is the best comprehensive expression of music in the eighteenth century, because he combined creative genius with a willingness to explore and express the best musical tenets of his time. For Barth, Mozart composes out of 'an objective "hearing" and "seeing" of reality. The vast, interconnected world of space and time standing over against the perceiving subject is the origin of musical impartiality'.[97] The influence of Hanslick's formalist aesthetics is clear, which converge with the theological frameworks Barth worked out of, underlining the priority of the divine over the human, and against the validity of an 'analogy of being' that allowed theology to work its way from the human to the divine. Barth reacted against the romantic expressionism of Rousseau underpinning Schleiermacher's concept of God and which, Barth thinks, 'found its disastrous end in Beethoven, Schubert, Mendelssohn, Wagner, liberal Protestantism, and royalist and Nazi absolutism'.[98]

However, in his appreciation and evaluation of Mozart's music Barth seems to contradict his own stated theological method, giving Mozart a place in the doctrines of creation and eschatology.[99] He concedes the possibility of what he called 'parables of God's kingdom' found in the world and names Mozart's music as one (in an essay eloquently entitled *How I Changed my Mind*): 'The golden sounds and melodies of Mozart's music have always spoken to me not as gospel but as parables of the realm of God's free grace revealed in the gospel – and they do so again and again with great spontaneity and directness.'[100]

Furthermore, Barth's love of Mozart was more than anecdotal preference but an intrinsic and reasoned element in his process of producing theological

---

[94]He wrote a series of essays on Mozart while in the process of writing the third volume of *Church Dogmatics*. Cf. Barth, *Wolfgang Amadeus Mozart*.
[95]Stoltzfus, 'Barth on Music', 114.
[96]Cf. Barth, *Wolfgang Amadeus Mozart*, 37, in *The Zwingli-Kalender* (Basel: Friedrich Reinhardt, 1956).
[97]Stoltzfus, *Theology as Performance*, 146.
[98]Stoltzfus, *Theology as Performance*, 138. According to Stoltzfus, Barth is strongly influenced by Eduard Hanslick, *On the Musically Beautiful: A Contribution towards the Revision of the Aesthetics of Music*, trans. G. Payzant, 8th ed. (Indianapolis: Hackett, 1986).
[99]Cf. Stoltzfus, 'Barth on Music', 147.
[100]Karl Barth, *How I Changed My Mind* (Richmond: John Knox Press, 1966), 71–2.

texts: 'I have for years and years begun each day with Mozart, and only then (aside from the daily newspaper) turned to my Dogmatics. I even have to confess that if I get to heaven, I would first of all seek out Mozart and only then inquire after Augustine, St Thomas, Luther, Calvin, and Schleiermacher.'[101] For those who have ears to hear, that awareness influences his writing style and method as 'quintessentially aesthetic' rather than 'scientific' (as Barth himself held),[102] in sonata form: 'first theme, second theme, exposition and development, recapitulation, and coda, ad lib'.[103] However, these musically attuned interpreters of Barth's theology are in the minority: as the impact of Mozart on Barth is immensely underestimated, most commentators sideline music to an anecdote or overlook it entirely.[104]

Hans Urs von Balthasar (1905–88) is a more complex figure (whose work is explored in chapter seven). An accomplished musician (reportedly able to play all of Mozart's piano pieces by heart and who had considered music as a possible career), Balthasar only wrote twice on music, but they are significant: his very first academic publication, called *The Development of the Musical Idea. An Attempt at a Synthesis of Music*,[105] and a short and intense *Tribute to Mozart*.[106] The former, while immature in comparison to his later opus, is perhaps a testimony to a first, if always undeclared, love?

> Music is the most incomprehensible art because it is the most immediate one. It questions us more directly, penetrating deeper in us than the others. But is it not perhaps this closeness that makes it an eternal enigma, which has always moved us to fix its limits, to regulate it, to force it into numbers and express it endlessly in laws?[107]

The second is a remarkable, unexplained ode to the music of Mozart as an echo of creation transfigured and redeemed, along the same lines as Barth (who was one of Balthasar's main theological influencers). Despite

---

[101] Barth, *Wolfgang Amadeus Mozart*, 16, quoting 'A Testimonial to Mozart', in the Round Robin in the *Neue Zürcher Zeitung*, 13 February 1955.
[102] Gill, 'Barth and Mozart', 403–11.
[103] George Hunsinger, *How to Read Karl Barth: The Shape of His Theology* (New York: Oxford University Press, 1991). Isolde Andrews, on the other hand, finds in Barth a 'latent deconstructive character' comparable to Derrida's approach to thought and grounds Barth's love of Mozart on his delight at the upsetting of expected forms. Isolde Andrews, *Deconstructing Barth: A Study of the Complementary Methods in Karl Barth and Jacques Derrida* (New York: Peter Lang, 1996).
[104] There are a few noteworthy exceptions: Arthur C. Cochrane's piece, 'On the Anniversaries of Mozart, Kierkegaard and Barth', in *Scottish Journal of Theology* 9 U956V. 2.51–63); Robert J. Palma, *Karl Barth's Theology of Culture: The Freedom of Culture for the Praise of God* (Eugene OR: Wipf and Stock, 1983).
[105] Hans Urs von Balthasar, *Die Entwicklung der Musikalischen Idee. Versuch einer Synthese der Musik* (Braunschweig, 1925). To my knowledge, this writing is as yet not translated into English.
[106] Hans Urs von Balthasar, 'Tribute to Mozart', *Communio* 28, no. 2 (2001): 398–9.
[107] Balthasar, *Lo sviluppo dell'idea musicale*, 13.

bringing theological aesthetics as a discipline back into the heart of Catholic systematic theology, Balthasar always remained suspicious of a theology grounded on anthropological premises or measured by human standards and never pulled the threads of the theological importance of music. The most he achieved was a metaphorical explanation of how a Christian worldview navigates diversity in an essay on truth as necessarily plural, or symphonic:

> In his revelation, God performs a symphony, and it impossible to say which is richer: the seamless genius of his composition or the polyphonous orchestra of Creation that he has prepared to play it. Before the Word of God became man, the world orchestra was 'fiddling' about without any plan: worldviews, religions, different concepts of the state, each one playing to itself. Somehow there is the feeling that this cacophonous jumble is only a 'tuning up': the A can be heard through everything, like a kind of promise. 'In many and various ways God spoke of old to our fathers by the prophets . . . ' (Heb. 1.1). Then came the Son, the 'heir of all things', for whose sake the whole orchestra had been put together. As it performs God's symphony under the Son's direction, the meaning of its variety becomes clear.[108]

His suspicion of the human underlies, perhaps, his position on artistic creativity, in which he poses the incompatibility of the artistic and Christian vocations, because the former demands complete surrender and obedience to God while the latter complete surrender to creative freedom.[109] Is it unreasonable to intuit here an internal conflict in the musical theologian Balthasar was? Balthasar knew that without beauty, theology was lame, unfinished, incomplete and yet could not reconcile, much less explain, the theological importance of music – be it that of Mozart or his own. In Balthasar, was the artist perhaps stifled by the theologian?

The last twentieth-century theologian that this chapter highlights brings a different musical influence on theological activity. Dietrich Bonhoeffer (1906–45) brought not only what we term the classics in music into theological reflection but also the 'spirituals' and other music of Afro-American roots which he encountered during his time studying in New York.[110] In fact, some link his exposure to Afro-American communities and music while in the United States to the sociopolitical awareness of his thought, as we shall see in chapter eleven. Another accomplished musician who considered a career as a pianist before choosing a life in ministry and theology, Bonhoeffer's love

---

[108]Hans Urs von Balthasar, Truth Is Symphonic: Aspects of Christian Pluralism (San Francisco: Ignatius Press, 1987), 8.
[109]Cf. Pierangelo Sequeri, *Anti-Prometeo. Il Musicale nell'estetica Teologica di Hans Urs von Balthasar* (Milano: Glossa, 1995), 72.
[110]Begbie, 'Three Musical Theologians', 141–62 (156–62).

for a variety of musical genres followed him his whole life. On the one hand, he had a pastorally informed position on music in church and worship, preferring the 'unity, clarity and simplicity' of unison singing in Christian worship, rejecting harmonization so as to prioritize words over music, and speaking of some music as appropriate to the church (referring to Bach) and others not so much (the Romantics).[111] On the other hand, he 'bemoaned the Nazis' demonic use of the romantic German tradition (Beethoven, Wagner, and others)'.[112] In his early writings, Bonhoeffer situated music in the first of Christ's four commands: labour, marriage, government and church. Later, he resituates it in the broad area of freedom, along with the other arts, education (or cultural formation), friendship and play. His commitment to justice ran also to his understanding of music's power: hymn-singing must serve truth and the struggle for freedom, and not decorate it: 'only he who cries out for the Jew may sing Gregorian chants'.[113]

It is towards the end of his life that we find the richest vein of theological thought influenced by music, emerging from time in prison for his part in an assassination attempt on Hitler. Bonhoeffer writes eloquently of musical memory, which seems to have accompanied his writing during that period: 'the music we hear inwardly can almost surpass, if we really concentrate on it, what we hear physically'.[114] He developed two notions with theological resonance: the *cantus firmus* of God's love that lays the foundation for all others, and what he called the 'polyphony of life'. The first compares one's love for God to the firm foundational tone that allows every other love take its place: 'God wants us to love him eternally with our whole hearts – not in such a way as to injure or weaken the other parts, but to provide a kind of *cantus firmus* to which the other melodies of life provide the counterpoint.'[115] This is developed into the interweaving of voices that polyphony develops, where various melodies can sound together without conflating into one but for the enhancement of the music, with a Christological application in terms of the divine and human natures: 'the two are "undivided and yet distinct" . . . like Christ in his divine and human natures'. He asks: 'May not the attraction and importance of polyphony in music consist in its being a musical reflection of this Christological fact and therefore of our *vita Christiana*?'[116]

---

[111] Dietrich Bonhoeffer, *Life Together* (London: SCM Press, 1954).
[112] Cf. Begbie, 'Three Musical Theologians', 141–62 (157).
[113] John W. De Gruchy, *Christianity, Art, and Transformation: Theological Aesthetics in the Struggle for Justice* (Cambridge, UK: Cambridge University Press, 2001), 138–9.
[114] Dietrich Bonhoeffer, *Letters and Papers from Prison*, ed. E. Bethge (London: SCM Press, 1971), 240.
[115] Bonhoeffer, *Letters and Papers from Prison*, 303.
[116] Begbie, 'Three Musical Theologians', 141–62 (156–62).

There are other voices we could hear, such as Ludwig Wittgenstein or Michel Foucault,[117] but I suggest the point is made: the inseparable nature of music, faith and theology challenges anachronic and historically biased positions which have allowed theology to marginalize music to spaces below or above itself (too worldly or too transcendent, depending on the tactic employed). Reunifying these realms, albeit with a historically systematic and integrated approach to theological method, is a core task if the theology of the future is to fulfil its role for the academy, the churches and society at large. But before I explore how, it is time to move to the other side of this history of theology, as seen through the lens of music.

Selected further reading

Balthasar, Hans Urs von. 'Tribute to Mozart'. *Communio* 28, no. 2 (2001): 398–99.

Barth, Karl. *Wolfgang Amadeus Mozart*. Translated by Clarence K. Pott. Grand Rapids, MI: William B. Eerdmans, 1986.

Begbie, Jeremy, and Steven R. Guthrie. *Resounding Truth: Christian Wisdom in the World of Music*. London: SPCK, 2008.

Benson, Bruce Ellis. *The Improvisation of Musical Dialogue: A Phenomenology of Music*. Cambridge: Cambridge University Press, 2003.

Chua, Daniel K. L. *Absolute Music and the Construction of Meaning*. Cambridge: Cambridge University Press, 1999.

Epstein, Heidi. *Melting the Venusberg: A Feminist Theology of Music*. New York: Continuum, 2004.

Lynch, Danielle Anne. *God in Sound and Silence: Music as Theology*. Eugene, OR: Pickwick Publications, 2018.

Schleiermacher, Friedrich. *Christmas Eve Celebration: A Dialogue*. Translated by Terrence N. Tice. Eugene, OR: Cascade Books, 2010. 1805.

Small, Christopher. *Music of the Common Tongue: Survival and Celebration in African American Music*. Hanover, NH: University Press of New England, 1987.

Small, Christopher. *Musicking: The Meanings of Performing and Listening*. Hanover, NH: University Press of New England, 1998.

---

[117]Cf. Tom Beaudoin, 'I Was Imprisoned by Subjectivity and You Visited Me: Bonhoffer and Foucault on the Way to a Postmodern Christian Self', in *Witness to Dispossession: The Vocation of a Postmodern Theologian*, 103–22 (Maryknoll, NY: Orbis Books, 2008).

3

Unsung sources

Theology in the public square of music-making

Unsung sources

We turn our attention now to this same history of theological thought from the perspective of music and as traced *by* music, seeking the oft-unknown theological dimensions of music's history and development. Music in theology tends to be classified as liturgical, sacred or secular, as if those boundaries were clear, but from a historical perspective, they are not. In fact, in the bigger picture and in line with our understanding of musicking as a relational and identity-constituting event, their histories overlap and intertwine in ways that defy the clear distinctions we place between current genres of music. Our focus here is broad: the theological history of music. This implies a particular focus on Western music as the context within which theology developed for centuries, but situated within the broader setting of music in the origins of human life and language, on the one hand, and the current global and plural phenomenon of contemporary musicking, on the other. When has theology influenced music in a way that we can name and map? There are composers some herald as theologians (although our approach would problematize this view) and genres we would not immediately associate with theology that have emerged from a context with deep theological resonances and as an explicit attempt to make sense of faith.[1] Other musical movements are theologically significant in how they distance themselves from the divine! Our

---

[1] In quite different ways, one can think of Bach, or Palestrina, or the gospel and blues music that emerged from Afro-American faith communities.

quest is to highlight key moments and movements – as in our last chapter, genres and figures – so as to bring to light that there is nothing untheological about the history of music and that its complete separation from theological investigation is a false position.

Our starting point is music's place in human communication and religious sentiment across the world religions: music is interwoven into the origins of language, in all likelihood preceding and facilitating its appearance. Music is also an inseparable element of every major world religion. As modernity unfolded against the backdrop of a Eurocentric world view, 'a small group of intellectuals decided that the irreligious condition of *man* is *his* natural condition',[2] but we have since come to realize that the sacred and secular cohabited happily for tens of thousands of years before secularization's relatively short lifespan, and in many parts of the earth, still do. Sound, rhythm, dance, chant and religion are essential and interwoven elements in every known culture across the world. This has oft been read through a classicist lens comparing myth-based rituals with the more 'sophisticated' musicking of developed religious systems – as if awaiting their development and imitation – but such a position is at worst, arrogant and at best, untrue. However, it is a deeply embedded bias that has shaped theology's understanding of music in manifold ways and inhibited its vision and understanding of what the musical world had and has to offer.[3] The culturally contextual nature of all theological investigation and the historically conditioned character of human understanding invite us to reach into musicking of all types to find its *theologal*[4] soul, without which it would not have come to be. As with chapter two, here too, I shall look at world views, musical trends and specific composers or musicians in three broad sections: the creation myths and understanding of music in world religions (including Christianity's first millennium); the history of 'classical' music in the second millennium CE;[5] and the reaction and responses of

---

[2] Cf. Pierangelo Sequeri, *La Qualità Spirituale: Esperienza nella Fede nel Crocevia Contemporaneo* (Casale Monferrato: Piemme, 2001), 58–9; translation and emphasis mine.

[3] Another bias or blind spot that has conditioned and limited the history of theologies of music is the lack of a feminist critical framework and analysis of both theology and musicology – not unlike the history of musicology, if slower to react. I shall return to this later in the chapter. Cf. Heidi Epstein, *Melting the Venusberg: A Feminist Theology of Music* (New York: Continuum, 2004).

[4] This word does not exist in English but is used in other Latin-based languages as distinct from theological to refer to those virtues explicitly dependant on God, rather than human reason. Faith, hope and charity, for example, are the *theologal* – not theological – virtues, in Spanish or Italian, finding their roots in the very same Latin word *theologia*, which in English becomes (only) 'theological'. The resonance is different. Since the notion of what is and is not currently understood as theological work emerged in the early Middle Ages and was consolidated in scholasticism, I propose the recovery of this broader meaning would be helpful.

[5] In referring to classical music, I am using the term in the broad, more generic sense of music born of the European-American tradition of music often understood as meaning the opposite of light or popular music. Cf. 'classical' in Kennedy, Michael, and Joyce Bourne Kennedy. *The Concise Oxford Dictionary of Music*. 5th ed. (Oxford: Oxford University Press, 2007).

modern music, from both within and beyond that same Euro-American music tradition.

In the beginning was sound

Let's start with creation myths. In *every* description of the genesis of the world, an acoustic element accompanies that moment, accentuating one of two symbolic elements, depending on the philosophical background within which it is expressed – energy (vibration) and harmony (order):[6]

> The source from which the world emanates is always an acoustic one: the profound abysm, the wide-open mouth, the singing cave, the *singing* or *supernatural ground* of the Eskimos, the crack in the rock of the Upanishad or the Tao of the ancient Chinese from which the world emanates 'like a tree', are images of the empty space or of the non being, from which the breath of the creature is exhaled.[7]

The Judaeo-Christian Scriptures resonate with this world view: it is the Word of God that calls forth creation from the Spirit-filled chaos, the Hebrew *DABAR* that 'does what it says', never returning to God without accomplishing that for which it sounded! God said, 'let there be . . . ', and it was so! (cf. Gen. 1.1-5; Isa. 55.10).

Another universal phenomenon shared by the world's religions is the bond between music and altered states of consciousness (trance, ecstasies, visions, mystical journeys, etc.), known as shamanism.[8] Twentieth-century interest in the shamanism of Siberia and regions of Asia led to the recognition of how widespread this practice was and is: similar beliefs and practices are found in Inuit and Yupik tribes of the Arctic, American and Australian Aboriginal tribes, and some tribes of Africa.[9] Aside from the practice of trance or healing rituals, the importance of music to the 'dreaming' or 'dreamtime' of

---

[6] Cf. Pierangelo Sequeri, *Musica e Mistica: Percorsi nella Storia Occidentale delle Pratiche Estetiche e Religiose* (Città del Vaticano: Libreria Editrice Vaticana, 2005), 20; translation mine. This section on music in other faiths draws mainly from chapter one of this book, entitled '*Divinizations of the Original Rhythm: Traces*'. Unfortunately, the book is not available in English.
[7] Schneider Marius, *La Musica Primitiva*, Adelphi (Milano 1992); quoted in Sequeri, *Musica e Mistica: Percorsi nella Storia Occidentale delle Pratiche Estetiche eReligiose*, 20.
[8] Shamanism comes from a Manchu-Tungus word drawn from the verb *ša-* 'to know', that is 'one who knows'.
[9] For example, the work of the Origins Centre at the University of the Witwatersrand, Johannesburg, focusses on reading history through the rock art of the San peoples of Southern Africa and uncovers the centrality of shamanic rituals (trance dance) in these images. Cf. J. Lewis-Williams and David Pearce, 'The Southern San and the Trance Dance: A Pivotal Debate in the Interpretation of San Rock Paintings', *Antiquity* 86, no. 333 (2012): 696–706. Cf. https://www.wits.ac.za/rockart/about-rock-art/rock-art-of-southern-africa/ (accessed 18 May 2020).

the Aboriginal peoples of Australia – the most ancient extant culture in the world – is also renowned.[10]

Music is omnipresent in all world religions. India's ancient *Vedic* religion, where Hinduism finds its roots, not only includes hymns and notations in its most sacred texts but places an original vibration at the origin of the world and sacred texts and music at the centre of its ritual practice: 'The sound of this creator Word is the sound of the Veda; its form is the visible world.'[11] In the two main styles of classical Indian music – Hindustani and Carnatic – music is *born of the temple* and central to their whole world view. It takes three fundamental forms: repetitive vocal prayer, known as mantras (of which the most venerated is the syllable OM, also prominent in Tibetan Buddhism); the inspired singing and playing of the independent and somewhat anarchic *baul* mystics (both Hindu and Muslim); and dance, the origin of which Hindu narratives place in creator god Brahma's unification of words, mime, music and feeling in their fifth *Veda*: the *Natyasastra* (from *natya*, evoking theatre and dance). Significantly, this third dimension of India's music – dance – is where mystical experience is opened to those of all casts. The chants and music created by Buddhist traditions include ritual performance and chants reserved for male voices, in some ways similar to Gregorian chant. At the heart of Islam is the psalmody revealed in the Koran, which although not understood as 'music' has rhythmic pauses in its liturgical recitation, and in Islamic culture, we find similar complexities as those facing Christianity in relation to music. Music is allowed, but a special place is reserved for what is called *samá* (a complex word signifying both music one listens to and the act of listening to it). Over the centuries, the development of the Islamic mystical tradition has maintained this *samá* – in music and ritual dance – at its centre;[12] and the importance of music in *Sufism* as a way to the divine is renowned.

As noted in chapter two, music is central to the beginnings of Christianity: in the first millennium of Christian life and well into the second, Christian thought developed alongside and in a symbiotic relationship with the music through which it prayed (*lex orandi, lex credendi*), which in turn helped express its identity and meaning. Even as it navigated the relationship between instrumental and vocal music, song was at the heart of Christianity's life and thought. A metaphor for Christian life, music is 'redeemed' by the

---

[10]The Australian Institute for Aboriginal and Torres Strait Islander Studies (AIATSIS) has an ongoing focus on the retrieval and recording of the culture, history and heritage transmitted through what they term 'songlines'. Cf. https://aiatsis.gov.au/research/research-themes/culture-and-heritage/songlines (accessed 18 May 2020).
[11]Swâmî Harihara Sarasvatî, quoted in Sequeri, *Musica e Mistica: Percorsi nella Storia Occidentale delle Pratiche Estetiche e Religiose*, 27.
[12]The most well known is that of the *Mevlevi* Order in Turkey (known as the whirling dervishes), disciples of master and poet, Jalal al-Din Rumi.

revealed word it carries.¹³ In terms of musical styles, Gregorian chant – best understood as a form of communitarian prayer rather than as a form of musical art¹⁴ – is our clearest expression of this reality, in which the 'content' of music is the text it transmits. 'Music does not modulate itself, but rather it modulates the Word of God.'¹⁵

From faith-shaped musicking to God-sized ventriloquism

Word and music: Inseparable rivals

Chant is at the origins of Western musical notation: the earliest musical 'writing' (known as 'neumatic notation') was the melodic recitation of the Christian Scriptures in Aramaic. And the inventor of notated staff music that led to music as we know it was eleventh-century Italian monk and music theorist Guido of Arezzo, whose work laid the foundations for the possibility of musical harmony and the development of Western music in the second millennium. This is not to say that Western music is paradigmatic for all musical development. The rhythmic and harmonic development of Chinese, Indian and African musicking, for example, is at least as complex as Western music. Our intent, quite simply, is to underline the Christian underpinnings of Western music from its very origins. The most complex harmonies of Wagner's *Tannhäuser* (Figure 3.1) owe its condition of possibility to the attempts of an Italian monk to music his monastery's prayer (Figures 3.2 and 3.3 on the next page).

The movement from Gregorian music (known as monophonic: with one melodic line) to melody accompanied by chords (homophonic), to polyphonic music parallels cultural developments in art and architecture in the second millennium CE. I would invite the reader to reimagine visits to churches the world over: the development from the simple lines of Romanic architecture through Baroque ornamentation to Gothic sophistication is mirrored in music's ever more complex melodic and harmonic lines. But it is a *theologal*, or even theological, journey: improvisation over authorized chants began as a kind of commentary or musical gloss on important passages, developing into more complex melodic combinations and the need to notate, regulate and preserve them. Composers at this time (inventors of the first harmonic tropes and descants) were doing a similar activity as their

---

¹³Cf. Sequeri, *Musica e Mistica: Percorsi nella Storia Occidentale delle Pratiche Estetiche e Religiose*, 46–8.
¹⁴Even as we recognize its subsequent gift to the world of music: cf. Katharine W. Le Mée, *The Benedictine Gift to Music* (New York: Paulist Press, 2003).
¹⁵Cf. Sequeri, *Musica e Mistica: Percorsi nella Storia Occidentale delle Pratiche Estetiche e Religiose*, 107.

FIGURE 3.1 *Four bars of Wagner's* Tannhäuser.

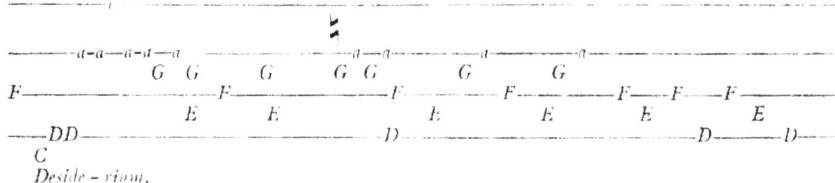

FIGURE 3.2 *An image of the four-line stave created by Guido d'Arezzo. From Guido D'Arezzo,* Micrologus Guidonis: Id Est Brevis Sermo in Musica, *ed. A. M. A. OSB (Romae: Desclee, 1904), 28. Public domain.*

scholastic theological counterparts: adding layers of interpretation on a central authoritative text – a musical 'commentary', if you will.[16] The creation of different voices with varying rates of motion also prompted the beginnings of rhythmic notation. Its development is linked to scholasticism's love of logic and order and Augustine's understanding of music as 'the art of measuring well'.[17] The 'motet' composers, for example, constructed their precise, rhythmic harmonies using the same principles as the architects of Gothic cathedrals. This music was not limited to the liturgical space, and reflects the interweaving of thought, art and culture of the time. Balthasar describes this historical shift from a linear understanding of music to harmony as one that

---

[16]These developments are closely associated with the Cathedral of Notre Dame, in Paris, and its two most well-known figures: Leoninus (1150–1201) and Perotinus (1200–30).

[17]In Latin, 'Musica est scientia bene modulandi', in Augustine, *De Musica*, ed. M. Jacobsson and L. J. Dorfbauer (Berlin: Walter de Gruyter, 2017), 1.2.

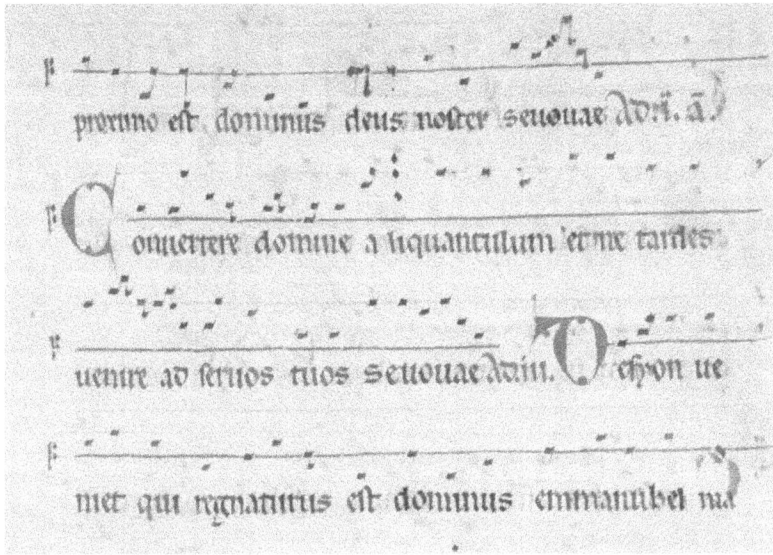

FIGURE 3.3 *Four-line stave in Cistercian Antiphonary for day hours. Twelfth-century notated music. https://www.loc.gov/item/2008562461/. Library of Congress Public Domain.*

reflected Western culture's understanding of relativity and space, coinciding with changes in cosmological world views. Harmony, he said, opened 'the space of music'.[18] Even a reader not trained in reading music can sense the process in its notated forms (Figures 3.4, 3.5 and 3.6 on the next page).

In the fourteenth century, as the Church began to lose its authority over the temporal world, the centre of musical innovation moves from the cathedral to the public square of courtly love and political satire – once again, an analogue shift to the visual arts and literature. Mass compositions were mostly polyphonic, ever increasing in harmonic and rhythmic complexity but, with the exception of England, the main hub of musical creativity were the courts. This continued into the fifteenth and sixteenth centuries, where the educational mindsight shifted from the abstract and logical to the humanities. The birth of musical print began the move from music as performance to music as commodity, and the themes reflected in music were often less about faith than life and love. This does not mean the Church abandoned the world of the arts, or vice versa (yet!). Music's importance in Church and society overlapped and interweaved, in much the same way as life did, and the Church developed a role in supporting and sponsoring the

---

[18]Hans Urs von Balthasar and Pierangelo Sequeri, *Lo Sviluppo dell'idea Musicale Testimonianza per Mozart Antiprometeo: Il Musicale nell'estetica Di Hans Urs von Balthasar* (Milano: Glossa, 1995), 30–2; translation mine.

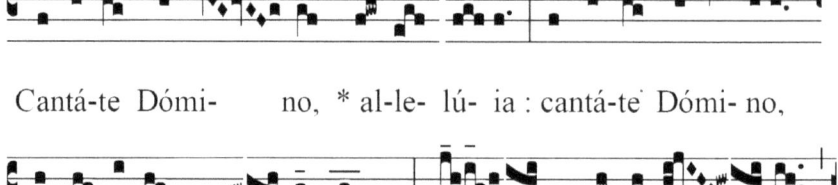

FIGURE 3.4 *'Cantate Domino'*. Transcribed by Nicola Amadio and edited by Giovanni Vianini. Creative Commons Attribution Non-commercial Share Alike 3.0: https://imslp.org/wiki/Cantate_Domino_(Gregorian_Chant).

FIGURE 3.5 *'Organum'* by Magister Perotinus. Public domain: https://musopen.org/music/10003-organum-triplum/.

FIGURE 3.6 Joaquin Des Prez's three evangelic motets. Public domain: https://musopen.org/music/10483-3-evangelic-motets/.

arts, music included. Many composers wrote music for Church, or even full masses, although not always intended for liturgical celebration.

There are a number of ways in which the development of music and music theory in this period is relevant to contemporary theology's understanding of the same. The Renaissance's turn to humanism, and the discovery of an expanded world beyond Europe led to interest in the composer as an individual. It also rediscovered and revived the ancient Greek writings on music theory, especially their belief in the effect of musical modes on human emotions and the corresponding need for care in the combination of words and music.[19] Both foci can be seen in contemporary attention to musical meaning, but it is the dialectic between words and music which had the most lasting effect on the history of music. Musical theory was developed based on a heritage in which the word had priority over music, notwithstanding the diversity of compositional strategies. It led to the fundamental argument (noted in chapter two) about the primacy of harmony or melody in musical composition that shaped the second millennium's approach to musicking and is reflected in the different styles of music emerging from French or Italian composers, respectively.[20] France will prefer music that values counterpoint, harmony and classic forms in *support* of words, which music is meant to carry and to which it is subordinated, while Italy, valuing the expressive power of vocal music *over* words, gives birth to opera. A key figure here is Claudio Monteverdi (1567–1643), who wrote a treatise differentiating the two compositional practices (called *prima pratica* and *seconda pratica*)[21] and composed one of the first known operas, *Orpheo*, in which music is personified on stage, singing her power: 'I am music.'[22] It is an about-face in terms of music's history and one that opens the door for the developments of the next centuries. It would be overly simplistic to suggest that Christianity's loss of power in the world is reflected in music's victory over the word in performed meaning. However, it is equally unacceptable to ignore the role music played in the emergence of the modern world – an essential aspect of the complex history of Christianity's self-understanding and its place in the world.

The ecclesial lungs of Western 'classical' music

The ecclesial worlds of the reformation and counter-reformation were another battlefield of theology's entanglement with music. The intra-ecclesial

---

[19]As with other aspects of Greek thought, the historical difference was often overlooked and conflated – in this case the difference between musical modes of ancient Greece (which would have been hard to know with precision) and contemporary Europe.
[20]The dilemma between harmony and melody is epitomized in the writings of Rameau and Rousseau.
[21]'First Practice' and 'Second Practice'. Cf. Claudio Monteverdi, *Fifth book of Madrigals* (16–5).
[22]The opera is also known as *La favola d'Orfeo* (*The Fable of Orpheus*) based on a libretto by Alessandro Striggio.

counterpart to madrigals and opera were the oratories, sacred concertos and cantatas. Organ music's importance finds its origins in the Lutheran areas of seventeenth- and eighteenth-century Germany, laying the foundations for the figure of Bach.[23] As noted in chapter two, music did not receive the same negative treatment as visual art in the reformers' theological positions and practices, and the differences in their positions emerged largely from the personal convictions of their founders. Luther was a singer, composer and admirer of polyphonic music: he maintained much of the Catholic music tradition, extended to include translations into the vernacular. John Calvin was wary of the power of music to distract and corrupt, and limited musical expression to texts found in Scripture: 'songs not merely honest but holy, which will be like spurs to incite us to pray and praise God'.[24] Only Ulrich Zwingli banished music from any liturgical setting. While at first, music in the Lutheran music remained close to its Catholic sources (albeit with vernacular translations), it soon expressed and shaped its own culture. Its most important form became the strophic hymn (*Choral* or *Kirchenlied* in German; *chorale* in English), meant for congregational singing in unison, a musical tradition with particular influence on German and Anglo worship on both sides of the Atlantic. The other musical influence that would reach the United States was that of the Puritans, who brought and developed Calvinist psalm singing.[25]

Also important in this tradition of the history of music is the influence of Moravian Piety and music on key thinkers of the Protestant reform and the musical cultures they engendered. I have already noted Schleiermacher as one figure, but brothers John (1703–91) and James Wesley (1707–88), the founder and most prolific composer of the Methodist Church, both had key conversion experiences in branches emanating from this Christian community. Moravians (otherwise known as Bohemian Brethren, or Hussites) inaugurated congregational choral singing fifty years before Martin Luther encouraged it. They adapted Gregorian and secular melodies for worship, created services made practically *only* of music (*Singstunden*) and initiated trombone assemblies (*Posaunenchor*), a tradition that was taken around the world, lasting (with some developments) until today.[26] Their influence on musical practice, religious expression and theological influencers is one of the unknown treasures of music's theological history.

The Council of Trent's (1545–63) response to the reformation touched only in passing on music, within the context of its concern for liturgical

---

[23]Barbara Russano Hanning, *Concise History of Western Music*, ed. D. J. Grout, 3rd ed. (New York: W.W. Norton, 2006), 146–61.
[24]Cf. John Calvin, Preface to the Psalter (1542).
[25]Mainly in New England.
[26]Moravians claim to be the longest established music institution in the United States, dating from 1745! Cf. Tim Dowley, *Christian Music: A Global History* (Minneapolis, MN: Fortress Press, 2011), 100–1.

abuses and clerical behaviour. The core issue once again revolved around the relationship between words and music: overly complicated polyphony obscured the texts! Most importantly, however, while there are various discussions on the topic of music in liturgy during the Council sessions, calling on music to support the words so that "the hearts of listeners should be ravished by longing for heavenly harmony and by contemplation of the joys of the blessed" [27], Trent *did not ban any genre of music*, referring only in general terms to everything 'lascivious or impure'. The Catholic tradition's emphasis on the sacramental nature of divine revelation in which matter is a channel for encountering the divine[28] places it as an ongoing, if at times controlling, friend of music.[29] The need for music and words in sacred polyphony 'in a new manner',[30] to serve the words, became the central intent of the sixteenth century's best-known composer, Giovanni Pierluigi da Palestrina (1567–1643).

In this way, the reformation and counter-reformation lay the foundation for some of the key genres and musickers[31] of the second millennium. There would be no Bach without Luther's love of Scripture and music; no Handel's 'Alleluia Chorus' without the reformers' emphasis on chorale and organ music; and no Baroque opera – 'the musical vocabulary of the affections'[32] – without the counter-reformation's commitment to winning back the faithful through the arts' effect on the senses and the soul.[33] It is this understanding of music's potential to move the emotions that led the way to the *separation* of vocal and instrumental music, in which the latter sought to emulate (and eventually replace) the expressive capacity of the human voice. We are reaching the crux (and cliff edge) of modernity's self-understanding, the scene set for the music of the next three centuries: Baroque moves through

---

[27] Quoted in K. G. Fellerer and Moses Hadas, 'Church Music and the Council of Trent', *The Musical Quarterly* 49, no. 4 (1953): 576–94 (576). For an excellent presentation of Trent's role in the history of polyphony, see Chiara Bertoglio, *Reforming Music: Music and the Religious Reformations of the Sixteenth Century* (Berlin: De Gruyter, 2017).
[28] Later encapsulated in Gerard Manly Hopkins' (1844–89), *God's Grandeur*: 'the world is charged with the grandeur of God'.
[29] As witnessed by Paul VI's homily quoted at the end of chapter two. Paul VI, *Homily, 'Artists' Mass' in the Sistine Chapel* (Thursday, 7 May 1964).
[30] Palestrina, in his dedication to the *Second Book of Masses* (1567).
[31] While the word may jar while speaking of those often referred to as 'the great composers', this *is*, in fact, the appropriate nomenclature, since despite our imaginings, in them the line between composition and improvisation is not always clear. Bach, for example, was better known in his lifetime for his virtuoso improvisation than for all the works we now recognize as born of that musicality.
[32] Barbara Russano Hanning, *Concise History of Western Music*, ed. D. J. Grout, Fifth ed. (New York W. W. Norton & Company, 2014), 240.
[33] The Baroque 'theory of affections', which is reflected in Descartes' *Passions of the Soul* (1645–6), is the theoretical backdrop to this approach in art, in which affection and the soul are directly linked and composers used rhythmic and harmonic musical gestures to not only validly interpret human experience but also provoke in listeners corresponding affections.

classical to romantic music, mirroring Enlightenment and Romanticism's respective emphases on how meaning and the transcendent can be accessed. The former enthrones reason as our access point to knowledge, the latter seeks to correct this imbalance by defending the role of the senses and feelings in understanding. This history of 'thought' is played out, quite literally, by composers such as Johann Sebastian Bach (1685–1750) in the Baroque period; the 'classical' music of Wolfgang Amadeus Mozart (1756–91), Franz Joseph Haydn (1732–1809) and Ludwig van Beethoven (1770–1827) in the eighteenth century; the latter of whom bridges and sets the scene in the nineteenth century for the romantic music of Franz Liszt (1811–86), Johannes Brahms (1833–97) and Claude Debussy (1862–1918), to name but a few. Its culminating chapter is best exemplified in the complex and contested figure of Richard Wagner (1813–83).

Musical figures of theology performed

As I focus briefly on some of these figures, it is how their music embodies the theological and doctrinal understandings of their time that is of interest. In each genre or composer represented, theology's presence and influence are not limited to one factor but weave together cultural and ecclesial backdrops and the intentionality of the composers, with how performance and notation were interpreted, received and understood by their contemporaries *and* those they influenced.

Bach is the musical figure who has most consistently drawn theology's attention.[34] Steeped in his Lutheran faith, Bach grounded his composing on a Scriptural understanding of the role of music in Christian faith and lived his life as a church musician, 'doing his job, day in, day out'.[35] Challenges about the sincerity of Bach's commitment to his faith have relented in recent years, due to the historical evidence of a personal library of Luther's Scriptural Commentaries with marginal notes in Bach's hand on biblical texts about music.[36] Through these annotations, we can see that he perceived music as a bearer of the Word of God, through which God's grace is known and received.[37] This intentionality is perhaps one reason he is hailed by some as 'Bach among the theologians' and his music as the 'ultimate Christian music' that 'reflects as no other human artefact ever has or could the Christian

---

[34]By way of example, Robin A. Leaver, *Music as Preaching: Bach, Passions and Music in Worship* (Oxford: Latimar House, 1982); Wilfrid Howard Mellers, *Bach and the Dance of God* (London: Faber, 1980); Jaroslav Jan Pelikan, *Bach among the Theologians* (Philadelphia: Fortress Press, 1986).
[35]Quoted in Pelikan, *Bach among the Theologians*, 140.
[36]Cf. Robin A. Leaver, *J.S. Bach and Scripture: Glosses from the Calov Bible Commentary* (St. Louis, MO: Concordia Publishing House, 1985), 11–21.
[37]Cf. Leaver, *J.S. Bach and Scripture*, 29.

vision of creation'.[38] However, while intentionality is important, my position is not to posit faith-inspired musical genius as a replacement for theology. 'If Bach's sense of his own vocation was to compose music to the glory of God, that sense of calling does not make him a traditional practitioner of theology (*fides quaerens intellectum*) comparable to Augustine, Anselm, Aquinas, Luther, or Calvin.'[39] It is what his music presents of the culture and understanding of the time that is important: 'Bach was first and foremost a musician whose engagement with theology was deliberate, sustained, and carefully designed. Theology was intrinsic to much of his work as a composer, and the relationship between music and theology can well be described as a harmonious whole.'[40]

Bach's theological import is more musical in nature. The compositional style of his musicking is an unsurpassed example of what was known as *inventio* and *elaboratio*.[41] The terms derive from classical rhetoric and in Bach's time were widely used as a metaphor for the basic musical idea (*inventio*), an idea that was capable of being developed in a variety of ways (*elaboratio*). For Bach 'crafting a workable idea, one that unlocks the door to a complete musical work', was inseparable from thinking about how it might be developed.[42] In fact, Bach was better known in his lifetime for his virtuoso improvisation and criticized as 'behind the times' in not following the trend of enlightenment understandings of aesthetics. He only came to fame with Felix Mendelssohn's recovery of Bach's *St Matthew Passion* in 1829. However, his music has drawn theological attention since then for a variety of reasons. One is his capacity to balance natural and artistic beauty:[43] rather than pitting the composer-genius against God in trying to compose-from-nothing, he emerges as one who welcomes given themes and performs/reforms them in an infinite number of ways. A case has been made for interpreting Bach's musicking as a nuanced critique of modernity – *not* as a conscious, rationally elaborate framework of thought-made-music, but rather in its style – by trusting in music as gift from God alongside performance as the space of its elaboration. This approach to Bach's music,

---

[38]David Bentley Hart, *The Beauty of the Infinite: The Aesthetics of Christian Truth* (Grand Rapids, MI: William B. Eerdmans, 2003), 282–5, (83).
[39]Richard J. Platinga, 'The Integration of Music and Theology in the Vocal Composition of J. S. Bach', in *Resonant Witness: Conversations between Music and Theology*, ed. J. Begbie and S. R. Guthrie, 215–39 (220) (Grand Rapids, MI: William B. Eerdmans, 2011).
[40]Platinga, 'The Integration of Music and Theology in the Vocal Composition of J. S. Bach', 215–39 (220).
[41]Cf. Laurence Dreyfus, *Bach and the Patterns of Invention* (Cambridge, MA: Harvard University Press, 2004).
[42]Jeremy Begbie, 'Created Beauty: The Witness of J. S. Bach', in *Resonant Witness: Conversations between Music and Theology*, ed. J. Begbie and S. R. Guthrie, 83–108 (97) (Grand Rapids, MI: William B. Eerdmans, 2011).
[43]Begbie, 'Created Beauty: The Witness of J. S. Bach', 83–108 (108).

as interpretation and development of the musical form, has found traction with the emergence of historical consciousness.[44]

If the aim of Baroque music was to glorify God and move the emotions, 'classical' music – thus named to evoke ancient Greek and Roman culture – sought ways to construct an ideal, universal vision of life and nature in tune with Enlightenment goals of realism, harmony and order.

> Writers held that the language of music should be universal rather than limited by national boundaries and should appeal to all tastes at once, from the sophisticated to the untutored. The best music should be noble as well as entertaining, expressive within the limits of decorum, and 'natural' – free of technical complications and capable of immediately pleasing any sensitive listener.[45]

Despite the difference in styles, these are values embraced by both Mozart and Haydn, for example. I already noted that Barth's enthusiasm for Mozart rested precisely in the fact that it was not self-expression, but rather a perfect incarnation or expression of the musical form. However, in music as well as thought – and we cannot forget that Romanticism's thinkers were often musicians and poets as well – Enlightenment thinking generated its own pushback, with composers and audiences making space for feelings, emotions and personal expression. Composers began incorporating national traits in song, instrumental music and opera. By the end of the eighteenth century, the 'persistent, rationalistically biased Enlightenment view of instrumental music as a "deficient mode" (song without words) gave way [or birth?], to the idea of a language "above" speech, a language that transcended the vulgar world of empirical reality and fixed signs'.[46] Under the influence of Schopenhauer's understanding of the human will, music is taken more seriously than ever before and the classical music prodigy of Mozart is replaced by the inspired, tormented, solitary, creative artist (epitomized by Beethoven) who suffers courageously to bring humanity a glimpse of the divine through music. 'The modern artist', says Friedrich Schlegel (1772–1829), must 'work out from the inside' to produce 'new creation from nothing'.[47]

---

[44]This is the creative theological metaphor found in the Goldberg Variations by Anthony J. Godzieba, '"And Followed Him on the Way" (Mk 10:52): Unity, Diversity, Discipleship', in *Beyond Dogmatism and Innocence: Hermeneutics, Critique, and Catholic Theology*, ed. A. J. Godzieba and B. E. Hinze, 228–54 (Collegeville, MN: Liturgical Press, 2017).
[45]Hanning, *Concise History of Western Music*, 311.
[46]Thomas S. Grey, *Wagner's Musical Prose Texts and Contexts* (Cambridge and New York: Cambridge University Press, 1995), 7.
[47]Daniel K. L. Chua, 'Music as the Mouthpiece of Theology', in *Resonant Witness: Conversations between Music and Theology*, ed. J. Begbie and S. R. Guthrie, 137–61 (155) (Grand Rapids, MI: William B. Eerdmans, 2011).

You will ask me whence I get my ideas. That I am not able with certainty to say. They come unbidden, indirectly or directly; they are so palpable that it seems I could seize them with my hands while I am out walking, in the open fields or in the forest, in the dead of night or early in the morning, stirred into being by moods such as are converted by the poet into words but by me into tones; they sound, roar, and storm until at last they stand before me in musical notes.[48]

Enter the notion of absolute music, in which vocal expressivity gives way to instrumental symphony as the ultimate expression of transcendent meaning: free, pure and true to nothing but itself. The notion of 'absolute music' was first used by music theorist and critic Eduard Hanslick[49] (1825–1904) but made famous (or infamous) by Wagner's critique of the notion.[50] And once again, we find a co-relation to musicking in the world of conceptual thought! Absolute music is the musical reflection of Kantian aesthetics: 'Music, following the subject, was made to empty its content in order to mime the noumenal world of Kantian freedom and morality. The autonomy of music is therefore tied up with the autonomy of the subject, and the aesthetic was a way of bringing them into recognition as brothers of invisibility.'[51]

This position will have lasting effects on Western culture and theology's understanding of music. Although the ahistorical nature of 'pure' music sits uneasy with contemporary historical consciousness, the words below resonate with how theological circles often uncritically think about music as pure, inaccessible, mysterious and ultimately, unthinkable (or un-thoughtworthy):

> Just try interrogating absolute music's purity. What is it? What does it mean?. . . . There is no answer; or, at least, when asked to disclose the criteria for musical purity, absolute music deliberately draws a blank. Its signs signify nothing. Indeed it cleverly champions this nothingness as its purity . . . the meaning of absolute music resides in the fact that it has no meaning; the inchoate and the ineffable become synonymous. . . . This is why its purity is not a fact that is open to investigation, but a secret

---

[48]Quoted in Max Unger, 'From Beethoven's Workshop', *The Musical Quarterly* 24, no. 3 (1938): 323–40.
[49]In Eduard Hanslick, *On the Musically Beautiful: A Contribution towards the Revision of the Aesthetics of Music*, trans. G. Payzant, 8 ed. (Indianapolis: Hackett, 1986).
[50]In an open letter on Franz Liszt's symphonic poems, which can be found in English in Richard Wagner. *Judaism in Music and Other Essays*. University of Nebraska Press, 1995, Wagner negated its interpretation as espoused by formalist music theorists. It was a term he himself had previously used in relation to Beethoven's Ninth Symhpony. Cf. Daniel K. L. Chua, *Absolute Music and the Construction of Meaning* (Cambridge, UK: Cambridge University Press, 1999), 230; Grey, *Wagner's Musical Prose Texts and Contexts*, 1–3.
[51]Chua, 'Music as the Mouthpiece of Theology', 137–61 (155).

whose power resides in the inaccessibility of its sign. No wonder the early Romantics venerated instrumental music as a mystery that wraps mysterious things in a mysterious language.[52]

Music became transcendent, without ever offering an adequate definition of the word. A universal language, a meaning one cannot quite put one's finger on, and therefore both all-powerful and weak (woman and woman*ly*), essential and useless, especially to conceptual understanding. As the revealed God fades from view – missed only by madmen[53] – music replaces divine presence with infinite and unnamed longing. Music is not a side story in the emergence of our world, but rather its theological centre! The convergence between Philip Stoltzfus and Daniel Chua is striking, as they name the centrality of music in the very construction of modernity:

> From 'I am who I am' (Exodus 3:14) to 'the Word [Logos] was God' (John 1:1), Western theology has celebrated the presence of Word. The three hundred year tradition of Western instrumental music has celebrated the absence of word. As the so-called 'logocentric' discourses of classical, medieval, and enlightenment thought have been put to the test by nineteenth- and twentieth Century concepts of 'absolute music' and musical performance, music has come to rival word as a location for philosophical reflection and theological construction.[54]

> Music, with its god-like aura, is employed by the ventriloquists[55] to articulate the theological consequences of modern thought. Indeed, the resonances between music and its discourses are like harmonics to the 'fundamental bass' of theology. . . . Music, acting as a kind of divine surrogate . . . can be heard as a mode of 'secular theology' that exposes some of the major theological issues of our times.[56]

Modernity's breakdown is heralded – despite himself – by Richard Wagner, considered 'the father of twentieth-century music'[57] and a controversial

---

[52]Daniel K. L. Chua, 'On History', *Absolute Music and the Construction of Meaning*, 1–7 (4–5): (Cambridge, UK: Cambridge University Press, 1999).
[53]Such as Nietzsche's madman in the square, lamenting more than proclaiming the death of God: 'Do we not feel the breath of empty space? Has it not become colder? Is not night continually closing in on us?. . . . God is dead. God remains dead.' F. Nietzsche, *The Gay Science* (1882, 1887), paragraph 125; *Thus Spoke Zarathustra*, tr. J. Hollingdale (London: Penguin Classics, 2003), 181–2.
[54]Philip Edward Stoltzfus, *Theology as Performance: Music, Aesthetics, and God in Western Thought* (New York: T&T Clark International, 2006), 242.
[55]A veiled reference to Nietzsche's accusation of Wagner of trying to be the 'ventriloquist of God'.
[56]Chua, 'Music as the Mouthpiece of Theology', 137–61 (138).
[57]Cf. Wicks, Robert, "Arthur Schopenhauer", The Stanford Encyclopedia of Philosophy (Fall 2021 Edition), Edward N. Zalta (ed.), URL = <https://plato.stanford.edu/entries/schopenhauer/>.

figure whose nationalistic anti-Semitic writings have historically tainted (to this day) his musical brilliance. In line with Romanticism's atheistic quest for the infinite, Wagner deliberately attempts a sacrality without God, a secular sacred, earning the title of 'God's ventriloquist' from Nietzsche![58] This operatic reform-theorist who viscerally challenged the Romantics' autonomy of music (even while still being held by some of its main tenets, not least through the influence of Schopenhauer) considers himself Beethoven's true successor. His musical style introduces the use (if not the description) of *leitmotifs* in music – small musical themes that personify themes or characters – which were immensely influential in twentieth-century film music. Wagner calls for a new era of music, in which poetry, drama and music come together in the fullest expression of meaning. The grandiosity of his thought is perhaps a harbinger of its demise:

> This last symphony of Beethoven's is the redemption of music out of its own element as a universal art. It is the human gospel of the art of the future. Beyond it there can be no progress, for there can follow on it immediately only the completed artwork of the future, the universal drama, to which Beethoven has forged for us the artistic key. . . . Man as artist can be fully satisfied only in the union of all the art varieties in the collective artwork [*Gesamtkunstwerk*]; in every individualization of his artistic capacities he is unfree, not wholly that which he can be; in the collective artwork he is free, wholly that which he can be.[59]

The paradoxically universalist while still nationalist position of Wagner, and his suggestion that the only way forward is into a new artform that supersedes all past forms, epitomizes – or rather caricaturizes – the peak of nineteenth-century modern thought at its cracking point. This complete and empty pinnacle of meaning had nowhere to go except the myriad of directions twentieth- and twenty-first-century musicking led us. Our next section will sketch two strands of that development – one emerging from Europe and influencing the Americas; the other more global but equally (and inversely) as influential. But before I leave this more specifically 'Western' history, and lest the point of this fascinating story is missed: at this stage, we have reached and started to move beyond the time in which *theology found the form that now defines it*. From here, it will open up to (or project itself into) the various contextual strands and theological explorations of

---

[58]This history of Wagner and Nietzsche's friendship and estrangement is, in itself, of interest in the development of thought. Cf. Daniel W. Conway, 'The Case of Wagner and Nietzsche Contra Wagner', in *A Companion to Friedrich Nietzsche*, ed. P. Bishop, 279–307 (Rochester and New York: Boydell & Brewer, 2012).
[59]Richard Wagner, *The Artwork of the Future* (1850) quoted in W. Oliver Strunk and Leo Treitler, *Source Readings in Music History*, Rev. ed. (New York: Norton, 1998), vol. 6, 66–70.

twenty-first century. We can argue about who led whom, but in the history of Western music, we have the perfect mirror – some would say muse – of its philosophical and theological counterparts.

The counter-reform of music: Postmodern and post-tonal musical movements

As with other thought-strands in the modern to postmodern shift, music is contextually sensitive fragmentation at its best, with all the push-and-shove for space that constitutes human life and thought in our plural world. There are two interweaving perspectives which, from very different theoretical and practical starting points, converge in pushing back at the tonal hegemony of Euro-American classical music's self-understanding: on the one hand, its own 'internal' reaction to tonal harmony as expressed in modernism and experimental music; and on the other, the explosion of new music, faith and thought (intrinsically intermingled) that flooded the world from the Afro-American roots of blues, jazz and rock.

The avant-garde spirituality of post-tonal music

The first strand pursued a parallel trajectory to other forms of modernist thought and art. Modernism 'on the whole continued and radicalised the Wagnerian enterprise',[60] emerging under the influence of Henri Bergson's (1859–1941) philosophical distinction between *elán vitale* and duration of time (*durée*), Edmund Husserl's (1859–1938) ecstatic temporality and Heidegger's (1889–1976) understanding of our mortality in time (*Dasein*). Art shifts from trying to evoke the beautiful and resonate with listeners' sensibilities, to music-forms that sought to challenge and at times shock them into reinterpreting what they heard and the world they lived in. Post Holocaust and Hiroshima culture was a counterstatement against the ideologies and tonalities that harmonized with (and supported?) the horrors seen and experienced. Music, of course, is perfectly suited to express and explore these dimensions.

The foremost innovation is the twelve-tone scale and compositional method invented by Arnold Schoenberg (1874–1951), in a clear move away from known tonal musical expressivity. 'Atonal' music – although Schoenberg preferred to speak of the 'twelve-tone technique', or dodecaphony – lacks a

---

[60]Cf. Catherine Pickstock, 'Quasi Una Sonata: Modernism, Postmodernism, Religion, and Music', in *Resonant Witness: Conversations between Music and Theology*, ed. J. Begbie and S. R. Guthrie, 190–211 (191) (Grand Rapids, MI: William B. Eerdmans, 2011). It is a thesis argued in Roger Scruton, *Death-Devoted Heart: Sex and the Sacred in Wagner's Tristan and Isolde* (Oxford: Oxford University Press, 2003).

tonal centre and therefore does not 'resolve' in the same way as tonal music does. It is a compositional method based on using all twelve notes in the chromatic scale (although the chromatic scale had already been used by Wagner and others of the late romantic movement). This led to serialism, the famous Darmstadt School[61] and total serialism, a musical form in which it is not only tone and melody that are 'de-hierarchized' but other aspects of musical form, such as rhythm, dynamic, colour, intensity, attack, duration and polytonality.[62] Avant-garde composer Erik Satie (1866–1925) – more known in mainstream musical appreciation for his elegant *Gymnopédie* – began to explore the distinction between music, sound and noise, including car horns, sirens, typewriters or modified pianos. The very notion of musical performance is stretched to breaking point.

Some examples might be helpful to intuit the deliberate strangeness of these innovators: Satie's composition *Vexations* is 180 notes long, repeated 840 times. In 1963, it took a relay team of 10 pianists over 18 hours to perform it! Luigi Russolo (1885–1947), a key early figure of futuristic music with his 1913 manifesto *The Art of Noises*,[63] proposed that all music be destroyed and that new instruments reflecting the current technological age be built. Following his own advice, he built machines and performed them, although they were destroyed during the First World War. Both Satie and Russolo influenced John Cage (1912–92), whose most famous work challenging the division between music and noise is *4'33"*, a three-movement piece, 'for any instrument or combination of instruments', during which not one note it played: the content of the piece is that of the sounds of the environment that the listeners hear during the performance. These are perhaps the most notorious innovations emerging from the cultural melting pot of late nineteenth and early twentieth century music, but it is fair to say that most composers of that time explored non-tonal music in some way, seeking and often creating their own, recognizable musical style. They include Igor Stravinsky (1882–1971), Claude Debussy (1862–1918), Sergei Rachmaninoff (1873–1943), Amy Marcy Beach (1867–1944) and Ralph Vaughan Williams (1872–1958).

Where faith and religion fits in this postmodern musical world is a fascinating question.[64] While there are composers who inhabit the 'spiritual but not religious' zone, such as Ralph Vaughan Williams (1872–1958) or Benjamin Britten (1913–76), almost despite itself, music continues to serve as a vehicle for the most explicit belief and Christian expressions of

---

[61] The Darmstadt School refers to a group of influential composers of the twentieth century. The name was born of a series of International Summer Courses for New Music in the 1950s and 1960s, in Darmstadt.
[62] Pickstock, 'Quasi Una Sonata', 190–211 (196).
[63] *L'arte dei rumari*, in the Italian original.
[64] For an informed and insightful reflection on this theme (some of which is reflected here), see Pickstock, 'Quasi Una Sonata', 190–211.

faith. Major innovators in music-making from either Jewish or Christian faiths include Stravinsky, Schoenberg, Oliver Messiaen (1909–92), Alfred Schnittke (1934–98), Galina Ustvolskaya (1919–2006) and Arvo Pärt (born 1935), to name a few. From a Catholic perspective, Messiaen stands out: arguably the most influential composer of the Darmstadt School – despite his *explicitly* Catholic positioning (for which he distanced himself from total serialism, to maintain his ideological freedom). While Schoenberg believed God is unrepresentable, Messiaen held that God is present everywhere and in all sounds – from the roar of an orchestra to the songs of exotic birds.[65] Before being celebrated, his compositions were attacked by the musical world for their religious text and by the religious for its dissonances![66] He considered himself a theological composer, rather than a mystical one. Strongly influenced by Thomas Aquinas, Messiaen quotes Aquinas' recognition of the weakness or limitation of reason to comprehend divine truth and its ensuing need for symbolic modes, of which music is one. For Messiaen, music provided a *more* rather than *less* exacting means of saying things than the words of language.[67] Exploring the etymology of the word 'music' he concludes:

> The fact that the word music belongs to: I) the same root as mind, memory, muse, man – means that it belongs to the same order as thought, to the divinities of thought, and to the thinking being; 2) the same root as divination, prodigious – means that it belongs to time and to the supernatural; 3) the same root as love – means that it belongs to the grandest of sentiments. All this clarifies our conception of music: it is a thinking art, intellectual, abstract, immaterial, an art of time (this speaks to the importance of rhythm in music), a supernatural art (this speaks to religious aptitudes and the psychic power of music). It is then an art of love, capable of expressing love – and this last point thrills me.[68]

Music comes to the aid of humanity's sunken reality, disillusioned by the failed empty promises of the Enlightenment, and the task of a theological music is to impart a veritable *éclairage de l'âme* (a cathartic awakening of the soul) to humanity's soul lost in the abysm.[69] Messiaen became both

---

[65] Dowley, *Christian Music*, 201.
[66] Dowley, *Christian Music*, 201.
[67] Pickstock, 'Quasi Una Sonata', 190–211 (192).
[68] Olivier Messiaen and Melody Ann Baggech, 'An English Translation of Olivier Messiaen's *Traite De Rythme, De Couleur, Et D'ornithologie* (University of Oklahoma, 1998), 49.
[69] 'The metaphor that Messiaen often used in connection with the realization of God's grace and truth is that of the abyss [l'*abîme*], a concept he borrowed from the Bible and the nineteenth-century theologian and writer Ernst Hello (1828-1885).' Robert Scholl, 'The Schock of the Positive: Oliver Massiaen, St Francis, and the Redemption of Modernity', in *Resonant Witness: Conversations between Music and Theology*, ed. J. Begbie and S. R. Guthrie, 162–89 (172) (Grand Rapids, MI: William B. Eerdmans, 2011).

revered and influential for many composers of the twentieth century, whom he taught for years at the Paris Conservatory.

So, theology is alive and well in this strand of musicking, belying the lie of religion's disappearance from music's horizon.[70] This music is characterized by a rediscovery of the spiritual, according to Sequeri, who speaks of the 'post-tragic mystical dramatization' of Cage and Karlheinz Stockhausen (1828–2007); the 'luminous vibration *from* silence and *of* silence' of Pärt; the humble transition from dogmatism's disillusion to invocation of Luigi Dallapiccola (1904–75) and the mysticism born of knowing human suffering in Krzystof Penderecki (born 1933). For Sequeri, in this music we find a necessary bridge and condition of possibility for the spiritual quality of culture and Christian faith into the future. Of all the arts, music is the one that most resists the separation between the worlds of art and religion! Nowhere better is Nietzsche's aphorism proven correct: 'Art raises its head where religion withdraws.'[71] However, for the most part, this is a music of the elite, unconcerned still about the musicking of the masses, to which I now turn.

The time-honoured tradition of music's mutiny

When I listen to hip-hop, I hear a theological cry. The prophets are speaking.

RALPH BASUI WATKINS[72]

The second strand of twentieth-century musicking that theology cannot ignore emerges from the Afro-American spirituals, tracing a path through blues, ragtime, jazz, rock and roll, hip hop and pop, to the myriad of ways musicking currently meets and cross-fertilizes around the globe. Each one of these music styles and their representatives are the focus of current theological study, at times for their theological content,[73] but more

---

[70]Cf. Pierangelo Sequeri, 'Iniziazione, Invocazione. Contemporaneita', *Musica e Mistica: Percorsi nella Storia Occidentale delle Pratiche Estetiche e Religiose*, 426–504 (Città del Vaticano: Libreria Editrice Vaticana, 2005).
[71]Quoted in Sequeri, *Musica e Mistica: Percorsi nella Storia Occidentale delle Pratiche Estetiche e Religiose*, 510; translation mine.
[72]Ralph Basui Watkins, *Hip-Hop Redemption: Finding God in the Rhythm and the Rhyme* (Grand Rapids, MI: Baker Academic, 2011), 133.
[73]By way of example: for a study of the Scriptural references in contemporary pop music, see Philip Leroy Culbertson and Elaine Mary Wainwright, *The Bible in/and Popular Culture: A Creative Encounter* (Atlanta: Society of Biblical Literature, 2010); an exploration of religious themes is the focus in Carl Olson, *An Introduction to Religion and Religious Themes in Rock Music* (Lewiston, NY: Edwin Mellen Press, 2011); Gilmour takes this approach to a broad range of popular music in his work, for example: Michael J. Gilmour, *Call Me the Seeker: Listening to Religion in Popular Music* (New York: Continuum, 2005); Michael J. Gilmour, *Gods and Guitars: Seeking the Sacred in Post-1960s Popular Music* (Waco, TX: Baylor University Press, 2009).

frequently for the *implicit* doctrinal resonance of 'secular' music, often situated in studies on faith and culture. However, an overemphasis on the lyrical content misses the main point of music (and of this book's quest): words are not the primary carriers of meaning in musicking, which is why 'pop music and culture' tend to be studied together.[74] Jon Spencer's claim – under the title of *theomusicology* – that all popular music is theological because people are inescapably religious, constantly exploring the meaning of their finite existence, encapsulates an intuition underlying many studies of contemporary music. Popular music gives access to a 'more honest religious discourse' than explicitly Christian worship music.[75] Specific genres, such as blues,[76] rhythm and blues, soul, rock,[77] country,[78] heavy metal,[79] hip hop,[80] rave[81] and jazz,[82] are studied for their approach, theological underpinnings,

---

[74]For example, Tom Beaudoin, ed., *Secular Music and Sacred Theology* (Collegeville, MN: Liturgical Press, 2013). Mike Grimshaw, ed., *The Counter-Narratives of Radical Theology and Popular Music: Songs of Fear and Trembling* (New York: Palgrave Macmillan, 2014); Christopher H. Partridge, *The Lyre of Orpheus: Popular Music, the Sacred, and the Profane* (Oxford: Oxford University Press, 2014); Gordon Lynch, *Understanding Theology and Popular Culture* (Malden, MA: Blackwell Pub., 2005); Kelton Cobb, *The Blackwell Guide to Theology and Popular Culture* (Malden, MA: Blackwell Pub., 2005); Christian Scharen, *Broken Hallelujahs: Why Popular Music Matters to Those Seeking God* (Grand Rapids, MI: Brazos Press, 2011).
[75]Cf. Jon Michael Spencer, *Theological Music: Introduction to Theomusicology* (New York: Greenwood Press, 1991); *Blues and Evil* (University of Tennessee Press, 1993); *Theomusicology* (Durham, NC: Duke University Press, 1994); Watkins, *Hip-Hop Redemption*.
[76]James H. Cone, *The Spirituals and the Blues: An Interpretation* (New York: Seabury Press, 1972).
[77]J. Ardui, 'Truth, Rock Music and Christianity: Can Truth Be Maintained in the Dialogue between Theology and Rock Music?', in *Theology and the Quest for Truth: Historical- and Systematic-Theological Studies*, ed. M. Lamberigts, L. Boeve, and T. Merrigan, 199–212 (Leuven: Leuven University Press, 2006); Roberto Avant-Mier, *Rock the Nation: Latin/O Identities and the Latin Rock Diaspora* (London and New York: Continuum, 2010); Mina Carson, Tisa Lewis, and Susan M. Shaw, *Girls Rock!: Fifty Years of Women Making Music* (University Press of Kentucky, 2014); Gillian G. Gaar and Yōko Ono, *She's a Rebel: The History of Women in the Rock and Roll* (Seattle, WA: Seal Press, 1992); David Nantais, *Rock-a My Soul: An Invitation to Rock Your Religion* (Collegeville, MN: Liturgical Press, 2011). Nantais' book is an exceptionally clear introduction to a theology of rock, a spirituality of rock and roll.
[78]David Fillingim, *Redneck Liberation: Country Music as Theology* (Macon, GA: Mercer University Press, 2003).
[79]Robert Walser, *Running with the Devil: Power, Gender, and Madness in Heavy Metal Music* (Middletown, CT: Wesleyan University Press, 1993); Mark LeVine, *Heavy Metal Islam: Rock, Resistance, and the Struggle for the Soul of Islam* (New York: Three Rivers Press, 2008).
[80]Watkins, *Hip-Hop Redemption*.
[81]Graham St. John, *Rave Culture and Religion* (London and New York: Routledge, 2004); Gordon Lynch and Emily Badger, 'The Mainstream Post-Rave Club Scene as a Secondary Institution: A British Perspective', *Culture and Religion* 7, no. 1 (2006): 27–40.
[82]For an excellent overview of recent writings in this field, see Bradley K. Broadhead, *Jazz and Christian Freedom: Improvising against the Grain of the* (Eugene, OR: Pickwick Publications, 2018). Other focussed studies include Bruce Ellis Benson, *The Improvisation of Musical Dialogue: A Phenomenology of Music* (Cambridge: Cambridge University Press, 2003); 'Improvising Texts, Improvising Communities: Jazz, Interpretation, Heterophony, and the *Ekklesia*', in *Resonant Witness: Conversations between Music and Theology*, ed. J. Begbie and S. R. Guthrie,

social critique or compositional style. And the theological attention given to groups like U2[83] or musicians like John Coltrane's 'A Love Supreme'[84] rivals that garnered by Bach or Mozart.

Each musicker, group and genre would merit attention, but that is not the aim of this book. What *is* important, where possible, is to trace the big picture underpinning music-making and its theological relevance, and the reality in this group of genres is that we are not talking about completely separate and diverse phenomena: in terms of genesis, they share a point of origin and a confrontational approach to sociopolitical forces. Each genre is recognized to share musical traits we can trace back to African music, such as syncopation, multiple layers of rhythm with beats in some instruments (or handclapping or foot-stomping) and off-beats in others, improvisation based on a simple formula that allows wide-ranging variation and bending pitches or sliding from one pitch to another.[85]

> Such seemingly disparate musics as, say, country and western, reggae, jazz, punk rock, Broadway popular songs and calypso were all in fact aspects of one brilliant tradition, which resulted from the collision in the Americas, during and after the times of slavery, between two great musical cultures (perhaps one should say, groups of cultures) that of Europe and that of Africa, a tradition which partakes of the nature of both but is not the same as either. . . . [They] are not separate musical categories, however much the analytical temper of Europeans would have it so, but are constantly shifting and interacting facets of the great tradition, meeting and flowing into one another, grouping and regrouping with dizzying rapidity, and without regard for the labours of specialists or archivists.[86]

This birth-place allows us to perceive family traits: from our perspective of the social relationships this stream of music establishes, they are forms of musical resistance to sociopolitical systemic pressures, *and* they generally work in the opposite way that Euro-American classical musicking did. Small's analysis of the characteristics of Afro-American musicking is fascinating:

295–319 (Grand Rapids, MI: William B. Eerdmans, 2011). The importance of how jazz works as a paralogical form of knowing is being applied to other areas of human life: Frank J. Barrett, *Yes to the Mess: Surprising Leadership Lessons from Jazz* (Boston, MA: Harvard Business Press, 2012).

[83]For example, the U2 conference and network of scholars, fans and those working in the media industry created in 2009 and still active: https://u2conference.com/.

[84]Cf. Jamie Howison, *God's Mind in That Music: Theological Explorations through the Music of John Coltrane* (Portland, OR: Wipf and Stock Publishers, 2012).

[85]Cf. Hanning, *Concise History of Western Music*, 535.

[86]Christopher Small, *Music of the Common Tongue: Survival and Celebration in African American Music* (Hanover, NH: University Press of New England, 1987), 3–5.

1. First, this musicking 'is not exclusive. The gift of musicking is open to all' (and Afro-American musicians work just as hard at their art as do those of the European classical tradition, even if less time is spent in solitary practising).
2. Second, 'all performance carries within it an element of original creation, however modest; it is not just the recreation of another person's composition' or genius.
3. Third, 'relationships between the participants in a performance are not hierarchical; the performers do not dominate the audience, nor are they dominated by any outside person such as a composer or conductor. Nor is the performance dominated, or the relationships mediated, by a written score'.[87]

This is musical creation from the bottom up, not top down:

> from Great Composers (or Great Songwriters) via Great Performers to the ordinary music lover. In Afro-American music, as we have seen many times – it is without doubt its greatest strength – new musical styles originate at the bottom of society and work their way upwards, reaching the ears of the middle and upper classes, generally through the medium of records, and often in diluted form, quite possibly around the same time as their anonymous creators (anonymous to us maybe, but not to their community) are abandoning them for something new.[88]

The difference between musical traditions and performance cultures is stark, especially in light of the fact that African slaves used *music* to resist the way their 'owners' told the Christian story as a mechanism of control. Compare this approach with Schoenberg's description of modernist art – 'If it is art, it is not for all, and if it is for all, it is not art'[89] – or Princeton professor Milton Babbitt's writings on 'The Composer as Specialist' (first published as 'Who Cares If You Listen?' in 1958):

> Why should the layman be other than bored and puzzled by what he is unable to understand, music or anything else? It is only the translation of this boredom and puzzlement into resentment and denunciation that seems to me indefensible. . . . I dare suggest that the composer would do himself and his music an immediate and eventual service by total, resolute, and voluntary withdrawal from this public world to one of private performance and electronic media, with its very real possibility of complete elimination of the public and social aspects of musical composition. By so

---

[87]Cf. Small, *Music of the Common Tongue*, 464–5.
[88]Small, *Music of the Common Tongue*, 465.
[89]Arnold Schoenberg, *Style and Idea: Selected Writings of Arnold Schoenberg*, ed. L. Stein, Rev. paperback ed. (London: Faber, 1984), 124.

doing, the separation between the domains would be defined beyond any possibility of confusion of categories, and the composer would be free to pursue a private life of professional achievement, as opposed to a public life of unprofessional compromise and exhibitionism.[90]

These are polar opposite understandings of music and musicking, reflective of the thought-systems of each culture and more importantly their underlying understandings of being and the divine. Afro-American musicking, as a key space of self-identification and community building, is the resource of a culture which, even as it has advanced and adapted, has manifested the resilience and creativity necessary to cope, survive and thrive. Interestingly – and returning to our notion of music as *theologal* – it resists not only unjust relationships but also the underpinning sense of the transcendent that sustains those systems. Once again, the fundamental question is what image or understanding of God underpins our musicking.

Small's final chapter, provocatively entitled 'Confronting the Rational God',[91] is not an attack on Christianity but on a form of rationalizing an unjust economical system that is European-American Industrialism and how certain forms of musicking supported or challenged it. Through the work of Albert Murray, Small argues that African-American culture works with different metaphysical conceptions of change, time, continuity and permanence.[92] That this challenge is formulated in musical terms leads him to a difficult question:

> *Is there something built into the nature of classical works that makes performing and listening to them under any circumstances go counter to the way I believe human relationships should be?* Do they sing a siren song? Or to put it in newspaper headline terms, *Was even Mozart wrong?* Many people whose views I respect would answer those questions with a firm yes.[93]

Why? Because of the kinds of relationships that are reflected and established. It is important to emphasize that Small is not advocating Afro-American music against classical music. He himself was known to play and perform classical music in his local community and his commitment is to a descriptive rather than evaluative understanding of how musicking is taking place.[94]

---

[90]Milton Babbitt, 'The Composer as Specialist', in *The Collected Essays of Milton Babbitt*, ed. S. Peles, et al., 48–54 (51–3) (Princeton: Princeton University Press, 2003).
[91]Small, *Music of the Common Tongue*, 461–83.
[92]Small, *Music of the Common Tongue*, 243.
[93]Christopher Small, *Musicking: The Meanings of Performing and Listening* (Hanover, NH: University Press of New England, 1998), 16; emphasis in original.
[94]For example, he notes that in eighteenth- and nineteenth-century classical performances, an improvisational space was left for the soloist to show his or her own inventiveness ... known as a cadenza, something which current performance culture could not imagine. Cf. Small, *Music of the Common Tongue*, 282.

The issue is about how music is made in their performances, jazz club versus symphony hall, if you like, and the mode of relationships they emulate and effectuate. Critical reflection is required on what each style of musicking models and makes present.

From a theological perspective – which was not Small's – there are further questions to be asked in relation to the Afro-American music tradition (in all its forms), such as what lies behind its ongoing influence among millions of peoples who have had little or no contact with the experience of Black people in America or elsewhere. It is facile and classicist to continue defending certain kinds of music as a kind of opium of the unthinking masses or proof of higher thought processes! 'Black music is not the universal unconscious or the primitive body projected by romanticists of various stripes but rather a highly disciplined set of practices.'[95] Another issue is what the essential difference in compositional mode between these musical traditions of the twentieth- and twenty-first centuries say about the enculturated nature of human thought *and* the underlying sense of the divine. Take jazz, for example, a music form that is currently a major focus of contemporary theology studies into music.[96] Jazz emphasizes performance and freedom – or rather the held tension between a shared musical 'idea' or riff and the necessary skill, spontaneity and *risk* of the performer of getting it wrong! It is not just content that jazz methods and improvisation bring to the theological table but rather a different way of thinking about music and theology! 'Jazz says we don't know until we can do.'[97] Compare this to modernist music, which – for all its harmonic innovation – still holds tight to the control of its compositional form. Messiaen was adamant: 'the values are always notated exactly; hence ... the reader and the performer have only to read and execute *exactly the values marked*'.[98] More fundamental and perhaps subversive questions include musical styles and their corresponding metaphysical imaginations, such as is there an 'image' of God underlying different styles of musicking and how does it relate to the God revealed in Jesus? And – returning to chapter two – what does the preference of modern aesthetic theory and specific theologians for certain music styles says about their understanding of human and divine relationality?

---

[95] Susan McClary and Robert Walser, 'Theorizing the Body in African-American Music', *Black Music Research Journal* (1994): 75–84 (76).

[96] Broadhead, *Jazz and Christian Freedom*; Carl F. Ellis Jr, *Free at Last?: The Gospel in the African-American Experience* (Downer's Grover, IL: InterVarsity Press, 1996); Ann Pederson, *God, Creation, and All That Jazz: A Process of Composition and Improvisation* (St. Louis, MO: Chalice Press, 2001).

[97] Broadhead, *Jazz and Christian Freedom*, 7–8, commenting on Robert Gelinas, *Finding the Groove: Composing a Jazz-Shaped Faith* (Grand Rapids, MI: Zondervan, 2009).

[98] Olivier Messiaen, *The Technique of My Musical Language*, trans. J. Satterfield (Paris: Alphonse Leduc, 1956), 14.

These issues have long been emerging and named in the interdisciplinary field shared by New Musicology's cultural approaches to musical meaning[99] and feminist analyses of music theologies.[100] Their insights will take a while to trickle through the resistant bastions of theology's modus operandi and the insecurity of some Church authorities. That is not my main focus in this book. But there are too many convergences between the exclusion of female voices from all things ecclesial and theological, suspicion about bodies and embodiment in Western culture, and music's historical marginalization from thought to ignore. In theology's resistance to performing the logos with other than words, I see an echo of the above persistent attempts to control meaning, identity and the relationships communities establish among themselves and with the Transcendent (named or unnamed), also through music. This is a costly journey and one in which the ecclesial cultures framing theology are (once again) trailing behind social sciences, in which 'it is quite possible that gender has already ceased to be a principal focus in and of itself, as more and more scholars observe gender-related issues in their research as a matter of course'.[101] Theology that doesn't include the methodological paradigms necessary to theologize as required will find itself increasingly skirting the outside of cultural discourse, and as a result, left out of the conversation. To this problem, chapter four offers a reflection.

A coda: Theological endings?

We have come full circle, in two ways. First, if Western music (and thought) began in Europe and influenced the Americas in both their classical and ecclesial musicking, it is now the multiple genres born of this Afro-American tradition that hold sway over the majority of musicking in the West and across the world today. 'Blues, jazz, rhythm and blues, soul, rock, and rap are among the American-born music forms that have had a vast impact on the musical cultures of the world.'[102] Arguably, this is the same trend we

---

[99]Susan McClary's work still stands out today as groundbreaking in this field: Susan McClary, *Feminine Endings: Music, Gender, and Sexuality* (Minneapolis: University of Minnesota Press, 2002); '"Feminine Endings" at Twenty', *TRANS-Transcultural Music Review* (2011); '"Feminine Endings" in Retrospect', *Feminine Endings: Music, Gender, and Sexuality*, ix–xx (Minneapolis and London: University of Minnesota Press, 2002). She builds on the work of Joseph Kerman and others, in, for example, Joseph Kerman, *Contemplating Music Challenges to Musicology*, ed. S. American Council of Learned Societies (Cambridge, MA: Harvard University Press, 1985).

[100]Heidi Epstein's rewriting of music theologies over the history of its existence should be obligatory reading for every theologian even minimally interested in the field, including those suspicious of some of her positions in relation to feminist and queer theologies. See Part I of her book Epstein, *Melting the Venusberg*, chapters 1–3.

[101]McClary, '"Feminine Endings" in Retrospect', ix–xx (xviii).

[102]Jon Michael Spencer, 'Overview of American Popular Music in a Theological Perspective', *Black Sacred Music: A Journal of Theomusicology* 8, no. 1 (1994): 205–17 (205).

see in current religious and theological hubs, where the Global South and racial diversity are taking the lead. Second, much of these musical traditions resist and refute Western 'secularizing' narratives that enthrone thought over feeling and reason's maturity over religion. The faith-filled resistance of Afro-American spirituals and blues resonates with our starting point: the essentially religious and musical nature of human life across the globe, and the contribution music has to offer theological discourse. It is ironic, bordering on unbelievable, that 'each of these types of music has tended to be perceived by Westerners as being unreligious and therefore incapable of revealing people's religious cosmology'.[103] The question of which image of God music reflects is omnipresent!

Before moving on to chapter four in which I make a specific proposal as to how music and theology could fruitfully interact, I would propose that with all we have discovered, Chua's claims about absolute music – that it 'cannot be confined to the history of music as if it were purely musical'[104] – could be stated about all musicking. Chua speaks of a 'necessary and unresolved dissonance' at the core of Western knowledge.[105] The histories of music in theology and theology in music narrated in chapters two and three may not resolve how to move forward, but they do, I maintain, prove the theological nature of musicking, tout court. By way of coda, a conversation between writer Toni Morrison and philosopher Cornel West on blues and jazz[106] is apropos:

> CW: You've got a blues sensibility, don't you?
> TM: A very complicated sense of blues as it morphed or changed or influenced jazz. . . . The blues is about some loss, some pain and some other things. But it doesn't whine; even when it's begging to be understood in the lyrics, the music contradicts that feeling of being a complete victim and completely taken over. There's a sense of agency, even when someone has broken your heart. The process of having the freedom to have made that choice is what surfaces in blues.
> CW: There's no vengeance and bitterness in the blues, even though there's a dogged determination. And when you respond to terrorism, if what is motivating you is the bitterness and the vengeance, then Shakespeare says vengeance is sweet but short-term, whereas the blues folk say it's about justice and it's about looking beyond so you don't reinforce the cycle.

---

[103]Spencer, 'Overview of American Popular Music in a Theological Perspective', 205–17 (205).
[104]Chua, *Absolute Music*, xii.
[105]Chua, *Absolute Music*, xii.
[106]Cornel West, *Race Matters, 25th Anniversary: With a New Introduction* (Beacon Press, 2017).

I want to make a distinction between 'childish' and 'childlike.' You see, the blues and jazz are childlike, the sense of awe and wonder and the mystery and perplexity of things. 'Childish' is immature. And what we have now, we have the imperial elite who are adolescent and immature because they perceive their crude interests to be protected only by might, only by force. . . . The blues tradition that goes, let's say, from Leroy Carr to your own work is not just music, it's an idiom; it's a way of being in the world, it's mature, and it takes unbelievable courage, persistence, practice, discipline, energy to be a mature, compassionate, decent person. And that's exactly what the blues fish is trying to get us to be because you can't have a democracy without it.

And the question is what role do, first, the artists, play, then the activists, and the intellectuals, for the larger citizenry?[107]

Selected further reading

Beaudoin, Tom, ed. *Secular Music and Sacred Theology*. Collegeville, MN: Liturgical Press, 2013.

Broadhead, Bradley K. *Jazz and Christian Freedom: Improvising against the Grain of the West*. Eugene OR: Pickwick Publications, 2018.

Carson, Mina, Tisa Lewis, and Susan M Shaw. *Girls Rock!: Fifty Years of Women Making Music*. Lexington: University Press of Kentucky, 2014.

Cone, James H. *The Spirituals and the Blues: An Interpretation*. New York: Seabury Press, 1972.

Dreyfus, Laurence. *Bach and the Patterns of Invention*. Cambridge, MA: Harvard University Press, 2004.

Ellis Jr, Carl F. *Free at Last?: The Gospel in the African-American Experience*. Downer's Grover, IL: InterVarsity Press, 1996.

Gelinas, Robert. *Finding the Groove: Composing a Jazz-Shaped Faith*. Grand Rapids, MI: Zondervan, 2009.

Godzieba, Anthony J. 'And Followed Him on the Way (Mk 10:52): Unity, Diversity, Discipleship'. In *Beyond Dogmatism and Innocence: Hermeneutics, Critique, and Catholic Theology*, edited by Anthony J. Godzieba and Bradford E. Hinze, 228–54. Collegeville, MN: Liturgical Press, 2017.

Lynch, Gordon. *Understanding Theology and Popular Culture*. Malden, MA: Blackwell Pub., 2005.

Messiaen, Olivier. *The Technique of My Musical Language*. Translated by John Satterfield. Paris: Alphonse Leduc, 1956.

Nantais, David. *Rock-a My Soul: An Invitation to Rock Your Religion*. Collegeville, MN: Liturgical Press, 2011.

---

[107] West, *Race Matters, 25th Anniversary: With a New Introduction*.

Partridge, Christopher H. *The Lyre of Orpheus: Popular Music, the Sacred, and the Profane*. Oxford: Oxford University Press, 2014.
Schoenberg, Arnold. *Style and Idea: Selected Writings of Arnold Schoenberg*, edited by Leonard Stein. Rev. paperback ed. ed. London: Faber, 1984.
Spencer, Jon Michael. *Theomusicology*. Durham, NC: Duke University Press, 1994.
West, Cornel. *Race Matters, 25th Anniversary: With a New Introduction*. Boston: Beacon Press, 2017.

4

From theory to interiority

When is song-writing theological?

I will solve my riddle to the music of the harp . . . Ps. 49.4

Up to this point, the focus has been on musicking as a social and identity-making activity and the interweaving of theology and music in the emergence of the Christian world as we know it. In this chapter I turn my attention more explicitly to the *theological potential* of Christian songwriting for the future of theology.[1] It is an explicit attempt to bridge the gap between a world gone by and one that is emerging – how music and theology have interacted until now and what might need to happen to build its future. For that reason, this is necessarily a more theoretical chapter than those before or after it, because it seeks to create a recognizable framework for the discipline of theology within which music has a place. We have seen how there are a variety of perspectives from which musicking can be of theological import. At this stage, the question focuses on how musick*ing* and theologiz*ing* might aid one another in theological investigation; that is to say: how the activity of intentional Christian musical composition can function as a form of theological activity and in what way. Therefore, in hermeneutical terms, the

---

[1] At the heart of this chapter is the work of James Maher MSC in James Maher, 'The Christian Songwriter as Theologian: Giving Voice to the Converted Heart and Mind' (MCD University of Divinity, 2013). James died prematurely before being able to promote and publish his work further, but conversations with him before his passing have enriched my own explorations, for which I am deeply thankful. I am also grateful to Kathleen Williams RSM of Yarra Theological College for her advice and encouragement in taking this forward.

chosen perspective is that of 'behind the text': the activity of the theologian or theological community *in formulating theological understanding*.

To further concentrate our attention, while much of what is said can be applied to a variety of styles of music with or without lyrics, the genre or type of musical composition I focus on specifically is that of the 'Christian song' – that is to say, when the symbolic forms of words and music come together as a whole in an intentional practice of expressing or conveying religious experience towards a greater understanding of truth, in the light of Christian revelation. By song I mean 'a piece of music for voice or voices, whether accompanied or unaccompanied',[2] not explicitly composed for use in liturgy or at least leaving aside the question of whether and in what situations this might be appropriate. When and in what way can songwriting be considered a theological act and an explicit part of the collaborative and interdisciplinary discipline of theological reflection? When and how can or *should* it be included in and as theological investigation?[3] In this way, the chapter completes Part I of the book and lays the foundations for Part II, in which each chapter presents the theological insights of a range of thinkers through the complementary lenses of music and words.

A theological method with space for the arts

In what ways, within our current understanding of the discipline, can we call music *theological*? Is that not asking too much of music? In the words of Paul Westermeyer, 'theology is a reflective process that demands words, music a performing process that demands sound. Theology reflects on music (and everything else), and music sounds. Let the two be what they are'.[4] Westermeyer is drawing on a common conception of theology as 'words about God' (*theologos*) that limits theology to 'discursive language' and thereby excludes music from theology. It also overlooks the nature of sound implicated in words.[5] In this paradigm, 'we can only re-admit it by demonstrating music's language-like capacities'.[6] But music,

---

[2] Geoffrey Chew et al., 'Song' (Oxford University Press).
[3] We need to keep in mind that musical production involves not only the inspiration, genius or expertise of one person or group but tends to be the fruit of a process, including composition, arrangement, performance and production. The myth of the individual genius is waning in current research. See David W. Galenson, *Old Masters and Young Geniuses: The Two Life Cycles of Artistic Creativity* (Princeton, NJ: Princeton University Press, 2006).
[4] Paul Westermeyer, 'Reflections on Music and Theology', *Theological Education* XXXI (1994): 183–9 (189).
[5] Cf. Stephen H. Webb, *The Divine Voice: Christian Proclamation and the Theology of Sound* (Grand Rapids, MI: Brazos Press, 2004).
[6] Maher, 'The Christian Songwriter as Theologian', 8.

in my opinion, is not a language. Even claims to its universality in terms of affect or feeling are misplaced when one starts to explore the diversity of musical genres and tonal systems.[7] Given the non-referential nature of the musical symbolic form, the significance of music for theology needs a different approach.

The issue depends on how we think about and organize theological research, which in one sense is a known and defined field but in another is constantly developing in relation to the needs of the context and its subject matter. A recent study into the current state of theology worldwide and how it is shaped by the institutions that 'host' it described theology as a discipline with multiple self-defined fields of study, subdivided 'by subject matter, source materials and/or as a web of related subfields'.[8] In the current climate of specialized knowledge, it is the last option that holds more promise for a theology in which music's theological potential is recognized. Understood in this way, theological research flourishes when it reflects on how each subfield relates to and interacts with others, for the critical accountability of each and the advancement of theological knowledge as a whole.[9] It is worth noting that extra-theological studies into musical meaning also tend to be interdisciplinary in nature due to the variety of angles from which music can be studied.[10]

The problem is not limited to theology, as other areas of research in the humanities seek paradigms to include 'the role of artists in proposing new concepts for the problems of contemporary society and their ability to offer alternative solutions, or at least to propose new questions, based on non-exclusive rational modes of thought'.[11] Seeking to articulate the difference and connecting points between what is commonly understood as academic research and the type of research specific to artistic activity, experts working in what is variously named as 'arts-based research', 'research-led practice', 'practice-as-research' or 'research-creation' are focussed on 'the bi-

---

[7]The universality of music is more accepted in relation to the activity of music-making, even while its meaning and role may differ. Cf. Jean-Jacques Nattiez, *Music and Discourse. Toward a Semiology of Music* (Princeton, NJ: Princeton University Press, 1990).
[8]Cf. at *The Syndicate* https://syndicate.network/symposia/theology/syndicate-project-on-the-state-of-theology/ (accessed 6 May 2021).
[9]Discovery of the fruitfulness of interdisciplinary collaboration and delimitation of fields is evident across the board in academic research. In many ways, theology is coming late to the party. See, for example, Walter S. Gershon, *The Collaborative Turn: Working Together in Qualitative Research* (Rotterdam: Sense, 2009); Vera John-Steiner, *Creative Collaboration* (New York: Oxford University Press, 2000).
[10]For example, David J. Hargreaves, Dorothy Miell, and Raymond A. R. MacDonald, *Musical Imaginations: Multidisciplinary Perspectives on Creativity, Performance, and Perception* (Oxford: Oxford University Press, 2012); Eric F. Clarke, Nicola Dibben, and Stephanie Pitts, *Music and Mind in Everyday Life* (Oxford: Oxford University Press, 2010).
[11]Ruben López-Cano, 'Art Research, Music Knowledge and the Contemporary Crisis', *Art Research Journal* 1 (2015): 69–94 (69).

directional nature of collaboration between artistic practice and research'.[12] Their methodological organization is based on the understanding that there are investigative questions that can only be answered by the type of activity and knowledge born of artistic activity.[13] Importantly, it is the questions being asked that mark the investigative form, and the quest is to define and accompany how this takes place, and in what way it interacts with other investigators. These are similar quests to the one I am proposing for theology, which exemplify a differentiation of roles necessary to the accumulation and transmission of knowledge.[14] Opening a space for music in theology is not to say it can substitute words, but rather that there is a role for music in theology that is distinct and that theology will be poorer if it continues to be sidelined. This is not the only field seeking to cultivate the intersection between theological investigation and praxis,[15] and there have been collaborative projects with more or less success over the past few decades.[16] But it needs a more formulated and systematic organization if it is to be effective.

The theological framework I have chosen as a channel to identifying where music fits and functions in theology is that of Bernard J. F. Lonergan and the research centres that apply and develop his approach.[17] I am aware of the, at times visceral, reactions to Lonergan's method, perhaps based on a rigid understanding (or implementation?) of his work; or the effort it takes to study his rather comprehensive underlying epistemology;[18] or his at times black-and-white language; but I think we are at a stage in the battle for

---

[12]Hazel Smith and R. T. Dean, *Practice-Led Research, Research-Led Practice in the Creative Arts* (Edinburgh: Edinburgh University Press, 2009), 1.

[13]Cf. Sophie Stévance and Serge Lacasse, 'Research-Creation in Music as a Collaborative Space', *Media-N Journal of the New Media Caucus* (2015); Sophie Stevance and Serge Lacasse, *Research-Creation in Music and the Arts: Towards a Collaborative Interdiscipline*, Sempre Studies in the Psychology of Music (London, UK: Taylor & Francis Ltd., Routledge, 2019); Smith and Dean, *Practice-Led Research, Research-Led Practice in the Creative Arts*; Rubén López Cano and Úrsula San Cristóbal Opazo, *Investigación Artística en Música: Problemas, Experiencias y Propuestas* (Mexico: Fondo Nacional Para la Cultura y Las Artes).

[14]'Occasionally, one or a group of collaborators may be active in both creative work and research, but more often several people with differentiated roles interact effectively with each other.' Smith and Dean, *Practice-Led Research, Research-Led Practice in the Creative Arts*, 8.

[15]It is a large focus of practical theology. Cf. Joyce Mercer and Bonnie Miller-McLemore, *Conundrums in Practical Theology* (Leiden: Brill, 2016).

[16]By way of example, the aforementioned search by Jon Michael Spencer for a theologically informed musicology: Jon Michael Spencer, *Theological Music: Introduction to Theomusicology* (New York: Greenwood Press, 1991). And the *Music Theology* network spearheaded by Bennet Zon at Durham University: https://www.dur.ac.uk/musictheology/.

[17]Such as the Lonergan Centres and Institutes in Boston College, Massachusetts: https://bclonergan.org/; Regis College, Toronto: http://www.lonerganresearch.org; Loyola Marymount University, Los Angeles: https://bellarmine.lmu.edu/lonergan/; Dublin: https://lonerganmorin.wordpress.com/2007/03/04/dublin-lonergan-centre/; and at the Pontifical Gregorian University, Rome: https://www.unigre.it/it/ua/facolta/teologia/progetto-lonergan/.

[18]Cf. Bernard J. F. Lonergan, *Insight*, ed. F. E. Crowe and R. M. Doran, *Collected Works of Bernard Lonegan* (Toronto: University of Toronto Press, 1957).

theology's sustained influence in the humanities to put aside our differences and draw the best insights out of every thinker, beyond personal preference. While I am sure much of what I have to say can be translated and adapted to other frameworks, I have not found a clearer way to introduce it. So, this chapter clearly names and explains music's role in theology within a Lonerganian framework and using his terminology. I believe a greater understanding of this approach and insights would serve our students and future theologians well, for a variety of reasons.

First and foremost, how it frames the history of thought and the stages of meaning through which we have passed, shaping how theology works as we go. Lonergan identifies three broad 'eras' in the development of Western culture within which theology and philosophy have grown: myth, theory and interiority. Myth is the practical, pre-philosophical phase in which cultures navigate worlds of meaning through the creation of mythical narratives, so as to organize and control life. Philosophy marked the emergence of the second stage – theory – and it is here that the doctrinal and theoretical norms that guide theology were adopted and framed. However, cultural shifts worldwide have not remained in that space. The stage in which we currently find ourselves Lonergan calls 'interiority', and describes it as one in which historical consciousness, and both personal and shared contextual meanings ground every attempt to name truth. In these shifting sands of current cultural awareness and modes of learning, it is clear that forms of theologizing that draw on the lived experience of people of faith beyond, or rather to inform, the theoretical are needed. This implies integrating the way meaning manifests itself beyond or often before, in time *and* genesis, words.[19] We are symbolic beings and make sense of things in a variety of ways. It is not only words in explanatory discourse that break through human experience to make present a dimension and direction that lead us elsewhere, but also other human forms of expression, such as art, gesture, taste, friendship, poetry, stories and memory. Furthermore, as symbols follow the laws of image and feeling rather than logic, they can bring together what logical discourse struggles with – the tension of opposites and incompatibilities – before dialectical discourse tackles them.[20] Songs combine artistic, symbolic, intersubjective (especially when performed) and linguistic meaning, even if at times lyrics are more exploratory than explanatory. The combined work or trajectory of an artist or group carries incarnate meaning, which is important for a theology of witness, and raises the issues of style, taste, culture and differentiations of consciousness. Is there any doubt that songs

---

[19]The shift from defining humanity as rational to relational, or symbol-maker, reflects that awareness. Susanne K. Langer, *Philosophy in a New Key: A Study in the Symbolism of Reason, Rite, and Art*, 3rd ed. (Cambridge, MA: Harvard University Press, 1957); Cf. William A. Van Roo, *Man, the Symbolizer* (Rome: Gregorian University Press, 1981).
[20]Cf. Bernard J. F. Lonergan, *Method in Theology* (New York: The Seabury Press, 1972), 64–7.

effectively communicate meaning that in some way shapes identity? 'Let me write a nation's songs, and I don't care who writes her laws.'[21]

Further to this, Lonergan's approach to theological method identifies the epistemological challenges facing theology, leaves space for diverse forms of awareness and thought, and allows *how* we address the issues at stake be led and shaped by the questions being asked. Four connected aspects of his thought are presented in the following section, a necessary premise to explaining the particular role of music-making I am proposing: his understanding of the proper function of theology in relation to culture; the different tasks, or 'specialities', needed for theology to function effectively; the hinge-point moment or task in theological method known as 'Foundations', and the complementary dynamics of knowledge at play in theology in connection to a multiform approach to conversion in theological investigation.

A theological method defined by questions

Theology in culture

The broadest and perhaps most inclusive definition of theology is John Macquarrie's concise description: 'God-talk'.[22] This is the one adopted by the aforementioned *Syndicate* study to include the broad spectrum of work in this field. I would suggest that theology is best understood when its overall aim is also clear. My chosen method describes theology as reflection on religion[23] which, in every context in which it finds itself, '*seeks to mediate between that cultural matrix (or matrices) and the significance and role of a given religion in that matrix*',[24] for the purpose of the human good of each individual and society. It has a bridging role between religion and its surrounding worlds. As such, theology is distinct from religion itself; it promotes the religion it studies, but it does not constitute religious events.[25] It does, however, have an aim that is consonant with the intentionality of the religion upon which it reflects. Therefore, rather than assuming the commonplace distinction between theology as 'faith seeking understanding', from within, and religious studies as its exploration 'from outside' religious belonging, it is possible to build a 'structure' in which the perspectives of both can (and should) feed into its overriding aim.

---

[21] Attributed to John Fletcher (1655-1716) and quoted in Bernard J. F. Lonergan, 'Art', in *Collected Works of Bernard Lonergan. Vol. 10: Topics in Education*, ed. R. M. Doran and F. E. Crowe, 208–32 (221) (Toronto: University of Toronto Press, 1993).
[22] John Macquarrie, *God-Talk: An Examination of the Language and Logic of Theology* (New York: Seabury Press, 1979).
[23] Lonergan, *Method in Theology*, 267, 355.
[24] Lonergan, *Method in Theology*, xi; emphasis mine.
[25] Lonergan, *Method in Theology*, 170.

Theology's functional specialities

How? By subdividing its tasks and recognizing the many and varied areas of religious studies that relate to the exploration of religion, from any number of positions on faith and religious belief, as well as identifying more clearly when and where an explicitly faith-oriented or ecclesial viewpoint is necessary. We are used to the division of labour in theological investigation, but it usually corresponds to subject areas: Scripture or doctrines, morality or interreligious dialogue and so on. Lonergan suggests that within these themes, a focus on the questions needing to be answered offers greater precision and overall results. Which task each individual or group is performing and how it interacts with the rest will depend upon the questions to which they are seeking an answer – that is to say, the intentionality that frames and guides their research. By distinguishing and separating the interlocking stages and specific methodological approaches required for the overall process to achieve its end, 'from data to results',[26] spaces are opened for the expertise of a broad spectrum of scholars. Lonergan names these different tasks or intents 'functional specialities' and identifies eight: Research, Interpretation, History, Dialectics, Foundations, Doctrines, Systematics and Communications.[27] The questions guiding Research and Communications are about human experience: 'What is happening or happened?' The questions guiding Interpretation and Systematics seek to interpret whatever research comes up with in a way that respects the cultural and historical context of the data. History and Doctrines explore what is changing or needs to be changed or expressed differently, as well as the interconnection between themes or doctrines. Dialectics and Foundations do the hard work of explaining contradictory opinions and grounding theology's reinterpretative task for the cultures within which it works, respectively. Furthermore, theological method is divided into two phases: mediating and mediated. This is important, because it makes space for the differences between faith traditions, leaving room for them to explore and make explicit their particular worldview and intentionality. The first phase (Research, Interpretation, History and Dialectics) continually studies and gathers the sources of religious practice and research from past and present;

---

[26]Lonergan, *Method in Theology*, 125.
[27]The wonder of discovery can conceal convergences with other approaches. Many current areas of theological research could easily be recognized in some of these fields. For example, in Research, much of Scripture scholarship and archaeology; in Interpretation, hermeneutics applied to the emergence of doctrines; in History, historical theology and philosophy. Foundations is the task that adds something new, which can be related to what Europe calls fundamental theology but is framed differently. Doctrines is the ongoing development of themes of dogmatic theology between which Systematics draws the connections and organizes. Communications has a lot in common with pastoral and some forms of practical theology. However, it is how they interrelate and the overall intent that is important.

the second (Foundations, Doctrines, Systematics and Communications) mediates the results of this research into the present and future of theology's service to religion and culture.

It is the watershed moment between these two phases that holds a place for Christian songwriting, the point at which all the gathered data of research is compared, aligned and decided upon. That is not to say music cannot be a focus in other stages of this methodological approach: on the contrary! There are many ways in which musicking can shed light on theological themes and their development. For example, research into the music of any given moment in history can shed light on the faith practice of a given culture, or lack thereof; writings on the interpretation of music or musical performance in a given denomination can speak to their approach to doctrines; the continuity or changes of music style over time in a given culture can speak to how doctrine develops and complements insights from other areas of the framework of theological research. In past work, I have made a case for music as an effective means of mediation into the presence of the risen and ascended body of Christ in a way that contemporary culture can grasp.[28] While these studies can allow us to navigate the style differences we face and to reflect upon effective communication of Christian faith, they do not fully explain what is happening when music is composed *with the intention of making sense of Christian experience and seeking a greater understanding of Christian faith*. Music is left as an optional means of pastoral application – post-theological, in a unidirectional movement from theology to Church – rather than how many people experience it: as a moment of meaning-making within faith which brings with it theological insights that otherwise might not emerge, *faith making sense of itself through a combination of music and words*. This is why the hinge moment between what theology gathers from the past and how it positions itself into the future, from a faith perspective is where Christian music-making fits. Within Lonergan's structure, this is called Foundations, the fifth moment of theological method.

Foundations: Finding our theological feet

Foundations speaks to theology's need to ground itself afresh amid cultural shifts that challenge its claims to truth, as explored in chapter one.[29] The

---

[28]Cf. Maeve Louise Heaney, *Music as Theology: What Music Has to Say about the Word* (Eugene, OR: Pickwick Publications Wipf and Stock, 2012); Maeve Louise Heaney, 'The Eloquence of Music in Contemporary Culture', *Theology* 114, no. 3 (2011): 198–206; Maeve Louise Heaney, 'Music and Theological Method: A Lonerganian Approach', *Theological Studies* 77, no. 3 (2016): 678703.

[29]A short essay on theology in our changing times explains this need. Cf. Bernard J. F. Lonergan, 'Theology in Its New Context', in *A Second Collection. Papers by Bernard J. F. Lonergan S.J.*, ed. F. J. Ryan and B. J. Tyrell, 55–68 (London: Darton, Longman and Todd, 1974).

epistemological dilemma contemporary culture inherited from the shifts of modernity to current postmodern uncertainty includes the possibility of our accessing truth about anything, never mind the divine. It is an issue which has implications for our understanding of revelation itself. In the current realm of meaning – 'interiority' – the propositional foundations upon which philosophy and metaphysics rest no longer resonate or fulfil their purpose.[30] Most of the current debates around the human capacity to know and affirm the divine are a symptom of this crisis. The very role of philosophy within theology is not fully understood without an insight into this shift of realms, because if the religious experience which provokes the theological quest does not find an echo in how philosophy makes sense of life and faith, then apologetics, the reasoned account of the hope that sustains us (1 Pet. 3.15), is useless. Correct, perhaps, but useless as a means of making sense of God's entry into the world of human meaning.[31] And two wings without connection or coordination can't take flight![32] New foundations for the whole enterprise are needed, and this, Lonergan proposes, in a similar way to the foundations of modern science is not some ultimate verified theory but the expertise of the scientific community in ongoing critically verified accumulation of knowledge. This may seem like a challenge to the metaphysical tenets of Christian philosophy and theology, but it is not. Instead, the issue is about *how we access them*! It marks a transition from metaphysics as first philosophy to metaphysics as a heuristic principle and hermeneutical task. The only 'mind' with twenty-twenty vision is God's. As human beings with limited perspectives, critical reflection on our horizons, assumptions, prejudices and thought processes is essential to our quest for truth.

This position echoes insights from the disciplines of hermeneutics and spirituality in which the perspective as well as *involvement* of the scholar or interpreter is not marginal but an essential element of human understanding. Theological sources are not merely rational data but reflect and open worlds of meaning, and if understanding takes place, human worlds are enlarged and transformed, whether the text at hand be a biblical one or a truth developed and

---

[30] For an overview of contemporary views on and challenges facing metaphysics, see John R. Betz, 'After Heidegger and Marion: The Task of Christian Metaphysics Today', *Modern Theology* 34, no. 4 (2018): 565–97; Michael R. Slater, 'Theology, Metaphysics, and Realism about Truth', *Modern Theology* 35, no. 2 (2019): 244–67. Lonergan addresses this issue by looking at the 'realms of meaning' within which people make sense of life and faith, and assessing its place in the stages of Western culture through which Christianity has developed: common sense, theory and interiority (as seen earlier). The current challenge facing theology is the adequate 'translation' of metaphysical meaning into terms that can be understood in contemporary culture.
[31] Cf. Lonergan, 'Theology in Its New Context', 55–68 (62).
[32] Reference to the image given in *Fides et Ratio* on the complementary nature of faith and reason in guiding us to the contemplation of truth. Cf. John Paul II, *Fides et Ratio: Encyclical Letter of the Supreme Pontiff John Paul II, to the Bishops of the Catholic Church on the Relationship between Faith and Reason* (Strathfield, NSW: St. Paul's Publications, 1998), Introduction.

handed down over time.³³ For this reason I suggest that Christian songwriting is an exercise in Foundations with some elements of what Lonergan called Doctrines. The focus of the book is on a specific type of song-writing. As with other activities in theological investigation, prior and informed knowledge is essential to the specific quest for a role *in* theology for music. The Christian artist who makes music combined with words is reaching for a meaning born within known doctrines, even if trying to read them afresh.³⁴ Each of the songs in Part II of the book seeks an attentive reception of and critical reflection on the thought of the author presented, as well as a personalized, second naïveté, fresh interpretation of some core aspect of faith, in musical form. In this way, songwriting can play a part in the traditioning of faith and the development of theological insight, because it bridges not only the texts but the worlds within which they are born and received.

The complementary dynamics of theological knowledge

Theologies of revelation involve two interweaving sources and dynamics of human knowledge: the human quest for knowledge and divine revelation. The first is the knowledge of reality within which a person lives when as a self-transcending subject, she is attentive to, intelligent about, reasonable and responsible with the internal and external phenomena experienced.³⁵ Lonergan calls this process of attentive self-reflexivity 'self-appropriation'. Attentiveness to the performance of these operations constitutes and grounds meaning in our post-theoretical theological and philosophical worlds. In fact, in a world in which our access to the metaphysical is questioned, the only fixed point is precisely the self-appropriated subject herself, in dialogue with other equally self-appropriated subjects. This is a radical statement (in its etymological sense pertaining to 'forming the root' of something). And in fact, it is also a costly one. Self-appropriation is hard work. It is the commitment of each theologian to be ever attentive to her own operations of experiencing, questioning, understanding, verifying, deciding and acting out in accordance with what emerges.

---

³³Cf. Ricoeur's mapping of the process of human understanding, from first naïveté, through critical inquiry and understanding of the meaning of a text to second naïveté appropriation when that meaning is actualized in and for the interpreter, in Paul Ricoeur, *Interpretation Theory: Discourse and the Surplus of Meaning* (Fort Worth: Texas Christian University Press, 1976).
³⁴Cf. George Steiner, *Real Presences: Is There Anything in What We Say?* (London: Faber, 1991), 195.
³⁵Lonergan refers to these 'operations' of the human person as the 'normative pattern of the recurrent and related operational patterns of the human cognitional process', calling it 'intentionality analysis'. Cf. Lonergan, *Method in Theology*, 24. In philosophical terms, it is a critical-realist position that says *all* human knowledge, albeit in different patterns, follows these steps.

But not everything about our knowledge is human: to this 'upward' dynamic of seeking knowledge we must add the 'downward' gift of God's grace and love by the universal gift of the Spirit to and among human beings. This is experienced in the many ways love floods our lives, the implications of which we 'work out' through personal and *responsible* reception, *reflecting upon* the experience *reasonably* to *understand* what has happened and uncover enriched colour and dimension to every internal and external sensor *experience*.[36] This 'downward' dimension of knowing is the living out of faith, 'the knowledge born of religious love',[37] and colours every subsequent question and quest for knowledge. I would change or even reverse the images of 'upwards' and 'downwards' as unhelpful to contemporary understanding or imagination of the world: Whence is the divine revealed to the human spirit? Perhaps God's gift emerges within the depths of ourselves and we descend there to open to them, or at the very least we seek from within what reaches us from beyond ourselves. However, distinguishing these two dimensions is important: the intertwining of what is given to us and that which we seek in our quest for knowledge.

The notion of conversion in theological method is important to both. As a theme, conversion is gaining momentum in theological discussion,[38] but it is important here to resist a narrow understanding of conversion involving more piety and prayer in theological work (without suggesting this would be a bad thing!). Conversion provokes a shift in the worldview or horizon of a person,[39] an 'about face' that changes and refutes some features of the previous one.[40] And this in various dimensions of the human experience in such a way that it affects how we experience, understand, reflect and act upon our faith. In Lonergan's framework, four conversions or dimensions of human life that have direct consequences on theological thought are named as religious, moral, intellectual and psychic.[41]

---

[36]The words in italics – to experience, to understand, to reflect upon and responsibly act upon – reframe the terminology lonergan uses for the process of human knowing, in the 'opposite' direction.
[37]Lonergan, *Method in Theology*, 115.
[38]This was spearheaded by the work of Groupe des Dombes; Groupe des Dombes, *Vers Une Même Foi Eucharistique: Accord Entre Catholiques Et Protestants* (Taize: Les Presses de Taize, 1972); Groupe des Dombes, *For the Conversion of the Churches* (Geneva: WCC Publications, 1993); Catherine E. Clifford, *The Groupe Des Dombes: A Dialogue of Conversion* (New York: Peter Lang, 2005). Lonergan recognized influence of Rosemary Haughton on his own thought. Cf. Rosemary Haughton, *The Transformation of Man: A Study of Conversion and Community* (London: Chapman, 1967).
[39]A horizontal exercise of freedom for Lonergan is one that moves within the same horizon. A vertical one moves us from one horizon of comprehension to another.
[40]Cf. Lonergan, *Method in Theology*, 237.
[41]The inclusion of psychic conversion was, in fact, an insight of Lonergan scholar Robert Doran, which Lonergan recognised as a useful addition to the other three. Some scholars subdivide these into further nuances, such as subdividing moral conversion into individual ethical conversion and a sociopolitical one; or further developing the notion of religious conversion.

- *Religious conversion* is the reality provoked by the love of God poured out into our hearts, leading to a response of abandonment and surrender, dedication of one's whole life in loving God with all one's heart, soul, mind and strength. It is 'being grasped by ultimate concern'.[42]
- *Intellectual conversion* situates itself on the level of our cognition and consists in the self-appropriation of our process of knowing as described earlier: overcoming the myth of empiricism, or a non-critical type of 'realism' that would have us believe (perceive and think) that 'knowing is like looking, that objectivity is seeing what there is to be seen and not seeing what is not there'.[43] The real world is that of a person in the midst of the world with the meaning that they give it, a meaning which is not invented, either, but rather received from and in the midst of a community which transmits that meaning to its members, who then further develop their own. Knowledge is much more complex than we may imagine it to be.
- *Psychic conversion* refers to the healing of our 'sensitive consciousness', the affective 'aesthetic undertow' of our spiritual being, and touches on aspects of the human experience such as affectivity, symbolic perception and intuition. It is related to the areas of feelings and values, and the integration of our embodied existence.[44] Psychic conversion heals the direction of our desire and our attentiveness.
- *Moral conversion* is the ongoing exercise of human freedom in moving from choices guided by satisfaction to those guided by values. In fact, fundamentally it is the change from choosing one thing over another to the awareness that we are entrusted with deciding about our very beings: 'one has to find out for oneself that one has to decide for oneself what one is to make of oneself'.[45] Significantly, this commitment extends to revising not only one's personal authenticity but that of the tradition one belongs to,[46] the common meaning one has inherited.

Cf. Donald L. Gelpi, *Encountering Jesus Christ: Rethinking Christological Faith and Commitment* (Milwaukee, WI: Marquette University Press, 2009), 614–21. Another proposal is that of aesthetic conversion: Richard Viladesau, *Theological Aesthetics: God in Imagination, Beauty, and Art* (New York: Oxford University Press, 1999), 210. The central point here is to note that conversion is not simply about more piety before God but a transformation of various dimensions of human living and knowing.

[42] Lonergan, *Method in Theology*, 240.
[43] Cf. Lonergan, *Method in Theology*, 238–9.
[44] Cf. Robert M. Doran, *Theology and the Dialectics of History* (Toronto, Canada: University of Toronto Press, 1990), 46–53.
[45] Lonergan, *Method in Theology*, 121.
[46] Lonergan distinguishes between what he calls minor and major authenticity, the first being one's authenticity within and to a certain tradition, the second being the very authenticity of

The majority of people may not be consciously aware of the horizons they inhabit or just drift into them, but each of these dimensions of human life and knowledge affects how we think about faith, *especially* when they are not conscious. While conversion is intensely personal, it is not private, as it implies not only a personal change of horizon but also belonging to a group tradition or changing *how* we belong to one.[47] In a recent book on theological foundations, Neil Ormerod and Christiaan Jacobs-Vandegeer explore the effects of each of these conversions on theological investigation and doctrinal development, identifying four examples of how they affect its outcomes. They explain how intellectual conversion helps clarify the doctrine of Eucharistic real presence; religious conversion could inform biblical discussions on the historical Jesus; moral conversion illumines philosophical positions used by liberation theologies; and psychic conversion could shed light on the issues of religious violence and the discernment of good and evil. So once again, it is the central role of theological investigation in our understanding of faith that concerns us here and how the presence or absence of each of these 'about-turns' affects our world view.

Returning to the overall structure of theological method, in Foundations, theology becomes personal, because here theology shifts from gathering data on a given theme to taking a stand[48] – that is to say, 'from the *indirect discourse* that sets forth the convictions and opinions of others (in mediating theology) to the *direct discourse that states what is so* (in mediated theology)'.[49] It is hard to overstate how important this introduction of a specific place and role for conversions into theological method is *for the theological mediation of Christian meaning*; and the familiarity of the term 'conversion' makes the specificity of each harder to grasp. This is not only about the need for faith in theology, as an ecclesial act. Neither is it the intuition that the lives of the saints and mystics who are closer to the source can in some way give us data on how the human can experience something of the divine. Rather, it is one way of working out of Vatican I's formidable balancing act between faith and reason, natural and supernatural knowledge (admitting those terms now need 'translation' to continue to serve their purpose), by which theologians take position in relation to the information gathered from those researching and gathering the history of a given theme's interpretation over time. It asks theologians to 'own' and make explicit the underlying convictions and horizons that colour their opinions and their stance in relation to these four coordinates, as well as their influence on theological positions.

---

that tradition, which is judged definitively by history and God. Cf. B. Lonergan, Bernard J. F. Lonergan, 'Existenz and Aggiornamento', in *Collection. Papers by Bernard Lonergan S.J.*, ed. F. E. Crowe and R. M. Doran, 240–51 (246–7) (New York: Herder and Herder, 1967).
[47]Lonergan, *Method in Theology*, 169.
[48]Neil Ormerod and Christiaan Jacobs-Vandegeer, *Foundational Theology: A New Approach to Catholic Fundamental Theology* (Minneapolis MN: Fortress Press, 2015).
[49]Lonergan, *Method in Theology*, 267; emphasis mine.

While this is not completely new – liberation, feminist and contextual theologies have been calling theology to an awareness of its underlying biases and privileges for years – the novelty here is double: on the one hand, the 'content' or specific dimensions of the call to self-appropriation which go beyond sociopolitical, racial or gender awareness to include a reflection on the process of human knowledge in relation to core experiences and tenets of Christian life itself; and on the other, the structured way this reflection is framed into a methodological whole with the rest of theological disciplines. Theologians are asked to identify and name, *for themselves, first and foremost*, and then transparent to the academic community, the worldview within which they live in these four dimensions: what religious experience underlies their position; what values or interests are at stake in those opinions, both personally and for the tradition within which they are reflecting; what epistemology underpins their understanding of the world and the categories with which they are explaining themselves, and how their own psyche – in its affective and symbolic resonances – could be affecting what they choose to perceive, attend to and defend. In Lonergan's words, Foundations '"objectifies" the horizon effected by intellectual, moral, religious, [and psychic] conversion'.[50] To 'objectify' is an unhappy word against which personalist sensibilities may push against, but the point is about bringing to awareness how these dimensions colour our perception and understanding. In fact, without that awareness, the probability of bias and mistaken judgement is heightened.

My reason for emphasizing and explaining at such length this moment in theological method is because I propose that music, and indeed more broadly the arts, has an important role to play here, in two ways.

- First, because of how musical meaning works, it can help us gain access and bring to conscious expression the underlying horizons constituted by conversions. Therefore, the act of Christian songwriting can function theologically as an exercise of objectifying conversion (religious, first and foremost, but also potentially others), and as such needs to be adequately framed within the overall theological enterprise.

- Second, investing in the patterns of consciousness that music and other forms of artistic activity bring to human knowledge and Christian meaning-making can help the theologians of the present, and perhaps especially the future, to live and think out of conscious, self-appropriated, authentic subjectivity. In other words, that music and the arts more broadly have a role to play in enabling the conversions identified in Foundations – specifically, I would suggest, intellectual and psychic conversion.

---

[50]Lonergan, *Method in Theology*, 355. An alternative word to explain what is meant by 'objectifies' is hard to find. It seeks to name the process of the person becoming aware and naming the underlying shifts that affect their positions.

Accessing Foundations: The sense music makes of faith

Does songwriting aid us in accessing our consciousness, being present to the work of the Holy Spirit within and how that presence transforms our way of being, understanding and action in the world? Can it exteriorize the transformative effect of welcoming the gift of God's love within? The point is not whether every piece of music does this. I would venture that music emerges from preconceptual areas of our being and therefore, in some primordial sense, 'does not lie', in that it transmits the elemental meaning whence it emerged. So, making a case for music as theological does not negate the complexity and ambiguity of the musical form. It can also be the expression of a disoriented life! Music's dangerous influence on the human mind has been recognized in most of the main strands of philosophical and religious thought.[51] Therefore, the question being asked here is not about all music but about the *potential* of music born with the explicit intent of communicating something of a religious experience, with the added factor of lyrics, which is not insignificant for a word-based discipline such as theology. To make this clear: Does Arvo Pärt's *Da Pacem Domine* explore something of the peace it speaks of?[52] Does it add anything? Does James McMillan's setting of the 'Seven Last Words from the Cross' bring anything new or significant to any (other) theological interpretation of the meaning of those seven phrases?[53] Do the complex and at times invasive tones of Oliver Messiaen's exploration of the Resurrection bring the biblical texts and allusions he uses to our awareness with any more strength than if we read them?[54] And so as to avoid classicism, does Matt Maher's exploration of Paul's notion of strength in weakness in 'Empty and Beautiful'[55] or Audrey Assad's take on Henry Francis Lyte's 'Abide with Me' allow us to participate more fully in

---

[51]Cf. Edward Foley, 'Liturgical Music: A Bibliographical Essay', in *Liturgy and Music: Lifetime Learning*, ed. R. A. Leaver, J. A. Zimmerman, and J. F. Baldovin, 411–52 (438–9) (Collegeville, MN: Liturgical Press, 1998).

[52]*Da pacem, Domine, in diebus nostris / Quia non est alius / Qui pugnet pro nobis / Nisi tu Deus noster; Grant peace, Lord, in our time / for there is none else / who would fight for us / if not you, our God.* Arvo Pärt, 'Da Pacem Domine' (Universal Edition, 2004), © Copyright 2004 by Universal Edition A.G., Wien. This version: © Copyright 2008 by Universal Edition A.G., Wien. See https://www.arvopart.ee/en/arvo-part/work/182/.

[53] James McMillan, 'Seven Last Words from the Cross', (1993): https://www.boosey.com/cr/music/James-MacMillan-Seven-Last-Words-from-the-Cross/6108.

[54]I could ask a similar question of his orchestral music that names themes to be explored without words, such as his 'Quartet for the End of Time' or 'The Ascension – Four Symphonic Meditations', but the chosen genre here is song – music with words.

[55] Matt Maher, 'Empty and Beautiful', in *Empty and Beautiful* (Essential Records, 2008): https://mattmaher.lnk.to/EmptyAndBeautifulWE.

what they might mean?[56] The question is not whether they communicate what we already know, in a nicer way, but whether they thematize what is underlying and not yet fully grasped.

The fact is that we are more than aware that 'something happens' in and through music that does not happen through words alone. The more insightful question may be why theology is taking so long to access and understand why.[57] In part, the answer has to do with how we understand meaning. From a Christian perspective, revelation is the personal entry of God into the world of human meaning,[58] which takes place in and through the ways in which human beings *make* meaning.[59] Theology is *reflection on* what that entrance means as it is received and develops over time. The question about the theological significance of music and Christian songwriting is one about what kind of meaning can emerge and be transmitted in music and in music combined with lyrics, and about its connection with conversion.

If we think about the four dimensions of conversion and ask which kind of carrier of meaning might help us gain access to them, the potential of music as a means of 'objectifying' the experience of unconditional love to which we surrender (religious conversion) or the healing experienced as we awaken to the biases of our symbolic awareness and are freed to a new attentiveness to the world (psychic conversion), proves hopeful. Take, for example, the classic Christian conversion song, 'Amazing Grace'.[60] The first verse of John Newton's (1725–1807) famous hymn articulates, in poetic language, the Christian doctrine of grace and original sin. Subsequent verses give further expression to this doctrine.[61] There is perhaps no Christian

---

[56]*Abide with me; fast falls the eventide / The darkness deepens; Lord with me abide / When other helpers fail and comforts flee, / Help of the helpless, O abide with me....* The lyrics are by Henry Francis Lyte (1847), and this version can be found at Audrey Assad, 'Abide with Me', in *Inheritance* (2016): https://www.musicbed.com/songs/abide-with-me/21748.

[57]Practical theology also recognizes the need to broaden the sources and order of theological work to recognize this fact. Cf. Ruth Illman and W. Alan Smith, *Theology of the Arts: Engaging Faith* (New York: Routledge, 2013).

[58]Cf. Lonergan, 'Theology in Its New Context', 55–68 (62).

[59]The importance of songs (reception) and song-making in how contemporary culture understands itself is a focus of studies in popular culture. This is particularly true in how young people forge their identities through music and gain perspectives on the world. Cf. Tia DeNora, *Music in Everyday Life* (Cambridge: Cambridge University Press, 2000); Christopher H. Partridge, *The Re-Enchantment of the West: Alternative Spiritualities, Sacralization, Popular Culture, and Occulture*, vol. 1 & 2 (London and New York: T&T Clark International, 2004–2005); Gordon Lynch, 'The Role of Popular Music in the Construction of Alternative Spiritual Identities and Ideologies', *Journal for the Scientific Study of Religion* 45, no. 4 (2006): 481–8; Tom Beaudoin, *Virtual Faith: The Irreverent Spiritual Quest of Generation X* (San Francisco: Jossey-Bass, 1998), 21–36.

[60]*Amazing grace! How sweet the sound / That saved a wretch like me! / I once was lost, but now am found, Was blind but now I see*. John Newton, 'Amazing Grace', *in As One Voice* (Dee Why, NSW: Willow Connection Pty Ltd, 1992), 29.

[61]The melody most commonly used today for 'Amazing Grace' is called 'New Britain', and this tune passed through several composers' hands during the nineteenth century before settling

song that more powerfully communicates this central doctrine of Christian theology, yet we don't even get past the first verse without realizing that the power of Newton's hymn is not in its articulation of the doctrine of grace per se, but rather in its articulation of *his experience* of grace. *In foundations, theology becomes personal*.[62] Even without prior knowledge of Newton's life story of involvement in and conversion from the slave-trade, the listener and the singer can relate, at some level, to the experience being expressed:

> Newton is giving witness to his own religious conversion and professing the faith that has thus been born in his heart. Not all hymn texts are as personal as this, and not all hymns succeed in moving people as does 'Amazing Grace', but this enormously popular and enduring hymn demonstrates clearly that something more foundational than doctrine is being expressed in such a song. A religious experience is being articulated, which is somehow connected to doctrine, but is more elemental than doctrine, and in fact provides the context within which doctrine may be apprehended.[63]

The fact that it focusses on personal conversion without mention of its ecclesial mediation or that its style is one that some composers consider unworthy of their liturgies does not efface this fact. It can serve a theological function. The meaning it communicates has been effective, constitutive of Christian identity, and at least to some degree, cognitional. A similar reflection about the cognitive and effective meaning communicated in a song like 'Abide with Me', by Scottish Anglican Henry Francis Lyte (most often sung to English composer William Henry Monk's tune entitled 'Eventide'), might illustrate and perform the bonds of music with memory and feeling in relation to the human experience of mortality and Christian hope in the face of death.[64] Or the expression of moral conversion implicit and explicit in the incarnate style of the music of John L. Bell and the Iona Community.[65]

---

into the melodic shape we know today. Certainly, the tune 'New Britain' was unknown to John Newton. Cf. Tim Dowley, *Christian Music: A Global History* (Minneapolis, MN: Fortress Press, 2011), 124–5. A point of interesting research is the fact that in the past, hymn words could be sung to many tunes in the same meter. The perceived inseparable unity of words and music seems to be a fairly recent development.

[62]This is important because we are accessing the conversion experience which constitutes that doctrine. We get access to *why* a doctrine is true and real, and not just *what* it is.

[63]Maher, 'The Christian Songwriter as Theologian', 6.

[64]Alongside the music itself, such an analysis would need to take into account the accumulated meaning attributed to songs in human memory in relation to context.

[65]For example, John L. Bell, 'The Summons', in *Heaven Shall Not Wait: Songs of Creation, the Incarnation, and the Life of Jesus* (Iona Community: Wild Goose Resource Group, 1987): https://hymnary.org/text/will_you_come_and_follow_me.

When can we say Christian songwriting is theological? In the measure that it objectifies, that is to say, exteriorizes, thematizes and makes present to the artist *and* to those who listen to them the reality of religious conversion or other dimensions of our ongoing multiform conversion to the fullness of Christian living. It does not have to be a full theological treatise to serve this purpose. It is obvious that discursive language explains and defines with more clarity, but there is a need for this one form of theological discourse to be enhanced and complemented. Perhaps the distinction between exploratory and explanatory meaning is a helpful one, as long as we don't explain away the complexity of meaning available to theological thinking. While the role of discursive language in *defining and explaining* Christian truth is essential to theology and doctrinal clarity, *its description, exploration* and *participatory potential* through music are no less important. Howard Gardner's groundbreaking work on the various forms of intelligence through which human beings work could, once again, prove useful to theology.[66] The implications of this gap are not innocent. In what modes and patterns are people formed, whether they are aware of this or not? There is power in knowledge and in the hands of its gatekeepers.[67] It is time to recognize and implement the benefit different patterns and modes of awareness could bring to theology.

Patterns of consciousness in theological self-appropriation and authenticity

Thinking theologically is not easy. Whether one is studying out of interest in the things of faith to prepare oneself for the ministry of leadership in an ecclesial community, or to teach religion in the Catholic education system, it is clear that the 'enlargement of mind'[68] that true knowledge reaches for is an arduous quest. And the framework outlined in this chapter, in one sense, makes it no easier, but it does help us clarify how. The self-appropriation of the theologian is slow-cooked. Part of the problem is the desire to know – essential to human existence but fragmented and frayed in

---

[66] Howard Gardner, *Frames of Mind: The Theory of Multiple Intelligences* (New York: Basic Books, 1983); and his follow-up work on mapping these intelligences in major thought leaders of Western culture, in Howard Gardner, *Creating Minds: An Anatomy of Creativity Seen through the Lives of Freud, Einstein, Picasso, Stravinsky, Eliot, Graham, and Gandhi* (New York: BasicBooks, 1993).
[67] In relation to the connection between power, knowledge and the visible, see Margaret Ruth Miles, *Image as Insight: Visual Understanding in Western Christianity and Secular Culture* (Boston: Beacon Press, 1985).
[68] Cf. John Henry Newman, *The Idea of a University* (New Haven, CT: Yale University Press, 1996), Discourse Six.

today's silence-averse forums of everyday life.[69] Another is the oft-hidden constraints of the structures we live in.

> The subject's performance is massively conditioned by education, socialisation and acculturation. These networks constrain us almost always to handle the non-coincidence of ourselves with ourselves by faking roles that do not really mean what we feel and think internally. It is perhaps only rarely that such subjects reach what Lonergan calls 'the critical point', when subjects realise that their existence is at issue, at stake.[70]

This 'non-coincidence of ourselves with ourselves' is a serious problem for philosophical and theological education. It is the issue of 'subjectification' or 'subject-making': what are the power plays and controls of knowledge at work in what we teach *and how we teach it*. 'A dominative pedagogical power has forced theologically inflected voicings of protest knowledge to operate only on the fringes of theological teaching and learning.'[71] Now more than ever we need to pay more attention to the diversity of ways in which human beings make sense of the world. The recurrent operations of human knowing unfold in a variety of patterns of experience and consciousness, and the intellectual one out of which most theology makes sense of things is, at times, a thin thread.

What could the aesthetic and artistic patterns bring to theological investigation? The aesthetic pattern is characterized by an unlimited openness to wonder. Situated between the biological and the intellectual patterns as receptivity to a form of meaning that is symbolic and elemental, aesthetic patterns are a source of liberating, spontaneous, 'self-justifying' joy, through which we are led to speak of 'experience for the sake of experience'.[72] The mode of the aesthetic pattern frees us from practical or intellectual constraints and invites us to participation rather than explanation, 'straining for truth and value without defining them'.[73] Such a pattern in theology could be a compelling provocation. We think of art as an extra, a luxury for

---

[69]While the notion of fragmented can be taken as positive in terms of theology's humble recognition of its limits of each perspective, even this recognition implies a degree of self-awareness. Cf. Kenneth L. Woodward, 'Interview with David W. Tracy', *Commonweal* 146, no. 15 (2019): 54–61.
[70]Frederick G. Lawrence, 'Grace and Friendship. Postmodern Political Theology and God as Conversational', *Gregorianum* 85, no. 4 (2004): 795–820 (797).
[71]Tom Beaudoin, 'Multiple Theological Intelligences: An Inquiry', in *Witness to Dispossession: The Vocation of a Postmodern Theologian*, 13–27 (26) (Maryknoll, NY: Orbis Books, 2008). In this chapter, Beaudoin critically assimilates Gardner's approach intelligences and explores its implications for a fruitful integration of music into theological investigation and teaching.
[72]Lonergan, *Insight*, 207–8.
[73]Lonergan, *Insight*, 410.

those who have time and money, but what if it is more essential than that, even to our thought processes?

> Art is relevant to concrete living, that is, it is an exploration of the potentialities of concrete living. That exploration is extremely important in our age, when philosophers for at least two centuries, through doctrines on politics, economics, education, and through even further doctrines, have been trying to remake [humanity], and have done not a little to make life unliveable. The great task that is demanded if we are to make it liveable again is the re-creation of the liberty of the subject, the recognition of the freedom of consciousness.[74]

The artistic pattern is even more relevant to our quest for the craft of theology. If the aesthetic pattern portrays what we could describe as elemental meaning, the making of art is 'the *exercise of intelligence in discovering ever novel forms* that unify and relate the contents and acts of aesthetic experience'.[75] In the artistic pattern, the one creating 'beholds, inspects, dissects, enjoys and repeats' the patterns of experience in order to 'objectify, unfold and make it explicit' in a work of art, abstracting the form, not conceptually but by doing.[76] There is real intentionality in the artistic pattern of consciousness, which aligns it with the intellectual while broadening its scope. This is why 'artists and writers find their place among those who have expressed strikingly the human questing that draws attention to the presence of God'.[77]

Furthermore, the artistic pattern of experience is related by Lonergan intrinsically to how we construct our lives (the dramatic pattern of existence). Would its inclusion in academic research, at some level, aid in the self-appropriation necessary for theological thought in our current cultural contexts? Most thinkers who identify or resonate with Lonergan's school of thought seem to name intellectual conversion as the most difficult to attain. Accustomed to living in a world in which knowledge is equated with some form of empirical given, the shift to appreciating the role of our minds in constituting what is real is named as strange, slow and demanding, a hidden-in-broad-daylight invitation to discover oneself. And where it emerges, it does so as a result of a quest for insight, self-affirmation and appropriation.[78] But perhaps it is also because we need to bridge theoretical

---

[74]Lonergan, 'Art', 208–32 (232).
[75]Lonergan, *Insight*, 208.
[76]Lonergan, 'Art', 208–32 (217–21).
[77]Gerald O'Collins, *Revelation: Towards a Christian Interpretation of God's Self-Revelation in Jesus Christ* (Oxford: Oxford University Press, 2016), 65.
[78]See, for example, Richard M. Liddy, *Transforming Light: Intellectual Conversion in the Early Lonergan* (Collegeville, MN: Liturgical Press, 1993); Richard M. Liddy, *Startling Strangeness: Reading Lonergan's Insight* (Lanham, MD: University Press of America, 2007).

patterns with others that could heal and hold our attention more. Robert Doran noted that intellectual conversion could be strengthened by the healing of our psyche,[79] so although art is not usually related to intellectual conversion, I suggest this is a significant oversight.

Caveats and consequences: Foundations, doctrines and the community of faith

In conclusion: this chapter seeks to articulate a place for music in theological activity. It is *not* saying that *anything* musical can be called theology, implying that theology loosens or renounces on its parameters and standards, but rather inviting theology to face the contemporary scenario in all its complexity, and seek appropriate ways of moving forward. In decades past, a key question was about the sources of theology, and the quest to include human experience as one of them something that needed proving. Currently, the challenge is methodological interdisciplinarity, not only of areas but also of modes and patterns of experience and intellectual activity, each with their own contribution to the whole.[80] Rahner laid down that challenge decades ago: 'theology cannot be complete until it appropriates these arts as an integral moment of itself and its own life, until they become an intrinsic moment of theology itself'.[81] The challenge of finding a way to do so is not to conflate spirituality with theology but to further differentiate and enrich academic questioning and the shape of its answers.[82] Naming songwriting as an act of Foundations and an aid to theological formation does not mean it can accomplish everything theology needs to do, but that it can do some aspects better than words alone, and in doing so bring a qualitative difference to the effectiveness of our insights. Neither does this position contend that all Christian music expresses good theology. In the same way as words written by theologians need to pass through the

---

[79]Doran suggested that the precariousness of intellectual conversion is due in part to the need for more awareness of the psychic elements of our knowing and that sustained growth in self-transcendence through the workings of intentional analysis is sustained also by the healing of our psyche in psychic conversion. See Doran, *Theology and the Dialectics of History*, 52–3.
[80]This is implicit in Lonergan's intuition that the polymorphism of consciousness is 'the only solution to philosophy'. Lonergan, *Insight*, 452; Gerard Walmsley, *Lonergan on Philosophic Pluralism: The Polymorphism of Consciousness as the Key to Philosophy* (Toronto: University of Toronto Press, 2008). The distinction, definition and overlap between 'researcher-creator' and 'creator-researcher' found in the aforementioned 'Research-Creation' paradigm could be helpful. Stevance and Lacasse, *Research-Creation in Music and the Arts*.
[81]Karl Rahner, 'Theology and the Arts', *Thought* (1982): 24–5.
[82]It is a challenge being negotiated by other sciences as well. Bruno Latour, *Science in Action: How to Follow Scientists and Engineers through Society* (Cambridge, MA: Harvard University Press, 1987).

verification of the academy and the *sensus fidelium*, so the reception of music by theology's various audiences is essential.[83] If 'genuine objectivity is the fruit of authentic subjectivity',[84] it follows that also here the 'genuine objectivity' of theological development is a shared task, with due control of process and meanings discovered. However, control of meaning and constraint to the point of exclusion of the aesthetic and artistic modes of human interpretation and understanding – including the compositional process – are quite different things!

There are aspects not covered in this chapter. The hermeneutical question surrounding all knowledge applies equally to music: Where does the meaning of a song lie – in the composer, the receiver, between them both? There are well-developed frameworks for the hermeneutical understanding of music that are beginning to bear fruit,[85] and examples of contextually sensitive analyses of music that give us greater access to the musical meaning of a piece and its effect on surrounding culture;[86] and there are tools from the social sciences we can use to access both the meaning underlying a song (ethnography and autoethnography) and the story that music combined with words itself tells (musicology and musical semiotics).[87] Phenomenological explorations into the process of making and producing music will also be helpful.[88]

I finish with two complementary challenges, from within and beyond the Lonerganian approach to theological method, one in relation to the arts in general; the other music more specifically. They speak for themselves.

> Critically grounded systematic theology, however rigorous, indeed however brilliant, is hardly the apex of Christian experience. Ask Thomas Aquinas. Any method that would see only a one-way street between the aesthetic and dramatic, on the one hand, and the theoretical and the systematic on the other, such that the latter is always a development on

---

[83] One would also hope that more awareness of the theological importance of songwriting 'ad-intra' might also help us understand the importance of music written for those on the edge or beyond the explicitly Christian experience, in whatever medium and genre through which God calls forth.

[84] Lonergan, *Method in Theology*, 292.

[85] For example, Jean Jacquez Nattiez's tripartitional method for the analysis of musical meaning. Cf. Nattiez, *Music and Discourse. Toward a Semiology of Music*. See also chapter two of Heaney, *Music as Theology: What Music Has to Say About the Word*.

[86] See, for example, the politically contextualized biblical and theological analysis of Mozart's opera in Steffen Lösel, 'Clemency and Conversion: Theological Reflections on Mozart's La Clemenza di Tito', *Modern Theology* 34, no. 4 (2018): 637–56.

[87] Cf. Willem Marie Speelman, *The Generation of Meaning in Liturgical Songs* (Kampen: Kok Pharos Publishing House, 1995). Speelman's musical semiotics form the basis of my understanding of musical symbolism and action. See chapter three of Heaney, *Music as Theology: What Music Has to Say About the Word*.

[88] Cf. Bruce Ellis Benson, *The Improvisation of Musical Dialogue: A Phenomenology of Music* (Cambridge: Cambridge University Press, 2003).

the former, is in fact so seriously in error that it may at least be incipiently heretical.[89]

Musicality may fail to appear to most theologians as a mode for theology not because of music's inherent deficiencies as a cognitive practice, but because of the reigning knowledge paradigms in which modern theology and theological education are invested. . . . What seems to be needed is much more time to allow nondominant domains of knowledge an extended opportunity to make real contributions to theology. Some sort of 'affirmative action' for these heretofore nondominant domains may be programmatically required in order to give them a fair chance at proving their truth-bearing possibilities.[90]

That is the attempt of each chapter in Part II of this book: to bring together the exploratory dimensions of the aesthetic and artistic patterns of human creativity with explanatory discourse, each chapter focussed on the life and questions of groundbreaking thinkers in the history of Christian theology. The hope is it will advance this process.

Selected further reading

Beaudoin, Tom. 'Multiple Theological Intelligences: An Inquiry'. In *Witness to Dispossession: The Vocation of a Postmodern Theologian*, 13–27. Maryknoll, NY: Orbis Books, 2008.
Lawrence, Frederick G. 'Grace and Friendship. Postmodern Political Theology and God as Conversational'. *Gregorianum* 85, no. 4 (2004): 795–820.
Liddy, Richard M. *Startling Strangeness: Reading Lonergan's Insight*. Lanham, MD: University Press of America, 2007.
Lonergan, Bernard J. F. *Method in Theology*. New York: The Seabury Press, 1972.
Lonergan, Bernard J. F. 'Theology in Its New Context'. In *A Second Collection. Papers by Bernard J. F. Lonergan S. J.*, edited by F. J. Ryan and B. J. Tyrell, 55–68. London: Darton, Longman and Todd, 1974.
Lonergan, Bernard J. F. 'Art'. In *Collected Works of Bernard Lonergan. Vol. 10: Topics in Education*, edited by R. M. Doran and F. E. Crowe, 208–32. Toronto, ON: University of Toronto Press, 1993.
Maher, James. 'The Christian Songwriter as Theologian: Giving Voice to the Converted Heart and Mind'. Masters of Theology, MCD University of Divinity, 2013.

---

[89]Robert M. Doran, 'Lonergan and Balthasar: Methodological Considerations', *Theological Studies* 58, no. 1 (1997): 61 (82).
[90]Beaudoin, 'Multiple Theological Intelligences: An Inquiry', 13–27 (162, notes 66 and 72). Beaudoin's challenge includes a thorough case both *against* and *for* the continued reign of linguistic discourse over other forms of intelligence and names the lack of intimate cross-disciplinary collaboration as one of the main difficulties.

McMillan, James. *Seven Last Words from the Cross*. London: Boosey & Hawkes, 1993.

O'Collins, Gerald. *Revelation: Towards a Christian Interpretation of God's Self-Revelation in Jesus Christ*. Oxford: Oxford University Press, 2016.

Ormerod, Neil, and Christiaan Jacobs-Vandegeer. *Foundational Theology: A New Approach to Catholic Fundamental Theology*. Minneapolis: Fortress Press, 2015.

Viladesau, Richard. *Theological Aesthetics: God in Imagination, Beauty, and Art*. New York: Oxford University Press, 1999.

PART II

Musicking theology
A theopoetical weaving of Christian thinkers through music

Introduction to Part II

We move to the second part of the book, which is an attempt to implement or *perform* the thesis presented in Part I. Each of the twelve chapters in Part II explores a key issue, doubt or question in life that presents a challenge to Christian faith or to our image of God. These issues are addressed in two ways: through the life and thought of a theologian who voices that question and responds to it in thorough, audacious or creative ways, and through an original song (music with lyrics).

Each chapter focusses on *one* core issue or aspect of a theologian's thought, arguably to the detriment of others, but it would be impossible to do justice to the whole of each person's work, nor is that the aim of this book. Our intent here is to learn to think theologically, through words and music, from those who have done it well, and this is best served by focussing on one issue in each. I do, however, situate that issue in the context of their lives and theological work, and at the end of each chapter, some resources are offered to facilitate further exploration of their contributions to Christian thought.

There is a clear connection between the life and work of each theologian or thinker (as some do not necessarily fit solely into the category of 'theologian', either because they pre-date that disciplinary definition or because they bring other fields of expertise into their theological work). In fact, the book challenges a commonplace supposition that theory and practice are separate. Our opinions and options are always informed by worldviews and value systems, be they implicit or explicit. For that reason, the second part of each chapter presents a brief overview of each person's life and thought, as a fellow-questioner who dared to ask difficult questions and worked to pull out of the best tradition of Christian thought 'old insights and new'. And I have tried to make explicit that connection between life and thought: whence those questions arose, why they are important and even the humanity – brilliant and blessed, incomplete and imperfect – of those we are studying. It does not help to set those thinkers apart who are to be our mentors and guides, for the aim is that we might do the same, differently. God has chosen humanity as the pathway to a transformed or divinized life (as the Eastern traditions would name it). We need to embrace the shadows and lights through which we learn and grow.

The first chapter focusses on someone we have already extensively drawn from in Part I: twentieth-century Canadian Jesuit Bernard J. F. Lonergan. His thought (interwoven with that of those who accept and develop his theological method) provides the framework of the whole book and indeed my understanding of the theological role of music-making, as explained in chapter four. For this reason, chapter five focusses specifically on the role of art and artistic experience in meaning-naming and truth (an aspect of his thought he is not particularly well known for). And as a theme, it also provides a framework for *how* to interact with the songs linked to each chapter. My understanding of the role of music and art in human life is influenced by Lonergan's critical realist epistemology, within which art works at the first stage of human knowing: an expression of elemental meaning in experience, *prior* to understanding, reflection and deliberation about what the experience might imply. In this light, the inclusion of a piece of music is an invitation to the reader to enter into and re-experience something of the question being addressed. It seeks to open a theopoetical space to experience and think afresh these themes, so we might hear again that which we already knew, or to open our minds to issues we may not have broached yet. They are situated at the end of each chapter but could perhaps more fruitfully be taken as the chapter's entry point. The lyrics (also included) do not exhaust the meaning of the song nor are they intended as a control of meaning, but rather to exemplify *one* theopoetical engagement with the question being posed, alongside and complementary to other, verbal and non-verbal, interpretations. In fact, 'what does it mean?' is the wrong question to ask of a song! The songs interpret – in a similar *and* different way to how words work – the central theme being explored, as I *experience* and *interpret* it. For this reason, the written part of the final section in each chapter is more personal than the rest of the chapter, as it seeks to introduce you to *one* access point to what the songs might mean: in this case, my own. In other publications, I have sought to analyze further the music from the perspective of musical semiotics, (in the case of the songs of chapters six and eight, for example). This exceeds the scope of this book, but remains a potentially useful task for the future. But the aim here is to open a world into which readers and listeners are invited as fellow 'musickers', capable of recognizing surplus of meaning and multiplying it, all towards our shared worlds of truth and purpose, the Reign of God, ever bigger than how we imagine it. Tradition is a living beast.

For this reason, I would suggest some points of awareness that might guide your listening to these theological musickings:[1]

1. Reject the inner voice telling you to hurry up and get to, or stay with, the main point of the chapter, as if listening to music were secondary to the point of theological reading. The Word, in Scriptural and Christian terms, has always been more than a source of information, but rather a dynamic expression and means of accessing the very life of God, embodied and transformative. Take time to open your incarnated mind and spirit to what might happen in and through music.

2. Be aware of your own experience and opinion. There is no single take on any piece of music – even that of its composer/s.

3. Style is essential to human existence and is pluriform. You do not have to 'like' every musical style to receive from it, but classicism (which comes in all shapes and forms and could be defined as the preference of one style over others to the point of making it an absolute standard of excellence) *can* rob us of the capacity to hear and appreciate styles of music, art, theatre, literature, etc. *other* to our taste. Christianity is multi-cultural and so *must* find expression in that diversity, or it will not affect and effect change! So, although you really do not need to *like* the songs, I would nonetheless invite you to open yourself to them.

Each chapter is not long, in comparison to those of Part I, as they are not seeking to be comprehensive but to open and allow space for thought on key figures and the questions they tackle. They can be read in any order, and

---

[1]The foundation of these points can be found in chapters two and three of Maeve Louise Heaney, *Music as Theology: What Music Has to Say about the Word* (Eugene, OR: Pickwick Publications Wipf and Stock, 2012). Respectively, they explore the multidimensional nature of musical meaning, guided by Canadian musicologist Jean-Jacques Nattiez, and the musical semiotics of Willem Marie Speelman in how it differs from and complements verbal comprehension.

the book is written in a way that would allow readers to start with Part II and work back to the foundations laid in Part I, if you wish. I also attempt to bring some of the authors' own writings into each chapter, especially those who might be less known to contemporary readers, in the conscious attempt to move us from reading *about* important theologians of the past to reading their own words. The link to the music specific to each theologian can be found towards the end of each chapter. However, in case useful, a link to the archive of all the songs can be found here: bloomsbury.pub/suspended-god

A final note on my choice of theologians. Except for one, all are Catholic authors, and while they have obviously all influenced my own thought, they have also been important in the shaping of theology and Christian doctrine today. They address issues that were important enough to draw the attention of the academic community in a sustained way and to evoke music from this songwriter's creative energies. I chose to trust my creative gut here as well. There are many others I could have inserted and indeed find missing to complete the picture, but the intent here is to open a pathway, not to finish a marathon. I have chosen to recognize these incomplete and somehow suspended openings as a value: awaiting other contributions – both musical and theological – to further music's contribution to Christian thought.

Furthermore, while I focus on each person through the lens of a question they raise and to which they respond in theologically significant ways, no theologian lives in an island, uninfluenced by the sociopolitical context and theological movements of their time. Most of our theologians live and work during or after the Second Vatican Council. Some were personally involved in the events and documents emerging from that Council (such as Lonergan and Rahner, who were theological 'experts' [*periti*] there), while others take particular aspects of its teaching as their lens or the hermeneutical key of their work (e.g. *Gaudium et Spes* for Elizabeth Johnson and the Council's teaching on Scripture for Sandra M. Schneiders). Sobrino's theology emerges from the historical-geographical context that gave birth to the liberation theologies of Latin America, and strongly influenced contemporary contextual theologising and Schneiders, Johnson and Haughton interact in different ways with the emerging awareness of women's role in the Church and world. In each chapter, limits of space allow me to give only a brief explanation of this context in how it affects the life and thought of the theologian under discussion but I point to recourses for further exploration. Some of the authors are alive. Where possible, I have sought their feedback about my take on their lives. I am grateful for those who have interacted with me about their work.

5

Can the arts contribute to our knowledge of truth?

What place do music and the arts have in human life and knowledge?

Within a vision of life that sees in the human an imprint of God's image, what is the point of the arts? This is the first issue I am going to deal with, and it is a foundational one, since the whole book is an attempt to explore one art form's contribution to theological knowledge and truth. If chapter four looked at the issue of music-*making*, this one asks about our interaction with the arts, from an aesthetic (receptive), rather than artistic, perspective. It's a huge question, and one that is not limited to music but to all art forms, which is addressed here from a specifically theological viewpoint. What use are the arts? How essential are they to the common good, to the betterment of life around the globe, to the education of our children and the shape of our towns and cities? For some, this is not an important question or perhaps not even a question at all, either because the arts are low on their value scale or the question is not asked or thought necessary, so central to their existence is music, painting, dance or other artistic dimensions of life (including style of dress, rituals, etc.).

The issue is both personal and social. We have one life: although beautiful, it is short, fragile, limited – in the sense that we do not have unlimited options about how to invest it. Each decision rules out a myriad of others. So, in the words of poet Mary Oliver, 'what is it you plan to do with your one wild and precious life?'[1] Apart from its being a financially questionable option, is a life pursuing artistic creativity a well-spent life? Rilke suggested a poet's life was one to be chosen *only* if one could not *not* write poetry, which

---

[1] From 'The Summer Day', in *Truro Bear and Other Adventures: Poems and Essays*, ed. Mary Oliver (Boston: Beacon Press, 2008), 65.

touches, I would say, on the internal, vocational source of artistic creativity and suggests it is a hard option both to take and to avoid! But what about its social and cultural relevance? There must be something important about art when we find its traces at the very origins of the emergence of human consciousness. Paintings, music, dance have been a characteristic of human activity from the moment the capacity for human symbolization appears.[2] Current studies recognize that human beings love symmetry. What does this mean? What benefits do the arts reap for society, culture and the world around us? What do the arts contribute to the shared venture of human life? Funding and educational trends across much of the world would suggest very little, but it is hardly credible to state that the results in intellectual and cultural development bear out that position![3]

Why? What do the arts bring that we need? Responding to the question implies defining or at the very least offering some kind of explanation of what we mean by the arts: What are they? What activities do they include and more importantly, what is happening within and among us when engaged in the arts? This latter question is where Lonergan's work is helpful; the former on what *is* art is one we need to delimit. It presents a similar dilemma to the one addressed in chapter two in relation to music. In the broadly defined West, to speak of 'the arts' evokes a certain kind of activity – somewhat high-brow and exceptional – reserved to those who have the time and financial stability to afford it. In this paradigm the arts are valued, but unnecessary: a special dimension of a privileged life, but unessential for the 'normal' everyday individual. In fairness, this understanding of the arts is a result of its historical development in Western thought and belongs more to late modernity. A succinct and fairly accurate account of the history of Western thought on what the arts are can be found in the provocatively entitled *Bloomsbury Guide to Human Thought*, which finishes with the suggestive description that 'the arts . . . are actually simple, among the most remarkable manifestations of the human intellect and human spirit, and available for the excitement, uplift and satisfaction of everyone who approaches them'.[4] Although the attempt seems to be that of freeing the arts for access to us all, it begs the question about where our bodies, affectivity and emotions fit, and remains somewhat intellectualist and extrinsic, as if art is not already part of human presence and activity in the world.

However, a classicist notion of the arts is fading fast in the face of multifaceted challenges and developments in contemporary culture. First,

---

[2]Cave art dates to the Upper Palaeolithic period spanning roughly 50,000–10,000 years ago, when symbolic, functional and ritual behaviours are also evidenced. Cf. Stephen Davies, 'Defining Art and Artworlds', *Journal of Aesthetics & Art Criticism* 73, no. 4 (2015): 375–84 (376).
[3]Furthermore, it is hard to ignore how the creative spirit pushes back when mainstream cultures try to ignore it, in a similar way in which spirituality fills the gap religion leaves as it withdraws from a culture's self-understanding.
[4]"The Arts', in *Bloomsbury Guide to Human Thought*, ed. Kenneth McLeish (London: Bloomsbury, 1993).

from within the arts themselves, as they open and adapt to the ever-plural and experimental fruits of human creativity. Second, due to exposure to the plethora of cultures for whom the arts are second nature and never relegated to the outskirts of life, with the growing awareness of, and access, to different forms of entertainment and artistic creativity by a broader range of people. Our understanding of the arts is on the move.

On the quest for a definition

Defining the arts is not simple – so much so that it may be easier *not* to do so. The Australia Council for the Arts simply describe what they do:

> Our focus is on increasing the visibility of Australia's vibrant arts and culture, and recognising the evolving way that Australians make and experience art. Our role is to support the unimagined along with the reimagined, the unknown and experimental along with the keenly anticipated. We are a champion for Australian arts both here and overseas. We invest in artistic excellence through support for all facets of the creative process, and are committed to the arts being accessible to all Australians.[5]

The *Webster* online dictionary speaks of

> the expression or application of human creative skill and imagination, typically in a visual form such as painting or sculpture, producing works to be appreciated primarily for their beauty or emotional power ... the various branches of creative activity, such as painting, music, literature, and dance ... subjects of study primarily concerned with human creativity and social life, such as languages, literature, and history (as contrasted with scientific or technical subjects) ... a skill at doing a specified thing, typically one acquired through practice.[6]

It is a broad, inclusive definition touching on both activities or products of artistic activity and the expertise needed to achieve them. The *Oxford Dictionary of English* addresses or avoids the issue by subdividing art into categories such as the 'beaux arts', the 'decorative' arts, the 'industrial', 'liberal' or 'performing' arts and so on.

---

[5] https://www.australiacouncil.gov.au/ (accessed 4 January 2021). Interestingly, the Council recently developed a three-part series of conversations precisely on the value of the arts and their influence on social cohesion, mental health and well-being, rebuilding economic recovery and resilience. Cf. https://www.australiacouncil.gov.au/programs-and-resources/in-conversation-with-the-australia-council/
[6] Cf. http://www.webster-dictionary.net/definition/Arts.

From a more academic perspective, an interesting and relatively comprehensive definition of 'the arts' is presented by Stephen Davies, as follows:

> I propose that something is art (a) if it shows excellence of skill and achievement in realizing significant aesthetic goals, and either doing so is its primary, identifying function or doing so makes a vital contribution to the realization of its primary, identifying function, or (b) if it falls under an art genre or art form established and publicly recognized within an art tradition, or (c) if it is intended by its maker/presenter to be art and its maker/presenter does what is necessary and appropriate to realizing that intention.[7]

It is interesting because it is both precise and broad enough to allow us to include art that emerges before human beings were conscious of it, art that is recognized as such by others, independent of the maker's intention, and the art-worlds as they have unfolded over time, in all their diversity, while keeping giftedness and excellence at the heart of the description. It also leaves space for other possible 'functions' of art, alongside its identity as an artwork, such as its place in education, cultural development, sociopolitical awareness, to name but a few.[8] The elite and untouchable 'art for art's sake only' is suitably marginalized.

How do I define the arts?

In theological terms, the arts are usually linked to the notion of beauty – both divine Beauty and its reflection in humanity and the world – and are an essential element of the theme of human freedom in theological anthropologies, and studies on faith and culture. They appear – often in polemic terms, sadly – in liturgical studies as an important element of ritual, liturgy and sacramental theology. But the contribution of the arts to theology, knowledge and truth can only be found, in my opinion, by exploring how the arts work in human living, knowing and culture, or we shall ever be in danger of reductionism or classicism, valuing art according to its recognized value or 'use' to Christian faith. Instead, we need to know how art works in and for human living. To do so implies overcoming historical Christianity's suspicion of the body (especially female), the flesh and the senses (in particular that of some forms of Catholic culture), and embracing our incarnated existence. God had no qualms doing so. It is appropriate we follow suit in this as well. To that end, I would invite you to an exercise of imagination, in two moments:

---

[7] Davies, 'Defining Art and Artworlds', 375–84 (377–8).
[8] For an interesting debate on the characteristics influencing support of the arts, see Therese Filicko and Sue Anne Lafferty, 'Defining the Arts and Cultural Universe: Lessons from the Profiles Project', *Journal of Arts Management, Law & Society* 32, no. 3 (2002): 185.

1. How and where do you rest? What do you love to do? What relaxes your mind after (or before) a day's work? What's your favourite place on earth? Where's your favourite room in your house? Who's your favourite artist or band? Could you imagine a world without them? Would you want to?
2. Think of the music you listen to, the concerts you've paid for, the art galleries you've walked through, the museums you've visited, the liturgies that led you to prayer. Think of the clothes you choose to wear, the books you read, the comic strip that makes you laugh out loud, the films you watch, the play you still remember, the gospel story that tells your life. Imagine your life without them! What would be left? Who would you be?

As I write, all eyes in the world are on the researchers working on the vaccine for Covid-19, because we *know* the value of health and have seen too much death. It must be so, and I am as grateful as everyone else for their dedication and the government and private-sector finance invested to back them. But it is also true that while funding was made available to most sectors, in one way or another, the arts sector was one of the hardest hit. Musicians had gigs cancelled (the main source of income for most since online streaming substituted appropriately paid music-sales), art galleries and performance venues were closed – some permanently – and actors and orchestra members lost their jobs. And yet, all through 2020 and 2021 violinists played on balconies, choirs harmonized through Zoom and FaceTime Live performances multiplied. Because the arts will never die. They are an essential form of human expression and creativity that not even dictators could quash[9] (who arguably understood their worth better than contemporary democratic capitalism)! So, what are we missing? We fail to understand both what our lives would be like without art and what they *could* be if we comprehend better its role and take it more seriously. Enter a theologian who explores how human knowing and understanding works.

Bernard Lonergan, SJ: An 'orthodox who thinks a lot!'

I have already presented certain aspects of Lonergan's theology in chapter four, including:

- his understanding of the importance of culture in theology's task and the shift in eras over history affecting how human beings make meaning;

---

[9] And dictators *do* target their artists and intellectuals first and foremost, as the history of Spain, Russia and El Salvador, for example, can attest to.

- the notion of questions as the defining source of learning;
- the proposal that theology be subdivided not by themes but by the tasks needing to be accomplished – which he called 'functional specialities' – a proposal he thought best implemented the insights of the Second Vatican Council;
- a multiform dynamic of conversion as foundational to theological discourse;
- some elements of the aesthetic and artistic patterns of knowing that open a space for musical composition as a theological act.

This chapter focusses the lens on his work from the perspective of art: what we can glean from his thought about the role and importance of art for human life, Christian faith and theology. But before I do so, who was Bernard J. F. Lonergan? What is the life underpinning this man's work?

Bernard Lonergan was born in Canada in 1904 in a loving family, with two brothers. His father was an engineer, and his mother is said to have had a love of music and art. In 1922, at the age of seventeen, he entered the Society of Jesus (the Jesuits) known for their in-depth education and strong spirituality, both of which are reflected in his life's work. His insistence on the importance of questions in knowledge reflects his own approach to studies in both philosophy and theology, in which he reached for answers well beyond the material taught in Heythrop College (philosophy) and the Gregorian University in Rome (theology).[10] This was fed by his awareness of the huge cultural changes surrounding and affecting the Church, as well as what he considered an inadequate and outdated manualist approach to philosophy and theology.

In England, he not only studied philosophy but also received a degree in mathematics. Unconvinced by the conceptualist neo-scholastic metaphysics of his time, he explored the classics and discovered the thought of John Henry Newman, whose introspective approach to writing echoes Augustine's *Confessions*. He read Newman's *Grammar of Assent* six times. Newman influenced Lonergan's own notion of self-appropriation, as well the attention paid to *how* one comes to faith and knowledge. At the Gregorian, despite or in addition to the influence of some noteworthy professors,[11] Lonergan's

---

[10]For an insightful presentation of his educational pathway, and philosophical and theological influences, see Fergus Kerr, 'Bernard Lonergan', *Twentieth-Century Catholic Theologians: From Neoscholasticism to Nuptial Mysticism*, 105–20 (Malden, MA: Blackwell Pub., 2007). For an accessible introduction to his theological approach, see Michael Paul Gallagher, 'Bernard Lonergan', *Faith Maps: Ten Religious Explorers from Newman to Joseph Ratzinger*, 72–86 (New York: Paulist Press, 2010).

[11]In particular, Peter Hoenen's writings on Aquinas seem to have initiated his lifelong interest in Thomas' thought. Cf. Peter Hoenen, *Reality and Judgement according to St Thomas*, trans. H. F. T. S.J. (Chicago: Regnery, 1952).

interest in Aquinas seems to have been for the most part self-taught or at the very least critical of the neo-scholastic filters and interpretations through which it was often taught. His doctoral thesis on the concept of grace in St Thomas Aquinas[12] was undertaken at first 'under obedience', since he had wanted to write a philosophy of history to address misconceptions affecting the history of philosophy and epistemology in the second millennium, but the centrality of Aquinas to his work was one Lonergan later recognized and never regretted. Lonergan had a lifelong interest in mathematics and science that comes through in his writing, for both its systemic thoroughness and a carefully grounded challenge to the division between knowledge and belief. Lonergan was cognizant that all knowledge, including that of the sciences, is grounded on and develops through probability and faith.[13]

Over the course of his life, Lonergan worked and taught in Montreal, Toronto, Massachusetts (Harvard and Boston College) and Rome (Gregorian University) on areas of philosophy and theology. In fact, he is probably claimed more by philosophers than theologians, as the bulk of his work was spent in studying how the human mind comes to knowledge, although his ultimate aim was always its application to theology. In this, as we shall see, he played the long-game. He was well known during his life, and featured on the cover of *Time* magazine in 1970 as one of the finest philosophical minds of his time. He was not as well known or influential in the European hubs of theological development, however, mainly due to an illness in 1965, which forced him to leave his teaching post in Rome and return to Canada.

Major theological themes and works

What aspects of his life would I highlight as interesting or important for theology in the twenty-first century? First and foremost, his passion for big-picture thinking and finding the roots of problems[14] and a corresponding commitment to solid – often slow – research into and development of adequate, systemic responses that grounded a shift in the discipline.

> Just as Theology in the 13th century followed its age by assimilating Aristotle; just as Theology of the 17th century resisted its age by retiring into a dogmatic corner, so Theology today is locked in an encounter with

---

[12] It can be found in Bernard J. F. Lonergan, *Grace and Freedom: Operative Grace in the Thought of St. Thomas Aquinas*, ed. F. E. Crowe and R. M. Doran, vol. 1, *Collected Works of Bernard Lonergan* (Toronto, ON: University of Toronto Press, 2000).
[13] Cf. Bernard J. F. Lonergan, 'Belief: Today's Issue', in *A Second Collection. Papers by Bernard J. F. Lonergan S. J.*, ed. F. E. Crowe and R. M. Doran, 87–99 (London: Darton, Longman and Todd, 1974).
[14] It is said he spent over twelve years studying the reasons behind the Wall Street Crash, before giving up due to the lack of reception to his results! This was many years before the global financial crisis of the early twenty-first century!

its age. Whether it will grow and triumph or whether it will wither to insignificance depends in no small measure on the clarity and accuracy of its grasp of the external cultural factors that undermine its past achievements and challenge it to new endeavours.[15]

He took this big-picture and long-term approach in both philosophy and theology, and their intersection points. His first major book, *Insight*, was the fruit of eleven years work on how the mind comes to know, re-exploring and drawing Aquinas' epistemology into what he called a 'critical realist' approach to knowledge that sought to resolve a five-hundred-year-old epistemological conundrum between idealism and empiricism about whether and how subjects can *know* anything outside themselves. 'In this work his aim was nothing less than to redirect the course of modern philosophy and to provide at the same time foundations for a Catholic theology that would be truly "at the level of its times."'[16] His second book, *Method in Theology*, a post illness (cancer) work, took him another eleven years exploring recent philosophical, scientific and historical frameworks in order to apply his findings in *Insight* to what he perceived to be the crumbling structure of Catholic theology. The book brings together the immensely fragmented world of theological disciplines into a theological method that seeks to enable theology do the work it is meant to do.

Both are ambitious projects – unpopularly so. Philosophy does not always like someone claiming to have fully solved a major problem. Theology does not tend to welcome someone revolutionizing and restructuring its whole approach to every discipline area and how they interact. And yet, this is his claim. In *Insight*, by calling thinkers (not only philosophers, as he will extend this invitation to all theological work proper as well) to authentic subjectivity through awareness and self-appropriation of how human knowing works – attentive to experience, intelligent in questioning it, reasonable in reflecting on it and responsible in dealing with it – Lonergan claims to have found the ultimate foundation to human understanding: 'Thoroughly understand what it is to understand and not only will you understand the broad lines of all there is to be understood but also you will possess a fixed base, an invariant pattern, opening upon all further developments of understanding.'[17] The age-old and contemporary issue of 'what is truth' beyond each subject's apprehension about it is solved, he says,

---

[15] Lonergan, 'Theology in Its New Context', 55–68 (58).
[16] Gerard Whelan, SJ, 'The Continuing Significance of Bernard Lonergan', *Thinking Faith*, September 23 (2008).
[17] Bernard J. F. Lonergan, *Insight*, ed. F. E. Crowe and R. M. Doran, *Collected Works of Bernard Lonegan* (Toronto: University of Toronto Press, 1957), 22.

through the enterprise of shared authentic subjectivity: 'genuine objectivity is the fruit of authentic subjectivity'.[18]

Similarly (or even more ambitiously) Lonergan addresses the *whole* theological endeavour, stating that theology has shifted from being deductive, static and universal to being empirical, dynamic and integrative of the historical totality of particulars, and that these changes are here to stay; and that its new vocabulary – historicist, personalist, phenomenological and existentialist reflection – is also here to stay.[19] His solution is as radical as his diagnosis: 'This development necessitates a complete restructuring of Catholic theology.'[20] We find this restructuring in *Method in Theology*: 'Part One: Background', introduces the reasoning and overall structure in chapters on 'Method', 'The Human Good', 'Meaning', 'Religion' and 'Functional Specialities'. 'Part II: Foreground', contains nine chapters on the eight areas of theological method: 'Research, Interpretation', 'History', 'Dialectics', 'Foundations', 'Doctrines', 'Systematics' and 'Communications' (with history getting the attention of two chapters). Problem solved.

But as will be obvious, although Lonergan (a rather unknown expert at Vatican II) felt his methodological approach to theology was an appropriate implementation of the documents that emerged from the Council, and was disappointed at how philosophy developed afterwards, theologians and theology faculties did not fully understand, welcome and implement this 360-degree shift in their organization. And Lonergan's pretension to complete clarity about cognition and metaphysics has often been strongly criticized, if not simply ignored. There are other reasons at play in this as well: he was not working or teaching in Europe, where most of the advances in Catholic theology were taking place; his actual theological work (on themes that would have interaction with people working in that field) was not prolific, due to his preference for long-term goals; the ways in which his work was presented by those who accepted his premises may not always have been nuanced enough; perhaps he was ahead of his time, or we are behind it! Frederick Crowe described him as a theologian of the future rather than of the present:

> To withdraw from the hunt when there is quarry immediately before one, to postpone the pursuit while giving oneself to the forging of a new and vastly superior instrument, to be willing, and entirely to determine, to spend one's entire life at that task (hoping the long-term benefit will make it worthwhile but knowing with certainty that one will not see the full harvest and realising that at best one's effort will be appreciated by only a

---

[18]Bernard J. F. Lonergan, *Method in Theology* (New York: The Seabury Press, 1972), 292.
[19]Cf. Lonergan, 'Theology in Its New Context', 55–68 (55–67).
[20]Lonergan, 'The Future of Christianity', 149–63 (161).

small band of attentive readers and students) ... is not the act of a drifter or a self-seeker. It is an act of notable self-transcendence.[21]

From where I am standing, however, I need to say that in most of what he achieved, I believe he was right, and we need more of the same. Here are some reasons why.

1. *His Understanding of Tradition*: Lonergan had a balanced and careful approach to tradition that is hard to find. His lucid appreciation of the state of things and the need to move forward *carefully*, with discernment and creativity, so as not to lose what is essential while still maintaining our dialogue with modernity, is rare.

   > Our disengagement from classicism and our involvement in modernity must be open-eyed, critical, coherent, sure-footed. If we are not just to throw out what is good in classicism and replace it with contemporary trash, then we have to take the trouble, and it is enormous, to grasp the strength and the weakness, the power and the limitations, the good points and the shortcomings of both classicism and modernity. Nor is knowledge enough. One has to be creative.[22]

   Our Church – and with it, at times, our theological societies – is plagued by ideological stances that are well intentioned but not invested in this kind of careful openness and faithful exploration. Hasty conclusions and lazy analyses leave people in the pews or in our formation centres exposed to superficial teaching and inadequate instruments to deal with life as it is actually is. His predictions are scarily accurate:

   > Classical culture cannot be jettisoned without being replaced; and what replaces it cannot but run counter to classical expectations. There is bound to be formed a solid right that is determined to live in a world that no longer exists. There is bound to be formed a scattered left, captivated by now this, now that new development, exploring now this, now that new possibility. But what will count is a perhaps not numerous centre, big enough to be at home in both the old and the new, painstaking enough to work out one by one the transitions to be made, strong enough to refuse half-measures and insist on complete solutions even though it has to wait.[23]

---

[21]Frederick E. Crowe, *Method in Theology: An Organon for Our Time* (Milwaukee, WI: Marquette University Press, 1980), 57.
[22]Lonergan, 'Belief: Today's Issue', 87–99 (98–9).
[23]Bernard J. F. Lonergan, 'Dimensions of Meaning', in *Collection. Papers by Bernard Lonergan S.J.*, ed. F. E. Crowe and R. M. Doran, 252–67 (267) (New York: Herder and Herder, 1967).

It is in this context we can understand his anecdotal quip when asked by his provincial (who would be his direct 'superior' or 'supervisor' in the Jesuits) on his orthodoxy: 'I am orthodox, but I think a lot!'

2. *The Importance of Philosophy for Theology*: The way Lonergan integrates philosophy and theology in theological research is both critical *and* thorough. His methodological framework for the study of theology allows us to address in a systematic way the oft-unspoken issues our students have with philosophy as we were taught it. Let me name two: I can remember the concerted effort I made to enter into and grasp the philosophical arguments in metaphysics and natural theology – including various arguments for the existence of God – and working them out more than sufficiently for the grade I was used to achieving, all the while thinking: so what? My way of understanding life, meaning and faith does not relate at all to the way these arguments are presented. That God may exist, but He [*sic*] does not affect my existence or draw my attention. It is an experience I often observe in my students, unless they are enamoured with a certain kind of logical thought, which is helpful for them, but does not assure me the right connections are being made.[24] Philosophy is essential to theology. It gives us the language and categories to grasp and speak about the divine, but *how* in each time and place? Another obvious difficulty is that not every culture approaches thought and faith with the categories that have shaped Western culture, and yet we have been teaching philosophy and theology in the same way for centuries. I am not suggesting we relativize the importance of philosophy – most of the issues in evangelization and mission are more epistemological and philosophical than theological – but rather that we rethink *how* these are structured, taught and integrated into the overall project of theological method. Lonergan's method does this: his interpretation and translation of Aquinas' categories placing cognitional theory and epistemology as the entrance point to metaphysics ground the latter in personally appropriated knowledge. It allows us to rethink and reorganize philosophical education accordingly.

3. *Historical Consciousness*: Lonergan's theology echoes the way the Spirit was leading the Church before, during and since the Second Vatican Council, anticipating the importance of historical studies in every aspect of human life, including doctrine and

---

[24]This is not completely new. Michael Buckley's work in this area has long revealed that the origins of modern atheism were found in the inadequate categories with which theology sought to defend him. Cf. Michael J. Buckley, *At the Origins of Modern Atheism* (New Haven: Yale University Press, 1987). Others have continued this line of thought. The novelty here is how Lonergan integrates philosophy into theological method *without* undermining its importance.

theology. 'The meaning of Vatican II was the acknowledgement of history.'[25] His proposal of a new foundation for theology is based on the shift in understanding of revelation in one of its most foundational documents: *Dei Verbum*. When Revelation was understood as transmitted through perennial concepts valid always and everywhere, definitions and dogmas were a valid foundation for theological work, but where we have moved to a personalist, empirical and historical paradigm, talking about 'Jesus of Nazareth ... mighty in word and deed', theology needs to ground itself elsewhere. Drawing on his scientific background and study on the human mind, Lonergan offers the simple but clear move from concepts, considered as the 'objects' of study of theology, to the subject. In an analogous way to which the basis for scientific investigation is not a set of rules or laws but the person of the scientist who implements and 'guarantees' them, the foundation of all the statements of theology is the stating subject, the community of theologians in multiform and ongoing conversion.[26] This is the backdrop to which he offers the conversion of the theologian as a new foundation for theology.

4. *Ongoing Communitarian Endeavour*: Lonergan's proposals, while ambitious, are neither easy nor complete in themselves. *Insight*'s position is not a theory to be accepted but an invitation to appropriated self-knowledge, which takes time and effort. Nor is it a solitary journey. Lonergan is one of the thinkers of the twentieth century who most clearly understood the communitarian and social nature of human life and thought: the community comes first. The worlds of meaning we access as we grow into personhood are not our own inventions but of the cultures of meaning we are introduced to by the community who speak that language, long before we make our own determinations. Similarly, his method is unthinkable individually. It grounds and implies the ongoing work of a diverse, interdisciplinary academy of thinkers. And where his thought is applied this is often what you find: a community of thinkers from a broad range of philosophical and theological fields, collaborating with each other and people from other disciplines whose expertise contribute to the process.

5. Finally, as we shall see in the next section of this chapter, his epistemology identifies the place of art, aesthetic experience

---

[25] Quoted by F. Crowe in Frederick E. Crowe, *All My Work Has Been Introducing History into Catholic Theology* (Lonergan, 28 March 1980)', *Lonergan Workshop* 10 (1994): 49–81 (49). It is interesting that although he was in Rome during the Second Vatican Council and officially an expert for the same, he seems to have been involved less than others. Perhaps this can be explained by his overarching need to build a long-term solution to the issues facing Catholic theology.
[26] Cf. Lonergan, 'Theology in Its New Context', 55–68 (67).

and artistic creativity in human knowledge in a way I have not found elsewhere and which echoes true to my own experience of musicking.

There are a few other elements of his thought I would name, in passing, since I have already dedicated an entire chapter to his thought:

- The priority of love over knowledge, in relation to God, whom we receive and love before we understand. There is a presence of God that precedes 'knowledge', and provokes faith, which he defines as 'the knowledge born of religious love'.[27]
- His reversal of how we imagine how we come to know God. We speak of the story of salvation as one revealing, over time, God as Creator, Redeemer, and Spirit, but we access or experience triune love the other way around: from reception of unconditional love (the Spirit) to its recognition through the Word proclaimed (Jesus), all towards the ever-beyond us knowledge of God Creator/origin, laying the foundations for innovative spaces of theological reflection on interreligious and comparative theologies.

It has been noted that Lonergan's thought develops over time. These later insights were developed after his brush with cancer and the care received to overcome it, especially, by a female nurse who is mentioned as being important to him. As a religious in a male community in the early twentieth century, before many of the developments in human and spiritual formation for someone in such a walk of life were understood and implemented, it is not beyond imagining that these human experiences, of frailty and the care of a woman to recover, would have contributed to this awareness and development. He died in 1984.

Look, sense, breathe: Stretching human experience so God can break in

So how does Lonergan help us answer our question about art? Aesthetic insight is not immediately associated with Bernard Lonergan's approach to philosophy or theology,[28] but then he has also been accused of being intellectualist, which I think reflects a superficial reading of the succinct, Anglophone way of stating facts of this theologian also trained as a

---

[27]Lonergan, *Method in Theology*, 115.
[28]Exceptions include Hilary A. Mooney, *The Liberation of Consciousness: Bernard Lonergan's Theological Foundations in Dialogue with the Theological Aesthetics of Hans Urs von Balthasar* (Frankfurt: Knecht, 1992). John D. Dadosky, *The Eclipse and Recovery of Beauty: A Lonergan Approach* (Toronto: University of Toronto Press, 2014).

mathematician and scientist. Lonergan's theology takes Romans 5.5 as its foundation – the love of God poured out freely into human hearts – and identifies clear roles for religious experience, affectivity, felt-values, freedom, the common good and the progress of society in general within its framework. Hardly the outlook of a narrow intellect!

Lonergan is the perfect thought-companion for the question about art's role in human knowing because of how thoroughly he explores the different dimensions of human life and knowledge, and how they contribute to the whole.[29] Here I explore what art and the aesthetic mean to him, where they fit into the human process of grasping truth and the theological implications of his position, for art as a whole and music in particular. In light of what I have explained previously about his understanding of thought (philosophical *and* theological) as a journey of personal self-appropriation, at every stage of this chapter I would ask you, the reader, to test what is being said in your own experience: be attentive to what you are being told and make spaces to reflect, test out and verify or quarrel with what I am explaining. If not, you may end up 'knowing' both more and less than you did: unappropriated theory can be damaging or paralysing, especially when we do not realize what we do not know.

To start the process, I would also invite you to listen to the song that accompanies this chapter, once or twice. Take your time, stop everything else you are doing and make sure your speakers or your earphones are of good quality: this is not about listening to the music as you continue reading but finding a time and place to enter into a musical experience, relevant to the theme at hand, but in need of its own space of meaning. As you do so, listen to what you *feel*, how you receive it, what it evokes or provokes in you. What if you don't like it? Listen to that as well: it could be an issue of taste – a style you dislike or are unfamiliar with (which at times, coincides) – or it could be because you do not like how your body feels in this interaction. The most important aspect of this exercise is that you don't pre-judge your experience or interpretation of the song. Just hold the space, the feelings and thoughts that emerge, for the moment. And reflect upon them. We shall return here shortly.

Lonergan's critical realist epistemology

The fundamental concern of all Lonergan's work is about truth: how it is grasped and how it is transmitted. *This* is why he spent his life dedicated to *how* we come to know and applying it to how theology discovers and

---

[29]I have explored this theme more thoroughly, with an explicit focus on music and music-making, in Maeve Louise Heaney, 'Music and Theological Method: A Lonerganian Approach', *Theological Studies* 77, no. 3 (2016): 678–703. This chapter maintains a focus on the role of art-reception (which obviously also grounds the need for artistic creativity but which has been more thoroughly explored in relation to music in Part I).

transmits truth. One of the core questions in addressing this is where experience fits in. Remember that the philosophical backdrop during the two centuries prior to him oscillated between *all* experience (empiricism) and *no* experience (idealism) being real. So, what is 'experience' for Lonergan? He comments that while for most people experience is a form of knowledge, for him it is an infrastructure of knowledge. He fits in with the line of Anglo-American thinkers who challenge the original notion of experience as that of objects, or self as object, to that of our experiencing ourselves. But experience is only the first step in what he calls 'intentional consciousness' (also called 'intentionality analysis').

Lonergan analyses the operations and process of human knowing, and classifies them into four stages, or levels, of consciousness: empirical, intellectual, rational and responsible. In the first we experience; in the second we seek to understand what it is we experience: what is it? (*quid sit, cur ita sit*); in the third we reflect on what has been understood to verify its truth and reality: is it really so? (*an sit*); and finally we decide on its value and on what will we choose to do with it (*an honestum sit*). It is on this final level that the reality of our decision and freedom comes more specifically into play. This process is the same in every kind of knowledge, from the most banal to the most important.[30] So, for knowledge to be authentic, we must be attentive to our experiences, be intelligent about what they might mean and reflect upon what we think is at play, and then be reasonable about how we deal with them. From a theological perspective, this process achieves its ultimate fulfilment in the 'fifth level',[31] which he calls 'being-in-love', provoked by an unconditional experience of being loved – the Holy Spirit poured out into the human heart (Rom. 5.5) – described as 'the efficacious ground of all self-

---

[30] I invite the reader to explore the thesis that all knowledge follows these three questions. For example: you shiver. You notice that you shiver – that is the experience – *and ask why: what is it?* Are you cold? Or scared? Or feeling feverish? You might immediately have a sense of which and why: the door is open, you are alone at night in a dark alley or there's a flu making the rounds in your family, for example. But you might need to verify further: *Is that really the cause?* Have you got a temperature, for example? Once you are pretty sure what it is, you can take steps: *What does this mean? Or what do I do now?* Do I put a coat on, get out of that alley or take some medicine? This banal example works pretty much the same with more important insights: you feel sad, and ask yourself why: Was it something someone said? Or memories of a lost relative, a broken heart, a failure or loneliness . . . ? You reflect upon what might have provoked this feeling (a conversation, perhaps, or the time of year?) so as to verify what's happening and decide what to do about it. You might talk to a friend, read a book or pray, etc. This is the process of human knowing and acting, if our interaction with the world around us and ourselves is one that seeks to be authentic and in conscious freedom. We can also choose to ignore negative feelings, or supress them, resulting in the drifting lives of those who never really know why they do what they do.

[31] In some writings and interpreters, this is called the fulfilment of the fourth level, rather than an extra level, but I think it is clearer to separate it as it influences all levels of knowing, not just the deliberative (fourth) stage.

transcendence'.³² This gift of God's love is the principle of movement behind the whole dynamic process. Therefore, for Lonergan 'experience' properly expressed (which can be both external and internal) constitutes the first part of the fourfold process of knowledge. The quest for truth implies that we 'be attentive, be intelligent, be reasonable, be responsible, be in love'.³³ This structure of human knowing explains why Lonergan rarely speaks of experience of God ('we have no data on God' was one of his known quips!), but rather experience of the divine or of grace. It also lays the foundations for understanding the complexity and slow-cooked nature of theological work: true and 'correct' knowledge always implies the interaction of all four levels, bathed in and fulfilled in the fifth.

Art and the aesthetic in Lonergan's epistemology

What is the place and role of art and aesthetic experience in this framework? I will let his own words lead us into the answer, since although he is known to be both exceedingly complicated and extremely clear, at different times, this is an example of the latter. The context of the statement is that of a conference for educators tasked with creating a 'philosophy of education':

> What I want to communicate in this talk about art is the notion that *art is relevant to concrete living*, that it is an exploration of the potentialities of concrete living. That exploration is extremely important in our age, when *philosophers for at least two centuries, through doctrines on politics, economics, education, and through even further doctrines, have been trying to remake man [sic], and have done not a little to make life unlivable*. The great task that is demanded if we are to make it livable again is the re-creation of the liberty of the subject, the recognition of the freedom of consciousness.³⁴

His point is clear: art is not an extra, optional and superfluous to the real substance of things but necessary and relevant to all concrete living. Furthermore, it has something philosophy has not and can complement one-sided approaches to life and education which relate to the essence of human life and Christian anthropology: our conscious freedom.

---

³²Lonergan, *Method in Theology*, 241. As explored in chapter four, this being-in-love is the essence of religious conversion, without which theology proper, for Lonergan, is impossible. It is, however, also a universally accessible experience, often implicit in human knowing before its source is named and recognized.
³³Lonergan, *Method in Theology*, 268.
³⁴Bernard J. F Lonergan, 'Art', in *Collected Works of Bernard Lonergan. Vol. 10: Topics in Education*, ed. R. M. Doran and F. E. Crowe, 208–32 (232) (Toronto: University of Toronto Press, 1993); emphasis mine.

Why? Lonergan situates art on the first level of consciousness, that of experience, and has the function of stretching and enriching human experience *before* the mind moves on to the next steps of understanding, judging and acting on what we have experienced. It invites us to stop, taste, and see the moment we are experiencing! This fact makes attentiveness to aesthetic experience central, which was my attempt in inviting you to be attentive to the song 'Come Alive' and how you experienced it *before* you sought to understand, interpret and come to a judgement about its meaning for you. Only in this way do we allow art to fulfill its purpose. Be attentive! How art enriches human experience relies on two other elements of his thought: his definition of art and the different modes and patterns of activity through which human beings live in the world. I will briefly explain these before returning to his claim about art's role in human consciousness, freedom and truth.

Art and the aesthetic pattern of human consciousness

Lonergan's definition of art is influenced by Susanne Langer's philosophy of art[35] and those who viewed the role of art as expressive of meaning rather than imitative of beauty. He describes art as 'the objectification of a purely experiential pattern',[36] where the emphasis is on the pattern being *purely experiential, elemental, without interpretations or objectifications* alien to it. Art is situated on the first level of the process of human knowing: experience, without any type of instrumentalization.[37] It provokes a release of meaning which is, however, elemental; that is to say, meaning in which subject and object are not yet differentiated. 'Lonergan describes "experiential" and "elemental meaning" as of the seen as seen, of the heard as heard, of the felt as felt.'[38]

Depending on the context or the nature of what we are doing, human beings inhabit and interact with the world in different ways, or with different patterns, such as common sense or practical, theoretical, mystical/religious, artistic and aesthetic. Lonergan calls this the 'polymorphic' nature of human consciousness.[39] Each of these patterns follows the levels of consciousness unfolding from experience into understanding, judgement and decision-making, but *each in and according to its own pattern*. The aesthetic pattern of experience, which is our focus here, is situated between the biological and the intellectual patterns, and therefore has the potential to liberate the

---

[35] Cf. Susanne K. Langer, *Feeling and Form: A Theory of Art Developed from Philosophy in a New Key* (London: Routledge and Kegan Paul, 1953).
[36] Lonergan, *Method in Theology*, 61.
[37] Cf. Lonergan, 'Art', 208–32 (213).
[38] Cf. Lonergan, 'Art', 208–32.
[39] Cf. Lonergan, *Insight*, 452 and; Gerard Walmsley, *Lonergan on Philosophic Pluralism: The Polymorphism of Consciousness as the Key to Philosophy* (Toronto: University of Toronto Press, 2008).

process of human knowing from the pull of biological needs on the one hand and the constraints of intelligence and the intellectual patterns of experience on the other. This is why art helps to keep us human! It allows us to inhabit, symbolise and imagine the world afresh; with room to move, since the meaning it grasps is symbolic and incomplete, communicating 'subtly' rather than to giving definitive or absolute answers.[40]

This is how art can be transformational and contribute to an expanded awareness of life and its meaning or truth. Art invites to participation rather than explanation, 'straining for truth and value without defining them'.[41] Aesthetic experiences force us to withdraw from practical living to 'explore the possibilities of fuller living in a richer world', a world which 'may be regarded as illusion, but it also may be regarded as more true and more real': 'a transformed subject in [her] transformed world'.[42]

This is why he relates art to the re-creation of the liberty of the subject, the recognition of the 'freedom of consciousness'.[43] We can't control it, scary as that might seem to our control-friendly educational disciplines. Art is linked to the imaginative capacity of the human mind to play, to explore, to reinvent ourselves and the world we live in: 'experience for the sake of experience at the service of everyday living'.[44] We need it! Human knowledge is less than it could be without art. Theology is narrower, less human and therefore less divine than it should be without the aesthetic and artistic dimensions of human life and understanding of truth. I invite you to return to the questions earlier in this chapter, this time in light of our understanding of human knowledge: What would your world, and your life, be without the aesthetic experiences you have had? And take it a step further: Where do they lead me? Our patterns of knowing move through experience, understanding, reasoning and action, so our knowledge and grasp of its meaning will be enriched if we are critically reflective at each stage.

Come Alive

I turn now to the piece of music offered as a space to better experience and access some of what I have been explaining. At this stage, if you have not taken time for an attentive listen to the song, now would be the moment to do so. All I intend to do, at this stage, is to express some of what – in my

---

[40]Lonergan, *Insight*, 207–9.
[41]Lonergan, *Insight*, 208.
[42]Lonergan, *Method in Theology*, 63–4.
[43]Cf. Lonergan, 'Art', 208–32 (232).
[44]Lonergan, 'Art', 208–32 (217). Lonergan briefly explores how different art forms affect human consciousness, exploring visual art, sculpture, architecture and music in their relation to our experience of space and time, but it is a topic that has been developed much further and elsewhere since then.

understanding – the music and lyrics seek to express and what the song means to me. I share this *not* to control its meaning or to place the source of the song above the experience, felt meaning and interpretation each reader and listener may have. But it is *one* perspective and can be helpful for a fuller overview of its potential interpretations.[45]

The music for this song emerged first, and very quickly, in comparison to others, and without any words. Songwriting for me can go both ways: from a text that inspires me to music that expresses it, or vice versa, when music emerges from or around something I am living and then I seek the words that seem to fit that experience. In this case, the latter was true. For a long time, this was piano-based tune, with harmonies included, that I would play each morning, as if opening a door to the day. It slowly built up to the song you hear, with multiple layers and contributors. It is one of the most 'produced' songs I have, with suggestions at the pre-production and production stage, which to my mind have enriched the whole immensely. Music is always a collaborative venture, but at times this is more obvious.

It is what I would call my most 'spatial' piece of music, which I will explain. Music is often linked to time: it develops and unfolds over time, with a meter, that measures it out and carries it (and us) forward. This meter can feel 'quick' or 'slow', although these are metaphors, as time moves at the same rate all through. But music is also spatial: it affects the spaces we inhabit and how we experience them (be they shopping malls or churches) and ourselves as we pass through them: music fills the space in and through which it sounds. This song seeks to do this, in the recognition that art affects human experience of the world and of our own lives and bodies: Come alive! The first time I performed this was at an event at the Jesuit School of Theology, at Santa Clara University, California. To make this spatial point, we had musicians enter into the music from every corner of the room, dancers emerge from the audience and an artist paint live in front of us, so that the whole space echoed this truth: art can bring us alive, stretching us towards new awareness. Be attentive! Art can change your mind. As I hear it, the fullness of sound in this song is essential. Music is the most embodied of the arts: sound vibrating right through us, which is why it is so hard to not move when you listen to or play music. The underlying beat – of drums both live and electronic – and the overlayered voices are meant to move you, physically and in other ways.

This is what the lyrics seek to express as well. Lonergan's critical realism, which allows the body and the senses to mediate insight and knowledge to us, was in my heart and mind as I wrote it, as well as the Ignatian spirituality

---

[45]I have presented at length a potential approach to musical meaning, which explores the various hermeneutical perspectives at play in musical meaning. Jean-Jacques Nattiez breaks open the usual threefold perspectives in literary criticism to allow for the non-verbal dimensions of musical meaning, by which its meanings are more complex and multi-dimensional than words, especially theoretical discourse (as poetry also often plays with sound and multiple meanings).

he grew out of: 'to find God in all things'. Those who have done the Ignatian month of spiritual exercises might recognize the second-week invitation to imaginative contemplation: enter into the scene, touch, smell, taste, watch! Because all knowledge comes through the senses – even knowledge of God, since faith comes through the Word (Rom. 10.17). Christianity has a paradoxical relationship with the body and the senses, but none of them permit us to negate its worthiness to receive an incarnated God and be transformed into that likeness. Every one of us is loved, and all of us can be an access point to truth. My favourite part of the lyrics and one of the strongest, I would suggest, from a theological perspective, is the line at the end of each verse:

> *Don't name it, or claim it, just stay put and let the new . . . break through,*

and

> *Don't tame it, before it's her time, don't wake up the truth is we still don't know.*[46]

Don't close down the quest for truth before time! Don't be scared of unfinished thought! (The echo of John Henry Newman's words that 'to live is to change; to be perfect, to have changed often' is clear). Don't decide your life before you know it! Don't conform to less than you can be! And for heaven's sake, don't reduce God to your own image and likeness or that of anyone else! Awaken, and imagine the faces you could recognize! Maybe even your own or that of your God! The link to the song is in the note.[47]

'Come Alive' lyrics[48]

> *Come alive! Change your mind!*
> *Awaken the spaces, the shapes and the places;*
> *Imagine the faces you once recognized . . .*
> *Taste and See / Touch . . . hold . . . feel!*
> *Don't name it, or claim it, just stay put and let the new . . . break through.*
> **Come alive! Change your mind!**
> **Awaken the spaces, the shapes and the places;**
> **Imagine the faces you once recognized**

---

[46] The reference to the Song of Songs is clear.
[47] The link to 'Come Alive': https://res.cloudinary.com/bloomsbury-online-resources/video/upload/v1639138277/Suspended%20God/Come_Alive.wav
[48] Where applicable, the repeated chorus of the song is in bold, and therefore not fully written out more than once.

Awaken the spaces, the shapes and the places;
Imagine the faces you could recognize
Look . . . sense . . . breathe / Hush . . . hold . . . still
Don't tame it, before it's her time, don't wake up the truth is we still don't know.
Come alive . . .

©MAEVE LOUISE HEANEY, 2020.
Strange Life, The Music of Doubtful Faith

Selected further reading

For an introduction to Bernard Lonergan's life and theology

Gallagher, Michael Paul. 'Bernard Lonergan'. In *Faith Maps: Ten Religious Explorers from Newman to Joseph Ratzinger*, 72–86. New York: Paulist Press, 2010.

Kerr, Fergus. 'Bernard Lonergan'. Chap. Seven In *Twentieth-Century Catholic Theologians: From Neoscholasticism to Nuptial Mysticism*, 105–20. Malden, MA: Blackwell Pub., 2007.

For an introduction to his theological method

Crowe, Frederick E. *Method in Theology: An Organon for Our Time*. Milwaukee, WI: Marquette University Press, 1980.

Good starting points for Lonergan's thought

Lonergan, Bernard J. F. 'Dimensions of Meaning'. In *Collection. Papers by Bernard Lonergan S. J.*, edited by F. E. Crowe and R. M. Doran, 252–67. New York: Herder and Herder, 1967.

Lonergan, Bernard J. F. 'Theology in Its New Context'. In *A Second Collection. Papers by Bernard J. F. Lonergan S. J.*, edited by F. J. Ryan and B. J. Tyrell, 55–68. London: Darton, Longman and Todd, 1974.

Lonergan, Bernard J. F. 'Pope John's Intention'. In *A Third Collection. Papers by Bernard J. F. Lonergan*, edited by F. E. Crowe, 225–38. New York: Paulist Press, 1985.

Lonergan on Art

Lonergan, Bernard J. F. 'Art'. In *Collected Works of Bernard Lonergan. Vol. 10: Topics in Education*, edited by R. M. Doran and F. E. Crowe, 208–32. Toronto, ON: University of Toronto Press, 1993.

6

Is Scripture a world for women?

The issue of women and Scripture: A foundational problem

For most women, at some stage in their life, reading Scripture – the central and foundational text of Christian revelation for all Christians (independent of or integrated with their understanding of tradition) – is problematic. This experience is felt differently across the world, depending on a myriad of factors, including but not limited to cultural understandings of the role of women and men, education and theological literacy, and the major differences in how gender plays out in language. But it is no longer true to say that this is a Western problem.[1] At some stage of most women's lives, reading or hearing the male-gendered language applied to God, and the male-centred focus of God's redeeming love, makes reading Scripture and finding one's place in the praying heart of Church a viscerally felt challenge. This experience is often linked to one's personal experience of belonging to or exclusion from the Church, in one way or another. As a female theologian, my own experience might prove helpful: I was born to faith during the 1980s in a community dedicated to training women for preaching, a space in which my voice had equal resonance as any man's (except perhaps, and understandably, the community's founder). During the 1990s, as that openness began to shift, and the willingness to let us preach was questioned,

---

[1] In 2014, in response to a request of Pope Francis for theology to engage in this issue, the International Network of Societies for Catholic Theology (INSeCT) took 'A question of gender justice: the role of women in decision-making in different areas of church and society' as its research project across the world. In 2017, I was at the meeting leaders of Catholic Societies of Theology from across the five continents presenting the results of this research, listening to a rare convergence of concerns emerging from radically different particular contexts. For a summary of their theological position on this issue, see https://www.insecttheology.org/post/a-question-of-gender-justice

my awareness of where women stand in the history of the Catholic tradition and the Christian Scriptures began to emerge.[2] It was a painful and unsought awareness, in which the safe spaces of revelation and prayer began to look unrecognizably strange and unwelcoming. I would like to suggest (and believe), albeit polemically, that the same applies to theologically aware men who have women in their lives that they appreciate: sooner or later the tone-deaf texts of Scripture grate against the lived experience that women are equally loved and called by God, and that this recognition is essential to Christianity's present and future.

Our focus in this chapter is the reality of Scripture and its interpretation in addressing this problem. It is one issue, among many, related to women's place in the history of salvation and their inclusion in, or exclusion from, decision-making processes in Church and State. As such, given the cultural shifts across the world in relation to women's dignity and leadership, from where I am standing, it is also about the future of the Church tout court. This is not a hope*less* statement or a denial of our faith that the Spirit will accompany us to the end of time, and that truth will win: my faith in this is miraculously firm. But it expresses a call to responsibility for the people we leave by the wayside as a consequence of our lack of attentiveness and responsibility in reading the signs of the times: our world does not accept complacency about the role of women in the Church. Our commitment to the mission of the Church obliges us (much as it did Paul) to reflect on this theme, informed by the best scholarship we can. In other words, it *is* about faith transmission, and evangelization, and the possibility that future generations might hear words of eternity life.[3]

As I enter into the theme, a few caveats are necessary and a plea. I will start with the plea: I ask the reader to *not react for or against* this theme without being open to reflect upon it. The issue of women in the Church has become dangerously polarized in recent decades. In part, this is due to the complex interweaving of secular and ecclesial awareness over the nineteenth- and twentieth centuries in relation to the role of women in both society and Church. Significant movements in history are always difficult to navigate, and the dual-but-opposite temptation to stick our heads in the sand in relation to obviously necessary changes or throw the baby out with the bathwater is ever at play. In other words, neither fear nor undiscerned overconfidence will serve us well, theologically, to map the development of tradition. Fear is a bad advisor, and ignorance an unwise guide. So, the

---

[2] For a more complete presentation of this story and struggle, see Maeve Louise Heaney, 'From the Particular to the Universal: Musings of a Woman Theologian', in *Catholic Women Speak: Visions and Vocations*, ed. T. Beattie and D. Culbertson, 211–19 (New York, Mahwah, NJ: Paulist Press, 2018).

[3] The expression is taken from Johannine scholar Mary Coloe as a better description of the gift of life in offer in Jesus than that of 'eternal life', which evokes continuation and more of the same, in the future, rather than qualitatively different life now and forever.

attempt here is to improve our awareness of the history of this issue and more clarity about the nuances of what is at stake. The caveat I need to name is that I do not yet have a specific 'outcome' in addressing this issue. It is unpopular and perhaps unambitious to be unfinished in one's thought processes, but in this space, I am and will remain so. Some of the authors I present have more clearly defined and decided on the necessary steps to be taken. I present them because they make a good case for their claims *and* because I am convinced interacting with and understanding their thought is essential to the future of theology and the Church. But where this will lead, I am not going to guess – sometimes because I honestly do not know; others because I don't feel we are ready for what I intuit might need to happen. But in all cases, the need to theologize clearly and courageously about these issues is non-negotiable, for the reason stated earlier: our faith and the faith of the future generations.

The emergence of feminist awareness and theology

The 'and' in this heading – feminist awareness *and* theology – serves to separate and distinguish two categories that while linked are not the same. Cultural awareness of women's rights in the world and theological reflection on their identity and role in a Christian world view in light of a theologically informed anthropology are distinct, if overlapping, themes. This is the case in every area of Christian living: the complex, mutually enriching and challenging spaces of faith and culture contextualize tradition, and it has always been so. But here it is perhaps more visible, and somehow more threatening, than others, given its potential to critique, challenge and revise a broad spectrum of theology's sources and thought. However, it is the theological insight we are seeking even as we trace the cultural movements that overlap and affect it.

Most introductions to feminist theology speak of three strands or waves of feminist awareness, although they are not solely chronological and overlap with one another.[4] The first emerged in the nineteenth century, lasted until the mid-twentieth century and is linked to the slavery abolitionist movement and a growing awakening of human rights and the equality of all human beings (even if its implementation in terms of racial awareness was uneven

---

[4]For a brief introduction to the emergence and focus of feminist theologies, see Rosemary Radford Ruether, 'Feminist Theology', in *The New Dictionary of Theology*, ed. M. Collins, D. A. Lane, and J. A. Komonchak, 391–6 (Collegeville, MN: Liturgical Press, 1987). Stanley J. Grenz and Roger E. Olson, 'Feminist Theology: The Immanence of God in Women's Experience', in *20th Century Theology: God & the World in a Transitional Age*, 224–36 (Downers Grove, IL: InterVarsity Press, 1992); Mary M. Veeneman, 'Feminist Theologies', in *Introducing Theological Method: A Survey of Contemporary Theologians and Approaches* (Grand Rapids, MI: Baker Academic, 2017).

and slow). Its promoters were mainly white, middle-class, well-educated North American women who understood patriarchy as illegitimate, even though it defined society in such a way that women were marginalized and dominated. Key figures at this time were Elizabeth Cady Stanton (1815–1902), Lucretia Mott (1793–1880), Susan B. Anthony (1820–1906) and Charlotte Perkins Gilman (1860–1935); and a defining event was the first Woman's Rights Convention at Seneca Falls, New York, in 1840.

Second-wave feminism is marked by the growing dissatisfaction felt by women due to their lack of social power and political influence, and their attempt to raise awareness of the systemic oppression of women by the cultural, political and ecclesial structures in which they lived. One of its paradigmatic texts is that of Betty Friedan entitled *The Feminine Mystique*,[5] and 'the personal is political' sums up the position of this phase. However, it was not monochrome and included a variety of strands which Maria Riley differentiates into four: liberal feminism, which focussed on legal issues; cultural feminism, which accentuated the difference between the male and the female, at times in terms of moral superiority; radical feminism, which sought systemic change and the rooting out of patriarchy; and socialist feminism, focussed on race and class analyses.[6] It was a multifaceted, cultural tidal wave (or tsunami?) which affected all areas of the Western world (as it was still *mainly* led by white or Western educated women). It is at this stage we begin to see 'feminist theologies', properly speaking, since prior to this time, women did not have access to theological education and therefore could not develop the vocabulary to understand and express their experiences and insights. Key figures here include the historical work of Gerda Lerner,[7] Elisabeth Schüssler Fiorenza's work on the writing out of women in Scriptures and the early Church[8] and Rosemary Radford Ruether's analogue scholarship on women in Christian tradition and doctrine.[9] Sandra Marie Schneiders and Elizabeth A. Johnson, as we shall see, represent a maturation and development of these and other thinkers.

Third-wave feminism, in an analogue way to postmodern shifts away from universal statements to contextual sensibility, is attentive to difference and the particular. The inclusion of women's experience in theological research developed into the consciousness that the different contexts in

---

[5] Betty Friedan, *The Feminine Mystique* (New York: Norton, 1963).
[6] Cf. Maria Riley, *Transforming Feminism* (Kansas City, MO: Sheed & Ward, 1989), 46–63; Anne M. Clifford, *Introducing Feminist Theology* (Maryknoll, NY: Orbis Books, 2001).
[7] Gerda Lerner, *The Creation of Patriarchy*, ed. S. American Council of Learned Societies (New York: Oxford University Press, 1986).
[8] Elisabeth Schüssler Fiorenza, *In Memory of Her: A Feminist Theological Reconstruction of Christian Origins* (New York: Crossroad, 1983); Elisabeth Schüssler Fiorenza, *Bread Not Stone: The Challenge of Feminist Biblical Interpretation* (Edinburgh, Scotland: Clark, 1990).
[9] Rosemary Radford Ruether, *Sexism and God-Talk: Toward a Feminist Theology. With a New Introduction*, 10th anniversary ed. (Boston, MA: Beacon Press, 1993).

which women live lead to different theologies, in which not only gender but also race and class are a factor of exclusion. So we see the birth of 'Womanist' theology emerging from African or Afro-American experiences, 'Mujerista' or 'Latina' feminist theology and various Asian, African and Native American contextualized theologies by and about women's experience and understanding of faith. It is a further shift from the centre towards the margins. Current scholarship has also broadened to address issues of our understanding of gender, sexuality and intersectionality (understood as the interconnected nature of social categorizations such as race, class, gender and disability).[10] This is less about overcoming feminist theology as broadening further a critical analysis of power mechanisms at the basis of separation, hierarchization and sexualization of experience and conceptual worlds, affecting everyone.[11]

Shared approaches, positions and themes

In the midst of this plurality and process of development and despite their particular accents, the following traits can be named as shared convictions and approaches to theology by a broad spectrum of feminist theologies:

- *The importance of women's experiences as a source for theology*: the reality of 'experience as source' for theology is a relatively new, if largely accepted, dimension of current theological *loci*,[12] but feminist work has awakened us to the fact that up until recently, male experience and forms of expression have been accepted unquestioningly as paradigmatic of all human experience to the point of substituting those of women (children, minorities, differently abled etc.). This has extended to shaping both the content and the form of theology. For this reason, most theologizing influenced by feminist awareness speaks of 'women's experiences and theologies' rather than 'woman' and 'theology of woman' in a pushback to universal essentialist (and unembodied) interpretations of reality.

- *Knowledge as embodied:* the importance of particularity and bodies, and by way of a reaction to the simultaneous exclusion and sexual objectification of women, has led women and feminist theologians to emphasize the embodied nature of Christian faith and life, as well

---

[10]For an insightful overview of current work in this field, see a dedicated volume of *Concilium* in 2012: Lisa Sowle Cahill, Diego Irarrazaval, and Elaine Mary Wainwright, eds., *Gender in Theology, Spirituality and Practice* (London: SCM Press, 2012).

[11]Regina Ammicht Quinn, 'Dangerous Thinking: Gender and Theology', *Concilium Special Edition on Gender in Theology, Spirituality and Practice* 4 (2012): 13–25 (15).

[12]Cf. Dermot A. Lane, *The Experience of God: An Invitation to Do Theology* (New York: Paulist Press, 2003).

as alternative, less abstract forms of theologizing (including but not limited to the arts and music).[13]
- *The importance of narrative in theology*: storytelling as a form of access to experience and understanding is a central tenet and consequence of taking women's experience seriously. One needs to listen to and hear the story of a people or a person, before theologizing about it.
- *Patriarchy/kyriarchy as structural and systemic:* the recognition that the key sources of Christian revelation were written and handed on by men living (albethey unaware) in a patriarchal society, with the ensuing need to reread and rediscover what was written and what was left out of these stories. The aim is to access Jesus' intentionality and vision of the Reign of God. Despite its name, patriarchy in many contemporary authors is not confined to the oppression of women by men but all structurally blind bias and marginalization (such as white privilege or postcolonial advantage), which is best described with Schüssler Fiorenza's term 'kyriarchy'.[14]
- *Historical awareness:* rereading and rediscovering the reality of women's contribution to the story of salvation and history of the Christian churches as a logical consequence of the above. This includes studies into ancient documents of the early churches (including the excluded apocryphal writings) and what can be known about the roles of women in the medieval Church.
- *Ecological/ecofeminist consciousness:* many feminists and other theologians who accept their premises have developed thought on ecological consciousness. An awareness is growing that 'the same systems that oppress women also oppress and exploit the environment to the detriment of both nonhuman animals and marginalized people ... any move toward the liberation of women is incomplete without an accompanying move toward the liberation of the earth'.[15]

The shared intent of all of these theologies can be described as a threefold task: first, to unveil the patriarchal and misogynistic bias of the Christian tradition; second, to draw on these alternative sources and ways of theologizing, so as to (third) re-envision and reconstruct core theological themes in a way that is liberating, rather than oppressive.[16]

---

[13]The work of Sallie McFague here is important. For example: Sallie McFague, *The Body of God: An Ecological Theology* (London: SCM Press, 1993); Sallie McFague, *Life Abundant: Rethinking Theology and Economy for a Planet in Peril* (Minneapolis, MN: Fortress Press, 2000).
[14]Cf. Elisabeth Schüssler Fiorenza, *Jesus, Miriam's Child, Sophia's Prophet: Critical Issues in Feminist Christology*, 2nd ed. (London, England: Bloomsbury T&T Clark, 2015).
[15]Veeneman, 'Introducing Theological Method', 147, quoting Clifford, *Introducing Feminist Theology*.
[16]Cf. Ruether, 'Feminist Theology', 391–6 (392).

The issue of women and/in the Scriptures

A golden thread in and through *each and every* stage and particular expression of feminist or women-centred theology is the challenge of Scripture! Long before nineteenth-century feminist Elizabeth Cady Stanton proposed that Bible teachings degrade women from Genesis to Revelation and pulled together a 'Revising Committee' to evaluate the Judaeo-Christian legacy and its impact on women through history, Margaret Fell, cofounder with George Bell of *The Society of Friends* (Quakers), developed a Scriptural hermeneutic supporting women preachers, in 1667.[17] Stanton and her co-workers produced a *Women's Bible*,[18] a text that sought to comment on and revise 'those texts and chapters directly referring to women, and those also in which women are made prominent by exclusion'.[19] While dated, it is a fascinating read. For example, on the creation stories

> All the commentators and publicists writing on woman's position, go through an immense amount of fine-spun metaphysical speculations, to prove her subordination in harmony with the Creator's original design. It is evident that some wily writer, seeing the perfect equality of man and woman in the first chapter, felt it important for the dignity and dominion of man to effect woman's subordination in some way. To do this a spirit of evil must be introduced, which at once proved itself stronger than the spirit of good, and man's supremacy was based on the downfall of all that had just been pronounced very good. This spirit of evil evidently existed before the supposed fall of man, hence woman was not the origin of sin as so often asserted.[20]

This was only the first of an ongoing river of books, commentaries and resources created to help women interact with Scripture in accessible and prayerful ways.[21] The problem is that the Scriptures – the foundational revelatory text for every Christian denomination – was born of and written by a culture and people imbued with a patriarchal world view. Women are ignored, marginalized, or worse, in both the Hebrew and Christian writings. It is anachronistic to expect that they *not* reflect the language and mentality of the time, but it is equally unfair to these writers and those who approach Christian faith now to ignore this conditioning. The ongoing influence of male images of the divine and the absence of female leadership clearly leave

---

[17]Cf. Margaret Fell. *Womens Speaking Justified, Proved, and Allowed by the Scriptures*. London: Early English Books Online, 1666.
[18]Elizabeth Cady Stanton and the Revising Committee, *The Women's Bible* (1896–1898).
[19]From the preface of Stanton and Committee, *The Women's Bible*.
[20]Stanton and Committee, *The Women's Bible*, 21.
[21]A current intent worthy of mention is Liturgical Press' Wisdom Commentary Series: https://litpress.org/wisdom-commentary-series

women struggling to 'imagine' their roles as anything but subordinate and secondary to men. But these are texts we profess to be inspired! This is a foundational issue because of the importance of Scripture in Christianity's self-understanding and development. In the words of Rosemary Reuther, one of the most important theological voices of twentieth-century feminist theology: 'It is one thing to critique the tradition as flawed, but on what basis can one speak of Scripture as distorted by sexist bias and still regard it as an authoritative source of revelation?'[22] This is the question at the centre of this chapter.

In the history of feminist research into Scripture, we can identify three ways to deal with this issue, although properly understood they reflect a dynamic spectrum, rather than static alternatives:[23] 'reformist Christian feminist theologians' view the biblical text and the Christian tradition as fundamentally liberating for all and situate the problem in its interpretation; revolutionary feminist theologians reject both Scripture and the tradition it has given birth to as 'irredeemably patriarchal', by which the only way forward is outside and beyond Christianity;[24] and in between these two extremes we find 'reconstructionist Christian feminist theologians', who recognize that while the biblical text contains passages that are deeply problematic, there is the possibility of recovering the silenced presence and downplayed voices of women who were and are part of the heritage of Scripture and Christian tradition.[25] As we shall find, Sandra Schneiders' work is firmly situated in this third group.

Each of the women and some of the men in this book can be better understood in relation to this mapping of feminist theology. In fact, the awareness or lack thereof in each of our authors of the mega-phenomenon that is women's self-understanding and emergence into theological scholarship is one lens through which they could be studied, and although this is not the core aim of this book, where relevant, each chapter points out if their theology overlaps or intersects in some way with the theme. Of course, not everyone agrees with any of these feminist interpretations of Scripture and tradition. The well-known 'theology of the body' grounded on Hans Urs von Balthasar's anthropology and ecclesiology, which became

---

[22]Ruether, 'Feminist Theology', 391–6 (394); Ruether, *Sexism and God-Talk*.

[23]These categories are presented in chapter one of Clifford, *Introducing Feminist Theology*.

[24]This is the position Mary Daly comes to embrace. See Mary Daly, *The Church and the Second Sex* (New York: Harper & Row, 1968); Mary Daly, *Beyond God the Father: Toward a Philosophy of Women's Liberation* (Boston: Beacon Press, 1985). This approach proposes other forms of religious affiliation, exploring ancient versions of goddess worship, and 'woman-Church'. A well-known theological description of this position is that of Mary Daly, in *Beyond God the Father: Toward a Philosophy of Women's Liberation*. Boston: Beacon Press, 1985.

[25]A foundational text that explores the early history of the Church as counter-cultural and subversive of contemporary hierarchical sociopolitical structures in relation to the role of women is Schüssler Fiorenza, *In Memory of Her: A Feminist Theological Reconstruction of Christian Origins*.

prominent during the papacy of John Paul II,[26] promotes an alternative hermeneutic of Scripture that emphasizes essential differences between men and women and promotes 'feminine genius' as a particular contribution of women to the Church and the world that complements male leadership. This approach usually implies that making changes in authoritative roles in the Church is unnecessary for real influence.[27] (I will address this position in chapters seven on Balthasar and sixteen on Haughton.) Other attempts at articulating complementarity between genders that include a clear challenge to power structures are also being developed,[28] and analyses of the limits of feminist theology and the need for fresh approaches to its underlying concerns are also emerging.[29]

However, no one in the Church denies the marginalization of women in society, about which the Church has gradually spoken out since the Second Vatican Council. John Paul's *Letter to Women* in 1995 challenges the history which has been 'an obstacle to the progress of women ... [in which] women's dignity has often been unacknowledged and their prerogatives misrepresented; they have often been relegated to the margins of society and even reduced to servitude'.[30] And more recently, Pope Francis identified the need 'to create still broader opportunities for a more incisive female presence in the Church' and explicitly asked pastors and theologians to explore 'the possible role of women in decision-making in different areas of the Church's life'.[31] But awakening to the reality of structural injustice is never easy, and the language of 'gender' still provokes an allergic reaction in many ecclesial circles. In fact, gender is one of the most polarized terms in church circles today.[32] One of the reasons for this difficulty is the overlap of

---

[26]Cf. John Paul II, *Mulieris Dignitatem: On the Dignity and Vocation of Women* (Vatican: Vatican Press, 1988).
[27]For example, Congregation for the Doctrine of the Faith, *Collaboration of Men and Women in the Church* (13 July 2004); Michele M Schumacher, *Women in Christ: Toward a New Feminism* (Grand Rapids, MI: William B. Eerdmans, 2004).
[28]For example, Benedito Ferraro, 'Theology in the Context of Reciprocity and Complementarity between Men and Women', *Concilium Special Edition on Gender in Theology, Spirituality and Practice* 4 (2012): 36–45 (37), referring to the work of Rose Marie Muraro and Leonardo Boff.
[29]For example, Susan Parsons speaks of the need to '"think anew what it is to be orthodox, to be informed by a tradition and embodied in its thinking, and to engage in a work of apologetic theology for our day that is sensitive to the feminist critique".' Cf. Tina Beattie, *New Catholic Feminism: Theology and Theory* (New York, NY: Routledge, 2006), 8, quoting Susan Frank Parsons, 'Accounting for Hope: Feminist Theology as Fundamental Theology', in *Challenging Women's Orthodoxies in the Context of Faith*, ed. S. F. Parsons (Aldershot: Ashgate, 2000). Beattie's book presents a brilliant, if challenging, exploration into the theme.
[30]John Paul II, *Letter to Women* (Vatican 1995).
[31]Francis, *Apostolic Exhortation Evangelii Gaudium* (Vatican City: AAS, 2013), 103 and 104.
[32]An insightful attempt to bring together diverse and opposite opinions can be found in Elizabeth A. Johnson, *The Church Women Want: Catholic Women in Dialogue* (New York: Crossroad Pub. Co., 2002). A more recent one focussing on the issue of how we name God is Celia Wolf-Devine, *Naming God: Selected Readings Representing Differing Perspectives* (New York:

some of the concerns between women's equality movements and women in Christian theology,[33] which at times has led to a conflation of the differences between them. But more fundamentally, the genesis of social and ecclesial discourse on gender has been hijacked, and war is waged under the banner of 'gender ideology' – of which there are more than one! – without a serene and nuanced study of the terms and their meanings, in relation to Christian truth.[34] However, outright rejection of all feminist or gender theology insights (because of elements one does not agree with), on the one hand, or of all Scriptural revelation (because of other elements one cannot accept), on the other, leads us nowhere. So, the issue for many women and a growing number of men about how to 'rescue' Scripture for the life of the church, remains. We turn to the life and work of Sandra Schneiders to address it.

Sandra Marie Schneiders: 'Some woman for one woman!'[35]

If the connection between life, questions and theology is one of the threads that weaves through this book, few hold these together more clearly than Sandra Marie Schneiders, IHM. Born in Chicago in 1936, Schneiders felt the call to religious life at the age of six, a vocation that developed alongside a constant thirst to read and question beyond her years. By the time she finished high school, she had founded an unofficial newspaper that critiqued the administration, the curriculum and the teachers at her school – in the

---

Crossroad Publishing Company, 2019). In my opinion, the latter book fails, however, in its intent, due to the woefully mismatched academic and theological quality of some of the contributors.

[33]In this regard, the *Madaleva Manifesto* is interesting, in which a group of important, mainly Catholic, theologians made a statement about the *theological* significance of theologizing from a feminist perspective as essential to a full understanding of the gospel. Cf. 1985–2001 Madaleva Lecturers in Spirituality, 'The Madaleva Manifesto: A Message of Hope and Courage' (2000).

[34]For an excellent overview of the history of the emergence and definitions of 'gender' in Catholic ecclesial world, see Rebeka Jadranka Anić, 'Gender, Politics and the Catholic Church', *Concilium Special Edition on Gender in Theology, Spirituality and Practice* 4 (2012): 26–35. It includes an insightful overview of the origin and sources underpinning the widely translated Dale O'Leary, The Gender Agenda: Redefining Equality (Lafayette: Vital Issues Press, 1997). For a theological exploration aiming to avoid the extremes of both gender essentialism and complete gender fluidity, proposing a form of 'heteronormativity that is statistically structured allowing for a greater flexibility than suggested by gender essentialism, while still constraining the social and cultural construction of gender within certain biological realities', see Jonathan Heaps and Neil Ormerod, 'Statistically Ordered: Gender, Sexual Identity, and the Metaphysics of "Normal"', *Theological Studies* 80, no. 2 (2019): 346–69.

[35]This is an Irish expression, the origin of which I could not find, but in a matriarchal Ireland of strong women, it is one of our highest compliments to women whose achievements stand out as more than what one person is usually capable of.

legitimate spirit of freedom of the press – and was considered somewhat wild for religious life! However, enter she did! In 1955, at the age of eighteen, Schneiders joined the Sisters of the Immaculate Heart of Mary (IHM), a life-option that made possible, grounded and oriented much of her intellectual work and achievements. Her commitment to the living out and understanding of faith through a life transformed in the Spirit, and the felt belonging to the Church as a member of that walk of life that is religious life breathes through every dimension of her writing.

After the Second Vatican Council, the Sisters of the IHM were one of the congregations in the United States that had the insight and vision to educate a certain proportion of sisters with higher degrees in theology. Local theology faculties were not so quick to read the signs of the times and therefore were not yet open to women students, so Schneiders was sent to the Institut Catholique of Paris to do her licentiate (completed in 1971) and the Pontifical Gregorian University in Rome for her doctorate (completed in 1975), one of the first women to receive a doctorate in theology from a pontifical university. Therefore, and by her own admission, the Second Vatican Council set the context for her work: '"The church in its previous 500 years had become pretty fixed in its identity, theology, organization, and engagement with world," Schneiders said. "When I look back at my career, which certainly I hope is not over, I can really say it has been deeply shaped by the Council's effect on the church."'[36]

Twelve days after leaving Rome in 1976, she began teaching at the Jesuit School of Theology at Berkeley (which has since become part of Santa Clara University) as their only female faculty member and later the first non-Jesuit and female professor there to be tenured. She stayed there for over forty years, teaching long after she became emeritus, and only recently returned to Michigan, from where she continues to write and speak. It is not possible to list here all her achievements, publications and awards, but in 2016, not only was an archive created for her work at Santa Clara University[37] but an exhibition was created to showcase her contribution to the fields in which she works.[38]

Her contribution to theological thinking can be broadly divided into three fields: biblical studies and hermeneutics, Christian spirituality, and religious

---

[36]Cf. 'Faithful Feminist' at https://www.scu.edu/news-and-events/feature-stories/2016/stories/faithful-feminist.html (accessed 7 February 2021).

[37]Cf. https://scu-aspace.libraryhost.com/repositories/3/accessions/148 and https://www.scu.edu/library/asc/exhibits/schneiders/ (accessed 3 February 2021).

[38]'To Trace the Course of Wisdom: The Prophetic Spirituality of Sandra M. Schneiders Illuminated Through the Saint John's Bible'. I am grateful to Kelci Baughman McDowell, the Research & Instruction Services Coordinator of Archives & Special Collections at Santa Clara University Library, for her help in accessing these and other files of interest in relation to Sandra's work. This exhibition identified five pillars of her spirituality and work: biblical hermeneutics, Christian spirituality, feminism, propheticism and religious life.

life.³⁹ As we shall see, her contribution to each of these fields is not incidental or minor. One of the characteristics of Schneiders' work is that it is question-led, slow-cooked and thorough. She never writes about anything without first exploring and defining her terms in relation to the contemporary understanding, achievements and challenges of that academic discipline.⁴⁰ This humility and thoroughness in the quest for understanding mark all of her work and make it groundbreaking and foundational for the rest of us. Her questioning spirit and capacity to open new areas of theological exploration are present from her very first contribution to theological research. Her doctoral thesis, for example, went beyond the contemporary focus on historical-critical methods of Scriptural investigation to literary-critical approaches to Scriptural analysis and symbolism.⁴¹ Even at that early stage, her work pulled together interdisciplinary threads of philosophy, the emerging field of hermeneutics and biblical exegesis to answer questions that could not be explored from solely one perspective.

Her work on biblical scholarship – in particular the Gospel of John – is obligatory reading for any exploration of Johannine literature.⁴² That Scripture is the soul of theology (cf. *Dei Verbum* 24) is not an abstract or general notion in her writings but one that is fleshed out in every area of her work: in her theological commitment to the lens of faith in Scriptural text as inspired and canonical while holding fast to the most thorough of biblical exegesis; in her understanding of Christian spirituality as experience *and* discipline that informs and frames the questions she asks and the answers she finds; and in her forty-year commitment to the reality and implications of the resurrection narratives that open into the clearest, systematic defence of the resurrection of the body, Christian anthropology, eschatology and the possibility of embodied knowing that I have read. That consistency in taking seriously the embodied reality of the risen Christ continues to push her into new fields of phenomenological and theopoetic approaches to Scripture, spirituality and theology.⁴³

---

³⁹These three were the subject of a tribute organized for Schneiders at the American Academy of Religion by publishers, colleagues and friends in 2016.

⁴⁰I have personal experience of this approach to her writing: barely out of my doctorate and one week into a fellowship at the Jesuit School of Theology in Berkeley, *she* found and quizzed *me* for my understanding and definitions of key concepts and themes in theological aesthetics and artistic activity, an area she was beginning to explore.

⁴¹Sandra M. Schneiders, *The Johannine Resurrection Narrative: An Exegetical and Theological Study of John 20 as a Synthesis of Johannine Spirituality* (Pontificia Universitas Gregoriana, 1975).

⁴²Sandra M. Schneiders, *Jesus Risen in Our Midst: Essays on the Resurrection of Jesus in the Fourth Gospel* (Collegeville, MN: Liturgical Press, 2013).

⁴³Her current work *Risen Jesus, Cosmic Christ* gathers her prior work in what she describes as a hermeneutical circle of the major issues of her scholarship. 'It will bring together the themes of revelation and resurrection, the Christian experience of transformation, mystical prayer and religious life.' Cf. Jamie Manson, 'Biblical Scholar Sr. Sandra Schneiders Celebrates Four Milestones', *Global Sisters Report*, 25 January 2017.

Led by questions about and insights into the significance of the biblical text for lived faith and spirituality, Schneiders helped define Christian spirituality as an advanced, academic and multidisciplinary field of study.[44] Her approach is shaped by a phenomenological approach to the exploration of religious experience as it presents itself historically in personal and shared lived experience, open to comparison and in dialogue with a plurality of religious experiences. With quintessential thoroughness, she defines spirituality as 'the actualization of the basic human capacity for transcendence ... the experience of conscious involvement in the project of life integration through self-transcendence toward the horizon of ultimate value one perceives'[45] This understanding of spirituality can be defined as Christian when the Triune God revealed in Christ is the ultimate concern of one's life, self-transcendence refers to modelling one's life after the life of Jesus, and the 'spirit in spirituality is identified with the 'Holy Spirit', all lived out in the community of the Church.[46] Schneiders was instrumental in establishing the United States' first doctoral programme in Christian spirituality at the Graduate Theological Union in Berkeley, and co-founding the Society for the Study of Christian Spirituality.[47] Some would say she brought spirituality *into* the Academy!

Her contribution to the understanding of religious life is equally foundational. Her trilogy on religious life is unique in its exploration of the three evangelical counsels *as lived out* in the specific walk of life that is religious life.[48] Her insight into the cultural shifts affecting the Church and religious life before and after the Second Vatican Council,[49] combined with an understanding of its prophetic role in the Church,[50] has led her to be an authoritative voice for religious across the globe. She became particularly

---

[44]Sandra M. Schneiders, 'Spirituality in the Academy', *Theological Studies* (1989): 676–97.

[45]Sandra M. Schneiders, 'Approaches to the Study of Christian Spirituality', in *The Blackwell Companion to Christian Spirituality*, ed. A. Holder, 15–33 (16) (Oxford, UK: Blackwell Publishing Ltd., 2005).

[46]Cf. Schneiders, 'Approaches to the Study of Christian Spirituality', 15–33 (17); Sandra M. Schneiders, 'Biblical Spirituality', *Interpretation: A Journal of Bible and Theology* 70, no. 4 (2016): 417–30 (417).

[47]For an insightful presentation of her work in the field of Christian spirituality and some of the threads stemming from that work in current scholarship, see Bruce H. Lescher and Elizabeth Liebert, eds., *Exploring Christian Spirituality: Essays in Honor of Sandra M. Schneiders* (New York: Paulist Press, 2006).

[48]Sandra M. Schneiders, *Finding the Treasure: Locating Catholic Religious Life in a New Ecclesial and Cultural Context* (New York: Paulist Press, 2000); *Selling All: Commitment, Consecrated Celibacy and Community in Catholic Religious Life* (Mahwah, NJ: Paulist Press, 2001); *Buying the Field: Catholic Religious Life in Mission to the World* (New York: Paulist Press, 2013).

[49]Sandra M. Schneiders, *Beyond Patching: Faith and Feminism in the Catholic Church* (New York: Paulist Press, 2004).

[50]Sandra M. Schneiders, *Prophets in Their Own Country: Women Religious Bearing Witness to the Gospel in a Troubled Church* (Maryknoll, NY: Orbis Books, 2011).

influential in the years between 2009 and 2011 when, for a variety of complex and questionable reasons, women religious in the United States became an object of a visitation (read 'investigation') by the Vatican.[51] Her clear, unmistakeably informed authority guided many religious communities and leaders through this time of discernment and dialogue. This was not coincidental eloquence in times of deficit, but rather an already established voice whose understanding of religious life mapped its meaning and the gift it brings to the Church and the world. These include an exploration of the cultural shift affecting the human and ecclesial contexts of religious life,[52] celibate chastity lived in community as its essence,[53] and evangelical poverty and obedience as enabling culturally informed prophetic freedom, necessarily outside hierarchical ecclesial structures, as an ongoing reminder of the eschatological resonance of the Reign of God.[54]

Where does Schneiders situate herself within the landscape of feminist approaches to theology we explored briefly earlier? She very clearly identifies the emergence of the feminist awareness that runs through her scholarship from her time in Rome. 'It doesn't take long to become a feminist when you live in Rome. . . . Everything was so structured to oppress women that you would have to be blind to think there was anything normal about this.'[55] But it was not until she returned from Rome that she began to develop a vocabulary with which to understand and express this awareness. She describes feminism as much more than a movement for women's rights and equality as a result of individual or even shared experiences of limitation or injustice, but rather the awareness that emerges when one becomes conscious that the limitations experienced are the result of systemic oppression, based on sexism (patriarchy), which will only be changed by embracing an alternative vision for humanity and the earth and commitment to structural social change. 'Raised consciousness, i.e.: feminist consciousness, is the *sine qua non* of feminist commitment.'[56] This leads to an analysis and critique of the cause and the commitment to a different vision and hope for human connectedness and the Reign of God. For Schneiders, this is a fully theological quest, consisting in

> the explicit recognition by feminist Catholics that what they are talking about and promoting is not a baptized version of secular feminism but 'evangelical' or '*Gospel feminism.*' In other words, women who have

---

[51]The Apostolic Visitation of Institutes of Religious life in the United States was concluded in 2012 and its final report published in 2014: Congregation for Institutes of Consecrated Life and Societies of Apostolic Life, *Apostolic Visitation Final Report* (Vatican 2014).
[52]Schneiders, *Finding the Treasure*.
[53]Schneiders, *Selling All*.
[54]Schneiders, *Buying the Field*; Schneiders, *Prophets in Their Own Country*.
[55]Cf. Santa Clara University, 'Faithful Feminist', in *Feature Stories* (Santa Clara, USA, 2016).
[56]Sandra M. Schneiders, 'Feminist Spirituality', in *The New Dictionary of Catholic Spirituality*, ed. M. Downey, 394–406 (395) (Collegeville, MN: Liturgical Press, 1993).

remained faithful participants in the Church while becoming ever more committed feminists have come to an explicit awareness that they are not simply trying to achieve in the Church and for Catholics what feminists in general are trying to achieve for women in society. They are claiming as their own the agenda of Jesus in the Gospel, what he called 'the coming of the reign of God,' and insisting that feminist commitment is not just compatible with but is integral to commitment to the Gospel.[57]

When depth of knowledge and freedom come together, it is a wondrous and scary thing! The combination of her extensive work on Scripture, her understanding of Christian spirituality and commitment to religious life, all underpinned by feminist consciousness, gives a depth and freedom to her work that is both rare and challenging. Simply by way of example, in relation to laments about vocations to religious life, Schneiders maintains that the precipitous drop in membership is not an unhealthy sign, but rather a normal consequence of the overabundance of sisters entering communities after Vatican II: 'a large number of people ended up in religious life and didn't belong in religious life. . . . If there had been other opportunities for women at that time, we would not have had such a stupendous influx of numbers'.[58] With similar clarity, she names the challenge of religious life by Church authorities as a consequence of their engagement with 'on the ground' issues, as opposed to theoretical conundrums:

> Religious are not under suspicion because they are debating the internal processions of the Trinity or the philosophical understanding of transubstantiation. They are on the front lines in regard to homosexuality, inter-religious dialogue, the identity and roles of women in the life and ministry of the Church, the realities of marriage and procreation within the framework of a patriarchal moral theology, mandatory singleness and sexual apartheid in ordained ministry that is causing eucharistic famine throughout the Church, ecclesiastical elitism and exclusivism in relation to other Christian tradition, intellectual freedom in theology and freedom of conscience in religion, and numerous other issues that the Vatican would like to declare 'settled,' or 'closed,' or 'forbidden'.[59]

Similar (if less explicitly challenging) clarity can be found in all of her work. She is, in my Irish mind and language, 'some woman for one woman'! Her approach to and work on Scripture is the perfect lens for the theme of this chapter.

---

[57]Schneiders, *Beyond Patching*, xv, emphasis in original.
[58]Manson, 'Biblical Scholar Sr. Sandra Schneiders Celebrates Four Milestones'.
[59]Schneiders, *Prophets in Their Own Country*, 25.

Colliding worlds: From claimless to powerful[60]

Before I explore Schneiders' approach to rereading women in Scripture, we need to understand her overall approach to biblical studies and its intersection with spirituality. As mentioned previously, none of Schneiders' work is improvised or superficial, but rests on an integral approach to the premises and methods of academic expertise. In a recent book gathering much of her work on the resurrection in the fourth gospel, Schneiders summarizes the presuppositions and methodological principles underlying her approach to Scripture as follows:[61]

Principles and methodological presuppositions

- *The canon of Scripture and intertextuality:* while the books have different authors and genres, they form, for Christians, a whole which is the 'canon' of Scripture. This theological lens means that beyond the context and intentionality underlying their origin, *in its current state*, the Scriptural texts relate mutually to each other and form a whole (intertextuality), which affects our interpretation and understanding of each of them.
- *Interpretative presupposition:* taking the final text as an integral whole, notwithstanding the importance and relevance of where it came from and the intentionality that brought it to birth, she adopts a literary-critical approach, rather than a historical-critical one. The inspired and therefore revelatory text of Scripture can and should be interrogated by the best means of literary criticism, making story, plot and characters as or more important than historical facts.
- *Theological presupposition:* the text, as text is revelatory. That is to say: 'the *locus* of revelation is not the historical events that the gospel text recounts, nor even the intention of the author, but the text itself ... what the inspired biblical authors wrote for the sake of our salvation'.[62] While research into and an understanding of what *actually happened* is important, and at no stage does she relativize the importance of the historical foundations of Christian revelation, fact is not the same as truth. Even during his life when people could *actually see* Jesus, not everyone believed. The question 'what is the text trying to tell us?' and paying attention to the symbolic

---

[60] A fuller presentation of this section, as well as a semiotic analysis of the song itself, can be found in Maeve Louise Heaney, 'A Hermeneutical Exploration of the Revelatory Text of John 4:1–42, in a Performative Key', *Theological Studies (Baltimore)* 81, no. 2 (2020): 278–302.
[61] Schneiders, *Jesus Risen in Our Midst*, xii–xviii.
[62] Schneiders, *Jesus Risen in Our Midst*, xv–xvi, emphasis in original.

and metaphorical language used by its inspired authors may get us further than the ever-elusive quest for 'which words or deeds are factually more correct?' It is a position that echoes and applies what *Dei Verbum* teaches on Scripture, Inspiration and Tradition.

- *Hermeneutical presupposition:* if the text is revelatory, the *event* of revelation takes place between the text and reader, that is, in the reading (or hearing) by which one interprets and understands the text. The encounter that takes place between the text and the reader when she or he interpret that text is transformative, and this is her ultimate aim: 'to facilitate the transformative encounter with the word of God in the interaction between the reader and the text'.

Questions define method: The development of biblical hermeneutics

This intention to open a space of transformation is front and centre in all of Schneiders' work, and it was there from the very start of her academic formation. Question defines method, and Schneiders entered the world of biblical studies led by the question about inspiration: What difference does it make to our interpretation of the text of the Old Testament that we consider it to be inspired?[63] That is to say, alongside historical-critical analysis' quest to find in the text 'what really happened?', Schneiders adds the question about how our understanding of these books *as inspired and therefore a source of revealed truth* affects our lives and our scholarship. This does not mean she relativizes the historical truth or 'factual' relevance of what Scripture narrates – although we need to ask what 'historical' means in relation to transhistorical events such as the incarnation and the resurrection – but rather that she brings two essential aspects of Christian faith and spirituality into the heart of Scriptural studies: first, the recognition that Scripture is a culturally conditioned literary text which we also believe to be *inspired*, a foundational source of Christian revelation. Therefore, *how* can we approach it in a way that is faithful to that belief, as well as to the best resources of scholarship at our disposal? Second, Schneiders introduces the personal faith of a researcher as a 'contributing partner in the academic enterprise',[64] *necessary* for the fullest knowledge of its meaning. It is somehow analogue to what Lonergan sought to do by making conversion foundational to theology and consistent with feminist

---

[63]Cf. Sandra M. Schneiders, *The Revelatory Text: Interpreting the New Testament as Sacred Scripture* (Collegeville, MN: Liturgical Press, 1999), 2.
[64]Schneiders, *The Revelatory Text*, xxxvi. This text of *The Revelatory Text* presents the fullest explanation of Schneiders' methods and their origin.

theology's insight that 'experience' is a source for theology. Schneiders articulates a position that honours both the integrity of research and the self-involvement of scholars in their research.[65] In biblical studies, this was novel, but she is clear:

> Many biblical scholars regard this kind of engagement with the text as non-scholarly devotionalism. In fact, *experiencing* the text is as integral to the work of biblical interpretation as hearing a Mozart symphony played in concert is integral to the work of the music critic or as seeing *Hamlet* in the theatre is to the work of the literary scholar.[66]

To arrive at her approach, Schneiders draws strongly on Gadamer's work on historical consciousness, the ontological nature of human understanding, the centrality of aesthetic experience in human comprehension and the 'truth claims' of the classics.[67] Inspired Scripture is *also* a classic, with transformative potential when grasped (interpreted) by human understanding. Paul Ricoeur's understanding of the world that texts produce, open and project on their readers resulting in the enlargement of human horizons, as well as his development of the steps required in the human interaction with and understanding of a text[68] are clearly influential on Schneiders' approach. The biblical text opens up a world of meaning into which the reader is invited to enter into a 'fusion of horizons' that leaves neither text nor interpreter unchanged. That the world opened by Scripture is one experienced through the lens of faith does not imply the text no longer functions as written works of literature do. The process of interpretation of the text involves first naïveté interpretation, distanciation, critical analysis and finally aesthetic re-surrender to the world in front of the text, in second naïveté transformation. This 'world' which Scripture opens and invites us into could be named as life in the Spirit, the body of Christ or the call to discipleship, but its *understanding passes through the text as text and as classic*. Space does not allow us to explore further the development of her thought, but the thoroughly interdisciplinary nature of her work is obvious.

---

[65] Cf. Lescher and Liebert, eds., *Exploring Christian Spirituality*, 4–5. This is further explored in the book by Belden C. Lane, 'Writing in Spirituality as a Self-Implicating Act. Reflections on Authorial Disclosure and the Hiddenness of the Self', in *Exploring Christian Spirituality: Essays in Honor of Sandra M. Schneiders*, ed. B. H. Lescher and E. Liebert, 53–69 (New York: Paulist Press, 2006).
[66] Schneiders, *The Revelatory Text*, 173, emphasis in original.
[67] Cf. Hans Georg Gadamer, *Truth and Method*, trans. J. W. a. D. G. Marshall, Second Revised ed. (New York and London: Continuum, 2004).
[68] Paul Ricoeur, *Interpretation Theory: Discourse and the Surplus of Meaning* (Fort Worth: Texas Christian University Press, 1976).

Based on this understanding of the 'revelatory text', Schneiders develops a threefold, hermeneutical understanding of the discipline of biblical spirituality:[69]

- Behind the text, the spirituality *which produced the text* is the object of study of exegesis and criticism;
- The spirituality *in the text* is the object of study of biblical theology;
- The spirituality *the text produces in readers* by their interaction with it is the object of study of hermeneutics.

Although interpretation and what she calls 'transformative understanding' takes place *before the text*, it presupposes the other two hermeneutical perspectives. *Only* after responsible scholarly interrogation of the text with a critical lens in line with the researcher's question, and verification of the validity of one's understanding through that critical analysis can one advance to the ultimate goal of biblical interpretation: aesthetic surrender to the text and critical existential interpretation of the same. The question one brings to the text will determine which methods of analysis one employs, but these questions are all some form of this one: What is the meaning of the text for the believing community, here and now?

Women in and in front of the biblical text

We are now in a position to find out how Schneiders asks and answers the questions about women in Scripture. It is clear that she perceives the difficulties Scripture can present, from prejudices embedded within the text itself, where women are presented as marginal or inferior; or prejudices developed over the history of their interpretation, by which they have been used (consciously or not) to justify and perpetuate unjust or un-evangelical positions and practices. In the last chapter of *The Revelatory Text* – in which she presents her method of Scriptural hermeneutics in a comprehensive way – she applies that method to the text of Jn 4.1-42, commonly known as the text of the Samaritan woman or the woman at the well. While this is but one text of Scripture in need of exploration, her analysis is paradigmatic of what is possible with others.

The fourth chapter of the fourth gospel is a textbook example of the trivialization of women in Scripture and its interpretation, which has at times participated in, or legitimated, ongoing oppressive practices towards women

---

[69]See Schneiders, 'Biblical Spirituality: Text and Transformation', in *The Bible and Spirituality: Exploratory Essays in Reading Scripture Spiritually*, 128–50; 'Biblical Spirituality'. *Interpretation: A Journal of Bible and Theology* 56 (2002): 133–42, hereafter 'Biblical Spirituality' (2002) and 'Biblical Spirituality'. *Interpretation: A Journal of Bible and Theology* (2016): 70 (417–30).

within the Church. We do not know her name. We only 'know' she must have been unfaithful and the text sits as an uncomfortable if attractive conversion story that seems to move the people of Samaria towards Jesus. Schneiders, faithful to her understanding of Scripture as inspired and seeking to rescue the text from its history of interpretation and misinterpretation so that it *can* continue to mediate transformative, divine revelation to men and women alike, comes to the text with the following question: *What is the role and identity of the woman* in this missionary story? *Can* this biblical text function as revelatory text, as a locus of salvific encounter with God, for women and men once their feminist consciousness has been raised?[70] Accordingly, she chooses 'feminist critical analysis' as her lens of suspicion and retrieval. I would strongly recommend a slow and thorough reading of Schneiders' analysis.[71] Here, I can only present some of the insights her analysis uncovers:

1. The text is a symbolic 'type story', rather than historical narrative: the woman is not a historical person but a nameless symbolic figure, who can, therefore, represent collectivities. The reasons Schneiders gives are multiple, but they include the historical improbability that a woman of that time and culture 'wed' five times; the underlying symbolism of betrothal evoked by its setting at Jacob's well and that the depth and theme of their highly theological conversation evoke the religious history of Samaria as a fivefold story of adultery, with considerable symbolic accuracy.

2. Taking the text *as it is*, and as inspired, it presents a deeply religious and theological discussion, in which Jesus not only questions but is, in turn, questioned, by the woman, about his identity and the place of Samaria in the history of salvation.

3. In this text, for the first time in the Gospel of John, we find Jesus' self-revelation as the 'I am' – '*Ego Eimi*' – and this to a woman, in the context of a dialogue of mutual discovery. Let me repeat: in the Gospel of John, inspired by the Holy Spirit and received in the Church as an authoritative source of divine revelation, the *first person* to whom Jesus personally reveals his identity as the unnameable *I Am* is an unknown woman whose name did not make it into the gospels.

4. Therefore, she concludes, this text is probably a recognizable story (for those who wrote it and their contemporaries) about the history of Samaria and the validity of the Christian community there, as well as an implicit statement about the role of women in the community at Samaria.

---

[70]Schneiders, *The Revelatory Text*, 181.
[71]Schneiders, *The Revelatory Text*, 180–99.

Schneiders completes her analysis by talking about the potential fruits of a hermeneutical appropriation of this analysis, asking: In light of this newly gained insight and knowledge, what are the transforming effects of our encounter with the world of this text ? She enunciates two:

- The inclusivity of the kingdom, even of the unnamed and marginalized;
- The eschatological tension of that very inclusivity: an already inaugurated although not yet fully manifest revelation.

It would appear that this is no longer a text about mission with a passing unknown woman who makes us as uncomfortable as the disciples were when they found him alone with her, but an audacious, identifiable (for their contemporaries) presentation and possible defence of both the Christian community of Samaria and the role of women as leaders therein.

Nameless

We move to the song that seeks to open a space and enable us to enter into and savour this theological and Scriptural issue. Once again, the song will speak to you in ways it does not to others. In fact, that is the point of music and art. The various perspectives of whence it emerged can give light, however, so I would explain how I went about composing 'Nameless'[72] and what Schneiders herself has to say about the song. I do so in the conviction that the creative process has much to offer theological thinking and that theology tout court might be well served by people disclosing more about their creative writing process. I present it following the steps Schneiders describes as intrinsic to an interpretative process that leads to transformation: first naïveté interpretation, distanciation, critical analysis and aesthetic re-surrender to the world in front of the text, in second naïveté transformation.

1. *First naïveté interpretation*: This is a very important text for me. My first naïveté, pre-critical experience and discovery of meaning with Jn 4.1-42 led me to what I interpret as my first contemplative experience of the living presence Jesus Christ. Through the words of verse 10: 'if only you knew . . . ', I was held by, and tasted something of the 'love beyond all telling' that called me to religious life, to be exclusively dedicated to loving Jesus and those he placed into my hands. For me this text has always been revelatory and transformative.

---

[72]I have presented elsewhere the hermeneutical perspective of Jean-Jacques Nattiez for the exploration of musical meaning. Cf. Chapter two of Maeve Louise Heaney, *Music as Theology: What Music Has to Say about the Word* (Eugene, OR: Pickwick Publications Wipf and Stock, 2012).

2. *Distanciation*: However, life, time, education and the experience of being marginalized from the very mission I felt called to by Jesus led me to take distance from the text. It became increasingly difficult to re-access that foundational experience and interpretation – often despite rather than through my theological training.
3. *Critical analysis and aesthetic re-surrender*: Schneiders' analysis of Jn 4.1-42 had two discernible effects on me:
   a. It enabled me to return to the text for a refreshed understanding, mediating a deepened transformative encounter, again and for the first time. The experience of Jesus' eternity life and the call to be his were returned to me, this time as an older, theologically informed woman and leader in the community of the Church, who needed to know that Jesus continued to voice that call to my life. The text makes sense to me, in a new and transformed way.
   b. It led me to a process of musical creativity, this time following an artistic pattern of experience, as opposed to theoretical, although coloured by the insights identified earlier.

I started this chapter with the suggestion that sooner or later women can find Scripture challenging. This song seeks to open the text to women and men in new ways.

From a different perspective, Sandra Schneiders is still very much with us, so I asked her to say something about the song for its launch in December 2020. Sharp as ever, these were her words when asked 'what does the song mean?':

> What does it mean? I suggest that it invites the hearer to get into the dynamic of the text, and that the oscillation between the nameless and the blameless is initiating us into the question that was raised by the whole episode. It doesn't give us an answer; it is initiating us into the question which dominates that whole scene: here's this famous or infamous rabbi; here's this questionable woman and these clueless disciples being caught up in the mystery of the name of God, which reverberates in *anyone* who is serious about the spiritual life. You can't really interpret the song. You can only enter into it, and feel it expressing the questions that anyone who seriously thinks about Jesus is going to ask – because it raises the question of who they are. The song doesn't actually mean. It invites you into the question.[73]

I invite you to do just that. The link to the song is in the note.[74]

---

[73] Livestreamed on 6 December 2021 at the launch of album *Strange Life. The Music of Doubtful Faith* at The Cave Inn, Woolloongabba, QLD, Australia.
[74] 'Nameless': https://res.cloudinary.com/bloomsbury-online-resources/video/upload/v1639138146/Suspended%20God/Nameless.wav

'Nameless' lyrics

I am ... You are ... nameless, claimless still ...
You are ... I am ... shameless, faceless, if ... only you knew
You interrupt her and she interrupts you right back.
The time and the place for eternity life to make sense:
The right kind of a space for a scene
What is she doing here? Rabbi, you've got to eat!
How dare you speak to me?
How dare you cross the line that was drawn and still drawn;
Give me something to drink – I am tired. ... It is the 6th hour, 'cos
I am ... You are ...
You have no bucket, she cut through the small talk and called you to honour an overdue covenant:
One of those conversations that mark a world;
One of those rare occasions where time stands still
And the truth that was claimed as their two worlds collide and change shape, is she's more than a match for your mind: she can find her way through all the clues to your truth and your power, for now is the hour of
I am ... You are ...
If only you knew ... If only you knew ... If ... ἐγώ εἰμι,
I am ... You are.

©MAEVE LOUISE HEANEY, 2020.
Strange Life, The Music of Doubtful Faith

Selected further reading

Biblical hermeneutics

Schneiders, Sandra Marie. *The Revelatory Text: Interpreting the New Testament as Sacred Scripture*. Second ed. Collegeville, MN: Liturgical Press, 1999.

Schneiders, Sandra Marie. *Jesus Risen in Our Midst: Essays on the Resurrection of Jesus in the Fourth Gospel*. Collegeville, MN: Liturgical Press, 2013.

Schneiders, Sandra Marie. 'Biblical Spirituality'. *Interpretation: A Journal of Bible and Theology* 70, no. 4 (2016): 417–30.

Christian spirituality

Schneiders, Sandra M. 'Spirituality in the Academy'. *Theological Studies* (1989): 676 – 97.

Schneiders, Sandra M. 'Approaches to the Study of Christian Spirituality'. In *The Blackwell Companion to Christian Spirituality*, edited by Arthur Holder, 15–33. Oxford: Blackwell Publishing Ltd, 2005.

Religious life

Schneiders, Sandra Marie. *Beyond Patching: Faith and Feminism in the Catholic Church*. New York: Paulist Press, 2004.

Schneiders, Sandra Marie. *Prophets in Their Own Country: Women Religious Bearing Witness to the Gospel in a Troubled Church*. New York: Orbis Books, 2011.

Feminist theology and spirituality

Schneiders, Sandra Marie. *Women and the Word: The Gender of God in the New Testament and the Spirituality of Women*. Madeleva Lecture in Spirituality. New York: Paulist Press, 1986.

7

Is beauty superfluous to human life and Christian faith?

When did we lose sight of God's beauty and power of attraction?

'That's just aesthetics', we are told when something is not considered important; or 'appearances are skin deep', the implication being that the substance of something is what's important, not how it's presented. So with regard to food, it's the nourishment value and not the taste or how it looks; with regard to a person, it's their character, not their face or their figure; and in Christian living, it's our faith and our acts that matter, not our style. And yet, there is a whole other dimension to life that is left out with this presumption, and losing it is something that has cost Christianity dearly.

What about the human love of beauty, of natural spaces that are peaceful or impressive in their grandeur or of architectural places that open the senses to what is possible? When you walk into a well-made building – past or present – the body *feels* differently. We are not always aware of what is happening, but as embodied beings, how something looks and feels affects what we perceive and know. We have explored the role and importance of art for human life in chapter five. Here I go a step further and perhaps deeper, by asking what the aesthetic sensibility and need for beauty that is simply part of our embodied lives say about the One in whose image and likeness we are made: Is God beautiful? Can God be attractive? The question might be jarring for some, but it did was natural for the ancient world: 'Late have I loved you, beauty so ancient and so new; late have I loved you.'[1]

---

[1] Augustine, *Confessions*, trans. H. Chadwick (Oxford: Oxford University Pres, 1992), Book X.27.38.

I invite you to read slowly the rather long quotation below from Augustine's *Confessions*. It is one of the most famous segments of an immensely influential book of the early centuries of Christianity. More poetry than prose, it needs to be savoured, not read at speed, and the length of the quotation invites us to read outside of our comfort zone, since Augustine was born in the fourth century of the Christian era, but this classic allows us enter into how he felt and experienced the world and God. Augustine is explaining his quest for God, whom he already senses lovingly close, but whom he is seeking to grasp and understand more:

> My love for you, Lord, is not an uncertain feeling but a matter of conscious certainty. With your word you pierced my heart, and I loved you. But heaven and earth and everything in them on all sides tell me to love you ...
>
> But when I love you, what do I love? It is not the physical beauty nor temporal glory nor the brightness of light dear to earthly eyes, nor the sweet melodies of all kinds of songs, nor the gentle odour of flowers and ointments and perfumes, nor manna or honey nor limbs welcoming the embraces of the flesh; it is not these I love when I love my God. Yet there is a light I love, and a food, and a kind of embrace when I love my God. . . . That it is that I love, when I love my God.
>
> And what is this object of my love? I asked the earth and it answered, 'It is not I'; I asked all that is in it, and they made the same confession. I asked the sea, the deeps, the living creatures that creep, and they responded: 'We are not your God; look beyond us.' I asked the breezes which blow, and the entire air with its inhabitants said: 'Anaximenes was mistaken; I am not God.'[2] I asked heaven, sun, moon, and stars, they said: 'Nor are we the God whom you seek.' And I said to all these things in my external environment: 'Tell me of my God who you are not. Tell me something about him.' And with a great voice they cried out:
>
> 'He made us.' (cf. Ps. 99(100):3) My question was the attention I gave to them, and their response was their beauty.[3]

Augustine, after reflecting for a while on the mystery of the human mind and self as more than the mind can grasp, and the power of memory to hold and remember images, colours, tastes and more, then prays:

> Late have I loved you, beauty so ancient and so new; late have I loved you! And see, you were within me and I was in the external world and sought you there, and in my unlovely state I plunged into these lovely

---

[2] Anaximenes of Miletus was a sixth-century BC pre-Socratic philosopher, who taught that air is divine and that all reality is air at different degrees of density.
[3] Augustine, *Confessions*, X.6.8–9.

created things which you made. You were with me and I was not with you. The lovely things kept me far from you, though if they did not have their existence in you, they had not existence at all. You called and cried out loud and shattered my deafness. You were radiant and resplendent, you put to flight my blindness. You were fragrant, and I drew in my breath and now pant after you. I tasted you, and I feel but hunger and thirst for you. You touched me, and I am set on fire to attain the peace which is yours.[4]

Augustine's longing is palpable and his logic irresistible: it is the beauty of creation that both draws Augustine and leaves him wanting. For someone with Neoplatonic influences and a certain suspicion of the senses, this text reads as an exceptionally eloquent testimony to the importance of beauty, in the world and in God. 'In what is arguably the most beautiful passage of the *Confessions* we have a summary of the effects of Divine Beauty on Augustine's soul.'[5]

So what happened? Where did this kind of sensibility go? Christianity used to be a patron of the arts, deeply aware of the beauty of the world it lived in as a reflection of divine beauty. And yet somehow, over the centuries of doctrinal and theological development, the importance of God's beauty was forgotten. Moral duties and defence of truth moved centre stage, and this thirst for a beauty to satisfy the soul was sidelined as secondary and non-essential.

Why is the importance of God's beauty and the world as its mirror not an essential element of theological formation and Christian worship? That is the question that Swiss theologian Hans Urs von Balthasar (1905–88) grappled with during the twentieth century. It is a question that is essential for these postmodern worlds in which we live. Modernity emerged, in part, out of humanity's growth in knowledge, power and production, but the limits of that mind frame predicted its own demise. Michael Paul Gallagher's classic book on faith and culture, *Clashing Symbols*,[6] explores the different sensibilities that characterize modernity and postmodernity. He situates it within an understanding of 'post'-modernity as growing out of modernity, both its consequence *and* as a counterreaction to its excesses.[7] Postmodern sensibility has been much maligned as unstable, fragmented and unfriendly to Christian narratives, but that is not the whole story. The human (embodied) spirit has a way of pushing back at trends that ignore or suppress essential

---

[4]Augustine, *Confessions*, Book X.27.38.
[5]Notation by Michael P. Foley in Augustine, *Confessions* (Indianapolis: Hackett Publishing Company, Inc., 2007), Book, X.27.38, note 88.
[6]Michael Paul Gallagher, *Clashing Symbols: An Introduction to Faith and Culture* (London: Darton, Longman & Todd, 2003).
[7]He also differentiates between postmodernism as a philosophical mindset and postmodernity as a cultural sensibility, albeit fragmented. It is the latter meaning that sheds light on this theme.

elements of its make-up, and postmodernity is no exception. With all its limitations, there are gifts in this era for humanity and theology in relation to our theme of beauty. Postmodernity is suspicious of an overvaluation of reason and science's 'naive claims to progress, and insensitive dominance of the earth' that alienate the self from a more whole sense of itself. With renewed awareness about ecology, feminism and the return of spirituality, postmodern sensibility invites us to recover a more humble sense of wonder, gratitude and beauty that integrates the aesthetic and creative dimensions of life and thought.[8] In this context, Balthasar's thought on beauty can be read as a prophetic anticipation of this return to beauty and aesthetic celebration as essential dimensions of human life and Christian faith.

And as the witness of Augustine shows, a consideration of beauty's role in Christian faith is not only about adapting to a changing future but recovering a forgotten dimension of who God is. Contemporary 'atheism' – apart from a small vociferous minority – is more about sensibility than about reasons. Most people are not particularly interested in reasons for or against God's existence when they find it hard to *imagine*, *experience* and *want* the presence of the God under discussion. Opening spaces of beauty, and understanding why these might be essential rather than superficial and expendable, is a central theological theme. Where is the intersection between beauty and Christian faith?

Hans Urs von Balthasar: Theology on our knees

The theologian who was instrumental in reminding us of this truth is one I have interacted with before in the book: Hans Urs von Balthasar. We explored his writings on music and its cultural development in chapters two and three. We know he was a passionate musician who wrote only a few, if significant, pieces on the philosophical and theological significance of music. In this chapter, my focus is different: his contribution to a theology of beauty as essential to Christian faith and where it came from. Balthasar is an unlikely theologian, in some ways. There are stories about his aversion to the theology he was taught, to the point of putting wax in his ears during class and reading books he found interesting under the desk:

> My entire period of study in the society of Jesus was a grim struggle with the dreariness of theology, with what men had made out of the glory of revelation. I could not endure this presentation of the Word of God. I could have lashed out with the fury of a samson.

---

[8]Cf. Gallagher, *Clashing Symbols: An Introduction to Faith and Culture*, 105–10.

Something of the personality of this famous man runs right through his life and works. It is not surprising that his theology has been both acclaimed and criticized for different reasons, both during his life and after it. But his contribution to theological aesthetics and the subsequent development of the arts in theology are undeniable. The full picture of his background and spirituality is rarely explored, however, so in this section, I shall look at influences on his life and thought, some of his core writings, as well as an evaluation of his theology and how it has been used.

Life and influences

Hans Urs von Balthasar was born in the Swiss city of Lucerne on 12 August 1905 and entered the Society of Jesus in 1928. He studied German literature and philosophy and had a lifelong interest in literature and music, all of which had obvious and lasting influence in his writings. Balthasar lived for a time in Lyons, a hub of thought for the Nouvelle Théologie which raised deep questions about the neo-scholastic doctrine of grace and nature. He worked for a while on the Jesuit journal *Stimmen der Zeit* (loosely translated as *Notes, or Signs of the Time*). In his early Jesuit life, he worked with Rahner on a new schema for the study of theology, which Rahner published but which reflects their shared work.[9] It reflects the frustration of both with an outdated theological apparatus. His theological influences include Erich Przywara's work on the *analogia entis* (the analogy of being), which helped him discover an understanding of being as dynamic and love, responding to and channelling his dislike of neo-scholasticism. Jean Daniélou, Gaston Fessard and Henri de Lubac stoked his interest in the Church Fathers (in particular Irenaeus, Origen, Gregory of Nyssa and Maximus the Confessor). This interest in Patristic theology influenced Balthasar's conviction about the universal salvific will of God. Henri de Lubac contributed to his sense of the catholicity of the church. One of the most important theological influences was that of Karl Barth. As well as his Christ-centred and biblical understanding of revelation, Balthasar said he owed Barth 'the vision of a comprehensive biblical theology'.[10] In terms of literature, Balthasar met and translated the poetry of Paul Claudel (1868–1955) into German and also loved the works of Charles Peguy (1873–1914), Johann Wolfgang von Goethe (1749–1832) and Pedro Calderón (1600–81), some of whom he also translated. De Lubac is quoted as having called him 'the most cultured man of his time'. I think it is fair to say that this would refer, consciously or

---

[9]Karl Rahner, 'A Scheme for a Treatise of Dogmatic Theology', in *Theological Investigations I: God, Christ, Mary and Grace*, ed. Cornelius Ernst, 19–36 (London: Darton, Longman & Todd, 1974).
[10]Hans Urs von Balthasar, *My Work: In Retrospect* (San Francisco, CA: Communio Books, 1993), 89.

unconsciously, to a classic if not classicist understanding of Western European culture as standard and measure. Balthasar celebrated the Baroque as a full-bodied proclamation of the Catholic spirit.

Alongside these theological and cultural influences, there is the presence of and collaboration with the Swiss physician and mystic Adrienne von Speyr (1902–67). Balthasar met her in 1940 when he was the student chaplain in Basel. He accompanied her in becoming a Catholic and was moved by the depth of her understanding and her mystical experiences, which multiplied after entering the Catholic Church.[11] His accompaniment of her spiritual life led to a shared mission to found a secular institute (whose members live in the world but according to the evangelical counsels) called *The Community of Saint John* (*Johannesgemeinschaft*), which for both of them was inspired in the life and teaching of Ignatius of Loyola.[12] It led to his painful departure from the Society of Jesus in 1950, since they did not accept his involvement in this mission as a Jesuit. He would later insist that their theological work together was part of an inseparable whole, of which her contribution was the more important: 'Her work and mine are neither psychologically nor philologically to be separated: two halves of a single whole, which has as its centre a unique foundation . . . the greater part of so much of what I have written is a translation of what is present in more immediate, less technical fashion in the powerful work of Adrienne von Speyr.'[13] Because of Balthasar's own witness to her influence and the works that emerged from both of them, and its contested reception in scholars on Balthasar, I have dedicated a section below on her life, spirituality and influence.

Balthasar was incardinated in the diocese of Chur in 1956 and continued writing his whole life. He never held an academic chair in theology and was not invited to the Council as an expert, but his thought was well known. He strongly criticized Rahner's anthropological approach to theology,[14] founding the journal *Communio: International Catholic Review* with Daniélou, de Lubac and Ratzinger, in 1972 as a reaction to the journal Rahner helped establish, *Concilium*. He also distanced himself a little from Barth, although it was the latter who remained suspicious of how Balthasar interpreted his analogy of faith. Towards the end of his life, his theology found favour with Joseph Ratzinger and John Paul II, leading the latter to integrate much of Balthasar's anthropology and ecclesiology into his understandings of gender

---

[11]For Balthasar's own introduction to Adrienne von Speyr, see Hans Urs von Balthasar, *First Glance at Adrienne Von Speyr* (San Francisco: Ignatius Press, 1981).
[12]Quoted in Patrick W. Carey and Joseph T. Lienhard, *Biographical Dictionary of Christian Theologians* (Westport, CT: Greenwood Press, 2000), 46. For an insightful reflection on her Easter visions and the mystery of atonement, see Aidan Nichols, 'Adrienne Von Speyr and the Mystery of the Atonement', *New Blackfriars* 73, no. 865 (1992): 542–53.
[13]Balthasar, *My Work: In Retrospect*, 105.
[14]His most famous criticism being that of Rahner's notion of 'Anonymous Christianity' in Hans Urs von Balthasar, *The Moment of Christian Witness* (San Francisco, CA: Ignatius Press, 1994).

and a theology of the body. Balthasar was a member of the International Theological Commission from 1969 to 1988 and died a few days before officially accepting the title of cardinal.

Adrienne von Speyr

There are varying opinions on the importance of Adrienne von Speyr's influence on Balthasar's theology, which could be divided into three groups: the first has a certain respect for the influence she had over him, without any further scholarly engagement with relevant themes or topics. This has constituted the majority of scholars, in whose writings she may or may not be named; the second either rejects the relationship as having any impact on von Balthasar or has distaste for it as deformative of his theology; a third group considers that von Speyr's relationship with von Balthasar is 'essential to understanding him *and* deserves serious scholarly engagement'.[15] For the reasons outlined below, the only sensible option is that of the third group. Therefore, a brief overview of her life and spiritual experience is essential.

Born in 1902, von Speyr's family was one of medics, leading her to discover a gift of ministering to the physical and mentally ill and to become a doctor. Her journey was not an easy one, due to a difficult relationship with her mother, the early death of her father and of her first husband, as well as her own ill-health. Born into the independent Reformed church, Balthasar accompanied her into the Catholic Church and formed a lasting friendship with her which changed the course of his own life. Von Speyr was a mystic whose experiences and visions started early in life, becoming much more frequent and intense after becoming a Catholic and towards the end of her life. Her mystical experiences were often in the form of angels visiting to explain things to her, and she would pray during much of the night, finding herself present to many places and situations in the word in need of prayer.[16] However, more importantly, every Easter she would enter into a trance from Good Friday to Easter Sunday and experience the passion with Jesus. This included his 'descent into hell', an element of the Apostolic Creed to which she gives a particular focus and interpretation. These visions were not an external viewing of what happened as much as 'an experience of the interior sufferings of Jesus in all their fulness and diversity – whole maps of suffering were filled in precisely there where no more than a blank space

---

[15]Cf. Sutton Matthew Lewis, 'Hans Urs von Balthasar and Adrienne Von Speyr's Ecclesial Relationship', *New Blackfriars* 94, no. 1049 (2013): 50–63 (especially 56–9).

[16]Some of the places named are concentration camps, religious houses where prayer itself had grown cold, confessionals where confession was simulated or lukewarm or the priest was not up to the needs of his penitents, seminaries, the offices of the Roman Curia, and empty churches. Cf. Nichols, 'Adrienne Von Speyr and the Mystery of the Atonement', 542–53 (546).

or a vague idea seemed to exist'.[17] The influence of these experiences on Balthasar's writings on the mystery of the atonement, salvific universalism and understanding of revelation is undeniable.[18] Other areas of influence include

> Jesus' Sonship as obedience to the point of powerless identification with the Godforsaken, faith as Marian womb-like receptivity, virginity as spiritual fruitfulness for the world, personhood as unique sending from God, the vicarious representative character of prayer and suffering in the Church, the bodiliness of Christian existence, the naked standing before God and the Church in the sacramental act of confession as expressing the fundamental Christian attitude.[19]

An understanding of the importance of prayer and the role of the laity in the Church is another point of von Speyr's influence on Balthasar's understanding of spirituality, theology and the Church.[20] Before the Vatican Council, Balthasar wrote critically of the fortress mentality of the pre-Conciliar church. He sought a Christianity open to the world, supporting the role of the laity as witnesses in the world. Although he was critical after the Council of its accommodation to the world, his belief in the presence of Christians in the world, based on charity and prayer, emerges in a variety of writings. His focus is on the reality of the Christian as 'elected', chosen in Christ, and he develops a theology of the different states of life with a particular emphasis on the evangelical counsels and the priesthood.[21] This vision, drawn from and shared with von Speyr, involves an understanding of new forms of life in the church with their roots in the Johannine and Ignatian traditions of spirituality. [22]

Alongside the different theological positions in relation to Adrienne von Speyr's influence on Balthasar and the importance or consequences of her spirituality on Balthasar's theology, there is the simple reality of a 'friendship in the Lord', to use an Ignatian expression, which Balthasar testifies to being central to his immense theological enterprise. This friendship and

---

[17]Balthasar, *First Glance at Adrienne Von Speyr*, 35.
[18]Hans Urs von Balthasar, *Mysterium Paschale* (San Francisco, CA: Ignatius Press, 2005); Hans Urs von Balthasar, *Dare We Hope That All Men Be Saved? With a Short Discourse on Hell* (San Francisco, CA: Ignatius Press, 1988).
[19]John J. O'Donnell, *Hans Urs von Balthasar* (London: Chapman, 1992), 5.
[20]Hans Urs von Balthasar, *Razing the Bastions: On the Church in This Age* (San Francisco, CA: Ignatius Press, 1993).
[21]For example, Hans Urs von Balthasar, *Love Alone Is Credible* (San Francisco, CA: Ignatius Press, 2004); Adrienne von Speyr, *The Christian State of Life*, ed. H. U. v. Balthasar (San Francisco, CA: Ignatius Press, 1986).
[22]See Hans Urs von Balthasar, *Our Task: A Report and a Plan* (San Francisco, CA: Ignatius Press, 1994). The book is a comprehensive overview of the inspiration, vision and programme of the community.

collaboration developed and grew over the years. Ill-health forced von Speyr to give up practising medicine in 1954. She had married again, although at some stage it seems they opted, by mutual agreement, to live their relationship as brother and sister. Balthasar lived with them for a time, which allowed him to attend to her visions and to reflect theologically on them. For years, Balthasar would personally write down the dictations of these visions every day. She died at the age of sixty-five on 17 September 1967, the feast day of another mystic of Catholic history, Hildegard von Bingen This was an intense, long-standing friendship. What does it say about our understanding of theology that we can ignore, sideline or even criticize it as having held him back? From where I am standing the oversight reflects two costly deficits in Christian theology: first, a disembodied understanding of theology that has still to integrate what Metz understood decades ago and autoethnographical studies are seeking to further: all theology is biographical;[23] and second, the ongoing separation of mystical experience from theology '*proper*', whatever that might mean.

In chapters ten and twelve, I speak further about how to understand mysticism and its contribution to theology, especially in light of the female Doctors of the Church named in the twentieth century who bring their experiences to theology. But here I would suggest that reading Balthasar *without* von Speyr is manifest and public bias, in the Lonerganian sense of a blind spot that impedes our access to truth. This is not to say that everything should be called theology, *or* that her writings should not be read with a contextually critical lens, but to ignore her influence and with it the role of such writings in the theological life of the Church will only serve to accentuate the narrowing range of theology's sources and influence, as the world sails on.

Theological works and background

Balthasar never accepted an academic position as a theologian, but he is the author of eighty-five separate volumes, over five hundred articles and contributions to collected works, almost a hundred translations, and editor of sixty volumes of the works of Adrienne von Speyr and other pieces.[24] His largest and most well-known works are a voluminous trilogy on the theological meaning of the transcendentals in Christian theology, starting

---

[23]Cf. Johann Baptist Metz, 'Excursus: Theology as Biography', in *Faith in History and Society: Toward a Practical Fundamental Theology*, 219–28 (London: Burns and Oates, 1980). Metz is referring mainly to the non-extraordinary mystical biography of Rahner which underpins his whole theological enterprise, but the point is the same.

[24]Peter Henrici S. J., 'A Sketch of von Balthasar's Life', in *Hans Urs von Balthasar: His Life and Work*, ed. D. L. Schindler, 7–43 (31) (San Francisco: Ignatius Press, 1991).

with seven volumes on beauty: *The Glory of the Lord*,[25] five volumes on the good: *Theo-drama* and three on truth: *Theo-logic*. While my focus in this chapter is mainly on his approach to beauty, as we shall see, for Balthasar, they go together. In fact, 'the transcendentals are inseparable . . . neglecting one can only have a devastating effect on the others'.[26] Other shorter but important writings can be found in his *Explorations in Theology: The Word Made Flesh; The Spouse of the Word; Creator Spirit;* and *Spirit and Institution*. These are not a systematic presentation on one theme but separate articles gathered under the central title of each volume. There are other writings of a more pastoral nature, some of which have already been named. While the trilogy is considered his most important work overall, as I will explain later, his method and underlying approach to these themes are as important as their content. This is found as much in his shorter and collected writings as in these more theological contributions, and is important for both appreciating his theological contribution and evaluating its value.

In light of all the above, I would name two major theological contexts or influences that are essential to understanding Balthasar and his theological writings. One is the catholicity of Christian faith and the ecclesial nature of the theological task therein, including the role of the mystics in theological development, clearly visible in his interaction with von Speyr and his writings on saints, holiness and theology.[27] The other is what has been called dialectical theology and in particular the thought of Karl Barth. A brief word on both, starting with dialectical theology.

Dialectical theology is described by David Ford in *The Modern Theologians: An Introduction to Christian Theology in the Twentieth Century* as that strand of theology which finds its foundation *not* in what God and humanity have in common but in their contrast and difference. God is *other* to humanity, unknowable except through revelation in Christ. This contrast plays out in every sphere of life: gospel and church, sacred and secular history, God's hiddenness and self-communication. In this outlook and influenced by Kierkegaard's 'infinite qualitative distinction' between time and eternity, Christ is the sole Mediator and connection point between the sphere of humanity and that of God. Barth, its most prominent representative, rejected the 'analogy of being' embedded in a

---

[25] Hans Urs von Balthasar et al., *The Glory of the Lord: A Theological Aesthetics* (Edinburgh: T&T Clark, 1982–1989).

[26] Hans Urs von Balthasar, *The Glory of the Lord: A Theological Aesthetics. Vol. 1, Seeing the Form* (Edinburgh: T&T Clark, 1982), 9.

[27] Alongside his commitment to and comments about the connection between von Speyr's work and his own, see, for example, Hans Urs von Balthasar, 'Theology and Sanctity', in *Explorations in Theology 1: The Word Made Flesh*, 181–209 (San Francisco, CA: Ignatius Press, 1989); Hans Urs von Balthasar, *Two Sisters in the Spirit: Thérèse of Lisieux & Elizabeth of the Trinity* (San Francisco, CA: Ignatius Press, 1992).

Catholic understanding of God's communication, by which human beings are open towards the transcendent and can somehow grasp something of God's revelation. He defended instead the 'analogy of faith', by which our *only* access point to God's revelation is through the *sole* person in whom the union of human and divine natures takes place: Christ.[28] Balthasar – a friend of Barth's in both theology and musical taste – embraced much of this Christ-centred approach of dialectical theology, although he never rejected the analogy of being and gave his theological endeavour a deeply Catholic ecclesial dimension. He was, however, adamant that the *only* measure of all things human – goodness, truth, beauty – is Christ, the *apex* of human existence in whom we can see who we are called to be. From here we can understand his insistence that his work in *The Glory of the Lord* is a 'theological aesthetics' and not an aesthetical access point to theology nor a theology of art. His *Theo-drama* series reflects Barth's insistence on the personal and historical nature of revelation and the interaction of human and divine freedom. *Theo-logic* explores the Triune God in whom being is truth mutually surrendered in love and our reference point for all human life.

The second influence mentioned earlier is that of the ecclesial nature of the theological task and the place of contemplation, holiness and mysticism therein.[29] While influenced by Balthasar's aforementioned relationship with von Speyr, this goes further. The identity of the theologian and the role of theology between spirituality and dogmatics are Balthasar's underlying concerns. He speaks of the distance between contemporary theology and the 'complete' theologians of the past, who were also pastors and saints and for whom theology meant 'to expound revelation in its fullness', not only through their teaching but also through lives which 'reproduced the fullness of the Church's teaching'.[30] He laments the historical split between dogmatic theology and spiritual masters as a 'divorce that has sapped the vital force of the Church of today and the credibility of her preaching of eternal truth'.[31]

> Theology and spirituality have become, as it were, each a world of its own, with hardly any point of contact, and so the saints and spiritual writers are more and more ignored by theologians. What modern treatise of theology, which adduces as its highest authority, next to the Bible, the great saints of the patristic and Scholastic ages, feels equally obliged to cite any of the three above-mentioned doctors [Teresa of Avila, Hildegard

---

[28]Cf. Chapter one of Part I in David Ford, *The Modern Theologians: An Introduction to Christian Theology in the Twentieth Century*, 3rd ed. (Oxford and New York, NY: Blackwell, 2013).
[29]Cf. Balthasar, 'Theology and Sanctity', 181–209; Antoni Sicari, OCD, 'Hans Urs von Balthasar: Theology and Holiness', in *Hans Urs von Balthasar: His Life and Work*, ed. D. L. Schindler 121–32 (San Francisco: Ignatius Press, 1991).
[30]Balthasar, 'Theology and Sanctity', 181–209 (181).
[31]Balthasar, 'Theology and Sanctity', 181–209 (193).

von Bingen, Catherine of Siena], or to accord them equal weight, not to mention the numerous other later saints, such as John Vianney and Thérèse of Lisieux? Where theology is concerned, they hardly exist; they are left for 'spirituality' to plunder. And spirituality hardly exists any longer for theology.[32]

He is not suggesting that theology *not* be intellectually rigorous and is also critical of a holiness that does not seek to be theologically informed. It is the separation that is being challenged. By way of contrast, he reflects upon Anselm's prayerful approach to theology 'on his knees':

> As time went on, theology at prayer was superseded by theology at the desk, and this brought about the cleavage now under discussion. 'Scientific' theology became more and more divorced from prayer, and so lost the accent and tone with which one should speak of what is holy, while 'affective' theology, as it became increasingly empty, often degenerated into unctuous, platitudinous piety.[33]

He took the claims of the mystics seriously, placing their vision at the foundation of his theology. He focussed on the lives of saints and women mystics such as Hildegard of Bingen, Mechthild of Magdeburg, Therese of Lisieux and Elizabeth of the Trinity, because of his conviction that the saints are not given to us to admire for their heroic powers, but that we should be enlightened by them on the inner reality of Christ, both for our better understanding of the faith and for our living thereby in charity.[34] In this way, 'his work attempts to return the evidence of the saints and mystics to the theological conversation'.[35]

Influence and evaluation

It is clear that Balthasar's influence has been tremendous. As mentioned at the beginning of the chapter, positions are varied: some consider him the greatest theologian of the twentieth century, others are much more critical of his conclusions in areas such as anthropology, ecclesiology and theology of atonement. His theological method is also questioned. Before I explore this chapter's theme of Beauty through Balthasar's lens, some attention needs to be given to these limitations and challenges.

---

[32] Balthasar, 'Theology and Sanctity', 181–209 (191).
[33] Balthasar, 'Theology and Sanctity', 181–209 (208).
[34] Balthasar, 'Theology and Sanctity', 181–209 (204).
[35] Cf. Carey and Lienhard, *Biographical Dictionary of Christian Theologians*, 48.

One clear area of difficulty is how he understands women and how this view transfers to other themes such as theological anthropology and the Church. This challenging area of his thought is the focus of an extensive exploration into the psychosexual underpinnings of Balthasar's thought by Tina Beattie.[36] She also explores its connection with the intense, long term and intimate-if-spiritual relationship with von Speyr. 'The shadow is as long as the tree is tall', according to an Italian proverb, and such is the case here. I speak elsewhere in this book about the benefits of friendship in spiritual life and here it is obvious. But if the depth of their friendship *cannot* be overlooked in relation to the spiritual and theological insights born of that collaboration, neither can the questionable interpretation of gender difference and the role of Mary as the bride of Christ linked to their understanding of the meaning of their work.[37] Von Speyr understands a stigmata under her breast as a wound received to suffer vicariously for Balthasar, and she compares their shared mission as the one of the Church and Christ: as the Church is given to Christ, so she is given to Balthasar 'to be his companion on earth in order that he may have on earth a sign of the presence of the Father'.[38] Their relationship also typifies Balthasar's ecclesiological Marian principle: woman is the 'answer' to men's need for fulfilment and completeness, and should relate to men as all humanity should relate to God. The implicit and explicit supposition in Balthasar's writings is that women contribute the passive fruits of their spiritual insights and men contribute intellectual acumen![39] Whatever his admiration for the spiritual insights of women both past and present, the distortion of women's contribution to *any* aspect of the world or the Church on this premise is guaranteed.

The most balanced and incisive critique of his work is that of Karen Kilby's *Balthasar: A (Very) Critical Introduction*.[40] In fact, I suggest that it is essential reading for someone interested in any aspect of Balthasar's theology. She recognizes the creativity, freshness and possibilities to be found in aspects of Balthasar's vast enterprise, but also presents a thorough

---

[36]Tina Beattie, *New Catholic Feminism: Theology and Theory* (New York, NY: Routledge, 2006).

[37]For an insightful *and* disturbing exploration of their relationship and its theological implications, see Johann Roten S. M., 'Two Halves of the Moon: Marian Anthropological Dimensions in the Common Mission of Adrienne Von Speyr and Hans Urs von Balthasar', in *Hans Urs von Balthasar: His Life and Work*, ed. David L. Schindler, 65–86 (San Francisco: Ignatius Press, 1991). He describes their relationship as one of 'objective intimacy'.

[38]Quoted in S. M., 'Two Halves of the Moon: Marian Anthropological Dimensions in the Common Mission of Adrienne Von Speyr and Hans Urs von Balthasar', 65–86 (73).

[39]For an exploration of the potential and blind spots of Balthasar's theology for feminist theology, see Michelle A. Gonzalez, 'Hans Urs von Balthasar and Contemporary Feminist Theology', *Theological Studies (Baltimore)* 65, no. 3 (2004): 566–95.

[40]Karen Kilby, *Balthasar: A (Very) Critical Introduction* (Grand Rapids, MI: William B. Eerdmans, 2012).

and convincing critique of key aspects of his theology. Some of this relates to themes, such as the omnipresence of his particular take on gender and sexual difference as a paradigm for *much* of his thought, or his understanding of the inner life, love and suffering of the Trinity. However, most of it pertains to the very way in which he theologizes, which she describes as contradictory. He often speaks of catholicity: the need to seek the whole as bigger than and unifying the parts. And yet, he seems to situate himself above each God-centred theme, describing with certainty – without ever specifying how he knows[41] – things which are the subject of theological discussion.[42] For good and for bad, Balthasar was an 'unfettered' theologian, never accountable to the academy, publishing his own books without peer review or correction. His brilliance had no contemporary checks and balances.

One of the key problems, in my view, is how we consider the place of Balthasar's theology in Christian thought. Balthasar's position on gender, for example, was extremely influential on Pope John Paul II's 'theology of the body', but there are significant difficulties with both his anthropology and his theological method. Commenting on von Speyr's influence on Balthasar, Fergus Kerr is critical of her excessive influence, because Balthasar takes a 'familiar theological and iconographical topos' (in this case Jesus' descent into hell) and radically revises it 'principally on the strength of von Speyr's private revelations'. This, he says, 'is not a very traditional way in which to develop Catholic doctrine'.[43] But Balthasar is theologizing, *not* developing doctrine! It is perhaps a slip of the tongue in an otherwise insightful overview of how their thought interacts, but the point is important. Balthasar's thought sat well with certain magisterial positions and in my opinion has been prematurely assumed as a quasi-magisterium in the mind of many without due attention to the feedback of the academy and the long-term reception of the *sensus fidelium* of the Church, both essential to the development of doctrine.[44]

The approach to Balthasar that Kilby suggests is that of carefully addressing aspects of Balthasar's theology, rather than adopting his theology as a whole:

> Balthasar in fragments is important and worth pursuing, for there is much to learn from, to borrow, to think about, to develop. But Balthasar as a whole ... as a contemporary church Father ... becomes dangerous.

---

[41]Kilby, *Balthasar: A (Very) Critical Introduction*, 146.
[42]Kilby identifies one book as an exception: Balthasar, *Dare We Hope That All Men Be Saved? With a Short Discourse on Hell*.
[43]Fergus Kerr, 'Adrienne Von Speyr and Hans Urs von Balthasar', *New Blackfriars* 79, no. 923 (1998): 26–32 (32).
[44]Cf. Ormond Rush's foundational exploration of the theme in chapter nine of Ormond Rush, *The Eyes of Faith: The Sense of the Faithful and the Church's Reception of Revelation* (Washington, DC: Catholic University of America Press, 2009).

If there is much to learn from Balthasar, the one thing in view one ought *not* to learn from him is how to be a theologian.[45]

I think this is a fair and insightful appraisal of Balthasar's work. His approach to the theme of beauty is one of these fragments worth thinking about, and for which theology is in debt to him. For that reason and in this spirit, I turn to Balthasar's contribution to the central question of this chapter: the conviction that God is the supreme Beauty'[46] It is undeniable that this aspect of his work is extremely valuable.

Eyes closed to see: Beauty, glory and the crucified Christ

Oscar Wilde once said to a journalist referring to a city whose name I won't reveal: 'I wonder your criminals don't plead the ugliness of your city as an excuse for their crimes.'[47] It is irreverent Irish humour, which holds a truth nonetheless. There is a link between behaviour and beauty, between truth and our desire to apprehend it. How does Balthasar approach the issue of beauty and what light does it give us about the role and importance of beauty in human living and Christian faith? In chapter one, I named Balthasar as the main figure responsible for bringing the notion of beauty back into systematic theology. Given my attempt to allow each chapter a certain independence, a brief recap is not out of place.[48]

God as beauty

One of Balthasar's greatest insights was to realize that in its journey through the ages, theology and Christian practice had forgotten about and marginalized the concept of beauty from its world view. The philosophical and theological term 'transcendental' is used to refer to that which is intrinsic and essential to being, and traditionally has included beauty alongside the

---

[45]Kilby, *Balthasar: A (Very) Critical Introduction*, 167.
[46]O'Donnell, *Hans Urs von Balthasar*, 18.
[47]Quoted in Roy Morris, *Declaring His Genius: Oscar Wilde in North America* (Cambridge, MA: Belknap Press of Harvard University Press, 2013), 111.
[48]Balthasar is a theologian on whom I have written before, given his role in bringing theological aesthetics back into a central position in systematic theology. A more comprehensive presentation of his thought on theological aesthetics and music can be found in Maeve Louise Heaney, *Music as Theology: What Music Has to Say about the Word* (Eugene, OR: Pickwick Publications Wipf and Stock, 2012), 192–210. Any overlap is used by permission of Wipf and Stock Publishers: www.wipfandstock.com.

concepts of one, true and good as essential aspects of the divine.[49] However, somewhere along the way, theology continued to speak of God as true, or the Truth, with a corresponding dedication to formulating and developing doctrine; it also continued to refer to God as the Supreme Good and the basis for the moral implications of faith; but the understanding of God as beautiful, or Beauty, got lost, and with it, an essential dimension of Christian faith. In Balthasar's far-reaching statement:

> Beauty is the last thing which the thinking intellect dares to approach, as only it dances as an uncontained splendour around the double constellation of the true and the good [. . .] Beauty is the disinterested one, without which the ancient world refused to understand itself, a word which both imperceptibly and yet unmistakably has bid farewell to our new world, a world of interests, leaving it to its own avarice and sadness.[50]

The loss leaves humanity without a fundamental element of its approach to life and God, because the transcendentals are inseparable. 'In a world without beauty . . . in a world which is perhaps not wholly without beauty, but which can no longer see it or reckon with it: in such a world the good also loses its attractiveness, the self-evidence of why it must be carried out.'[51]

The point is simple: it is not enough to know what I should believe and how I should act: I need to *want* to live in such a way. It is postmodern sensibility's continuous challenge to mission, which in various ways expresses the following stance: 'if I do not like the look of it, or don't feel drawn to try it out, then I shan't'. In light of this, we need to open spaces that draw people in. We are wired with a sensibility to what attracts the eye, and our apprehension of the beautiful, according to Balthasar, is not external or superficial, but rather united to our understanding of the good and the true. It is beautiful 'only because the delight that it arouses in us is founded upon the fact that, in it, truth and goodness of the depths of reality are manifested and bestowed, and this manifestation and bestowal reveal themselves to us as being something infinitely and inexhaustibly valuable and fascinating'.[52] It cannot, therefore, be understood on its own, and its comprehension is linked with our perception of being itself. But what do we mean by beauty?

---

[49]Some authors name only oneness, truth and goodness, but most include beauty, although there are differences in *how* beauty was considered alongside the others. However, the basic statement stands.
[50]Balthasar, *The Glory of the Lord I*, 18.
[51]Balthasar, *The Glory of the Lord I*, 19.
[52]Balthasar, *The Glory of the Lord I*, 118.

What kind of beauty?

'What beauty will save the world?' Fyodor Dostoevsky asks in his novel *The Idiot*,[53] a classic work of literature with a similar awareness as Balthasar that 'there is only one positively beautiful figure on earth and that is Christ'.[54] How do we reconcile the idea of God as Beautiful with such a broken and at times ugly world? By maintaining a standard of beauty not set by the world but by the God revealed in Christ: 'God's greatest work of art',[55] and this refers to a crucified and risen Christ. The Incarnation is vitally important to Balthasar, because our salvation is not dualist or spiritualist but one of our whole human existence. Yet the Incarnation points towards Jesus' passion and death. From the very introduction of his work *Mysterium Paschale*, Balthasar insists that the incarnation is ordered to the Passion. Situating himself in continuity with Scripture and the testimony of the Fathers of the Church, he states: 'there can surely be no theological assertion in which East and West are so united as the statement that the Incarnation happened for the sake of man's redemption on the Cross'.[56] The centre of Balthasar's whole theology – including this understanding of beauty – is a crucified God. And while our eyes have become used to the image and are now drawn by its meaning, we cannot forget that this was a brutal, humiliating form of death that provoked horror in those who witnessed it. 'If theology is to be Christian, then it can only be a theology which understands in a dynamic way the unsurpassable scandal of the Cross.'[57]

Why a crucified beauty? Because the humanity that Christ assumes in the incarnation is a sinful humanity, marked by the enigma of death. Only by entering totally into that brokenness could Jesus re-insert us into the heart of the Trinity. In fact, Balthasar believes that in the history of theology the consequences of sin are often overloooked or avoided, and merit more attention. The 'no' to God of humanity in sin took us out of our relationship with God, which is our home. The only possible way back was the life of Jesus in complete obedience to God. For Balthasar, how the Trinity reveals Godself in history mirrors the inner workings of Triune love: the kenosis of the incarnation implies the eternal *kenosis* or mutual self-emptying of the divine persons in their loving relationship. Therefore, the guiding thread of Jesus' life from intra-Trinitarian existence, throughout his incarnate life, to

---

[53] Fyodor Dostoyevsky, *The Idiot* (London: Heinemann, 1913), 366, in the dialogue of Hippolyte with the Prince.

[54] From a letter to Dostoyevsky's niece, quoted in Gray Brett Christopher, 'Clones, Princes, and Beautiful Parodies: Rowan Williams' Negative Literary Christology', *Literature & Theology* 29, no. 3 (2015): 284–97 (287).

[55] Balthasar, 'Revelation and the Beautiful', 491–502 (117).

[56] Cf. Balthasar, *Mysterium Paschale*, 11–41.

[57] Balthasar, *Mysterium Paschale*, 56.

and through the cross and the abyss of Holy Saturday to the Resurrection is his utter loving obedience to the Father.

> Jesus proclaims himself with his teaching, he is essentially 'handed over' in it.... And by casting himself, in gratuitous freedom into this unimaginable abyss (death as abandonment by God or as followed by the underworld, bereft of all hope) ... he makes himself into an indispensable sacrificial food for all ... not in the freedom of creative genius but in straightforward obedience. (Jn 10.18)[58]

Freedom, for Balthasar, is also a key related theme, understood not as self-determination but as surrender of self. This handing over is double: the Father 'does not spare' the Son (Rom. 8.32) and the Son hands himself over freely for the sake of humanity. We are in the heart of Catholic teaching on redemption as 'representation' – *admirabile commercium* (admirable exchange) – in which Jesus takes our place. God's love holds together merciful faithfulness and justice. Infinitely loving humanity as a chosen covenant partner, God utterly rejects sin, and Jesus in his death on the cross assumes sin with all its consequences, including the abyss of death. Without a doubt, one of the most beautiful and most profound aspects of Balthasar and von Speyr's soteriology is their perception of Jesus' descent into the abyss and silence of Holy Saturday. It speaks about the hiatus between Good Friday and Easter, during which Jesus enters the abyss of the impotence of the sinner, in total abandonment by God and lack of hope: the Word becomes silent. 'This is the plunging down of the 'Accursed One' (Gal. 3.13) far from God, of the One who is 'sin' (2 Cor. 5.21) personified, who, falling where he is 'thrown' (Rev. 20.14), 'consumes' his own substance (Rev. 19.3).[59] This aspect of their theology has been both lauded and strongly contested and will continue to draw theological discussion into the future, but its depth and power are undeniable.

Jesus takes our place. The 'no' of humanity to God is experienced, embraced and overcome in the 'yes' of Christ's obedient acceptance of death. 'On the cross Jesus bears the negativity of sin but without inner division ... the cross signifies not contradiction but love in the midst of contradiction.'[60] And it is Jesus' singular death for all, and God's answer to that self-giving, in Jesus' prototypical Resurrection, which is the turning point between the old aeon and the new, which becomes an efficacious principle affecting the being of all things.[61]

---

[58] Balthasar, *Love Alone Is Credible*, 85–6.
[59] Balthasar, *Mysterium Paschale*, 50.
[60] O'Donnell, *Hans Urs von Balthasar*, 104.
[61] Cf. Balthasar, *Mysterium Paschale*, 53.

When faith becomes worship

In this sense, what is Christian salvation? Provoked by the utterly free initiative of God's love, it is where God sets us free to live in thanksgiving within Christ's own relationship with the Father through the Spirit. It is freedom from sin and death for life in Trinitarian life, overcoming the enigma of death. It is insertion into the body of Christ, which is the Church, in the womb of Mary's *fiat* to God. Salvation includes an integral conception of human life, of our whole existence. Salvation even includes the redemption of time, and yet it is eschatological, in hope. 'Earthly time *is* blown apart.'[62] Eternal life is another concept of time touching history. Salvation unfolds into a life of loving, which is not an ethical system but a response to the free love of God.

One final, audacious element of Balthasar and von Speyr's theology of redemption is their conviction – or hope – in a universal salvation of all peoples and realities of all times and spaces. It is not that they underestimate freedom. In fact, the drama of human freedom and the gravity of sin are centre stage in their theology: hell must be a possibility because human freedom is not a game and there is a real chance that a person can decide to close to love. But what witness is there to deny that hell may be empty? Hope would not be hope that excluded someone.

> Just as God so loved the world that he completely handed over his Son for its sake, so too the one whom God has loved will want to save himself only in conjunction with those who have been created with him, and he will not reject the share of penitential suffering that has been given him for the sake of the whole. He will do so in Christian hope, the hope for the salvation of all men, which is permitted to Christians alone. Thus, the Church is strictly enjoined to pray 'for *all* men' [sic] (and as a result of which to see her prayer in this respect as meaningful and effective).[63]

We come full circle back to back to Augustine and the kind of Beauty that merits our love: 'Two trumpets sound in a different way, but one and the same Spirit blows air through them. The first says: *Beautiful, the most beautiful of the children of man;* and the second, with Isaiah, says: *We have seen him: he had no beauty, no dignity.*'[64]

---

[62]Balthasar, *Mysterium Paschale*, 67.
[63]Balthasar, *Love Alone Is Credible*, 97. Despite the non-inclusive language, Balthasar is referring to any believer, woman or man. While normal at the time, the contrast with his clear genderization of the Church is striking.
[64]Pierangelo Sequeri, *L'estro di Dio: Saggi di Estetica* (Milano: Glossa, 2000), 3, quoting Augustine In Io. Ep. 9,9.

It is a strange beauty that presents itself as crucified, but when grace opens the eyes of faith to see how loved we have been, then the normal response is one of gratitude and love. The *Oxford Dictionary of English* defines 'worship' as the 'feeling or expression of reverence and adoration for a deity'. It is a term I have long struggled with: Why would God require our adoration? And yet, when 'the immeasurable gulf between the world as it is and as it ought to be for God, is endured to the end, answered for, and – in the ultimate existential engagement of the Word of God – bridged over'[65] by a life given unto death, then the only adequate response is one of absolute love. 'We call this response "worship", the pure "thanks-giving" that gives glory . . . that gathers up and gives meaning upon one's entire existence.'[66]

Every Moving Light

This worship song seeks to reflect two key aspects of Balthasar's approach to theology: the centrality of contemplation to theological investigation and the crucified Christ as the measure of beauty and love, both human and divine. I will admit that every time I listen to it, the opening feels slow and somehow tired – but that may be because it evokes in my memory the song's birthplace. After a long, difficult week of work, followed by a particularly demanding weekend retreat for people seeking a first experience of faith, I found myself late on Sunday evening in a chapel in Southampton, England, in front of a large crucifix, on my knees, feeling drained, and lost, and alone. It was not one of those moments of prayer in which one feels welcomed, loved and fruitful, but rather one of emptiness, silence and sheer exhaustion. In my case, this can come with a certain amount of self-doubt: here we are: was that any use? Am I doing what You want of me? Where are You in all of this? I think it is one of the most subtle temptations of apostolic life: that of doubting your worth and weighing with human measures the fruitfulness of your efforts. In moments like these, when I feel like I cannot pray, music often comes to my aid, like an escape valve or a side-door into some kind of meaning or presence. My tired guitar and voice came up with the opening bars of this song: *After the grain of wheat has died; after loving You with every living breath . . . every moving light recalls your name.*

My community was born in Spain, where spirituality is passionate, crucifixes are big and bloody, and obedience is radical: follow me! Leave everything! Die to yourself in order to rise into life! And I know this is part of the universal gospel, but those who have lived in Spain will know what I am trying to say: there is something *clear* and *total* about how Spanish

---

[65]Balthasar, *Love Alone Is Credible*, 115.
[66]Balthasar, *Love Alone Is Credible*, 107–8.

culture and language gives you access to Jesus. My foundational experience of faith and Jesus was forged in this space of total trust and surrender to the will of God: 'if the grain of wheat does not fall into the ground *and die*, it bears no fruit' (Jn 12.24). And to die is to *feel* that death, to let go, lose, abandon oneself, one's plans, one's health, one's need to succeed and get it right. I have since developed and complemented that spirituality with the recovery of an Irish sense of space, some Sabbath spirituality and a time-aged recognition that accessing 'all' to give it to God takes a lifetime. But I treasure this foundational 'Spanish' impulse of complete abandon before an abandoned God as sure ground to walk on. Nothing can separate us from the love of Christ: 'neither death, nor life, nor angels, nor rulers, nor things present, nor things to come, nor powers, nor height, nor depth, nor anything else in all creation' (Rom. 8.38-39). *After all is said and done, it is in losing You have won, it is in being broken we perceive your wholeness.* God is holy, Other, Beautiful, glorious in the most accessible and humble way we could *never* have imagined.

I have presented in this chapter the life and thought of a brilliant and talented man whose life was lived radically in obedience to what he perceived to be the will of God. Balthasar's theological opera is tremendous, and it is flawed, but at its heart, there is the gem of a crucified Triune Love who pour themselves out for the salvation of *all*. The logic of the cross – which is completely absurd, or 'other' to how one could imagine redemption – makes sense, when people love. When you love someone, you *would* prefer to suffer than to see them in pain. Balthasar and von Speyr's theology of atonement give us access to imagining a Love that can and does actualize that desire. Through the cross and the silence of a Godless world – and there are echoes of a Johannine understanding of the Jesus' death as his moment of glory in this theology – we are loved back into where we belong: inside Love. This song is born of one moment of letting go, getting on my knees and resting in that knowledge. The link to the song can be found in the note below.[67]

'Every Moving Light' lyrics

After the grain of wheat has died
After loving you with every living breath . . .
Every moving light recalls your name
After all is said and done, it is in losing You have won,
It is in giving we receive, in being broken we perceive your wholeness
Holy, You are Holy, You . . .
Holy . . . are You. Glory to You!

---

[67]'Every Moving Light': https://res.cloudinary.com/bloomsbury-online-resources/video/upload/v1639138260/Suspended%20God/Every_Moving_Light.wav

Now you've brought me to my knees;
My eyes are closed so I can see the You I know, turn up in places I don't think to go.
Now that all is said and done, I surrender: You have won!
My hands are open to hang on to what I can't afford to lose: this moment
Holy, You are Holy . . .

©MAEVE LOUISE HEANEY, 2020.
Strange Life, The Music of Doubtful Faith

Selected further reading

On Balthasar's life and theology

Kilby, Karen. *Balthasar: A (Very) Critical Introduction*. Grand Rapids, MI: William B. Eerdmans, 2012.
O'Donnell, John J. *Hans Urs von Balthasar*. London: Chapman, 1992.

Balthasar's writings

Balthasar, Hans Urs von. *First Glance at Adrienne Von Speyr*. San Francisco: Ignatius Press, 1981.
Balthasar, Hans Urs von. *The Glory of the Lord: A Theological Aesthetics. Vol. 1, Seeing the Form*. Edinburgh: T&T Clark, 1982.
Balthasar, Hans Urs von. *Love Alone Is Credible*. San Francisco, CA: Ignatius Press, 2004.
Balthasar, Hans Urs von. *Mysterium Paschale*. San Francisco, CA: Ignatius Press, 2005.

On the significance of his writings

Nichols, Aidan. *Divine Fruitfulness: A Guide to Balthasar's Theology beyond the Trilogy*. London and New York: T&T Clark, 2006.
Schindler, David L. *Hans Urs von Balthasar: His Life and Work*. San Francisco: Ignatius Press, 1991.

8

How to believe in God in such an unjust world?

Poverty and faith in God: A different reading

This book is about how questions lead theology, opening us to new pathways of thought. What is equally true is that certain realities and life experiences can turn questions on their head and change our perspective on things. Such is the case with this chapter's central theme. One of the biggest issues Christian faith faces is that of how God can be credible in the light of human suffering. On a personal level, we instinctively turn to God in pain and protest when something negative cuts through our lives or the lives of those we love with a 'why?'; or 'why did this happen to us when we have tried our best . . . ?', as if being good should shield us from the pain life brings. On a broader scale, however, the access to and awareness of what happens around the world has amplified the issue. Large-scale events of human suffering, such as natural disasters, war, the holocaust of the twentieth century and ongoing genocides around the world, interrupt every trusting fibre of our being and force us to rethink meaning at its very core. At times and at a safe distance, the issue of suffering, or justice, is used to bolster a case for the implausibility of a provident God. The authors promoting current positions on 'new atheism' take a step further by pointing out the damage religion does *in the name of* God. But they can overlook that the question is not alien to those who self-identify as believers, whose faith can also waver in the face of such suffering.

There is nothing new about this issue: holding together the reality of a broken world in which goodness, sin and evil coexist is one of the questions Scripture has always battled with, even before the coming of Christ. From the creation narratives to the struggle of the Jewish people to make sense of suffering and death, this is the core issue.[1] And it was only accentuated with the life and death of Jesus: the chosen One of God, innocence incarnated, was not spared the suffering of the prophets but *passed through* the weight of injustice in order to birth the transformative grace of resurrection life. Theodicy, the area of theology that defends the existence, goodness and power of God in the face of suffering and evil, was named by Gottfried Wilhelm Leibnitz (1646–1716), but the theme runs right through the development of Christian thought from its beginnings. Christianity has struggled with a myriad of dualistic or gnostic philosophies that could not conceive contact or interaction between an eternal, unchangeable God with a broken, sinful and at times evil world, without compromising that very Being in the process. Over the centuries, theology has offered different responses, such as defining evil as absence or privation of being due to humanity's turning away from God (as in Augustine and Aquinas, for example); eschatological perspectives on the redemptive effect of suffering on humanity's journey towards God as the Omega point when all of creation will be *in* Christ (e.g. Jürgen Moltmann and Teilhard de Chardin, although in *very* distinct ways); or redefining God's power as omni-persuasion in the evolutionary process towards liberation (as in some process theologies). However, the question remains, in part because there *is* no straightforward answer. The existence of sin and evil is a mystery, about which Scripture evokes even God's consternation.[2] Furthermore, part of the problem are the negative consequences of facile or theoretical argumentations in the face of that which does not make sense: human pain. Reasons for, or 'proofs' of, God's existence and power in spite of human suffering can too often betray a lack of awareness of and empathy with the actual victims and what they are going through. Theoretical responses to real questions are never going to suffice.

So how can theology seek a way forward? Or rather, how do theologians who are faced with situations of immense suffering theologize? What answers do they find and where do they find them? This is our approach to this chapter's question. It is no one's role to compare and judge levels of suffering, since each life is unique and only those who live it, and the Spirit of God within, really understands what is happening. But it is also true that the issue of suffering as it is experienced in some contexts has a whole different meaning, and this is when the reality of poverty and injustice is a systemic presence in the everyday lives of millions of people. What are the questions someone asks when their whole lives – and even religious

---

[1] How could God allow the people of Israel to suffer and die? The figure of Job is outstanding in this regard, as is the story of the seven brothers in 2 Maccabees 6.7–7.42, where the theme of trusting in the midst of suffering opens into the issue of life after death as the reward for faithfulness to God.

[2] All theological language is analogical, but the puzzlement of God in the face of the lack of fruit produced by the people of Israel is a compelling image (Isa. 5.1-5).

belief system – have taken shape within colonial or neocolonial structures that ignore and thwart human freedom and development? What styles of Scriptural exegesis and interpretation guide a people who do not always recognize in their pastors the echo of a saving voice, and yet have been born into a deeply felt Christian world view? Or is the issue not only about their questions to God but also about the ones *they* pose *us* when their faith in God does not vacillate as easily as the long-standing doubt of the comfortable West?[3]

The theologian I turn to here is Spanish Jesuit Jon Sobrino SJ who has spent most of his life in El Salvador, theologizing in and for the reality of Latin America, taking their reality and questions seriously. In a similar way to the feminist theologians presented in other chapters, Sobrino is part of a broader movement of theological awareness that emerged in the twentieth century challenging the normative interpretation of Western European theology of the Christian sources, this time from a geographical region with a particular history and lived experience of Christian faith: Latin America. The strand of theology is known as 'liberation theology', or rather 'theologies', because at this stage there are a range of theologies, born of different contexts, that identify with both the name and much of the underlying theological method. However, it is fair to say that the Church in Latin America – pastors and theologians – opened up new pathways in theology which have catalysed similar contextualized reflections around the world. While there is much variety in how each theologian works, an introduction to the history and premises of liberation theology is important to understand Sobrino's life and thought.

The emergence of liberation theologies and method

Context and experience are foundational to theological method. This is not to say they are more important than Scripture or Tradition, but rather that the culture within which life and faith are experienced and received will mark how theology makes sense of Scripture, tradition and faith *for that culture*. This has always been the case, even when we were unaware of it. Two characteristics stand out at the origins of liberation theologies in twentieth-century Latin America: the first is the reality of poverty lived by a large majority of people, that is 'endemic, pervasive and imposed'.[4] This is not the accidental and marginal poverty of some within an otherwise functioning society. It is the majority state of entire peoples who were the source of

---

[3]This will be a key focus in this chapter, as I am very aware that I am writing this chapter about a reality I have not lived.
[4]Stanley J. Grenz and Roger E. Olson, 'Latin American Liberation Theology: Immanence in Liberation', in *20th Century Theology: God & the World in a Transitional Age*, 210–24 (216) (Downers Grove, IL: InterVarsity Press, 1992).

another world's wealth when first colonized and the continued source of wealth for others when 'liberated' politically while remaining financially oppressed by a global financial system that maintains its hold, from within and beyond national borders. The second characteristic is the position of the Church in these countries, in the double sense of the strength of the lived faith of the people in those countries on the one hand and the presence and power of the ecclesial structures in its history – prophetic or complicit – on the other. The extension and strength of Christian faith in Latin America are felt across the world, replacing Irish or Polish Catholicism in its felt immigrant and inculturated presence, wherever they find themselves. These are Christian countries; their leaders are often practising Catholics. Therefore, the question of how faith addresses poverty is very different to how it might emerge in other places. The complicity of the Church in protecting the status quo of rich, influential political leaders in these countries is a relatively well-known fact. The prophetic stance of the Latin American Episcopal Conference (CELAM) and its influence on the emergence and development of liberation theologies, however, is unfortunately somewhat less known.

In a gathering in Medellín in 1968, which took place only three years after the last session of the Second Vatican Council and the publication of *Pastoral Constitution on the Church in the Modern World Gaudium et spes*, the bishops of CELAM denounced the Church's traditional alliance with the ruling classes and challenged what it described as the 'institutionalized violence' against the people of their countries, perpetuated by its political leaders.[5] The statement was considered revolutionary and is often interpreted as the beginning of liberation theology in Latin America. In 1979, they gathered again, in Puebla, this time to assess, and perhaps balance, the liberation theology that had emerged and spread during the 1970s. In this meeting, their position included reflections on God's preferential option for the poor, the positive valorization of the 'base communities' born during the 1970s and a critique of military dictatorships.[6] All in all, despite the limitations of any given theological stance and the opposition – in particular from the Vatican – to methods employed and extreme positions taken by some liberation theologies – it stands out as a movement born of pastoral and theological concern for the realities born of systemic social injustice and its causes. But what is liberation theology? How does it work? Questions lead theology, so this explanation of the position of Gustavo Gutierrez[7] (one of its most influential founding thinkers) is insightful:

---

[5] Cf. https://www.celam.org/conferencias_medellin.php (accessed 30 March 2021).
[6] Cf. https://www.celam.org/conferencias_puebla.php (accessed 30 March 2021).
[7] Cf. Gustavo Gutiérrez, *The Power of the Poor in History: Selected Writings* (Maryknoll, NY: Orbis, 1983); Gustavo Gutiérrez, *A Theology of Liberation: History, Politics and Salvation*, Rev ed. (London: S.C.M., 1988); Gustavo Gutiérrez, *We Drink from Our Own Wells: The Spiritual Journey of a People* (Maryknoll, NY: Orbis Books, 2003).

According to Gutierrez, a major difference between European and North American theologies on the one hand, and Latin American theology on the other, arises from their different 'interlocutors.' The North Atlantic theologies, whether liberal or conservative, have been shaped by the questions of modern Western nonbelievers. The main question they ask focuses on how to speak of God in a secular world. The task of Latin American theology, in contrast, is not conditioned by the nonbeliever's questions, but by the question of the 'nonperson': 'the human being who is not considered human by the present social order – the exploited classes, marginalized ethnic groups, and despised cultures. . . . Our question is how to tell the nonperson, the nonhuman, that God is love, and that this love makes us all brothers and sisters.'[8]

If this is their starting point, what are the premises of their theological method? In brief:[9]

1. Theology *must* be contextual and is never universal. In Latin America, theology is done by and with the poor. This is linked with the praxis of the 'base communities' that gather to explore and interpret the Word of God from within their situation, creating a new or different experience of what being church means;
2. An analysis of the structural poverty of Latin American countries as provoked by *external* influences of North America, Europe and multinational corporations and the *internal* 'institutionalized violence' of ruling minority oligarchies and military dictatorships;
3. Scripture witnesses to a God who has a preferential option for the poor, not because they are morally or spiritually superior but in the quest for justice and the full flourishing of *all* human beings. The Church must therefore take a prophetic stance for the poor and against oppression;
4. Theological method is critical reflection on praxis, meaning that theoretical reflection *follows* theology's first act, which is the praxis of commitment to the liberation of the poor. In this context,

---

[8]Grenz and Olson, 'Latin American Liberation Theology', 210–24 (215), Gutiérrez, *The Power of the Poor*, 93. This question could just as well come *from* the 'non-person' as from those who see their suffering, since the faith of the 'non-person' excluded from society can be stronger than the faith of the privileged.
[9]This short description is taken from Grenz and Olson, 'Latin American Liberation Theology', 210–24. See also Juan Luis Segundo, *Liberation of Theology* (Dublin: Gill and Macmillan, 1977); Gutiérrez, *A Theology of Liberation*; Leonardo Boff, *Introducing Liberation Theology*, ed. C. Boff (Maryknoll, NY: Orbis Books, 1987). Segundo's earlier work witnesses to a transitional moment between a European approach to theology and that of liberation theologies: Juan Luis Segundo, *A Theology for Artisans of a New Humanity* (Maryknoll, NY: Orbis Books, 1973).

'critical' – a descriptor theology is familiar with – has sociopolitical connotations and not merely epistemological ones. The central concern, therefore, is not orthodoxy but orthopraxis,[10] and the central theme is liberation, as witnessed in the history of salvation in Scripture;

5. Liberation theology draws on Marxism as a 'tool of analysis' and aid to Christian praxis, by far the most contested aspect of this theological method, although drawing the response that this is comparable to the use of Greek philosophy by European theology;
6. Salvation is understood as integral liberation, including this-worldly, intra-historical, social transformation;
7. Christian mission as liberating praxis, which had led to the problematic issue of whether the use of violence can ever be justified when faced with the reality of violent oppression by the ruling powers.

Our intent here is not to enter into a critical reflection on this theology, except to note that the reactions to this powerful incarnation of theology's attempt to mediate religion and culture have been passionate, both for and against.[11] Nonetheless, it is undeniably one of the most significant theological movements of the twentieth century, which has matured and developed in many directions since then.[12] For the reader who is less familiar with both the context and the method of liberation theologies, I would also warn against trying to understand or prematurely react to a theology without a serious attempt to grasp the contextual and cultural factors that gave birth to it. As a European theologian currently working in Australia, it seems to me that the first step in this chapter and in the context of a book on theological questioning is to ask about what others are living and what questions they are asking. Or even further, what happens to our questions about God's existence when the reality of the poor is taken seriously as an integral part of our faith?

---

[10] This description is coined by Argentinian Methodist theologian José Míguez Bonino, in José Míguez Bonino, *Doing Theology in a Revolutionary Situation* (Philadelphia: Fortress Press, 1975), 81.

[11] Of particular note is the reaction of the Congregation for the Doctrine of the Faith, led by the then Cardinal Ratzinger, entitled 'Instruction on Certain Aspects of the "Theology of Liberation"' (1984), and the silencing of theologian Leonardo Boff for a year. Equally important is another instruction from the same Congregation, which also highlighted positive contributions of liberation theologies, entitled 'Instruction on Christian Freedom and Liberation' (1986). The latter can be read as the 'completion' of a hermeneutic circle in which key concepts of liberation theology – including a love of preference for the poor – are fully welcomed into Catholic social teaching.

[12] For an insightful exploration of the perspective of liberation theologies on some central themes, see Jon Sobrino and Ignacio Ellacuría, eds., *Systematic Theology: Perspectives from Liberation Theology* (London: SCM Press, 1996).

Jon Sobrino SJ: When suffering wakes up knowledge

> The work of Jon Sobrino of El Salvador indicates the radical transformation of Christianity and of theology that liberation theology represents.[13]

Sobrino is one of the theologians who is still alive and active in the theological world. Born in 1938 in Spain's Basque region, he currently lives and works in the Oscar Romero Centre in San Salvador. In a recent book entitled *Jon Sobrino: Spiritual Writings*,[14] he has given extensive and generous access to his own life, journey, influences and theology. This chapter will name briefly key steps of his life and some of the core aspects which ground and influence his work, before looking at his theological reflection on the questions and contributions of the poor to theology and, in the context of this chapter, theodicy.

Sobrino's life's journey is one that is embedded in and witnesses to the emergence of liberation theology as described earlier, interwoven with the Church in Latin America's preferential option for the poor initiated in Medellín (1968) and continued in Puebla (1979). He entered the Jesuits in 1956 and was sent to El Salvador in 1957 as a second-year seminarian, so Sobrino's connection to the people of El Salvador started early, although his awakening to a theological understanding of that reality would, of course, take time. He began undergraduate studies in Havana, Cuba (1958–60), and later completed a BA and a licentiate in philosophy (1963) and a master's in structural engineering (1965) at St Louis University, Missouri. After teaching for a year at the University of Central America (UCA) and the diocesan seminary, he then went to Frankfurt, Germany, for doctoral studies, where he was also ordained a priest (1969). His doctoral dissertation 'A Comparison of the Christologies of W. Pannenberg and J. Moltmann' (1975) began a lifelong interest in and dedication to Christology. Moltmann's influence on Sobrino is also lifelong, especially palpable in his book *The Crucified God*.[15] Other influences include Karl Rahner, Ignacio Ellacuría and through him the epistemology of Spanish philosopher Xavier Zubiri, as we shall see. However, Sobrino insists that by far the greatest influence on his life and thought has been the reality of people – friends, companions and the

---

[13] David Ford, *The Modern Theologians: An Introduction to Christian Theology in the Twentieth Century*, 3rd ed. (Oxford and New York, NY: Blackwell, 2013), chapter 17: 'Latin American Liberation Theology'.

[14] Jon Sobrino, *Jon Sobrino: Spiritual Writings*, ed. R. Lassalle-Klein (Maryknoll, NY: Orbis, 2018).

[15] Jürgen Moltmann, *The Crucified God: The Cross of Christ as the Foundation and Criticism of Christian Theology* (London: SCM Press, 1974).

suffering people of El Salvador – who have lived their lives as witnesses to the gospel.

Sobrino's life and thought breathe a refreshing openness to the influence of the people and events around him. He describes his spiritual and theological journey as one of a series of awakenings:[16] the first, during his studies in Germany, forced him to demythologize his faith and wake up from the 'dogmatic slumber'[17] of naïve understandings of faith, an awakening which he describes as painful. He recalls the positive influence of Karl Rahner's thought in navigating his way through that period. It is an influence that can be seen, from time to time, in his writings. The second, after his return to El Salvador in 1974, was provoked by his life open and committed to the people of El Salvador, with the realities of cruel suffering, and grace, experienced through them. He calls it an 'awakening from the sleep of inhumanity', provoked by actually seeing the world of the poor . . . the 'real world', in his terms. There are particularly strong moments in Sobrino's life: the conversion and courageous prophetism of Saint Oscar Romero and his murder in 1980;[18] being one of the first witnesses to the bodies of four North American women – Maura, Ita, Jean and Kathy – missionaries who were raped and murdered by the Salvadoran National Guard in 1981; the shooting and killing of his whole Jesuit Community at UCA along with two women who worked there by order of the military regime while he was doing pastoral in Asia in 1986; along with the multitudes of people killed or disappeared during that brutal regime. It is unsurprising that martyrdom is a key theme in Sobrino's theology, from initial dedications of his work to the memory of fallen friends and companions to explicit writings on the theme.[19] He frequently names the 'cloud of witnesses' who have marked his life, faith and hope. Some of these were close to him, but others are unknown. The reality of the unnamed, non-personhood of those oppressed and dying in the poor countries of the world (in contrast to how loss of life is marked in affluent countries) is an ongoing theme.[20] They are the 'crucified people', the sign of the times par excellence for theology in Latin America and the world. And this centre of his theological thought also emerged gradually and under the influence of the people around him. A watershed moment seems to be when Romero travels to the region where murdered Jesuit priest Fr Rutilio

---

[16] Cf. Jon Sobrino, 'Awakening from the Sleep of Inhumanity', *Christian Century* 108, no. 11 (1991): 364.
[17] An expression taken from Kant.
[18] Cf. Jon Sobrino, 'In Archbishop Romero God Passed through El Salvador', in *Fathers of the Church in Latin America*, ed. S. Scatena, J. Sobrino, and L. C. Susin (London: SCM Press, 2009).
[19] Cf. Jon Sobrino and Ignacio Ellacuría, *Companions of Jesus: The Jesuit Martyrs of El Salvador* (Maryknoll, NY: Orbis Books, 1990); Jon Sobrino, *Witnesses to the Kingdom: The Martyrs of El Salvador and the Crucified Peoples* (Maryknoll, NY: Orbis Books, 2003).
[20] Cf. Sobrino, *Witnesses to the Kingdom: The Martyrs of El Salvador and the Crucified Peoples*.

Grande, SJ, worked for three months, and in the homily proclaimed to the people there: 'You are the image of the pierced savior . . . who represent Christ nailed to the cross and pierced by a lance.'[21] Shortly after this, Ellacuría reframes Moltmann's image of 'the crucified God' as 'the crucified people' for the bishops preparing for a CELAM meeting in Puebla in 1978. This becomes the centrepiece of Sobrino's theology, which he describes as quite simply raising the reality we are living to the level of a theological concept.[22] 'Christology is also the Christology of the "body of Christ"' who is to be found in the oppressed majorities: 'the crucified people who are the historical continuation of the suffering servant of Yahweh'.[23]

In Sobrino, theology is undergirded by a *Spirituality of Liberation*[24] that has sociopolitical dimensions and aims to transform the secular reality. He defines spirituality as 'the spirit of a subject – an individual or a group – in its relationship with the whole of reality'[25] which, while simple, maintains both the personal or particular dimension of Christian spirituality and its connection with the whole. And while spirituality is always historically situated, Sobrino's understanding includes an awareness of what *life with spirit* implies. Sobrino names three important characteristics:

1. The spirit of Jesus' practice can be found in the Sermon on the Mount, with its emphasis on poverty – both material and spiritual – and the purity of heart needed to live it out. I shall explore in the next section how Sobrino understands poverty;
2. Spiritual life must have historical efficacy, both in itself and in the action it seeks to initiate, in the quest for justice;
3. Life with spirit must be expressed in, and enabled by, spiritual practices, 'especially those that touch on the deepest roots of the Christian life, such as the eucharist, prayer, spiritual exercises or retreats, discernment, and the like'. [26]

While he names the need for spirituality to find personal expression and motivation, Sobrino challenges individualistic notions of Christian holiness predominant in the history of Catholic praxis and in many treatises on salvation and grace. The alternative is what he calls 'political holiness',

---

[21]Sobrino, *Jon Sobrino: Spiritual Writings*, 18.
[22]Cf. Jon Sobrino, *Jesus the Liberator: A Historical-Theological Reading of Jesus of Nazareth* (Maryknoll, NY: Orbis Books, 1993), 8.
[23]Cf. Sobrino, *Jesus the Liberator: A Historical-Theological Reading of Jesus of Nazareth*, 26, quoting an expression of Ellacuría.
[24]Jon Sobrino, *Spirituality of Liberation: Toward Political Holiness* (Maryknoll, NY: Orbis Books, 1988).
[25]Sobrino, *Spirituality of Liberation: Toward Political Holiness*, 13.
[26]Cf. Sobrino, *Spirituality of Liberation: Toward Political Holiness*, 5–6.

which is much more than a presumed or contested connection between faith and politics.

> By holiness I mean the outstanding practice of faith, hope, and especially charity and the virtues generated by the following of Jesus. By politics I mean action directed toward structurally transforming society in the direction of the reign of God, by doing justice to the poor and oppressed majorities, so that they obtain life and historical salvation.[27]

Political holiness is a dimension of charity that involves an awakening and conversion to the call of God from within a particular historical reality of suffering, to see the structural causes of a situation and work effectively to change them. It is *love* invested in effective structural change.

The beauty of Sobrino's work is that it is not simply exhortative but offers an informed challenge to epistemologies that leave us unengaged with reality. For this he draws on Ellacuría's knowledge and appropriation of Zubiri's 'sentient intelligence',[28] in which human intelligence is fundamentally a biological activity which adapts constantly to the world around it, even in its most abstract operations; involves historical activity, since historicity pertains to the very structure of intelligence; and most importantly, has as its core function not to grasp meaning as most Western philosophy would understand it, but to apprehend, and to confront oneself with, reality.[29] Ellacuría claims that 'confronting oneself with real things' comprises three steps: (1) grasping what is at stake in reality (*hacerse cargo de la realidad*), (2) assuming responsibility for reality and paying the price for it (*cargar con la realidad*) and (3) taking charge of reality (*encargarse de la realidad*).[30] Building on this foundation and in direct relation to these three moments of intelligence, Sobrino proposes that any genuine spirituality will demand (1) honesty about the real, (2) fidelity to the real (no matter where it leads you) and (3) a certain 'correspondence' by which we permit ourselves to be carried (or swept) along by the 'more' of the real.[31] This final moment, according to Sobrino, is the dimension of grace.[32] Only in this way, with

---

[27]Sobrino, *Spirituality of Liberation: Toward Political Holiness*, 80.
[28]For a fascinating exploration of the life, thought and influence of Ignazio Ellacuría, see Kevin F. Burke and Robert Anthony Lassalle-Klein, *Love That Produces Hope: The Thought of Ignacio Ellacuría* (Collegeville, MN: Liturgical Press, 2005).
[29]Robert Lasalle-Klein, 'Awakening from the Sleep of Inhumanity: The Spirituality of Liberation', in *Jon Sobrino: Spiritual Writings*, ed. Sobrino, 25.
[30]Cf. Ignazio Ellacuría, 'Hacia Una Fundamentación Del Método Teológico Latino-Americano', *Estudios Centroamericanos* 30 (1975): 409–235, quoted in Sobrino, *Jon Sobrino: Spiritual Writings*, 24–25.
[31]Cf. Sobrino, *Spirituality of Liberation: Toward Political Holiness*, chapter 1: 'Presuppositions and Foundations of Spirituality', 13–22.
[32]Jon Sobrino, 'The Crucified People and the Civilization of Poverty', in *No Salvation Outside the Poor: Prophetic-Utopian Essays*, 1–18 (2) (Maryknoll, NY: Orbis Books, 2008).

our feet firmly in the historical reality of the present moment and the sociopolitical reality we have access to, can we begin to speak of experience of God. Revelation is always in history. Having relaid the epistemological foundations of human interaction with reality, Sobrino also redefines the activity of theologizing. Instead of St Anselm's 'faith's intelligence' or 'faith seeking understanding', Sobrino suggests 'love seeking understanding' or 'the intelligence of love', mercy or justice: *intellectus amoris, intellectus misericordiae, intellectus iusticiae*.[33] His theology has had a lasting influence on many major contemporary theologians and themes.[34]

It is hard to appreciate the radicality of these insights and their challenge to theology for those of us who are accustomed to the language and ethics of Christian and Catholic social teaching and commitment. But theologizing on themes of the social and structural dimensions of sin, studied through the lens of a preferential option for the poor, was both challenging and scandalous to a Church for whom these claims were new. Sobrino's theological epistemology is one in which the poor are the space within and from which we theologize. The interweaving of praxis and theory intrinsic to liberation theologies in Sobrino becomes the commitment of mercy to the crucified peoples to take them down from the cross upon which social sin and unjust structures have placed, and maintain them.[35] But such a position has a cost. Sobrino rereads the central themes of Christian theology, with a particular focus on Christology. He explains the life of Jesus of Nazareth against the background of the suffering and injustice of Latin America, on the premise that God, in Jesus, was and is on the side of the poor.[36] His ecclesiology is essentially linked to this lens of the historical Jesus and the chosen paradigm of the Church as *of*, not only for or in support of, the poor.[37] It is hardly surprising that the cost to be paid for grasping what is at stake in reality and assuming responsibility for it would also affect his theological work. Two of Sobrino's writings were the object of an investigation by the Congregation for the Doctrine of the Faith (CDF): *Jesus the Liberator: A Historical-Theological Reading of Jesus of Nazareth* and *Christ the Liberator: A View from the Victims*. The CDF wrote what is called a 'Notification' on certain elements of his Christology and theological method.[38] A notification

---

[33] Cf. Jon Sobrino, *The Principle of Mercy: Taking the Crucified People from the Cross* (Maryknoll, NY: Orbis Books, 1994), 27–46.
[34] Cf. Stephen J. Pope, *Hope & Solidarity: Jon Sobrino's Challenge to Christian Theology* (Maryknoll, NY: Orbis Books, 2008).
[35] Cf. Sobrino, *The Principle of Mercy: Taking the Crucified People from the Cross*.
[36] Jon Sobrino, *Christology at the Crossroads: A Latin American Approach* (London: SCM Press, 1978); Sobrino, *Jesus the Liberator: A Historical-Theological Reading of Jesus of Nazareth*. Jon Sobrino, *Christ the Liberator: A View from the Victims* (Maryknoll, NY: Orbis Books, 2001).
[37] Jon Sobrino, *The True Church and the Poor* (Maryknoll, NY: Orbis Books, 1984).
[38] Cf. Congregation for the Doctrine of the Faith, *Notification on the Works of Father Jon Sobrino SJ*, 26 November 2006. http://www.vatican.va/roman_curia/congregations/cfaith/docu-

does not silence or impede a theologian from teaching, but rather averts to certain questioned or contested aspects of a person's theological writing, ostensibly for the good of the Church. The protective dimension of the magisterium is an essential element of its authority and therefore necessary. For theologians who exercise a different kind of responsibility within the teaching authority of the Church, it can, however, be deeply painful. Ecclesiologist Richard Gaillardetz's balanced and insightful reflection on the roles and responsibilities of both magisterium and theologians (in relation to another case) is apropos.[39] Jon Sobrino has only recently published in full the letter he sent to his Superior General in response to the critiques and issues raised by the Congregation.[40] An excellent response to this notification attempting to take seriously 'both the concerns of the CDF and the theological insight offered by Sobrino to the church' can be found in *Hope & Solidarity: Jon Sobrino's Challenge to Christian Theology*.[41]

For the purpose of this chapter, the notification was the immediate provocation for the composition of the song linked to this chapter. Before explaining this musical exploration of his theology, however, let us take a closer look at what Sobrino's theology has to offer our question of God's existence in the face of suffering, or rather, how the question itself is transformed in this space of the poor.

Between you and I: No salvation without the poor

With Sobrino and through the lens of a theology that makes space for the real world of the poor, we return to our question about faith in God in such an unjust world, only to find that we need to shed the skin in which it makes sense in order to see things from another's viewpoint. As a first step, who *are* the poor, in Sobrino's theology? The density of Scripture's understanding

---

ments/rc_con_cfaith_doc_20061126_notification-sobrino_en.html (accessed 29 March 2021). It was made public in early 2007.

[39]Cf. Richard R. Gaillardetz, 'By What Authority? Foundations for Understanding Authority in the Church', online resource (189 pages) (Collegeville, MN: Liturgical Press, 2018); Richard R. Gaillardetz, *When the Magisterium Intervenes: The Magisterium and Theologians in Today's Church. Includes a Case Study on the Doctrinal Investigation of Elizabeth Johnson* (Collegeville, MN and Adelaide: Michael Glazier and ATF, 2012).

[40]Jon Sobrino, 'Letter to Fr. Kolvenbach, S.J., Explaining Nonadherence to "Notification" from the Congregation for the Doctrine of the Faith", in *Jon Sobrino: Spiritual Writings*, ed. R. Lassalle-Klein, 189–204 (Maryknoll, NY: Orbis, 2018).

[41]Cf. Pope, *Hope & Solidarity: Jon Sobrino's Challenge to Christian Theology*. In particular, the contributions of William Loewe, 'Interpreting the Notification: Christological Issues' (158–167) and James T. Bretzke S.J., 'The Faith of the Church, the Magisterium, and the Theologian: Proper and Improper Interpretations of the Notification' (186–199).

of poverty and the rich development of its various dimensions over time[42] make it necessary to define and clarify a term which is at risk of being over-spiritualized. Starting with the materially poor (and with explicit reference to Medellín and Puebla) Sobrino develops several aspects and steps in understanding poverty:

- The materially, or economically, poor, who struggle to live and 'who die before their time';
- The dialectically, or sociologically poor, who have been marginalized, oppressed or denied and robbed of that which was duly theirs: 'those who have no name either in life or in death';
- The consciously poor, 'who have awoken' from the lie (the dogmatic dream) that their poverty was natural or even God-willed;
- The freedom-seeking poor, who have moved from being conscious to working with others towards changing their situation;
- The spiritually poor, or the 'poor-with-spirit' (a phrase taken from Ellacuría), who live their material lives with generous and open hands, trusting in a provident God.[43]

He completes this description with biblical and theological perspectives on the poor as the beloved of God, the preferred ones. Not only did God reach out to an enslaved and oppressed people, but it was done *through* prophets and voices that were poor or young, weak or vulnerable: the *anawim* of God who attract God's gaze. This *modus operandi* continued with the Incarnation, not only because God became human but because of the type of human Jesus was: 'who . . . in the form of God, did not regard equality with God as something to be exploited, but emptied himself, taking the form of a slave' (Phil. 2.6-7). God reveals Godself as a servant, who preached to poor, chose disciples from among the poor, and continues to be present and real now in and through the poor: 'for I was hungry and you gave me food, I was thirsty and you gave me something to drink, I was a stranger and you welcomed me, I was naked and you gave me clothing, I was sick and you took care of me, I was in prison and you visited me' (cf. Mt. 25.31-46).

On this basis, the question Sobrino asks is what the poor can teach us? Take note: not what we can give the poor or how we can educate them – both worthy and necessary tasks – but what we can learn from them. And he names various key aspects of life and faith in which the poor have

---

[42]For example, literature on poverty and religious life has a long tradition of exploring dimensions of evangelical poverty.
[43]Cf. Jon Sobrino, *The Eye of the Needle. No Salvation Outside the Poor: A Utopian-Prophetic Essay* (London: Darton, Longman and Todd, 2008), 57–8. He insists upon the need to understand the diversity and depth of the poor seen through a Christian lens. See also Sobrino, 'Depth and Urgency of the Option for the Poor', 19–34 (22–5).

revelatory potential, such as who God is, who we are in light of that God, what redemption actually implies and perhaps most importantly here, what questions we should really be asking. Let's begin with the last: *the poor teach us to ask the right questions*! Instead of the understandable but superficial reaction to need (when we actually see it) of 'what should be done?' Sobrino suggests that openness to grasp reality as the poor live it implies asking instead: What do I actually know? What can I hope for? What *must* we do?[44] So rather than joining us in our questioning of God *in their name*, their challenge goes deeper, towards what image of God we are interacting with:

> The poor have no problems with God. The classic question of theodicy – the 'problem of God,' the atheism of protest – so reasonably posed by the non-poor, is no problem at all for the poor (who in good logic ought of course to be the ones to pose it). The poor have no magician-type God, no *Lückenbüsser* (stopgap) God, and no killjoy God like the one Bonhoeffer was so rightly concerned to dissipate. The God the poor believe in is a God dwelling in their midst with good news. Their faith in God is not naive, although the external expressions of that faith may make it look as if it were. The faith of the poor is deeply dialectical: the poor believe in a liberator God, crucified. It is in virtue of the equilibrium they maintain between these two poles that the poor maintain the stubbornness of their faith.[45]

So who is the God they present? One who is near, who is victim and who has suffered their fate! It is that nearness that makes God credible, not God's power but because 'on the cross, God's love may look impotent but it's believable'.[46] And that presence is perpetuated in his body, Head and members, *who they are*, crucified with and *in* a crucified God. So *the poor are the ones who*, in the words of Paul, complete in their sufferings 'what is lacking in Christ's afflictions for the sake of his body' (cf. Col. 1.24). *They* have a role to play in the mystery of redemption, not by accepting it as in the past they have been taught, in the hope of some other-worldly salvation, but by awakening and challenging the inconsistency of unjust structures and apathy with the life and love of such a God. However, this always comes with a cost: 'by its nature, redemption is a struggle against evil, not only from outside but from within: we have to shoulder the responsibility for it'.[47] The insight reminds us of the late Archbishop Don Hélder Câmara's well-known description of the suspicion that haunts those who challenge injustice that when he fed the hungry, they called him a saint, but when he asked why people are hungry, they called him a communist! Similarly, Sobrino identifies

---

[44]Cf. Sobrino, *The Eye of the Needle*, 59–63.
[45]Sobrino, *Spirituality of Liberation: Toward Political Holiness*, 167.
[46]Cf. Sobrino, *The Principle of Mercy: Taking the Crucified People from the Cross*, 9.
[47]Cf. Sobrino, *The Eye of the Needle*, 56.

the strength of the shadow side of the redemptive process: 'Mercy and anti-mercy are real. Let mercy be reduced to sentiments or sheer works of mercy, and anti-mercy will be tolerant enough. But let it be raised to the status of a principle, and anti-mercy will react.'[48] In the midst of this, the faith of the poor is not without hope. To the questions raised above to which the poor invite us, Sobrino adds, 'What can I celebrate?' in the recognition that the poor often carry a joy for life and hope that makes little sense in relation to what they suffer, but which is grace-filled and contagious.

Finally, this understanding of God and redemption also reveals us to ourselves, not primarily in how we resemble God's image but in how we fail to. The poor are a kind of reverse mirror revealing the underside of the world we have become. By way of contrast, they tell us of our own sickness. Taking an image from Ellacuría, Sobrino speaks of *coproanalysis:* the analysis of human faeces which detect a sick humanity.[49] So redemption, 'taking the poor down from the cross', is not something we do *for* the poor. It needs to come from them, precisely because of how they grasp the reality of God and the human reality. As such, they are a necessary part of the way forward. This is where Sobrino's central thesis about redemption rests: '*extra pauperes nulla salus*' – there is no salvation outside of, or without, the poor.[50] The phrase is adapted from Origen and Cyprian's '*extra Ecclesiam nulla salus*' – there is no salvation outside of the Church – which has had its own embattled history, as we know. It was reframed and adapted by Edward Schillebeeckx to emphasize the importance of the world in a Christian understanding of salvation: there is no salvation outside of the world – *extra mundum nulla salus*. Sobrino takes this decisively a step forward: *extra pauperes nulla salus*. Sobrino traces and explains the immediate influences on his formulation,[51] and it is important to understand that Sobrino is not idealizing the poor or suggesting they are automatically or necessarily morally superior, but rather that for all of the above, we cannot grasp or access the fullness of Christian salvation without the reality of the poor. Because God is *in* their suffering, and Christian redemption includes them, or more, comes *through* them.

It is provocative and lapidary, and true. (And incidentally, not one of the aspects questioned by the CDF, although it is a consequence of raising the situation of millions – the majority of human beings in the world – to the condition of visible members of the body of Christ!) The poor are in the body, so there is no salvation without them. For those who might find it challenging, it is worthwhile remembering that salvation in Scriptural and Christian terms was *never* about the escape of the soul from the body to an individual eternal bliss, but rather the promise that Christ would be all in

---

[48]Sobrino, *The Principle of Mercy: Taking the Crucified People from the Cross*, 19.
[49]Sobrino, 'The Crucified People and the Civilization of poverty', 1–18 (5).
[50]Cf. Sobrino, *The Eye of the Needle*.
[51]Sobrino, 'Extra Pauperes Nulla Salus: A Short Utopian-Prophetic Essay', 35–76 (70–1).

all: that one day 'every tear will be wiped from our eyes. . . . Death will be no more; mourning and crying and pain will be no more' (Rev. 21.4). This was the original vision, which Paul described in terms of the end of time (which he believed was imminent): 'For the trumpet will sound, and the dead will be raised imperishable, and we will be changed' (1 Cor. 15.52). Together: the mystery of God's will is 'to gather up all things in him, things in heaven and things on earth' (Eph. 1.10). Over time, as Christianity realized the end was *not* imminent, it had to deal with the problem (and whereabouts!) of those who have died; and it is beautiful, and possible, and theologically rich to imagine and trust in God's welcome to each loved one into an eternity that is outside of our time. However, our understanding of a personal eternal life after death in God *now*, while comforting, is incomplete, unChristian and untheological if we lose sight of the communitarian, shared and social dimensions of the life of the whole Christ.

This is true in relation to the end of times. However, in the now – the meantime – the point being made is that we do not grasp, understand or have access to the fullness of that life without, or outside of, the poor: *extra pauperes nulla salus*. That is the quintessential message of Christian faith.

> This is the marrow of liberation theology . . . that the crucified people themselves are bearers of salvation. The one chosen by God to bring salvation is the servant, which increases the scandal. We sincerely believe that theology does not know what to do with this statement.[52]

Jerusalem: Salvation in the Poor

This song has a very specific birthplace and motivation: Lent of 2007, a few days after the notification about Sobrino's theology went public. I was doing research for my doctorate at the Jesuit School of Theology in Berkeley, in which many of the scholars were Sobrino's friends or colleagues, or drew upon his theology and other theologies of liberation in their work. The collective reaction was one of pain and exhaustion at the ongoing difficulty to appreciate what theologies like Sobrino's bring to the table. There was also a certain awareness that underlying this notification there could be more than simply doctrinal issues: Sobrino and his collaborators in El Salvador had a long history of challenging social and ecclesial structures to be more prophetic for the poor of the nation. This could not go unchallenged. In that moment, staff and students sought intelligent and scaffolded ways to accept, read, assimilate and channel the aspects of Sobrino's theology being questioned and the meaning of the notification. I was only beginning to

---

[52]Sobrino, *The Principle of Mercy: Taking the Crucified People from the Cross*, 53.

realize the potential of music at the service of theology, but my experience of the Church at that time (and now), in various settings and countries, was that the atmosphere among students was often polarized and intolerant.[53] It never fails to astonish me that such a universal Church can be so deeply opposed to experiences and thoughts outside its comfort zone, but so it is. Therefore, in part because I process things through music, and in part as a conscious decision to enshrine some of his insights in a piece of music, I wrote 'Jerusalem: Salvation in the Poor'.[54]

A song speaks for itself, but for those interested in music analysis, this is one of the pieces I have analysed more fully using a form of a musical semiotics that explores the combined meaning of music and lyrics.[55] The chapter also made a case for music as an aid to the kind of epistemological challenges found in Sobrino's work, because of the different way in which we interact with reality *in* and *through* music. Taking this further and for our purposes here, from behind the text, that is to say, from my perspective, there are two images underlying this song: Jesus 'setting his face' towards Jerusalem (Lk. 9.51) and his tears as he looks over Jerusalem and senses the people's blindness to what God was really doing: 'If you, even you, had only recognized on this day the things that make for peace! But now they are hidden from your eyes' (Lk. 19.41-44). So the core of the song for me is Sobrino's challenge to the epistemological illiteracy of un-awakened and therefore unaware lives, theology, and leadership: when our hearts are not touched our mind simply cannot *know* God, others, the world, ourselves, in the biblical sense in which knowing and loving are of a piece. Liberation theologies challenge a Christianity that is complicit in unjust structures and their consequences on the disenfranchised and defenceless. In our contemporary globally interconnected world, this is the reality of every developed country in the world, because of *how* our markets work. Either we take a position against it and in favour of fairer and more sustainable structures, or we insulate ourselves from the voices we are meant to hear.

For me, Sobrino's theology constitutes a personal challenge. As a religious belonging to a community with presences worldwide – struggling and developed – I have always been sent to mainly Western,

---

[53] By way of example, I remember one first-year theology student taking issue with what he called the over-influence of Rahner's theology of revelation over Balthasar's in *Dei Verbum*, *when it was obvious he had no real knowledge of either*. I suggested he could revisit that thought once he had actually read the writings of both and learned to appreciate the role of an ecumenical Council in the life of the Church.

[54] The link to the song 'Jerusalem: Salvation with the Poor' is here: https://res.cloudinary.com/bloomsbury-online-resources/video/upload/v1639138281/Suspended%20God/Jerusalem-_Salvation_in_the_Poor.wav

[55] Cf. Maeve Louise Heaney, 'Mercy, Music and the Prophetic Voice of Theology', in *Music, Theology, and Justice*, ed. M. Connor, H.-A. Kim, and C. Labriola, 43–62 (Lanham: Lexington Books, 2017). This study would be impossible without the expertise and collaboration of theologian, semiotician, (and friend), Willem Marie Speelman, Director of the Franciscan Study centre at Tilburg University.

rich, countries, for a variety of reasons which have always made sense. But there are aspects of Sobrino's awareness I reach for, because they have not touched my skin, although I try to live coherently with the options taken. But knowing is (also) biological and contextual, so this is a real limitation. The song is about the body of Christ: life, death, Eucharist, suffering past and ongoing, in his Body. It is both lament and celebration. If the path Jesus walked took him to his death, ours is that same one, but we walk in hope because that life won, because what *we* could not see was recognized by God as his beloved suffering Servant: our no became God's yes. And yet, the entrance point, the access point between us and that Life, are the ones who understand and live *this kind of humanity*, in which wrong is right, up is down, weak is strong and poor *is* rich, the authentically poor.

'Jerusalem' lyrics

You set your face towards Jerusalem / Finally the beginning of the end
The path you've taken is the ground beneath our feet
So, tell me why so often we lose sight of this . . .
Forgive us Lord for hearts of stone!
Our eyes don't cry; our minds don't know
Forgive us Lord, and don't give up!
We still don't know what we're doing
Have mercy on Jerusalem!
Blessed are those who draw your gaze on them
The 'anawim' you choose to call your friends
Between you and I are those of whom the Kingdom is
My heart needs to stretch and break to let them in . . .
Forgive us Lord for hearts of stone!
Our eyes don't cry; our minds don't know
Forgive us Lord, we haven't learnt!
We still don't know what we're doing
We're so in need of *You*
Wrong is right, and weak is strong, and stupid is wise
Poor is rich, and up is down, and You are Real . . .
So, thank You Lord for losing all!
For unashamedly being on the side of your people
Thank You Lord, for giving all!
For unreservedly being broken and given . . . thank you, Lord!
Jerusalem. A peace that fights, a word that bites and heals within . . .
Jerusalem
A freedom that enchains us to reality . . . Jerusalem . . .

©MAEVE LOUISE HEANEY, 2020.
Strange Life, The Music of Doubtful Faith

Selected further reading

On liberation theology

Gutiérrez, Gustavo. *A Theology of Liberation: History, Politics and Salvation*. London: S.C.M., 1988.

Sobrino's life and thought

Sobrino, Jon *Spiritual Writings*, edited by Robert Lassalle-Klein. Maryknoll, NY: Orbis, 2018.

On a spirituality of liberation

Sobrino, Jon. *Spirituality of Liberation: Toward Political Holiness*. Maryknoll, NY: Orbis Books, 1988.

Sobrino's approach to liberation theology

Sobrino, Jon. *The Principle of Mercy: Taking the Crucified People from the Cross*. Maryknoll, NY: Orbis Books, 1994.
Sobrino, Jon. *No Salvation Outside the Poor: Prophetic-Utopian Essays*. Maryknoll, NY: Orbis Books, 2008.

9

Is original sin an outdated doctrine?

When new life is so heartbreakingly beautiful, why do Christians talk about sin?

This chapter's question is one which pastoral attentiveness is already working out on the front lines of ministry and outreach, but it is a textbook example of how a core truth of faith can be true but also need rephrasing and reframing in language that better expresses what it means. New life is beautiful, perhaps the most universally recognized reality worthy of love and protection: babies from the moment they are born – red, bloody and wrinkled – are beautiful, helpless, innocent and life-changing: magnets of human attention. As a friend of mine (who is deeply in love with his wife, by the way) described fatherhood to me on the birth of his first child: 'suddenly, there is someone in the world more important than you!' Life turns on its axis towards this being who is loved before she or he even *begins* to unfold their lives into who they shall become.

And yet, not so long ago, the first thing a midwife would do if a newborn was sick or in danger of not making it was to take some water and baptize them in the name of the Father, of the Son, of the Holy Spirit: an impromptu but *valid* baptism for the good of the child's salvation. Why? Because of the doctrine we call 'original sin', which basically states that human beings enter into a fallen reality which affects them even before they are capable of exercising their free will to choose between right and wrong, good or evil. Also underlying this practice is the broader issue of salvation outside the Church and the necessity of baptism – that is to say, explicit and confessed belonging to the Church – for salvation. This second question is one I address with Karl Rahner in chapter ten. Here, the specific focus is the anthropological question of how human beings as *good*, made in the image and likeness of a God who is One, Good, Truth and Beauty, can *need* to be saved before they have even begun to have an awareness of the world into which they have arrived.

The origin of the doctrine on original sin is Scripture-based, especially the second creation story of how Adam and Eve turned away from friendship with God (cf. Gen. 3.1-24) and Paul's interpretation of our solidarity in sin since Adam: 'just as sin came into the world through one man, and death came through sin, and so death spread to all'. Interestingly, Paul's starting point in understanding this doctrine is not sin itself but the universal salvation achieved in Christ. If all are saved in Christ, Paul thinks, then all must have fallen in Adam (cf. Rom. 5.12-21). However, its development over time has focussed on sin and its effects on humanity, in different ways.[1] The most influential source of this teaching is Augustine, who situated sin in the realm of human will and love, where creatures or self can take the place of God in human loving. His thought on original sin emerged from his defence of child baptism against Pelagianism, which taught that human beings were naturally good and could achieve their own salvation, and that Adam's sin was simply a bad example that did not affect the natural capacity of human will to choose good.[2] Against this position, Augustine maintained that although infants cannot commit personal sins, all of humanity inherited what he described as the congenital effects of original sin, requiring baptism for its removal. Augustine's underlying suspicion of the body and sex is a clear influence in his consideration of this theme. Even after baptism, the effects of sin, which became termed 'concupiscence' (a disordered desire that turns the will away from God), remain as an ongoing tendency towards sinful acts. However, in his view, concupiscence was not considered 'sin' but rather a weakness or 'aftereffect' left once sin is forgiven and removed by the grace received in baptism.

The theological history of this doctrine is colourful and multifaceted. Aquinas developed it further, maintaining the biological transmission of sin. Lutheran theology radicalized the negative effects of sin on human will, maintaining that the remaining effects of sin in the person after baptism *are* still sin, on the basis that human beings always remain sinners before God. Modernity emphasized the importance of free will and self-determination in a person's development and life of faith, making belief in prior guilt hard to receive. Liberation and social justice movements of the twentieth century introduced a different emphasis by challenging the overly individualistic development of the doctrine and Christian salvation as a whole. Original

---

[1] For an clear oversight of the origins and development of the doctrine of original sin, see 'sin' in Ian A. McFarland et al., *The Cambridge Dictionary of Christian Theology* (New York: Cambridge University Press, 2011).

[2] Pelagius was a fourth-century monk from Ireland or Britain who taught in Rome and North Africa, and whose teaching was ultimately not accepted as orthodox. The influence, however, of such an understanding, remains.

sin, in this framework, comes to be linked with social structures of sin into which we are born and participate in, complicit to the extent in which we do not actively challenge and oppose them. The discovery of the evolutionary dynamics intrinsic to the creation of the planet compounded the awareness that suffering, death and brokenness are part of how things have *always* worked, dismissing ideas that there ever was a prelapsarian idyllic state evoked by the Garden of Eden. Feminist perspectives in theological anthropology have challenged understandings of the foundational sin as one of disobedience born of pride as being a particularly male way of understanding sin. It would suggest that avoidance, omission, trivialization and not taking responsibility are other dynamics in need of consideration. In all of this, however, the foundational belief that human beings are sinful and intrinsically in need of salvation is unquestioned by Christian theologies of all denominations. How to frame it is another issue.

It is important to say that a basic understanding of humanity as fallen and that this affects the whole of creation is not something that requires much proof. I have often found that it is one of the truths of Christian faith which is least questioned, even by those outside a Christian worldview, except perhaps to ask *how* God could have created something so 'wobbly' to begin with, to use a term this chapter's theologian likes. Perhaps most important of all is to state that in any case, sin is always a revealed reality: anyone can perceive right and wrong, as well as the effects of unethical human choices upon the world and humanity. But to call it 'sin' is to enter into the realm of our relationship with God and our turning away from that Love, each other, the world and ourselves. Furthermore, the reality of the body of Christ in whom we are united gives a theological depth and challenge to understanding how sin, as well as grace, might affect all the members.

Our focus here, however, is on children, and one aspect of the history of theological thought on this theme speaks to this directly. During the Middle Ages, Roman Catholic theologians developed the theory that unbaptized children went to what was called a *limbus puerorum* (children's limbo) which was a place of natural happiness, but not yet in full union with God until the end of times. I should mention that this was consistent with other aspects of Catholic theology about the necessity of Christ for salvation, such as what happens to those who lived *before* Jesus' incarnation, and the necessity for all of us to be purified in order to be united with God (unhappily named as purgatory), but it is more challenging given our sense of a child's innocence. It is incomprehensible to contemporary sensibility to think of those tiny bundles of joy and sleepless nights we bring into the world as *not* having quick access to God, but rather going to some kind of divine waiting room until things get sorted out. Theology on limbo never entered into the dogmatic definitions of the magisterium but was mentioned in ordinary Church teaching up until the Second Vatican Council and was common knowledge (or fear) in Catholicism until relatively recently. In 2007, the International Theological Commission endorsed dropping it completely, in a document that received the approval of Pope Benedict XVI in the same year. They described their work as an exercise and example of the historical development of the faith as described in *Dei Verbum* 8: 'there is a growth in the understanding of the realities and the words which have been handed down' achieved through the reflection and the study of the faithful, the experience of spiritual things and the teaching of the magisterium.[3]

So, doctrine develops, and attention to the sense of the faithful (*sensus fidelium*) is part of how that happens. And our understanding of human life also grows, as well as the tools we have to grasp and develop our lives and those of the ones we love. Is there a perspective on human life, growth and psychology that can shine a different light on the reality of human beauty and fragility 'from birth', as it were? Is the concept of original sin simply that: a concept we know and defend as true but only on an intellectual level, but which does not really colour or even resonate with how we experience our lives (and those of our children)? How is humanity beautiful and broken?

To answer this question, I turn to one of the few theologians in the twentieth century who brought together psychology and theology in the quest for insights into Christian theological anthropology: Sebastian Moore, OSB. His thought is complex and ever in development, as most of those who value his theology admit, and the weaving of his theological journey into a full, systematic picture is a bigger project than this book attempts. Instead, I have chosen particular writings relevant to our theme to highlight both his approach to theology and his contribution to rethinking Christology, anthropology and with it the notion of original sin. But who was he?

Sebastian Moore: Taking human experience seriously

Charles Patrick Moore (1917–2014) was born in British India in 1917, only taking the monastic name of Sebastian upon entering the novitiate for the Benedictines in 1938. He was a monk of the Abbey of St Gregory the Great, known as 'Downside Abbey', and did his doctoral studies in Rome in Patrology, after which he went back to England to study and teach at Downside Abbey. Although he spent his first years as a monk there, and Benedictine religious vows include a commitment of stability to one's monastery, he lived much of his life outside the monastery in England and abroad – *ex claustro* (outside of the cloister) – as a pastor, teaching,

---

[3]Cf. International Theological Commission, *The Hope of Salvation for Infants Who Die without Being Baptised* (2007). https://www.vatican.va/roman_curia/congregations/cfaith/cti_documents/rc_con_cfaith_doc_20070419_un-baptised-infants_en.html

lecturing and writing in Cambridge, Rome, Liverpool, Milwaukee and Boston. He returned home to Downside Abbey for another twenty-two years, however, before he died in 2014. We know a lot about his personal and theological journey, due to the honesty shot through his own writings and the dedication and writings of his friends, colleagues and students.[4] Due to how interwoven his life and thought is, I reflect on that journey before exploring his theological method, style and contributions.

From personality to theological explorations of psychology

One of Moore's books is called *The Inner Loneliness*,[5] and in an interview towards the end of his life, he recognized this reality of human aloneness as his constant foundational experience: 'my starting point is loneliness. My starting point is me and myself'. He links this with his option for life alone as a monk, and friends recognized that although he was a warm, charming and much-admired person in all his activities, he may have struggled to hold together his thirst for intimacy and the introspective nature of his personality.

> His prolonged introspections yielded him many insights, for his writing as well as his biographical narratives, though they also marked off the distance he maintained from even the closest companions. In many respects, this vivacious and entertaining figure remained a soul in solitude, concerned to communicate with himself and with God, excluding others even as he faced a deep, inner loneliness. He considered such isolation to be also a necessary condition of those who traversed unknown ground, along a frontier of new understanding.[6]

His capacity to charm was linked, in his mind, with the need for approval and attention, a theme which will become an essential aspect of his reflections on human anthropology in terms of the human desire for and need of self-esteem, self-righteousness and the accompanying dark shadow of self-contempt.

Moore's interest and interaction with psychology and Freudian-Jungian psychoanalysis dated from a mental breakdown in 1953 after the death of his

---

[4]A symposium hosted by the monastic community of Downside in 2017 to celebrate the centenary of Sebastian's birth led to a dedicated issue of the *Downside Review* in 2018 with various articles on his life and thought. They are a source for some of what is presented here. See *Downside Review* 136, no. 3 (2018).
[5]Sebastian Moore, *The Inner Loneliness* (London: Darton, Longman & Todd, 1982).
[6]Joseph Melling, 'Sebastian Moore: A Life in Movements', *Downside Review* (2018): 1–4 (2).

mother, and he remained a lifelong adherent to the Freudian model of child development and sexual maturity, as we shall see in the third section of this chapter. This was also linked with his own sexual orientation as homosexual and his fears about how that would affect his life as monk and theologian. Moore lived through the enormous changes in society and church during the twentieth century. It is hard to overestimate how deeply this surrounding context would influence such a reflective and intelligent person: a gay man whose life spanned the pre-Vatican II rules and lifestyle of monastic celibate life, the sexual revolution and challenges of the 1960s, and later attempts to reframe our thinking about a myriad of social, religious and theological issues. In the 1960s, Moore would initiate and lead what was called an 'experimental' parish team in Liverpool for nine years, with which he became deeply involved but which also led to personal stress and challenges he was not equipped for. Again, psychological support helped him through this stage. During these years, his discovery of psychological categories and explorations of human development gave him 'a new vocabulary of ideas and understanding about his family history and the growth of his consciousness'.[7] I think it would also ground his evident ongoing receptivity to ideas and insights from the world outside Christian thought.

Context and influences

Apart from thinkers in psychology and psychoanalysis – which included Otto Rank (1884–1939) and Karl Jaspers (1883–1969) – Moore's first major writings drew upon and responded to the influential figure of Ernest Becker (1924–74), in particular his work *The Denial of Death* exploring the human quest for meaning and contemporaneous denial of finitude and death. Moore describes the human person as both 'God-directed' and 'God-alienated' on a quest for significance which, however, can only come from Another. Another significant influence was the Ignatian month of Spiritual Exercises he did in 1973 in the United States after leaving his monastery in difficult circumstances and finding ministerial refuge teaching at Marquette Jesuit University in 1971. This returned Moore to his contemplative centre and led him to request a transfer from the Benedictines to the Jesuits. The request was ultimately denied, but it attests to the effect of this spirituality on his life and thought.

During his time in the United States, he met and interacted with two groups of scholars invested in the thought and method of Bernard Lonergan in centres at Marquette University and Boston College. Lonergan is deeply influential in Moore's understanding of and approach to theological method, as we shall see. He also became friends with Robert Doran, the

---

[7]Melling, 'Sebastian Moore: A Life in Movements', 1-4 (2).

foremost editor of Lonergan's opus *and* proponent of including psychic conversion as foundational to theological method (see chapter four). There are suggestions that conversations between Moore and other scholars on themes at the intersection of psychology and theology may have influenced Doran's important insight.[8] Other more contemporary influences and dialogue partners were René Girard's notion of mimetic desire as the root of violence, James Allison, who continues and develops Girard's work, and Eckhart Tolle's *The Power of Now*.[9] As is clear, Moore's openness to question and learn from life and contemporary thought colours both his thought and his theological style, to which I now turn.

Theological approach and style

Psychology is a relatively new science, and Moore was one of the first in the twentieth century to make a serious attempt at reflecting on theological themes in light of the insights of psychology. His thirst for understanding and openness to learn continuously from what he read is one of the reasons, to my mind, for the difficulty in grasping his thought. He not only constantly cites the authors who are currently helping him name issues he is grappling with, but his honesty and commitment to self-awareness lead him to detract previous positions he came to, as he further clarifies what he thinks! His works read more as a work in progress than a finished statement. Having said that, his insightful and creative approach to the themes of Christology, salvation and theological anthropology through the lens of desire led him to be a much-read author during the twentieth century. And there is a clear line of development and growth in his theology over the years. Some situate his work as a contribution to fundamental theology due to his focus on areas of human life that serve as entry points or preconditions to explicit faith.[10] In a Lonerganian framework, his work fits into the functional speciality of Foundations because of his attempt to give expression to the experience of conversion.[11] Neil Ormerod describes his work as sitting 'in a twilight zone between academic theology and spirituality'.[12] Others describe it as a form of psychological theology or theological psychology. What is certain is that it represents a serious attempt to pay attention to human experience in light

---

[8]Cf. William P. Loewe, 'Sebastian Moore, Redemptive Transformation, and the Law of the Cross', *Downside Review* 136, no. 3 (2018): 178–85 (180).
[9]Eckhart Tolle, *The Power of Now: A Guide to Spiritual Enlightenment* (Sydney, NSW: Hodder Headline Australia, 2004).
[10]Cf. Michael Paul Gallagher, 'Contexts and Horizons of Desire: Sebastian Moore's Contribution to Fundamental Theology', *Lonergan Workshop* (1998): 59–72.
[11]Neil Ormerod, 'Sebastian Moore: Psychological Theology', in *Introducing Contemporary Theologies: The What and the Who of Theology Today*, 71–80 (Alexandria, NSW: E.J. Dwyer, 1997).
[12]Ormerod, 'Sebastian Moore', 71–80 (71).

of the insights of psychology and bring them into the investigation of key themes of Christian doctrine.

A word on his theological method and chosen pathway of theological reflection. His first book, published in 1967, is entitled *God Is a New Language*.[13] It predates his more well-known work on desire, which I shall look at shortly, but marks an interesting start to his theological endeavours. Moore's central concern is that of turning away from conceptual explanations of God that have little or nothing to do with people's actual life experience.

> Christians, who normally deal in stocks and shares and politics and love and friendship, talk together about salvation, the coming of God, the love of God and the love of neighbour, and so forth. In this game, they do not ask 'What does it all mean, really?' because they do not need to. They know the rules. They know the language. And it is the old language, a dead language.[14]

Through reflections on various aspects of Christian life, and in poetry as much as prose, he seeks to wake people up to the reality that we either understand God through our conscious, dynamic life experiences and awareness, or we have not understood at all. His concerns echo those of the first authors in theopoetic movements I spoke about in chapter one, on the quest for language, because 'anyone who talks of the divine encounter without at least wishing he [sic] could write poetry is talking about nothing at all . . . guilty of the supreme conceptualism, offering something apparently alive, which is worse than offering something manifestly dead. He [sic] is opening up before the thirsty wanderer the mirage that is the final exacerbation of thirst'.[15] It is not surprising that Moore would resonate with Lonergan's grounding of theology in an ever-dynamic and multifaceted conversion. In fact, he also understood in a similar fashion to Lonergan the stages of theology over time and saw his own quest to bring the insights from psychology and psychoanalysis to bear on Christian dogmas as part of a quest for unity necessary in a theology expressed in terms of interiority. He describes four moments in theology's development in history: in Patristic theologizing, the Fathers of the Church used all the arts of storytelling, myth and imagination to tell the salvation story; scholastic theology received and responded to the need to reason about the core concepts of our faith, introduced by the Greeks; a third moment emerges with Luther and the shift from a question about what the Christian story *is* to 'what does the story mean in terms of human self-awareness? What's it *like* to be lost?'; at this point, the immense complexity of human contexts and experiences overloads

---

[13]Sebastian Moore, *God Is a New Language* (London: Darton, Longman & Todd, 1967).
[14]Moore, *God Is a New Language*, 9.
[15]Moore, *God Is a New Language*, 143–4.

the theological quest for understanding, in his opinion, leading to the fourth moment we find ourselves in now, in which there is a need for 'deeper unity in human experience. Is there some state of being which everybody wants?'[16] This turn to the inner life of the subject is not something new, he suggests, but rather honesty with what has ever been the case: theology has to be autobiographical because it has always been that way, 'each one pushing his or her own story, so that the next step will be to be honest about this'.[17] Doing so implies a focus on human symbolization:

> What ended the medieval and began the modern period in our understanding of everything was the newly felt need to understand ourselves. What this means for theology is the shift from thinking systematically about the great symbols in which our faith is contained, to attending to and coming to understand ourselves in our response to these symbols, and indeed as productive of them.[18]

Moore brought this concern and intent to key areas of Christian theology and anthropology, developing what Ormerod describes as an 'existential Christology'. His quest to understand Jesus sits at the intersection of anthropology and Christology, in the attempt to discover how Jesus responds to the core questions afflicting human existence. *The Crucified Jesus Is No Stranger* (1977)[19] responds to Becker's work on finitude and death and strands of depth psychology by exploring the meaning of the death of Christ when it is experienced in human existence. The focus here is less on the meaning of Jesus' historical life, death and resurrection than on the self as crucified or crucifier, depending on our experience of ourselves, the world and forgiveness, or lack thereof. *The Fire and the Rose Are One* (1980) turns its focus to the historical Jesus as the sinless One who saves us by exploring and interpreting the experience of the disciples of Jesus' life, death and resurrection. *The Inner Loneliness* (1982) explores the human condition as one of a 'cosmic loneliness' characterized by three basic human experiences: our discomfort with sexuality, which despite every desire confirms us in our ultimate 'common aloneness'; our dependence on the planet for survival; and our mortality. However, his main focus is that of sexuality, ending with a brief account of the Trinity as 'the Infinite Unloneliness'. *Let This Mind Be in You: The Quest for Identity through Oedipus to Christ* (1985) focuses more specifically on original sin but needs to be understood in light

---

[16]Sebastian Moore, *The Fire and the Rose Are One* (London: Darton, Longman & Todd, 1980), 3–4.
[17]Sebastian Moore, 'Four Steps Towards Making Sense of Theology', *Downside Review* 111, no. 383 (1993): 79–100 (82).
[18]Sebastian Moore, 'The Girl Next Door', *The Irish Theological Quarterly* 62, no. 1 (1996): 49–69 (50).
[19]Sebastian Moore, *The Crucified Jesus Is No Stranger* (New York: Paulist, 1977).

of his previous thought, building on them and integrating about-turns and developments with quintessential honesty, poetry and aplomb.

Before I move to the third section offering some light to our understanding of both the potential and the fragility of human life, a word on Moore's reception and influence. Sebastian Moore is currently not as well known as he was a few decades ago. There are different reasons for this, to my mind, including the complexity of his thought, the specific knowledge of psychological categories presumed in his books and his eccentric combination of prose, colloquialisms and poetry. He could have done with a more ruthless editor, to enable the originality of his insights to be carried through more easily. Another problem is the constant integration in his writings of new authors that (perhaps) better explain what he is trying to express, which makes it hard to situate: psychology is a new science whose methodologies are still on the move. Critiques of his work by younger theologians can be negative or flippant in their assessment of Moore's theological approach, especially his later writings, such as the brilliantly named *The Contagion of Jesus: Doing Theology as If It Mattered*.[20] For me, these criticisms reflect more their authors' own ignorance of the context in which Moore wrote and the challenges he faced *and* managed to think through than a balanced theological assessment of his work. The range of people who respect and value his thought shows how broadly his theology reached.[21] A person's thought does not have to be perfect to have something to teach us. In Sebastian Moore we have

> a brilliantly eclectic thinker who possessed the capacity to integrate ideas and insights from a wide variety of disciplines to throw fresh light on the most important questions of Christian witness . . . his intention was always to communicate inter-subjectivity, as he wrote in the Preface to *Let This Mind Be in You* (1985), 'This book, I hope, is about you. It is certainly about me'.[22]

We all change names: The original blessing of (God's and our) goodness

In this section on how new life can help us reframe our understanding of original sin, and precisely because of the complexity of Moore's writing, I

---

[20]Sebastian Moore, *The Contagion of Jesus: Doing Theology as If It Mattered*, ed. S. McCarthy (Maryknoll, NY: Orbis, 2007).
[21]For insight into some of these theologians and areas they cover, see William P. Loewe and Vernon J. Gregson, eds., *Jesus Crucified and Risen: Essays in Spirituality and Theology in Honor of Dom Sebastian Moore* (Collegeville, MN: Liturgical Press, 1998).
[22]Joseph Melling, 'Sebastian Moore: Beyond Piety', *Downside Review* 136, no. 3 (2018): 145–7 (147).

am going to interweave accessible segments of his writings with an attempt to translate key notions of Moore's mature theology into contemporary terms. The golden thread running right through his work is desire: 'Desire is probably his most fundamental category, but it is more than a category: it is an ocean of energy, the realm of crucial acceptance or refusal of ultimate love.'[23] The human person longs for love, to be recognized and valued. In fact, our self-esteem is not something we can give to ourselves but is rather drawn from our desirability for others. The fact is that we *are* loved. This is his foundational starting point: we are desired into existence by a God who enjoys life and wants us to share in that enjoyment. While the more minute development of the meaning of original sin is dealt with in *Let This Mind Be in You*, two chapters in *The Inner Loneliness*, suggestively entitled 'God the Hedonist: 1' and 'God the Hedonist: 2', make the point with unusual clarity:

> The most important fact about the human condition is that, at root, self-love and self-gift are one, that self-love flowers in self-giving, flowers *as* self-giving. This radical oneness between the way pleasure works and the way self-gift works makes it to be the case that pleasure finds its full intensity only in self-gift, and self-gift loses every last trace of moralism and condescension in pleasure. . . . Our biggest obstacle to believing in God is our innate distrust of happiness. This is a disbelief in our goodness. We do not easily believe that, through no work or merit of ours, our deepest desire is to make another person happy. We do not believe in this spontaneous goodness of ourselves.[24]

He questions whether the root of this distrust in happiness is because of our need to control things: Do we choose a thin and cramped vision of life because we have more control over it than an abundant one surrendered to Another? It is a fascinating challenge to the hegemony of freedom over life understood as living-for-others and Another.

However, the foundation is that we are loved. We have an original blessing of goodness and capacity to enter into the joy of goodness, as described by Meister Eckhart, a mystic of the fourteenth century Moore quotes often: 'God enjoys himself and wants us to join him [sic].'[25] In this light, Christian faith is the farthest thing possible from a crutch for the weak but an audacious trust in the overabundance of life and love that is *possible* and for which we were created! In light of this, the shadow side of human existence is our difficulty in believing this intrinsic goodness and value we

---

[23]For an insightful exploration of this area of his thought, see Gallagher, 'Contexts and Horizons of Desire: Sebastian Moore's Contribution to Fundamental Theology', 59–72.
[24]Cf. Moore, *The Inner Loneliness*, 24–9.
[25]Quoted in Moore, *The Inner Loneliness*, 25.

hold in God's eyes. It is a 'closing up of the self',[26] a 'radical alienation from God, a primal guilt, our original cosmic love affair with God gone sour, a deep sense of having failed the other, a disaffection with creaturehood'.[27] The felt guilt underpinning the human reality at the thought of life as happiness – epitomized in our 'this is too good to be true' reactions – is a symptom and expression of the deep underlying turning away from the mystery of unlimited Love that is our origin. And Satan is true to the etymology of the word, 'the accuser', attacking our basic need for self-esteem and love in and for which we were made.

To explain the human dynamic of awareness that manifests this reality, he refers to the crises through which the human condition came about. First (although Moore's literary order is eclectic) is the recognition of the evolutionary processes of human development, specifically the moment of coming to human consciousness. Remember that Moore's theological method is focussed on the subject and on the need to (re)discover the original and originating symbols of life and our response to them. So, the question, for him, is some form of 'what did it *feel like* to become human?'. He describes this in terms of our step into consciousness: the self-awareness that we actually *are*:

> The difference between an animal existence not aware of itself and a self-aware existence is so vast, so absolute, that it is difficult to think of any psychic continuity through the change, of any 'subject' to which the change happened. Yet a failure to stretch our minds at this point will mean that we shall never understand our human plight, potential and destiny. . . . Our deepest memory is that we are an animal species that became conscious. That has to have been a shattering experience.[28]

From there he turns to ask about what is most significant about the process of human growth and reflects upon Freud's amazement at the dramatic nature of human development in comparison to our animal counterparts. Animals develop automatically into 'adulthood', whereas human beings *only* do so through the traumatic events of separation (from the mother) and the Oedipal crisis. Drawing on the work of Margaret Mahler in *The Psychological Birth of the Human Infant*[29] and other authors within or connected to Freudian analyses, he explores how a child starts to 'practice' who she is through the discovery that motor skills *work*! 'I am, because I

---

[26] Moore, *The Fire and the Rose Are One*, 71.
[27] Cf. Ormerod, 'Sebastian Moore', 71–80 (74).
[28] Sebastian Moore, *Let This Mind Be in You: The Quest for Identity through Oedipus to Christ* (Minneapolis: Winston Press, 1985), 78.
[29] Margaret S. Mahler, *The Psychological Birth of the Human Infant Symbiosis and Individuation*, ed. F. Pine and A. Bergman (London: Karnac Books, 1985).

work, this works.' It is the obvious and delightful dynamic of every child learning to walk. And what happens next? She looks to Mum for affirmation. This leads to the rapprochement phase in which a child turns to her mother for corroboration.

> As the most alarming thing, 'conscious separate existence', really gets under way, the need for support becomes enormous. And not for a support of the crutches type that would *mitigate* the venturesomeness of individual reality, but for a total *encouragement* in it. The first powerful sense of self looks ecstatically to the mother for support in an incredible adventure.[30]

So the mother has to combine encouragement and support of the child's self-discovery with a pushing away *so that the* child can become herself, in separate-although-loved existence.

This is followed by a second separation from the mother: the entrance and presence of the father, which leads the child, in Moore's terms, into 'very strange waters'. According to Freud, a child's love for its mother is huge – the greatest love human beings experience – and it demands complete reciprocity. The entrance into consciousness of the father introduces the double reality of someone else in my mother's world who needs her in a different way than the child does. In this school of thought, it is here that sexual identification begins, as the crisis is only mitigated or balanced with the 'promotion' of the child into the adult world of sexual identity: I am a girl (like mum) or a boy (like dad)! I am not arguing for the complete adoption of this analysis, and theology needs to collaborate with experts in this field and others on gender development to find an intelligent way forward. But Moore's point in relation to original sin versus original blessing is that 'the child's total zest for life, the sense of being welcome everywhere without strings attached, meets its first great disappointment in the mother's commitment to an "other" in an "other" way'. Enter disappointment. Enter a world view which begins to distrust desire and longing, to know frustration and to accept it as the norm. It is worth listening to Moore a bit more fully on this point:

> The most radical experience we have of original sin is the memory of beginning to realize that desire could not be trusted. The reason desire cannot be trusted is that I am beginning to doubt my desirability. The sense of desirability, that directed me happily through life in infancy, now no longer works for me, for I am no longer just 'this body' . . . I don't feel good with any conviction, and therefore I don't *do* what is good. So not

---

[30]Moore, *Let This Mind Be in You*, 71.

feeling good is the origin of the *sin* of not doing what is good. It is the 'original sin', the origin of sin.[31]

That is clear as far as it goes. The problem is that Christian theology (and its unhappy expression in some doctrinal statements) turned this around, confusing the real foundations of sin: 'how easy it is to *blame* the sense of being good and desirable that seems to have let us down. So we get the opposite version of what original sin is: original sin is the feeling of being good, it is 'pride', it is 'hedonism'. For Moore, this is the complete reversal of the doctrine of original sin.[32]

> Because this mistake is so easily made, it has pervaded the Christian moral tradition, which has come to place original sin in feeling good instead of in feeling bad, which is where it should be placed, and the Christian moral tradition has laid itself open to those critics who accuse it of propagating the very disease it claims to be curing.[33]

What disease? That we are not loved, loveable, desirable, fantastic, originally blessed and meant to feel glorious about it! Is it any wonder Marianne Williamson's famous passage resonates deeply with so many people?

> Our deepest fear is not that we are inadequate. Our deepest fear is that we are powerful beyond measure. It is our light, not our darkness that most frightens us. We ask ourselves, 'Who am I to be brilliant, gorgeous, talented, fabulous?' Actually, who are you not to be? You are a child of God. Your playing small does not serve the world. There is nothing enlightened about shrinking so that other people won't feel insecure around you. We are all meant to shine, as children do. We were born to make manifest the glory of God that is within us. It's not just in some of us; it's in everyone. And as we let our own light shine, we unconsciously give other people permission to do the same. As we are liberated from our own fear, our presence automatically liberates others.[34]

Our original and originating sin or 'no' to God is the 'no' to ourselves. It says:

> No, the Oedipal arrangement is absolute and final. Self-repression is what life is all about. . . . Visions are moonshine. We are only half desirable,

---

[31] Moore, *Let This Mind Be in You*, 83.
[32] From a different starting point, this converges with feminist analyses of the insufficiency of limited understandings of pride as the founding sin.
[33] Moore, *Let This Mind Be in You*, 83.
[34] Marianne Williamson, *A Return to Love* (New York: Harper Collins Publishers, 2005).

and half is OK. Sin is the refusal to grow. It is the canonizing of the status quo. It outlaws forever the child's sense of being all-desirable. Thus sin is not the *feeling* the child gets of not being all-desirable. It is the universal decision that this feeling is correct, is the thing to live by. Sin is self-denial. And this is the denial of God.[35]

For Moore, this does not mean that salvation or the return to a blessed sense of ourselves is something we can attain by ourselves. The drama of human life is one we are born into, larger and prior to us. 'Christian tradition has a name for the spiritual inertia that is woven into the human condition over and above personal: original sin.'[36] And this is where Moore's Christology and anthropology come together. Sin is a revealed reality, as discussed in chapter eight. It is not the simple realization that good is preferable over bad. Moore explores the life of Jesus as 'the sinless One', whose whole life radiated the trust and confidence born in his intimate knowledge of how loved he was by his Abba. We easily relate to Jesus as 'like us in all things but sin' (*Gaudium et spes* 22, quoting Heb. 4.15), but can forget that in some ways, Jesus *was not a bit like us*. For example, he mentions the repeated refrain from the Sermon on the Mount in which Jesus challenges Jewish law by placing his own authority over God's word as given in the law: 'it was said of old . . . but *I say* . . . ' (cf. Mt. 5.21-22, 27-28, 31-32, 33-34, 38-39, 43-44 etc.).[37] The life of Jesus was uninhibited by the shadow of doubt about his worth before God. Based on that trust, he *also* broke through every other kind of social and cultural distortion and marginalization of women, children, outcasts and sinners. Drawing on the Scripture studies of his time (albeit with freedom and perhaps overextending, slightly, his psychological conclusions), Moore describes the effect Jesus' life, death and subsequent resurrection must have had on the disciples. As the sinless one, 'Jesus enabled the disciples to experience the yes of God in an unparalleled way. With the whole of their religious faith caught up in the ecstatic experience of following Jesus of Nazareth, the disciples could experience his failure and tragic death only as the death of God.'[38] The experience of the resurrection, according to Moore, lays the foundation for the Council clarifications and declarations of the early Church. It was the birth of a completely new religious awareness:

> The new people who ran around saying 'Jesus is Lord' were giving expression to a new religious consciousness, an awareness of God

---

[35]Moore, *Let This Mind Be in You*, 77.
[36]Sebastian Moore, 'Jesus the Liberator of Desire: Reclaiming Ancient Images', *Downside Review* 108, no. 370 (1990): 1–19 (4–5).
[37]Cf. Moore, 'Jesus the Liberator of Desire: Reclaiming Ancient Images', 1–19 (8).
[38]Denis Edwards, 'Sebastian Moore', in *What Are They Saying about Salvation?*, 46–60 (54) (New York: Paulist Press, 1986).

without guilt. God was no longer culture's 'God': he had 'come out' from the corner of the soul where guilt locks him up; he was human, physical. But he didn't stop being mysterious, ultimate. To the consciousness of God as both mysterious and human at the same time they gave a special name. It was the name of the Holy Spirit, a super-consciousness in which everything came together and all people came together. . . . This is the origin of the two central Christian doctrines, of Incarnation and Trinity.[39]

It is *in and from* this experience of the risen Christ that the awareness of original sin is born. Only in the realization of what a free and forgiven world feels like could the early Christian Church *name* that originally, before this experience, things were not as they should be. They intuited an abyss of separation between the Creator and disharmony with each other and the world: 'They called it original sin. They saw it as something much more radical than the sins that people, even peoples, commit. It was a cut-off-ness from God that was somehow woven into the human condition and had been so since the beginning of human time. This is the doctrine of original sin.'[40]

Coming full circle to our question about whether original sin is an outdated doctrine which should be ditched, it would appear that the reality of human life and experience has much to offer Christian understanding. There is something deeply Spirit-led about humanity's fascination with children, the love between parents and their newborns, and our silent or spoken 'envy' of their exuberant ambitions. Chesterton's exploration of the 'Ethics of Elfland' and the truth of what we imagine is apropos: there is a certain way of looking at life, which was created by fairy tales and lets us imagine that what could happen *might just* happen, if we rethink how we see reality![41] Children return us to our sense of what *could* be. However, this truth of Christian faith needs reframing, and approaching it as repression (understood by psychoanalysis as forgetting plus forgetting that we forgot!) of our original blessedness is a wonderful starting point. And further theological exploration of how children image and reflect the likeness of God *in their own right* is necessary. Current theological explorations into the theological value and agency of children are promising.[42]

Moore's contribution is not perfect: some have described his approach to the human condition as overly 'male' and his use of Scripture overextended

---

[39] Moore, *The Fire and the Rose Are One*, 94–5.
[40] Moore, *Let This Mind Be in You*, 87.
[41] Cf. Chapter four of G. K. Chesterton, *Orthodoxy* (Garden City, NY: Image Books, 1959).
[42] Cf. James Gerard McEvoy, 'Theology of Childhood: An Essential Element of Christian Anthropology', *Irish Theological Quarterly* 84, no. 2 (2019): 117–36; James Gerard McEvoy, 'Towards a Theology of Childhood: Children's Agency and the Reign of God', *Theological Studies* 80, no. 3 (2019): 673–91.

in relation to interpretations of Jesus' effect on his disciples. However, his insights and contribution are compelling. In fact, the basic tenet of Moore's theology applies to a myriad of issues. We can find answers and pathways to theological insights *through*, and only through, human experience, not by working around it. They say that Sebastian Moore, with all his struggles and mental fragility, was curious, joyful, outspoken and enthusiastic to a ripe old age. Childlike, even, in some ways. Theology is autobiographical.

Song Unfolding (for Julian)

This song has a very specific origin. It was written for Julian, the first child of friends of mine in Australia who asked me to be his godmother. Two human experiences unfolded before my eyes during that time. The first was how this couple sought to prepare themselves for parenthood. The second, watching Julian in his first weeks of life and taking care of him, from time to time. The song tries to express what I saw and felt in that experience, so it is as much about being parents as about the wonders of new life.

The first verse focusses on the parents. Watching this couple prepare for the arrival of their son was moving. Alongside their joy and excitement, I saw the growing awareness of two emotionally intelligent people of what was on the horizon. I used to love the antics of an Argentinian comic strip character created by cartoonist Quino (Joaquín Salvador Lavado Tejón) called *Mafalda*, a compassionate and intelligent little girl who had simple opinions and questions about life and the world as she saw it. It became very influential in Argentina during the 1970s. In one of them she is arguing with her mother: 'Why do I have to do it?', she asks. 'Because I told you to and I am your *mother*', the mother's voice comes back. 'Well if it's a question of titles, I am your *daughter*!', she yells back, 'and we both graduated on the same day, right?'[43] And ain't that the truth? *By night awake . . . we all change names*. If anything should affect your sleep, it is walking through the door into being a parent. Everything will change, for the rest of your life. I asked Julian's father, David, to introduce the song for the CD launch. These were his words:

> It's a song written by a godmother for her newly born godson, but it is also much more than that. It captures all of the challenges and also all of the joys that come from new life, as *one hand uncurled conducts a world*. We don't get to choose our family, but we do get to choose every day, to recommit to love them. Because love always protects, always trusts,

---

[43]I have translated this comic strip from memory.

always perseveres; love never fails. Love remains. And he still has that clear smile, cool frown, deep sigh. This song is a lullaby. This song is an anthem.[44]

Is there a human love more like God's own than parenthood? *We'll do right by you. We'll always be here for you. Only love can stay your fears.* Admittedly, in other chapters and through the eyes of different theologians, I highlight the potential of friendship, and passion, to explore and even enter us into an experience of divine love, but parenthood seems to go that step further into the whole dynamic of self-giving that is the essence of a Creator God whose love *simply does not run out*. I am not a mother. I have helped many people come to life in faith and the bond feels mother*ly*, with a responsibility to nurture, care for, and protect, but I cannot express what human motherhood, an identity and role one takes on for life, feels like. I am a daughter, however, and the longer I live, the more I realize the ground upon which I walk is the unconditional love and commitment my parents showed and show me still. I have not given them the easiest pathway to walk: when one's youngest daughter leaves home at barely seventeen to explore a life as alien as missionary life was to Dubliners of the 1980s, you know loving and being loved by this daughter is not going to be how you thought it might. But that unconditional love, the choice they made once and for all, as well as daily, to love me is like a solid ground underpinning everything I experience, understand and decide, and has got me through *many* an existential crisis. David and Katrin have no idea who Julian will be and what he will do over the course of his life. But he and his siblings will *always* be the centre of their lives. And he was the one who gave them that gift, first. Parenthood is a theological space we need to listen to and explore more *in order to understand* the very life and love of God.

And then there is Julian: that explosion of life, love, joy and needs that one small, blue-eyed, blond boy can be! What is it about new life that makes human beings smile, react and stand in awe? Is it a window into God's abundance of life? Is it a mirror of how your own life once was and is perhaps still meant to be, because 'unless you change and become like children' (cf. Mt. 18.3), you will never know what life could be. We have no idea who children will become. Their personality emerges more quickly than expected as you watch someone being and becoming themselves, all at the same time. And there is no need to be naïve: we did not need Girard to tell us that children can be selfish and motivated by envy and selfishness, as we all are at times, but the point stands: new life both expresses and touches in all of us something pure, essential and human. One experience in particular lies behind the second verse: my experience of babysitting him for the first

---

[44] I am grateful to David Kirchhoffer and his wife Katrin Potthast, not only for these words but for having access to the world that the love they share opens for their family and beyond.

time – a sign of trust on the part of the parents, I knew. So, while trying to not disturb his sleep, every now and again (which was *often*) I would creep into the room to listen for life, and hear ... first silence ... and then a short but deep sigh, which mingled with my own. Phew! He's fine: *sleep tight!*[45]

'Song Unfolding' lyrics

And who are we, to feel so deep, for one unknown ...
... who'll call us home
Who are we ... new life to give? By night awake ... we all change names
And only love remains; We'll watch and wait as life takes shape
And only love will stay (yours fears)
So, sleep tight! Don't cry! Love life! Dream high, ..
And we'll do right by you ..
Blue eyes, clear smile, cool frown, deep sigh!
We'll always be here, for you.
So, who are you? So small, so new?
One hand uncurled conducts our world ...
We only have one rule in life: with open minds and hopeful hearts ...
To humbly walk with God;
And try to love what's right, and not lose sight (of what we know):
Only love prevails. So, sleep tight ...

©MAEVE LOUISE HEANEY, 2020.
Strange Life, The Music of Doubtful Faith

Selected further reading

For an introduction to Sebastian Moore's life and theology

Edwards, Denis. 'Sebastian Moore'. In *What Are They Saying about Salvation?*, 46–60. New York: Paulist Press, 1986.

Melling, Joseph. 'Sebastian Moore: A Life in Movements'. *Downside Review* (2018): 1–4.

Melling, Joseph. 'Sebastian Moore: Beyond Piety'. *Downside Review* 136, no. 3 (2018): 145–47.

Ormerod, Neil. 'Sebastian Moore: Psychological Theology'. In *Introducing Contemporary Theologies: The What and the Who of Theology Today*, 71–80. Alexandria, N. S. W.: E. J. Dwyer, 1997.

---

[45]'Song Unfolding' is here: https://res.cloudinary.com/bloomsbury-online-resources/video/upload/v1639138268/Suspended%20God/Song_Unfolding_For_Julian.wav

On Original sin

Moore, Sebastian. *Let This Mind Be in You: The Quest for Identity through Oedipus to Christ*. Minneapolis: Winston Press, 1985.

Moore's Existential Christology

Moore, Sebastian. *The Fire and the Rose Are One*. London: Darton, Longman & Todd, 1980.

His poetic approach to various theological themes

Moore, Sebastian. *The Contagion of Jesus: Doing Theology as If It Mattered*, edited by Stephen McCarthy. Maryknoll, NY: Orbis, 2007.

On the significance and influence of his theology

Loewe, William P. 'Sebastian Moore, Redemptive Transformation, and the Law of the Cross'. *Downside Review* 136, no. 3 (2018): 178–85.

Messias, Teresa. 'Desiring and Being Desired by Christ: Sebastian Moore's Notion of Desire in Dialogue with Ignatian Spirituality'. *Downside Review* 136, no. 3 (2018): 148–64.

Roy Op, Louis. 'Sebastian Moore's Spiritual Vision and Christological Project'. *Downside Review* 136, no. 3 (2018): 165–77.

10

Who's going to go to Heaven?

What will happen to those we love who are not Christians?

When I lived in England, where Saturday afternoon and soccer are synonyms, there was always a person in the crowd with a flag that was different from everyone else's. It was never commented on by officials and always carried the same message: Jn 3.16. You will also find Jn 3.16 inscribed on the soda cups of the *In-N-Out* fast-food chain in the United States. It is one of the most well-known readings from the Gospel of John which summarizes, in a way, the central message of the Christian Scriptures: 'For God so loved the world that he gave his only Son, so that everyone who believes in him may not perish but may have eternal life.' It evokes the central truth of the Christian story: The world exists because God loved it into existence, and is committed to enabling our life to the full. Somehow this world turned its back on the life and love for which it was created (the theme of chapter nine). However, God did not give up, initiating instead a story of salvation with us. This history began with the people of Israel and culminated with the sending of the second Person of our Triune God, who came, lived and loved, taught and healed, died and was risen from the dead. In that process of incarnating, dying and being risen to new life, we have been given the possibility of sharing that same eternal life: 'For God so loved the world . . .'.[1]

The two key notions of Christian faith here are 'eternal life' and what 'not perishing' means, which in the Christian tradition is usually described with the word 'salvation'. They are two of the most important words in Christian

---

[1] Although we do not address it in this chapter, it is worth noting that our understanding of eternal life as a continuation of our lives here is incomplete. It would be better to speak of 'eternity life' (a phrase coined by Johannine scholar, Mary Coloe), which better evokes the reality of the gift of God's life within that transforms our lives now, and which never ends.

theology, and yet somehow, they have often not been well understood. Unpacking this chapter's question implies exploring them more but let me first explain this chapter's fundamental question in the terms in which it has often been formulated and why it is so important. Christians believe in life after death; that when we die, it is not the end, but rather the beginning of a better life, without pain, or suffering, with God. The key to 'getting in' to this eternal life, as the passage notes, is faith in Jesus. I cannot buy my way in, nor is it a question of being good so that I can get rewarded, although all Christians would recognize that faith finds expression in a life of love and charity. We trust that after a life attempting to be open, and loving, lived in friendship with God, this will continue. Therefore, what happens to those who do not believe? Or, because where it cuts most is in relation to those we love, what happens to those we love who do not believe in Christ? If faith is the key to salvation, are they to be lost, whatever that might mean? Will they suffer? Are we never to see them again?

I have no doubt that this was one of the motivating forces behind someone who would spend their time during a football match holding an unpopular banner. They have come to experience something of the life to be found in Christianity and want others to access and know that life. Because the stakes are high, because being lost is a possibility. This is also the reason for the Church's mission: 'the Church exists to evangelise'[2] because what is at stake is the quality of life – now and forever – of humanity.

For a long time, in Christendom – when Christian culture and secular culture overlapped – this understanding of eternal life was taken for granted. Life was lived in the awareness that there was a God who could see the heart and to whom we are accountable, and whatever we might get away with during life, at the end of it, there was Someone we could not fool who would judge us. The options were three: reward in 'heaven', the place where God lives in an eternal joy in which we are allowed to share; punishment in an eternal hell of separation from God (which was imagined in terms of flames and torture); or purgatory, an intermediary punishment or preparation for heaven for those who were neither ready for heaven nor condemned to hell. Most Christian living was understood as a means to this end: a life of virtue fed by the sacraments as our 'ticket' through the Pearly Gates. This may seem alien to us now, but it was the real context of many people in the last century, including the parents of many of us working in theology now. So it is not far from memory or experience, and our focus here is on how this real question was dealt with and, I suggest, transformed by the thought and influence of this chapter's theologian.

The problems with this understanding of Christianity are legion: 'What kind of a God would send people to eternal suffering?' is the most central

---

[2]Paul VI, *Apostolic Exhortation Evangelii Nuntiandi* (Vatican City, 1976), 14.

one people ask. How can we reconcile that teaching with the good news of a loving God? It has led to theologians proposing that hell exists – since the real possibility of people turning their backs on God is a condition of human freedom – but it might be empty: a merciful God would surely never reject true repentance of a sinner! And there are other issues: What is Christian salvation? If it is mainly an other-worldly reward for good behaviour, then perhaps Marx was right that religion is the opium of the masses if it teaches people to *not* rebel against unjust action now, as *now* is not as important as *then*. Slave owners across the globe combined slavery with weekly Christian worship perfectly well, as do many of the 10 per cent of people owning 80 per cent of the world's riches, without a second thought about the potential unfairness of the system upon which our wealth is based. And what about those who have never heard about Christ and who therefore could *not* have faith in Christ? What about the people of other faiths, who were born into a culture in which news about Jesus was simply not available? Or those for whom Christianity has been a source of oppression and pain, making faith in Jesus untenable or inaccessible, due to no fault of their own? The questions can be posed in many ways, but ultimately, we all know people who are *good*, and open, generous and loving, who seem to be able to forgive and with whom we have deep connections that edify our own lives. It seems unthinkable that they would be 'outside' the reach of grace and of God's life.

Once again, there is a background of doctrine and thought underpinning this theme of which we need to be aware, in relation to the central Christian concepts of salvation, eternal life, heaven, human freedom and the identity of God as love. Salvation or redemption – as they are often used interchangeably although they have different nuances – refers to the need human beings have to be saved, or delivered, from a situation of slavery, or sin, by Another. Etymologically, salvation means 'to deliver from some danger and bring to safety' from the late Latin *salvare* 'make safe, secure' and the old French *sauver*. 'To redeem' is drawn from the Latin *redimere* 'to redeem, buy back' and could also mean to make amends. These connotations have played a part in the long history of theology's developing understanding of *how* Jesus' life, death and resurrection saved us from sin and give us eternal life.[3] But the core message is clear and undisputed: Jesus' life, lived out in complete openness to God even unto losing his life as a cost of that faithfulness, restored humanity to itself. It is a present reality and future hope. Christianity – and this deeply hopeful and seemingly impossible truth at times needs to be stated – holds that there *will* come a time in which pain, suffering, wars, injustice and death will pass; that there will be winners and losers: sin and evil will lose, and Life will win. That is what salvation means. Underlying each of these concepts

---

[3] One of the most influential *and* contested notions has been St Anselm's 'theory of satisfaction', according to which God's offended honour could only be satisfied by the sacrifice of the God-man, Jesus Christ. It is, however, a theme for another chapter!

is an understanding of the human person and community as created in and for freedom. Made in the image and likeness of a God who loves, we are free (even though that freedom may be a wounded one, in need of help, but God will not force us to receive life): we can open to God's grace, or we can remain closed to it. The Church's defence of the possibility of someone *not* being saved (that is to say, the notion of hell or eternal separation from God) is simply the consequence of taking freedom seriously: we can refuse help.

The issue is *who* can be 'saved' and *how*? Herein lies our question, and again, it is not a new one. The first theologians of the early centuries of Christian thought (known as the Fathers of the Church) were already asking about the generations *before* Jesus' coming. If faith in Jesus is the premise, are they irredeemably lost? This seemed untenable and in various ways they answered in the negative, united in the faith that God's divine plan was working in an invisible way. An example of this is Justin's 'seeds of the logos' present in creation or the Apostolic Creed's description of Jesus 'descending into hell' to retrieve those who had been lost before his coming. Later, the attempt to say that human nature was not really so affected by sin that we should *need* grace as a free gift emerged with Pelagianism and semi-Pelagianism, but they were rejected as heresies. Grace is necessary for salvation, and grace is a free gift received through faith and baptism into the body of Christ.

The biggest issue has been played out in relation to the Church. The life of grace as one received and lived out in the community of the Church is an essential dimension of Christian faith from the beginning: 'He who believes and is baptized shall be saved, but he who does not believe shall be condemned' (Mk 16.16). Origen (*c.* 184–*c.* 253) was the first to formulate the dogmatic axiom *Extra Ecclesiam Nulla Salus* (no salvation outside of the Church), and although it was never fully accepted by all as referring to the physical and historically identifiable reality of the Catholic Church, much ink has been poured out debating just what 'the church' could mean here and how salvation could be received by those who did not join it. Some denominations take quite literally that whoever does not explicitly confess faith in Jesus is automatically condemned. Conversely, in such a belief system, whoever does confess Jesus is automatically saved. A minimally attentive look at the lives of many Christians makes this second statement at least as problematic as the first! Ironically, it is not a very well-known fact that for Catholics, such a statement would be heretical: we have no guarantee of our salvation but God's goodness, so our faith is one of trust, as only God knows the human fate. However, the role of the Church in our salvation is a doctrine of faith: the Church is necessary for salvation. It has been stated often in the history of Church tradition, so the theological question is how to understand it: What happens to those we love who do not belong to the Church?

Our lens for this question is Karl Rahner, SJ. My aim in this chapter is to show not only how he theologizes on the issue but also how his work witnesses to how theology can mark Church teaching and spirituality. Rahner is one of the most important theologians of the twentieth century on whom many others have built their thought. We speak a lot about him, but I fear that his writings are accessed less than they used to be, so where possible and within the limits of space, I have sought to quote him directly.

Karl Rahner, SJ: Our 'last' systematic theologian?

Karl Rahner was born on 5 March 1904 in Freiburg in Breisgau, Germany.[4] He joined the Society of Jesus in 1922 at the age of eighteen and studied philosophy and theology from 1924 to 1933. He started a doctorate in Philosophy at Freiburg in 1934 and although he took classes with Heidegger, he chose to do his thesis under Martin Honecker. Honecker eventually failed Rahner's dissertation on knowledge in Thomas Aquinas, terminating his doctoral studies. It is helpful to know about such a 'failure' in the life of arguably the most important Catholic theologian of the twentieth century! He was successful the second time around at Innsbrück, with a dissertation on the Church as second Eve issuing from the wounded side of Jesus in Jn 19.24, although Rahner himself is somewhat scathing about the quality of that work.[5] Despite aspiring to be a pastor, Rahner was assigned to teach theology, and from early on began to distance himself from neo-scholastic approaches to theologizing, preferring biblical and Patristic sources. His interest in the theme of grace – arguably the most central theme of his theology – developed early as well. He described grace as 'God's self-communication to human beings'. Bear in mind that this was still more than twenty years before the Second Vatican Council's Constitution on Divine Revelation *Dei Verbum*!

Rahner lived through two world wars: during the first he was still at school, but it affected his family insofar as one of his brothers was injured in it. He was teaching at Innsbrück in Austria when the Nazis closed it in 1938, whereupon he did pastoral work until he returned to teaching. The concerns he was exposed to during this time of pastoral ministry and postwar Germany are easily seen in his approach to theology over the course of his life. He will dedicate himself to bridging the gap between the world and the Church. Rahner taught at Innsbrück from 1948 until 1964. He spent three years at the University of Munich (1964–7) before taking a Chair in the University of Münster, in 1967, until 1981. He died in 1984.

---

[4]There are many exceptional introductions to Rahner's life and thought. I recommend Herbert Vorgrimler, *Understanding Karl Rahner: An Introduction to His Life and Thought* (London: SCM Press, 1986); John J O'Donnell, *Karl Rahner* (Rome: PUG, 1986); Harvey D. Egan, *Karl Rahner: Mystic of Everyday Life* (New York: Crossroad Pub. Co., 1998).
[5]Cf. Karl Rahner, *The Origin of the Church as the Second Eve from the Side of Christ the Second Adam: An Investigation of The Typological Significance of John 19:34* (Innsbruck, 1936).

Rahner and the Church

Rahner's whole theological enterprise is one lived out in the service of the Church and Catholic theology. Since his contribution to the Church is one of our subjects in this chapter, it is helpful to note his experiences of and interaction with the Church over the course of his life. During his first theology studies in the Netherlands, the Church was still in defensive mode towards the challenges of modernist ideas, and all of his lecturers had to take the Oath against Modernism. However, despite the fact that much of Rahner's work involved an attempt to help the Church dialogue with the world rather than react against it, most of his writing and teaching was well received. Jesuit writings always go through an internal censorship process, which tends to help avoid most issues, but at times his interest and freedom in seeking to reinterpret aspects of Catholic teaching led the Vatican to pay him more attention. He had minor skirmishes, such as when he questioned the logic behind each priest saying 'his own Mass' daily in favour of concelebration.[6] He was vetoed from writing on the theme by Pope Pius XI. His essay on what the dogma of the perpetual virginity of Mary might actually mean[7] also led to his writings drawing more careful scrutiny and censorship. However, in 1963 he was named a *peritus* (expert advisor) to the Second Vatican Council by Pope John XXIII, and as I explore in the next section, he left his mark on its most significant documents. During and after the Council, Rahner became well known outside Germany, mainly through his work there and the translation of some of his work into English. In later years, Rahner would comment on the failure of the Church to implement the spirit of the Council and his disappointment at what he called a 'wintry season' of the world *and* Church.[8] He was a man of Church, as fierce in his sense of belonging as he was in his call for it to change. This piece on not stifling the Spirit's action in the Church reflects well both his position and his passion:

> Where is the courage we need to become engaged in the questions of our time, really to face up to them, really to feel the burden of them? . . . . We are passing through a revolutionary change in the times, a change which we certainly do not over-estimate, but rather underestimate . . .
>
> It is extremely painful and bitter to put forward accusations when one does not know how to alter the state of affairs which is being complained

---

[6]Only later translated and published as Karl Rahner, *The Celebration of the Eucharist* (New York: Herder and Herder, 1968).
[7]Karl Rahner, 'Virginitas in Partu', in *Theological Investigations IV*, 134–62 (London: Darton, Longman and Todd, 1974).
[8]Cf. Karl Rahner, *Faith in a Wintry Season: Conversations and Interviews with Karl Rahner in the Last Years of His Life*, ed. P. Imhof, H. Biallowons, and H. D. Egan (New York: Crossroad, 1990).

of. Nor do these observations of mine imply that everything in every department of the Church's life is in a bad state. On the contrary there is much that is filled with the Spirit and alive with divine life, love, faithfulness, patience in bearing the Cross, apostolic work which is full of self-sacrifice, youthful courage, theological acumen, a determination to tackle fresh problems and much else besides of which the Spirit is the prime dispenser . . .

Today, when we are struggling to solve the real problems which confront us, we should not, properly speaking say: 'How far must I go?' because the very nature of the situation itself absolutely compels us to go at least as far as possible. We should be asking ourselves, rather: 'How far can we go by taking advantage of all the possibilities in the pastoral and theological spheres?'[9]

In the words of Johann-Baptist Metz: 'In good Jesuit fashion, Rahner seems almost like a natural churchman. So he has this Church in his guts, and feels its failures like indigestion.'[10]

Theology in collaboration

Over the course of his life, Rahner worked with some major theological and ecclesial figures of the twentieth century: as a young lecturer, conversations with Hans Urs von Balthasar formed the basis for a piece entitled 'A Scheme for a Treatise of Dogmatic Theology',[11] since both young Jesuits were of the view that the neo-scholastic theology they had received needed reformation. During the Council, Karl Rahner and Joseph Ratzinger, both experts aiding the bishops, wrote a document that was instrumental in changing the direction of conversations on revelation and shaping what later became *Dei Verbum*.[12] Johann-Baptist Metz was a student of his who explored the political and social dimensions of grace. Some of these collaborators moved in different directions to Rahner during his life, challenging the influential theology of grace he developed: Ratzinger because of his more negative view of modern culture after 1968; Balthasar for what he thought was too anthropological an approach to theology and his notion of 'anonymous Christianity';[13] and Metz for what he perceived as an overly individualistic

---

[9]Karl Rahner, 'Do Not Stifle the Spirit!', in *Theological Investigations VII*, ed. D. Bourke, 72–87 (77–81) (New York: Seabury, 1977).
[10]Quoted in Vorgrimler, *Understanding Karl Rahner*, 37.
[11]Publishing in Karl Rahner, *Theological Investigations I: God, Christ, Mary and Grace*, ed. C. Ernst, (London: Darton, Longman & Todd, 1974), 19–37.
[12]Later published as Karl Rahner and Joseph Ratzinger, *Revelation and Tradition* (New York: Herder and Herder, 1966).
[13]Cf. in particular Hans Urs von Balthasar, *The Moment of Christian Witness* (San Francisco,

notion or understanding of grace.[14] Rahner, however, names Metz as a colleague and friend all his life, and his influence is perceptible in some of his writings. He strongly challenged Ratzinger in a public letter when the latter blocked Metz's appointment to a Chair in Munich, in 1979.[15]

He is said to have valued friendships dearly. Later in life – and in connection with a theme of friendship that I speak to in the final section of this chapter – Rahner speaks of life as one in companionship. The image is a military one, with those who form part of your life marching in your column and the unfillable loss felt as you lose them. The piece, called 'God of the Living', is moving:

> I should like to remember my dead to You, O Lord, all those who once belonged to me and have now left me. . . . When I look back in this way, I see my life as a long highway filled with a column of marching men. Every moment someone breaks out of the line and goes off silently, without a word or wave of farewell, to be swiftly enwrapped in the darkness of the night stretching out of both sides of the road. The number of marchers gets smaller and smaller, for the new men coming up to fill the ranks are really not marching in my column at all . . . for the only ones making the pilgrimage with me are those with whom I set out together, the ones who were with me at the very start of my journey to you, my God.[16]

One of his last acts – in the troubled 1980s – was to write to the bishops of Peru in support of Gustavo Gutierrez's theology of liberation.[17]

Rahner's theology and writings

Rahner has hundreds of titles to his name, so it is challenging to represent fairly the breadth of his knowledge and theology. At this stage, perhaps his most well-known writings are a large series of theological explorations on a breadth of themes published in a series called *Theological Investigations*. In the original German there are sixteen, in English, twenty-three. In chapters of varying length, they cover a legion of theological themes, with impressive expertise and dominion of each. The richness of these writings, which I draw from in the next section, is Rahner's capacity to name the

---

CA: Ignatius Press, 1994), frequently cited using part of its original title: *Cordula*.
[14]Cf. Johann Baptist Metz, *Faith in History and Society: Toward a Practical Fundamental Theology*, ed. N. D. Smith (London: Burns and Oates, 1980), 154–68.
[15]Cf. John L. Allen, *Pope Benedict XVI: A Biography of Joseph Ratzinger* (New York: Continuum, 2000), 124–5.
[16]Karl Rahner, *Encounters with Silence* (Westminster: Newman Press, 1960), 53–4.
[17]Cf. Fergus Kerr, 'Karl Rahner', in *Twentieth-Century Catholic Theologians: From Neoscholasticism to Nuptial Mysticism*, 87–104 (90) (Malden, MA: Blackwell Pub, 2007).

issue at stake, describe the teaching of the Church on the issue, including its historical development, and offer balanced and nuanced positions that even now, when some of the themes are dated, make sense. It is this breadth of knowledge and capacity of drawing a broad spectrum of teaching to bear on any given issue which earned him the title of this section, as least as a question: Is he the last 'systematic theologian' who can write so well about theological themes without needing to recur to other experts? The lack of reference notes in his writings is a point in fact. He himself admitted the shifts in theological expertise and the multiplication of knowledge in the twentieth century:

> Forty years ago the ratio between what I knew, and the problems, available information, and methods, was maybe 1:4; today it's more like 1:400.[18]

And he was aware of the fact that there were new methods and approaches to theology he could not integrate. The future of the Church and theology would be global; others would take his thought further than he could, and different contexts would give birth to new theologies, but he continued to do what he did, writing on just about everything with thoroughness and thoughtfulness: the last 'systematic theologian' of a certain kind.

The background to that breadth of knowledge may be Rahner's editorial involvement in a series of large compendiums, encyclopaedias and dictionaries of theology that demanded of him a thorough knowledge of a broad area of fields. These include a *Handbook of Creeds, Definitions and Declarations* called the *Enchiridion symbolorum definitionum et declarationum*, known as the 'Denzinger' after its first editor; a *Lexicon for Theology and Church* (thirteen volumes); a *Handbook for Pastoral Theology* (five volumes); *Mysterium Salutis – The Mystery of Salvation* (five volumes), to name a few.[19] Rahner's first major published work is his failed philosophy dissertation on Thomas Aquinas, published as *Spirit in the World*[20] in the original German *Geist in Welt* in 1939. Based on his analysis of Aquinas' thought, the thesis defended the human capacity to 'know' God, due to an innate restlessness that attracts them to God in a dynamic apprehension of reality. The influence of Kant is clear here, although underlying influences also include Belgian Joseph Maréchal's (1878–1944) understanding of Kant and interpretations of Aquinas' thought by French Jesuit Pierre Rousselot (1887–1915).[21] His second major book, *Hearers of the Word*, was born of

---

[18]Rahner, *Faith in a Wintry Season*, 19.
[19]It gave him an overview of core themes that laid a solid foundation for future thinking. In the age of the internet, where everyone has an opinion on everything and authority is self-made, this is a useful piece of information. As a theology lecturer, it baffles me how hard it is to make students understand the importance of a good theological dictionary and handbook.
[20]Cf. Karl Rahner, *Spirit in the World*, trans. W. Dych, ed. (London: Sheed & Ward, 1968).
[21]This classic work by a man who died very young has had major influence on our theology of

his lectures on 'Foundations of a Philosophy of Religion' in Innsbrück. It explores what it is to be a human person, inhabiting the world as embodied while open and receptive to 'hearing' the Word. He became known in the English-speaking world for the translation of a work summarizing his approach entitled *Foundations of Christian Faith: An Introduction to the Idea of Christianity*.[22] It has been understood and read as a synthesis of his thought, although for Rahner himself it was, as its subtitle suggests, an academic introduction to Christianity.

In terms of style, Rahner's work in these books is generally complex and highly philosophical in tone.[23] The influences of Heidegger and Kant are clear, and some criticize the lack of biblical references and Scriptural analysis (a gap he was aware of and chose to leave to others). However, the complexity of some aspects of Rahner's terminology and philosophical underpinnings does not paint the full picture of Rahner's writings. At times there is magnificent prose interwoven in his theology, and the more poetic and spiritual writings provide a good entry point to his intentionality and achievements.

His first known writing at the age of twenty-two was entitled *Sehnsucht nach dem geheimnisvollen Gott* (*Longing for the Mysterious God*) and is a simple and unacademic exhortation to prayer.[24] It is always interesting to note the first theme a person writes on, as it often shows something of the underlying motivation and passion that moves them. In Rahner, this is also the case: his writings on prayer are beautiful and reveal much of the underlying motivation for the theology he dedicated his life to. Two examples suffice to make my point: 'Prayer for Creative Thinkers' is a two-page prayer-manifesto on the need for creative thinkers,[25] begging God to raise them up. *Encounters with Silence*[26] is a series of chapters written completely *to* God about various dimensions of life and faith, such as God's love for him, his daily routine, his difficulties in hearing answers to his prayer, death, and so on. Each chapter begins with prayed evocation of God: 'God of . . . '. Some commentators refer to Rahner's prayer-life as his *leitmotif*, the recurring theme underpinning his theology of grace and an access point to his theology: 'Karl Rahner the human being expresses

---

faith. Cf. Pierre Rousselot, *The Eyes of Faith*, trans. Joseph Dunceel SJ (New York: Fordham University Press, 1990).

[22]Cf. Karl Rahner, *Foundations of Christian Faith: An Introduction to the Idea of Christianity*, ed. W. V. Dych (London: Darton Longman & Todd, 1978).

[23]His brother Hugo (also a Jesuit) allegedly quipped that in his retirement he would translate Karl into German!

[24]It is partially reproduced as 'Why We Need to Pray' in Karl Rahner, *Spiritual Writings*, ed. P. Endean (Maryknoll, NY: Orbis Books, 2004), 31–3.

[25]Cf. Karl Rahner, 'Prayer for Creative Thinkers', *Theological Investigations V*, 130–1 (London: Darton, Longman and Todd, 1971).

[26]Cf. Rahner, *Encounters with Silence*.

himself in his prayers, with his disappointments and his longings, with his theology, with his human heart in which there was love and from which anger could arise. The prayers are therefore an appropriate approach to Karl Rahner.'[27] The conviction that God could touch and be experienced in human life is the golden thread of this theology: 'his key theological insights revolve around the intuition that all men and women have the capacity to have an experience of God, indeed an immediate experience of God'.[28]

This 'everyday mysticism'[29] symbolizes his theological conviction that God could be found in human life and in fact that human life itself was an expression of God's grace. His lapidary statement is well known: 'the devout Christian of the future will either be a "mystic", one who has "experienced" something, or he will cease to be anything at all'.[30] What is less known is the context within which it was said and the meaning it held for him. Rahner is not denying that there are 'mystics' with a special type of vision and experience, but he is bringing personal experience of God into the heart of Christian living as essential to its continuation and growth. His underlying concern is pastoral: the future of Christian living in a rapidly changing culture: 'For devout Christian living as practised in the future will no longer be sustained and helped by the unanimous, manifest and public convictions and religious customs of all, summoning each one from the outset to a personal experience and a personal decision.'[31] Essential elements of this 'everyday mysticism' include:

1. Direct personal relationship with God, in which we maintain a constant closeness to this God;
2. Recognition of the world as a place of God's implicit presence and active responsible action towards that end: 'Wherever secular life is lived with unreserved honesty there *ipso facto* an essential element in religious life is already present because God loves the world in itself, endows it with grace in itself and in no sense regards it as a rival to himself [sic] as though he [sic] were envious of it.';
3. A new asceticism to guide our lives and enable us to love God since 'moderation is no longer imposed from without'.[32]

---

[27]Vorgrimler, *Understanding Karl Rahner*, 10.
[28]O'Donnell, *Karl Rahner*, 7–8.
[29]Karl Rahner, *Everyday Things* (London: Sheed and Ward, 1965). Egan, *Mystic of Everyday Life*.
[30]Rahner, 'Christian Living Formerly and Today', 15.
[31]Rahner, 'Christian Living Formerly and Today', 15.
[32]Rahner, 'Christian Living Formerly and Today', 11–20. In this quest, he saw the emerging phenomenon of the secular institutes as key to testing out and developing new ways of Christian living.

This call to an awareness of the presence of God in the everyday and to experience that God is, in Rahner's own understanding, the centre of his life's work. He pens a reflection by Ignatius of Loyola (one of the founders of the Jesuits, initiator of the Spiritual Exercises and the understanding of spirituality as finding God in all things) which he later calls his spiritual testament: 'Ignatius of Loyola Speaks to a Modern Jesuit.'[33] In a tribute to Rahner on his seventieth birthday, Metz places Rahner's mystagogical approach to theology at the centre of his life's work, calling it a 'biographical dogmatic theology' or a 'mystical biography of the Christian believer today', because of how he had taken 'the many and varied needs and questions of others' into a theological mediation between biography and dogmatic theology.[34]

One final word about Rahner's writing, and it is linked to his awareness of the effects of cultural changes on language and their capacity to 'speak' to the human reality. Rahner perceived an internal tiredness and deafness to the word that is particularly challenging for Christianity, 'as the religion of the word proclaimed, of faith which hears and of a sacred scripture, has a special intrinsic relationship to the *word*'.[35] So he has numerous writings on the need for poetry and creativity, both in the world and in theology.[36] 'Rahner wanted to begin at the deepest dimension, the deepest desires of men and women, and formulate the answer in the most contemporary language possible, without repeating worn out, empty concepts.'[37] Underpinning these writings is a deep sense of the sacramentality of the Word:

> Our word is more than a thought: it is a thought become incarnate . . . the word is the embodied thought, not the embodiment of the thought.[38]
>
> Everything is redeemed by the word . . . which is 'the sacrament by means of which the realities communicate themselves to man, in order to achieve their own destiny'.[39]

---

[33]Karl Rahner, 'Ignatius of Loyola Speaks to a Modern Jesuit', in *Ignatius of Loyola*, ed. H. N. Loose, R. Ockenden, and P. Imhof (London: Collins, 1979); quoted in Rahner, *Spiritual Writings*, 35.
[34]See the expansion and development of that tribute in Johann Baptist Metz, 'Excursus: Theology as Biography', *Faith in History and Society: Toward a Practical Fundamental Theology*, 219–28 (London: Burns and Oates, 1980).
[35]Karl Rahner, 'Poetry and the Christian', in *Theological Investigations IV*, ed. H. F. Tiblier 357–67 (357) (London: Darton, Longman and Todd, 1974).
[36]Cf. Karl Rahner, 'Priest and Poet', in *Theological Investigations III*, 294–316 (London: Darton, Longman & Todd, 1967); 'Poetry and the Christian', 357–67; 'The Task of the Writer in Relation to Christian Living', in *Theological Investigations VIII: Further Theology of the Spiritual Life*, ed. D. Bourke, 112–29 (London: Darton, Longman and Todd, 1971); 'Prayer for Creative Thinkers', 130–1.
[37]Vorgrimler, *Understanding Karl Rahner*, 130–1.
[38]Rahner, 'Priest and Poet', 294–316 (295).
[39]Rahner, 'Priest and Poet', 294–316 (300–1).

He talks of the depth of the human word, referring to what he calls 'primordial words' (*Urworte*), the words of poets in which 'there is signified a piece of reality in which a door is mysteriously opened to us into the unfathomable depths of true reality in general'.[40] Hence the need for writers, ministers, artists, poets, theologians and priests 'endowed with creative powers' who grapple with the meaning of words: 'We have need of them!'[41]

Standing in the gap as theology becomes Church teaching

We return to the question of salvation this chapter poses: Who will be saved? And can there be salvation outside the Church? It is a question Rahner struggled with as well, as is clear from the sheer volume of articles on themes of faith, belief and atheism.[42] The central one raising our question is called 'The Christian among Unbelieving Relations'.[43] In fact, he considered bridging the gap between the grounds of credibility of Christian revelation and the actual decision to believe as an essential emerging task for theology.[44] His response to whether there is salvation outside the church is a resounding yes, based on a carefully constructed theology of grace. His basic tenets, which ground everything, are clear:

1. *God's universal will of salvation*: God 'desires everyone to be saved and to come to the knowledge of the truth' (1 Tim. 2.4). So, since God *wants* all people to be saved, transforming grace is offered to *all*, often in hidden and unseen ways;

2. *Transcendental or implicit revelation*: the offer of grace to every person in an implicit way constitutes the very nature of their personhood; and human beings respond to grace – affirmatively or negatively – in every act of knowing and loving;

3. *Categorical or explicit revelation*: the explicit revelation of Jesus Christ in and through the witness and preaching of the Church, to which human beings respond with Christian faith, baptism and entry into the community of believers.

---

[40]Rahner, 'Priest and Poet', 294–316 (298).
[41]Rahner, 'Prayer for Creative Thinkers', 130–1 (130).
[42]By way of example, Karl Rahner, 'The Faith of the Christian and the Doctrine of the Church', in *Theological Investigations XIV*, ed. D. Bourke, 24–45 (New York: Seabury, 1976); 'Thoughts on the Possibility of Belief Today', in *Theological Investigations V*, ed. K.-H. Kruger, 3–22 (London: Darton, Longman & Todd, 1975); 'Faith between Rationality and Emotion', in *Theological Investigations XVI*, ed. D. Morland, 60–78 (London: Darton, Longman and Todd, 1979); 'Intellectual Honesty and Christian Faith', 47–71.
[43]Rahner, 'The Christian among Unbelieving Relations', 355–72.
[44]Rahner, 'Reflections on a New Task for Fundamental Theology', 156–66 (164).

God wants all humanity to be saved, and if salvation implies faith which is a gift of grace, then that grace has to be made available to the immense amount of people who, for many reasons, do not have the chance of explicitly hearing about or accepting the Christian message. Every person lives within the presence or horizon of grace as an offer or invitation, which they can accept or reject. In his own words:

> Because God in his grace wills the salvation of all of humankind there can really be no night of atheism which would not be pierced within by a ray of light as long as human beings do not close themselves off to God by an act of ultimate culpability. . . . Atheists gaze inculpably into their night. They do not reflect that on the horizon behind them the sun is already rising and that for this reason their night is not as absolutely pitch black as it would be if God and his grace were not at work behind them, thus giving witness to himself as they stand with their backs turned gazing in the other direction.[45]

God's universal offer of supernatural grace floods human existence even when it's not recognized. Grace lights up human existence as human, and we accept or reject that grace in our knowing and loving. In theological terms, Rahner links this understanding of grace with what theology has called 'habitual grace' and 'actual grace'.[46]

This leads Rahner to he calls transcendental or implicit revelation. Transcendental is understood here in the Heideggerian sense of it being an inalienable structure of the human life while still being utterly free and universal. Rahner calls the presence of grace in the human person that constitutes their being 'supernatural existential'. Human beings receive this grace (even if not explicitly recognized as such) to make available faith in revelation and reach their supernatural destiny. This grace is intrinsic to the anthropological structure of humanity as transcendent, open to and tending towards God, in the living out of everyday life, whether the content of their knowledge or actions be explicitly religious or not. Such grace transforms human consciousness. It is Rahner's contested – and ill-named – 'anonymous Christianity': those who orientate their lives in an implicit but real way open and responsive to this grace make up the group of what he called 'anonymous Christians'.[47]

> Even if a man does not think of God as part of his conscious vocabulary or even feels he has to reject such a concept as self-contradictory, he

---

[45]Karl Rahner, 'The Church and Atheism', in *Theological Investigations XXI: Science and Christian Faith*, ed. H. M. Riley, 137–50 (145) (New York: Crossroad, 1982).
[46]Cf. Karl Rahner, 'On the Theology of Worship', *Theological Investigations XIX*, 141–9 (London: Darton, Longman and Todd, 1984).
[47]Karl Rahner, 'Anonymous Christians', *Theological Investigations VI*, 390–8 (London: Darton Longman & Todd, 1969).

is nevertheless always and inevitably involved with God in his secular awareness.[48]

There must be a Christian theory to account for the fact that every individual who does not in any absolute or ultimate sense act against his own conscience can say and does say in faith, hope, and love, Abba within his own spirit, and is on these grounds in all truth a brother [sic] to Christians in God's sight. This is what the theory of the anonymous Christian seeks to say, and, in so far as it is valid, what it implies.[49]

He did not leave it there, as if implicit knowledge were enough and mission not necessary! This implicit revelation tends to and is completed by the explicit proclamation of Jesus (which he calls categorical revelation), and in fact, *all* grace, in Rahner's view, is Christ-centred, even when one is unaware of it:

Everyone who is saved is saved only through the grace of Christ. There is no work which might be of use for eternal life unless it is accomplished in the grace of Christ. But this does not mean that all this happens only where the man himself [sic] expressly knows that it happens in the grace of Christ in the sphere of his objective, conceptually articulated knowledge.[50]

However, this theology was challenged, at first, in very strong terms. Some took exception to his anthropological starting point,[51] others to his interpretation of Kant, and others to the perceived relativization of the church and mission in its mediation of salvation. The charge is that emphasizing the implicit openness of the human person (and communities) to God relativizes the uniqueness of Christian revelation and is too anthropocentric.[52] In my opinion, Rahner's position is too ecclesial and his perception of grace too Christ-centred to uphold these accusations. For Rahner, grace is not a 'natural' opening to God; it is fruit of God's reaching out to humanity in Jesus and the very sign of the presence and invitation of grace.

---

[48]Rahner, 'Anonymous and Explicit Faith', 52–9 (55).
[49]Rahner, 'Observations on the Problem of the Anonymous Christian', 280–94 (294).
[50]Rahner, 'The Christian among Unbelieving Relations', 355–72 (365).
[51]The most vocal and famous opposition came from Balthasar, who accused him of anthropological and subjectivist reduction of theology and Christianity. For a comprehensive and balanced response to these critics, see Francis P. Fiorenza's Introduction to Rahner, *Spirit in the World*, xix–xiv.
[52]Of these criticisms, the most famous is that of Hans Urs von Balthasar. For a balanced appraisal and critique of the positions of Rahner and Balthasar, see Eamon Conway, *The Anonymous Christian – a Relativised Christianity? An Evaluation of Hans Urs von Balthasar's Criticism of Karl Rahner's Theory of the Anonymous Christian* (New York: Peter Lang, 1993).

I would suggest that the title 'anonymous' Christians is misleading, if not a bit patronizing, in that those who do not call themselves Christians are not likely to want us to call them so. But hindsight is twenty-twenty, and Rahner's was another time. He was trying to name and theologically ground the reality that grace is at work in people before and as they hear the Word, and before they are baptized.[53] This is not new teaching. When 'no salvation outside the Church' was interpreted as no salvation outside of the walls of the Roman Catholic Church, that church itself recognized it as heresy. However, a theology of grace that enables us to understand and recognize what might be happening in the world and in each person before they are baptised was necessary, and Rahner's gives us that.

Rahner sought to respond to misunderstandings about his theology of anonymous Christianity in many writings, but one stands out: *Reflections on the Experience of Grace*. In it, he is trying to explain how that hidden grace in an anonymous Christian's heart is not a lowering of Jesus' standards of love but a real and active presence, even when unnamed:

> Have we ever kept quiet, even though we wanted to defend ourselves when we had been unfairly treated? Have we ever forgiven someone even though we got no thanks for it and our silent forgiveness was taken for granted? Have we ever obeyed, not because we had to and because otherwise things would have become unpleasant for us, but simply on account of that mysterious, silent, incomprehensible being we call God and his will? Have we ever sacrificed something without receiving any thanks or recognition for it, and even without a feeling of inner satisfaction? Have we ever been absolutely lonely? Have we ever decided on some course of action purely by the innermost judgement of our conscience, deep down where one can no longer tell or explain it to anyone, where one is quite alone and knows that one is taking a decision which no one else can take in one's place and for which one will have to answer for all eternity?[54]

God's grace poured out in Christ is at work in these moments, whether or not we name it thus.

Rahner's theology of grace and Church teaching

The tasks of the magisterium of the Church and of theology are different, even though they both pertain to the prophetic and teaching dimensions of Christian ministry: the former is necessarily more protective and pastoral, the latter more forward looking and creative in the attempt

---

[53]The church has long recognized a baptism of 'desire' in those who want to be Christians before they become one or despite never reaching that step.
[54]Rahner, 'Reflections on the Experience of Grace', 86–90 (87).

to bridge Christianity and culture. It is moving to see how theology can and does influence and inform Church teaching, not only when we work collaboratively together but also in our writings and teachings. This is the case with Rahner's theology of grace. He does not name his own influence, but he does identify that the Council was surprisingly receptive to a hopeful and inclusive understanding of salvation:

> This optimism concerning salvation appears to me one of the most noteworthy results of the Second Vatican Council. For when we consider the officially received theology concerning all these questions, which was more or less traditional right down to the Second Vatican Council, we can only wonder how few controversies arose during the Council with regard to these assertions of optimism concerning salvation, and wonder too at how little opposition the conservative wing of the Council brought to bear on this point, how all this took place without any setting of the stage or any great stir.[55]

It is hard not to recognize an authoritative echo of his voice in the following statements of the *Pastoral Constitution on the Church in the Modern World, Gaudium et spes* 22, on the redemption of humanity in the person of Christ:

> All this holds true not only for Christians, but for all men [sic] of good will in whose hearts grace works in an unseen way (cf. *LG* 16). For, since Christ died for all (cf. Rm 8: 32) and since the ultimate vocation of man [sic] is in fact one, and divine, we ought to believe that the Holy Spirit *in a manner known only* to God offers to every man the possibility of being associated with this paschal mystery.

This paragraph of *Gaudium et spes* refers back to paragraph sixteen of the *Dogmatic Constitution on the Church, Lumen gentium*, which describes a long list of those who are 'related in various ways to the People of God': the people of Israel, those of other faiths who believe in one God, all those who 'in shadows' seek an unknown God and those who no fault of their own do not know the gospel or the Church and strive to live a good life, 'for it is God who gives to all men [sic] life and breath and all things, and as Saviour wills that all men be saved (cf. 2 Tim. 2.4).

Just as significant and even more explicit are John Paul II's words on mission in *Redemptoris missio* 10:

> The universality of salvation means that it is granted not only to those who explicitly believe in Christ and have entered the Church. Since salvation

---

[55]Rahner, 'Observations on the Problem of the Anonymous Christian', 280–94 (284).

is offered to all, it must be made concretely available to all. But it is clear that today, as in the past, many people do not have an opportunity to come to know or accept the gospel revelation or to enter the Church. The social and cultural conditions in which they live do not permit this, and frequently they have been brought up in other religious traditions. For such people salvation in Christ is accessible by virtue of a grace which, while having a mysterious relationship to the Church, does not make them formally part of the Church but enlightens them in a way which is accommodated to their spiritual and material situation. This grace comes from Christ; it is the result of his Sacrifice and is communicated by the Holy Spirit. It enables each person to attain salvation through his or her free cooperation.

For this reason the Council, after affirming the centrality of the Paschal Mystery, went on to declare that 'this applies not only to Christians but to all people of good will in whose hearts grace is secretly at work. Since Christ died for everyone, and since the ultimate calling of each of us comes from God and is therefore a universal one, we are obliged to hold that the Holy Spirit offers everyone the possibility of sharing in this Paschal Mystery in a manner known to God.' (cf. *Gaudium et spes* 22)

I am not suggesting that only one person was responsible for these texts, but I am proposing that when a theologian can name an issue that limits or hinders the living out of Christian life and work out a way to make sense of it; when that theologian receives and addresses criticisms of his position and works out responses that explain and clarify that position; and when that work resonates enough with the *sensus fidelium* of the church – the sense of faith of the people of God 'from the bishops down to the last lay faithful' (*Lumen gentium* 12) – to become an element of Church teaching, then we are in the presence of greatness. It is not unreasonable that he was called, at times, a 'quiet mover of the Catholic Church'.[56] From a personal perspective, I find the combination of common sense and Catholic belonging both attractive and moving. It echoes the kind of common sense and capacity to question we find in passages of Aquinas' work, another 'systematic theologian' who wrote on just about everything! He clearly identified what was central to Catholic dogma and doctrine and pruned away all the nonsense so that faith *could* understand and recognize itself. For all of this, I am indebted to this man, as well as for the understanding of mission and friendship his theology has allowed me develop, which comes through in the chapter's next section.

---

[56]Egan, *Mystic of Everyday Life*, 19.

Meet My Friend

The idea for this book was born after a conversation with a stranger on a plane on the way to Uluru: Australia's red centre. He was an open soul: interested, intelligent, funny, suitably surprised when he learned I was a theologian; and he was an atheist, or so he thought. By the end of the flight, we had kind of come to the agreement that he was more an agnostic than an atheist. This song, and this chapter, is for people like him.

The song is called 'Meet My Friend', but it has a hidden subtitle: 'Song for my Anonymous Christian Friend' and is a clear attempt to put into song everything Rahner's theology has to offer. I wrote it as an assessment piece for my thesis director, mentor and friend, Michael Paul Gallagher, SJ, in a course on 'Faith and Unbelief'. The song not only seeks to reflect Rahner's theology but also my own understanding of the heart of Christian mission after years of dedicating my life to bridging the gap between God and others. Because friendship *is* the only heart of mission: 'I call you friends' (Jn 15.15).

This chapter's song is a theology of friendship, or rather, a theology of *mission* as friendship: not as a kind superficial and interested trap in which we befriend others so that they may come to Jesus. It is offensive to suggest the ulterior motive of wanting others to know God allows us to not *see* and welcome others for who they are. Each life has intrinsic value and beauty, and if we cannot see that, then we have no business trying to proclaim a God that gave them life and loves them.

There are two extremes often found in Christian approaches to mission, which miss the mark. The first holds that God is good and therefore anything goes, and so as long as everyone is doing their best, then we have no right to interfere. It calls us to 'respect' others, and the term is understood as tolerating anything and questioning little. The problem is that everyone is *not* doing alright, and if the gospel is good news and Jesus is life, then they have a right to know it. Furthermore, the word 'respect' comes from the Latin *respicere* 'look (back) at, regard, consider' and *specere* 'to look', meaning that to respect implies to look at or to consider again, attentively, not to look away and let be when they do things we would do differently or that do them harm. The issue is how loving or authentic our interaction with others is. The second extreme holds that God is good and has saved us in Jesus and that anyone who does not explicitly profess Christ is not saved, be they non-believers from another faith or in some cases, another Church! So mission is absolutely imperative, because the life of others depends on it. The danger here is the presupposition that the ones doing mission are already saved, know the complete truth and have nothing to learn from the world, and the ones they are approaching are lost, wrong in everything and have nothing to give. There is a whole continuum of possible positions in between these two, of course, but they are not invented caricatures. Interestingly, while opposites in a way, they can both end up with a similar position of not really seeking, meeting and loving people where they are! They risk underestimating the graced value of genuine friendship.

I am blessed by all of my friendships, including and at times especially, those who are not Christians. They accept in me the whole package of what Christianity and the church mean to me. No small feat! And I find in them access to an understanding of the world I would not have without them. In terms of faith, in our shared care for one another, a bridge is built between God and us, because if there is love, then Jesus is there, and I am blessed in that space: *I'm standing here in the gap, holding you both within; no words will ever say just how graced I feel, tapping into the ebbs and the flows of it all we are richer, we are blessed.* Life is richer when we are not fearful of people's worlds and all they bring us. Such is the sacramental mystery of friendship, which Paul applied to marriage between a believer and non-believer, but which is broader and mutual, because, in Rahner's terms, the hidden presence of the grace of God is mysteriously present.

Let's recall Rahner's writing on the experience of grace that enables us to live open, forgiving, loving beyond our means. We all know people like this, and if we are lucky, they are friends, because our horizons of comprehension drew us to one another. The Spanish have an expression: '*Dios les crea y ellos se juntan*' (God creates them, and they find one another). The step from implicit to explicit faith often happens through a friend, because *the shared love is already an expression of the yes of both to the love being offered.* And of course, we want them to take that step to explicit knowledge of God, and when the time is right to introduce them to one another, explicitly! And it *is* a question of timing, and witness, and genuine friendship. We need to realise that, in some ways, the tables are now turned: people are not so scared of death and punishment, and crying out for salvation. It is God who needs defending, voices to present that Love beyond all telling, as Rahner intuited: 'We live in an age in which the question is not so much how as sinners we may gain access to a gracious God who will justify us; on the contrary the impression is that it is God – if there is a God – who must justify himself to his creatures in their distress.'[57]

We do this in our genuine friendships. This chapter's song is a bit tongue-in-cheek. It came out in 3/4 timing – not one I often compose in – but I am suggesting that while Jesus can seem radical, and scary, '*his heart is in the right place*'. I am pretty sure Jesus, in his wisdom, does not mind taking himself lightly. The stranger on the flight to Uluru became a friend and I hope is not quite so clear whether he's agnostic or not. I *do* know that Jesus is in our friendship and that we are both a little more saved because of it. The link to the song can be found below.[58]

---

[57]Rahner, 'Christian Living Formerly and Today', 12.
[58]Link to 'Meet my Friend': https://res.cloudinary.com/bloomsbury-online-resources/video/upload/v1639138154/Suspended%20God/Meet_My_Friend.wav

'Meet My Friend' lyrics

Meet my Friend! You will like one another . . .
You've common ground!
You feel the same in so many ways.
Your horizons have colours that match!
Meet my friend! I know he can be outspoken and radical,
But his heart's in the right place.
He is open inside like you are . . .
Underground Café with wine that is seasoned by people whose eyes open into their souls and
forgiving against all odds, giving despite the cost,
Trusting again and again and again . . .
Meet my Friend . . .
I'm standing here in the gap, holding you both within;
No words will ever say just how graced I feel,
tapping into the ebbs and the flows of it all we are richer, we are blessed
Have you met, someplace, sometime . . . ?
Meet my Friend . . .

©MAEVE LOUISE HEANEY, 2020.
Strange Life, The Music of Doubtful Faith

Selected further reading

On the life and development of Rahner's theology

O'Donnell, John J. *Karl Rahner*. Rome: PUG, 1986.
Vorgrimler, Herbert. *Understanding Karl Rahner: An Introduction to His Life and Thought*. London: SCM Press, 1986.

On spirituality and mysticism

Egan, Harvey D. *Karl Rahner: Mystic of Everyday Life*. New York: Crossroad Pub. Co., 1998.
Rahner, Karl. *Encounters with Silence*. Westminster: Newman Press, 1960.
Rahner, Karl. *Spiritual Writings*, edited by Philip Endean. Maryknoll, NY: Orbis Books, 2004.

On anonymous Christianity

Rahner, Karl. 'The Christian among Unbelieving Relations'. In *Theological Investigations III* 355–72. London: Darton, Longman & Todd, 1967.

Rahner, Karl. 'Reflections on the Experience of Grace'. In *Theological Investigations III*, 86–90. London: Darton, Longman & Todd, 1967.
Rahner, Karl. 'Anonymous Christianity and the Missionary Task of the Church'. In *Theological Investigations XII*, 161–78. London: Darton, Longman & Todd, 1974.

On creativity and poetry in Christian life and theology

Rahner, Karl. 'Priest and Poet'. In *Theological Investigations III*, 294–316. London: Darton, Longman & Todd, 1967.
Rahner, Karl. 'Prayer for Creative Thinkers'. In *Theological Investigations VIII*, trans. David Bourke, 130–1. London: Darton, Longman and Todd, 1971.

11

What is it with Christianity and martyrdom?[1]

What can one life achieve in such a messed-up world?

At first glance, this is a simple question. It addresses our contemporary awareness of just how large and interconnected the issues facing our world are. What can one life do, in the midst of this messed-up world? What should we try to do? Is real, definitive change possible in this world, and from where will it emerge? It is an anthropological question that colours our lives from very early on, in the child's questioning of every living thing and the adolescent's quest for selfhood, although we rarely recognize this as anything more than basic human curiosity or overly idealistic youthful dreams. However, our self-understanding, and with it some elements of our personal vocation in this universe as we grow and begin to see the world and ask real questions. At first, we build our worlds of meaning based on the communities we belong to. In Lonergan's terms: 'the community is prior' to the individual. We learn about language, meaning, history and values from those we live with. But there is also the unique, different, sometimes strange particularities that colour each person's worlds of interest and how they deal with them. In the midst of those questions, one usually finds various forms of 'Why is it like that?' 'Why is there poverty?' 'Why do those people suffer?' 'Why is that species dying?' and so on. It depends, of course, upon the formation and capacity for critical reflection and dialogue of parents and educators, which is where family and educational background are not insignificant factors of *anyone*'s life, but even so, some form of questioning

---

[1] I am grateful to Bonhoeffer scholar and friend, Gunter Prüller-Jagenteufel, for conversations and insight into Bonhoeffer's life and thought, as well as his invaluable feedback on this chapter.

is usually present. From a theological perspective, two points here are significant: first, we often find in these early questions the seeds of the particular shape of that person's mission in the following of Christ. Second, the world would be a different place if we did not stifle these questions and callings by suggesting young people push them back until they have more knowledge, money, influence or wisdom. The spontaneous, human and Christian desire to change what is wrong can be very quickly drowned by a received message that there is no real point trying, because some things are bigger than we are.[2]

The question is also an ecclesiological one about the Reign of God, Jesus' favourite theme, whether that is God's work or ours, and what do its fruits look like? Is the call to follow Jesus a personal one, or a sociopolitical one, or both? How do we recognize the Reign of God in the Church and in the world? For centuries the Church spoke as if the two were identical: the Church was the presence of the Reign of God in the world, the 'great and perpetual motive of credibility' of God's existence,[3] which only the very sinful could miss. Contemporary ecclesiology has reframed this understanding of the Church with the notion of sacramentality: the Church as sign and presence of God's grace in the world. But how God's grace and our efforts interact has been a theological and doctrinal conundrum for centuries. And while to a large extent, it is theologically 'resolved', in that most denominations articulate some form of grace acting in and through humanity in the world, the need for a more comprehensive and coherent approach to the range of themes and issues addressed by Christian social teaching could not be more obvious.[4] I like to imagine what the world would look like if all Christians – or since 'charity starts at home'– if the *circa* billion Catholics in the world took their role in the building of the Reign of God on earth seriously. How do faith and action interact and imply one another? This is a central theme of reflection for many strands of contextual and political theology today, and here I am not attempting to address it in all its complexity, but in the life and work of this chapter's theologian in focus, Dietrich Bonhoeffer, we find one of the first coherent, theological reflections

---

[2] A moving example of this early clarity and its fruitfulness is that of Greta Thunburg, whose single-minded vision and action seem to epitomize the human capacity to accept a call to change what is wrong.
[3] *First Vatican Council, Dogmatic Constitution 'Dei Filius'*. 1870.
[4] There is a myriad of unjust and oppressive political regimes around the world, in which faith of various kinds intermingles with politics, to the detriment of both. I write this in the aftermath of the 2020 election results and subsequent 2021 protests in the United States – a nation whose 'Christian' rhetoric underpins much of its political discourse about human rights and democracy. The various and challenging positions of Christian ministers in contemporary politics were international public consumption during and after those election tensions. It manifests that an intelligent and balanced negotiation of the interaction between State and Church is far from achieved. There is, unfortunately, more to learn from Bonhoeffer's position in relation to Hitler's German National Socialism than we might think.

on the theme – and one that ends in death, which brings us to the theme of martyrdom. How can we understand the value Christian Tradition gives to this reality? Is it heroism? Or the value of eternity over the insignificance of life in this world?

I think the issue about the meaning and personal vocation of our lives underpins Christianity's essential link with martyrdom, and is, therefore, our best entry point to a thoughtful and responsible reflection. It is too easy to spiritualize the image of the martyr when the person is not close to us. We often quote the words of Tertullian (*c.* 155/160–after 220), one of the first Christian theologians, as he made sense of the suffering of those who were persecuted: 'the blood of martyrs is the seed of the Church; blood of martyrs, seed of Christians'.[5] We pray for the persecuted Church, which from afar seems like a minority, when the truth is that the twentieth century had more martyrs for Christian faith than any other of the previous nineteen.[6] We develop a theology of witness (the etymological meaning of martyr) and ground it in the reality that Jesus came to die for our salvation, because 'unless a grain of wheat falls into the earth and dies, it remains just a single grain' (Jn 12.24). *All of which is true*! But incomplete, unless we also remember that Jesus came to *live*, as well as to die, to reveal humanity to us, as well as to redeem it, because those thirty odd years Jesus walked this earth are not insignificant. It is *that life* in whom God rejoiced: 'this is my Son, my beloved, listen to Him!' (Lk. 9.35); *that* image of God we could not reconcile with our own and therefore killed; *that* man who prayed to his God that such a death might not come his way 'if it were possible . . . ' (cf. Mt. 26.39). When we lose touch with the Jesus whose *life* and death is our access point to everything, we sterilize the faith we hold. Death is always an unspeakable loss, the hardest goodbye, which is why mourning is so essential to human living. A culture that mourns well is a healthier one than those that hide death behind sterilized walls. And some deaths are tragic, before their time, unjust, unwanted, by us and God, *even if* we can also say and trust with all our beings that God is present and pray: 'God's will, even through this, be done'!

The contradiction I have just defended will be a key theme of this chapter, but the starting point is this: every life has an irreplaceable place in the world and the advancement of the Reign of God. And every life is both a gift received and a task that will only become all that it is meant to be and could be if we take our freedom seriously: we are responsible for who we become, and no one on earth can live, be and do what each one of us can. Our mission is unique, necessary, desired and depends on both God and us!

---

[5]Cf. Tertullian, *Apology De Spectaculis*, ed. M. Minucius Felix, T. R. Glover, and G. H. Rendall (Cambridge, MA: Harvard University Press, 1931), XLIX.13.
[6]Cf. George Carey, 'Enthronement Sermon Canterbury, England Friday, April 19th 1991', *Evangelical Review of Theology* 16, no. 1 (1992): 4–7 (3,4).

Why, if not, is survival one of our most basic instincts? Why do we lament more than anything else the loss of young lives? That unfulfilled potential of what we imagined but could not yet be seen and will *never* be seen! The loss, or abuse, or oppression of any life is to truncate the love whence life came and the dream that each life was invited to imagine, and develop, in co-creativity with the God whose image and way-of-being is imprinted in who we are. Martyrdom is the opposite of giving up or not wanting to live and it is *never* to be sought.[7] It is far from a lack of appreciation of human life but rather its contradiction; and in and through this tragedy we believe in the goodness of God, *who will make right this wrong*!

So how do we make sense of a death born of loving in theological terms? Is there a theological word that could help those who have loved and lost someone who died for their faith, which goes beyond the access to eternal life explored in chapter ten (with all the nuance introduced about what eternity life is). It is for this that I turn to someone whose life and thought, as pastor, theologian and martyr, open a remarkable pathway to explore. There would be much to learn from the life of any person whose life of faith and fidelity led to them paying the ultimate price of their lives, but in Dietrich Bonhoeffer we find his thought and death linked. As he struggled with the circumstances he lived through, we watch him choose to stay where God planted him and reach for theological meaning as he develops his thought – an incomplete life's work but one with treasures for our questioning.

Dietrich Bonhoeffer: When thought costs a life

Who was Dietrich Bonhoeffer? I shall start and end with this question. I have already mentioned some of his thought on music, but who was this vivid man who stands out like a lighthouse in the storm of mid-twentieth century, war-torn Europe, hanged at the age of thirty-nine on 9 April 1945 with the express consent of Hitler, a week before his prison camp was liberated and three weeks before Hitler himself committed suicide?

Bonhoeffer: Pastor, martyr, academic theologian

Dietrich Bonhoeffer was a pastor, an academic theologian, a seminary director and finally, a martyr. It is the way he made sense of this journey, which makes his theology fascinating for this book, because his thought was the source of his end, not its contradiction: a theologian from start to

---

[7]The witness of Thomas More is eloquent in this: he tried hard to not say the words that would cost him his life. And in the end, it was the lie of a betrayer that condemned him to death, although he accepted it.

finish, he was martyred for his life's consistency with his thought. But who was he? The most comprehensive biography and closest hermeneutic of his life come to us through his student and friend Eberhard Bethge,[8] but there are others,[9] and current research suggests the need to complement Bethge's widely accepted authority with other perspectives that are, as yet, less known or explored.[10]

Bonhoeffer was born into a large and loving family of eight siblings, in Breslau in 1906. His father was a prominent physician and later professor of psychology and nervous diseases at the University of Berlin; his mother was of aristocratic background with prominent intellectuals and theologians in her family. While the family was not particularly practising of their Christian faith, their background came from the Old Prussian Union (a mixture of Reformed and Lutheran churches), and his mother was keen to instil in her children Christian prayer and practices. His decision at the age of fourteen to become a theologian would have been odd in that context of intellectual and cultural conversation with no particular respect for contemporary Church practice, but his mother's ancestry could be one influencing factor, as well as the quality of the intellectual and cultural conversation in the household. He became engaged to be married later in life, at the age of thirty-six, but would be separated from his fiancée soon afterwards, when imprisoned. He was precociously intelligent, musically talented and quite brilliant in his academic thought and writing, as his short but swift career manifest.

At seventeen, he started theological studies at Tübingen, where he studied the biblical texts with Adolf Schlatter, and came to know the liberal Protestantism of Friedrich Schleiermacher and Albrecht Ritschl under Karl Heim, from 1923 to 1924. He did his doctoral studies at the University of Berlin from 1924 to 1927, defending his doctoral thesis on '*Sanctorum Communio* [The Communion of Saints]: *A Dogmatic Enquiry into the Sociology of the Church*'[11] at the age of twenty-four. During his time there,

---

[8]Eberhard Bethge, *Dietrich Bonhoeffer: Theologian, Christian, Contemporary* (London: Collins, 1970).
[9]For example, Ferdinand Schlingensiepen, *Dietrich Bonhoeffer, 1906–1945: Martyr, Thinker, Man of Resistance* (New York: T&T Clark, 2010). Sabine Dramm, *Dietrich Bonhoeffer: An Introduction to His Thought* (Peabody, MA: Hendrickson Publishers, 2007); Christiane Tietz, *Theologian of Resistance: The Life and Thought of Dietrich Bonhoeffer* (New York: Fortress Press, 2016). The introductions and texts of Dietrich Bonhoeffer, Clifford J. Green, and Michael P. DeJonge, *The Bonhoeffer Reader*, ed. C. J. Green and M. P. DeJonge (Minneapolis, MN: Fortress Press, 2013) are also an excellent and up-to-date presentation of his life and thought.
[10]This emerges clearly in a developing podcast series called 'The Bonhoeffer Podcast' in a conversation entitled 'The Church for the World' with Jennifer McBride, 24 June 2019. It is understandable that such a fascinating and brilliant life has drawn the attention of so many that other, less prominent characters and players in the epoch-changing movements of Germany and the German Church of the 1930s and 1940s have been overlooked or underplayed. Cf. https://player.fm/series/the-bonhoeffer-podcast/dr-jennifer-mcbride-the-church-for-the-world
[11]Which he studied under Reinhold Seeberg.

he came to know theological liberal thought through Arnold von Harnack and studied Martin Luther under Karl Holl; he also thoroughly dived into the theology of Karl Barth. This dual underpinning of the Lutheran tenets of faith (*sola fede, sola gratia* and *sola scriptura*) and the theology of Barth remains during his life, although he will challenge the absolute transcendence of Barth's theology of revelation as 'positivist' and insufficient to understand the presence of Christ in the church (and in a broader sense, the world).[12] From 1929 to 1931, he worked on a second dissertation (entitled *Habilitationsschrift* in Germany and required for accreditation to teach) on the philosophy of Martin Heidegger in connection to theology and ecclesiology, published as *Act and Being*, and began teaching at the University of Berlin. Bonhoeffer was an avid and personally motivated thinker and writer.

Between and after these intense academic experiences, Bonhoeffer's travel and work abroad left a mark on his life and thinking. He travelled to Italy and North Africa with his brother in 1924 and commented on how, despite his aversion to what he saw as Roman dogmatism, it was on a Palm Sunday in Rome that he sensed 'something real' in Catholicism – the concept of Church.[13] In 1928 he worked in Barcelona as curate for the German-speaking Lutheran church, and in 1933–5, he worked in London as a minister to two German-speaking communities, where he met and established a significant friendship with Bishop George Bell of Chichester. But it was his postdoctoral time in New York as the Sloane Scholar at Union Theological Seminary in New York that seems to have left the deepest mark on his life and writings. He came under the influence of French Lutheran pacifist Jean Lassere[14] and became friends with an Afro-American minister and student, Frank Fisher, which led him to spend a lot of time at the Abyssinian Baptist Church in Harlem, at a time when the plight and fight for Afro-American rights were at his heights. The influence of Lassere in learning to read the beatitudes as the essence of Christian discipleship, and the Afro-American faith and positioning in the face of their struggles would awaken Bonhoeffer to the realities of racism and deeply affect his position and theological reflection on resistance to Hitler's oppression of the Jews.[15] This time in the United

---

[12]Cf. Dietrich Bonhoeffer, *Letters and Papers from Prison*, ed. E. Bethge, *Enlarged* ed. (London: SCM Press, 1971), 280, 86. Philip Kennedy, 'Dietrich Bonhoeffer: 1906–1945', in *Twentieth Century Theologians: A New Introduction to Modern Christian Thought*, 85–99 (97) (London: I.B. Tauris & Co. Ltd., 2010).

[13]Cf. Kennedy, 'Dietrich Bonhoeffer: 1906–1945', 85–99 (88).

[14]Cf. Schlingensiepen, *Bonhoeffer, Martyr, Thinker, Man of Resistance*, 65.

[15]Cf. Clifford J. Green's Introduction to *Ethics* in Dietrich Bonhoeffer, *Dietrich Bonhoeffer Works. Vol. 6, Ethics*, ed. C. J. Green et al., *Ethik* (Minneapolis, MN: Fortress Press, 2009), 3–4; Reggie L. Williams, *Bonhoeffer's Black Jesus: Harlem Renaissance Theology and an Ethic of Resistance* (WACO, TX: Baylor University Press, 2014); Reggie L. Williams, 'Developing a Theologia Crucis: Dietrich Bonhoeffer in the Harlem Renaissance', *Theology Today* 71, no. 1 (2014): 43–57. This was not his only exposure to opposition to German National Socialism.

States provoked a profound change in Bonhoeffer, which Bethge describes as the transition from theologian to Christian, and Bonhoeffer seems to link with taking Scripture seriously.[16]

On 30 January 1933, Hitler came into power as the Chancellor of the Third Reich. On 1 February 1033, Bonhoeffer challenged Hitler's form of leadership[17] on a public radio transmission which was cut off before he finished.[18] In 1933, Hitler introduced 'the Aryan clause' into German law (entitled the 'Law for the Re-establishment of the Professional Civil Service'), which forced civil servants to prove they were of Aryan descent. Pastors of the German Lutheran Church – a state church – could be considered obligated to adopt the law, which Bonhoeffer vehemently opposed. However, the clause was adopted by a Synod of the Old Prussian Union in September 1933. It is at this moment that Bonhoeffer leaves for London. When he returns to Germany (partly at the urging of Barth) he is an influential member of an organization called 'The Confessing Church', set up as a counterpart to the church in Germany because of their complicity with anti-Semitism, renouncing, in his eyes, their true Christian identity and heritage. He became director of its clandestine and illegal seminary for preachers (first in Zingst, then in Finkenwalde), which was shut down in 1937.[19]

Although he left Germany to accept an invitation to go to Union Theological Seminary, in New York, he lasted a month, famously explaining his return in the following words: 'I have made a mistake in coming to America. I must live through this difficult period of our national history with the Christian people of Germany. I will have no right to participate in the reconstruction of Christian life in Germany after the war if I do not share the trials of this time with my people.'[20]

Bonhoeffer becomes part of the resistance in Germany by publicly being a civilian member of the Abwehr (the military intelligence) while secretly labouring with the underground resistance movement. Although banned from writing and teaching, he managed to travel and get work done (such as smuggling out Jews and communicating with contacts in the British Allies), as he slowly came to the realization of a call to actively work against Hitler. He participated in the planning of two attempts to kill Hitler, which led to

---

His family also resisted Hitler, and one of his grandmothers took a courageous anti-Nazi stance in relation to Jewish marginalization when she refused to stop buying at their shops once it was banned.
[16]Schlingensiepen, *Bonhoeffer, Martyr, Thinker, Man of Resistance*, 93–6.
[17]Cf. 'The Führer and the Individual in the Younger Generation', in Bonhoeffer, Green, and DeJonge, *The Bonhoeffer Reader*, 359–69.
[18]This has long been interpreted as a censorship move. There is, however, the possibility it was due to his having gone over time. Bonhoeffer, Green, and DeJonge, *The Bonhoeffer Reader*, 359.
[19]This notion of a 'seminary' was a novel notion in German culture.
[20]Quoted in Kennedy, 'Dietrich Bonhoeffer: 1906–1945', 85–99 (93).

his imprisonment and eventual death. During his years of imprisonment, he continued to think and write – not only theology but letters, poems and a novel. His last words in Flossenbürg, as a message sent to his friend, George Bell, are recorded as 'This is the end, for me the beginning of life.'[21]

Theological thought and development

This rather detailed account of his life explains the context and emphases of his theology.

- *An incomplete theology:* The first necessary comment on Bonhoeffer's thought is to state that it is incomplete. To ignore this is to risk (over)interpreting thought-provoking aspects of his writings which, while incisive, are not finished, and taken out of context can say more about the position of the interpreter than of Bonhoeffer himself. We have some finished works, such as his doctoral and *Habilitation* dissertations; writings born of his time as director of the seminary at Finkenwalde (arguably his most well known): *Discipleship* and *Life Together*; and the transcript of his lectures on *Creation and the Fall*. His *Papers and Writings from Prison* are fascinating, but must be read as what they are: a luminous attempt to make sense of immensely difficult and demanding conditions, smuggled out with the help of a sympathetic guard and never written for publication. Other writings, including *Ethics*, which he considered the culmination of his theological and personal journey, were unfinished and gathered, edited and published by his student and friend Eberhard Bethge.
- *Context and thought:* Bonhoeffer does theology within two overlapping contexts he finds himself in which were the emerging secularism of the early twentieth century with which most contemporary Western theology was grappling, and life near the centre of the Hitler regime. The former, for the first time in Western Christianity, faces the reality of a world that understands itself without God, and theological greats (such as Paul Tillich, Rudolf Bultmann and Karl Barth), in different ways and with very dissimilar conclusions, precede Bonhoeffer in reflecting upon the meaning of the world, the secular, and religion. The dilemma of how to negotiate the transcendence and immanence of God is fresh and polemic, a theological counterpart, if you will, to philosophy's pendulum

---

[21]Cf. 'S. Payne Best to George K. A. Bell' in Dietrich Bonhoeffer, *Dietrich Bonhoeffer Works. Vol. 16, Conspiracy and Imprisonment, 1940–1945*, ed. M. S. Brocker, L. E. Dahill, and D. WStott (Minneapolis, MN: Fortress Press, 2006), 468.

between what the mind can and cannot know. The latter – Hitler and German National Socialism – is the *locus theologicus* of all of Bonhoeffer's later thought: his life is marked by his theology, as his theology reflects his life.

Eberhard Bethge identifies three stages and core concerns in the process of his thought:

1. Church as community, from his time teaching (the theme of his doctoral dissertation, but also an ongoing question about what the church *is*, in Christ);
2. Costly discipleship, during his work with the Seminary of the Confessing Church, which gives birth to his two most well-known writings: *Discipleship* (later published and known as *The Cost of Discipleship,* in recognition of how it had cost Bonhoeffer his life) and *Life Together;*
3. Worldly holiness, from his work in the resistance to Hitler (which *Ethics* and *Papers and Writings from Prison* reflect).[22]

However, in and through each of these stages, there are constants in Bonhoeffer's work, in terms of both themes and the way he approaches them, that need to be named.

- *Core themes and approach:* Bonhoeffer's thought is fully theological, with Christ as its starting and end point, often led by the question: 'Who is Jesus Christ, for us, today?'[23] Even when dealing with the most sociopolitical situations imaginable, the lens with which he approaches them is a Scripturally based faith in Christ (echoing one of the Pauline phrases he loves: 'in Christ'). *The Cost of Discipleship*, for example, is an extended commentary on Jesus' call to his disciples and the Sermon of the Mount, in which the figure of Christ manifests absolute, complete and compelling authority. Christian life is lived out in obedience to God's call. In fact, faith and obedience are two sides of the one reality: 'only those who believe can obey, only those who obey can believe'.[24]

This leads to a theology that makes for prayerful and challenging pastoral reading, not in terms of pious platitudes to console mediocre living but as a Church theologian profoundly in touch with an ever-present call to respond with one's whole person to the person of Christ. The felt presence

---

[22]Cf. Kennedy, 'Dietrich Bonhoeffer: 1906–1945', 85–99 (95).
[23]Cf. Stanley J. Grenz and Roger E. Olson, *20th Century Theology: God & the World in a Transitional Age*, Twentieth-Century Theology (Downers Grove, IL: InterVarsity Press, 1992), 149.
[24]Dietrich Bonhoeffer, *The Cost of Discipleship* (London: SCM Press, 1959), 60.

of Christ compels us, even while leaving us ever free: '*if* someone would follow me . . . ' (Mt. 16.24). Based on his understanding of God as *imago relationis*, 'an image of relationship', Jesus is God-for-us, and 'Man-for-others', who calls us to discipleship, understood by Bonhoeffer as 'costly grace', the opposite of our oft-invoked compromises with God's ultimacy:

> Cheap grace is the mortal enemy of the church. Our struggle today is for costly grace. Cheap grace means grace as bargain-basement goods. . . . Cheap grace is preaching forgiveness without repentance, it is baptism without the discipline of community; it is the Lord's Supper without the confession of sin; it is absolution without personal confession. Cheap grace is grace without discipleship, grace without the cross, grace without the living, incarnate Christ.[25]

This notion of cheap grace, he maintains, is born of misunderstanding the central Lutheran theology of justification: when justification of sin is proclaimed without the justification of the repentant sinner!

All other themes (ecclesiology, ethics, anthropology, community etc.) build upon God's revelation through the incarnated Christ and the call to be faithful to discipleship. The world is our access point to God because God became incarnate: there is no other way to God except through Christ, and the call to follow Jesus is to follow him *back into the world*. This means that reality, for Bonhoeffer, is a theological place, a *locus theologicus* outside of which there is no Christian life.

> In Christ we are invited to participate in the reality of God and the reality of the world at the same time, the one not without the other. The reality of God is disclosed only as it places me completely into the reality of the world.[26]

Bonhoeffer's understanding of the world resonates, from a Catholic perspective, as deeply sacramental. He uses two terms to explain his understanding of life: 'penultimate' and 'ultimate'.[27] God is the *only* ultimate. Everything else is penultimate in the sense that it derives its meaning only and always from that which is ultimate. *However*, the ultimate has already touched us, in Christ. In fact, we *are*, in Christ. It is the eschatological 'already yes, but not yet'. God is enmeshed in human existence, but full

---

[25] Bonhoeffer, *The Cost of Discipleship*, 35.
[26] Bonhoeffer, *Ethics*, 55.
[27] Cf. Gunter Prüller-Jagenteufel, '"Restraining Power" against Evil and "Scarring Over" of Guilt: Bonhoefferian Remarks on "Penultimate" Steps toward Reconciliation', in *Reconciliation: The Way of Healing and Growth*, ed. J. Juhant and B. Žalec, 169–77 (Wien-Berlin: LIT Verlag, 2012).

transformation will only take place in the fullness of time. This position implies taking this world seriously, in both its redemption and its sinfulness. Sin, for Bonhoeffer, is the opposite of who Jesus as Man-for-others is: sin is egocentrism, the turning away from God. Humanity is both justified and sinner at the same time, *simil iustus et peccator*, in this penultimate reality. Complete forgiveness is eschatological, and while we can and must work for the reconciliation of the world, full atonement here is not possible. This anthropology grounds his ethics: as humans, we cannot see the ultimate good, since we are always and everywhere justified *and* sinful, but we can, as Jesus did, take on the guilt of others and are called to resist evil, which he calls the 'scarring over of guilt'. This implies risk: there is no ultimate security in the penultimate, so we have to risk. As our whole lives are situated in time and space, the question for ethics is not 'how to be good?' or 'how to do something good?' but 'what is the will of God, today and right here?' God is ultimate and therefore to do good is to seek God's will *in the present time and the current situation* because the good is penultimate and only takes meaning from the ultimate.

Bonhoeffer's ecclesiology reflects these themes. He was always fascinated with the notion of how church was community, herself also holy and sinful (*simil iusta et peccatrix*), rejecting solitary or private notions of Christian life. 'The Church is only the church when it exists for others.'[28] The church, for Bonhoeffer, is the community of succession of Jesus, who enables us to discover the will of God (ecclesial hermeneutic) and the realization of that will in the world: 'the place where Jesus Christ's taking form is proclaimed and where it happens'.[29] Theologizing at a time when our understanding of the church and the world was shifting, he maintained a stance one could call 'in-between': fully in the world while not of the world (cf. John 17): 'I fear that Christians who stand with only one leg upon earth also stand with only one leg in heaven (12 August 1943).'[30] He compares these two positions on grace with two well-known characters of Miguel de Cervantes: Don Quixote and Sancho Panza – the former always chasing other-worldly dreams, the latter an epitome of cheap grace, trying to balance his master! But the position of a mediocre mediating stance will not work: the church is called to a radical response to God in response to the world as it is in the here and now: a 'world come of age'.

---

[28]Bonhoeffer, *Letters and Papers from Prison*, 382.
[29]Bonhoeffer, *Ethics*, 102.
[30]Maria von Wedemeyer-Weller, 'Appendix: The Other Letters from Prison', in *Letters and Papers from Prison*, ed. E. Bethge, 412–19 (415), (London: SCM Press, 1971).

Later themes

This theme of the world come of age together with that of religionless Christianity and secret resistance are perhaps his theological explorations that have been least understood, most loved and often extrapolated, all at the same time. By way of background, there are echoes of Barth's rejection of 'natural religion' as a valid means of access to God, but it goes further. During his time in prison, Bonhoeffer writes of a world that no longer turns to what he refers to as a 'working hypothesis' called 'God' to solve problems already accessible through science and our growth in the understanding of how the world works. It is a world 'come of age'. He is once again asking about Jesus and the church, in the here and now in which people live, without religion: In what way could the historical form and language around church be transient? Could there be a Christianity without 'religion' as it has been lived and understood for nineteen centuries? His awareness of the incarnated Christ also pushes against binary thinking in relation to sacred and secular, Church and State.

> Thinking in terms of two realms understands the paired concepts worldly-Christian, natural-supernatural, profane-sacred, rational-revelational, as ultimate static opposites that designate certain given entities that are mutually exclusive. This thinking fails to recognize the original unity of these opposites in the Christ-reality and, as an after-thought, replaces this with a forced unity provided by a sacred or profane system that overarches them. Thus the static opposition is maintained.[31]

This leads to his underdeveloped notion of 'secret discipline' taken from the early church's reserve placed on baptized Christians to not reveal Christianity's hidden mysteries to non-Christians. It seems to lead Bonhoeffer to say that this time was not one for proclamation, a theme that was very present in his writings on discipleship and community life, but rather than now, this 'hidden source' is not to be displayed as a form of identity or principled justification for our deeds. The will of God is the source of Christian living, and our trust in God cannot be replaced by trust in 'religion'. Furthermore, in a time in which the world is living without religion and talk about God has lost its meaning, 'traditional churchy language must remain silent, so that our being Christians today will consist in only two things: in praying and in doing justice among people'.[32] The position sounds problematic

---

[31] Bonhoeffer, *Ethics*, 58–9.
[32] Cf. Grenz and Olson, *20th Century Theology*, 155, paraphrasing Bonhoeffer, *Letters and Papers from Prison*, 286, 300. I have changed the translation of this quite particular text from that of Grenz and Olson, 'working on behalf of others' to 'doing justice among people', since Bonhoeffer only rarely uses the term 'justice' in this way, connected with God's justice. The meaning here is quite specific. Once again, I thank Gunter Prüller-Jagenteufel for this insight.

from the perspective of Christianity's commitment to proclamation and evangelization, but this is the same theologian who challenged preachers to preach in a way that lets those who are being alienated from the church find Jesus, rather than mere words:

> It is simply not true that every word critical of our preaching today can be taken as a rejection of Christ or as anti-Christianity. Today there are a great number of people who come to our preaching, want to hear it, and then repeatedly have to admit sadly that we have made it too difficult for them to get to know Jesus. Do we really want to deny being in community with these people?.... Nothing would contradict our own intention more deeply and would be more ruinous for our proclamation than if we burdened with difficult human rules those who are weary and heavy laden, whom Jesus calls unto himself. That would drive them away from him again.[33]

The call to secret discipline is the apologetics of a man who has seen Christianity gradually sidelined as an intelligent interlocutor for the advancement of society, and who has seen churches and church leaders back Hitler or leave him unopposed, and his world reduced to a cell. Jesus does not come to fill what is missing, a God of stopgaps coming to tell people what they are not. Instead, God has something to offer people at their strongest: 'It always seems to me that we leave room for God only out of anxiety. I'd like to speak of God not at the boundaries but in the Center, not in weakness but in strength, thus not in death and guilt, but in human life and human goodness.'[34]

Influence and limitations

The context and times within which historical figures live help us to understand and learn from them – both in what they did and said, and in what they left out. In considering the contributions and limitations of a theologian, it is important to avoid being anachronic in our expectations and assessment of their work. It is clear that the religion about which Bonhoeffer is writing and with which he is concerned is Christianity. It is missing the interreligious considerations later decades would bring forward. In fact, although his stance in favour of the Jews was exceptional, it has been noted that his theological reasons fell short of a true appreciation of

---

[33]Bonhoeffer, *The Cost of Discipleship*, 29–30.
[34]Cf. Grenz and Olson, *20th Century Theology*, 152, quoting Dietrich Bonhoeffer, *Letters and Papers from Prison*, ed. J. W. De Gruchy et al., 1st English language ed. (Minneapolis MN: Fortress Press, 2010), 366–7.

the role of the Jews in salvation history but was rather concerned with the Christianity of his people. Another significant shortcoming is that not only is there no concern for women in his Scriptural reading[35] or the feminist issues which were already emerging in his time.[36] His theology is strangely and strongly classical and patriarchal.[37]

> For Bonhoeffer, women are not, like men, separate persons with a variety of vocations, but are indistinguishable members of a homogenous group with a standardized vocation of subordination.[38]

Although this emerges from his understanding of the four 'orders' of humanity that are mandated (his word) structurally in an organization that is gendered, it sits ill with the radicality of his understanding of Christ's universal grace and his rejection of norms beyond discipleship. For this reason, his work has long been ignored by feminist movements, although some strands of fruitful interaction are emerging.[39]

The 'Death of God' movement of the 1960s 'discovered' Bonhoeffer's writings and refers to him as a point of inspiration and influence, a fact which has influenced his reception. However, Bonhoeffer never went as far as these theologians did in his understanding of the world. The centrality of Christ in Bonhoeffer's thought belies any possibility of a 'Christ-less' world. He was, however, one of the first to seriously engage with modernity and secularity in a fully theological attempt to think Christologically about the world, even in its rejection of religion.[40] This brilliant theologian was often ahead of his times. His doctoral thesis interacted with a sociology of the Church before that discipline was even established[41] for example, and the seminary community he directed was utterly unlike anything Germany was used to seeing, in terms of an attempt at a holistic formation of leaders for a Church in the secular world. The pathway to becoming a minister in

---

[35] Not only is all the language utterly non-inclusive, but even the female presences in the gospel – for example at the cross – seem to be invisible to him.

[36] For example, the question of the ordination of women in the confessing Church is not one he gives any attention to, despite it already being a theme in discussion.

[37] Cf. 'A Wedding Sermon from a Prison Cell' in Bonhoeffer, *Letters and Papers from Prison*, 41–7.

[38] Jennifer M. McBride, 'Bonhoeffer and Feminist Theologies', in *The Oxford Handbook of Dietrich Bonhoeffer*, ed. P. G. Ziegler and M. G. Mawson, 365–84 (6) (Oxford: Oxford University Press, 2019).

[39] Renewed attention is being given to retrieve some aspects of his thought. Cf. Lisa Elaine Dahill, 'Reading from the Underside of Selfhood: Bonhoeffer and Spiritual Formation,' (ProQuest Dissertations Publishing, 2001); McBride, 'Bonhoeffer and Feminist Theologies', 365–84.

[40] For a thorough evaluation of this aspect of the theology of Bonhoeffer and the theologians who refer to his work (such as William Hamilton, Thomas Altizer, John A. T. Robinson and Harvey Cox), see Grenz and Olson, *20th Century Theology*, 156–69.

[41] Cf. Kennedy, 'Dietrich Bonhoeffer: 1906–1945', 85–99 (89).

Germany at the time was university education, not shared life in a monastic-inspired community. However, Bonhoeffer thought it was the only way to work towards fully Christian living and leadership: forming the whole person into shared living in Christ.

It is a tragic loss to theology that we did not see the further fruits of this theologian's mind at the service of Christian faith. Our Christian awareness that 'all things work together for good for those who love God, who are called according to his [sic] purpose' (Rom. 8.28) would be ill served by our passing too quickly over this *loss* of life. In fact, it is our felt experience and appreciation of loss that allows us intuit what lies at the heart of this chapter's theme. What light does Bonhoeffer's life and 'ethics of responsibility' bring to our question of the value and influence of our lives, and the meaning of losing it, for Christ?

One Life: Faith in the public square of the Body of Christ

The man who acts out of free responsibility is justified before others by dire necessity; before himself he is acquitted by his conscience, but before God he hopes only for grace.[42]

There are authors who wake you up to something within oneself. I remember reading Helder Camara's *The Desert Is Fertile*[43] at the age of fourteen and knowing my eyes had been opened to an awareness I could not block out: I was one of those being called by God to do something about the world. Camara's thesis is simple but clear: God could have chosen to hand out gifts and callings in equal portions, with everyone's role and duty being exactly the same. But that is not how God decided to do things. From the very beginning of the history of salvation revealed in Scripture we see a God who calls a few for the many, who risks seeming unfair by lavishing gifts on people in different measures: to some, one, to others, five, or ten talents, each invited to invest all, to be a 'good and faithful servant'. And I knew that I was one of those to whom much had been given for the good of many, for whom surrender to that generosity of life and heart was to be the only way in which life would feel like life! This is how Bonhoeffer's writings hit you: they are a window into a vision of reality that has Christ at its core and centre, written by a man who seems to breathe the presence and person of Jesus more easily than air. His writing is clear and compelling, relentless but

---

[42]Bonhoeffer, *Ethics*, 14.
[43]Hélder Câmara, *The Desert Is Fertile*, ed. D. Livingstone (London: Sheed and Ward, 1974).

irresistible, Jesus-focussed and reality-centred, in a way that pulls you under its surface to the hidden life in Christ that is Christian discipleship, at the same time as forcing you to open your eyes to the here and now in which God is calling you to see and respond.

I name this experience as one of awakening to the deepest meaning of human freedom: your life is in *your* hands *to become* the child of God you have the potential to be. It echoes Lonergan's moral conversion from drifter to authenticity – the realization that you can make of your life what you will – except this time with a Christological lens: God in Jesus is the *only* Absolute who merits the response of complete obedience and surrender as the form this authentic living takes. And that call to surrender to Jesus' call is one that implies and requires freedom from *all* that would tie us to the world.[44] The fact that behind the words is a life that paid the ultimate price for that faith may contribute to the strength of his writings, but it is also, I believe, simply the grasp of truth that underpins his theology, which gives it such resonance. What does it tell us of about our human life?

Becoming human

One of the greatest dangers Christianity has faced and fallen into, at times, over its two millennia of history is that of relativizing life and history in the light of eternity life to come. As mentioned earlier, the categories Bonhoeffer uses to explore how the reconciliation of the world is achieved in Christ are those of ultimate and penultimate: we live in a penultimate reality that is touched by God, whence it draws its meaning. But this does not mean that this life, the here and now, is disposable. On the contrary, the importance of our lives now is increased:

> From this follows now something of decisive importance, that the penultimate must be preserved for the sake of the ultimate. Arbitrary destruction of the penultimate seriously harms the ultimate. When, for example, a human life is deprived of the conditions that are part of being human, the justification of such a life by grace and faith is at least seriously hindered, if not made impossible. . . . Given this fact, in addition to proclaiming the ultimate word of God – the justification of the sinner by grace alone – it is necessary to care for the penultimate in order that the ultimate not be hindered by the penultimate's destruction.[45]

That is to say, what is at stake now is who we are now, and somehow, also, who we shall be in the ultimate reality towards which we journey. He does

---

[44]Cf. Bonhoeffer, *The Cost of Discipleship*, chapter three.
[45]Bonhoeffer, *Ethics*, 160.

not attempt to limit God's mercy – as everything is given, even the call – or to guess how exactly that correspondence happens. But our life in the here and now and our life in God are not separate entities: God calls us to become a selfless person-for-others.

This importance of each and every human life in its present and its fullness is, once again, grounded on his understanding of Christ. He assumes but inverts Anselm's response to the question of why Jesus became human ('that humanity might become divine') to note that God, in Jesus, made humanity who we are called to become.

> Bonhoeffer's premise is that the name of Jesus Christ means first, foremost, and above all *God's becoming human*. This phrase recurs throughout the manuscripts like a litany. Bonhoeffer's distinctive emphasis is summed up in the German word he uses consistently, *Menschwerdung*, 'becoming human'. It is a striking feature of *Ethics* that Bonhoeffer does not use the word that was readily available and is commonly employed in this topic of theology, namely, *Inkarnation*, 'incarnation.' Not, of course, that he questions in the least the true and full humanity of Jesus Christ, including the real bodily, fleshly existence of Jesus of Nazareth – that is never in doubt. The emphasis, however, is not on enfleshment per se but on *humanity* and *humanization*. . . . God's being-for-humanity has a purpose and an end – it is the promise and offer to human beings of a new humanity, indeed the renewal of humanity both personally and corporately – the restoration of true humanity.[46]

Any ensuing theology of redemption widens our attention (without removing it) from the cross to include the life that was crucified, and the lives we are called to live, in the here and now of our concrete realities. So, what is my fully human life?

A life-for-others

A fully Christological focus changes that question, because as soon as my focus is the person I want to be, I have once again about-turned to face myself and the self is in command, not God's call. And it risks becoming theoretical and stagnant, as if our salvation were a theory to be applied, or a holiness to be achieved, rather than an unmarked pathway along which I follow Someone, in obedience to the voice leading. And it misunderstands

---

[46] Clifford J. Green, 'Editor's Introduction to the English Edition', in *Dietrich Bonhoeffer Works. Vol. 6, Ethics* (6), ed. C. J. Green (Minneapolis, MN: Fortress Press, 2009). Emphases mine. This introduction to Bonhoeffer's papers on ethics is an insightful summary of his 'ethics of responsibility' and their Christological foundations.

freedom. He differentiates clearly between the 'ethical' and the Christian, precisely in the fact that the ethical appears as an 'ought' to the conscience in a boundary situation whereas the Christian

> rests not on principles and norms revealed in the conscience's experience of the ought but in God's command. And God's command differs from the ethical imperative because it supplies not only prohibitions and obligations, but also permission. God commands *freedom*. Thus while God's command does indeed concern the boundary situations of life … it concerns much more: the fullness of life.[47]

'The commandment of God is permission to live before God as a human being. God's commandment is permission. It is distinguished from all human laws in that it commands freedom.'[48] It is both more exciting and more frightening to hold our freedom in our hands than a list of laws and guidelines – albethey challenging – to follow, but this is the dynamic of life in the world as a Christian.

This is why the question to be asked is not that of 'what is good' but rather: What is God's will *now* for me and in relation to this situation in which I am living? Because an ethics of responsibility plays out in the realm of a situated freedom: the body of Christ. For Bonhoeffer, Christ is the centre of history and nature, and the centre of the Church as the hidden centre of the world, in the sense of the sociopolitical reality in which one finds oneself.[49] There is no discipleship 'outside of' or 'without' the world, because I cannot access Jesus except through the world assumed in Him.

> What matters is participating in the reality of God and the world in Jesus Christ today, and doing so in such a way that I never experience the reality of God without the reality of the world, nor the reality of the world without the reality of God.[50]

So how do we take seriously the reality we live in? Bonhoeffer's attempt to reflect theologically on this, in the concrete circumstances in which he lived, can be found in *Ethics*. Two overlapping motivations underpin these writings: his desire to contribute to the reconstruction of life in Germany and the West in the peace that would follow the war, and his attempt to reflect upon his own decision-making, as a pacifist who chose to support the assassination of Hitler. He does not try to defend his decision as 'good' or 'better'. He does not draw upon previous theologies of 'just war' to justify

---

[47] Cf. Green, 'Ethics' (667); emphasis mine.
[48] Bonhoeffer, *Ethics*, 681.
[49] Cf. Green, 'Ethics' (5).
[50] Bonhoeffer, *Ethics*, 55.

the removal of 'the tyrannical despiser of human beings', the barely veiled way he describes Hitler in his writings. The following elements form part of that theologizing.

First, he challenges various principles that comprise an 'ethics of nobility' as inadequate to the situation he found himself in: reason, principle, conscience, duty, absolute freedom and private duty – these are the ethics of a 'noble humanity' but they are insufficient. Rather it implies a free responsible action 'that rests solely on [one's] own responsibility, the only sort of action that can meet evil at its heart and overcome it'. Such an act:

1. takes the risk of a vicarious representative action that assumes the guilt of another as one's own. 'It may be better to do evil than be evil';
2. must *correspond with the reality: 'in the course of history there are occasions when the raw necessities of human life are at stake. Such situations of ultimate necessity transcend all principles, laws, norms, and rules, appealing instead to 'the free responsibility of the one who acts, a responsibility not bound by any law'*;
3. implies the willingness to take on guilt as an act of repentance, in which the act is not justified, but rather takes on not only the guilt of his own action but that of his Church and his nation;
4. emerges from authentic freedom.[51]

The theological density with which we sense Bonhoeffer struggling with the realities he and those he collaborated with is moving. But its gift is not a justification of his actions, and to read as such would convert them into autobiography. Their gift is that of challenging us to re-understand the nature of Christian living, to overcome all false dualisms between the private and public spheres, and to assume an adult faith in a paradoxical world that is spiralling out of control while still being held in Christ: the public square is *in* Christ's body and the church exists *only and always* to witness to the full humanity that is Christ, even as we sense the reality of our own limitations and sin.

Strange Life

I wrote this song after the death of my thesis director and mentor, Michael Paul Gallagher, SJ,[52] just one person in my life whose presence made a difference and whose absence is felt.[53] I think his death was particularly

---

[51]For this summary of his thought, see Green, 'Ethics' (13).
[52]Michael Paul Gallagher, *Into Extra Time: Living through the Final Stages of Cancer and Jottings Along the Way* (London: Darton, Longman & Todd, 2016).
[53]Of course, when my father died, the cut was even deeper, and he has his own song.

hard because he was one of the people who saw who I was and invited me to theologize from that space and not another. A conversation in the halls of the Gregorian on how he liked my music and 'why did I not write more about it in my theology?' changed my thesis theme and theological journey, for life. We only have one life, and *'no one in this universe can do the things that you might do. One life . . . Can't buy . . . extra time'*. Therefore, as we move to the musical space for this theologian's thought, instead of starting with the music, I invite you to read, and try and imagine this one life cut off before full-time, through the lens of the more informal, personal thoughts we have access to through his copious letter writing, both before and during his time in prison. We see a man utterly grounded in a loving family, thanking them for every letter and package, where even knowing they were outside the prison gave him joy. We see a family struggling with his imprisonment hoping every week for his safe return – tragic reading when one knows the end! We see a man who loved life, the sun, sleep and the pleasure of good dreams. We see a man in love, drawing life from every word and detail he receives from or about his fiancée, Maria; and being teased by her about his incapacity to dance or ride a horse and drawing strength from dreams of when it might be over.

> Again I've had a marvellous letter from Maria. The poor girl has to keep on writing without getting a direct response from me. That must be hard, but I delight in every word about her and every small detail interests me because it makes it easier to share in what she is doing. I'm so grateful to her. In my bolder dreams I sometimes picture our future home. *Letter to his parents, Whit Sunday*, 14 June 1943[54]

We are given access to the agonies of falling in love and the gratitude and joy following a declaration of 'yes'.

> I sense and am overwhelmed by the awareness that a gift without equal has been given me – after all the confusion of the past weeks I had no longer dared to hope – and now the unimaginably great and blissful thing is simply here, and my heart opens up and becomes quite wide and overflowing with thankfulness and shame and still cannot grasp it at all – this 'Yes' that is to be decisive for our entire life. If we were now able to talk in person with each other, there would be so infinitely much – yet fundamentally only always one and the same thing – to say! . . . your faithful Dietrich. *Letter to Maria von Wedemeyer*, 23 January 1943[55]

---

[54] Bonhoeffer, *Letters and Papers from Prison*, 54.
[55] Bonhoeffer, *Dbwe Vol. 16 Conspiracy and Imprisonment*, 386.

It is the tenderness of a fully fledged feeling of human passion.⁵⁶ We see the same relentless stubbornness in trying to move the marriage forward and the sadness felt when it came too late:

> There was no urgency on his part, although. . . . After our engagement Dietrich became less cautious. He had at first accepted a waiting period out of respect to my family, but soon he objected, clearly, decisively, and repeatedly in letters and telephone calls to me. When we succeeded in changing the dictum, it was too late; he had been imprisoned.⁵⁷

We see a man whose commitment to worldly holiness unfolds in his commitment to that love: 'I discovered later, and I'm still discovering right up to this moment, that is it only by living completely in this world that one learns to have faith'.⁵⁸

We sense a man who others see as deeply joyful and present to others, who can accept and laugh even with his guards when Maria brought a Christmas tree that would only have fit into his room if he moved the bed out and stood for the whole Christmas season! A deeply human person who felt the struggle of inner doubts and self-questioning by the very fact that he is in prison. Bonhoeffer found being in prison humiliating, even as he recognized the respect he seemed to receive.

> Am I then really that which other men tell of?
> Or am I only what I myself know of myself?
> Restless and longing and sick, like a bird in a cage,
> Struggling for breath, as though hands were compressing my throat,
> . . . Faint, and ready to say farewell to it all.
> *Who am I? They mock me, these lonely questions of mine.*
> *Whoever I am, Thou knowest, O God, I am altogether thine.*⁵⁹

And we watch the end coming, as his fiancée cannot find which prison they have moved him to, writing to her mother: 'Unfortunately my whole journey to Bundorf and Flossenbürg was completely in vain. Dietrich isn't here at all. Who knows where he is. In Berlin they won't tell me and in Flossenbürg they don't know. A pretty hopeless situation. But what am I supposed to do now?'⁶⁰ Neither she nor his family learnt of his death until months after the fact.

---

⁵⁶Cf. Dietrich Bonhoeffer and Maria von Wedemeyer, *Love Letters from Cell 92. The Correspondence between Dietrich Bonhoeffer and Maria Von Wedemeyer, 1943–1945*, ed. R.-A. V. Bismarch and U. Kabitz (Nashville, TN: Abingdon Press, 1995).
⁵⁷Wedemeyer-Weller, 'Appendix: The Other Letters from Prison', 412–19 (413).
⁵⁸Bonhoeffer, *Letters and Papers from Prison*, 369.
⁵⁹For the full version of this beautiful poem, see Bonhoeffer, *Letters and Papers from Prison*, 459.
⁶⁰Letter from Maria von Wedemeyer to Ruth von Wedemeyer from Flossenbürg on 19 February 1945, in Bonhoeffer, *Letters and Papers from Prison*, 556.

As you listen to the song, perhaps one question to ask is this: What Germany of the Second World War would look like without a life like this (and all the connections, collaborators, loved ones that make such a life possible)? What kind of darkness would still colour European Christianity without the lightning strike of thought such as this? The first time I went to visit a concentration camp, the one clear thought remaining as I left was that if one life could engender that kind of evil, then only a life utterly surrendered to God and dedicated to good could merit the name of Christian: a life that has become itself, a life that knows what it wants, even when what that looks like makes no sense. Ours is *a strange life*.[61]

'Strange Life' lyrics

It's a strange life . . . Are you alright?
Sorry may be hard to say . . . til you try goodbye.
Take your time! You gotta slow right down to get things right
Be yourself! You're the only one who can work that out!
No one in a hundred thousand years has ever looked like you
No one in this universe can do the things that you might do
One life . . . Can't buy . . . extra time; Heartbeat, hold me near!
Close your eyes: You can see what's true best when it's dark
Search inside . . . be one of the few who know what they want.
Life is too real to not imagine what it's meant to be . . .
Life is way too short to waste on anything except your dreams
Strange life . . . we try . . . to walk in style; Beauty, help me feel!
Take your time! You gotta slow things right down to get them right
Become yourself! Ain't no one but you can work that out!
It's a strange life . . . Are we alright?
Sorry may be hard to say . . . til you try goodbye.

©MAEVE LOUISE HEANEY, 2020.
Strange Life, The Music of Doubtful Faith

Selected Further Reading

For an Introduction to Bonhoeffer's Life and Thought

Bethge, Eberhard. *Dietrich Bonhoeffer: Theologian, Christian, Contemporary.* London: Collins, 1970.

---

[61]The link to the song 'Strange Life' is here: https://res.cloudinary.com/bloomsbury-online-resources/video/upload/v1639138179/Suspended%20God/Strange_Life.wav

Dramm, Sabine. *Dietrich Bonhoeffer: An Introduction to His Thought*. Peabody, MA: Hendrickson Publishers, 2007.

Tietz, Christiane. *Theologian of Resistance: The Life and Thought of Dietrich Bonhoeffer*. New York: Fortress Press, 2016.

Bonhoeffer's Spirituality and Understanding of Ministry

Bonhoeffer, Dietrich. *The Cost of Discipleship*. London: SCM Press, 1959.

Bonhoeffer's Correspondence:

Letters and Papers from Prison, edited by De Gruchy, John W., Ilse Tödt, Renate Bethge, Eberhard Bethge and Christian Gremmels. 1st English language ed. Minneapolis, MN: Fortress Press, 2010.

Bonhoeffer's Theology of Reconciliation

Prüller-Jagenteufel, Gunter. '"Restraining Power" against Evil and "Scarring over" of Guilt Bonhoefferian Remarks on "Penultimate" Steps toward Reconciliation'. In *Reconciliation: The Way of Healing and Growth*, edited by Juhant, Janez and Bojan Žalec, 169–77. Wien-Berlin: LIT Verlag, 2012.

Bonhoeffer's Major Works

Bonhoeffer, Dietrich, Clifford J. Green, and Michael P. DeJonge. *The Bonhoeffer Reader*, edited by Green, Clifford J. and Michael P. DeJonge. Minneapolis, MN: Fortress Press, 2013.

Dietrich Bonhoeffer Works. Vol. 16, Conspiracy and Imprisonment, 1940–1945, edited by Brocker, Mark S., Lisa E. Dahill and Douglas W. Stott. Minneapolis, MN: Fortress Press, 2006.

On the Influence of Afro-American Spirituality on Bonhoeffer

Williams, Reggie L. *Bonhoeffer's Black Jesus: Harlem Renaissance Theology and an Ethic of Resistance*, WACO, TX: Baylor University Press, 2014.

12

Is celibacy ever a good idea?

Why would Christianity bless an option to *not* love?

One of the points made in various chapters of this book is that creation is good, human beings are well made and sexuality is a central part of human anthropology that theology and Church teaching need to interact with more intelligently than has been manifest in the past. Chapter sixteen will address this in relation to sexual relationships and marriage, drawing on the life and thought of Rosemary Haughton. Here I tackle a different pathway in the living out of sexuality: that of celibacy and its contribution to the life of the Church and theology. My approach here is slightly different from other chapters, because instead of studying a known theologian of the recent past, I am looking at this issue through the lens of the life and writings of women who lived in the sixteenth century and who was not technically a theologian: Spanish Carmelite Teresa of Avila (1515–82). Why? First and foremost, because not only does her life, thought and writings address the theme but also because of a gradual awareness of how much lives and writings like hers have to offer the theological task of the Church. In 1970, Paul VI gave Teresa of Avila the title of 'Doctor of the Universal Church'. In fact, during the last century, three other women were also accorded the title: Hildegard of Bingen (1098–1179), Catherine of Siena (1347–80) and Thérèse of Lisieux (1873–97).[1] A focus on one will help us imagine similar explorations of the other three. Before I focus on Teresa, an overview of what the title of 'Doctor of the Church' involves is important.

---

[1] For a fascinating account of the objections to, and finally acceptance of, women as doctors of the Church, see Keith J. Egan, 'The Significance for Theology of the Doctor of the Church: Teresa of Avila', in *The Pedagogy of God's Image: Essays on Symbol and the Religious Imagination*, ed. R. Masson, 153–71 (Chico, CA: Scholars Press, 1981).

Doctors of the Church

The criteria for receiving this title are three: holiness of life; service to the Church in the form of insight into Scripture and theological knowledge (referred to as 'eminent doctrine expressed in a significant body of writings'); and official approval by a Pope or Council. In this way, they are given, as it were, to the Church and theology as a witness of holiness and as an authoritative source of thought and insight. Work on the contribution of these women to Christian thought was already in progress before they were named Doctors, but the move has catapulted them into theological discourse in rich ways. They provide theology with both new impulse and disruption in how we understand theological activity. The former because they give us access to 'data' on the experience of the divine we can trust and explore. The latter because they upset the cart of theology's history and self-understanding. In and through these women from the twelfth, fourteenth, sixteenth and twentieth centuries, we get access to a world of thought and forms of writing which have been absent from mainstream theology as it has been understood, and we are poorer without it.

In this chapter, I focus on the issue of celibacy in light of the life and work of one of them: Teresa of Avila, but before I do, what are some of the themes these 'accidental theologians' bring to theology?[2] We have already addressed Hildegard of Bingen's musical contribution to theology in chapter two but beyond this, her theology of the Holy Spirit, her integral approach to human living and the notion of the *'viriditas'* in and of life in God (translated as greenness or simply viridity, because of how hard the word is to translate), cosmic regeneration and healing are themes being explored. Her image-led theology challenges and enriches both the content and style of theologizing. Catherine of Siena was the first woman whose writing was published in vernacular language in Italy, and her writings include letters, prayers and a work called *The Dialogue*. Her prose is vivid, concrete and Christ-centred, contributing to a rich theology of the Incarnation expressed in images of life such as blood, food, eating, nursing, engagement and marriage. Both Hildegard and Catherine were powerful prophetic voices in the conflicts of their world – within the Church and between Church and State – witnesses to the presence and influence of women in Christendom we can lose sight of. Thérèse of Lisieux's thought on the Eucharist, the gifts of the Spirit and her understanding of the mystical body of Christ, the communion of saints and a theology of the cross are some of the current foci of interest. This chapter will focus on Teresa of Avila's understanding of prayer and life in Christ, but her underlying grasp of the Church, the Trinity, the human person,

---

[2] Elizabeth Dreyer, *Accidental Theologians: Four Women Who Shaped Christianity* (Cincinnati, OH: Franciscan Media, 2014). Dryer's insightful work is a source for this chapter.

the Eucharist, Christology, suffering, and the Resurrection are some of the themes being explored in current studies of spirituality and theology.[3]

All of this is to say that there is a wealth of knowledge and teaching to be gleaned from these doctors of the Church, although their work is not in the discursive form we are used to in theology. Because of their exclusion from theological education, their writings draw on the resources that they had at their disposal: Scripture, *lectio divina*, spiritual writings, imagination, and symbols drawn from their life of prayer and daily experience. Their contributions are narrative, mystical, symbolic, imaginative and prophetic, bringing to theology a much-needed antidote *and* complement to the discursive methods of a theology shaped in scholastic times. Their methods are not reserved to women, of course. The rediscovery of St Ephrem's contribution to poetic theology is a case in point,[4] but the recognition by the Church of these writings is an invitation to theology to recover and *aggiornare* its understanding of how truth has been revealed, in light of them.

It is also interesting that all four women lived out their lives in celibacy 'for the reign of God' in distinct ways. Hildegard was a Benedictine nun and founder of two monasteries. Catherine was a Third Order Dominican laywoman, a form of commitment and belonging that embraced the evangelical counsels of poverty, chastity and obedience but did not imply living in community. Teresa belonged to and reformed the Carmelites, the Order to which Thérèse also belonged. I am in no way suggesting that they *had* to be celibate in order to be theologically fertile and to be named doctors. I am sure there are married men and women whose lives and thought could and should be added to the list (since there are currently none!). The Church is often more comfortable with celibate women in their theological and doctrinal circles, until that very freedom becomes an issue, of course. However, the reality is that these women *were* celibate, and in their time, this gave them the space, education, time and to a certain degree and not without caveats, the authority to speak and teach which they would otherwise not have had.

---

[3]Cf. Massimo Marcocchi, 'Spirituality in the Sixteenth and Seventeenth Centuries', in *Catholicism in Early Modern History: A Guide to Research*, ed. J. W. O'Malley, 163–92 (St. Louis, MO: Center for Reformation Research, 1988). Peter Tyler and Edward Howells (eds), *Teresa of Avila: Mystical Theology and Spirituality in the Carmelite Tradition* (New York: Routledge, 2017).
[4]Sebastian P. Brock, *The Luminous Eye: The Spiritual World Vision of Saint Ephrem* (Kalamazoo, MI: Cistercian Publications, 1992).

The issue of loving a greater love?

So, let's name this chapter's question! It is a complex one, because most of us have mixed memories of, and reactions to, the issue of religious life. For those within the Catholic Church, we know that much of our current education and health system owes its origins to the selfless and prophetic commitment of women and men of the past to serve the poor in their time. There are sisters, brothers, missionaries or priests whose life and presence made a difference for us. There are also too many people whose memory is of horror and pain, because the hurt suffered by someone who actually *symbolized* God's presence for them has done incalculable damage to their lives and faith in that God.[5] But even apart from this, in our contemporary world the thought of someone freely choosing *not* to live a sexually active life with another human being is simply strange: Why? What's the point? This is compounded by the historical preference of the Church for virginity over marriage as a pathway to holiness and its obvious difficulty in providing balanced and nuanced moral guidance in relation to sex. Many people's Christian formation of conscience revolved around *anything* sexual being sinful. This is not the case, of course, and as we explore in other chapters, the Christian understanding of sexuality is a beautiful and visionary one,[6] but that *is* how the Church left its mark on many people and cultures, and how it continues to be perceived, in the main. So, a world that cannot conceive life without sex sees a life-option without it as frustrated, and either demands of us more humanity or dismisses us as out of touch. And yet there continue to be people who freely choose this life-option.

Before going any further, I would clarify that this chapter is *not* about whether priests should be allowed to marry or not. The practice of celibacy in priesthood is one the Church values and defends, but it is a Church law that developed over time and therefore could be changed. Neither will I address here the issue of sexual abuse – a theme that is too important and complex to be dealt with in one chapter. That being said, a greater understanding of the meaning and contribution of the vocation to consecrated life – or what the church has called 'celibacy for the reign of God' – is a necessary element of an understanding of celibacy and will help us cut to the core of what would *actually* provoke change. The rediscovery of women in positions of authority and exercising influence in reforming the church offers some clues as to how power that avoids abuse could be imagined differently.

However, the focus of this chapter is on one small aspect of that bigger picture: the specific call to and living out of what we call consecrated celibate

---

[5] Cf. Marie Keenan, *Child Sexual Abuse and the Catholic Church: Gender, Power, and Organizational Culture* (Oxford: Oxford University Press, 2012).
[6] See chapter sixteen on Rosemary Haughton.

life by those who have felt it as their Christian vocation.[7] It is characterized by a lifelong commitment to three counsels, or vows – poverty, chastity and obedience – through which a person commits to giving up material possessions, a loving and intimate partnership with another person and control over their own decisions, in order to 'more closely follow Jesus, poor, chaste and obedient'. The commitment is often combined with an option for shared life in community, although it can also take the form of a personal option in the midst of the world and society. The question is *why*? And what does it contribute? To many, it looks like a rejection of human love, so why would Christianity value, and even bless, such a way of life?[8] Before I turn to our theological source, some background on its origins and meaning is necessary.

Background and meaning of consecrated life

There is a long history of people and groups who have chosen a celibate pathway since the event of Jesus' life, death and resurrection: Paul was single and encouraged people to not get married so as to remain focussed on Jesus, because he thought that 'time was short' (cf. 1 Cor. 7.29); the hermitic life and writings of Anthony of Egypt and the Desert Fathers and Mothers, who challenged a church becoming mainstream to maintain the values Jesus lived and preached; the Benedictine monastic tradition that emerged in the sixth century; the mendicant orders of the twelfth and thirteenth centuries including the Dominicans, Franciscans and the Sisters of St Clare; a myriad of apostolic orders from the sixteenth century onwards; and more recently, the reality of secular and new forms of consecrated life. The list *is* endless. But what does this life mean?

A theology of consecrated life developed over time, but some of its key points are these: it finds its first foundation in the life and witness of Jesus, whose relatively short life was celibate and poor, an option which was counter-cultural in Jewish mentality. Contemporary attempts to explore or give the historical Jesus a romantic story or a hidden wife seem implausible, although this does not mean the gospels and the tradition of the church did not overlook or even hide aspects of the human dimension of Jesus'

---

[7] I use the term 'consecrated life or celibacy' to distinguish it from the option for single life, which some people, for a variety of reasons, choose or find themselves in. This is another pathway which has long been overlooked by Church teaching and spirituality as if such lives were incomplete or frustrated version of life's normal pathways. The oversight has been a painful one, for many. Cf. Susan Muto, *Celebrating the Single Life: A Spirituality for Single Persons in Today's World* (New York: Crossroad, 1989).

[8] It is worth remembering that there are similar options in other religions or philosophies, such as Buddhism, Hinduism and the celibate Essenes and monks of the Qumran, in Judaism.

life and his friendships with, and trust in, women.⁹ Jesus chose to live alone in company. The felt meaning of this option of Jesus – and those who feel called to consecrated life – is the dual call to love God exclusively and with no human mediation, and in that love to keep one's life open and free to love and serve those who most need it. This is why history often finds religious women and men in remote parts of the world doing things for people who are marginalized or forgotten. The option for religious life was born as a charismatic and prophetic call to the Church to be authentic to its truest values. Poverty, chastity and obedience are not strange values invented by a Church that enjoys saying 'no' but counsels, or guidelines, drawn from Jesus' life and teaching, which in some form we are all called to live:

1. open to God and others, in material and spiritual willingness to receive and give without possessing, in the understanding that God is provident and material security is not everything (poverty);
2. pure in heart and body, so as to live with integrity and wholeness whatever way of life we choose to live (chastity);
3. seeking God's will, as our best chance at getting right a full life (obedience).

Without separating the counsels, Schneiders is right in identifying celibate chastity as the most essential element of religious life.¹⁰ Jesus' counsels to live open (poor), and seeking God's will (obedient) are for all disciples of Christ, and are often lived just as or more radically by those living them out *with and through another*. But consecrated celibacy is for those called to this way of life. Religious life took these counsels a step further by creating a 'way of life' in community through the vowed commitment to these values for life. In this option of life, the vow of poverty involves an option to not own anything material but to share all in common for the sake of a shared mission. Celibate chastity is the commitment to a life loving God and those in need – according to the specific mission of the community – instead of a

---

⁹Cf. Elisabeth Schüssler Fiorenza, *In Memory of Her: A Feminist Theological Reconstruction of Christian Origins* (New York: Crossroad, 1983); Sandra M. Schneiders, *The Revelatory Text: Interpreting the New Testament as Sacred Scripture* (Collegeville, MN: Liturgical Press, 1999), especially the final chapter on John 4. A recent film on Mary Magdalene, while theologically weaker than it could have been in relation to what we know about women in Scripture and early Christian communities, is a moving imaginative exploration of women's presence in Jesus' life and ministry. Cf. *Mary Magdalene* (2018), https://www.imdb.com/title/tt5360996/.

¹⁰Sandra Schneiders' trilogy on religious life – which we spoke about in chapter six – is built around the parable of the hidden treasure: 'a man finds treasure hidden in a field, and to ensure he can keep it, sells everything to buy the field' (Mt. 13:44). Sandra M. Schneiders, *Finding the Treasure: Locating Catholic Religious Life in a New Ecclesial and Cultural Context* (New York: Paulist Press, 2000); *Selling All: Commitment, Consecrated Celibacy and Community in Catholic Religious Life* (Mahwah, NJ: Paulist Press, 2001); *Buying the Field: Catholic Religious Life in Mission to the World* (New York: Paulist Press, 2013).

human partner. And obedience involves the option to seek in all things the will of God, made concrete in obeying the legitimately elected leaders of the community in which one commits to God. Each community of people committed to this lifestyle gathers around a particular task, or mission, which the church calls a charism. This explains the variety of forms of institutes of consecrated life existent in the Church: they arise as a response to a need, and new ones are still emerging, even as the world asks: 'What for?'. Finally, and from a theological perspective, as well as witnessing to what matters now, consecrated life is understood to be a prophetic witness of life to come, our eschatological union with God which, while shared in the body of Christ, is also deeply personal.

> By the profession of the evangelical counsels *the characteristic features of Jesus* – the chaste, poor and obedient one – *are made constantly 'visible' in the midst of the world* and the eyes of the faithful are directed towards the mystery of the Kingdom of God already at work in history, even as it awaits its full realization in heaven.[11]

The point is that despite our bonds to the ones we love and our hope of meeting again after this life, each one of us shall face God alone, in the end. Consecrated life offers us a witness that says: 'everything will be alright!'

My lens in this chapter is the life, spirituality and writing of Teresa of Avila. We are not looking for how she addresses the question of celibacy as a theological theme. We cannot expect a sixteenth-century woman to ask our questions. But we can look to how her living out of that pathway and writings contribute to a theological understanding of celibate chastity. From her life we shall glean what poverty, chastity and obedience can *look* and *feel* like when lived at depth and with courage. Within her thought, I focus on her understanding of friendship with God as the heart of Christian spirituality and how that enriches a theology of consecrated life.

Teresa of Avila: From friend of God to doctor of the Church

Context is important. At times the lives of saints or mystics are treated as extraordinary phenomena and written into the books of the lives of saints in a manner that makes them seem 'supernatural' and far above ordinary mortals.

---

[11]Cf. John Paul II, *The Consecrated Life: Post-Synodal Apostolic Exhortation Vita Consecrata* (Homebush, NSW: St. Pauls, 1996), 1. This Post-Synodal Apostolic Exhortation, published twenty-five years ago, provides an excellent oversight of the main principles and theological tenets of consecrated life.

Without taking away from the wonder of their lives, this is unreasonable and contrary to how God usually interacts with humanity, attentive to and within our worlds of meaning. Therefore, the more distant the historical context is, the more important it is to try and bridge that gap. Given the plethora of sources for comprehensive biographies on Teresa,[12] my focus here is on the key aspects of her experience that influenced her thought and writings. What made this sixteenth-century Spanish woman a formidable reformer, founder of seventeen convents and a doctor of the Church?

Teresa of Avila: Life and context

Teresa of Avila was born in 1515 as Teresa de Cepeda y Ahumada to a mother whose lineage was noble and a father who was a successful merchant and of Jewish descent. This mixed heritage, between the honour-obsessed nobility and what was considered in Spain at that time questionable ancestry, marks both her spirituality and her choices later on. But before that, Teresa's achievements and troubles are best understood against the backdrop of the cultural and ecclesial contexts underpinning her life. Spain was moving from a time of great flourishing and interaction with renaissance culture and other countries in Europe to one of defence and suspicion. This included suspicion of the *conversos* (Jews converted to Catholicism but not of an old tradition). It was the time of Martin Luther and the Reformation, and alongside this challenge, a defensive Church and country were wary of the influence of what were called the *Alumbrados* (the Illuminated), a spiritual movement that accentuated personal prayer and special illumination. While there were different groups under this banner and not all of them were deemed equally dangerous, their existence led to the disapproval and suspicion of the practice of mental prayer and spiritual writings describing ecstatic experiences, especially when written by women, who were untrained and considered gullible. This suspicion of mental prayer is one Teresa will address directly. She lived in the time of the Catholic Inquisition, in which the imprisonment and/or burning of 'heretics' and 'witches' was a real possibility. Church and royalty were invested in protecting and restoring 'Catholic Spain'. So, when Teresa began to experience visions, she and those who advised her knew she needed to be careful. But Teresa's commitment to her Catholic faith ran deep, and in that broad setting she speaks of a 'world in flames'. It was unlikely that she was familiar with Reformation theology, but she was deeply troubled by this opposition to Catholicism and aware of the need to reform *and* defend the faith. She was also conscious of the

---

[12]For an insightful reading of her life, context and spirituality, see Rowan Williams, *Teresa of Avila* (London: Geoffrey Chapman, 1991).

attempts being made in Spain's colonies to convert the peoples there, by which her convents provided prayer-support for those efforts.

What about Teresa's personality and vocation? Vivid stories about Teresa's life reveal her to be a passionate and fun-loving woman. At nine, fed by stories of the martyrs, she tried to escape with her brother Rodrigo to be beheaded for the faith. A few years later, she is devouring romantic novels and sent to board at a convent for eighteen months to avoid the scandal of compromising herself and her family. During her time there and after a period of illness and reflection, she decided to enter the convent and 'take the veil' in 1536, against family wishes, at first. By all accounts including her own, her first twenty years as a nun were sincere but average, in an atmosphere wherein convents were also places of social visits and status. Teresa was a sought-after interlocutor at convent gatherings, and she tells of how her prayer-life, which could be consoling, was intermittent and even absent during some of these years. She lived a life torn between a desire to be faithful and the company and approval of those who surrounded her. She was also plagued by illness, at times severe. Her slow journey of growth was fed by reading contemporary spiritual authors who influenced her understanding of prayer and spiritual life. This is important to note, because although the prime matter of writings will be the expression of her own experience, underlying these are books by authors of the time on methodological mental prayer, liturgical piety and spiritual exercises,[13] as well as translations of classics by Augustine, Gregory the Great, Bonaventure and Catherine of Siena, to name a few. It is not easy to identify everything Teresa read that influenced her, as she had 'an amazing capacity for assimilation and invention', but the sources are beginning to be identified and explored.[14]

Teresa says her first deeper experience of prayer took place during the Lent of 1554 (eighteen years after joining the convent). It was a vision of Christ suffering and wounded. She also describes another vision historically close to that one, which she calls her 'spiritual betrothal', in 1556. These catapult Teresa into a quest for faithfulness and, as part of that, the attempt with some other nuns to reform the Carmel through the foundation of convents that would return to a simpler life and the observation of the original constitutions. This began with the Convent of St Joseph in 1562. Hers was not an easy life. She suffered opposition from the Church, the Nuncio, the male provincial, the locals and her own sisters. Her books were sent to bishops for scrutiny of their orthodoxy. She battled with illness her whole life, succumbing in 1582 after a visit to one of her foundations. Yet, through all of this, her personality shines through, known and remembered

---

[13] Such as García Jiménez de Cisneros, Bernardino de Laredo and Francisco de Osuna, for example. We know that Teresa read Osuna's *The Third Spiritual Alphabet* during one of her periods of illness and was familiar with *The Imitation of Christ*, Augustine's *Confessions* and Gregory the Great's *Moralia in Job*.
[14] Cf. Marcocchi, 'Spirituality in the Sixteenth and Seventeenth Centuries', 163–92 (164–7).

for her intelligence, humour, freedom and practical wisdom. There are many stories of her wit. Some recount her discussions with Jesus: complaining to Him about her sufferings, she hears him respond: 'this is how I treat my friends', to which she retorts: 'and that is why you have so few!'. Others tell of her common-sense wisdom in orientating her convents. My favourite reached me as oral tradition from my time in Spain. Upon meeting the king, he tells her that he has heard of her fame as 'beautiful, intelligent and holy'. Her answer is: 'Beautiful? What your majesty sees. Intelligent? I'm not stupid. And as for holy? Only God knows'. Whether true or not, this is how the Spanish remember and revere her.

Teresa's identity as both noble *and* of Jewish descent came to bear on how she led her life and the reform she initiated. The former led her to interact with many powerful men and women during her life, including King Phillip II, whose support she sought and used. The importance of the latter and its influence on her spirituality and style of leadership have only recently been discovered.[15] As a person of Jewish descent, she was a 'displaced person' in the Spain of her day, ever aware of the fragility of status, and the stigma of being a 'convert' to the faith rather than an 'old Christian': *conversos* were considered impure and lacking in honour. Some elements of Teresa's reform were directly impacted by this awareness, such as the inclusion of *conversos* in her convents, the reluctance to receive endowments for foundations to avoid the expectations this imposed on them and the insistence on the equality among nuns, without titles or differences in work duties. Wary of human honour, from the start of her reform, she became known simply as 'Teresa of Jesus'.

Teresa's writings

Teresa writes because she is asked to by those who accompany her (confessors and advisors). Aware of the risks, her books are carefully vetted and presented to the authorities for approval. While she does not appear to be overly concerned by this, it is hard to underestimate the real danger she faced at that time in writing of her prayer experiences. Women mystics defending mental prayer were a concern for Church authorities, and while this feels offensive from a contemporary perspective, given the mentality of the time and the lack of theological education they were allowed access to, it is hardly surprising. A brief overview of her main writings shows a journey in her own understanding of what Christian prayer is and how it evolves.[16]

---

[15]Cf. in particular Williams, *Teresa of Avila*.
[16]Teresa's translated writings are gathered in three volumes: Teresa of Avila, *The Complete Works of St Teresa of Avila. Volume 1*, ed. E. A. Peers (London and New York: Burns & Oates, 2002); Teresa of Avila, *The Complete Works of St Teresa of Avila. Volume 2*, ed. E. A. Peers (London and New York: Burns & Oates, 2002); Teresa of Avila, *The Complete Works of St Teresa of Avila. Volume 3*, ed. E. A. Peers (London and New York: Burns & Oates, 2002).

The Book of Her Life is her first attempt to describe her journey and understanding of prayer for the benefit of Church authorities and at the request of her confessors and supporters. *The Way of Perfection* is a presentation of life in the convent as a way of prayer-life understood as friendship with God and with each other. It portrays a clear understanding of the connectedness of human affect and friendship with each and with God – without ignoring the pitfalls. It includes a careful introduction to mental prayer, not as an optional extra or a suspicious rarity but simply 'prayer that is conscious of what it is'.[17]

> Mental prayer, in my view, is nothing but friendly intercourse, and frequent solitary converse, with Him Who we know loves us.[18]

The conversations she used to seek and enjoy with others are now to be found in prayer: 'I will have thee converse now, not with men, but with angels.'[19] In light of this understanding of the centrality of friendship, Teresa insisted on convents being small, in part to avoid the multiplication of visitors and other tenants who were hosted in her old convent, making it a social hub, but mainly to promote genuine friendship among the sisters.

Her *Meditations on the Song of Songs* are an audacious commentary on a few verses of that famous biblical text – to which she herself would have had only limited access. The presumption of writing not only on Scripture but on *this* Scripture, as a woman and for the instruction of her nuns, led to attempts to have all copies burned. Thankfully, her nuns managed to send one to someone they knew would keep it safe!

> Let Him kiss me with the kiss of His mouth. O my Lord and my God, what words are these for a worm to use to its Creator! Blessed be Thou, Lord, Who hast taught us in so many different ways! Who would dare to use these words, my King, save by Thy permission? It is an astounding thing – and it may well be thought astounding for me to say that they may be used by anyone whatsoever. It will be said that I am a stupid creature, that the Bride does not mean this at all, that these words have many meanings, that it is obvious we could not address them to God, and that for this reason it is well that such things should not be read by simple-minded people. I confess that the words may be taken in many senses, *but the soul that is afire with love so that she hardly knows what she is saying is interested in none of them, but wishes only to repeat the words themselves.* Yes, and the Lord does not forbid her to. Dear God!

---

[17] Williams, *Teresa of Avila*, 88.
[18] Teresa of Avila, 'The Life of the Holy Mother Teresa of Avila', in *The Complete Works of St Teresa of Avila. Volume 1*, ed. E. A. Peers (50) (London and New York: Burns & Oates, 2002).
[19] Avila, 'The Life of the Holy Mother Teresa of Avila' (155).

Why should we be astounded at this? Does not the reality give us greater cause for wonder? Do we not approach the Most Holy Sacrament? I have even wondered if the Bride was asking here for this favour which Christ afterwards gave us. I have also wondered if she was asking for a union as great as that of God being made man.[20]

Over the next few years, she writes on her reform of the Carmel in *The Book of Her Foundations*. The book portrays her continued insistence on the importance of prayer and the quest for God, if also a matured awareness of the dangers of self-delusion and the parameters of a mature spiritual life. She is particularly wary of the excessive focus of some nuns on getting lost in contemplation. Apparently, they would fall into long periods of absorption that left them unable to attend to anything else:

> I have been trying very hard to discover the source of a deep absorption which I have seen in certain persons to whom the Lord gives great joy in prayer and who leave nothing undone in order to prepare themselves for the reception of His favours.... In my opinion, their love would be much better if they did not allow themselves to be carried away, for at this stage in their prayer they are quite capable of offering resistance.... It would be more to the point to use the time well rather than to spend so much of it in a state of absorption. Much more merit can be derived from a single act, and from the frequent arousing of the will to love God, than from the abandonment of it to this state of inertia. So I advise prioresses to make all possible efforts to prevent these long swoons, for in my opinion they do nothing but paralyse the faculties and senses and hinder them from fulfilling the commands of the soul; and in this way they deprive them of the advantage which, if they proceed with care, they generally gain. If a prioress finds that this is caused by weakness, she must dispense from fasts and disciplines ... and give such persons duties to do so as to distract them from thoughts of self.[21]

After about ten years *The Interior Castle* is written, her most mature and developed work. It describes in vivid terms the journey of the soul towards the God who dwells within with the image of a crystal palace with seven rooms, or mansions: 'I began to think of the soul as if it were a castle made of a single diamond or of very clear crystal, in which there are many dwelling places, just as in Heaven there are many mansions.'[22]

---

[20] Teresa of Avila, *Song of Songs. Conceptions of the Love of God*, 363–7. The description of herself as a 'worm' is shocking to contemporary ears, but Teresa both genuinely affirms her poverty *and* portrays herself as authorities are more comfortable seeing her.
[21] Teresa of Avila, *The Book of Her Foundations*, in *chapter VI*, 26–8.
[22] Teresa of Avila, 'Interior Castle', in *The Complete Works of St Teresa of Avila. Volume 2*, (201), ed. E. A. Peers (London and New York: Burns & Oates, 2002).

In this book, we find one of her best-known comparisons of the steps of prayer with how we draw water. For example, in the fourth mansion, in which the soul is learning to let God lead in prayer:

> To understand it better, let us suppose that we are looking at two fountains, the basins of which can be filled with water. There are certain spiritual things which I can find no way of explaining more aptly than by this element of water. . . . These two large basins can be filled with water in different ways: the water in the one comes from a long distance, by means of numerous conduits and through human skill; but the other has been constructed at the very source of the water and fills without making any noise. If the flow of water is abundant, as in the case we are speaking of, a great stream still runs from it after it has been filled; no skill is necessary here, and no conduits have to be made, for the water is flowing all the time . . . direct from its source, which is God, and, when it is His Majesty's will and He is pleased to grant us some supernatural favour, its coming is accompanied by the greatest peace and quietness and sweetness within ourselves – I cannot say where it arises or how. [23]

Teresa was also an avid letter writer, to her sisters, friends and those who supported her. Her friendship with John of the Cross is one that has always drawn interest, a male mystic and counterpart in the reform of the male Carmelites. More recently, her letters to a friend and advisor called Gracian have drawn the interest of scholars. The affection, intimacy and spontaneity expressed in these letters prove scandalous to some, but to my mind reflect the fullness of life and love possible in a life lived in open and honest friendship with Christ. Loving God exclusively cannot mean loving others less. A letter asking him *not* to read her letters to the nuns he helped accompany in Seville shows a keen awareness of the challenges of leadership alongside the need for discretion. She often carefully refers to Gracian with pseudonyms, in this case, Paul:

> There are many reasons why I may feel and express affection for you and why all the sisters may not do the same: nor are all superiors like my father [refers to Gracian himself], towards whom they can act with perfect simplicity. . . . You and I are charged with a heavy burden of which we must render an account to God and man. Knowing the love that prompts my words you will forgive me and grant me the favour I asked before – that of not reading my letters in public. People's minds differ, and there are some things that superiors should never say outright. I should not like anyone to overhear what I say to God nor to disturb my intercourse with Him, and it is the same as regards Paul.[24]

---

[23] Teresa of Avila, 'Interior Castle' (236–7).
[24] Teresa of Avila to Father Gracian, Seville, From Toledo, November 1576, 126–8.

Teresa's writing style

Teresa's writing style is original and accessible. Even as she writes of the heights of union with God open to a Christian, she insists on service and charity to others as its only guarantee, the dangers of confusing distraction with rapture, and a good meal as an important remedy to taking one's own holiness too seriously. She is a woman writing in a man's world, and for the contemporary reader, her frequent dismissal of her own expertise as that of a 'weak woman' susceptible to the devil with no qualification other than that of her history of weakness and temptation makes for strange reading today. It is, however, at least in part, a rhetorical trope to lessen the sense of threat of a woman's intelligence in her readers (who were also her superiors), as Teresa speaks more than once about the access Jesus gave to women and the fact that he let them comfort and support him. And the demands of her friendship with Jesus take precedence over any attempt to impede her work (as in the case where she tells of how it is the voice of Jesus himself in prayer that brushes aside a Pauline rebuke to women teaching: 'Tell them they shouldn't follow just one part of Scripture, . . . and ask them if by any chance they can tie my hands?'.[25] Unfortunately, even now, the skill of finding ways to get one's thoughts through the censorship of male authority and insecurity is often necessary. In *The Way of Perfection* Williams invites us to recognize in its tone 'a certain degree of deliberate and almost provocative irony. . . . It is a conversation between Teresa and her sisters carried on before a rather suspicious audience; we should expect to find a certain degree of faintly conspiratorial wit, the amused sideways glance to see if the audience is paying attention'.[26] Teresa was also a woman of her time, however, who while courageous in the aims and extent of her reforms and critical of much of the lack of true leadership she saw in the Church, did not question its right – including that of the Inquisition – to verify the truth of someone's teachings.

From that position, her work is impressive: sophisticated, symbolic and imaginative. The steps of prayer are compared to different and increasingly more fruitful ways of watering a garden; the journey to God passes through mansions, each with specific traits; the soul coming into union with God is like the caterpillar entering into a cocoon to be reborn; union with God is compared to a drop of water getting lost in the ocean. It is clear that her spiritual gifts were accompanied and enhanced by an acute intelligence and capacity to creatively explore the realities of faith she experienced.

---

[25]Cf. Williams, *Teresa of Avila*, 164, quoting 'Spiritual Relations XIX' in Teresa of Avila, *The Complete Works of St Teresa of Avila. Volume 1*, 344.
[26]Williams, *Teresa of Avila*, 79–80.

You complete me: When love demands the consecration of one's whole being

What is there in Teresa's life and thought that helps answer our question about the point of consecrated celibacy? First, we need to be aware that her understanding of religious life was progressive. It seems that her first motive for entering was somewhere between awareness that it was a good way to serve God and fear of damnation and hell, which in the spirituality of the time would have been normal. But Teresa's self-awareness and honesty – even of her mediocrity – led her forward. A good place to start is how she herself lived the three counsels that frame consecrated life: poverty, obedience and chastity.

1. In Teresa, we see a clear option for poverty. She resisted contemporary offers of endowments for her reformed convents, certain that she needed to live a simple lifestyle that witnessed to God's providence and a willingness to work to support themselves. The equality of the sisters in sharing that work was also essential to her vision, which might sound normal to us now but different classes and lifestyles of nuns in convents were common in her time.

2. She also witnesses to obedience on a variety of levels. Teresa is an intelligent, faithful, courageous woman whose experience of God led her to step out of line *many times* to be faithful to that God, often against or despite the lack of support of those around her. She insisted on the need for effective spiritual accompaniment for herself and others. She argued with Jesus when she felt what He was asking her was too difficult, and she trusted an imperfect Church in less than easy times as her spiritual home, even as she reformed it. Her life helps us to rethink this most misunderstood of vows. The word 'obedience' evokes images of submissive and blind relinquishing of one's capacity to think or decide for oneself, an understanding which has done much damage over time. But for Teresa, to obey implied a tremendous amount of freedom, starting with the freedom of self and others to listen attentively what was *happening* in the encounter with God, so as to discern what the will of God might be in any given moment. Then, to obey implied verifying that option, in which the advice of others and the guidance of the Church was essential, only after which there is the living out of that will. From her life we learn that obedience *can* imply surrendering one's will at times, not due to a lazy or insecure sense of self but rather based on trust in God and others, and never once and for all.

3. It is in Teresa's understanding of celibate chastity that we find her standout contribution to consecrated life and Christian spirituality more broadly, specifically in her experience and understanding of

affection, intimacy and friendship with the person of Jesus. Teresa's sustained focus on the humanity of Christ as the sole focus of her love, and his will as her only measure, witness to the heart of this vocation.

The first 'conversion' experience Teresa relates is provoked by the image of the suffering Jesus with his wounds. Her feelings of ingratitude and 'culpable indifference' are gradually replaced by a growing sense of Jesus needing her and of her wanting to be present to him in Gethsemane: 'she does this from a conviction that Christ in his vulnerability cannot refuse her presence, her "consolation", however unworthy she may be, so great is his need: "He had to accept me."'[27] From a theological perspective, this is Teresa's pearl of great price: the experience of the risen Jesus as friend. This sense of mutual presence and of Jesus needing her form the axis of her Christology. God, who is God, does *not* maintain distance but seeks mutual and reciprocal friendship. The familiar terms in her writing about honour and referring to Him as 'Majesty' reflect the society of her time, but categories are turned on their head in Jesus, who in becoming human for love of humanity needs her. This is her anchor.

Teresa clearly and decisively rejects tendencies of spiritual writings of her time to move through and beyond the humanity of Christ in the ascent of spiritual life towards union. The humanity of Christ sits at the centre of her understanding of prayer, because

> We are not angels and we have bodies. To want to become angels while we are still on earth, and as much on earth as I was, is ridiculous. As a rule, our thoughts must have something to lean upon . . . when we are busy, or suffering persecutions or trials, when we cannot get as much quiet as we should like, and at seasons of aridity, we have a very good Friend in Christ. We look at Him as a Man; we think of His moments of weakness and times of trial; and He becomes our Companion. Once we have made a habit of thinking of Him in this way, it becomes very easy to find him at our side.[28]

It is a fascinating witness to her grounded sense of life and an incarnated God that the importance of friendship with God extended for her into the friendship she wanted the sisters to have with each other. Teresa insisted on two hours recreation a day – a commitment many might call excessive, but she wanted them to be friends! It was also the main reason she wanted communities to be small, so that friendship rather than small groups or factions could characterize her convents.

---

[27]Williams, *Teresa of Avila*, 52.
[28]*The Life of the Holy Mother Teresa of Avila*, in Teresa of Avila, *The Complete Works of St Teresa of Avila. Volume 1*, 140–1.

Teresa is considered a mystic, in that particular sense of someone gifted with extraordinary access to experiences of the divine. Her visions are vivid, her experiences of God intimate, her writings audacious, prophetic and practical. There are many descriptions of the term 'mysticism' in writings in spirituality and theology, but the two main strands are characterized by whether mysticism is defined by an altered state of consciousness that transcends normal experience provoked by a special kind of vision or union with God (ecstasy), or something all Christians can access: to use Rahner's words, an 'everyday mysticism'. My own position, and that of a growing number of scholars, is that there is a continuum between what people such as Teresa seem to have experienced and the relationship with God that we are all called to. It is clear that she writes not only to verify her own experiences as orthodox within and for the Catholic Church but to teach a pathway to union with God. She helped define mysticism, and this is supported by her experiences and visions, but she does not mark a path for the special and the gifted. Rather, she helps us see what is possible or rather what is *essential* in our Christian experience of the person of Christ and where that experience can lead a life.

In chapter one, I spoke of the need for theology to explore and integrate different forms of expression and the growing strand of theology known as theopoetics. Spirituality scholar Sandra Schneiders situates Teresa's extraordinary imaginative contribution to theology in this field. In her view, Teresa is a theopoet, whose imaginative and intellective grasp of the risen humanity of Jesus is essential to the broader work of theology. The quote is long, but worthwhile in understanding the potential of mystical experience to inform, refresh and stretch theological understanding:

> The mystics ... are not interesting oddities who are decorative and even fascinating but non-essential to the Christian story, any more than are artists in a culture. Religious mystics are essential to the Church's faith life and to its theological enterprise, just as artists are essential to humanity's historical life, both personal and political, because there is a dimension of our faith life, as there is a dimension of our cultural life, that cannot be accessed nor made available by those powers and processes which we control, such as syllogistic reasoning, experiment, argument, and so on.
>
> The particular importance of Teresa of Avila's mystical experience for our time is that the Incarnation is the dimension of Christian faith and life that is most problematic, most 'incredible' for many contemporary believers. ... The direct experience of the mystics is not a dispensable decoration in relation to the reasoning of the theologians. It is necessary to assure us that there is indeed something *for* theology *to* explain. If there is no Jesus, alive and present and active in the 'now', there is no basis for Christianity as a living religion and no root of a cosmic Christ, however understood. Teresa says, 'I saw Him; I heard Him; He is alive.' And then she adds, if I may put words in her mouth, 'I leave it to the theologians to

explain this and will agree to whatever formulations they come up with or the Church teaches. That is their job, to explain the "how". But Jesus himself has assured me of the "that" and the "what."'[29]

Returning to the contribution of 'doctors of the Church' to theology, this book aims for a theology for the twenty-first century, in a stage of meaning of 'interiority' (Lonergan), in which Christians 'will be mystics or nothing' (Rahner). Perhaps the naming of such witnesses and writers as doctors of the Church is a recognition of theology's need to move in that direction. Their theology is fresh, experience-led and often symbolic and artistic in form.

While there are many canonized saints and respected theologians in the Church's history Doctors of the Church are recognized for the singular conjunction of extraordinary holiness with extraordinary theological brilliance. So, in a certain sense, the Doctors of the Church could be considered the models for scholars of religion in every age ... who aspire not only to faithfully transmit the tradition but to enhance it, and not only to teach but to live what they teach.[30]

I Think I Might

As we turn to the musical dimension of this theme, I will admit that this chapter cuts close to the bone, as it reflects my own calling and life-option, as well as some of its major influences. I felt called into and chose religious life in a community born in Spain with a lot of influence of Spanish mysticism and spirituality, especially that of Ignatius of Loyola and Teresa of Avila. Her definition of prayer is the one that marks my own understanding: to talk, often and alone, about friendship, with the One we know loves us.[31] To pray is to pass from talking *about* God to talking with God, from Jesus as Him to Jesus as 'You'! The song is a prayer and was composed in bits and pieces over more than twenty years. 'Take away the humanity of Christ, and I cannot pray' is the paraphrased refrain from Teresa of Avila's spirituality that underpins this song, along with an image from the Gospel of Mark as he calls

---

[29]Sandra M. Schneiders, 'The Jesus Mysticism of Teresa of Avila: Its Importance for Theology and Contemporary Spirituality', *Berkeley Journal of Religion and Theology* 2 (2016): 46–74 (69–71). On taking on Teresa's 'voice', I would point out that Schneiders' personality and that of Teresa show common traits of clarity and humour!
[30]Sandra M. Schneiders, 'The Jesus Mysticism of Teresa of Avila: Its Importance for Theology and Contemporary Spirituality', *Berkeley Journal of Religion and Theology* 2 (2016): 46–74 (49–50).
[31]'*Tratar, muchas veces y a solas de amistad con Aquel sabemos que nos ama.*' *Tratar*, in the original Spanish, is a difficult word to translate, as it gathers all types of presence and communication, not only those evoked by words or conversation.

someone who has come to be known as the 'rich young man': 'Jesus, looking at him, loved him and said, "You lack one thing; go, sell what you own, and give the money to the poor, and you will have treasure in heaven; then come, follow me"' (Mk. 10.21). He looked at him and loved him. Eyes are scary things: look for too long and you might fall in! This man did not, and he left.

It is a mystery that some people 'encounter' Jesus looking at them and are drawn into a way of loving that is exclusive, that leaves no space for another's eyes or a human partner, as it were, while others do not. It is clear that the commitment to loving God through another person in a loving relationship and family can be just as full as a life that gives up that option. But such is the mystery of vocation. For me, once I got hooked on seeking that face and that gaze – and there was a lot of seeking before any finding – that was it. There was no space for another. I understood that this was my life, that He was my life, and it demanded – and demand *is* the right word – my whole being. This is *not* because God does not leave us free. Scripture's exhortation to 'seek the face of God' (cf. Ps. 105.4) or to 'ask in order to receive' (cf. Lk. 11.9) is one manifestation of how God respects and will not barge down the gates of anyone's life. The Spirit needs an open door. But what this song seeks to express is that once the door is open, once God has taken residence in a life that has said yes, that love is all-consuming.

In various chapters of this book, we speak about falling in love: Lonergan uses the phrase to describe the Holy Spirit poured out freely into all open hearts (Rom. 5.5); Sequeri speaks of contemporary sensibility to affect and love as an apt shared language through which to develop a theology of faith; Haughton describes the human experience of breakthrough in falling in love as the most appropriate metaphor for God's love of humanity, expressed also in sexual loving. This song is a love song that explores what that love feels like when the form it takes is a call to celibacy, when loving God implies the consecration of one's whole being.

Vuestra soy, para vos nací, ¿qué queréis hacer de mí?[32]

And because the call to celibacy is not about loving less, but rather loving differently, you open a door to Jesus and those he brings home with him! It is a call to live your life open, dedicated not to a human family which rightly has the first claim on one's love but to those who need you most, without holding on to them or letting them hold on to you.

This song is embattled: '*You alarm and disarm me; You pull me apart and put me back together: I never stood a chance.*' Because the call to celibacy is not an easy vocation. There is a depth of love and peace to be found in the call to love God exclusively, but it comes with a cost of aloneness and

---

[32] 'I am yours; I was born for you: what do you want to do with me?'; translation mine. It has also been translated as 'what do you want me to do?', but I think this is closer to the original Spanish meaning.

loneliness. God gave Teresa friendships, and she instinctively understood how important they were to a healthy living out of God's love. But the freedom of a life in God, especially when it is also missionary, implies arriving, putting down roots, loving and moving on. Jesus is an attentive lover. Every thought, every feeling, every contact or lack thereof, is important. 'It's the little things that matter', they say, but we know well that there *are* no little things, when two people are intimate in love. How someone takes their coffee, what makes them laugh, pet hates and favourite small pleasures *are all part of the relationship* when people love one another. Well, if that intimacy is with Someone who dwells within and who sees every inner movement, feeling, thought and pain – 'in him we live, and move, and have our being' (Acts 17.28) – Scriptures' description of God as 'jealous' makes sense. There is nothing Jesus cannot touch and does not want to touch. Theologians can argue over how an eternal God can possibly connect with the transient, but the truth is that there is no lie, no hidden feeling, no powerful temptation, burst of happiness or broken promise that Jesus does not want to touch, converse about and bring into that relationship, because what stays outside is a wedge in-between. There is no one who sees us better than God.

That's why the song is both joyful and a bit tormented! Jeremiah speaks of being enticed, enraptured or deceived (my favourite translation of this text): 'Lord you have deceived me, and I was deceived; you have overpowered me, and you have prevailed' (Jer. 20.7). Because there is no going back when God has taken hold, without the agony of separation or the empty nothingness of mediocracy. '*I miss you*' because where love touches us, it leaves a mark – a God-shaped hole. We know this even in human love: you never forget someone you have loved, even if a friendship or relationship doesn't last or work out. Love goes deep. Consecrated life is meant to witness to the love of God for humanity.

At the start of the chapter I spoke about how every calling, every charism responds to a need, and over the centuries, there have been many. In my case, the cultural shifts of our times have made it harder not only to believe in God but also to imagine and feel God's presence, close to or in us. So, my focus is on enabling people to access an experience of God. Because it is possible to talk with God, it is possible to experience God, and it *can* be 'taught' or mediated. The theological foundation for this conviction and charism is the sacramentality of life and of words: God's love is mediated through matter, through the lives and the words of others: when someone has tasted the love of God – when it is real for them – they can mediate others into that experience, or rather, into their *own* experience, as Teresa sought to do.

After the words, only Jesus and the living experience of Christ should remain in the hearts of the listeners.

Constitutions of the Verbum Dei Community, 47

This is not limited to celibate living, of course: the closer to God we are, the more we can bridge others to that love.

This song has a chorus of 'oohs' instead of words. I never write choruses with no words, because they seem lazy to me, as if the composer ran out of creative steam or had to finish for a deadline. But this song was years in the making and simply no words fit. When I hear or sing it, it leads me to think of Augustine's 'jubilation': where the heart or rather the whole person – body, soul and spirit – sings without the need of naming why.

If I could finish this chapter on a personal note, I was educated by the Loreto nuns in Bray, Co Wicklow, Ireland. I think they did a good job, on the whole. I learned to think, question and speak freely, but I promised myself I would never be 'a nun', a celibate consecrated person. It made no sense to me, in part because I could not envisage life without human love and sex; in part because I did not see the need, in order to do what they did, which was to teach us. I do remember, however, that once a year one of their missionary sisters would come to speak to us. I have no recollection of the details of what they said, except that they were always working far away, in places of poverty, and I would feel like my day had been cut through with something real, each time. They were like a flash of light, of challenge, of awakening to need and life beyond my own imaginings. I credit them with sowing the first seeds of a missionary calling in me, to love beyond one's small circle. This and a myriad of other experiences tell me that while there is a need for many other callings in the life of the Church, and celibacy has often been wrongly overrated or badly lived, we shall always have a need for this vocation in the Church. And God will continue to call forth women and men to live solely of his love and for others, in whatever way is needed. I imagine that this will be in creative and new ways. The main thing, which I find consoling (in the Ignatian sense of a source of joy) is that this can still mean a wholeness of life and contribution to the Church and world that opens pathways, as Teresa did. The link to the song can be found in the note below.[33]

'I Think I Might' lyrics

You are, the air I breathe, the eyes I seek;
The words I speak when I am truthful
The one my bones ache for, the love my heart breaks for . . .
To hear your voice
And I miss you; I need You; I think I might . . .
You are the sacred space where truth awakes
My broken dreams are laid to rest in your arms

---

[33]Link to the song 'I Think I Might': https://res.cloudinary.com/bloomsbury-online-resources/video/upload/v1639138310/Suspended%20God/I_Think_I_Might.wav

You mourn in my dying,
You dawn in my crying your silent name
You calm my mind; You touch my lies; You know who I am . . .
You are . . . my ocean call: You rise, I fall,
Your waves caress and I lose my step, 'cos
You are that point of no return,
The still centre of my storm, when I am lost
And I miss you; I need You; I think I might love You . . .
You complete me; You deceive, you tie me in knots;
Your voice is stronger than my will;
Your love bodes ill for my plans . . . I think I might
You alarm and disarm me; You pull me apart and put me back together;
I never stood a chance
I think I might.

©MAEVE LOUISE HEANEY, 2020.
Strange Life, The Music of Doubtful Faith

Selected further reading

On Teresa's life and context

Dreyer, Elizabeth. *Accidental Theologians: Four Women Who Shaped Christianity*. Cincinnati, OH: Franciscan Media, 2014.

Williams, Rowan. *Teresa of Avila*. London: Geoffrey Chapman, 1991.

Teresa of Avila's writings

Teresa of Avila. *The Letters of St Teresa of Jesus*, edited by E. Allison Peers. London: Sheed and Ward, 1980.

Teresa of Avila. *The Complete Works of St Teresa of Avila. Volume 1*, edited by E. Allison Peers. London and New York: Burns & Oates, 2002.

On the significance of her writings

Schneiders, Sandra M. 'The Jesus Mysticism of Teresa of Avila: Its Importance for Theology and Contemporary Spirituality'. *BJRT @Graduate Theological Union* Issue 1 (2016): 46–79.

13

Where on earth is God?

Where on earth can God be found?

The question at the heart of this chapter takes on two forms that seem different but are really two sides of the same coin, from different cultural and faith perspectives. One is that of Western Christianity seeking to place the God it thinks it knows within a changing universe. We believe in the existence of God, somewhere, and we call it heaven ('our Father who art in . . . '), but where is that and how we can reach the God we imagine to be 'up there'? The question often emerges in specific times of suffering or simply when we face the hard or ugly side of life: Where is God *now?* The other form this question takes is broader and linked to our concern for a threatened planet and the viability of life as we know it, from within and beyond a Christian worldview: How does God relate to the world we live in? For those brought up within a Western anthropocentric world view in which the material world seems ordained to humanity, the issue involves an invitation to extend our moral consciousness beyond small circles and social concerns to our relationship with the planet. This is challenging because our individualistic formation of conscience to think of faithfulness to God as a private, inner relationship between God and each person has not yet fully integrated decades of social teaching aimed at broadening that awareness, at least not across the board. Extending it further to include non-human creatures is proving difficult. For all of us, including those who are not Christians, it is simply *the* global issue facing us now. In ethical terms, the question is what we should be doing so as to halt our current trajectory. In theological terms, it's about the place of the planet and the universe in God's loving plan of salvation, and the place of God in this world.

While the context is new, there are theological antecedents to this question in the history of thought. The intrinsically religious nature of human life has led us to seek answers to these questions from the very origin of human communities,¹ and it is clear that the more ancient and Indigenous cultures on earth have much to remind and teach us about a healthy relationship with the land that sustains us. Interreligious dialogue and comparative theologies have long explored the different ways in which religions approach the interaction between world and Spirit. In these conversations – the beginnings of which date back to biblical times – Christianity found its position in comparison with surrounding world views as they gradually discovered the God revealed in the Judaeo-Christian faith. Against dualist notions which postulated two opposing forces at the origins of the world – good versus evil – monotheistic religions came to the belief in one good and provident God, creator and point of origin of everything as good. The negative aspects of the created world were attributed to the mystery of a fallen reality, which we call sin. Against pantheism – that God and matter were *the same* – Christianity professed the reality of a God who is *Other* than the world and free from it. That is to say: to the question about why the world exists and its meaning, the answer Christianity offers is that of an underlying personal reality that is good and provident, whom we call God. The first thinkers understood this God as relational, Triune and creator of the world out of love and in freedom that we could experience the joy and life that the three Persons in our God *are*. Such is the central tenet of a Christian theology of creation. This leaves us with a myriad of issues about what went wrong (sin), and how this loving God and a created world interact. I addressed the question of the origins of sin in chapter nine with Sebastian Moore. My focus here is how God interacts with the created world, which we shall find also reveals much about *who* this God is. The particular focus of this age-old question is the value and place of the planet in God's story of salvation, because the history of Christian thought focussed more on how divine grace and humanity cooperate in the individual. A planet-sized creation theology is only slowly emerging and has therefore not really filtered down to the lived consciences of everyday Christians. Strangely, this neglect of the earth runs alongside and despite the sacramental principle intrinsic to faith in an incarnated God, which grounds the sacramental and liturgical conviction by which matter mediates Spirit.

There are many factors at play in this area, but one that needs to be named is the uneven way in which our awareness of the shape of the universe and our Christian imagination of the same have developed.² We are

---

¹In this context, by religious I am referring, first, to the etymological meaning of the word *religare* describing humanity's intrinsic tendency to relate to and connect with others, the land and the divine; and second, to the overwhelming fact that humanity across the planet seeks the spiritual, despite mainly Western philosophy's attempt of the last two centuries to pretend and prove otherwise. See chapter fifteen on Pierangelo Sequeri for further exploration of this area.
²I have written more fully about this in relation to music's role in experiencing the divine *in* the world in chapter six of Maeve Louise Heaney, *Music as Theology: What Music Has to Say about the Word* (Eugene, OR: Pickwick Publications Wipf and Stock, 2012).

a dot in an immense universe: a beautiful, mysterious *and* yet paradoxically increasingly *fathomable* expanding reality our minds can't really grasp. And yet, the core Christian doctrines that shape our life of faith and prayer were forged in and drawn from an ancient world view which identified the sky above them as where God lived. And it is worth noting that for the ancients, God *lived* in or just above the skies, out of reach but not totally out of touch. For the imagination of the ancient world, God's glory *could* descend from the heavens and effect change here on earth. Their imaginations were not tied down by Newtonian mechanics of material cause and effect. When Galileo di Vincenzo Bonaiuti de' Galilei (1564–1642) sought to bring into contemporary awareness Nikolaus Copernicus' (1473–1543) understanding that the world revolved around the sun and not vice versa – a notion Pythagoras had postulated in the sixth century BCE – it was not surprising that the Church pushed back, (although it *is* disappointing we took so long to admit the error). A helio-centred universe did not sit well with the understanding of the world and the language with which Christian faith was shaped. Galileo was condemned and only 'restored' three hundred years later by Pope John Paul II in 1983. It is one of the clearest episodes in history pointing to how essential ongoing and accurate collaboration between the worlds of faith and science are. There were at least two dimensions of Christian imagination that lagged behind science in that moment and in many ways even now. The first is how we imagine *where God is* in relation to the world: images of Jesus 'ascending' to sit at the right hand of God are built upon Scriptural images of God 'above'. But that worldview no longer holds. The second is related but distinct: as science began to understand 'cause and effect' in matter and biology, the possibility or probability of divine intervention came into question. Is a human experience of God *possible*? Both issues force us to rethink how we imagine and understand God's relationship to the world.

There is a lot of work emerging currently in this area, not least provoked by Pope Francis' epoque-changing (at least for Catholic teaching) encyclical *Laudato Si': On Care for Our Common Home*, which I look at later in this chapter. However, I turn to Australia for how the issues are both named and grappled with: a land forged by Irish-Anglo Catholicism against the backdrop of the ignored presence and suffering of the oldest surviving peoples on earth and at the intersection of a multicultural and climate-challenged Asia-Pacific. The quest for an integral spirituality that finds pathways forward is a hidden gem in this culture. A theopoetical space will help us intuit this more easily than trying to explain it. The poem is by Australian poet Lisa Jacobson and is entitled 'There are Stones that Sing':[3]

---

[3] Cf. Lisa Jacobson, *South in the World* (Crawley WA: UWA Publishing, 2014). I am grateful to the poet for her permission to reproduce the poem in full here.

> The churches are almost empty or sold,
> as if they've reached their tipping point,
> and from the pulpits, god slid out.
> And all that fanciful gold leaf
> on heaven's floor was incinerated
> by our telescopes, whose lenses caught
> it in the scope. And bits of tattered
> god fell down.
>
> I've heard that âme ('soul' in French)
> is the name of a wooden chip,
> very exposed and vulnerable,
> that violin makers insert into
> the bodies of their instruments
> to further enhance the sound
> So maybe that's where god
> lives now.
> If you ask a priest, he'll point up.
> If you ask black fellas, they'll point down
> to stones that sing and rivers
> vibrating underground.

Now, most priests would no longer point up, as in this poem, but it does evoke rather brilliantly the tides and currents of God's relationship to the planet, a spirituality born of a dualist world view in which spirit and matter interacted only awkwardly, and the contribution of Indigenous spiritualities to recovering an age-old awareness of matter as shot through with grace, from which contemporary Christian theology really should deign to learn. Other authors dealing with the same spiritual quest in Australia include David Tacey[4] and Hugh Mackay,[5] and I would contend this quest runs through their poets, authors and songwriters.[6] For a fascinating presentation of the depth and diversity of religious thought in Australia's history *and* present, Wayne Hudson's *Australian Religious Thought* stands out.[7] Against the backdrop of this rich and underestimated culture of spiritual quest, the life and work of Denis Edwards is our theological lens for the question of where on earth we find God.

---

[4]For example, David J. Tacey, *The Spirituality Revolution: The Emergence of Contemporary Spirituality* (Pymble, NSW: HarperCollins, 2003); *Religion as Metaphor: Beyond Literal Belief* (New Brunswick and London: Transaction Publishers, 2015); *The Postsecular Sacred: Jung, Soul, and Meaning in an Age of Change*, 1st ed. (New York: Routledge, 2019).
[5]For example, Hugh Mackay, *Beyond Belief* (Sydney, NSW: Macmillan, 2016).
[6]By way of examples, the work of Myriam Rose https://www.miriamrosefoundation.org.au/about-dadirri; Michael Leunig, http://www.leunig.com.au/; Tim Winton and Paul Kelly.
[7]Wayne Hudson, *Australian Religious Thought* (Clayton, VIC: Monash University Press, 2016).

Denis Edwards: A natural theologian

I am going to start at the end, because Denis Edwards is one of the theologians in this book I knew personally.[8] A key figure in the Catholic and ecumenical theological community in Australia, Denis died suddenly on 5 March 2019, the birthday of his most foundational theological source: Karl Rahner. Denis is both celebrated and sorely missed by friends and colleagues, and, as this chapter will show, was one of the key theological voices in a Church that has much to offer the world. My own memory of Denis is that of a gentle, attentive and welcoming presence at the Australian Catholic Theological Association, especially for younger scholars like myself. His humble wisdom personified the best of Australia's understated intelligence and allergy to unnecessary hierarchies.[9] It is both natural and poignant that a death brings forth our memories of a person's life and contribution to the world, so in this section to describe Denis' life, I draw from the reflections of his friends and colleagues in Adelaide.[10] Alongside comments from those who knew him closely, we also have Denis' own reflections on his journey and the meaning of his work, in a piece from a series of accounts of intellectual journeys in the field of science and theology. It is not usual to have access to a theologian's autobiographical understanding of their work, so I would recommend it in whole: 'Story of a Theologian of the Natural World'.[11]

Denis was born in 1943 in the South Australian city of Port Pirie, which stands on the very edge of the magnificent Flinders Ranges. He identifies this 'place of wordless peace, a place of God's Spirit' as a space in which 'the pressures of everyday life begin to lift and are replaced by a sense of wholeness'. These experiences, alongside walks with seminary companions through a nature reserve important to the Indigenous Kaurna people, now the Morialta and Black Hill Conservation Park, are important to his foundational awareness of the importance of the natural world for Christian life. We shall see later how this natural world will become the context and impulse for his eco-theological body of work. He had a 'deep personal love of landscape with its myriad life-forms, and from that love grew a practical and authentic commitment to ecological responsibility'.[12]

---

[8]I am grateful to Julie Trinidad, student, colleague and friend of Denis, for her insight into my work on this chapter.
[9]I have chosen to call Denis by his first name in this section for that very reason and move to using his surname in line with other chapters from then on.
[10]Specifically, the tributes and eulogy of Stephen Downs, Julie Trinidad, James McEvoy, Michael Trainor, and Dean Zweck.
[11]Denis Edwards, 'Story of a Theologian of the Natural World', in *God and the Natural World: Theological Explorations in Appreciation of Denis Edwards*, ed. T. Peters and M. Turner, 21–30 (Adelaide: ATF Press, 2020).
[12]Cf. Ted Peters and Marie Turner, *God and the Natural World: Theological Explorations in Appreciation of Denis Edwards* (Adelaide: ATF Press, 2020), 7, referring to the words of his niece Michelle Thomas, after his death.

Influenced by the faith of his family, he felt drawn to priesthood young, joining the seminary at twelve years of age. He was ordained a priest for the Archdiocese of Adelaide in 1966. The beginning and ongoing context of his theological life was pastoral, first as an assistant priest in parishes of Adelaide, youth ministry to the Young Workers Movement and chaplain to the Young Christian Students (YCS). But when he was asked to contribute to the field of adult education, he studied a Masters at Fordham University in New York and later completed a doctorate at the Catholic University of America under the direction of Avery Dulles. Denis' ecclesial belonging continued throughout his life and informed his theological activity:

> He had important roles in diocesan leadership, particularly in the various renewal movements through the decades: in the Diocesan Pastoral Renewal Program initiated by Archbishop James Gleeson in 1981; and as theological advisor to Archbishop Len Faulkner for the period of his leadership, 1986–2001. While committed to the Catholic church's sacramental view of ordained ministry and church leadership, Denis was deeply committed to fostering lay leadership in the church, and to urging the church to find practices which uphold and embody the equal dignity of women.[13]

Edwards' theological vision was ever at the service of faith formation, teaching and the promotion of theologically informed thinking at all levels. He chose to live in a public housing suburb to be in contact with the poor, and formed an intentional community with companion priests with whom he shared and grew over the years.

His ecumenical commitment was no less strong. He was the longest-standing member of the Lutheran–Roman Catholic Dialogue in Australia, serving for thirty-three years between 1983 and 2016, during which time the Dialogue group reached consensus and produced documents on major doctrines such as the Eucharist, church and ministry, justification, Scripture and tradition, and Petrine ministry.[14] His commitment to receptive ecumenism, a strand of theology which seeks to recognize the charisms and gifts given to a church's transformative journey through *other* churches, was patent.

Denis' identity as teacher and theologian was interwoven. His pursuit of accuracy in knowledge combined with careful and attentive support of those who sought him as a theological mentor led him to help people across the globe to find their theological voices: 'His advice was: believe in yourself

---

[13]James McEvoy, Eulogy for Denis Edwards at the funeral service in St Francis Xavier Cathedral on Tuesday, 12 March 2019.
[14]Dean Zweck's tribute to Denis Edwards at the Vigil service for Denis at Queen of Angels' Church, Thebarton, on Monday, 11 March 2019.

and what you have to say. Don't spend time with self-doubts. Denis was an uncompromising supervisor. He had high expectations of my writing output and yet such gentle ways of communicating and setting goals with me that made me want to do my very best.'[15] It was an approach to thought that guided his teaching *and* theological style:

> Denis loved teaching. Adept at understanding issues from students' perspectives, he could explain to beginners, step by step, even the most sophisticated line of thought, and help students discover how that understanding mattered to their lives. His books were written with that same skill – aimed at the 'average lay reader' yet also read by leading theologians. He was a clear thinker and a skilled communicator.[16]

Theological concerns and collaborations

This leads us to Denis' theological concerns, collaborations and writings. He is best known for his work on the relationship between science and theology and theology's response to the ecological crisis. His writings include fifteen books on themes ranging through Christology, the Trinity, theological anthropology, the Holy Spirit, creation, ecclesiology, inclusive ministerial practice, the relationship between science and religion, and the gift which theology could offer those seeking to bring the mystery of God into dialogue with the natural world, its beauty and struggles.[17] However, rather than seeing these solely as separate themes, or even intellectual developments, which of course, they are, I suggest the doorway to grasping his work is through the questions his experience of life led him to ask and the collaborative spaces he opened to answer them. The foundational work in his doctorate reflects the importance of spirituality and its theological understanding in a thesis on the dynamics of faith in Karl Rahner and John of the Cross. This intersection of spirituality and theology remained throughout his theological journey. His first book, *Human Experience of God*,[18] was born of classes taught on the topic over five years and applies the understanding of grace developed in his doctoral years to *how* to speak

---

[15]Julie Trinidad's tribute to Denis Edwards at the Vigil service for Denis at Queen of Angels' Church, Thebarton, on Monday, 11 March 2019.
[16]Stephen Downs' tribute to Denis Edwards at the Vigil service for Denis at Queen of Angels' Church, Thebarton, on Monday, 11 March 2019.
[17]Cf. Michael Trainor, 'In Memoriam: Denis Edwards (1943-2019)', in *God and the Natural World: Theological Explorations in Appreciation of Denis Edwards*, ed. T. Peters and M. Turner, 31–3 (31) (Adelaide: ATF Press, 2020).
[18]Denis Edwards, *Human Experience of God* (New York: Paulist Press, 1983).

about the experience of God in human life. Here as well, the seeds of his future work on the natural world *born of* experience can be seen:

> In many ways it was an attempt to interpret Rahner's thought, but while Rahner consistently refers to negative experiences of human suffering or emptiness when he gives examples of the experience of God ... many of my examples are positive, and unlike Rahner's, they are often experiences of God that occur in and through the encounter with the world of nature.[19]

In the 1970s, an awareness of the social dimensions of salvation grounded his ministry with workers and youth as well as his option to live in among the poor, influenced, among others, by the thought of the liberation theology of Gustavo Gutierrez.[20] It led to his second book on the theological explorations of salvation in the work of Rahner, Gustavo Gutierrez, Sebastian Moore and Edward Schillebeeckx, *What Are They Saying about Salvation?*[21] His questions were stretched, during the 1980s, by an awareness of the crises facing the natural world, which usually affect poor people and less-developed countries most. Influences and collaborators he names at this stage include Charles Birch and John Cobb,[22] Thomas Berry,[23] Sean McDonagh,[24] Paul Santmire,[25] Jürgen Moltmann,[26] Sallie McFague[27] and Gabriel Daly.[28] However, it is the influence of the Indigenous peoples of Australia that provoked in Denis his moment of 'ecological conversion':

> An important influence for me as an Australian was the voice of the Indigenous peoples of this land. Any talk of social justice in Australia had to address the extreme injustice experienced by many Aboriginal people. In thinking about this theologically, it seemed essential that we newcomers to this land adopt an entirely different stand before Indigenous Australians – we need to stand before them as learners. We need to learn

---

[19]Edwards, 'Story of a Theologian', 21–30 (23).
[20]Cf. Trainor, 'In Memoriam', 31–3.
[21]Denis Edwards, *What Are They Saying about Salvation?* (New York: Paulist Press, 1986).
[22]Cf. Charles Birch and John B. Cobb, *The Liberation of Life: From the Cell to the Community*, ed. J. B. Cobb (Cambridge: Cambridge University Press, 1981).
[23]In particular, Thomas Mary Berry, *The Dream of the Earth* (San Francisco: Sierra Club Books, 1988).
[24]Sean McDonagh, *To Care for the Earth: A Call to a New Theology* (London: Geoffrey Chapman, 1986).
[25]H. Paul Santmire, *The Travail of Nature: The Ambiguous Ecological Promise of Christian Theology* (Philadelphia: Fortress Press, 1985).
[26]Jürgen Moltmann, *God in Creation: A New Theology of Creation and the Spirit of God*, 1st Fortress Press ed. (Minneapolis, MN: Fortress Press, 1993).
[27]Sallie McFague, *Models of God: Theology for an Ecological, Nuclear Age* (Minneapolis, MN: Fortress Press, 1987).
[28]Gabriel Daly, *Creation and Redemption* (Dublin: Gill and Macmillan, 1988).

to respect their historical and ongoing role as custodians of this land, as people who know the spiritual significance of the land. . . . Listening to Aboriginal voices led me towards my own ecological conversion. [29]

In *Called to Be Church in Australia: An Approach to the Renewal of Local Churches*, Denis names the felt alienation of contemporary Australian culture as caused by the fact that the nation itself was built on a lie: that the land was empty – *terra nullius* (land of no one) – and therefore taken from the First Peoples.[30] This destroyed their cultures. He builds a theological framework for an apprenticeship to Aboriginal religiosity based on the pneumatology of the Second Vatican Council, which taught about the presence of the Spirit beyond the realms of the Church and the salvific potential in elements of other religions. In speaking of Christian witness, *Ad Gentes* invites believers to

> acknowledge themselves to be members of the group of people among whom they live; let them share in cultural and social life by the various undertakings and enterprises of human living; let them be familiar with their national and religious traditions; let them gladly and reverently lay bare the seeds of the Word which lie hidden among their fellows. . . . Even as Christ searched the hearts of men, and led them to divine light, so also his disciples, profoundly penetrated by the Spirit of Christ, should show the people among whom they live, and should converse with them, that they themselves may learn by sincere and patient dialogue what treasures a generous God has distributed among the nations of the earth.
>
> *Ad Gentes: Decree on the Mission Activity of the Church*, 11

He concluded that we need to listen for those elements of saving grace in the cultures and religions around us, and identified one we would receive from Aboriginal sensibilities, if we chose to learn:

> I believe that there is a providential grace, a revelatory word, that God has to give all Australian Christians. This word concerns the connection between the landscape and the Spirit. It can be given only when we begin to see the land as the Aborigines have learned to see it. This means a

---

[29]Edwards, 'Story of a Theologian', 21–30 (24), referring to an earlier piece of work: Denis Edwards, 'A Local Church in Apprenticeship to the Aboriginal View of the Land', in *Called to Be Church in Australia: An Approach to the Renewal of Local Churches*, 11-26 (Homebush, NSW: St. Paul Publications, 1987). Interestingly, for the purposes of this book, Denis also used Indigenous art in his teaching and had a particular liking for the work of Indigenous artist Gurrumil, using some of his music in his theology classes.

[30]For an overview on the history and recent debates on this issue, see the excellent commentary of long-time champion of Aboriginal rights and historian of forgotten Indigenous-settler conflicts, Henry Reynolds, 'A New Historical Landscape?', *The Monthly* 2006.

reversal of the paternalism by which Europeans have seen themselves as the ones with all the gifts to give. Many Aborigines, of course, rejoice in the Christian gospel and have received it as a gift from God (even as they reject the oppression and destruction of culture and lives that came with the European invasion). When non-Aboriginal Australians can approach Aboriginal attitudes to the land as apprentices in faith then we will be able to speak of true openness to the Spirit in this country.[31]

In the 1990s, under the impulse of an awareness that he did not know enough in the relevant areas of science to adequately address the questions he had about creation, cosmology and evolution, Denis sought and found international collaboration and learning in Robert John Russell, director of the Center for Theology and the Natural Sciences (CTNS) at Berkeley, and William Stoeger and George Coyne, two Jesuits at the Vatican Observatory. It gradually led to involvement with conferences spearheaded by the Templeton Foundation and the creation of the International Society for Science and Religion,[32] of which he was a founding member. Denis identifies Stoeger's work on a Thomist tradition of a God who acts through secondary causes that have their own integrity, as particularly influential.[33]

As he moved into the third millennium of Christianity, questions about the reality of suffering and evil in the natural world drew Denis' attention to the fact that 'the costs of evolution are built into the process – they are intrinsic to the emergence of life. Life evolves by processes that involve not only cooperation but also competition for resources, predation, death and extinction.'[34] The issue of suffering and death is built into creation's evolutionary dynamics. At this stage, Denis was involved in a conference in 2005 organized by CTNS and the Vatican Observatory on the problem of natural evil at Castel Gandolfo. In relation to his more recent work, Denis credits Celia Deane-Drummond as editor of *Ecotheology* with stimulating his thought on animal suffering and acknowledges his debt to Danish theologian Niels Gregersen for his thought on deep incarnation: 'an incarnation into the very tissue of biological existence, and system of nature'.[35]

From the fields of science, Denis brought into theological discourse the work of Steven Weinberg, Stephen Hawking, Paul Davies, John Barrow,

---

[31]Edwards, 'Apprenticeship to the Aboriginal View of the Land' (23).
[32]The International Society for Science and Religion was established in 2002 for the promotion of education through interdisciplinary learning and research in the fields of science and religion, conducted in an international and multi-faith context: https://www.issr.org.uk/.
[33]Edwards, 'Story of a Theologian', 21–30 (26).
[34]Edwards, 'Story of a Theologian', 21–30 (28).
[35]Niels Henrik Gregersen, 'The Cross of Christ in an Evolutionary World', *Dialog* 40, no. 3 (2001): 192–207; Niels Henrik Gregersen, 'Deep Incarnation: Why Evolutionary Continuity Matters in Christology', *Toronto Journal of Theology* 26, no. 2 (2010): 173–88.

John Gribbin, Martin Reese and evolutionary biologists including Ernst Mayr, E. O. Wilson, Richard Dawkins, Stephen Jay Gould, Ian Barbour, Arthur Peacocke and John Polkinghorne.[36] These, in his work, dialogue with great thinkers of the Christian theological tradition, from Scripture through Irenaeus, Athanasius, Augustine, Hildegard, Bonaventure, Aquinas, Martin Luther, John Calvin, Teilhard de Chardin, Karl Rahner, Jürgen Moltmann, Sallie McFague and Elizabeth Johnson. As is clear, he maintained 'constant interaction with some of the finest theological contemporary minds across the globe'.[37] This rather lengthy list of sources and interactions aim simply to foreground and bring to light the dedication and humble thirst for knowledge under the surface of a theologian of the quality of Denis Edwards. The extent of his influence can be seen in the breadth of themes covered in a recent tribute to, and exploration of, his work entitled *God and the Natural World: Theological Explorations in Appreciation of Denis Edwards*.[38] It is both moving and formidable to see so clearly the connected growth between life, thought and writings as it is in the life of Denis Edwards:

> grace-filled and gracious. He lived what he believed. He was faithful, thoughtful, gentle, humble, patient, kind, courageous in the faith, passionate about justice, friendly and loving (in a quiet kind of way), full of wonder about the cosmos and deeply caring of God's whole creation.[39]

He was indeed, in subject, content and form, a natural theologian.

Where are you and where am I? Finding God *in* the world

There are people who still take the creation stories in the Bible literally, as if every written word explains exactly how things happened. This is the case, despite all the evidence to the contrary on the birth and development of our planet and solar system billions of years ago; *plus* the fact that there are, in fact, two separate and different creation stories in Scripture, side by side, with a different order of things, that when taken literally contradict one another. Which is deemed to be correct? And more importantly, who was there to write things down? The problem with this kind of creationism is not only the kind of God it reveals but also how that affects the human capacity

---

[36] Edwards, 'Story of a Theologian', 21–30 (24–5).
[37] Cf. Peters and Turner, *God and the Natural World*, 8.
[38] Peters and Turner, *God and the Natural World*. The book brings together reflections from theologians all around the world on aspects of or intersecting with Edwards' work.
[39] Dean Zweck's tribute to Denis Edwards at the Vigil service for Denis at Queen of Angels' Church, Thebarton, on Monday, 11 March 2019.

and quest for truth. If in order to believe in the God of the Scriptures I need to close my eyes and ears to every finding of contemporary science, the kind of blind faith required inflicts more damage than any call to faith in a higher being we cannot see with our physical sense of sight could! And it puts in question our basic trust in humanity's capacity to seek and know the truth. Therefore, the issue I am addressing in this chapter is not only that of where and how God might show up in our world and we in God's, but also how *any* knowledge that human science discovers should be treated.

As discussed earlier, in Denis Edwards, we find a person who took seriously both faith in the God revealed in the Scriptures and scientific findings about human life and the universe, and spent no small amount of energy in accessing and updating that knowledge in order to make the conversation and dialogue possible. In that journey, Edwards identified three groups working in the area of science and theology: those who are specialists in both science and theology, those who are principally scientists committed to dialogue with people of religious faith and those who are principally theologians who see engagement with science as a fundamental part of their theological work. He situated himself in the third group. His endeavour to contribute to a twenty-first-century theology of the natural world is framed by this understanding:

> I am called to be part of a community of scholars seeking to build a theology of the natural world, one that can respond, on the one hand, to the insights of scientific cosmology and evolutionary biology, and, on the other, to the great issues we face in the global community of life Earth, such as climate change and the loss of biodiversity?[40]

To his mind, this quest was a natural consequence of three connected areas of global awareness in the twentieth century: social justice, feminism and the ecological movement, which were calling on Christianity to move from an anthropocentric world view to what he called an ethics of intrinsic value in relation to all of creation. I will present first something of the world view he adopted that became the context and framework for his whole work and then some key aspects of his theological approach relevant to our theme.

The bigger picture: An expanding universe in crisis

Two realities interweave in Denis Edwards' understanding of the world. The first is what Hawking described as 'one of the great intellectual revolutions of the twentieth century': that we live in an expanding universe.[41] Edwards

---

[40]Edwards, 'Story of a Theologian', 21–30 (21).
[41]Quoted in Denis Edwards, *Jesus the Wisdom of God: An Ecological Theology* (Homebush, NSW: St. Pauls, 1995), 12.

takes readers through the two strands of scientific investigation that underpin this discovery: one is theoretical and initiated by Einstein's General Theory of Relativity with his understanding of gravity as a stretching and curvature of space-time. The ensuing models of the universe (known as Friedmann-Lemaitre-Robertson-Walker models) led to the realization that the universe is expanding – a possible conclusion that horrified Einstein – and the theory of an initial Big Bang of a tiny dense heat as the origin of everything in the universe: that is to say, 'not an explosion in an already existing space and time, but the stretching and expansion of spacetime itself'.[42]

The other scientific strand that accompanies and verifies the theoretical is astronomical observation. Edwards describes four strands of observational evidence that support Big Bang cosmology: Hubble's discovery of other galaxies in the early twentieth century; the helium abundance of the universe born of that explosion; the confirmation in 1965 by Arno Penzias and Robert Wilson of the existence of cosmic background microwave radiation (which before this had been postulated as a necessary consequence of such an initiating explosion); and the discovery in 1992 by researchers in Berkeley of fluctuations in this radiation, consistent with the 'clumpy' ways in which matter emerged. These layers of scientific discovery led scientists to know that while there is still some speculation about the first second (literally) of our universe, there is general consensus about the moments after that. 'We can be fairly confident that we have the right picture, at least back to one second after the big bang.'[43]

Alongside this 'big picture' of the origins of the universe, Denis Edwards places his concerns for the tiny green and blue planet we can now see from a distance, whose development is in crisis due to the actions of human beings – only one of the millions of species that find their home here – radically affecting the earth's ecosystems and threatening its future. Current awareness of the elements affecting our planet is growing, thankfully, so an overview of these concerns is not necessary here, except to say that from his earliest writings in 1987,[44] and 1991,[45] it becomes a central feature of every theme he addresses. The clarity and relentless commitment to facing and broadening theological awareness is well exemplified in his focus on the rainforests in *Jesus the Wisdom of God: A Ecological Theology*:

> The reasons for the ecological crisis are many. They include rapid population growth in tropical areas, the desperate need for fuel of ordinary people around the globe, and misguided government

---

[42]Cf. Edwards, *Jesus the Wisdom of God*, 11.
[43]Stephen Hawking, *A Brief History of Time: From the Big Bang to Black Holes* (London: Bantam, 1988), 118, quoted in; Edwards, *Jesus the Wisdom of God*, 140.
[44]Edwards, 'Apprenticeship to the Aboriginal View of the Land'.
[45]Denis Edwards, *Jesus and the Cosmos* (Homebush, NSW: St Paul Publications, 1991).

development projects that attempt to 'open up' rain forests for the lumber industry and for cattle grazing. Often government thinking is restricted to short-term goals by the desperate need for hard currency. Behind these problems and fundamental to any solution of them is the structure of international debt, whereby the powerful and wealthy countries hold poorer countries in the economic bondage of runaway debts. The only human and ecological beginning to a solution is the writing-off or radical restructuring of dysfunctional and destructive debts.[46]

Rather than arguing simply for a more long-term but ultimately still instrumental view of the value of rainforests to human life, he suggests that the central truths of Christian faith push us further into the realization that 'the rain forest, and each species that makes it up, has value in itself, intrinsic value, which human beings need to take into account and respect'.[47] This leads him to formulate seven guidelines for ethical praxis:

1. The intrinsic value of all creatures in themselves and not just for humanity;
2. The unique value of human persons, with a priority for the poor of the earth;
3. Reverence for all forms of life;
4. The ethical weight of biological communities and their interconnectedness;
5. Level of consciousness as a criterion for ethical discernment;
6. Commitment to ecological sustainability in the use of resources;
7. A theology of companionship with other creature in an earth family.[48]

These two foundational realities – the mystery and challenge of *how the world came to be and how it works*, alongside the urgency of ecological crisis – form the context of all of Edwards' writings, in dialogue with a deep and broad understanding of the sources and central beliefs of Christian doctrine and theology.

Ecological theology and the Spirit in creation

In order to theologize about and respond to these questions Edwards chooses as his starting point *not* the creation stories – although these form

---

[46]Edwards, *Jesus the Wisdom of God*, 9.
[47]Edwards, *Jesus the Wisdom of God*, 9–10.
[48]Cf. Edwards, *Jesus the Wisdom of God*, 153–71.

part of his biblical explorations – but rather Christian faith in the crucified and risen Christ. That is to say, rather than retreating from the Christ event into creation stories, he sought to expand our understanding of the effects of that salvation on the created world. *Jesus and the Cosmos* weaves together in theological correlation the scientific account of the emergence of the universe, life on Earth and human consciousness with the story of Jesus of Nazareth. And *Jesus the Wisdom of God: An Ecological Theology* draws on the Wisdom Christology present in Scripture and theologies developed in the past, such as Richard of St Victor's concept of the Trinity as mutual Love and Bonaventure's notion of the universe as the self-expression of God. These are developed in conversation with contemporary theologians, including Walter Kasper and Elizabeth Johnson. Grounded on Rahner's understanding of God as divine self-communication *always* (self-giving relationality as the being of God *in* Godself and *as revealed to us*), he describes creation as ordered to the Incarnation of Christ. This echoes Rahner's premise that the economic Trinity (how we know God in the economy of salvation) and the immanent Trinity (how God is 'before' or outside our created universe) are one and the same. God acts as God is. Christ came to reveal and redeem us, not just as a solution to the fall and the brokenness born of sin but to show us who we are and to introduce us into the life of God. Contrary to theories of redemption that see Jesus' coming as a 'necessary if happy' remedy to a fault, this vision sees all of creation as part of God's plan from the 'beginning':

> He has made known to us the mystery of his will, according to his good pleasure set forth in Christ, as a plan for the fullness of time, to gather up all things in him, things in heaven and things on earth. (Eph. 1.9-10)

Creation was always meant to belong in God, through Christ. The question about where God is and where we are finds an answer in this vision of the Cosmic Christ.

To these Christological and Trinitarian perspectives, Edwards adds an extensive exploration of the person, presence and role of the Holy Spirit in Christian theology's understanding of God in the world. The absence of a developed theology of the Holy Spirit, of course, has been true mainly in Western theology. The Eastern approach to theology has a much more relational understanding of Trinitarian Being-in-Communion. Interestingly, rather than starting from the difference and conflict between East and West in his explorations, he starts with the great Eastern theologian of the Spirit, Basil of Caesarea (*c.* 330–379) – in particular, his understanding of the Trinity as Communion and of the Spirit as the Breath of God that always accompanies the Word. The role of the Spirit is precisely that of *dwelling in* the world, wakening and reawakening things from within. It is a theology of *theosis*: through Christ and the Spirit we participate in the divine life of God. But this refers not just to the communion in the Spirit of the Christian community but also to the Spirit's presence to all of creation. He proposes

> an understanding of the distinctive role of the Holy Spirit as the Creator and Life-Giver, immanent in creatures, who enables them to exist and evolve in an interrelated world, by bringing each creature into a communion with the dynamic Communion of the Three. . . . This is a differentiated communion, because each creature is loved and respected precisely for what it is, and for its own precise participation in the ecological whole. The Creator Spirit is present in every flower, bird, and human being, in every distant quasar and in every atomic particle, closer to them than they are to themselves, enabling them to be and to become.[49]

Underpinning this rich, fully Trinitarian theology of God continuously at work in creation through the Word and in the Spirit, Edwards draws on central figures of the Christian theological tradition to ask and respond to the questions formulated at the start of this chapter. How does God as *Other* to the world interact with it without compromising divine transcendence *and* human freedom? Based on Aquinas' understanding of God as primary cause at every stage of our ever expanding and evolving universe, and every other cause internal to space-time as secondary, Edwards paints a picture of an ever-patient God who is willing to limit Godself and wait on the natural process of things. God's enabling of human freedom is the ground for human existence and self-transcendence: the evolutionary emerging of the world as it evolves is all part of how God works. Edwards counters false images of an emperor-styled God who interferes with the workings of the world to the One revealed in Christ's kenosis. In Jesus, God is revealed as power-in-love who becomes defenceless to carve a pathway restoring life to what it was always meant to be: mutual self-emptying and giving.

And what of the groaning of this earth? *Where* is God when the evolutionary processes intrinsic to the whole dynamic are not just beautiful but also cruel and shot through with competitive resilience and death? Edwards is not naïve in how he sees and presents the suffering of the planet, which are not only an expression of sin but also intrinsic to the very dynamics of evolution:

> Christian theology has no theoretical answer to the issue of pain and death in nature. It simply has to face the fact that this is the way things are in this finite, limited, and evolving world. All Christian theology has

---

[49]Denis Edwards, *Breath of Life: A Theology of the Creator Spirit* (Maryknoll, NY: Orbis Books, 2004), 88.

to offer is its witness to the death and resurrection of Jesus. Here divine love is revealed as unthinkable compassion. The cross reveals a God who enters into the pain of the world, who suffers with suffering creation. In the resurrection and the outpouring of Spirit, new life is promised and in some way already given.[50]

So can God suffer? This is an ancient and still debated issue in Christian theology: how to understand a God who, unlike the tragic myths that shape gods in the image and likeness of human life and needs, is free in loving and creating us. But for Edwards, it is simply imperative that we can speak of God as suffering in and with the world, if we confess faith in a loving God. The solution, however, is clear and based again on Aquinas: all language is analogical, or comparative, which is a basic theological principle. We approach the reality of God with our language but never fully capture it. However, it is divine reality that is the paradigm! God as compassionate, the passion of God with and for humanity, reflected in the man-God on a cross, does not diminish or reduce God when understood as the overflow of divine creative love. Divine overflow is the measure of passion, not vice versa.

> If the statement 'God suffers with creation' is recognized as analogical language, then the statement is made on the understanding that God does not suffer with creation in a limited human way, but in the kind of identification with creation that is proper to God. God's capacity for being with creatures, God's capacity to love, God's capacity to feel with those who suffer, is *infinitely* beyond anything possible for human beings. Understood in this way, God's empathy and suffering with others are not to be thought of as diminishing God's transcendence. They are the very expression of God's infinite otherness.[51]

As a theological community, we are only beginning to explore the implications and future pathways of Denis Edwards' work. I have focussed here on some of his earlier work in the attempt to show whence his thought came and developed, but his later writings interweave and develop this theology eloquently. *Ecology at the Heart of Faith*[52] synthesizes the Christological and Trinitarian dimensions of ecological theology in relation to the Eucharist and to Christian spirituality. *Christian Understandings of Creation* traces thought on creation from Scripture through Irenaeus, Athanasius, Augustine, Hildegard, Bonaventure, Aquinas, Martin Luther, John Calvin, Teilhard de

---

[50] Edwards, *Breath of Life: A Theology of the Creator Spirit*, 79.
[51] Edwards, *Breath of Life: A Theology of the Creator Spirit*, 83.
[52] Denis Edwards, *Ecology at the Heart of Faith* (Maryknoll, NY: Orbis Books, 2006).

Chardin, Rahner, Moltmann, McFague and Johnson.[53] *How God Acts: Creation, Redemption and Special Divine Action* addresses more fully the problem of evil and the intrinsic suffering of the evolutionary process, and *Partaking of God*[54] integrates the more recent concept of deep incarnation into a new Trinitarian theology of the natural world, presenting 'the Spirit as the Energy of Love and the Word of God as the Attractor, in the evolution and final transformation of the universe of creatures.'[55] *Deep Incarnation: God's Redemptive Suffering with Creatures* was published after his death.[56] Ever concerned with the theological formation of the broader members of the Christian faithful, Edwards produced two books explaining his theological positions: *Made from Stardust*[57] and *Jesus and the Natural World*.[58] A good starting place for a mature overview of his work can be found in his book in the ATF Scholars series: *The Natural World and God: Theological Explorations.*[59]

In recent years, Denis Edwards reflected on the Pope's invitation to care for the earth in *Laudato Si'*. This is hardly surprising given the resonance of the 2015 text with Edwards' ecological conversion and writing in the 1980s. By way of conclusion, and as a demonstration of the prophetic nature of the life and thought of this theologian, ahead of his time in reading the signs of the times and listening to the Spirit, I shall let some texts of Laudato *Si'* (2015) and *A Local Church in Apprenticeship to the Aboriginal View of the Land* (1987) be read alongside one another:

> Saint Francis of Assisi reminds us that our common home is like a sister with whom we share our life and a beautiful mother who opens her arms to embrace us. 'Praise be to you, my Lord, through our Sister, Mother Earth, who sustains and governs us.'
>
> *Laudato Si'* 1

> In this sense, it is essential to show special care for Indigenous communities and their cultural traditions. They are not merely one minority among

---

[53] Denis Edwards, *Christian Understandings of Creation: The Historical Trajectory* (New York: Fortress, 2017).
[54] Denis Edwards, *Partaking of God: Trinity, Evolution, and Ecology* (Collegeville, MN: Liturgical Press, 2014).
[55] Edwards, 'Story of a Theologian', 21–30 (28).
[56] Denis Edwards, *Deep Incarnation: God's Redemptive Suffering with Creatures* (Maryknoll, NY: Orbis Books, 2019).
[57] Denis Edwards, *Made from Stardust: Exploring the Place of Human Beings within Creation* (North Blackburn, VIC: Collins Dove, 1992).
[58] Denis Edwards, *Jesus and the Natural World: Exploring a Christian Approach to Ecology*, ed. G. Corridon (Mulgrave, VIC: John Garratt Publishing, 2012).
[59] Denis Edwards, *The Natural World and God: Theological Explorations* (Adelaide: ATF Press, 2017).

others, but should be the principal dialogue partners. . . For them, land is not a commodity but rather a gift from God and from their ancestors who rest there, a sacred space with which they need to interact if they are to maintain their identity and values.

Laudato Si' 146

Beginning in the middle of the last century and overcoming many difficulties, there has been a growing conviction that our planet is a homeland and that humanity is one people living in a common home. . . . Interdependence obliges us to think of *one world with a common plan*.

Laudato Si' 164

Aboriginal spirituality can remind us of the Franciscan approach to creation, and lead us all towards a be-friending of the land in which we live. This will mean a recognition of our interdependence with soil, air, water and all living things. If the land is seen as mother then we move from a world-view in which the earth belongs to us to one in which we belong to the earth. We become conscious of sharing a common creaturehood with all of creation.

A Local Church in Apprenticeship to the Aboriginal View of the Land, 21

The questions raised at the start of the chapter are amply and intelligently explored in the breadth of Denis Edwards' work. Where is God? In our midst, midwifing a beloved but groaning earth to his fullness. Where are we? Imbedded into the very body of Jesus that died and was risen, entering us into a poured-out dynamic of living. Where is heaven? It is not a place we might 'go to' when we finish this life, but the new life we can access now, and which will reach its fullness, not only at the end of our lives but in space-time's fulfillment in Christ!

Meet You in the Middle of the Air

The song interpreting this chapter's question sits at the intersection of a lot of junctures. It is my interpretation of a song written by singer-songwriter Paul Kelly, perhaps the best-known interpreter of Australian culture through song. It is a conversation between Scripture and someone who questions God: *I am your true Shepherd – Where are You? Where am I?* It comes from a land of unspeakable beauty *and* unfinished healing of deep wounds. It is an attempt of this recently arrived immigrant to express how I see, sense, touch and feel this country that is *so* in tune with the earth God gave us. I do not pretend to capture all that is on offer here. I am one of the last through the door of this multicultural land distant from all that was familiar to me, but eight years are not water, and the song is one fruit of my time here.

The original song is a stunning rendition of Psalm 23, well worth a listen without my interpretation.[60] I will not attempt to suggest what might have been in Paul Kelly's mind when he wrote it, but it contains the psalm in full, the only addition being the intriguing refrain that resets and reframes the whole: variations on the words '*come and meet me in the middle of the air! I will meet you in the middle of the air*'. Art precedes thought: it is an evocative cosmological reshaping of an ancient prayer; I am not suggesting it is a developed theology of where God might be found. In fact, to my ears, it is somewhat ambivalent, or playful, as if to say: 'this is an issue, come and meet me in the space *between* where You and I are meant to be!'

There are a myriad of cultures in this country, and this song seeks to express and reflect something of that. On one level, the song is the prayer of someone who cannot find God or who struggles to. It's a song of longing – '*I wish I knew where ... I'd go anywhere*' – but also of challenge – '*We're stuck in life's shallows!*' It's an honest argument born in a country that values someone who 'calls a spade a bloody shovel!', because I think our Triune God can handle whatever we throw at them in the attempt to pray. Australia calls itself secular, but it is not nearly as secular as it believes. There are traces and hubs of spirituality shot through Australia's self-understanding, its education systems, its art-worlds, its seal-like attraction to pre-dawn surfing, its musicians and especially the cultural heritage of its First Peoples.

The first contact I had with Australian culture, a few days after arriving in Brisbane, was an evening on Reconciliation organized by the First Peoples Centre at Australian Catholic University. I remember listening to the story of the Indigenous peoples of this continent and how Australia had *come to be*, and thinking that it felt like Northern Ireland before the Good Friday Agreement: so much unrecognized pain under the surface. I taught a unit on sacramentality and the sacraments with an Indigenous friend and colleague and savoured the gentle way he would invite us to bend down, touch and 'introduce ourselves' to the land we were standing on.[61] This same friend took me to North Stradbroke Island and with permission of the elders there presented me to the sacred places on that island that, as a woman, I could meet. They have a special relationship with the land. In fact, in some ways this applies not only to the Indigenous peoples but to Australians in general.

---

[60] Paul Kelly introducing and singing it alone: https://www.youtube.com/watch?v=NvOZiKj2hU0 (accessed 12 January 2021).
[61] I am also grateful to my friend and colleague Ren Perkins, a Quandamooka man with connections to Minjerribah (Stradbroke Island), for his reading and advice on this chapter.

Australia is beautiful, but it is also formidable, with a tough climate and unpredictable weather systems, from drought to cyclones through fires: it is a country forged in connection with mother earth.

Most official events in Australia, big and small, start with either a 'Welcome to Country' by someone of the local Indigenous peoples or an 'Acknowledgement of Country', if none are present. In both, elders past and present of the peoples whose land it is are named as the traditional custodians of the land and waterways, and acknowledged, in gratitude for their wisdom, their continued care and spiritual connection to the land and those gathered. At times, these moments start with the beating of two sticks. I have wanted to replicate this in the song, along with the sound of the didgeridoo. I am told the meaning of the sticks varies from place to place but generally marks the shift to ritual, to ceremony. To my ears, it calls us to attention, opening our hearing to listen for and receive something deeper but present. Different places have distinctive sounds and smells: the sticks and the didgeridoo in this song are important, as they ground the song. They situate it. I need to say that I did not like the sound of the didge when I arrived: it felt harsh and unmelodic. Slowly, the sound has begun to resonate with me. My body recognizes it.

It is worth mentioning the efforts of a small group of elders in Queensland, in the 1990s, to express and develop a theology unique to this country. They called themselves Rainbow Spirit Elders, after the Creator Spirit at the heart of their creation or 'Dreaming' stories. Interestingly, this Rainbow Spirit lives *in* the land: always has and always will. A powerful image in their theologizing is that of the strangler fig, a parasitic plant of the rainforests that grows hair-like long roots at the base of the trunks of the trees they wrap around to grow, and which they slowly crush. This is compared to what Christian missionaries did to their culture by imposing the Christian message with its European wrappings and dismissing their own culture and spiritual heritage, rather than encouraging the seed of the Christian message here to grow and take on its own form in this new place.[62] The damage was conflated by the combination of religious and state power, of course, as in most colonial situations. Their challenge is hard to hear but necessary:

> The rule of the missionaries was supported by the power of the government – and its police force. Our elders had a sacred responsibility as caretakers of this land and its resources. Because they could no longer exercise this care, they lost their purpose in life. The core beliefs of our

---

[62]Cf. Philip Kennedy, 'The Rainbow Spirit Elders', in *Twentieth Century Theologians: A New Introduction to Modern Christian Thought*, 293–303 (294), (London: I.B. Tauris & Co. Ltd., 2010). This chapter is a clear and respectful introduction to this Indigenous Australian group of thinkers.

people were rejected. The self-esteem of our people was destroyed. And the spirit of our people was crushed.[63]

In light of all the above about the importance of the land and its care, the loss of this wisdom is something we are paying highly for. Part of any reconciliation process involves owning what went wrong, and there is much that the history and process of Christian mission has missed and repressed. I intuit this is also why the song is angry and questioning towards God. But perhaps, in a similar way to how Jesus on the cross assumes, silently, 'the sin of the world', God prefers our expressed anger at what we don't understand to respectful and apathetic distance. So, let's take God, and misguided missionary practices, and theology unworthy of the name, to task until we get things right. The link to the song is in the note below.[64]

Meet You in the Middle of the Air' lyrics

I am your true shepherd
Where are you and where am I?
I will lead you there
What to do when truth lies?
Beside still waters
I wish I knew where . . . I'd go anywhere
Come and meet me in the middle of the air / Could you meet me in the middle of the air?
I will meet you in the middle of the air / I would meet you in the middle of the air . . .

I will lay you down Walked so long with no rest
In pastures green and fair
Grass is greener somewhere
Every soul shall be restored
It's my body that's weak . . . (are) you above or within?
I will meet them in the middle of the air / I need to meet you in the middle of the air . . .
Come and meet me in the middle of the air

---

[63]Rainbow Spirit Elders, *Rainbow Spirit Theology: Towards an Australian Aboriginal Theology*, ed. G. Rosendale and F. Australian Theological, 2nd ed. (Hindmarsh, SA: ATF Press, 2007), 3.
[64]Link to 'Meet You in the Middle of the Air': https://res.cloudinary.com/bloomsbury-online-resources/video/upload/v1639138171/Suspended%20God/Meet_me_In_the_Middle_of_the_Air.wav

Through the lonesome valley / Through the lonesome valley
My rod and staff you'll bear / Your rod and staff I'll share
Fear not death's dark shadow / We're stuck in life's shallows
Come and meet me in the middle of the air / I will meet you in the middle of the air

With oil I shall anoint you Can you see what I see?
A table shall I prepare
Can you touch and taste me?
Your cup will runneth over
You in me and I in you everywhere
Come and meet me in the middle of the air / I will meet you in the middle of the air

In my house you'll dwell forever
Could I bear eternal?
You shall not want for care
This life ever turning?
Surely goodness and mercy will follow you
I don't know where I'd fit . . . this much I'll admit.
Come and meet me in the middle of the air / I will meet you in the middle of the air

©PAUL KELLY, EMI RECORDING

Selected further reading

On Denis Edwards' life and theology

Edwards, Denis. 'Story of a Theologian of the Natural World'. In *God and the Natural World: Theological Explorations in Appreciation of Denis Edwards*, edited by Ted Peters and Marie Turner, 21–30. Adelaide: ATF Press, 2020.

Eco-theology

Edwards, Denis. *Jesus the Wisdom of God: An Ecological Theology*. Homebush, NSW: St. Pauls, 1995.

Theology of the spirit

Edwards, Denis. *Breath of Life: A Theology of the Creator Spirit*. Maryknoll, NY: Orbis Books, 2004.

An overview of his theology of the natural world

Edwards, Denis. *The Natural World and God: Theological Explorations*. Adelaide: ATF Press, 2017.

On his approach to Christianity in Australia

Edwards, Denis. *Called to Be Church in Australia: An Approach to the Renewal of Local Churches*. Homebush, NSW: St. Paul Publications, 1987.

On the significance and influence of his theology

Peters, Ted, and Marie Turner. *God and the Natural World: Theological Explorations in Appreciation of Denis Edwards*. Adelaide: ATF Press, 2020

14

Is how we name God important?

Between past, present and future: 'What is your name'?

The Jews do not name God, as naming something, or someone, gives one power over it. That is the gift implicit in God's invitation to Adam to 'name' the creatures being created: a share in God's providence and oversight over creation. So, Jews found other ways to call out to God, in prayer, so as to avoid claiming authority over the all-powerful and provident Creator of all (such as Adonai, for example). The tetragram YHWH safeguards the sacred name of God, given in response to Moses' quest for *who* was sending him back into Egypt to free the people of Israel: *'ehyeh 'asher 'ehyeh*; 'I am who I am' (Exod. 3.14). There are exegetical complexities and different interpretations of this phrase. One says it's not an answer – a name that is not a name; another interpretation draws from the fact that in Hebrew there is no tense in these verbs, and therefore, I am who I was, who I am, who I will be: 'the God of your father, the God of Abraham, the God of Isaac, and the God of Jacob' (Exod. 3.6). God is as God does, in time and history. Another highlights simply the mystery of who God is, impossible to fully access. Scripture does, however, underline the importance of a name, especially the one by which we call God.

The importance of naming is a deeply human experience as well. We are named by others and yet grow into who we are. We can choose to reveal our name to others or not. Knowing someone's name gives us access to them, makes us a part of their life and we a part of theirs. In some cultures, the first name given is always the surname or family name, because allowing use of your personal name marks the stepping over of a barrier into the beginning of knowledge, trust or intimacy. In most cultures, naming is claiming, and knowing where I come from is belonging: Who are you? 'Who are your people?', the Indigenous peoples of Australia frame the question: 'Whose are you?' What is your name? Calling someone's name is a quasi-intimate thing. I am recognized, known, needed or at the very least invited in, without forgetting of course, that one can also be named in vain, slighted or slandered! It is interesting that not naming God in vain is one of the commandments; such is the importance of a name. It is this personal reality we are approaching in this chapter: Who *is* God? How can we rightly name God? How we ask and answer the question has consequences on the inner workings of Christian living and in our outreach and mission. This chapter is linked to chapter thirteen on where to find God, continuing and developing how human experience and understanding can source our theologizing.

Because of how it has emerged in past and contemporary theologizing, we need to revisit one of the particular issues I began to look at in chapter six when speaking about women in Scripture, because this was most strongly raised as an issue by feminist theologies and then carried forth, in various ways, by other strands of contextual theologies: How do we 'name' God?[1] Who is this mystery we seek to access in prayer and worship, understand in theology, and speak about in our teaching and preaching, mission and outreach? It has a particular emphasis in relation to women's experience and theologizing, due to the primacy of 'male' language in relation to all three persons of the Trinity. God as Creator, Origin and Giver of life is most normally named as Father; Jesus, of course, was a man, and the Spirit, well, floats between an uncomfortable 'he' and token 'she', although theology *and* doctrine are quite clear – and have been for many centuries – that neither the 'first' nor the 'third' member of our Triune God has ever had gender.[2] In relation to the second Person of the Trinity, already in the fourth century, St Ambrose was very clear that it would be heretical to say that because the Son of God is male in his incarnation it means the Logos of God was male before the Incarnation, because it would bring a human limitation – gender – into the uncreated God. And yet we are baptized 'in the name of the Father, and the Son, and the Holy Spirit'; we begin our prayer, 'in the name of the Father, and the Son, and the Holy Spirit', and in Anglo and Latin languages alike – despite their very different understandings of gender in relation to language and reality – 'He' is the normally accepted pronoun for God.

For some women, this is not a problem. But for others, it becomes one at some stage of their lives, as their experience and understanding of God develop, or when they reach a crisis point, or when their children dismiss God – and with 'Him' the Church – as too male and irrelevant.[3] But it *is*, *necessarily*, a central doctrinal and theological issue, and *not* a recent one.

---

[1] For some classic texts on this theme, see Martin Buber, *I and Thou* (New York: Scribner, 1970); Paul Ricœur, 'Naming God', *Union Seminary Quarterly Review* 34, no. 4 (1979): 215.
[2] The memory stands out from my theology lectures in Rome while studying Trinity that the one clarification the professor made in relation to the Spirit was that despite the neutral article in Greek, the Spirit was not female! No similar clarification was forthcoming about the non-gendered nature of God the Father, however.
[3] I explain my own experiential and theological encounter with this issue in the final section of this chapter.

The fallacy that gender has emerged as an issue due to current secular and anti-Christian tendencies in the world would be swiftly remedied if more people actually *read* what some of the Fathers – quite viscerally – had to say about women, humanity and salvation. We have thankfully moved beyond some of that rhetoric, although it merits attention. However, I would not dismiss it so easily as a culturally conditioned blip on the otherwise holy and wise landscape of their mercy-filled Christian writings![4] Could it not say something about the centrality of gender issues to our deeply incarnational faith, which we have yet to work through?

The most acute angle of this issue is framed in stark terms: What are the consequences of 'the maleness of Jesus' for the salvation of women? If all human beings are made in the image and likeness of God, what implication does the fact that our historical access to 'who God is' is revealed to us in and through the human presence of a *man* have for Tradition's understanding of the role of both men *and* women in the church and its ministries? For many of us, this may seem like an extreme, even unnecessary, question to address: we are all made in the image and likeness of God; we are all saved by Jesus' life, death and resurrection, and baptized into Christ's body. But from the very beginnings of Christianity, the understanding of church structures and ministries has been shaped and developed in reference to the maleness of Jesus' person and the maleness of the disciples he chose (although there are a growing number of challenges to the bias of those writing history on this point).[5] It is a theological issue which still draws quite different positions about why the Son of God appeared as a man. From an argued defence of the maleness (and masculinity) of Jesus that considers that 'it would have been monstrous if the Son of God had appeared as a woman',[6] to a compelling suggestion that perhaps it was necessary because the values God wanted to introduce us to of humility, service, and preference for the poor and the underdog – in fact the very revelation of God's face – would not have been clear if God had come as a woman, who was *expected* to live in that way:[7]

The issues at stake are legion: the cultural conditioning of revelation and tradition with the corresponding need for a hermeneutical approach to its reception and interpretation; the doctrinal weight of the names used in and transmitted by the stream of tradition in which we stand; the development of doctrine, at its most central axis of who God *is*; theological anthropology, not only in how women and men understand their identity but also in how

---

[4] Rosemary Haughton explores this further, as we shall see in chapter sixteen.
[5] Elisabeth Schüssler Fiorenza, *In Memory of Her: A Feminist Theological Reconstruction of Christian Origins* (New York: Crossroad, 1983).
[6] Manfred Hauke, Women in the Priesthood? *A Systematic Analysis in the Light of the Order of Creation and Redemption* (San Francisco: Ignatius Press, 1988), 267 quoting Louis Bouyer, Women and the Church (San Francisco: Ignatius Press, 1979).
[7] Cf. Sandra M. Schneiders, *Women and the Word: The Gender of God in the New Testament and the Spirituality of Women*, Madeleva Lecture in Spirituality (New York: Paulist Press, 1986), 50–63.

we face further questions concerning the identity and place of marginal groups (such as disabled, gay or transgender Christians); how we evangelize and preach – that is to say – how we speak of God and name grace for others; and at theology's heart and source, remembering that *lex orandi, lex credendi*: how we name God in prayer, personally and as the body of Christ in prayer constitutes our faith. The naming of God is no marginal issue, even when it places us at the frontiers of the challenges facing us.

Two caveats broaden our understanding of the question: first, the issue affects not only women but also our understanding of maleness and masculinity. A reduced or limited understanding of female means an equally incomplete understanding of male, in Archimedean correspondence. To return to our literature on the nature of knowledge in Part I of this book, if feeling and emotion are 'relegated' to the domain of women's contribution to society, and reason isolated and elevated as man's contribution to thought and progress, then both are reduced. A blindly androcentric approach to theological anthropology – one in which the male is normative – does not serve the future of the Church, or society, well. A growing body of literature and artistic explorations of the worlds of 'male' and 'masculinity' indicate the need for thought in this area. Second, this question is not limited to gender issues but addresses the reality of how we understand God, tout court. We are ever seeking a fuller understanding of the reality of God. Lonergan suggests our experience and knowledge of the divine starts with the Holy Spirit's silent work in human life, is followed by an explicit naming of God in Jesus through the preaching of the Church and ever progresses towards a Creator-God we *never* fully know. Rahner, in his exploration of the mystery of God, admitted that 'should the doctrine of the Trinity have to be dropped as false, the major part of religious literature could well remain virtually unchanged', so little does Triune faith seem to affect Christian life and practice.[8] The point is that God is ever greater than our minds and our words, meaning that in theological terms, we need to find ways that allow our understanding of our Triune God to be ever enriched. This also implies that we are willing to explore (doubt and question) the images we *are* using – where they came from and what they convey – as well as to develop discerned theological methods to do so.

Elizabeth A. Johnson, CSJ: On a quest for the living God[9]

Elizabeth A. Johnson is another of the theologians in this book who is still alive and abundant in her theological work and contributions. Born

---

[8]Cf. Karl Rahner, *The Trinity* (Tunbridge Wells, Kent: Burns & Oates 1970), 10–11.
[9]For explorations of her work, see Heidi Schlumpf, *Elizabeth Johnson: Questing for God* (Collegeville, MN: Liturgical Press, 2016); Neil Ormerod, *Introducing Contemporary Theologies:*

in Brooklyn, New York, in 1941, she is a religious of the Congregation of the Sisters of St. Joseph (CSJ). Her ministry started as a school teacher and moved to theology during and following the events of the Second Vatican Council. Her love for, and gift of, teaching seems to be one of the common denominators of Johnson's illustrious and ongoing career: she has a gift for grasping and explaining complex and historical issues in a way that is enriching and accessible to her students, as well as welcoming of questions and insights from wherever they arrive.[10] Her contribution to scholarship is no less important.[11] Johnson completed a doctorate at the Catholic University of America, where she taught for ten years before moving to Fordham University, where after years as Distinguished Professor of Theology, she is now Professor Emerita.

The questions leading Johnson's theological work are broad and constantly developing, placing her at the forefront of theological development in an ongoing way. In fact, questions are her entry point to theology, as she explained to her superior why she wanted to study theology:

> 'How could God be three persons in one divine nature? And how could Christ be one person in two natures, human and divine?' The elder nun said, 'If I questioned like that, I would lose my faith.' Johnson blurted out, 'If I did not question like this, I would lose my faith.'[12]

It is a position she remains faithful to over her whole career: 'The day we stop questioning is the day we're dead. . . . We have an infinite number of questions in us to ask, and each one is implicitly orienting us to the truth, the beautiful, and the good that is God.'[13]

However, the foundational concerns that led Johnson into theology relate directly to the one asked in this chapter about who God is and what God's relationship is to the world we live in. The dilemma of suffering and how God relates to it led to initial college studies and finds ongoing expression in her writings. In pursuing the quest for how to speak about God, she brought together Christological explorations with theories of religious language and what words about God really mean in her doctoral dissertation 'Analogy,

---

The What and the Who of Theology Today (Alexandria, NSW: E.J. Dwyer, 1997), chapter 15; Mary M. Veeneman, 'Feminist Theologies', in *Introducing Theological Method: A Survey of Contemporary Theologians and Approaches* (Grand Rapids, MI: Baker Academic, 2017).

[10]She received Fordham University's teaching award in 1998 and Professor of the Year award in 2011. Cf. https://www.fordham.edu/info/23704/theology_faculty/6347/elizabeth_a_johnson (accessed 21 February 2021).

[11]She has received fifteen honorary doctorates and was President of the Catholic Theological Association of America and the ecumenical American Theological Society.

[12]Schlumpf, *Elizabeth Johnson: Questing for God*, 26.

[13]Schlumpf, *Elizabeth Johnson: Questing for God*, 9.

Doxology and Their Connection with Christology in the Theology of Wolfhart Pannenberg'.

For Johnson, these questions are intrinsically related to the reality of the world. The concern to understand God in a way that explores and makes sense of human experience colours and grounds her theological approach in every theme she addresses. She links this explicitly to the Second Vatican Council and in particular, its *Constitution on the Church in the Modern World: Gaudium et Spes*.[14] Once again, we see life and thought overlapping. Johnson writes about her encounter with this document when she was preparing for final vows as a religious, before the world of female religious congregations had opened itself up to the invitation of the Council to its own renewal. In a cloister of 'world-denying asceticism' on the quest for a life of perfection that would 'save one's soul and the souls of others', she was struggling because of an intuition that a God who loved the world would want lives dedicated to God deeply engaged with that world. And then someone handed her a pamphlet with the draft version of *Gaudium et Spes*:

> The opening words riveted me: 'The joys and the hopes, the griefs and the anxieties of the people of this age, especially those who are poor or are in any way afflicted, these too are the joys and hopes, the griefs and anxieties of the followers of Christ.' . . . This document painted an image of God, defaced by the evil of sin, but redeemed by Christ and now led in history by the Spirit through the witness of the Church. This was a vision I had never before encountered, and it is was so beautiful. . . . On that hot summer day, my young questing spirit intersected with this Council document and found its life-long direction. In the decades since then, much has changed in myself, my religious community, the church, and the world, but the power of *Gaudium et Spes* to inspire and challenge me has not waned.[15]

While self-identifying as a feminist theologian whose work in this field I shall explore more fully, Johnson's approach to theology and work ranges through Christology,[16] salvation,[17] creation theology and environmental ethics,[18]

---

[14]Second Vatican Council, *Gaudium Et Spes: Pastoral Constitution on the Church in the Modern World* (1965).
[15]Elizabeth A. Johnson, 'Worth a Life – a Vatican II Story', in *Vatican II: Fifty Personal Stories*, Revised and expanded edition. ed. William Madges and Michael J. Daley (Maryknoll and New York: Orbis Books, 2012), 238–9.
[16]Elizabeth A. Johnson, *Consider Jesus: Waves of Renewal in Christology* (New York: Crossroad Publishing Company, 2017).
[17]Elizabeth A. Johnson, *Creation and the Cross: The Mercy of God for a Planet in Peril* (Maryknoll: Orbis Books, 2018).
[18]Elizabeth A. Johnson, *Women, Earth, and Creator Spirit* (New York: Paulist Press, 1993); Elizabeth A. Johnson, *Ask the Beasts: Darwin and the God of Love* (London: Bloomsbury, 2014); Johnson, *Creation and the Cross*.

Mariology,[19] *how* theology goes about its quest to understand God,[20] global perspectives on feminist theologies[21] and beyond. In some ways, she takes the baton from those who started out naming feminist concerns, maturing theological thought in directions that bridge feminist insights to theology's central themes and bring it into the heart of its research and teaching. At each step (and in relation to the overview on the stages or waves of feminist thought explored in chapter six), Johnson seeks to remain grounded in the teachings of the Catholic Church while challenging it to stretch itself, listen to and learn from the issues on the ground – in particular, the experiences and voices of women. In fact, a biography reveals her as nearly a reluctant feminist, or at least a slow-birthed one, midwifed into existence by the converging factors of a deep love of her call to religious life and of the Church, painful exposure to the defensiveness of the Church 'threatened by smart women saying challenging things' when applying for tenure at CUA[22] and genuine scholarly research into the best theological traditions in the light of the questions raised for herself and the world she lived in. Nowhere do these come together more fully than in her groundbreaking, and award-winning, work on naming God in *She Who Is: The Mystery of God in Feminist Theological Discourse*,[23] first published in 1992 but reprinted twice, ten and twenty-five years later. The insights of this book will be my main focus in the third section of this chapter, as it is there that Johnson more notably addresses the question being asked. However, it is important to begin by understanding her theological principles and method, all of which form part of the ongoing relevance of that response.

In her quest for 'right speech about God', Johnson firmly anchors her thought in dialogue with central figures of the theological tradition such as Aquinas, Augustine and Anselm.[24] Her interest in and study of the texts of Aquinas dates from her early theological studies and other, more contemporary influences include Rahner's definition of God as 'Infinite Holy

---

[19] Elizabeth A. Johnson, *Truly Our Sister: A Theology of Mary in the Communion of Saints* (New York– London: Continuum, 2003).
[20] Elizabeth A. Johnson, *Quest for the Living God: Mapping Frontiers in the Theology of God* (New York: Continuum, 2007).
[21] Elizabeth A. Johnson, *The Strength of Her Witness: Jesus Christ in the Global Voices of Women* (Maryknoll and New York: Orbis Books, 2016).
[22] While the reasons for this experience are complex, the named issue was an article published on Mary: Elizabeth A. Johnson, 'The Marian Tradition and the Reality of Women', *Horizons* 12, no. 1 (1985), 116–35. The article is challenging but clearly orthodox, but it led to some formal dialogues with bishops concerned about an application for tenure by someone writing on these themes.
[23] Elizabeth A. Johnson, *She Who Is: The Mystery of God in Feminist Theological Discourse*, Twenty-fifth Anniversary ed. (New York: Crossroad Publishing Company, 2017).
[24] Her book *Creation and the Cross* echoes both the theme and the style of Anselm's eleventh-century dialogue on the theme of why God became man: Anselm, 'Why God Became Man', in *The Major Works*, ed. B. Davies and G. R. Evans, 260–6 (Oxford and New York: Oxford University Press, 1998). Cf. Johnson, *Creation and the Cross*.

Mystery', Bonhoeffer's struggle for Christian living *in the world*, which she calls 'holy secularity', and the exploration of 'symbol' in both Paul Tillich and Paul Ricoeur. Her approach to the exploration of God in a way that affects how we act in the world can be found in chapter one of her book *Quest for the Living God: Mapping Frontiers in the Theology of God*, first published in 2007. She explores why the quest for an understanding of God is never-ending and her theological 'ground-rules' in terms of method. They are, interestingly, both 'triune' in nature. Three premises inform why we shall never end in our exploration of who God is:

1. God is limitless, unfathomable, beyond description. She echoes Augustine's 'if you have understood, it is not God' (*Sermon* 117, 5) to make the point that the temptation to make an idol out of our images or ideas is ever close;
2. The need and search of the human heart, made in God's image and likeness, is equally insatiable and will not conform to one encounter or felt meaning;
3. The changing history of human cultures, through which the experience of the divine is always mediated.

These three premises lead her to the conclusion that 'the profound incomprehensibility of God coupled with the hunger of the human heart in changing historical circumstances actually *requires* that there be an ongoing history of the quest for the living God that can never be concluded'.[25]

In seeking to pursue this quest, she proposes three theological principles for the naming of God:

1. 'The reality of the living God is an ineffable mystery beyond all telling.' As seen in St Augustine's image of a child trying to fit the sea into a hole made in the sand, God cannot fit into our categories;
2. 'No expression for God can be taken literally. None.' Drawing on the Fourth Lateran Council's statement in 1215 that 'between creator and creature there can be noted no similarity so great that a greater dissimilarity cannot be seen between them', the possibility of *any* concept being a literal explanation of God is rejected. Johnson explores the Catholic understanding of analogy as an access point to knowledge of God, (according to which the created world participates in God's goodness, truth and beauty); the notion of metaphor, more developed in Protestant dialectical theology (in which an image or word has revelatory potential by holding two realities in disparate tension); and the concept of symbol, which

---

[25] Johnson, *Quest for the Living God*, 13.

is a word, name, gesture or action that points beyond itself while participating in the reality it points towards. Useful as these are, in each case, we are naming 'towards' God, not nailing 'Him' down. The fact that no name exhausts the nature of God grounds her third theological principle:

3. 'We see the necessity of many names (*Summa Contra Gentiles* 1, 3:14).' There is a need for multiplicity of names for God, so that we might better attain to an enrichment of our understanding.[26]

Based on these premises, Johnson proceeds to explore a variety of issues, realities and experiences that raise questions about who God is and how divine love interacts with the world. Between the lines, one can read the feminist insight into human experience as a source for theological discourse, integrated alongside sources both old and new in the history of doctrine and its theological development to seek answers.

This book was the object of public questioning about its doctrinal content and mode of theologizing from the *United States Conference of Catholic Bishops' Committee on Doctrine* in March 2011, over three years after its publication. This is not the place to explore the stated and underlying issues behind the content and mode of acting of the committee about which much has been written.[27] Personally, I found nothing in the book that contradicted a Catholic understanding of who God is. On the contrary, I found it brought refreshing sources and language to name and shape Christian faith. Suffice to say, after reading the book, the critique and its various responses, I suggest the issues raised by the committee could have been more fruitfully addressed through timely conversation into varying theological and communicative positions rather than through a public dressing down that never reached the level of censorship or withdrawal of authorization to teach.[28] The pain inflicted on a faithful theologian's quest to help others in their understanding

---

[26] Cf. Johnson, *Quest for the Living God*, 12–22.
[27] Bradford E. Hinze and Christine Firer Hinze, 'The Elizabeth A. Johnson Case in the United States', in *Gender in Theology, Spirituality and Practice*, ed. L. S. Cahill, D. Irarrazaval, and E. M. Wainwright, 121–5 (London: SCM Press, 2012); Richard R. Gaillardetz, *When the Magisterium Intervenes: The Magisterium and Theologians in Today's Church. Includes a Case Study on the Doctrinal Investigation of Elizabeth Johnson* (Collegeville, MN: Adelaide: Michael Glazier–ATF, 2012).
[28] Guidelines on the interaction between bishops and theologians on doctrinal matters published in 1983 were approved, although not binding, by the USCCB in 1989. Cf. Joint Committee of the Canon Law Society of America and Catholic Theological Society of America, 'Doctrinal Responsibilities: Procedures for Promoting Cooperation and Resolving Disputes between Bishops and Theologians' (Appendix 1), Canon Law Society of America Proceedings 45 (1983): 261–84. For an insightful analysis of the issue from an ecclesiological perspective, see Richard R. Gaillardetz, 'Reflections on Key Ecclesiological Issues Raised in the Elizabeth Johnson Case', in *When the Magisterium Intervenes: The Magisterium and Theologians in Today's Church*, 276–94 (Collegeville, MN: Adelaide: Michael Glazier–ATF, 2012).

of God – whose intention, it was stated, was never in question – and the damage done to the credibility of the Church in North America in how it deals with its theologians, is somehow tragic. As noted by one author, 'much more is at issue here'.[29] Perhaps *one* of those things at issue is how one understands the role of theology itself. Pope Benedict, when visiting the Gregorian University in Rome in 2006, said that the mission of this university dedicated to forming theologians is

> at once easy and difficult: it is easy because you were founded to achieve this aim; it is difficult because it requires a constant fidelity to and rootedness in our Catholic history and tradition, never losing sight of these, and at the same time *an openness to the realities of our present day, attending to them with discernment and formulating creative responses to the need of the Church and the world.*[30]

Pope Francis, again in Italy, this time to a conference of theologians, called on them to foster in ever new ways the encounter of cultures with the sources of revelation and of tradition: 'a theological Pentecost' that permits the women and men of our day to hear in their own language. He notes that this work implies a measure of theological freedom, since

> without the possibility of experiencing new paths nothing new is created, and one does not leave space to the newness of the Spirit of the Risen One ... Among scholars, we should be able to go forward with freedom, and then, in the final instance, it will be the Magisterium that will say something ... [but] one cannot do theology without this freedom.[31]

It seems to me that Johnson is the very definition of a 'traditional' theologian: one eye on the past, the other on the future's 'questions arising', living the now in and through the presence of God at the very centre of her life: 'Is God a mystery beyond all comprehension, and if so what is the nature of our language about that?' Ever aware of the limits of what Aquinas called the fragility of thought, she requests: 'Just let my tombstone read: "She lost as gracefully as possible in the effort to understand God for the sake of resisting evil and healing the world."'[32] True as that may be, she left us with a formidable response to our question about how we might name God, to which I now turn.

---

[29]Hinze and hinze, 'The Elizabeth A. Johnson Case in the United States', 121–5 (125).
[30]Discourse of Pope Benedict to the Pontifical Gregorian University on 3 November 2006; emphasis mine.
[31]Francis, *Discourse at the Pontifical Theological Faculty of Southern Italy* (Vatican: Vatican News, 21 June 2019).
[32]Schlumpf, *Elizabeth Johnson: Questing for God*, 12.

She who is

Having presented the life and thought of Elizabeth A. Johnson, this section will focus explicitly on the question of how we name God, which she addresses in her book *She Who Is: The Mystery of God in Feminist Theological Discourse*.

We do not often have access to the experience underlying a given piece of writing, but the hermeneutical insights they provide when we do are noteworthy.[33] Johnson shares two memories in relation to *She Who Is*. Her unfair fight for tenure at the Catholic University of America is described as a 'radicalizing moment' in her awareness of the unjust treatment women have received over the course of the history of the Church. 'In former years they would be lighting the fire outside', to burn her at the stake, Johnson jokes. But this was serious: 'Even if you were doing everything right, you could still end up with your livelihood threatened.'[34] Her response to the exhausting affair was to apply for a sabbatical to research and write in order to respond to what she had seen. The second memory is her experience of exploring new ground in research and the consolation it brought to realize she was discovering new insights that had not yet been explored. While she was not the only theologian writing about female images for God, her pathway was particular: drawing (as usual) from Aquinas, along with the Wisdom tradition in the Scriptures, to seek other, non-male ways of addressing God. Once again, the spirituality at the centre of her theological work shines through:

> 'I knew I was walking a path that others weren't walking yet, and every day was a new discovery,' she recalls. Although it was intellectual work, writing *She Who Is* also was a tremendous spiritual experience. 'The dividing line between what's intellectual and what's spiritual dissolved,' she recalls. 'It was like a yearlong discovering of God.'[35]

This combination of spirituality and Catholic belonging, with sharp and thorough critical reflection on any given theme gives Johnson's theology a style that is balanced and respectful, even in its clear imperative to take up a form of critical rereading and retrieval:

> The feminist perspective, which honors women's humanity, women as *imago Dei*, finds this classical tradition [which continues to shape

---

[33] The issue of how a theologian self-implicates in their theology is one Schneiders addresses (chapter six). It is also an emerging theme in various fields of the social sciences and theological studies, under the title of autoethnography, a notion I shall explore further in the Coda.
[34] Schlumpf, *Elizabeth Johnson: Questing for God*, 41.
[35] Schlumpf, *Elizabeth Johnson: Questing for God*, 44.

contemporary language about God] profoundly ambiguous in what it has meant for female well-being. It has aided and abetted the exclusion and subordination of women, but *also sustained generations of foremothers and foresisters in the faith*. Along with the need for criticism of classical thought, my own inclination leads me in addition to give it a hearing, listening for wisdom that may yet prove useful.[36]

She who is: Imagining Wisdom Sophia

'To speak rightly about God' is both the title of the introduction and a reflection of an ongoing theme in Johnson's life. It is an issue that affects both our understanding of who God is and who we are, as human beings made in the image and likeness of that God. So it is both the identity and dignity of all human beings, in Church and society, and the very identity of the revealed God that is at stake. Her starting point is God as Holy Mystery and the possibility – or rather the obligation – of theology, and doctrine, to develop our naming and understanding of God over time and in history. It has ever been so. She begins by citing Thomas Aquinas' defence of the use of the un-Scriptural word 'person' for God, where he bases the validity of extra-biblical language about God on the grounds of historical needs and the sense of Scripture: 'The urgency of confuting heretics made it necessary to find new words to express the ancient faith about God . . . and the fact that it does not lead us away from the sense of Scripture.'[37] Theology today has the same call and responsibility, to dialogue and develop terminology for God that continues to grow our understanding of the revealed God who is also beyond all telling.

The underlying premise is about the symbolic power of language, and more precisely, the power of images, metaphors and names in human language and religious discourse. 'The symbol of God functions'[38] is the repeated mantra seeking to awaken us to the fact that it is not enough to 'explain' that God has no gender, that male pronouns are intended as inclusive – which, as noted earlier, works differently in some languages than in others – when the symbols we are using in prayer, everyday living and community worship evoke God as solely or mainly male.

> While officially it is rightly and consistently said that God is spirit and so beyond identification with either male or female sex, the daily language of preaching, worship, catechesis, and instruction conveys a different

---

[36]Johnson, *She Who Is*, 10; emphasis mine.
[37]Johnson, *She Who Is*, 7, referring to Aquinas, *Summa Theologiae*, 1 q. 29 a. 3.
[38]Johnson, *She Who Is*, 5, 6.

message: God is male, or at least more like a man than a woman, or at least more fittingly addressed as male than as female.

The symbol of God functions. Upon examination it becomes clear that this exclusive speech about God serves in manifold ways to support an imaginative and structural world that excludes or subordinates women. Wittingly or not, it undermines women's human dignity as equally created in the image of God.[39]

Underpinning this importance given to symbolic expression is Aquinas' epistemological approach to the role of images in knowledge and Paul Ricœur's exploration of the symbol as *prior* to thought: its source, rather than the other way around. As noted in chapter four, human beings are symbolic creatures before they are rational ones: art and creativity precede theory, which explains why Johnson would insist on the inclusion of images in her book, inviting the reader to dwell on them 'as examples of the power of image to move thought and praxis in specific directions'.[40] Insight, one could say, is dependent on the capacity for lateral and creative thinking. Tillich's understanding of symbols as growing from a deep level of the collective unconscious, pointing beyond themselves to something *other* in which they participate, opening up levels of reality that would otherwise remain untouched and unknown, is clear here as well.[41] Symbols give rise to thought because a true symbol participates in the reality it signifies, which Ricœur calls interpretation, 'for the possibilities abiding in a symbol are multivalent' – but they are not infinite. The inner structure of a symbol opens some possibilities and closes off others, requiring the work of critical thinking for awareness and development of the meanings enclosed.[42]

In Scripture there is a 'polyphony of discourse' naming God, each term contributing to our understanding of the referent 'God' revealed in their converging.[43] However, the ongoing preponderance of male images serves to justify and perpetuate societal structures in which male is normative and therefore superior.

> When God is envisioned in the image of one sex rather than both sexes, and in the image of the ruling class of this sex, then this group of men is seen to possess the image of God in a primary way . . . religious symbols

---

[39]Johnson, *She Who Is*, 5.
[40]Johnson, *She Who Is*, 300, n. 14.
[41]Johnson, *She Who Is*, 47, referring to Paul Tillich, *Dynamics of Faith* (New York: Harper & Row, 1957).
[42]Paul Ricœur, *The Symbolism of Evil* (Boston: Beacon Press, 1969). Also his exploration of categories by which God is named in Scripture: Ricœur, 'Naming God', 215.
[43]Referent is Ricœur's description on what a word denotes or 'refers' to.

are double-edged, directing attention both toward the infinite which they symbolise and toward the finite through which they symbolise it.[44]

In a culture and discipline influenced by modern theism which drew little from biblical images of God, and the absence of women to contribute a more balanced vision, in practical terms, God became male and theological anthropology became androcentric, a vision of humanity in which the female is always 'off-centre', in how we think, act and judge.

There are different options available to counter and complement this situation. One is to try and use neutral terms for God. While useful, given the power of symbols and the rich symbolic history of language about God, it is insufficient for the evocation of the personal God revealed in Scripture. Three options remain in the attempt to revalue the female, or feminine, in our naming of God: first, to discover and name the 'feminine' attributes of God (nurturing, compassion, gentleness etc.); second, to uncover a feminine dimension in God – usually located in the Spirit: that is to say, to construe the divine spirit in female terms; and third, to speak about God in a way that evokes the whole of God in which 'the fullness of female humanity as well as of male humanity and cosmic reality may serve as divine symbol, in equivalent ways'.[45] Johnson rejects the first two as unscholarly and insufficient. The third allows for the full range of naming God we can imagine, in line with Scripture's imaging of the revealed God.

Johnson therefore accepts that God can be named with male, female and other symbols and images that all contribute to a fuller grasp of who God is – she names the parables of the lost sheep and lost coin as an example of this complementarity – but historical reckoning leads her to favour a preference for female to correct the imbalance:

> Theoretically, I endorse the ideal of language for God in male and female terms, as well as the use of cosmic and metaphysical symbols. In actual fact, however, male and female images simply have not been nor are they even now equivalent. Female religious symbols of the divine are underdeveloped, peripheral and considered secondarily if at all in Christian language and the practice it continues to shape. . . . In my judgement, extended theological thinking about God in female images, or long draughts of this new wine, are a condition for the very possibility of equivalent imaging of God in religious speech.[46]

The rest of her book seeks a comprehensive response to this problem. Part I lays down the background and issues at stake, naming her concerns and her

---

[44]Johnson, *She Who Is*, 38.
[45]Johnson, *She Who Is*, 49.
[46]Johnson, *She Who Is*, 58.

chosen path, as described previously. Part II draws on women's multicultural experiences as a source for this reimaging, as well as Scripture, in which images of Jesus' *Abba*, the presence (*Shekinah*) of the Spirit in the world, the figure of Wisdom/Sophia and God as Mother emerge. From an exploration of what Johnson calls 'classical theology', she notes the usefulness of the notions of God's incomprehensibility, the value of analogy and the need for a myriad of names. Her choice of women's *experiences* also as a source for theology is not meant as an attempt to do theology from the margins but as a perfectly consistent recognition that faith, doctrine and the revelation of the divine are *always* mediated through historical experiences and understanding. It has never been otherwise; indeed, we even welcome some as foundational to Christianity and its development, such as the Jewishness of Jesus and the normativity of the first Councils in our understanding of Christ and the Trinity. Hence our need to better understand the Jewish symbolism and Greek philosophy underpinning our faith, as well as how doctrine and theology have developed over time.

Part III constitutes the centre of the book: a Trinitarian exploration of God as Wisdom: Spirit-Sophia, Jesus-Sophia and Mother-Sophia, in that order. Classical theology has tended to think about and present God as One and Triune, starting from the Origin and Creator – from whom all proceeds – through Jesus, to the Spirit, who can give the impression of an unknown and uncontrollable mystery of the kind homilies struggle with. Johnson's option to start with the Spirit is influenced by the 'sourcing of women's experiences' she includes as part of her theological method.[47] Spirit-Sophia pervades the world to revive and renew; Jesus-Sophia joins the world to heal, redeem and liberate, challenging androcentric Christological imagery; and Mother-Sophia, is an image of the Unoriginate Origin, immanent and transcendent, of Trinitarian Mystery.

In Part IV, Johnson returns, with her insights, to other theological explorations of Trinitarian theology. She laments the damage done by isolating definitions of God from any reference to human experience, as if the distance our language creates from ourselves makes statements more objective. In this last section she returns to Aquinas and the text this chapter began with: Moses' quest for God's name in chapter three of Exodus. The interpretations of this text are multiple, but Aquinas, drawing on the metaphysical instruments of his time, proposes 'He Who is' as the better

---

[47] It is interesting that for Lonergan – not particularly known for his feminist consciousness – also prefers this order. The Spirit is poured out into humanity and universally known implicitly in our experiences of unconditional love; Jesus, who we meet in the proclamation of the word of the Church, ever moving towards the unknowable Father, at least in fullness. Cf. Bernard J. F. Lonergan, 'Mission and the Spirit', in *Collected Works of Bernard Lonergan. A Third Collection*, ed. R. M. Doran and J. D. Dadosky, 21–33 (Lonergan Research Institute, Regis College, Toronto: University of Toronto Press, 1985); Frederick E. Crowe, 'Rethinking God-with-Us: Categories from Lonergan', *Science et Esprit* XVI, no. 2 (1989): 167–88.

definition of God's name. Johnson, as a result of her journey through the whole book and based on an alternative Latin interpretation to one rendered in an unquestioned androcentric universe, suggests otherwise:

> If God is not intrinsically male, if women are truly created in the image of God, if being female is an excellence, if what makes women exist as women in all difference is participation in divine being, then there is cogent reason to name toward Sophia-God, 'the One who is', with implicit reference to an antecedent of the grammatically and symbolically feminine gender. SHE WHO IS can be spoken as a robust, appropriate name for God.[48]

I am aware that to change, or even expand, how we name God is not simple or easy. In the section that follows, I explain my own attempt to do this. But the wisdom, thoroughness and vision in Johnson's work is undeniable. What is shocking, to my mind, is that this classic text is so little read and understood, and what is worrying is that its aim is as relevant now as it was then.

God by Any Other Name

At the start of this chapter I named prayer and worship as places where naming God can emerge as difficult. From where I am standing, this is the most essential one. I am a Christian because I can pray. I am a religious in the community I belong to because they taught me that dialogue with God was prayer. I am Catholic, and remain so, because I can pray, the Eucharist feeds me, the presence of God sustains me; my fumbling but vital friendships with the Persons of our Triune God hold me here. From my first experience of a silence filled with the presence of Jesus loving me, at the age of eighteen, life outside of God has not made sense. And I have *never* gone to God for an answer and not received one – although not always to my liking and at times only after a patient wait!

This song expresses my attempt to reach for that same God as I awoke to the reality that God (only) as Father no longer resonated as a sufficiently truthful way to name God, not only for the Church and the world – the future generations I want to help access the encounter with Life – but for myself. The strange, or somewhat sad, story is that I had to retrace steps I had somehow forced myself to take. My first conscious and foundational experience of God was Jesus-centred: first through the text of Jn 4.1-42 (see chapter six) and then other gospel passages, through a combination of *lectio divina* and Ignatian imaginative contemplation, my life unfolded as

---

[48]Johnson, *She Who Is*, 255–6.

friendship with Jesus, chosen and trusted, seated at his table, called to enable others access to that same friendship. I did not really relate to the Father. In fact, I could not imagine God as Father, perhaps because my own father was such a wonderful, loving, supportive presence, I did not need another. In hindsight and with the tools I have now, I realize I was seeking to give God attributes 'He' did not need, and I did not have words to name the immanent provident presence I *could* sense as the transcendent one I sought. The implicit influence of an image of God was too linked to that of modern theism's 'old man in the clouds' somewhere, controlling but not in control of the strings moving the cogs of our world.

But Jesus called God '*Abba*, Father!', so I sought somehow to access an experience of God the Father, through Jesus' experience and that helped forge my Trinitarian experience in God as greater than I, trustworthy, provident, origin of my being, who 'called me before I was born, while I was in my mother's womb' (Isa. 49.1). Trusting the Father whom Jesus trusted made sense and opened a space of presence. But slowly, the ever-present 'his' of the psalms I pray daily and the Eucharist I celebrate – also daily – found resistance from my spirit. The symbolic power of 'male' as the overriding evocative 'you' for God slowly became untenable for this theologian who knew the limits of language, but also its power. 'Words are not innocent', one of my most erudite professors at the Pontifical Gregorian University would say. So my capacity to name and access God as Creator became difficult. What does one do when the ground beneath one's feet shifts? I had worked hard to build a relationship with God as Triune – within the limitations of our human capacity to apprehend God – and this is the central relationship of my consecrated life. So losing it, or feeling it shake was, and is still, an uncomfortable experience, but one cannot go back to Egypt. Ahead lies only the desert, and the certain hope that things will change, that God as the God of all will prevail, that the Spirit of Love will help the Church discover and become reconciled with our unconscious fears of female symbols for God, to welcome a fuller expression of the One in whose image we are made.

The song – 'God by Any Other Name' – seeks to aid in that process. Symbols precede thought. They are prior, archetypal, generative of new words, understandings, theories and understandings. So, I took the two most central and instinctive prayers of any Catholic and tried to reclaim them in a broader way: how we start prayer and some Eucharistic texts that could express better the God revealed in Christ. The song *does not reject* God as Father. Any fair listener will have to accept that. In fact, I still call God 'Father' at times, as Jesus called God '*Abba*', something that was already a huge shift in the Jewish sense of God, in terms of its intimacy and trust. I intuit that I find it possible to still use 'Father' as a name, alongside others, because in *my* world, space is being made for women to lead, in different ways (as long as you have *significant* training and education). Contact with cultures in which women still suffer enormously from the male superiority complexes, or ones in which masculinity is unaware and toxic, reawakens my quest to symbolize differently this God who is the ground of our being. There is work still to be done.

The song tries to open that most sacred space that is our daily, instinctive naming of God to allow everyone in – including, if calling a name evokes a response even in God, a fuller sense of the presence of God. The invitation to the reader, as you listen to this song, is to pray with it and sense how it sits with *who God is* for you, with how you name God. It is dedicated to one of my nieces in her quest for the living God, with one foot in the Church and one in the world embracing the realities that have led her thus far. In that search, she begins life and prayer each morning with the words and gesture of 'In the name of the Father and the Son and the Holy Spirit; In the name of the Mother, the Daughter, and the Holy Spirit'.[49]

'God by Any Other Name' lyrics

In the name of the Father, the name of the Son, the name of the Holy Spirit
In the name of the Mother, the name of her Child, the name of the Living Breath, I pray . . .
Blessed are you God of all creation; Through you we receive . . . bread and wine
our gifts and labour . . . for the praise and the glory of God and the good of a Church . . .
gathered in your name.
In the name of the Father, the name of the Son, the name of the Holy Spirit
For the sake of my Mother, the sake of her Daughter, the love of the Living Breath,
I seek . . . your Face; I name . . . your grace.
Holy, Holy, Holy are You. Heaven and earth are alive with the glory of You
In the name of the Father, the name of the Son, the name of the Holy Spirit
In the name of the Mother, the name of her Child, the name of the Living Breath, I pray . . .
Hidden God with us; Loving God in us; Boundless God for ever. . . . Amen.
In the name of the Father, the name of the Son, the name of the Holy Spirit.

©MAEVE LOUISE HEANEY, 2020.
Strange Life, The Music of Doubtful Faith

---

[49]Link to the song 'God by Any Other Name': https://res.cloudinary.com/bloomsbury-online-resources/video/upload/v1639138246/Suspended%20God/God_By_Any_Other_Name.wav

Selected further reading

An introduction to her life and thought

Schlumpf, Heidi. *Elizabeth Johnson: Questing for God*. Collegeville, MN: Liturgical Press, 2016.

The naming of God

Johnson, Elizabeth A. *She Who Is: The Mystery of God in Feminist Theological Discourse*. Twenty-fifth Anniversary ed. New York: Crossroad Publishing Company, 2017.

Dialogue bringing together women of different theological approaches

Johnson, Elizabeth A. *The Church Women Want: Catholic Women in Dialogue*. New York: Crossroad Pub. Co., 2002.

Christology

Johnson, Elizabeth A. *Consider Jesus: Waves of Renewal in Christology*. New York: Crossroad Publishing Company, 2017.

Creation and eco-theology

Johnson, Elizabeth A. *Ask the Beasts: Darwin and the God of Love*. London: Bloomsbury, 2014.
Johnson, Elizabeth A. *Creation and the Cross: The Mercy of God for a Planet in Peril*. Maryknoll: Orbis Books, 2018.

Theological method applied to contemporary questions

Johnson, Elizabeth A. *The Quest for the Living God: Mapping Frontiers in the Theology of God*. New York: Continuum, 2007.

15

How can we know if God is trustworthy?

How do the 'reasons of the heart' fit into faith seeking understanding?

French philosopher Blaise Pascal (1623–62) famously challenged philosophical positions of his time with these words: 'The heart has its reasons, which reason does not know.'[1] Despite the romantic overtones of this well-known phrase that seem to corroborate contemporary tendencies to allow the heart rule over *every* other consideration, in its original context Pascal was actually proposing a theory of knowledge that integrated a form of 'intuition' alongside discursive reasoning. However, the phrase gives us an entry point to one of the longest and most costly reductive understandings of human life in the history of theology and philosophy: that of the marginalization and subordination of feeling to rationality effectuated during and after the Enlightenment. Part I explored some of the twists and turns of that process in what the disciplines of theology and philosophy call 'epistemology'. The etymology of the word is simple: *logos* and *epistome*, the study of knowledge – not in terms of the sum of all knowledge acquired (an impossible task) but rather of *how* we come to know. The aim of this chapter is not to revisit that history, but rather to pinpoint and shed light on a particular issue it has created, and a possible way forward through the work of Italian theologian Pierangelo Sequeri.

The question being raised is about the dynamic of Christian faith and has two sides to it: '*Is* God trustworthy?' That is to say: Who is the God we believe in? Is God on humanity's side, or are we somehow playing games

---

[1] Blaise Pascal, *Pensées* (New York: Philosophical Library: Open Road Integrated Media, Inc., 2016), 177.

with an unknown Being – or even worse, a despot – in a vain attempt to protect ourselves? And if God *is* trustworthy, *how do we come to believe in God?* That is to say: What is the nature of faith and trust, and how does it come about? Christian doctrine teaches us that faith is a mystery and a free gift. This has led some Christian denominations and theologians to the doctrine of predestination: there are those who are destined to believe and therefore be saved and those who are not, and since God is outside of space-time and sees all things, God therefore already knows who will be 'saved' and who will be 'lost'. But this makes a rather cruel game of our free will and is utterly incompatible with the image of a loving God who created us to share in life and joy and wants all to be saved and come to the knowledge of truth (1 Tim. 2.4).

I have dealt in other chapters with issues of salvation: guided by Rahner I looked at universal grace offered to all in the hidden dimensions of our freedom and knowledge, and Sobrino's theology opened up questions about the nature of salvation in the light of the world's poverty. My focus here is slightly more specific and at times 'technical', in that it asks about the link between the human dynamic of trust and faith in God, and the reasons necessary in order to take that leap of faith. How can we understand the process of a person coming to believe in God, in order to enable or support it? It underpins theologies of mission, but also our understanding of a theology of faith. It is an area of theology in development since the Second Vatican Council's Constitution on Divine Revelation *Dei Verbum*. The rich teaching and theology of revelation in this document include one, rather brief, number on faith:

> 'The obedience of faith' (Rom. 26.26; cf. Rom. 1.5; 2 Cor. 10.5-6) 'is to be given to God who reveals, an obedience by which the human person commits their whole selves freely to God, offering the full submission of intellect and will to the God who reveals', and freely assenting to the truth revealed by him [*sic*]. To make this act of faith, the grace of God and the interior help of the Holy Spirit must precede and assist, moving the heart and turning it to God, opening the eyes of the mind and giving 'joy and ease to everyone in assenting to the truth and believing it.' To bring about an ever deeper understanding of revelation, the same Holy Spirit constant brings faith to completion by his gifts.[2]
>
> *Dei Verbum 5*

While clear and gathering the elements of theological analysis of the act of faith consistent with Church teaching of the past, it really does not correspond to the Christological and anthropological density of the numbers

---

[2] The quotes refer back to statements on faith from the First Vatican Council's Dogmatic Constitution on the Catholic Faith *Dei Filius* and to the Council of Orange.

of *Dei Verbum* it follows. As a response to the revealing God, Christian faith merits more attention.

And there are other open questions. One of them pertains to a theological understanding of witness and the place of what are called the 'motives of credibility' in the human coming to faith. The history of Christian thought has always defended that faith is a gift from God, but that it also involves and integrates human freedom and knowledge. So, in coming to faith in Christ, there has to be something – a witness, a thought process, an experience of truth or love and so on – sufficient to invite a response while leaving us free to respond. How is this whole process enabled by grace while still leaving space for human freedom? The history of what theology calls the analysis of faith (*analysis fidei*) was disconnected in its understanding of how human beings come to believe and know. It defended the role of grace by undermining the subjective side of faith (*fides quae*), as was explained in chapter one, so faith could be blind and should not question; but at the same time, it defended the rational provability ('arguability') of why faith is credible (the motives of credibility) according to the models of scientific and philosophical reasoning of the epoque. The result was a theology convinced of the need to argue for the reasons of credibility according to the rules set by standards taken from outside of the realm of Christian anthropology. In other words, the rules of the quest to reach God were set by those not interested in joining the search. So common sense (which has its wisdom) rightly put down the option for faith to divine arbitrary and irrational impulses. Theology has long been lacking an updated understanding of *why* and *how* faith happens.

The question is being raised in an interesting way, I think, with the papacy of Pope Francis, or at least it underlies reactions to him. Within the Catholic Church, Pope Francis has his supporters and his opposers, those who understand and accept where he is seeking to lead the Church and those who think essential elements are being lost. I think the positions are unsurprising, if disappointing in their mode of expression. Popes Benedict and John Paul II had their supporters and naysayers as well, although opinions were less publicly and viscerally expressed, for a variety of reasons. However, more interesting, for our purposes here, are the reactions to Pope Francis of those outside or alienated from the Church, especially in relation to his positions relating to the poor and those in need. From the moment Francis was elected, people outside the Church have brought him into conversations as much or more than those I teach or work with. Why? Why was Pope Francis named 'Person of the Year' by the *Time* magazine in 2013? The image of the Church as a 'field hospital' and of Francis eating in lunchrooms for the homeless, or his response of 'who am I to judge?' when asked about gay people, have resonated around the world: Why?

I suggest that the real reason is not a fully formulated approval of a certain type of theology or Catholicism and much less a thought-through Christian moral code. I intuit, in a 'Pascalian' kind of way, that it has to do with witness and the 'motives of credibility' mentioned earlier. The majority of people outside Church do not find the Church credible or interesting enough to take part in the debate about minor or major aspects of Church teaching on marriage, sexuality or authority. Instead, it is the image of God that is presented in actions such as these of Pope Francis that resonate beyond Church walls. People on the edges of faith instinctively know that there is something authentic happening in such witness, because only such a God could be attractive or worthy of being believed in. Only a God who is merciful, compassionate, *more* capable than us of understanding and accepting the meanderings of the human heart is worth paying any attention to. This does not mean that his admirers *come* to Christian faith yet, but it carries an element of witness, one of the first elements of both a theology of mission and a theology of faith, as we shall see. In his refreshing and still relevant *Apostolic Exhortation Evangelii Nuntiandi*, Paul VI called Christians to create 'irresistible question marks' before speaking about Jesus: let the world ask 'why are they like this? Why do they live in this way? What or who is it that inspires them? Why are they in our midst?'[3] In relation to Francis' leadership, it is worth asking what it is about the image of God underlying these actions that people *outside* the Church as well as inside find fascinating. And how could this contribute to a theology of faith?

To explore this question, I turn to a theologian who is not well known in the English-speaking world but who has dedicated his life to these issues. His theology of faith and understanding of the process of human knowledge provide an insightful window into our question. He is also an expert in the area of theology and music, which explains my knowledge of his work, and how it contributes to and enriches his theology of faith, which is our main focus here. It is a pity that language barriers continue to inhibit the collaboration and cross-fertilization of good theology across the world. There are certainly differences between countries within the English-speaking world which cultural and ecclesial reflection cannot ignore, but when language is added to the equation, the challenge of mutual understanding and enrichment is not easy. But we live in a universal Church with a shared history, and some of the theological and ecclesial issues we face have similar theological roots. The more clearly we can grasp these roots and how they have been approached in the past, the easier our theological efforts at moving forward will be, *as well as* our shared understanding of and collaboration in where we are heading as a Church. Sequeri gives us a unique insight into the crises and challenges facing European culture and their theological origins. His theology of faith rereads *how* it came to be where it is, what was missing and what might contribute to the authentic development of a humanizing quality of culture that does not betray its origins. It also witnesses to what I

---

[3]Cf. Paul VI, *Apostolic Exhortation Evangelii Nuntiandi* (Vatican City, 1976), 21.

would describe as Italy's particular sensibility to its cultural heritage and the importance of human culture tout court, which when translated into English is refreshing in its depth and provocation. Alongside the necessary plurality of contextual theologies that make up Christian theology, it is an important element of our shared history.

Pierangelo Sequeri: Theologizing 'from the centre of the soul to one's fingertips'[4]

Pierangelo Sequeri was born in 1944 in Milan, a son of two musicians and himself a composer and musician. He was ordained a priest for the Archdiocese of Milan on 28 June 1968, and as a musician and composer, has written liturgical songs which are known and used in the Italian Catholic Church. In 1983, together with Professor Licia Sbatella, a bioengineer, clinical psychotherapist and musician, he pioneered a project of orchestral music-therapy with children and young people with learning difficulties called *The Esagramma Onlus Foundation*, which continues to thrive.[5] Sequeri is one of the best known and respected Italian theologians at present, renowned for his creative and original contribution to the theology of faith, among other areas. He has served as professor of philosophy and theology at the Major Seminary of Milan, musicologist of the *Biblioteca Ambrosiana* (Ambrosian Library), professor in charge of theological aesthetics at the Academy of Fine Arts of Brera, in Milan (*l'Accademia delle Belle Arti di Brera*), and most recently was the dean and professor of fundamental theology at the Theological Faculty of Northern Italy (*Facoltà Teologica dell'Italia Settentrionale*). He was the president of the Pontifical John Paul II Institute for Studies on Marriage and Family at the Pontifical Lateran University in Rome until September 2021, and at the time of writing this book, is a consulter of the Pontifical Council for Promoting the New Evangelization and a member of the International Theological Commission.

By way of background, Sequeri studied music and philosophy before obtaining his doctorate in theology at the Pontifical Gregorian University in Rome in 1972. This knowledge of music and philosophy forms an intrinsic part of his theological writings. His extensive knowledge of the history of Western theology makes identifying particular influences difficult, but his

---

[4] I have developed Sequeri's thought more fully in a previous, foundational exploration of authors working on the intersection of music and theology. Some of that work, in summarized form, is included here. The source is chapter five of Maeve Louise Heaney, *Music as Theology: What Music Has to Say About the Word* (Eugene, OR: Pickwick Publications Wipf and Stock, 2012), used by permission of Wipf and Stock Publishers: www.wipfandstock.com.
[5] Cf. https://esagramma.net/. Sbatella published a book on this project: Licia Sbatella, *La Mente Orchestra: Elaborazione della Risonanza e Autismo* (Milano: Vita e Pensiero, 2006).

approach to beauty echoes Augustine's and the influence of Balthasar in his understanding of theological aesthetics is important. In fact, some of his work can be understood as an attempt to continue or complete what he senses is missing in Balthasar's immense achievement. He is not well known in the English-speaking world, since he lives and works within the world of Italian theology, which historically interacts more with German schools of thought than with the world of English theology, and most of his work is not yet translated into English.[6] However, the combination of intellectual dexterity, spirituality and wisdom with which he addresses certain issues means he is an invaluable resource and guide for theology today. In what is presented further, unless drawn from the work of Irish Jesuit Michael Paul Gallagher, all of the translations of Sequeri's work are my own. At times, I have chosen to allow his words to speak for themselves, in an attempt to illustrate the particular eloquence and musicality of this Italian theologian's style. Sequeri writes on themes of spirituality and culture, theological aesthetics and art (with a focus on music), and a theology of faith and corresponding understanding of God. While these are interrelated in his approach, the last of these addresses our question more directly, so I will start with the others before exploring his theology of faith in the third section.

A cultural paralysis with theological roots

Sequeri's theological style is often conceptually dense, but the concern underlying it is far from intellectualist. In a Europe fast losing sight of its origins, he is concerned with the spiritual quality of human experience, culture and faith. In fact, he sees the need for a redefining and reconstruction of *what* spiritual quality is, as one step towards contributing to what he describes as cultural reconstruction. This is reflected in the titles of books such as *Spiritual Quality: Faith Experience at the Contemporary Crossroads*,[7] *Sensitive to the Spirit, Religious Humanism and the Order of the Affections*[8] or more recently *Technology and Meaning: Beyond the Human?*[9] As someone invested in placing theology at the service of a better society and world, he tries to find common ground by asking the question about what we can

---

[6] An accessible introduction to Sequeri in English can be found in Michael Paul Gallagher, 'Pierangelo Sequeri: Horizons of Trust', in *Faith Maps: Ten Religious Explorers from Newman to Joseph Ratzinger*, 119–31 (New York: Paulist Press, 2010). For an introduction to his theology of faith, see Michael Paul Gallagher, 'Truth and Trust: Pierangelo Sequeri's Theology of Faith', *Irish Theological Quarterly* 73, no. 1–2 (2008): 3–31.
[7] Pierangelo Sequeri, *La Qualità Spirituale: Esperienza nella Fede nel Crocevia Contemporaneo* (Casale Monferrato: Piemme, 2001).
[8] Pierangelo Sequeri, *Sensibili allo Spirito: Umanesimo Religioso e Ordine degli Affetti* (Milano: Glossa, 2001).
[9] Pierangelo Sequeri, *La Tecnica e il Senso: Oltre L'uomo?* (Milano: Glossa, 2015).

all think together or where we can meet in our understanding of 'spiritual life' or 'spirituality'.[10] Without this, we have no shared language through which to meet and dialogue. Sequeri is an acute observer of contemporary Western culture and situates the causes of the present situation in the double separation operated in the arrival of modernity and subsequently romanticism: the separation between reason and faith, and between theology and spirituality.[11] This has left contemporary culture with an awkward coexistence of calculating reason and uncontrolled sentimental and emotional thrust which are not integrated to work together.[12] While aware of the anthropological value of human affect and love, he challenges a sentimental thrust that does not integrate the bonds of charity (*agape*) worthy of human loving as not being a valid paradigm for Christian *or* human living. The result is a type of 'paralysis' of the conscience, which becomes incapable of discerning and less of deciding.

> Many no longer know either how to decipher their own feelings: they don't know if they love well or not, they don't know what they are scared of, they don't know what makes them euphoric at one moment and depressed at the next, they don't even know if they believe or not. They 'try out' [*provono*] all these feelings ('experiences' they say, but more than anything they are 'experiments' they do with themselves) and they are not capable of deciphering them.[13]

This is not only lived at an individual level but has forged the coordinates of our sociopolitical interactions. Sequeri is scathing about the presumptions of the present cultural (and political) situation in which the conscience is at the same time privatized and universally legitimized by which individual decisions are always right, irrespective of the quality of the conscience that decides. This has a double effect: on the one hand it empties and disempowers faith's contribution to society and culture, because either Christian faith has external effect and influence on the world around it or it is rendered useless and therefore meaningless. On the other, this privatization of conscience leaves 'culture' without external contrast.[14] For this reason, he is critical of the utilization of Christian voluntary work and social charities to cover up and legitimate the status quo of systems that control the economical-political laws. They use humanity's altruistic spirit to make up for institutional bias,

---

[10] Sequeri, *Sensibili allo Spirito*, 4.
[11] Cf. Sequeri, *La Qualità Spirituale*, 7–18.
[12] Cf. Pierangelo Sequeri, *L'estro di Dio: Saggi di Estetica* (Milano: Glossa, 2000), 14.
[13] Pierangelo Sequeri and Carlo Maria Martini, *L'oro e la Paglia: Meditazioni sull'educare alla Scuola della Parola di Dio* (Milano: Glossa, 1989), 110.
[14] Cf. Sequeri, *Sensibili allo Spirito*, 9–13.

leaving unjust systems unchallenged.[15] He is also critical of the religious coordinates of a 'politically correct' framework in its effect on culture:

> There are images of inter-religious dialogue that seem based more on disinterest for the quality of religion than on the common passion for truth. It is one of the effects of the so-called 'political correctness', already quite devastating for anthropological quality and culture.[16]

Spirituality, culture and aesthetics

This concern for culture is intrinsically linked to his work on aesthetics, which includes but is not limited to art-making and its reception. At stake for all of us is our embodied existence and the importance of the senses in our apprehension of reality. For this reason, he sees as important the cultivation of aesthetic perception, not as a pastime for the elite but in developing what he calls a 'spirituality of sensibility'.[17] In a beautifully written book whose title is difficult to translate, but roughly means *The Inspiration of God* (*L'Estro di Dio*),[18] Sequeri explores how 'the aesthetic is the recurring place of that question that the conscience rarely dares to formulate with the necessary seriousness: is this really the best of possible worlds?'[19] That is to say, aesthetic sensibility and art awaken in us desires about how the world could be and is perhaps meant to be. It opens a doorway to rediscovering the world in a different way. This is George Steiner's insight into the power of art to evoke other kinds of presences: when we encounter good art, it seems to ask us 'what do you feel, what do you think of the possibilities of your life, of the alternate shapes of being which are implicit in your experience of me, in our encounter?'[20] The exceptional artist or thinker reads being anew.[21] Is this the best world we could have? The answer art gives, according to Sequeri, is both yes and no, because it neither accepts that beauty cannot reflect itself in this world, nor that it be confined to the limits the world

---

[15]Cf. Sequeri, *Sensibili allo Spirito*, 79–114.
[16]Cf. Sequeri, *La Qualità Spirituale*, 61–2.
[17]The literal translation would be 'spirituality of the sensible', but the Italian meaning of *sensibile* and *sensibilità* is difficult to translate into English, as it seeks to evoke sensitive more than sensible, without the undercurrents of excessive reactiveness it carries in English. It refers to the whole realm of the senses: a spirituality that integrates the senses.
[18]Sequeri, *L'estro di Dio: Saggi di Estetica*. *Estro* is also translatable as gift, fancy or whim, the combination of which opens more space to intuit his intention.
[19]Sequeri, *L'estro di Dio: Saggi di Estetica*, 14. The question echoes Leibniz's foundational work in the early eighteenth century on the existence of God in the face of suffering: Gottfried Wilhelm Leibniz, *Theodicy: Essays on the Goodness of God the Freedom of Man* (Eugene OR: Wipf and Stock, 2001).
[20]George Steiner, *Real Presences: Is There Anything in What We Say?* (London: Faber, 1991), 142–3.
[21]Steiner, *Real Presences: Is There Anything in What We Say?*, 194.

imposes on it. Art pushes frontiers. He speaks of how imagination becomes corporal in aesthetic sensibility, awakening in a way that words struggle to, the awareness of another beauty. That is to say: What *could* this world be like? Let's imagine and recreate! In this sense, aesthetic sensibility is essential to the development of Europe into the future: 'The study of . . . the bonds between aesthetic experience and believing intelligence promises to have special importance in the slow reformation of a new way of considering the religious roots of Europe.'[22] And his modelling of beauty is not naïve. There are traces of Augustine in how he presents a Christian understanding of beauty: 'The Risen One is as beautiful as the crucified One is ugly.'[23]

Music sits centre stage in his thought on the arts. I drew on his exploration of the interweaving histories of Western culture and music in *Music and Mysticism*[24] in chapter three, but his translation of and commentary on Balthasar's first writing on music in *Anti-Prometheus: The Place of Music in the Theological Aesthetics of Hans Urs von Balthasar*[25] are the most insightful I have found on both Balthasar's contribution *and* deficit in relation to music in theology. He also explores the fascination Mozart held for some of theology's greats (in *Except Mozart: A Theological Passion*[26]). And it is from music that much of Sequeri's understanding of the centrality of aesthetics and the arts to human believing is derived. He observes a two-way bond between music and faith, in that religious inspiration seems to fascinate musical composition,[27] and faith, in turn, has never renounced on a special relationship with music and is at the core of much of its greatness. 'The contribution of the Christian Religion to the musical history of Occident is more profound, and propulsive, constant and decisive than in any other manifestation of the aesthetic.'[28]

As a musician, his understanding and explanation of *how music works* symbolically in human life are described in terms of relationality and operativity rather than semantics: 'there is a dimension of the symbolic, which human beings more typically live from, which has instead the form of action . . . it does not produce objects, it transforms subjects'.[29] In music, more than in any other form of expression or art, Christianity manages to say what it needs to say about the spirituality of matter and the materiality

---

[22]Sequeri, *L'estro di Dio: Saggi di Estetica*, 26.
[23]Sequeri, *L'estro di Dio: Saggi di Estetica*, 3.
[24]Pierangelo Sequeri, *Musica e Mistica: Percorsi nella Storia Occidentale delle Pratiche Estetiche e Religiose* (Città del Vaticano: Libreria Editrice Vaticana, 2005).
[25]Pierangelo Sequeri, *Anti-Prometeo. Il Musicale nell'estetica Teologica di Hans Urs von Balthasar* (Milano: Glossa, 1995).
[26]Pierangelo Sequeri and Vittorio Mathieu, *Eccetto Mozart: Una Passione Teologica* (Milano: Glossa, 2006).
[27]Sequeri, *Anti-Prometeo*, 109.
[28]Sequeri, *Anti-Prometeo*, 122.
[29]Sequeri, *L'estro di Dio: Saggi di Estetica*, 176–7.

of the Spirit. The essential *goodness* of matter and human love (*eros*), the holding together of senses and intelligence, is performed by music as nowhere else without, he says, falling into the heresy of denying either:

> Music, in itself, puts structurally in practice the *oxymoron* that represents the background of that truth of the Christian *logos*, but also its necessary effect: *the senses are also intelligent*, not only obtuse; *the spirit is also sensitive*, not only incorporeal. The Christian *logos* is not a naked truth without style.[30]

He seems to share in the admiration of Barth, Balthasar and Kierkegaard of Mozart but interestingly does not allow his appreciation for this style of music to enclose him in classicist understandings of the art of music. Instead, he calls for Christianity to pay attention to raising the level of artistic creativity in both ecclesial and cultural spaces by opening themselves in unprejudiced ways to the universe of artistic creativity, rather than trying to freeze its growth.[31] And the way forward is neither the identification or imposition of one style, nor the acceptance of any level of quality, but the promotion of the spiritual, human and Christian formation of artists necessary to nourish art, including finding forums for that to take place. It is a position born of the intrinsic unity of faith and art in Sequeri's thought. Building on the thought of Balthasar, he believes that the beautiful will return to theological discourse when Christians who are also artists 'experience the cosmos as revelation of an abysm of grace and an incomprehensible absolute love. Not only to believe but to experience'.[32] Then, 'convinced believers of passionate faith and real talent and formation' will be able to draw with them the interest of a culture.[33] In fact, between the sacred activities of ecclesial spaces and the world's sensibility to art, he identifies creative thinking as being able to open a 'third space' or way forward (which he calls third way – *terza via*) of dialogue between the Church and the worlds it inhabits. It is not hard to read his theological work as being precisely this kind of creative thought. His faith in, and commitment to, a qualitative theological contribution to culture runs right through his writings:

> I believe that a theology that is intellectually strong and creative, which thinks things and does not limit itself to explaining formulae, would be a *chance* also for this comprehensive culture. . . . Theology implies asceticism. Solid thought is built with time . . . a contemplative attitude

---

[30]Sequeri, *Anti-Prometeo*, 107.
[31]Sequeri and Mathieu, *Eccetto Mozart: Una Passione Teologica*, 11.
[32]Sequeri, *L'estro di Dio: Saggi di Estetica*, 102.
[33]Cf. Pierangelo Sequeri, 'Coscienza Cristiana, Ethos della Fede e Canone Pubblico', in *A Misura di Vangelo: Fede, Dottrina, Chiesa*, ed. M. Vergottini (29) (Cinisello Balsamo: San Paolo, 2003).

is indispensable for this exercise.... It must set its roots in the intimacy of a divine conversation that goes from the centre of the soul to one's fingertips.[34]

Let's turn now to his theology of faith in, and recognition of, the trustworthiness of God. In his work, we shall discover the (musical?) resonance of the human quality of a person in prayerful touch with the person of Christ, which allows us to understand that the perception as well as conviction of God's goodness is a powerful and eloquent theological source.

Show me your face: God as utterly trustworthy

We return to our question about *how* faith comes about and the need for a more adequate analysis and understanding of faith for contemporary culture that integrates our intuitive recognition of goodness and mercy as authentic signs of how God must be. Before entering into an explanation of his theology, I would like to clarify a keyword in Sequeri's theology that we have already encountered in relation to aesthetics but which in his theology of faith takes centre stage: *coscienza*, (conscience). It is important to understand how he uses this word if we want to grasp his central intent and thesis about the human capacity of trusting in God and the process by which this comes about. Translating the word as he means it needs the combination of the terms of conscience, consciousness and awareness. That is to say: it is both prior to and broader than the notion of moral conscience in English, because it includes both the human perception of truth and justice, and the realm of what he calls 'the order of the affects', which includes the whole realm of human affectivity, feelings, emotions and capacity for love and goodness. For that reason, I use both the terms 'conscience' and 'consciousness', according to the context and meaning. Importantly, the expression 'the believing conscience' does not seek to evoke the righteousness of someone with Christian beliefs, but rather to describe 'human consciousness as it believes'. The difference is immense.

Exploring the believing conscience

Implicit in Sequeri's thought is a basic trust in the human capacity of recognizing truth and justice, even when it is absent or incomplete. He refers to this as 'the truth of our experience'.[35] It is grounded on the conviction

---

[34]Sequeri, *La Qualità Spirituale*, 80–4.
[35]Cf. Pierangelo Sequeri, *Il Timore di Dio* (Milano: Vita e pensiero, 2008), 156.

that honest intelligence must take seriously the structure and process of human believing. We are capable of recognizing and responding to meaning. Further to this, of all the different human experiences, Sequeri identifies a shared space of meaning-making for an understanding of faith, as much for the believer as for those who are not: contemporary sensibility to love.

> In the present configuration of the modern city, the only universally 'sharable' consciousness of spiritual experience is today that which is written in the circle of individual emotion and feeling of love.[36]

Sequeri focusses on the human capacity to and process of trust that involves affectivity and feelings as well as reason, using the expression of 'order of the affects' for the sphere of human anthropology that brings together our perception of truth and justice. In fact, he challenges the separation of truth and freedom in human life *and* faith, as well as any separation between anthropology and theology. Interestingly, he relates this 'order of the affects' to the 'feelings' or 'mind' of Christ we are called to assume by Paul: 'have in yourselves the same mind as Christ' (Phil. 2.3-8).[37]

In this light Sequeri tends a theological bridge to Christian faith from within the human experience of faith. How? He starts with a critique of the epistemological heritage of the *analysis fidei* I mentioned earlier. In response to the eternal question of how to hold together respect for human freedom and the theological gratuity of grace, Sequeri believes that we *cannot* find a basis for Christian faith by analysing the believing conscience from the premises of a non-believing conscience, which is taken as 'objective' for the very reason of being non-believing! Nor can an authentic understanding of faith remain detached from the spiritual quality of human experience. Therefore, based on the existential personal nature of each person's reasons for and response in faith, he seeks to bring together how the process of human faith and trust play out and its connection with Christian faith. He identifies the task of theology as 'the *effective* re-composition of the unity of *theologal* and anthropological faith': 'a critical intelligence of the religious quality and Christian singularity of the believing conscience'.[38] That is to say, understanding how we come to *Christian* faith depends on a better understanding of how as beings made in the image and likeness of God, we believe and trust in our interpersonal relationships. This turns prior theological approaches to faith around. Instead of taking knowledge *not* linked to a Christian world view as the norm for theology, it explores the believing conscience as *theologal* (made in the image and likeness of God and therefore a theological place and access point to the divine) in all

---

[36] Sequeri, *Sensibili allo Spiritoo*, 13.
[37] Sequeri, *Sensibili allo Spirito*, 104, n. 29.
[38] Sequeri, *Il Timore di Dio*, 57–61.

spheres of life, an approach that will lead us to understand what is specific about the Christian act of faith.

From there, he offers an analysis of the believing conscience, which he identifies as a universal human reality, characterized by two fundamental elements: the perception of its finitude and the feeling of being 'unfounded', by which we know ourselves as mortal and apprehending the world as given, instinctively search for its meaning. This conscience is intrinsically capable of receiving what he describes as a *'notitia Dei'*, that is to say, information, or (good) 'news', of God, which can later lead us to a commitment to Christ. How does this 'news' or information reach us? He names three dynamics or areas of human awareness that work together in the reception of revelation: aesthetic, ethical and sacred (or religious), although this third follows the other two. These dimensions are fully human, and the process of faith passes *through* and not around them. Therefore, a sense of God can come in the form of an aesthetic mediation, by which reality appears 'loveable'; or by way of an ethical mediation, by which truth convinces freedom of its 'justice' and its need to be accepted. He gives major importance to the *symbolic* nature of this 'evidence' as part of the process of humans making sense of the world and our lives within it.[39] Integrating the dynamic of human symbolization is a key factor in explaining how divine grace and human perception meet in transformative ways. The step to Christian faith passes through the witness of the Church, by which this believing conscience becomes 'Christianly' constituted through the recognition of the truth and justice of the foundational event of Jesus Christ. But this coming into Christian faith follows the process of human faith, which is capable of recognizing truth and justice in the witness of the faith of the Church. In this way, through what he calls 'mediated immediacy', Christian faith becomes historically situated.

Of vital importance in his understanding is the unity of all the capacities of the human person: our perception of meaning, truth and justice, integrating the intellectual and affective dimensions of human life. I mentioned earlier that he identified love as an important shared space of understanding between faith and culture. This affective dimension of human life, with all its fluctuations, is central to faith: 'our life of feelings is the great river in which we learn to appreciate what is truly decisive for us, what touches us and convinces us, what asks for our commitment and calls forth our response'.[40] Sequeri talks about the disciples 'recognising themselves as recognised'[41] by the risen Jesus,

---

[39]Cf. Pierangelo Sequeri, Ezio Prato, and Pierluigi Lia, *Estetica e Teologia: L'indicibile Emozione del Sacro: R. Otto, A. Schönberg, M. Heidegger* (Milano: Glossa, 1993), 9–11.
[40]Pierangelo Sequeri, *Senza Volgersi Indietro: Meditazioni per Tempi Forti* (Milano: Vita e pensiero, 2000), 71.
[41]To actually see Jesus coincides with 'a resonance induced by being intentionally looked at and affectionately summoned by Him', in Jose Frazão, 'Penser la Dynamique Croyante de L'humain. La Foi Comme Nouveau Parcours de Théologie Fondamentale Chez Pierangelo Sequeri' Centre Sèvres, 2005); 86; translation mine.

by which they believe Him, revisit his memory and give credit to the revelation of God in Him. That happens by enacting the same human capacities that come into play in all our contact with and appreciation of reality.

Trust in a God who is on our side

But who is the God we recognize in Christ via the witness of the Church? Sequeri's theology of faith as described in a simplified way earlier is fully developed – in rich and often complex language – in two books: *The Trustworthy God*[42] and *The Idea of Faith: A Treatise on Fundamental Theology*.[43] However, part of the process of understanding a theologian, to my mind, is to identify their 'centre', the underlying image of God implicit or explicit in their work. I would suggest that in Sequeri, we find this pulse in a short but beautiful book written in 2008, entitled *The Fear of God* (*Il Timore di Dio*). The book is a form of narrative theology around key texts of Scripture, interpreted in light of a conviction in the profound goodness of God. One of the most telling chapters is how he interprets the story of the fall in Genesis. It is not the pride of Adam in wanting to be 'like God' or the temptation of Eve as the women (ever) at fault that is in the spotlight in this story, but rather distrust in the goodness of a God who has lovingly cared for them and provided for all they need. They are told not to eat of one tree in the middle of the garden, the tree of the knowledge of good and evil, or they would die. The temptation of the serpent unfolds in two steps: first, the provocation of asking why God has told them not to eat of *any* of the trees. Eve clarifies that this is not the case, but only one of them, and why: 'because they would die'. This explanation leaves room for the serpent to take another step which hinges on one intent: to sow a seed of doubt in the minds of Adam and Eve about God's motives: 'You will not die; for God knows that when you eat of it your eyes will be opened, and you will be like God, knowing good and evil' (Gen. 3.4-5). Sin's entry point, according to Sequeri, is not the desire to be like God actualized in the moment they eat the fruit of that tree but the prior, hidden entry of suspicion about God's good intentions into the mind, heart and imaginations of Adam and Eve.

> The religious relationship with God has been polluted, without reason and from the beginning, through the credit humanity gave to the fantasy of the serpent. And from then on, every religion will remain inexorably marked. . . In humanity's historical imagination, the idea of God is

---

[42]Pierangelo Sequeri, *Il Dio Affidabile*, Biblioteca Di Teologia Contemporanea (Brescia: Queriniana, 1996).
[43]Pierangelo Sequeri, *L'idea della Fede: Trattato di Teologia Fondamentale* (Milano: Glossa, 2002).

accompanied by the shadow of an arbitrary threat from which we must defend ourselves.[44]

This classic and brilliantly written text of ancient Scripture describes the key issue separating humanity from God: distrust, believing the lie that God was not fully on their side.

The story continues, and God appears on the scene again, oblivious and looking for their company for a walk in the afternoon breeze: 'where are you?' (Gen. 3.8), but they are hiding and shameful of their newly discovered nakedness. And still, the tenderness of a God, who will carefully sow and clothe them with garments made of skins, remains.

This is the image of God against which Sequeri rethinks the process of faith, and it leads him to talk of God in terms of trustworthiness, rather than credibility. It is the God we come to know in the kenosis of the Incarnation and in the life of Jesus and his witness of God as *Abba*, whom we are capable of recognizing and participating in: 'have in yourselves the same feelings as Christ' (Phil. 2.3-8). His is an explicitly Christ-centred theology. 'Nazareth is not a provisional experiment of the Son, it is a definitive style of God.'[45] Jesus is the one in whom and by whom God has challenged definitively the 'ambivalence of the sacred', with absolute trust in a God who is 'on the side' of humanity. Therefore, in this framework, the root of all evil can be found in our incomprehensible (for the human mind and God's also) definitive role reversal: the serpent is trusted, while God becomes an object of suspicion.[46] The redemption of that situation is effectuated by the crucified one, 'the revelation of the infinite capacity that God possesses of absorbing in Himself the negative'.[47] The faith of Jesus, which Sequeri is not afraid of talking about,[48] and in that faith the provocation of our own faith, is the counterpart or challenge to the despotism of the law, the magic of sacraments, the substitution of priests, the gnosticism of spirituality and the sectarianism of community.[49] Jesus' whole life and subsequent death was a challenge to false or incomplete images of God. So Job is commended for *not* accepting an image of God that is not worthy of Him.[50] God's anger and tenderness are expressions of a passionate love, both rooted in the 'depth

---

[44]Sequeri, *Il Timore di Dio*, 53.
[45]Sequeri, *Sensibili allo Spirito*, x.
[46]Sequeri, *Il Timore di Dio*, 51–72.
[47]Sequeri, *L'estro di Dio: Saggi di Estetica*, 6.
[48]'I see Jesus as electrified by an intuition or perception, one could even say by a faith in regard to God, as Father (I am not afraid of this term, since the Letter to the Hebrews speaks of the faith of Jesus, not in an intellectualist sense but as a relationship).' Cf. Gianni Vattimo, Pierangelo Sequeri, and Giovanni Ruggeri, *Interrogazioni sul Cristianesimo: Cosa Possiamo Ancora Attenderci dal Vangelo?* (Roma: Edizioni lavoro, 2000), 55, quoted in; Gallagher, 'Truth and Trust: Pierangelo Sequeri's Theology of Faith', 3–31 (23).
[49]Cf. Sequeri, *La Qualità Spirituale*, 65.
[50]Sequeri, *Il Timore di Dio*, 39–50.

of an affection that sweeps away the impassive marmoreal profile of the dignity of God' or that 'senile tolerance we dare to call mercy'.[51] And Jesus is amazed at our lack of trust! 'In fact, God considers immoral a faith that lacks intimate persuasion'.[52] It is a dynamic of trust *worthy* of human loving.

This compelling understanding of God's unspeakable compassion, and our corresponding capacity to recognize and believe in such a God, is the heart of Sequeri's theology. He places us before Jesus, his life, his faith, his faithfulness to the extreme to the God he knew was 'on humanity's side' against all pretension to the contrary, even (or especially) in the name of 'God'. In this theology, we are reminded that the humanity and faith of Christ will always imply the defence of the quality of human spirituality and faith, respectively. The goodness of all that is human will always be essential to our faith, even where we recognize that its discerning is not always transparent or simple. Still Jesus stands as the eternal witness to the goodness of God who is in favour of humanity and to just how far that God has gone to manifest that and to be accessible to us.

Sequeri also gives us what I would call keys for recognition. His is a contemplative and Christ-centred theology that invites us to recognize ourselves as recognized and loved by God in Christ, with keys to understanding how that happens and can happen. We may never fully understand how or even *when* grace enables Jesus to become the name and face we recognize: the integration of grace and free will always maintain some mystery. But this theology does allow us to intuit the richness and fullness of humanity involved. With Sequeri, we learn to recognize that a paralysed cultural sensitivity is still inhabited by a *human believing* consciousness, with all the density of that figure, and is *capable of recognizing* Jesus in the breaking of the bread, in the word explained, in his risen presence. It also grounds a theology of witness that calls out to our human condition on the quest for meaning. It is an invitation to be attentive to how love can be needed and recognized now, in both ethical and aesthetical areas, and to walk alongside the human culture we encounter now. Might this not be what is attractive about Pope Francis' attitudes and witness? Is there something about his embrace of the messy side of life that echoes with our instinctive quest for goodness, meaning and truth, and above all, mercy?

Lament: In the Pouring Rain

It is time to turn to a musical interpretation or access point to this theology of faith in a good God who wants nothing more than to meet

---

[51] Sequeri, *Il Timore di Dio*, 75.
[52] Sequeri, *Il Timore di Dio*, 75.

and walk with us in friendship. The song, from my perspective, is a series of encounters and intersections. First, between the music and the lyrics. It was born as a lament, without words. The chord progression came from a place of deep sadness – for what I honestly cannot remember – except the experience that, from time to time, my whole being can be sad. I know people who suffer from depression – that is not my cross – but I intuit the combination of Irish melancholy and artistic sensibility at times allows me to feel pretty deeply the 'river of feelings' and emotions Sequeri speaks of. And expressing that, in words and music, is a necessary and at times neglected part of Christian music. The text that made sense for the music is based, in part, on the prayer of Pope Francis for the year of mercy. Specifically, the phrase reflected in this chapter's question: *show us your face and we will be saved!* Jesus is the face of God's mercy, not coincidentally but as the very style of how God is. God is merciful, and there is no situation we walk through that will not draw that passionate and compassionate love of God who reaches out to heal our wounds and dress our nakedness.

The other point of intersection is between faith and culture: specifically, those in our contemporary culture that know the pain of depression. In Australia, one of the charities seeking to support those who suffer from depression is called 'Beyond Blue', and this seems to evoke well the unexplainable shadow that depression casts over a life, when things *'turn blue; dark colours washing through me'*. I have been told by friends that praying when you are actually depressed is really tough, so the song tries to express that. It also seeks to own the anger and frustration that the human condition can provoke in us, which *has a place in faith*. We do not need to hide what does not fit neatly into tidy versions of redeemed lives from the God who sees us more clearly than we do and loves who She sees. In chapter nine, Sebastian Moore's theology spoke of faith, not as a crutch or born of weakness but rather of an overabundance of life. However, it is also true that our fragility amid the hard experiences of life can open a space for us to reach out to the truth of how much we need God: in Sequeri's words, our 'unfoundedness'. And it is a false image of God that would lead us to hold back, or hold out, rather than allowing that love to reach, heal, support and rejoice in our company.

Finally, there is the intersection of languages and musical styles. I feel that currently, Latin has been semi-hijacked by a conservative wing who would prefer to avoid some of the questions this book asks. But, as those who know and love the history of our Church can tell us, it is also – or rather it is first – a language in which much of the history of our faith has been forged and therefore one that *should* also be able to bring us together. Therefore, part of the song is in Latin, in a quest to bridge distances from the past and across language divides in our world. But the main attempt of this song is to evoke and access the merciful face of God who is always on our side and worthy of our trust. In the words of Pope Francis in the prayer for the year of mercy (2016):

> Lord Jesus Christ,
> you have taught us to be merciful like the
> heavenly Father,
> and have told us that whoever sees you sees Him.
> Show us your face and we will be saved . . .
>
> You are the visible face of the invisible Father,
> of the God who manifests his power above all by
> forgiveness and mercy:
> let the Church be your visible face in the world, its
> Lord risen and glorified.
> You willed that your ministers would also be
> clothed in weakness
> in order that they may feel compassion for those
> in ignorance and error:
> let everyone who approaches them feel sought
> after, loved, and forgiven by God
> The link to the song 'Lament: in the Pouring Rain' is in the note.[53]

'Lament: In the Pouring Rain' lyrics

> *Osténde nóbis vúltum túum et sálvi érimus.*
> *Show us your face and we will be saved;*
> *We ask for this. We beg for this*
> *There's a place inside where I like to hide,*
> *but now it's turning blue; dark colours washing through me*
> *And I can't stand this, no man's land within me . . .*
> *I know that it's not fair: at times like this, I pray*
> *But maybe you don't mind; I don't know who I'll find here*
> *Touch this, lonely creature . . .*
> *Show me your face in the pouring rain,*
> *Can't you see my pain, from way out there?*
> *Show me my face, I got lost again, can't remember when I last saw*
> *me . . . it's dark again . . .*
> *Dómine Iesu Christe, Spiritum tuum mitte; nobis miserere*
> *Dómine Iesu Christe, tu vero es vúltus visíbilis Pátris, consecranos;*
> *Te rogamos, miserere nobis!*

---

[53]'Lament: In the Pouring Rain': https://res.cloudinary.com/bloomsbury-online-resources/video/upload/v1639138340/Suspended%20God/In_the_Pouring_Rain_Lament.wav

Show me your face in the pouring rain . . .
I'm trying to find my way home, not sure where I went wrong;
So, I'm down on my knees
Why do you feel so weak?
WCould you reach out and heal me, Lord of mercy?
Trying to see your face; find a way to make up.
Sorry's just not enough! Why does this feel so tough?
How long will you hold out when you know
I'm clothed in weakness now?
Osténde nóbis vúltum túum et sálvi érimus.

Based on Pope Francis' Prayer for Year of Mercy 2016
©MAEVE LOUISE HEANEY, 2020.
Strange Life, The Music of Doubtful Faith

Selected further reading

An introduction to Pierangelo Sequeri's theology

Gallagher, Michael Paul. 'Pierangelo Sequeri: Horizons of Trust'. In *Faith Maps: Ten Religious Explorers from Newman to Joseph Ratzinger*, 119–31. New York: Paulist Press, 2010.

Theology of faith

Gallagher, Michael Paul. 'Truth and Trust: Pierangelo Sequeri's Theology of Faith'. *Irish Theological Quarterly* 73, no. 1–2 (2008): 3–31.

An insight into his thought on music

Sequeri, Pierangelo. 'Music and Resurrection'. *Toronto Journal of Theology* 29, no. 2 (2013): 417–24, with an introduction by translator Paul Colilli.

A narrative reading of Scripture

Sequeri, Pierangelo. *Il Timore Di Dio*. Milano: Vita e pensiero, 2008.

16

What role does sexuality have in Christian faith?

Does Christian faith frustrate or empower romance and human sexuality?

The Catholic Church has a strange relationship with sex and sexuality. It has long suffered the effects of a Neoplatonist dualistic anthropology, in which the human 'soul', or spirit, is trapped in the body, and salvation its escape. Sexuality is currently hijacked by a long history of inadequate and polarized explorations on themes of sexual orientation and identity, in which even the terms are not clarified, making any form of sensible discussion difficult. The very mention of the term 'gender' draws forth heated responses from a melting pot of theological, sociopolitical and cultural positions that seem oblivious to their potential psychosexual underpinnings, and resistant to the necessary study and delineation of terms essential to any kind of reasonable pathway forward.[1] This chapter cannot address the full breadth of the issues related to sexuality and gender, although the life and thought of our theologian-in-focus provide insightful contributions to that conversation.

The issue here is specifically that of romance, passion and sexual relationships within a Christian world view and anthropology. As Chesterton

---

[1] The International Network of Societies for Catholic Theology (INSeCT) took the theme of gender justice as their three-year research project between 2014 and 2017, in the attempt to clarify terms and lay the foundations for future work. The need for such care in language and research into all dimensions of human anthropology is manifest in the document of the Catholic Congregation for Education, *'Male and Female He Created Them': Towards a Path of Dialogue on the Question of Gender Theory in Education* (Vatican City, 2 February 2019) cf. http://www.vatican.va/roman_curia/congregations/ccatheduc/documents/rc_con_ccatheduc_doc_20190202_maschio-e-femmina_en.pdf. While the intent is noteworthy, even the title is an ironic witness to the need for attention to how gender is translated from Latin or Italian into other languages. See chapter fourteen on how we name God.

pointed out, our fascination with particular issues often impedes our view of the more fundamental surprises of life.

> Ordinary things are more valuable than extraordinary things; nay, they are more extraordinary. Man is something more awful than men; something more strange. . . . Having a nose is more comic even than having a Norman nose.

So, in relation to sex (and in the context of debates on monogamy):

> I could never mix in the common murmur of that rising generation against monogamy, because no restriction on sex seemed so odd and unexpected as sex itself. To be allowed, like Endymion, to make love to the moon and then to complain that Jupiter kept his own moons in a harem seemed to me . . . a vulgar anti-climax. Keeping to one woman is a small price for so much as seeing one woman. To complain that I could only be married once was like complaining that I had only been born once. It was incommensurate with the terrible excitement of which one was talking. It showed, not an exaggerated sensibility to sex, but a curious insensibility to it.[2]

Below and before the issues of orientation and how we welcome and understand those who experience sexuality differently to how it 'should' be, there is the fact of sexuality, romance and passion *itself*: Why is it so central to human life? Why is it the first discussion point when anyone approaches the Church? Why does the Church seem so obsessed with sex when Jesus seemed to speak more about the social implications of his loving *Abba*? What does the reality of human sexuality say about who we are and *who God is*? And it is this last question that is the most important one, to my mind: the question is not only 'where does it fit?' but what does it add to our understanding of life and faith? How are we enriched by a proper understanding of sexuality and poorer in its absence?

This chapter intersects with and continues the issues raised in previous chapters: it presumes the centrality of affectivity to human thought (our focus with Sequeri in chapter fifteen) and the possibility of a life fulfilled in God *without* sex as a prophetic sign of our future becoming, just out of sight (explored with Teresa of Avila in chapter twelve). But I take it a step further *into* the reality of sexuality lived out with another, in what society and the Church call marriage. My guide here is a married, female theologian, mother of ten children of her own and others fostered and adopted, who dedicated much of her time writing about sexuality and marriage. The title of theologian is one she earned through the quality of her life's dedication to

---

[2]G. K. Chesterton, *Orthodoxy* (Garden City, NY: Image Books, 1959), in chapter four 'The Ethics of Elfland'.

public speaking and writing, rather than born of training 'in the academy', as many of the others in this book. But one of the core problems in relation to this chapter's issue is that most of our theological understanding of sexuality and marriage has been written by celibate men.[3] This does not necessarily make it wrong, but it does make it one-sided, incomplete and incapable of exploring the full range, depth and height of what reflection on human sexuality has to offer Christian life and thought.

The positive nature of sexuality is a Scriptural and theological given: made in the image and likeness of God, the human person is 'good', and that includes the capacity to love another in an exclusive way and, with her or him, to build a space for more life to emerge and grow. For St Paul, marriage was an image of the relationship of Christ with his Church (cf. Eph. 5.31-33). But theology has not often tackled the intricacy of human passion, the pull of sexual attraction and the life-determining experience of falling in love. The absence leaves sexuality vulnerable to being over-interpreted in light of the fall, the reality that we are well made but victims of our shared brokenness, as explored with Sebastian Moore in chapter nine. It seems as if the stronger human passions have little space in Christianity: anger is rarely righteous and love is meek and mild (like Jesus?). The infamous 'cleansing of the temple' scene where Jesus lets fly is sidestepped or theologized out of all human interpretation. The same with human passion: acceptable as long as one can hold it in check!

Clearly, this is not an adequate position. Scripture holds together remarkably well a prophetic welcome to an incarnated God – in the flesh – and an awareness that this changes all things material, including the understanding of our bodies and their coming together in intimacy. The evaluation of matter as created and good is foundational to our sacramental view of life. Matter mediates divine love, and hence we celebrate and ritualize the key moments of our lives: birth, death, life shared in friendship, maturity and the intimate love between two people. But Scripture's positive view of sexuality did not withstand the influences of the culture and philosophies through which thought developed over time.[4] Some of the Fathers considered that married couples temporarily 'lost' the Holy Spirit during sexual intercourse, whose presence there would not be fitting![5] For Augustine, marriage was a beneficial social institution, good despite the dangers of sex, which was sinful, although justifiable if done for the right reason.[6] Medievalists looked

---

[3] This is changing, of course, but the felt understanding of sexuality of most Christians on the pews (or in our streets) has been formed in this forge.

[4] For an overview of the history of marriage, see chapter eleven of Joseph Martos, *Doors to the Sacred: A Historical Introduction to Sacraments in the Catholic Church: Updated and Enlarged with Charts and Glossary* (Liguori, MO: Liguori Publications, 2014).

[5] Cf. Origen, *Homilies on the Book of Numbers*, 6.

[6] As usual, Augustine's brilliance sits alongside his blind spots. He also lays the first foundations of our understanding of marriage as *sacramentum*, a visible sign of the invisible union of Christ with the Church.

to the final aim of human sexuality as its justification – procreation – and this within the limits of their biological understanding of the human person, 'the depositing of semen in the vagina'.[7] Aquinas and Thomism followed suit, broadening the aims to include another: the mutual relationship of love. This second aim, however, remained just that in Catholic consciousness for a long time: secondary. Underpinning sexual morality during this period lies an understanding of the man as fully human and the woman as an incomplete, passive, receptor of the life (seed) poured into her but to which she contributes only her body as vessel. This limited understanding of human biology reinforced the natural double standard applied between men and women in all matters of faithfulness, adultery and divorce. Thankfully, the Second Vatican Council in *Gaudium et Spes* refused to hierarchize the goals of marriage and maintained the value of sexual relationships independent of their procreative outcome. However, in hidden and illogical ways, the remnants of this incorrect biology affect sexual morality to this day.

Sexuality is complex, and marriage is the last of the sacraments to be 'defined' as such – which within an understanding of developing doctrine and living tradition is perfectly acceptable. But the lentitude of the Church in navigating and growing in its understanding of this reality of human life stands out. Why has the Catholic Church policed sexual behaviour more than any other aspect of life? Why do all sexual sins seem 'serious' when in other areas we can grasp levels of gravity? This is not because sex is unimportant but because the integration of sexuality is *so essential* to human living and Christian spirituality. Paradoxically, it would seem that the Church's difficulty with sex – which could have been our leading question – 'Why is the Church so obsessed with sex?' – is something akin to the early church's struggles with the doctrine of the incarnation: Did God really become *human*? The utter materiality of Christianity is nowhere more clearly expressed than in human sexuality and sex. And the Church is still working this out. The solution is not to banalize it but to embrace it. The theologian explored in this chapter does just that.

Rosemary Luling Haughton: A fully lived life (1927–)[8]

This book highlights the link between life and thought in each of the theologians it presents, and in no one is this link more apparent than in

---

[7]Vincent J. Genovesi, SJ, 'Sexuality', in *The New Dictionary of Theology*, ed. M. Collins, D. A. Lane, and J. A. Komonchak, 947–54 (950) (Collegeville, MN: Liturgical Press, 1991).
[8]For an insightful and thorough presentation of Haughton's life and work, see Eilish Ryan, *Rosemary Haughton: Witness to Hope* (Lanham, MD: Rowman & Littlefield, 1997). Not only does Ryan explore some of the various writings which are now harder to get access to, but she

Rosemary Haughton. The richness of her theologizing and the journey of her thought map perfectly against her life experiences and stages of her calling. For that reason, I have chosen to interweave biography and thought together, so as to highlight that thought develops and matures *through*, not despite, our life's journey. I have also chosen to explain her life slightly more than with other theologians in the book, because of this connectedness and because she is not as well known as most of the others.

Haughton's early years: Called into Catholicism

Born in 1927 in Chelsea, London, to a North American father and English mother, Rosemary Luling's early years were somewhat unstable. Her father, a watercolour artist, was often absent and her mother's periodically successful career as a novelist, combined with the outbreak of the Second World War, led to a rather bohemian and unsettled childhood in which the most stable figure was her maternal grandmother, Ethel Thompson. Thompson's combination of structured discipline and loving encouragement of creative, intelligent freedom marked Rosemary for life. She grew up with an innate passion for art, reading and religion.

Her parents attended church only irregularly, but at a very early age, Haughton felt drawn to the Catholic Church, attracted by the 'strange holiness' of the saints – canonized and obscure – and the mystery of the candlelit churches she visited. She describes her childhood quest for God and the intuition of 'something important' in Catholicism rather vividly:

> Suddenly there flared up in my mind a great longing which I had known before, obscurely, but which I could not identify more nearly. I wanted to know this 'important something,' this thing that lived between the candles in the statues and in which the black-shawled women immersed themselves. I was filled with a curiosity, so strong it was more like being extremely hungry than like merely wanting information.[9]

This sense of a personal call to belong to the Church is one of the constants in Haughton's life. As a teenager, she sought instruction on Catholicism and her journey into faith was marked by weekly conversations with a Benedictine nun, Mother Raphael, on a plethora of books, followed by Compline and Benediction at Tyburn Convent. She was received into the Catholic Church in December 1943, at the age of sixteen.

---

interviewed and was given access to unpublished autobiographical writings of Haughton, making it an invaluable source for the study of Haughton's thought.
[9]Rosemary Haughton, 'Something Important', *Sign* 57 (1978) (17), quoted in Ryan, *Rosemary Haughton: Witness to Hope*, 33–4.

I became a Catholic at 16, drawn to it by a conviction that at [the] heart of this curious experience called 'the Church' there was to be found the possibility of an incredible richness of heroism, strangeness, beauty and a glory opening upon eternity. I never found a cause to doubt this.[10]

Two aspects apparent in this short paragraph run right through Haughton's writings. The first is her sense of being *called into faith* and an audacious promptness in responding to that call. Haughton's radical faithfulness to where she senses the Spirit leading her is both fascinating and daunting. It leads her into marriage, motherhood and an understanding of family life as open beyond its small inner circle. She feels called to found not one but two Christian communities over the course of her life, with shared but distinct aims. For most of her life, this call steers her between two continents. She is a woman who embodies that freedom of the Spirit that blows where it will and not without cost. The second element in the text is her sense of belonging to a rich, complex, Catholic tradition, whose truth needs to be mediated into and for the present world. Her thought can be described as an attempt to grapple with and work out the meaning of being Catholic in the world in which she found herself.[11]

The prophetic spirituality of family and community living

In 1948, Haughton married Algy Haughton, a teacher and adult convert to Catholicism. They were both passionate about education and fed by a desire to open their family life beyond the immediate family circle. They first attempted this in 1950, founding a family-style school for boys and girls in Wales, which failed due to lack of funding and left them financially precarious for a few years. Over twenty years later, with ten children of their own, two foster children and a family ethos committed to the hospitable welcoming of many others unnamed, they made their second attempt, buying land in rural southwest Scotland and moving to build an intentional, sustainable, Christian community based on Christian values, education and an alternative, less wasteful lifestyle. Lothlorien (named by previous owners after the Elves Forest in *Lord of the Rings*) was meant to be a place of healing and friendship for those who needed it, particularly the elderly and disoriented young people. Farming, prayer, joyful ritual celebrations of life

---

[10]Rosemary Haughton, 'We Caught the Touch of Incarnate Love', *National Catholic Reporter* 18 (1982): 8 October 1982 (15), quoted in Ryan, *Rosemary Haughton: Witness to Hope*, 43.
[11]For example, Rosemary Haughton, *The Changing Church* (London: Geoffrey Chapman, 1969); 'Saints Preserve Us', in *One Good Reason Why I'm Catholic*, 21–2 (Chicago: Claretian Publications, 1994).

and liturgy, and an attempt to live in harmony with the earth were the foci of this small, ecumenical open house.

Haughton's marriage was not always easy, affected first by her husband Algy's alcoholism (one unspoken reason behind the move to Lothlorien) and later struggles with his sexual orientation. They never divorced, maintaining a genuine friendship which, in her own words, their closer friends understood: 'Somebody, I think it was C.S. Lewis, talked about people facing ahead side-by-side rather than looking into each other's eyes. Ours has always been that kind of marriage.'[12] She did, however, feel called to leave Lothlorien, sensing that despite the ongoing love shared with her husband, they were moving in different directions. It was a slow, painful and discerned decision, which led her to the United States and ultimately a second intentional community in Massachusetts: *Wellsprings*.

Haughton's writing journey

Haughton's writing career began accidentally in 1954, with the illustration of children's books which later led to writing a book on St Thérèse of Lisieux for children. Over the years, it developed into a life of writing and lecturing which became a supplementary source of income for the family, as well as a means of exploring and expressing her spiritual quest and theological insights. Her writing is both original and deeply influenced by the legion of authors her intelligent and questing mind devoured. In her early years, these include Jacques Maritain, Gabriel Marcel, Charles Péguy, Etienne Gilson and Maurice Blondel. But it developed further through interaction with Karl Rahner, Edward Schillebeeckx and Elisabeth Schüssler Fiorenza. Whether she was influenced explicitly by Lonergan is not clear (although her position on many things is remarkably close) but that she influenced him is documented.[13] She is one of the few authors he explicitly names, describing her writing as an 'objectivation of religious experience' in terms of meaning-making in relation to Christian faith.[14] Although Lonergan does not seem to consider this theology *proper*, it is the task of the functional specialty 'Foundations', as seen in chapter four, so perhaps this contradiction in terms supports my position on the need to broaden the language of theological discourse and signals Haughton's success in doing so. Thomas Merton's life, spirituality, understanding of community and writings are another underlying influence

---

[12]Quoted in Ryan, *Rosemary Haughton: Witness to Hope*, 63.
[13]For example, Lonergan quotes Haughton's description of Jesus during his Passion as an example of what charity looks like, in Bernard J. F. Lonergan, 'Pope John's Intention', in F. E. Crowe (ed.), *A Third Collection. Papers by Bernard J. F. Lonergan*, 225–38 (232) (New York: Paulist Press, 1985), quoting Rosemary Haughton, *The Passionate God* (London: Darton Longman and Todd, 1982), 147–8.
[14]Ryan, *Rosemary Haughton: Witness to Hope*, 102, n. 34.

in Haughton's life. They met in 1967, and she impressed Merton as 'a quiet and intelligent lady, concerned about true contemplative life ... and also as being the first theologian he had met who was six months pregnant'.[15] By the mid-1990s, she is an authoritative commentator on the intersection of modernity, Christianity and theology.[16]

Haughton is a theologian *of* the Second Vatican Council, in the most challenging way possible, since her journey into the Church happened before that event and her writings embody the attempt to understand and translate the Council's vision and insight for herself and others. This can be seen not only in how she explicitly names themes and shifts introduced by the Council – especially in relation to sexuality and the laity – but also as a named motivation during the Second Vatican Council 'to *write in order to think through new ideas*'.[17] She speaks of how she moved from the comforting clarity of Catholic responses to questioning answers that avoid complex issues:

> One small black book of questions and answers about Catholicism was oddly engrossing ... 'the logic and reason was what I hungered for ... the dry-as-dust arguments gave my mind something to chew on – and I was too young to realise how the questions were restricted to the answer that would fit'.[18]

Once again, theology is led by questions. For Haughton, this is an essential dimension of being Catholic. In one of her most known books, she explores the reality of being Catholic through two allegorical figures: the twin sisters of 'Mother Church' and 'Sophia' (Wisdom), representing the structure of the Church and the living Spirit it enables us to encounter, respectively. Mother Church is famous: wise, earthy, experienced, skilled and protective, who uses her authority 'for their own good' and is suspicious of new ideas and swift in suppressing revolt. Her twin sister, Sophia, is a less known but loved presence, often called by other names or nicknames (mysticism, adventure, inspiration etc.) who 'Mother Church' finds embarrassing and difficult to handle, because she is so unpredictable, but knows, when honest, she could not live without. Both are essential to this thing we call the Catholic enterprise: 'the attempt to integrate the whole of human life in the search

---

[15] Cf. Ryan, *Rosemary Haughton: Witness to Hope*, 51, quoting John Howard Griffin, *Follow the Ecstasy: The Hermitage Years 1965-1968* (Fort Worth: JHG Editions/Latitude Press, 1983), 17.

[16] Cf. Rosemary Haughton, 'Transcendence and the Bewilderment of Being Modern', in *A Catholic Modernity? Charles Taylor's Marianist Award Lecture, with Responses by William M. Shea, Rosemary Luling Haughton, George Marsden, Jean Bethke Elshtain*, ed. J. Heft, 65–82 (Oxford: Oxford University Press, 1999).

[17] Ryan, *Rosemary Haughton: Witness to Hope*, 50; emphasis mine.

[18] Ryan, *Rosemary Haughton: Witness to Hope*, 42.

for the kingdom of God'.[19] Theology is often concerned 'with the antics of Sophia' but the strange essential interplay between the two is what gives 'the Catholic thing' its character.[20]

This is the setting of Haughton's theology, fed by her experience of and reflection upon the world she lived in. After the war in Paris, Haughton experienced Young Christian Student groups seeking ways to make sense of faith after the atrocities lived. In England and later in the United States, the quest for Christian communities that prayed Scripture and sought to live out their faith in service of the world fed her ongoing call to a spirituality that, while personal, is not self-serving but rather committed to prophetic service. Early in her marriage years and long before it became a theological focus of interest, she discovered, and emulated, communities seeking to incarnate a respectful relationship with the land. The plight of children and later homeless women and those affected by abuse became the focus of her attention, life and writing. In later years, her exposure to the effects of poverty in the United States on *women*, first and foremost, fuelled her interest in and perspective on feminist concerns and women. *Wellsprings* is the lived, community response to this issue.[21] Once again, Haughton's life is an incarnated witness to the concerns facing the church and world, in words and actions, a 'prophetic spirituality'.[22] Her life belies the myth of separation between commitment to prayer and social justice that fuels contemporary Catholic polarizations.

All of this is forged through difficult periods of life. Haughton identifies long periods of darkness and doubt in her prayer-life, during which she struggled to sustain her faith and hope. Her most acclaimed work, and the most developed theologically, *The Passionate God*, was written during the difficult discernment about leaving Lothlorien.

Haughton's theological method and style

Haughton's theological method is based on and provoked by experience: at every stage she reflects upon human experience, often choosing stories as her entry point to facilitate understanding. She is, in a sense, a precursor to contemporary approaches to narrative theology.[23] She explains, however,

---

[19]Rosemary Haughton, *The Catholic Thing* (Springfield: Templegate Publishers, 1979), 15–16.
[20]Cf. Haughton, *The Catholic Thing*, 11.
[21]Cf. Rosemary Haughton, *Song in a Strange Land: The Wellspring Story and the Homelessness of Women* (Springfield, IL: Templegate Publishers, 1990).
[22]Cf. Ryan, *Rosemary Haughton: Witness to Hope*, 155–78, for a fuller exploration of this understanding of Haughton's spirituality and thought.
[23]This is especially clear in her groundbreaking book on anthropology, community and conversion: Rosemary Haughton, *The Transformation of Man: A Study of Conversion and Community* (London: Chapman, 1967).

that this is not a new form of theology but essential to how the people of God have *always* made sense of faith, since '*all* good theology is, and always has been, a theology of experience'.[24] It is 'traditional' in the deepest sense of the word: 'for the true Christian, theological tradition requires that we constantly break new ground – the ground being man's [sic] experience of God at work in his [sic] life, which has a different impact in every age.'[25] This implies that theologizing implies a particular kind of awareness and knowledge of the experience of the grace of God at work, verifying the truthfulness of an experience and its theological expression over time, and a variety of forms of thinking about experience, both prophetic and reflective.

So theology has three aims: 'to reflect lucidly on the Christian consciousness gained from the experience of God's action in history, to communicate this reflection to others in an understandable way, and to interpret the Tradition through the study of doctrines developed in earlier periods of Christian experience'.[26] Far from being reserved to academics, it is an inescapable dimension of life, for 'there is scarcely a conscious act which does not express a theological position of some kind, and even unconscious motivations often grow from the theological views of our forefathers [sic]'.[27]

Haughton is particularly sensitive to the limits of language, advocating for poetic approaches to theology. In fact, for Haughton, theology *is* poetry, because of how it seeks to access questions of meaning, past and present, which are not obvious nor can be contained, as if complete, in conceptual statements: 'true answers to fundamental human questions must have the nature of poetry'.[28]

> Theology . . . is a particularly exacting kind of poetry. . . . This may appear to be one of those statements which are intended to provoke thought rather than to be taken seriously as a statement of fact, but it is a statement of fact which is important . . . for all thinking about religion, God, faith. There are 'areas of concern' which are so ultimate that they are literally out of sight.[29]

Theologians, with their words, open windows in the mind of the hearer 'unto the land whence culture draws its common life'.[30] This is a consequence of keeping experience at the centre of the theological task, because 'the poetry of good theology must grow from deep within the actual and concrete

---

[24] Rosemary Haughton, *The Theology of Experience* (Paramus, NJ: Newman Press, 1972), 9. It was first published under the title *The Knife-Edge of Experience*.
[25] Haughton, *The Theology of Experience*, 9.
[26] Ryan, *Rosemary Haughton: Witness to Hope*, 75.
[27] Haughton, *The Theology of Experience*, 31-2.
[28] Haughton, *The Passionate God*, 3.
[29] Haughton, *The Passionate God*, 5.
[30] Haughton, *The Passionate God*, 6.

experience of people, so deep that . . . they recognise in it both the accurate expression of their problems and hopes and loves and the evocation of deeper layers which they cannot touch but of which they are mutually aware, afraid and desirous'.[31]

This is precisely how Haughton's theology reads: a concrete, dynamic, at times intense, expression of well-understood Christian experience. In terms of style, one of the most attractive features of Haughton's work is the eloquent freedom with which she names things that could otherwise be negatively charged. An example from her writings on women in the early Church is apropos.

> At a certain point, Wisdom took flesh, became conscious, made decisions and shone with a light that enlightened the nations. . . . Women in the early Church had a new sense of themselves, and the men had this sense about the women, so they took on a new status and roles very quickly, but this did not last. It was one of those breakthroughs which comes too soon and cannot be assimilated into the rest of life.[32]

Yet another example is her description of intuition versus rational forms of understanding:

> The satisfactoriness of the intellect as a tool is the refrain of mystics and poets, and the occupational hazard of scientists and philosophers. Yet intuition is not normally regarded as of much practical use. The old joke about a woman's intuition being a way of proving she's right when she knows she's wrong is not so unjust, because what we know intuitively we have to translate by means of the intellect before we can make use of it, and in the translation is inevitably distorted by all sorts of unconscious motives and half-conscious preconceptions. . . . I am therefore suggesting that the human intellect, of which we are so proud, may be in fact a sort of evolutionary compensation for the loss (or the non-achievement?) of a more perfect kind of knowledge.[33]

The gentle irony with which she turns the tables on a negative charge against women, combined with a pretty scathing analysis of the history of reason's false hegemony over other thought-forms, is quite simply a breath of fresh theological air.

Before I look at some of the themes she explores, a word on the expressed limits of her theological style. Haughton's theology, while dealing with themes of universal appeal, is also contextual and local, precisely because

---

[31]Haughton, *The Passionate God*, 279.
[32]Haughton, *The Passionate God*, 263.
[33]Haughton, *The Theology of Experience*, 121–2.

she is so responsive to contemporary issues. She is speaking to a mainly middle-class audience of twentieth-century Britain and the United States, making sense of the cultural and political currents of that time. Some are critical of her apparently naïve use of Scripture, and in truth, at times the mind reaches for more analysis and comparison. But her focus is more literary and narrative than historical-critical, translating for understandable reading. It develops over time, although many of her insights have stood the test of time she herself demands of theology's self-evaluation.

Her writings explore themes of Christology (especially the Incarnation and Resurrection), theological anthropology and the quest for fullness of human living,[34] Mariology, ecclesiology,[35] sexuality,[36] marriage,[37] women's issues and homelessness[38] and parenting,[39] all through the lens of Christian spirituality. A brief further word on some of these themes, before focussing on the central question of the chapter:

1. *Ecclesiology:* Haughton's central image of the Church is the community gathered in Christ's body through baptism, fed by the Eucharist and at the service of the world. It includes an awareness of the Spirit of God at work in the world beyond church borders. She is acutely aware of the changing culture affecting the Church, as well as the polarized positions threatening that unity. Her descriptions – at times caricaturized – of both 'right' and 'left' and the shades in-between are insightful and challenging, unfortunately as relevant today as they were when she wrote them.[40]

   Her ecclesiology is practical, asking about the function of 'this Catholic thing' in our time, rather than why the Catholic Church exists.[41] Resting upon an understanding of Tradition as connected and continuous, in which 'the present searches the past for the sake of the future',[42] she seeks to bridge and build, with impressive balance.

2. *Formation and transformation*: Haughton's quest is for fully human living, understood as a process of formation and

---

[34] Rosemary Haughton, *On Trying to Be Human* (London: Geoffrey Chapman, 1966); Haughton, *The Transformation of Man: A Study of Conversion and Community*.
[35] Haughton, *The Changing Church*; Haughton, *The Catholic Thing*.
[36] Haughton, *The Mystery of Sexuality* (London: Darton, Longman and Todd, 1973).
[37] Rosemary Haughton, *Married Love in Christian Life* (London: Burns & Oates, 1966); Rosemary Haughton, *The Theology of Marriage* (Cork: Mercier Press, 1971).
[38] Haughton, *Song in a Strange Land: The Wellspring Story and the Homelessness of Women*.
[39] Rosemary Haughton, *The Children: Heirs of the Kingdom* (London: Darton, Longman & Todd, 1961).
[40] Cf. Haughton, *The Changing Church*, 10–15.
[41] Cf. Haughton, *The Catholic Thing*, 227.
[42] Haughton, *The Catholic Thing*, 17.

transformation in which the latter is the aim. She speaks frequently about the freedom of grace which builds on the pedagogy of the 'laws' and guidance of family, tradition, culture and education, but which needs to lead to transformation as the heart of Christian life.[43] Transformation (related to the concepts of conversion, eternal life and resurrection) rather than formation is the proper quest of Christianity and the reality of the Church: 'the community of the transformed'.[44] She distinguishes four stages in the pattern of a 'transforming breakthrough':

   a. The remote preparation, a probably lengthy process of normal life experience that inclines the individual towards transformation;
   b. An immediate preparation in which longing becomes intense passion at a weak or vulnerable spot in life at which breakthrough can occur;
   c. The actual breakthrough and often painful response to the offer of desired wholeness (usually identified as conversion);
   d. Finally, and frequently overlooked, the interpretation of the experience of breakthrough and its integration into the person's developmental process.[45]

3. *Mariology:* Haughton's understanding of Mary sits alongside her approach to women, the fullness of our sexual beings and her reading of how 'the feminine' and female has been seen and dealt with over history. She is clear that Christianity offers a new kind of existence to women (as seen earlier), but reads – with remarkable lucidity – the oppression, sidelining or repression of the feminine over history as something to be expected in the long journey towards balance. She reads two portraits of Mary in Scripture: 'the real woman who later disappeared from view, and the Mother of God, the God-bearer who afterward became clothed in layers of mystery'.[46] She situates the cult of Mary in the history of Catholic Tradition as one manifestation of the refusal of Catholic sensibility to renounce the role of the feminine in the Church.[47] Haughton's vision is not that women be equal to men but that the feminine take its place in a transformed body of Christ – including its structures.

---

[43]Cf. Haughton, *The Transformation of Man: A Study of Conversion and Community.*
[44]Haughton, *The Transformation of Man: A Study of Conversion and Community*, chapter VI.
[45]Cf. Ryan, *Rosemary Haughton: Witness to Hope*, 97–8.
[46]Ryan, *Rosemary Haughton: Witness to Hope*, 112.
[47]Haughton, *The Passionate God*, 263–70.

As is obvious, Haughton's writings could offer us answers to questions other than that of sexuality.[48] However, it is in her understanding of sexuality and God as passionate we see the heart of her thought and the depth that is possible when theology interacts consciously and seriously with human experience. She shares the same question that opens this chapter: 'How is it that for centuries the body was suspect to Christians, and sex at best a concession to the importune demands of a body we would be better without?'[49] And where does pulling the thread of this question lead us?

Come move in me: God is passionate

The Passionate God (1981) is the most mature presentation of Haughton's thought. However, it builds on and completes earlier writings on sexuality, sacramentality and marriage, because Haughton's writing is never divorced from life. For this reason, I begin with these earlier reflections, which are implicit in and form the foundation for her later writing.

Haughton's starting point is lived Christian spirituality and the sacramental nature of human life, both of which are grounded on the Incarnation. Jesus' mission was realized through words and deeds, and in his human life, he more often than not healed *through touch* alongside words.[50] His was a fully lived and loving life! By assuming humanity, God changed forever our relationship with matter: 'Christian mysticism is rooted in a tradition that sees the final freedom not as a liberation *from* the material but as a transformation *of* the material, which has in it already the seeds of eternal life.'[51]

This is true with every reality in human life, but, as the first section of the chapter has shown, nowhere has this *goodness* of human life been less assimilated than in relation to sexuality and sex.

> We have thought of sex as something which had to be sanctified, brought into the Christian life and made into a means of grace. . . . We must stop thinking in this way. We are not asked to sanctify sex or convert it to Christian use. What we have to do is to discover its sanctity, and find out what it tells us about the meaning of Christian living.[52]

---

[48]Cf. Dana Greene, 'Rosemary Haughton's Contributions to Catholicism Deserve Rediscovery', *National Catholic Reporter* (2018).
[49]Haughton, *Married Love in Christian Life*, 18.
[50]Cf. Haughton, *The Catholic Thing*, 15.
[51]Haughton, *The Catholic Thing*, 122.
[52]Haughton, *Married Love in Christian Life*, 69.

For this reason, Haughton frequently chooses to speak of 'sexual relationship', rather than 'marriage', because she wants to underline the fact that marriage is not a special or different kind of sexual relationship but the normal one, which is in need of better understanding.

And this is what she does, over a series of chapters, articles and books which avoid little related to the topic. *Married Love in Christian Life* (1966) is her first exploration of the theme of sexual love and the sacrament of marriage. This is also developed in two chapters in *On Trying to be Human* (1966): 'What God has Joined' looks at relationships as an essential source of self-discovery, and 'Two in One Flesh' explores her understanding of passion and its role in human maturity. In a chapter called 'Encounter' in *The Transformation of Man* (1967) she explores the process and transformative potential of falling in love. *Problems of Christian Marriage* (1968) speaks to the issues sexual love and marriage face in the contemporary world, such as having to prolong the time between falling-in-love and marriage due to economic reasons, pre-marital intimacy and the stress of an ever-reduced notion of the family unit on a couple's life. *The Gospel Where It Hits Us* (1968) continues her exploration of marriage as 'The Normal Sexual Relationship', bookended by a chapter on 'Marriage and Virginity' and one on 'The Nature of Woman' – an unhappy title for an insightful chapter exploring the qualities all humans need in different measures![53] 'The Hot Subject' in *The Changing Church* (1969) explores the challenges emerging in the sexual muddle of the 1960s in which the birth control controversy unlocked this hidden subject of sex for public discussion.[54] The next decade saw her grapple with the issues of divorce and contraception in *The Theology of Marriage* (1971),[55] explore understandings of sexuality in poetry in *The Theology of Experience* (1972)[56] and defend the potential of sexuality to help human beings become who they are in *The Mystery of Sexuality* (1973).[57] Ever led by life's experience and a commitment to those most in need, and under the evocative title of *Song in a Strange Land: The Wellspring Story and the Homelessness of Women* (1991), in later years Haughton's attention turns to the plight of women, in whom poverty and dispossession manifest in radical ways. Some of these books are small, but the number as well as range of her writings speaks to her dedication

---

[53]Cf. Rosemary Haughton, *The Gospel Where It Hits Us: Christianity and Contemporary Concerns* (London: Geoffrey Chapman, 1968), chapters one to three.
[54]Rosemary Haughton, 'The Hot Subject', in *The Changing Church*, 94–102 (London: Geoffrey Chapman, 1969).
[55]Haughton, *The Theology of Marriage*.
[56]Rosemary Haughton, 'The Intuitive Experience of Sexuality', in *The Theology of Experience*, 121–54 (Paramus, NJ: Newman Press, 1972).
[57]Haughton, *The Mystery of Sexuality*.

to this theme and the challenges it presents. What are the key elements of her theology?

Human beings as embodied and sexual

Haughton links sexuality and sex with her overall understanding of human development and fullness, which is both personal and shared: 'sexuality is a *quality of the human community*'.[58] We are our bodies, and any chance of maturity and growth implies changing the way we look at and think about sex. She revendicates sexuality as central to Christian holiness and eschews its marginalization and suspicion in Christian thought – 'the ugly sexphobia of the Christian tradition'[59] – much of it based on a misunderstanding of St Paul's writings on spirit and the flesh: 'The flesh and the spirit are, to him, opposed to each other not as two parts of a man [sic] but as two possible versions of what the *whole* man [sic] can be.'[60]

To address this, Haughton takes an explicitly theological lens. In fact, she echoes analogue challenges in theological reflection of her time to stop being hijacked unto foreign ground to explain and defend something that is a reality seen and experienced in faith. Sexual love is human, but *in Christ* its meaning – as with all the rest of life – is utterly transformed. Three key tenets underpin her thought:

1. *The unity and identity of knowledge and love in Christian life*: 'Love it is not a mental attribute; it is a searching for the other, it is a desire to discover the other, to communicate, to "know even as I am known."'[61] And in the same way in which we know what love is because God gave Godself to and for us in Christ's self-giving, so too we only *know another and ourselves* in total self-giving – not of a bit of ourselves but our whole person. Nowhere is this more clearly expressed than in sexual love.

2. *The Resurrection of Christ*: While sexual relations and marriage are an essential element of all human cultures – in one way or another – for Christians baptized *into* Christ's body and breathing his Spirit, *everything* takes on new meaning, because the reality of Love has broken through in us. His self-giving and risen life is paradigm and place for the full self-giving, in sexual love: dying to self, open to new life that may – or may not – emerge from the union.

---

[58]Haughton, *The Mystery of Sexuality*, 54.
[59]Rosemary Haughton, 'What God Has Joined: Relationships as Self-Discovery', in *On Trying to Be Human*, 76–91 (90) (London: Geoffrey Chapman, 1966).
[60]Haughton, *Married Love in Christian Life*, 35.
[61]Haughton, *Married Love in Christian Life*, 11–12.

> The Christian task ... [is] to judge any existing ethic by the standard of the full humanity which is in the risen Christ, and show how the fully human can be attained only by reaching beyond what any tribal ethic, however good, can manage to delineate as human.[62]

3. *Sexual love as a form of worship*: 'by the mercies of God, to present your bodies as a living sacrifice, holy and acceptable to God, which is your reasonable worship' (Rom. 12.1). In fact, it is the central and unifying dimension of love, not because it is easy or cannot be used selfishly – Haughton is remarkably realistic about the challenges of sex – but because

> In sexual intercourse, the couple express the passion which drew them together, and they express it in a practical and concrete way. In it, the quality of love is tested, and where it is lacking it can be improved. Selfishness will show up here, and if there is a real desire to unfold the implications of passion and not merely to enjoy its emotions, this is where selfishness can begin to be overcome ... [leading, when successful, to] ... not merely an increase of the physical sensation but an integration of the physical sensation into the whole personal exchange – so much so that there can be a feeling for the moment that the borderline between one person and another has actually disappeared. For that brief time they really 'know' each other.'[63]

> In sexual intimacy, as the rite of marriage expresses: 'With my body, I thee worship.'[64]

She describes the progress of a sexual relationship within the Christian paradigm (a foundation on which she will build her theology of God as passionate): first, normally, is the event we call 'falling in love', although she recognizes that sometimes sexual love develops more slowly within friendship. This transforming experience between two people opens them to wanting total and complete union with each other. Falling in love, which Haughton prefers to call passion, is the first step in the vocation to love. The expression of this love in physical intimacy, which can be gradual, finds its normal expression in sexual intercourse.[65] In the ongoing and everyday life of each particular couple (since love and the sacramental are *always*

---

[62]Haughton, 'The Hot Subject', 94–102 (100–1).
[63]Haughton, *Married Love in Christian Life*, 62–3.
[64]Haughton, *Married Love in Christian Life*, chapter 1, although the whole book unpacks Rom. 12.1-2 in steps.
[65]Haughton acknowledges and explores the fact that passion may not always express itself in sex – including but not limited to the religious vocation – but maintains that this is its normal and appropriate expression, without which other ways of enabling passion to lead us to self-giving and human fullness need to be found.

particular), sexual intercourse is the link between passion and daily life: 'a satisfactory sexual relationship is of its nature apt to bring about the synthesis between symbol of love and its practical working out.'[66] The opening of a couple to further new life is grounded on this understanding of self-giving. Haughton's ten children were less the result of a stance against contraception than a mutual understanding that children are one way in which sexuality continues its development in opening to others, beyond themselves.[67] Her observations on the pressure placed on couples who lack broader family circles and a community to support that journey are insightful. As with other vocations and pathways of holiness, sexual love also passes through 'dark nights', in which the emotion of passion grows less. Here as well, sexual love is sacramental and can 'recreate the sense of the reality of love, keep fresh the hope of earlier days, draw into itself the deepening insight and experience of life and love and then release them, transformed and purified, into the rest of life'.[68] A physical action symbolizes the love it expresses: it is a symbol that works!

In every step of this mystical and theological understanding of sex and Christian marriage, she witnesses to an understanding that would be impossible without its foundations in lived experience. In her framework – and here I come to her thought on God – she turns inside-out our classic understanding of *agape*-over-*eros* as the proper way of understanding both God and love. Instead, *eros* demands the true self of the spirit, and *agape* is a response to that demand.

God as passionate

We can now understand why understanding God as passionate is more accessible *after* exploring her theology of sexuality and marriage, rather than before. The temptation in Western theology is usually to sanitize God of any unreasonable feeling – protecting 'Him' from the vicissitudes and changeability of the world we are trying to escape. But God became human and lived, loved, laughed, suffered, died, was risen, ascended and 'the resurrection is bodily or it is nothing'.[69] With God at the centre of

---

[66] Haughton, *Married Love in Christian Life*, 55.
[67] As I write, the Catholic world is dealing with the response of the Congregation for the Doctrine of the Faith to the question of whether the blessing of same-sex unions is permissible. Cf. https://press.vatican.va/content/salastampa/en/bollettino/pubblico/2021/03/15/210315b.html (accessed 25 March 2021), and its annexed Explanatory Note: https://press.vatican.va/content/salastampa/en/bollettino/pubblico/2021/03/15/210315c.html (accessed 25 Mach 2021). With all her defence of a Catholic understanding of sexual love in marriage, it is interesting that Haughton invites us to recognize the good found even in relationships that do not conform to this ideal. Cf. Haughton, *Married Love in Christian Life*, 59.
[68] Cf. Haughton, *Married Love in Christian Life*, 68.
[69] Haughton, *The Passionate God*, 1.

our humanity, Haughton presents the passionate love between a man and a woman as *the most adequate* expression of love with which to try and comprehend God, not only as a comparison or metaphor – although all our language only attempts to name God – but as a transformed presence and manifestation of God's love. The omnipresence of 'feeling' and 'romance' in contemporary mythology about the meaning of human life is not despite Christianity but because of it. Haughton's theology converges with Sequeri's position that sensibility to love is a contemporary shared space in culture from which to begin a re-comprehension of faith. But her thought brings that intuition into the very understanding of who God is and who we are.

Three concepts underpin her thought on being and God and challenge the static image of eternal non-change that has hijacked philosophical terms used to explain God for centuries. Drawing from C. S. Lewis,[70] Charles Williams[71] and Dante's *The Divine Comedy*, she speaks of spheres, exchange and breakthrough. Being is exchange, or relationship, in the heart of the Trinity as they reach out to us; sin is the refusal and breakdown of that relationship, and romance – that particular understanding of love that emerged in Provence in the eleventh century – expresses love's breakthrough into human consciousness, as never before. Sexual love, or passion, is much more than 'the free play of instinct or lust' but rather that breaking-in of love into someone's life when a particular other becomes the centre of their universe, and the world is changed. The characteristics of passion – particularity, singleness, a capacity to change the face of reality and painfulness – express in human words the reality of how God in Jesus works. One falls in love with *a particular person in time*, as passion is not indifferent to who one wants to love! And that very awareness is both infused with glory and painful, because even as we love, we are made acutely aware of the fragility and temporal nature of human love.[72] Jesus is the particular human being who incarnates – literally – this passionate love of God for humanity. His appearance replicates or rather obeys the steps of transforming love we identified above: the history of God's chosen people is our long-term preparation, the silence of the prophets and disturbing experience of the Roman invasion, an immediate preparation for Love's breakthrough in a young, open and courageous girl named Mariam, the 'weak spot' through which the passionate love of God for humanity broke through.

> Mary is the 'handmaid', the slave of the Lord, she is one of the poor, the *anawim* of Yahweh, and so she is the weak spot where God's romantic

---

[70]In particular the last book of Clive Staples Lewis, *The Chronicles of Narnia* (New York: Harper Collins, 2001), in which the end of times is expressed with the notion of spheres.

[71]Insights from his novels run through Haughton's writings, but in particular, Charles Williams, *The Descent of the Dove: A Short History of the Holy Spirit in the Church* (New York: Oxford University Press, 1939).

[72]Cf. 'The Face of Beatrice' in Haughton, *The Passionate God*, 48–57.

passion for human beings, and through them all creation, could break through. She is earth, body, 'medium of exchange' . . . as conscious and fully willed, as active and sensitive, as real human life.[73]

It is impossible to do justice here to the depth, complexity and clarity of Haughton's exploration of the life of Jesus as Incarnated passion, himself also passing through the steps and stages of maturation in love. The invitation is to dive into this rich, slow-cooked theological feast of words seeking to take seriously our living God.[74]

Sexual love versus? celibacy

Before we move to the musical dimension of this chapter, a word on my own grasp of Haughton's thought. She regularly insisted on the holiness of marriage, challenging the long-held Catholic misconception that a married person's relationship with Christ is necessarily of 'a second best variety'.[75] This does not, however, lead her to undermine what consecrated virginity does bring to the Catholic table.

> When people love each other very much, there are moments when they know that their love is bigger than themselves. It is as if they were learning to know something beyond each other. This is a true feeling, real love shows the presence of God. Christian marriage makes this clear, shows people what their love means... It is often in moments of perfect stillness and peace that they realize most clearly the greatness their love – which is not 'theirs' but rather they are 'its.' So, throughout the history of the Church, there have been people who are, in their own lives, the sign of God with us. They are called to live this 'stillness' at the heart of things, to be witnesses of love itself which is deeper and greater and more intimate than sex. They are signs of *what it is* that makes sex in marriage, and good family life witnesses to the 'genuine nature of the Church'.[76]

I confess to being challenged by the radicality of her understanding of my own calling, but most of all grateful that her real experience of living faith within a call to marriage has found such intelligent expression.

> The theology of marriage might perhaps be written by a celibate theologian who had great powers of imagination, and who really tried to

---

[73]Cf. Haughton, *The Passionate God*, 129–40.
[74]Haughton, *The Passionate God*, 9.
[75]Haughton, *Married Love in Christian Life*, 38.
[76]Rosemary Haughton, *Problems of Christian Marriage* (New York: Paulist Press Deus Books, 1968), 51–2.

find out at second hand what marriage implies in practice. But ideally it should be written by one who has experienced it for himself.

Or herself. For it is hard to think of anyone better qualified to write this book than Mrs Haughton.

E. J. Yarnold, SJ[77]

Can I Have This Dance?

The song linked to this chapter has two versions, which speak directly to, or rather emerge explicitly from, two of the vocations to love open to Christians: marriage and consecrated celibacy. Since the entire theological project Haughton develops is grounded on reflection upon life experience and its call to fullness, I will start with the song that emerged from my own vocation – that of consecrated life – and point to how the wedding song emerged. My experience of life and of myself in it has always been in the awareness that sexuality is at the very centre of life, and the key element of religious life is celibate virginity. In this Schneiders is right: poverty and obedience are evangelical counsels which may have a particular vowed-form in religious life, but in real life are often practised much more by people in family life than any other. And while chastity is for all, celibacy – the renunciation of sexual intimacy and intercourse for life – is the defining factor of religious life.[78] If we do not embrace this reality, if affectivity and our emotional life and intelligence are ignored, or sidelined, or repressed, the result is a shrivelled life that witnesses to nothing but how selfish a person, or an institution, can become.

I mentioned in the chapter on Teresa of Avila that prayer without the humanity of Christ was, for her, impossible. For me, and this song is quite personal, the call to consecrated missionary life in an exclusive way has always been just that: an exclusive call to be loved by and love the person of Christ. The particularity I spoke of in relation to romantic love – that when we fall in love it is the face, the eyes, the movement of *one person* in time and space that pulls us beyond ourselves into them – for me, was Jesus: that man at the centre of every gospel story, the One who drew me to sit at the back of churches, asking a presence emanating from a tabernacle if I could please know Him. Despite the challenges – and there have been many! – the face of Christ, or rather the place I find when I connect with the way I am seen by Him, is my centre and my peace. 'Do you love me? . . . Do You love me? . . . Do you love me?' (Jn 21.15-19). '*Can I have this dance? . . . Can*

---

[77]Haughton, *The Theology of Marriage*, Preface, 11.
[78]Cf. Sandra M. Schneiders, *Selling All: Commitment, Consecrated Celibacy and Community in Catholic Religious Life* (Mahwah, NJ: Paulist Press, 2001).

I have this dance? . . . Can I have this dance?. . . .' Never-imposing but completely focussed is how I sense my human God, seeking my attention, my recognition, my smile, my humour, my body, my peace, all that I am. That is the experience underlying this song. Our God is a jealous God, and an intimate one.

Songs live beyond and outside themselves, but this was born as an offertory song for a sung mass entitled *Mass of the Ascension*: preparation for participating in and receiving the God who worships *us* with his body. We are adored by our self-giving God. This is why romantic and passionate love is the perfect paradigm within which to understand God's love: self-giving unto death is who God is, not in an abstract way but *to us*. Hence the insistent quest to gain our attention: 'do you love me?' 'Can I have this dance?' 'Stay awake with me!' (cf. Mt. 26.40).

Interwoven in the song are images evoking the body of Christ in whom we live, move and breathe (cf. Acts 17.28) from Gerard Manley Hopkins' 'As Kingfishers Catch Fire':

'for Christ plays in ten thousand places,
Lovely in limbs, and lovely in eyes not his',

and the poetic prose of Scripture scholar Jean-Pierre Sonnet in two small books called *Le Corps Voisé (The Voiced Body)* and *MEMBRA JESU NOSTRI: Ce que Dieu ne dit que par le corps* (The limbs of our Jesus What God Only Says with the Body).[79] Sonnet words the Incarnated God in ways that Haughton would relish. The song was written around the time of the 2011 translation of the Mass into English, in which some found the replacement of the words of the consecration: 'poured out for all' by 'poured out for many' hard to reconcile with God's universal will of salvation. Drawing on Hopkins' profound grasp of the Body Christ, I attempt to find a way between the words: '*poured out for as many . . . as the eye can see*'.

The second version of the song was not born of my experience but of that of young couples getting married. A friend of mine who was present at the premiere of *The Mass of the Ascension* got an early copy of this song and gradually couples who approached him for the sacrament of marriage would use it, in the Eucharist or as their first dance, so I found myself trying to express what that might mean or say about their love. The influence of Haughton's clear-sighted vision of sexual love is obvious. After, all, she is known to have compared the role of sex in marriage with that of going to mass in faith life. I will let the song speak for itself.

---

[79]Jean-Pierre SJ Sonnet, *Le Corps Voisé: Petite Suite Eucharistique* (Châtelineau: Le Taillis Pré, 2002); Jean-Pierre SJ Sonnet, *MEMBRA JESU NOSTRI: Ce que Dieu ne dit que par le corps* (Châtelineau: Le Taillis Pré, 2010).

A final word born of the song's reception. My family – who speak from within and beyond the Church's walls – love this song(s) but did ask the question about whether it portrays too passive an image of female self-giving in the mutuality of the loving relationship. Could it be misunderstood in a world in which women often feel obliged to submit and surrender too much? Time will tell and a song can be corrected. It was born of my own prayer-life, in which I am (finally!) becoming comfortable in letting Jesus take the lead, but that is only because of the freedom in which that call is delivered – *no one* understands 'consent' better than God! Furthermore, I thrive in the fact that this call draws out every latent capacity I have to follow *and* lead, as disciple *and* apostle. Haughton had little time for ideologies around gender. She knew women in Christ were called to freedom and roles of ministry and leadership, and that it was only a question of time until that happened. She also knew that the issue sits within the broader one of how we imagine leadership structures and that the sidelining of the feminine in men and the masculine in women maims human flourishing, theology, Church and society. I confess to having little time for those who try to name and define all that an abstract idea of woman might bring to the table, and am just as wary of the consequences of a one-sided or incomplete understanding of what it is to be a man. Our non-gendered yet male-incarnated God seeks only the fullness of who we are. The link to both versions of the song 'Can I Have this Dance?' is in the note below.[80]

Lyrics offertory version of 'Can I Have This Dance?'

Can I have this dance?
This is my body
Can I have this dance?
Broken for you . . .
Can I have this dance
The shortest route from me to You is unfolding right before my eyes
This is my blood
Can I have this dance?
Poured out for as many . . .
Can I have this dance?
As the eye can see, lovely in limbs, in eyes not his . . .
Magnify your voice in mine: so close to me, an echo free . . .
Can I have this dance? . . .

---

[80]The offertory version is here: https://res.cloudinary.com/bloomsbury-online-resources/video/upload/v1639138138/Suspended%20God/Can_I_Have_This_Dance.wav

The wedding version is here: https://res.cloudinary.com/bloomsbury-online-resources/video/upload/v1639138195/Suspended%20God/Can_I_Have_This_Dance_Wedding_Version.wav

Body sways, where words always fail: so, taste and see!
Come move in me
Can I have this dance? . . .

Lyrics wedding version of 'Can I Have This Dance?'

Wedding version

Can I have this dance?
This is my body
Can I have this dance?
(that) I give to you . . .
Can I have this dance
The shortest route from me to You is unfolding right before our eyes
Your life and mine
Can I have this dance?
Open and entwined
Can I have this dance?
. . . whatever life may bring, lovely in limbs, in eyes not his . . .
Magnify your voice in mine; So close to me . . . an echo free . . .
Can I have this dance?
This is my body
Can I have this dance?
(that) I give to you . . .
Can I have this dance
The shortest route from me to You is unfolding right before our eyes
Your blood and mine
Can I have this dance?
Face and race entwined
Can I have this dance?
(open to) whatever life may bring, lovely in limbs, in eyes not his . . .
Body sways, where words always fail; So, taste and see! Come move in me!
Can I have this dance . . . ?

©MAEVE LOUISE HEANEY, 2020.
Strange Life, the Music of Doubtful Faith

Selected further reading

An introduction to her life and thought

Ryan, Eilish. *Rosemary Haughton: Witness to Hope.* Lanham, MD: Rowman & Littlefield, 1997.

Sexuality and Marriage

Haughton, Rosemary. *Married Love in Christian Life*. London: Burns & Oates, 1966.
Haughton, Rosemary. *The Theology of Marriage*. Cork: Mercier Press, 1971.
Haughton, Rosemary. *The Mystery of Sexuality*. London: Darton, Longman and Todd, 1973.

Ecclesiology

Haughton, Rosemary. *The Changing Church*. London: Geoffrey Chapman, 1969.
Haughton, Rosemary. *The Catholic Thing*. Springfield: Templegate Publishers, 1979.

God as passionate love

Haughton, Rosemary. *The Passionate God*. London: Darton Longman and Todd, 1982.

Theological method

Haughton, Rosemary. *The Theology of Experience*. Paramus, NJ: Newman Press, 1972.

Coda

An invitation to autoethnography

Being an Irish theologian

Codas are not usually long (except those of homilists who have not learned to finish!), so this will not be long. This whole book has been about my attempt to grapple with what I understand theology should and could be, in the company of others whose wisdom and work form the backdrop of any theological understanding I have come to. So, to say that I am grateful for the lives and thought of each theologian presented is an understatement. During the book, I have moved between 'we' and 'I': partly because of the attempt to own my voice, but also in the recognition that we build on those who went before us: knowledge is never *only* one's own. But there is a time to own what you think, and at the end of each chapter, I have tried to do that. I do not apologize for the personalized tone it gave each theme, as I cannot see another way of trying to help us find the self-awareness and honesty necessary for the theology of the future. Lonergan called for an 'introspective attention' necessary for authentic subjectivity, aware that it is not common:

> Authors are always conscious of their intentional operations, but to reach knowledge of them there must be added introspective attention, inquiry and understanding, reflection and judgement . . . it leads to the impasse of scrutinizing the self-scrutinizing self and into the oddity of the author who writes about himself writing. Such authors are exceptional.[1]

---

[1] Bernard J. F. Lonergan, *Method in Theology* (New York: The Seabury Press, 1972), 166–7.

This Coda goes a bit further into the autobiographical background of my theology. Being this reflective and honest about the sources of my thought in what is an academic theology book does, at times, make one feel odd, but there is no progress without risk, and I am committed to this theological adventure God has led me into.

However, writing in this way also converges with current writings in the social sciences exploring the field of autoethnography as a means of including the perspective of the researcher in their studies, using narrative to ensure their personal voice is heard alongside others.[2] Stories complexify the process but raise (and expose) the profile and positioning of the person of the researcher behind every academic article – the underlying experiences and concerns that underpin their convictions. This is a dimension theologians among themselves are already usually aware of, anyway. It is just rarely named. I believe correcting this may be a necessary pathway for theologians into the future. 'In simple terms, there is an increasing weariness with the viability and attraction of a purely detached approach to theology.'[3] This is the sense I receive from *many* of my students, who come to theology with a clear and self-aware need for self-implication in what they are studying. In the words of Philip Sheldrake: 'theology involves becoming a *theological* person. Thus, theologians are those who *live* theology rather than "do" it as an activity divorced from who they are and from the vision of the world by which they seek to live'.[4] In one of his last speeches, suggestively entitled 'Experiences of a Catholic Theologian', Karl Rahner identifies elements he considers essential to doing Catholic theology.

I will mention them briefly, as they serve as a litmus test for whether my own theologizing measures up, and also help introduce the last song of this book:

1. *The analogical nature of all theological assertions*, since although we are required to seek as much clarity as we can in the language we use, the Fourth Lateran Council's apophatic stance still bears true: 'nothing substantial of a positive nature about God can be stated without, at the same time, perceiving the radical inadequacy of such affirmative statements'.

2. *The central statement of all theology is about God's grace given in Christ*: 'This sheer and unexpected miracle of God, a God who bestows God's very self and who turns such a love into the adventure that is God's own history. . . . If we accept this, then

---

[2] I am grateful to Dr Danielle Lynch for introducing me to this field of research in a shared passion for music in and as theology.
[3] Philip Sheldrake, 'Spirituality and Its Critical Methodology', in *Exploring Christian Spirituality: Essays in Honor of Sandra M. Schneiders*, ed. B. H. Lescher and E. Liebert, 15–34 (29–30) (New York: Paulist Press, 2006).
[4] Sheldrake, *Exploring Christian Spirituality*, 15–34 (25).

I think we can easily hold that God's self-communication to the creature is more pivotal than sin and the forgiveness of sin.'

3. *The affinity of theology to its spiritual source*, in this case, the *Society of Jesus* (Jesuits): 'I would hope that Ignatius Loyola, the great founder of my order, would recognize something of his own spirit and spirituality in my theology. At least I would like to think that that is the case!'
4. *The necessary humility of theology before the other sciences, including the arts*: 'If as a theologian I inquire not about an abstract concept of God, but wish to approach God directly, then absolutely nothing of what God has revealed as Creator of the world, as Lord of history, should be uninteresting to me.'[5]

Stretching theological 'language' towards musicking stands in continuity with the impossibility of fully naming God through words; I am convinced that music is one way in which God's ever-abundant grace is poured out. I hope this book helps us, as a Church, pay more attention to, and invest more resources in this universal form of making sense of life and faith. I too belong to a religious family, a *new form of consecrated life*, called the *Verbum Dei*. I too would like to think its founder – Jaime Bonet Bonet – might recognize something of his own spirit in my thought. I also hope my community do. I know that it would not have been imaginable without the spirituality and prayer-life into which they introduced me. Finally, this is quite simply an attempt to bring music into theological discourse proper, by listening first and foremost, to God's musical gift to me. I pray it encourages others more gifted than I to do the same, differently and better.

I have tried to present as clearly as I could the insights and the limits of each of the theologians in this book *and* the questions they wrestle with. But its central thesis is that we need not be scared of the limits of our knowledge. God is greater and deeper than our minds can know, and is not scared of what we bring to the conversation. Neither should we. God became known to us in Christ. The sheer radicality of God's emptying of self to meet us should ensure us that God's love for our lives and desire to be with us constitute the centre of every Christian statement, even about sin! We theologize because the world has the need and the right to know just how loved they are. In relation to his last point on other sciences and areas of knowledge might bring to theology in the future, Rahner names a number of challenges that were unthinkable in his time, including the possibility of a Pope resigning due to illness and for the betterment of the Church. And so things change.

---

[5]K. Rahner, D. Marmion, and G. Thiessen, 'Experiences of a Catholic Theologian', *Theological Studies* 61, no. 1 (2000): 3–15.

We need to think theologically in a way that prepares us for a future we cannot yet see, and to create pathways to theologize about what emerges. This implies interacting (also) with the musicality and musicking of the world we live in, *expecting* to learn about ourselves and the God we believe in.

Down Under

'Down Under' was written between two continents – Europe and Australia – when I knew that once again, I was pulling up my roots to go where I sensed God was sending me. In truth, the song is a plea to God to let me stay somewhere for a while, this time! After twelve years in Spain, seven in England, seven in Italy, one in the United States and half a year in Germany, I was ready to stay put for a while! I knew Australia was the place I was being called to, although I had never imagined my life would end up here. But the song is about being a missionary: that beautiful and challenging calling that implies arriving somewhere and putting your roots down to receive, listen to and learn from a culture; to love the people God places in your hands and let them love you; to give all you are and all you have; and all of this, ever in the freedom that you might one day be asked to pull them up again, leaving a part of you behind, and taking people and places with you. It is a costly vocation, for one's family as much as oneself. I do not regret it. I would not change it. My life has been and continues to be full and rich and unbearably loved. But it is not easy.

In this song, too, I have tried to be honest in expressing myself with God. I think taking songwriting into theology has to obey the rules of the genre: *say* what your mind and heart are thinking and feeling! And listen to the answer you intuit. So the song is a dialogue, not only about how I feel the cost of such a life but also about the grace received. And as I wrote it, *St Patrick's Breastplate* emerged as its, and perhaps, my *cantus firmus*, helping me realize that I am just one more Irish missionary in the history of Irish meanderings for whom the presence of Jesus is the ground we walk on, though light and shadows: '*Christ on my left, on my right, over me, under my feet, when I rise and I sleep . . . in the air that I breathe.*' Rahner names God's total self-giving into human history as the centre of every theological life. For me, in the midst of everything, my 'life is Christ' (Phil. 1.1) and worth the free fall.

The link to the song is given in the note.[6]

---

[6]'Down Under':https://res.cloudinary.com/bloomsbury-online-resources/video/upload/v1639138274/Suspended%20God/Down_Under.wav

'Down Under' lyrics

Living on the surface of me, maybe this time, I'll set my roots down . . .
The ground is moving under my feet:
Maybe this life, is meant to go round and round and
Never fear, never mind
I know you're feeling like a cloud that any wind can blow around . . .
Never fear, never mind:
I know you'd rather be a tree, with mighty roots to hold you still . . .
down under . . . up above . . .
Living on the edge of myself, trying to catch breath,
Pulled every which way but inward
I'm falling off the edge of my world:
Hard to let go – the only way out is free-fall
Never fear, never mind, when you get there you will recognize
Both of us growing there, both of us knowing where
Never fear, never mind:
Not a hair of yours falls to the ground, without my knowin' it,
without my growin' it . . . Down under . . . up above . . .
The ground beneath my feet moves like the sky above my head goes round and round . . .
The ground beneath my feet moves like the sky above my head goes is blue and brown . . .
I know if You go with me I'll be fine;
You know that I know that You're by my side
 Christ on my left, on my right, over me, under my feet
When I rise and I sleep. . . . In the air that I breathe . . .
. . . in the eyes, that can see [me]
[in] every ear that hears me
In the hearts that I feel. . . . In the words that I speak.

©MAEVE LOUISE HEANEY, 2020.
Strange Life, The Music of Doubtful Faith

BIBLIOGRAPHY

Allen, John L. *Pope Benedict XVI: A Biography of Joseph Ratzinger*. New York: Continuum, 2000.
Alves, Rubem A. *The Poet, the Warrior, the Prophet*. Philadelphia: Trinity Press International, 1990.
Alves, Rubem A. 'Theopoetics: Longing and Liberation'. In *Struggles for Solidarity: Liberation Theologies in Tension*, edited by Lorine M. Getz and Ruy O. Costa, 159–71. Minneapolis: Fortress Press, 1992.
Andrews, Isolde. *Deconstructing Barth: A Study of the Complementary Methods in Karl Barth and Jacques Derrida*. New York: Peter Lang, 1996.
Angelini, Giuseppe. *Una fede per tutti?: forma cristiana e forma secolare*. Disputatio. Milano: Glossa, 2014.
Anić, Rebeka Jadranka. 'Gender, Politics and the Catholic Church'. *Concilium Special Edition on Gender in Theology, Spirituality and Practice* 4 (2012): 26–35.
Anselm. *St. Anselm's Proslogion with a Reply on Behalf of the Fool*, edited by Anselm, M. J. Charlesworth, and Gaunilo. Notre Dame IN: University of Notre Dame Press, 1979.
Anselm. 'Why God Became Man'. In *The Major Works*, edited by Brian Davies and G. R. Evans, 260–56. Oxford and New York: Oxford University Press, 1998.
Ardui, J. 'Truth, Rock Music and Christianity: Can Truth Be Maintained in the Dialogue between Theology and Rock Music?'. In *Theology and the Quest for Truth: Historical- and Systematic-Theological Studies*, edited by M. Lamberigts, L. Boeve and Terrence Merrigan, 199–212. Leuven: Leuven University Press, 2006.
Augustine. *Confessions*. Translated by Henry Chadwick. Oxford: Oxford University Pres, 1992.
Augustine. *De Musica*, edited by Martin Jacobsson and Lukas J. Dorfbauer. Berlin: Walter de Gruyter, 2017.
Augustine. *Enarrationes in Psalmos*.
Augustine. 'Sermon 356'. In *The Works of Saint Augustine: A Translation for the 21st Century*, edited by John E. Rotelle. Translated by Edmund Hill, 167–71. Brooklyn, NY: New City Press, 1990.
Avant-Mier, Roberto. *Rock the Nation: Latin/o Identities and the Latin Rock Diaspora*. London and New York: Continuum, 2010.
Aydin, Mor Polycarpus A. 'From the Pauline Admonition to Remain Silent to St. Ephrem's Creation of Women's Choirs in the Liturgy'. In *Churches and

Moral Discernment: Learning from History, edited by Myriam Wijlens, Vladimir Shmaliy and Simone Sinn. Faith and Order Paper no. 229, 221–32. Oikoumene World Council of Churches Publications, 2021.

Aydin, Mor Polycarpus A. 'A Wedding Feast of Song': St. Ephrem and the Singing Ministry of Women in the Church'. In *Geschichte, Theologie, Liturgie und Gegenwartslage der Syrischen Kirchen. Beiträge zum Sechsten Deutschen Syrologen-Symposium in Konstanz*, edited by Dorothea Weltecke, 59–64. Wiesbaden: Harrassowitz Verlag, 2012.

Babbitt, Milton. 'The Composer as Specialist'. In *The Collected Essays of Milton Babbitt*, edited by Stephen Peles, Stephen Dembski, Andrew Mead and Joseph N. Stras, 48–54. Princeton: Princeton University Press, 2003.

Balthasar, Hans Urs von. *Dare We Hope That All Men Be Saved? With a Short Discourse on Hell*. San Francisco, CA: Ignatius Press, 1988.

Balthasar, Hans Urs von. *Die Entwicklung der musikalischen Idee. Versuch einer Synthese der Musik*; Bekenntnis zu Mozart. Einsiedeln: Johannes, 1998.

Balthasar, Hans Urs von. *First Glance at Adrienne Von Speyr*. San Francisco: Ignatius Press, 1981.

Balthasar, Hans Urs von. *Love Alone Is Credible*. San Francisco, CA: Ignatius Press, 2004.

Balthasar, Hans Urs von. *The Moment of Christian Witness*. San Francisco, CA: Ignatius Press, 1994.

Balthasar, Hans Urs von. *My Work: In Retrospect*. San Francisco, CA: Communio Books, 1993.

Balthasar, Hans Urs von. *Mysterium Paschale*. San Francisco, CA: Ignatius Press, 2005.

Balthasar, Hans Urs von. *Our Task: A Report and a Plan*. San Francisco, CA: Ignatius Press, 1994.

Balthasar, Hans Urs von. *Razing the Bastions: On the Church in This Age*. San Francisco, CA: Ignatius Press, 1993.

Balthasar, Hans Urs von. 'Revelation and the Beautiful'. In *Explorations in Theology 1: The Word Made Flesh*, 491–502. San Francisco, CA: Ignatius Press, 1989a.

Balthasar, Hans Urs von. 'Theology and Sanctity'. In *Explorations in Theology 1: The Word Made Flesh*, 181–209. San Francisco, CA: Ignatius Press, 1989b.

Balthasar, Hans Urs von. 'Tribute to Mozart'. *Communio* 28, no. 2 (2001): 398–9.

Balthasar, Hans Urs von. *Truth Is Symphonic: Aspects of Christian Pluralism*. San Francisco: Ignatius Press, 1987.

Balthasar, Hans Urs von. *Two Sisters in the Spirit: Thérèse of Lisieuz & Elizabeth of the Trinity*. San Francisco, CA: Ignatius Press, 1992.

Balthasar, Hans Urs von. *The Glory of the Lord: A Theological Aesthetics*, edited by Joseph Fessio S.J. and John Riches. Translated by Erasmo Leiva-Merikakis. Edinburgh: T&T Clark, 1982–9.

Balthasar, Hans Urs von and Pierangelo Sequeri. *Lo Sviluppo dell'idea Musicale Testimonianza per Mozart Antiprometeo: Il Musicale nell'estetica di Hans Urs von Balthasar*. Milano: Glossa, 1995.

Barrett, Frank J. *Yes to the Mess: Surprising Leadership Lessons from Jazz*. Boston, MA: Harvard Business Press, 2012.

Barth, Karl. *Church Dogmatics, Vol. 1 'the Doctrine of the Word of God: Prolegomena to Church Dogmatics'*. Translated by G. W. Bromiley, 1st American edn. Edinburgh: T&T Clark, 1975.
Barth, Karl. *Evangelical Theology: An Introduction*. Grand Rapids, MI: William B. Eerdmans, 1979.
Barth, Karl. *How I Changed My Mind*. Richmond: John Knox Press, 1966.
Barth, Karl. *Karl Barth's Table Talk*, edited by John D. Godsey. Edinburgh: Oliver and Boyd, 1963.
Barth, Karl. *Wolfgang Amadeus Mozart*. Translated by Clarence K. Pott. Grand Rapids, MI: William B. Eerdmans, 1986.
Bartleet, Brydie-Leigh and Carolyn Ellis. *Music Autoethnographies: Making Autoethnography Sing/Making Music Personal*. Bowen Hills, QLD: Australian Academic Press, 2010.
Beattie, Tina. *New Catholic Feminism: Theology and Theory*. New York, NY: Routledge, 2006.
Beaudoin, Tom. *Witness to Dispossession: The Vocation of a Postmodern Theologian*. Maryknoll, NY: Orbis Books, 2008.
Beaudoin, Tom. *Virtual Faith: The Irreverent Spiritual Quest of Generation X*. San Francisco: Jossey-Bass, 1998.
Beaudoin, Tom, ed. *Secular Music and Sacred Theology*. Collegeville, MN: Liturgical Press, 2013.
Begbie, Jeremy. *Resounding Truth: Christian Wisdom in the World of Music*. London: SPCK, 2008.
Begbie, Jeremy and Steven R. Guthrie. *Resonant Witness: Conversations between Music and Theology*. Grand Rapids, MI: William B. Eerdmans, 2011.
Bell, John L. 'The Summons'. In *God Never Sleeps*. Iona Community: GIA Publications, 1995.
Benedict XVI. *Meeting with Artists: Address of Pope Benedict XVI*. Vatican City: Libreria Editrice Vaticana, 2009.
Benson, Bruce Ellis. *The Improvisation of Musical Dialogue: A Phenomenology of Music*. Cambridge: Cambridge University Press, 2003.
Berry, Thomas Mary. *The Dream of the Earth*. San Francisco: Sierra Club Books, 1988.
Bethge, Eberhard. *Dietrich Bonhoeffer: Theologian, Christian, Contemporary*. London: Collins, 1970.
Betz, John R. 'After Heidegger and Marion: The Task of Christian Metaphysics Today'. *Modern Theology* 34, no. 4 (2018): 565–97.
Birch, Charles and John B. Cobb. *The Liberation of Life: From the Cell to the Community*, edited by John B. Cobb. Cambridge: Cambridge University Press, 1981.
Blacking, John. *How Musical Is Man?*. London: Faber, 1976.
Blackwell, Albert L. 'The Role of Music in Schleiermacher's Writings'. In *Internationaler Schleiermacher-Kongress Berlin 1984*, edited by Kurt-Victor Selge, 439–48. Berlin: de Gruyter, 1985.
Bochner, Arthur P., Carolyn Ellis and Symposium Couch Stone. *Ethnographically Speaking: Autoethnography, Literature, and Aesthetics*. Walnut Creek, CA: AltaMira Press, 2002.
Bochner, Arthur P. 'Criteria against Ourselves'. *Qualitative Inquiry* 6, no. 2 (2000): 266–72.

Boeve, Lieven. *God Interrupts History: Theology in a Time of Upheaval*. New York: Continuum, 2007.
Boff, Leonardo. *Introducing Liberation Theology*, edited by Clodovis Boff. Maryknoll, NY: Orbis Books, 1987.
Bonhoeffer, Dietrich. *The Cost of Discipleship*. London: SCM Press, 1959.
Bonhoeffer, Dietrich. *Dietrich Bonhoeffer Works. Vol. 6, Ethics*, edited by Clifford J. Green, Reinhard Krauss, Charles C. West and Douglas W. Stott. Minneapolis, MN: Fortress Press, 2009.
Bonhoeffer, Dietrich. *Dietrich Bonhoeffer Works. Vol. 16, Conspiracy and Imprisonment, 1940–1945*, edited by Mark S. Brocker, Lisa E. Dahill and Douglas W. Stott. Minneapolis, MN: Fortress Press, 2006.
Bonhoeffer, Dietrich. *Letters and Papers from Prison*, edited by John W. De Gruchy, Ilse Tödt, Renate Bethge, Eberhard Bethge and Christian Gremmels. 1st English-language edn. Minneapolis, MN: Fortress Press, 2010.
Bonhoeffer, Dietrich. *Letters and Papers from Prison*, edited by Eberhard Bethge. London: SCM Press, 1971.
Bonhoeffer, Dietrich. *Life Together*. London: SCM Press, 1954.
Bonhoeffer, Dietrich, Clifford J. Green and Michael P. DeJonge. *The Bonhoeffer Reader*, edited by Clifford J. Green and Michael P. DeJonge. Minneapolis, MN: Fortress Press, 2013.
Bonhoeffer, Dietrich and Maria von Wedemeyer. *Love Letters from Cell 92. The Correspondence between Dietrich Bonhoeffer and Maria Von Wedemeyer, 1943–45*, edited by Ruth-Alice Von Bismarch and Ulrich Kabitz. Nashville, TN: Abingdon Press, 1995.
Booth, Edward. 'Thomas Aquinas'. *The New Grove Dictionary of Music and Musicians*, edited by Stanley Sadie 1 (1980): 512.
Bowers, Jane M. and Judith Tick. *Women Making Music: The Western Art Tradition, 1150–1950*. Illinois: University of Illinois Press, 1987.
Boyd, Gregory A. *Benefit of the Doubt: Breaking the Idol of Certainty*. Grand Rapids, MI: Baker Books, 2013.
Brett Christopher, Gray. 'Clones, Princes, and Beautiful Parodies: Rowan Williams' Negative Literary Christology'. *Literature & Theology* 29, no. 3 (2015): 284–97.
Broadhead, Bradley K. *Jazz and Christian Freedom: Improvising against the Grain of the West*. Eugene, OR: Pickwick Publications, 2018.
Brock, Sebastian P. *The Luminous Eye: The Spiritual World Vision of Saint Ephrem*. Kalamazoo, MI: Cistercian Publications, 1992.
Brueggemann, Walter. *Finally Comes the Poet: Daring Speech for Proclamation*. Minneapolis: Fortress Press, 1989.
Buber, Martin. *I and Thou*. New York: Scribner, 1970.
Buckley, Michael J. *At the Origins of Modern Atheism*. New Haven: Yale University Press, 1987.
Buckley, Michael J. *Denying and Disclosing God: The Ambiguous Progress of Modern Atheism*. New Haven, CT: Yale University Press, 2004.
Buerkner, Paul. 'Embracing Uncertainty'. no. 18 November 2019.
Burke, Kevin F. and Robert Anthony Lassalle-Klein. *Love That Produces Hope: The Thought of Ignacio Ellacuría*. Collegeville, MN: Liturgical Press, 2005.
Buzard, James. 'On Auto-Ethnographic Authority'. *The Yale Journal of Criticism* 16, no. 1 (2003): 61.

Bychkov, Oleg V. and James Fodor. *Theological Aesthetics after von Balthasar*. Aldershot, England: Ashgate, 2008.
Cahill, Lisa, Diego Irarrazaval Sowle and Elaine Mary Wainwright, eds. *Gender in Theology, Spirituality and Practice*. London: SCM Press, 2012.
Câmara, Hélder. *The Desert Is Fertile*, edited by Dinah Livingstone. London: Sheed and Ward, 1974.
Cano, Rubén López and Úrsula San Cristóbal Opazo. *Investigación Artística en Música: Problemas, Experiencias y Propuestas*. Mexico: Fondo Nacional Para la Cultura y Las Artes.
Caputo, John and Catherine Keller. 'Theopoetic/Theopolitic'. *CrossCurrents* 56 (2007): 105–11.
Carey, George. 'Enthronement Sermon Canterbury, England Friday, April 19th 1991'. *Evangelical Review of Theology* 16 (1992): 4–7.
Carey, Patrick W. and Joseph T. Lienhard. *Biographical Dictionary of Christian Theologians*. Westport, CT: Greenwood Press, 2000.
Carson, Mina, Tisa Lewis and Susan M Shaw. *Girls Rock!: Fifty Years of Women Making Music*. University Press of Kentucky, 2014.
Chesterton, G. K. *Orthodoxy*. Garden City, NY: Image Books, 1959.
Chua, Daniel K. L. *Absolute Music and the Construction of Meaning*. Cambridge: Cambridge University Press, 1999.
Clarke, Eric F., Nicola Dibben and Stephanie Pitts. *Music and Mind in Everyday Life*. Oxford: Oxford University Press, 2010.
Clifford, Anne M. *Introducing Feminist Theology*. Maryknoll, NY: Orbis Books, 2001.
Clifford, Catherine E. *The Groupe Des Dombes: A Dialogue of Conversion*. New York: Peter Lang, 2005.
Cobb, Kelton. *The Blackwell Guide to Theology and Popular Culture*. Malden, MA: Blackwell Pub., 2005.
Collins, Mary, Dermot A. Lane, and Joseph A. Komonchak. *The New Dictionary of Theology*. Collegeville, MN: Liturgical Press, 1991.
Collins, Guy. *Faithful Doubt: The Wisdom of Uncertainty*. Eugene, OR: Cascade Books, 2014.
Cone, James H. *The Spirituals and the Blues: An Interpretation*. New York: Seabury Press, 1972.
Congar, Yves. *A History of Theology*, edited by Hunter Guthrie. New York: Doubleday, 1968.
Congregation for the Clergy. *The Gift of the Priestly Vocation. Ratio Fundamentalis Institutionis Sacerdotalis*. Vatican City: Osservatore Romano, 8 December 2016.
Congregation for the Doctrine of the Faith. *Collaboration of Men and Women in the Church*. 13 July 2004.
Congregation for Institutes of Consecrated Life and Societies of Apostolic Life, *Apostolic Visitation Final Report*. Vatican, 2014.
Conway, Daniel W. 'The Case of Wagner and Nietzsche Contra Wagner'. In *A Companion to Friedrich Nietzsche*, edited by Paul Bishop, 279–307. Rochester and New York: Boydell & Brewer, 2012.
Conway, Eamon. *The Anonymous Christian – a Relativised Christianity? An Evaluation of Hans Urs von Balthasar's Criticism of Karl Rahner's Theory of the Anonymous Christian*. New York: Peter Lang, 1993.

Crowe, Frederick E. 'All My Work Has Been Introducing History into Catholic Theology (Lonergan, March 28, 1980)'. *Lonergan Workshop* 10 (1994): 49–81.
Crowe, Frederick E. *Method in Theology: An Organon for Our Time*. Milwaukee, WI: Marquette University Press, 1980.
Crowe, Frederick E. 'Rethinking God-with-Us: Categories from Lonergan'. *Science et Esprit* XVI, no. 2 (1989): 167–88.
Culbertson, Philip Leroy and Elaine Mary Wainwright. *The Bible in/and Popular Culture: A Creative Encounter*. Atlanta: Society of Biblical Literature, 2010.
Dadosky, John D. *The Eclipse and Recovery of Beauty: A Lonergan Approach*. Toronto: University of Toronto Press, 2014.
Dadosky, John D. 'The Original Green Campaign: Dr. Hildegard of Bingen's Viriditas as Complement to Laudato Si'. *Toronto Journal of Theology* 34, no. 1 (2018): 79–95.
Dahill, Lisa Elaine. *Reading from the Underside of Selfhood: Bonhoeffer and Spiritual Formation*. ProQuest Dissertations Publishing, Graduate Theological Union, Berkeley, CA, 2001.
Daly, Gabriel. *Creation and Redemption*. Dublin, Ireland: Gill and Macmillan, 1988.
Daly, Mary. *Beyond God the Father: Toward a Philosophy of Women's Liberation*. Boston: Beacon Press, 1985.
Daly, Mary. *The Church and the Second Sex*. New York: Harper & Row, 1968.
Davidson, Robert. *The Courage to Doubt: Exploring an Old Testament Theme*. London: SCM Press, 1983.
Davies, Stephen. 'Defining Art and Artworlds'. *Journal of Aesthetics & Art Criticism* 73, no. 4 (Fall 2015): 375–84.
De Gruchy, John W. *Christianity, Art, and Transformation: Theological Aesthetics in the Struggle for Justice*. Cambridge: Cambridge University Press, 2001.
DeNora, Tia. *Music in Everyday Life*. Cambridge: Cambridge University Press, 2000.
Descartes, René. *Discourse on Method*. Translated by Laurence J. Lafleur. New York: Liberal Arts Press, 1970.
Deusen, Nancy Van. 'Material: Phillip the Chancellor and the Reception of Aristotle's Physics'. In *Resonant Witness: Conversations between Music and Theology*, edited by Jeremy Begbie and Steven R. Guthrie, 46–64. Grand Rapids, MI: William B. Eerdmans, 2011.
Doran, Robert M. 'Lonergan and Balthasar: Methodological Considerations'. *Theological Studies* 58, no. 1 (1997): 61.
Doran, Robert M. *Theology and the Dialectics of History*. Toronto, Canada: University of Toronto Press, 1990.
Dowley, Tim. *Christian Music: A Global History*. Minneapolis MN: Fortress Press, 2011.
Dramm, Sabine. *Dietrich Bonhoeffer: An Introduction to His Thought*. Peabody, MA: Hendrickson Publishers, 2007.
Dreyer, Elizabeth. *Accidental Theologians: Four Women Who Shaped Christianity*. Cincinnati, OH: Franciscan Media, 2014.
Dreyfus, Laurence. *Bach and the Patterns of Invention*. Cambridge, MA: Harvard University Press, 2004.
Dufourmantelle, Anne. *In Praise of Risk*. New York: Fordham University Press, 2019.
Edwards, Denis. *Breath of Life: A Theology of the Creator Spirit*. Maryknoll, NY: Orbis Books, 2004.

Edwards, Denis. *Christian Understandings of Creation: The Historical Trajectory*. New York: Fortress, 2017.
Edwards, Denis. *Deep Incarnation: God's Redemptive Suffering with Creatures*. Maryknoll, NY: Orbis Books, 2019.
Edwards, Denis. *Ecology at the Heart of Faith*. Maryknoll, NY: Orbis Books, 2006.
Edwards, Denis. *Human Experience of God*. New York: Paulist Press, 1983.
Edwards, Denis. *Jesus and the Cosmos*. Homebush, NSW: St Paul Publications, 1991.
Edwards, Denis. *Jesus and the Natural World: Exploring a Christian Approach to Ecology*, edited by Geraldine Corridon. Mulgrave, VIC: John Garratt Publishing, 2012.
Edwards, Denis. *Jesus the Wisdom of God: An Ecological Theology*. Homebush, NSW: St. Pauls, 1995.
Edwards, Denis. *Called to Be Church in Australia: An Approach to the Renewal of Local Churches*. Homebush, NSW: St. Paul Publications, 1987.
Edwards, Denis. *Made from Stardust: Exploring the Place of Human Beings within Creation*. North Blackburn, VIC: Collins Dove, 1992.
Edwards, Denis. *The Natural World and God: Theological Explorations*. Adelaide: ATF Press, 2017.
Edwards, Denis. *Partaking of God: Trinity, Evolution, and Ecology*. Collegeville, MN: Liturgical Press, 2014.
Edwards, Denis. 'Story of a Theologian of the Natural World'. In *God and the Natural World: Theological Explorations in Appreciation of Denis Edwards*, edited by Ted Peters and Turner Marie, 21–30. Adelaide: ATF Press, 2020.
Edwards, Denis. *What Are They Saying About Salvation?*. New York: Paulist Press, 1986.
Egan, Harvey D. *Karl Rahner: Mystic of Everyday Life*. New York: Crossroad Pub. Co., 1998.
Egan, Keith J. 'The Significance for Theology of the Doctor of the Church: Teresa of Avila'. In *The Pedagogy of God's Image: Essays on Symbol and the Religious Imagination*, edited by Robert Masson, 153–71. Chico, CA: Scholars Press, 1981.
Ellacuria, Ignazio. 'Hacia Una Fundamentación Del Método Teológico Latino-Americano'. *Estudios Centroamericanos* 30 (August–September 1975): 409–25.
Ellis, Carolyn, Tony E. Adams and Arthur P. Bochner. 'Autoethnography: An Overview'. *Forum Qualitative Sozialforschung / Forum: Qualitative Social Research* 12, no. 10 (2011): 273–90.
Ellis Jr, Carl F. *Free at Last?: The Gospel in the African-American Experience*. Downer's Grover, IL: InterVarsity Press, 1996.
Epstein, Heidi. *Melting the Venusberg: A Feminist Theology of Music*. New York: Continuum, 2004.
Faber, Roland, ed. *Theopoetic Folds Philosophizing Multifariousness*, edited by Jeremy Fackenthal, Perspectives in Continental Philosophy. Bronx: Fordham University Press, 2013.
Ferm, Vergilius ed. *Contemporary American Theology: Theological Autobiographies*, 2 vols. New York: Round Table Press, 1932–1933.
Ferraro, Benedito. 'Theology in the Context of Reciprocity and Complementarity between Men and Women'. *Concilium Special Edition on Gender in Theology, Spirituality and Practice* 4 (2012): 36–45.

Filicko, Therese and Sue Anne Lafferty. 'Defining the Arts and Cultural Universe: Lessons from the Profiles Project'. *Journal of Arts Management, Law & Society* 32, no. 3 (Fall 2002): 185.
Fillingim, David. *Redneck Liberation: Country Music as Theology*. Macon, GA: Mercer University Press, 2003.
Fiorenza, Elisabeth Schüssler. *Jesus, Miriam's Child, Sophia's Prophet: Critical Issues in Feminist Christology*, 2nd ed. London, England: Bloomsbury T&T Clark, 2015.
Fisichella, Rino. 'Beauty'. In *Dictionary of Fundamental Theology*, edited by Rene Latourelle and Rino Fisichella, 77–8. New York: Crossroad, 1994.
Flanagan, Sabina. *Hildegard of Bingen, 1098–1179 A Visionary Life*, 2nd ed. London and New York: Routledge, 1998.
Foley, Edward. 'Liturgical Music: A Bibliographical Essay'. In *Liturgy and Music: Lifetime Learning*, edited by Robin A. Leaver, Joyce Ann Zimmerman and John Francis Baldovin, 411–52. Collegeville, MN: Liturgical Press, 1998.
Ford, David. *The Modern Theologians: An Introduction to Christian Theology in the Twentieth Century*, 3rd ed. Oxford and New York: Blackwell, 2013.
Fowler, James W. *Stages of Faith: The Psychology of Human Development and the Quest for Meaning*. New York: HarperOne a Division of HarperCollins Publishers, 1995.
Francis. *Apostolic Exhortation Evangelii Gaudium*. Vatican City: AAS, 2013.
Francis. *Discourse at the Pontifical Theological Faculty of Southern Italy*. Vatican: Vatican News, 21 June 2019.
Francis. *Lumen Fidei: Encyclical Letter of the Supreme Pontiff Francis to the Bishops, Priests, and Deacons, Consecrated Persons, and the Lay Faithful on Faith*. Image, 2013.
Frazão, Jose. *Penser la Dynamique Croyante de l'Humain. La foi comme nouveau parcours de théologie fondamentale chez PierAngelo Sequeri*. Paris: Centre Sèvres, 2005.
Friedan, Betty. *The Feminine Mystique*. New York: Norton, 1963.
Fuentes, Agustin. *Why We Believe Evolution and the Human Way of Being*. New Haven: Yale University Press, 2019.
Gaar, Gillian G. and Yoko Ono. *She's a Rebel: The History of Women in the Rock and Roll*. Seattle, WA: Seal Press, 1992.
Gadamer, H. G. 'Artworks in Word and Image: 'So True, So Full of Being!' (Goethe) (1992)'. *Theory, Culture and Society* 23, no. 1 (2006): 57–83.
Gadamer, Hans Georg. *Truth and Method*. Translated by Joel Weinsheimer Marshall and G. Donald, 2nd revised ed. New York and London: Continuum, 2004 (1960).
Gaillardetz, Richard R. *By What Authority? Foundations for Understanding Authority in the Church*. Collegeville, MN: Liturgical Press, 2018.
Gaillardetz, Richard R. *When the Magisterium Intervenes: The Magisterium and Theologians in Today's Church. Includes a Case Study on the Doctrinal Investigation of Elizabeth Johnson*. Collegeville, MN and Adelaide: Michael Glazier and ATF, 2012.
Galenson, David W. *Old Masters and Young Geniuses: The Two Life Cycles of Artistic Creativity*. Princeton, NJ: Princeton University Press, 2006.
Gallagher, Michael Paul. *Faith Maps: Ten Religious Explorers from Newman to Joseph Ratzinger*. New York: Paulist Press, 2010.

Gallagher, Michael Paul. *Clashing Symbols: An Introduction to Faith and Culture*. London: Darton, Longman & Todd, 2003.
Gallagher, Michael Paul. 'Contexts and Horizons of Desire: Sebastian Moore's Contribution to Fundamental Theology'. *Lonergan Workshop* 14 (1998): 59–72.
Gallagher, Michael Paul. *Into Extra Time: Living through the Final Stages of Cancer and Jottings Along the Way*. London: Darton, Longman & Todd, 2016.
Gallagher, Michael Paul. 'Truth and Trust: Pierangelo Sequeri's Theology of Faith'. *Irish Theological Quarterly* 73, no. 1–2 (2008): 3–31.
Gallagher, Michael Paul. *What Are They Saying About Unbelief?*. New York: Paulist Press, 1995.
Gardner, Howard. *Creating Minds: An Anatomy of Creativity Seen through the Lives of Freud, Einstein, Picasso, Stravinsky, Eliot, Graham, and Gandhi*. New York: Basic Books, 1993.
Gardner, Howard. *Frames of Mind: The Theory of Multiple Intelligences*. New York: Basic Books, 1983.
Gelinas, Robert. *Finding the Groove: Composing a Jazz-Shaped Faith*. Grand Rapids, MI: Zondervan, 2009.
Gelpi, Donald L. *Encountering Jesus Christ: Rethinking Christological Faith and Commitment*. Milwaukee, WI: Marquette University Press, 2009.
Gerard Whelan SJ. 'The Continuing Significance of Bernard Lonergan'. *Thinking Faith*, 23 September 2008.
Gershon, Walter S. *The Collaborative Turn: Working Together in Qualitative Research*. Rotterdam: Sense, 2009.
Gill, Theodore A. 'Barth and Mozart'. *Theology Today* 43, no. 3 (1986): 403–11.
Gilmour, Michael J. *Call Me the Seeker: Listening to Religion in Popular Music*. New York: Continuum, 2005.
Gilmour, Michael J. *Gods and Guitars: Seeking the Sacred in Post-1960s Popular Music*. Waco, TX: Baylor University Press, 2009.
Godzieba, Anthony J. and Bradford E. Hinze. *Beyond Dogmatism and Innocence: Hermeneutics, Critique, and Catholic Theology*. Collegeville, MN: Liturgical Press, 2017.
Golden, Michael. 'Musicking as Education for Social and Ecological Peace: A New Synthesis'. *Journal of Peace Education: Music and Peace Education* 13, no. 3 (2016): 266–82.
Gonzalez, Michelle A. 'Hans Urs von Balthasar and Contemporary Feminist Theology'. *Theological studies (Baltimore)* 65, no. 3 (2004): 566–95.
Greene, Dana. 'Rosemary Haughton's Contributions to Catholicism Deserve Rediscovery'. *National Catholic Reporter*, 2018.
Gregersen, Niels Henrik. 'The Cross of Christ in an Evolutionary World'. *Dialog* 40, no. 3 (Fall 2001): 192–207.
Gregersen, Niels Henrik. 'Deep Incarnation: Why Evolutionary Continuity Matters in Christology'. *Toronto Journal of Theology* 26, no. 2 (2010): 173–88.
Grenz, Stanley J. and Roger E. Olson. *20th Century Theology: God & the World in a Transitional Age, Twentieth-Century Theology*. Downers Grove: InterVarsity Press, 1992.
Grey, Thomas S. *Wagner's Musical Prose Texts and Contexts*. Cambridge and New York: Cambridge University Press, 1995.

Griffin, John Howard. *Follow the Ecstasy: The Hermitage Years 1965–1968*. Fort Worth: JHG Editions/Latitude Press, 1983.
Grimshaw, Mike, ed. *The Counter-Narratives of Radical Theology and Popular Music: Songs of Fear and Trembling*. New York: Palgrave Macmillan, 2014.
Groupe des, Dombes. *For the Conversion of the Churches*. Geneva: WCC Publications, 1993.
Groupe des, Dombes. *Vers une Même Foi Eucharistique: Accord entre Catholiques et Protestants*. Taize: Les Presses de Taize, 1972.
Guido, D'Arezzo. *Micrologus Guidonis: id est brevis sermo in musica*, edited by O. S. B. Ambrosii and M. Amelli. Romae: Desclee, 1904.
Gutiérrez, Gustavo. *We Drink from Our Own Wells: The Spiritual Journey of a People*. Maryknoll, NY: Orbis Books, 2003.
Gutiérrez, Gustavo. *The Power of the Poor in History: Selected Writings*. Maryknoll, NY: Orbis, 1983.
Gutiérrez, Gustavo. *A Theology of Liberation: History, Politics and Salvation*. Rev edn. London: S.C.M., 1988.
Hadas, Moses and K. G. Fellerer. 'Church Music and the Council of Trent'. *The Musical Quarterly* 49, no. 4 (1953): 576–94.
Hanning, Barbara Russano. *Concise History of Western Music*, edited by Donald Jay Grout. New York: W. W. Norton & Company, 2014.
Hanslick, Eduard. *On the Musically Beautiful: A Contribution Towards the Revision of the Aesthetics of Music*. Translated by Geoffrey Payzant. 8th edn. Indianapolis: Hackett, 1986.
Hargreaves, David J., Dorothy Miell and Raymond A. R. MacDonald. *Musical Imaginations: Multidisciplinary Perspectives on Creativity, Performance, and Perception*. Oxford: Oxford University Press, 2012.
Harrison, Carol. 'Augustine and the Art of Music'. In *Resonant Witness: Conversations between Music and Theology*, edited by Jeremy Begbie and Steven R. Guthrie, 27–45. Grand Rapids, MI: William B. Eerdmans, 2011.
Harrison, Carol. *The Art of Listening in the Early Church*. Oxford: Oxford University Press, 2013.
Hart, David Bentley. *The Beauty of the Infinite: The Aesthetics of Christian Truth*. Grand Rapids, MI: William B. Eerdmans, 2003.
Haughton, Rosemary. *The Catholic Thing*. Springfield: Templegate Publishers, 1979.
Haughton, Rosemary. *The Changing Church*. London: Geoffrey Chapman, 1969.
Haughton, Rosemary. *The Children: Heirs of the Kingdom*. London: Darton, Longman & Todd, 1961.
Haughton, Rosemary. *The Gospel Where It Hits Us: Christianity and Contemporary Concerns*. London: Geoffrey Chapman, 1968.
Haughton, Rosemary. *The Changing Church*. London: Geoffrey Chapman, 1969.
Haughton, Rosemary. *Married Love in Christian Life*. London: Burns & Oates, 1966.
Haughton, Rosemary. *The Mystery of Sexuality*. London: Darton, Longman and Todd, 1973.
Haughton, Rosemary. *On Trying to Be Human*. London: Geoffrey Chapman, 1966.
Haughton, Rosemary. *The Passionate God*. London: Darton Longman and Todd, 1982.
Haughton, Rosemary. *Problems of Christian Marriage*. New York: Paulist Press Deus Books, 1968.

Haughton, Rosemary. 'One Good Reason Why I'm Catholic'. *U.S. Catholic* 59, no. 5 (1994): 18.

Haughton, Rosemary. 'Something Important'. *Sign* 57 (1978).

Haughton, Rosemary. *Song in a Strange Land: The Wellspring Story and the Homelessness of Women*. Springfield, IL: Templegate Publishers, 1990.

Haughton, Rosemary. *The Theology of Experience*. Paramus, NJ: Newman Press, 1972.

Haughton, Rosemary. *The Theology of Marriage*. Cork: Mercier Press, 1971.

Haughton, Rosemary. 'Transcendence and the Bewilderment of Being Modern'. In *A Catholic Modernity? Charles Taylor's Marianist Award Lecture, with Responses by William M. Shea, Rosemary Luling Haughton, George Marsden, Jean Bethke Elshtain*, edited by James Heft, 65–82. Oxford: Oxford University Press, 1999.

Haughton, Rosemary. *The Transformation of Man: A Study of Conversion and Community*. London: Chapman, 1967.

Haughton, Rosemary. 'We Caught the Touch of Incarnate Love'. *National Catholic Reporter* 18 (October 1982): 8.

Hawking, Stephen. *A Brief History of Time: From the Big Bang to Black Holes*. London: Bantam, 1988.

Heaney, Maeve Louise. 'Can Music "Mirror" God? A Theological-Hermeneutical Exploration of Music in the Light of Arvo Part's Spiegel Im Spiegel'. *Religions* 5, no. 2 (2014): 361–84.

Heaney, Maeve Louise. 'The Eloquence of Music in Contemporary Culture'. *Theology* 114, no. 3 (2011): 198–206.

Heaney, Maeve Louise. 'From the Particular to the Universal: Musings of a Woman Theologian'. In *Catholic Women Speak: Visions and Vocations*, edited by Tina Beattie and Diana Culbertson, 211–19. New York and Mahwah, NJ: Paulist Press, 2018.

Heaney, Maeve Louise. 'A Hermeneutical Exploration of the Revelatory Text of John 4:1–42, in a Performative Key'. *Theological Studies (Baltimore)* 81, no. 2 (2020): 278–302.

Heaney, Maeve Louise. 'Mercy, Music and the Prophetic Voice of Theology'. In *Music, Theology, and Justice*, edited by Michael Connor, Hyun-Ah Kim and Christina Labriola, 43–62. Lanham: Lexington Books, 2017.

Heaney, Maeve Louise. 'Music and Theological Method: A Lonerganian Approach'. *Theological Studies* 77, no. 3 (2016): 678–703.

Heaney, Maeve Louise. *Music as Theology: What Music Has to Say About the Word*. Eugene, OR: Pickwick Publications Wipf and Stock, 2012.

Heaney, Maeve Louise. 'Musical Space: Living in-between the Artistic and Christian Callings'. In *Secular Music and Sacred Theology*, edited by Tom Beaudoin, 16–31. Collegeville, MN: Liturgical Press, 2013.

Heaney, Maeve Louise and Roger Hillman. 'Music's Multilayered Subversion of the Word'. *Literature and Theology* 31, no. 2 (2017): 200–14.

Heaps, Jonathan and Neil Ormerod. 'Statistically Ordered: Gender, Sexual Identity, and the Metaphysics of "Normal"'. *Theological Studies* 80, no. 2 (2019): 346–69.

Hecht, Jennifer Michael. *Doubt: A History: The Great Doubters and their Legacy of Innovation, from Socrates and Jesus to Thomas Jefferson and Emily Dickinson*. San Francisco: Harper, 2003.

Hildegard. *Hildegard of Bingen's Book of Divine Works: With Letters and Songs.* Santa Fe, NM: Bear & Co., 1987.

Hildegard of Bingen. 'Ordo Virtutum: The Play of the Virtues by Hildegard of Bingen'. In *Nine Medieval Latin Plays*, edited by Peter Dronke, 147–84. Cambridge: Cambridge University Press, 1994.

Hinze, Bradford E. and Christine Firer Hinze. 'The Elizabeth A. Johnson Case in the United States'. In *Gender in Theology, Spirituality and Practice*, edited by Lisa Cahill, Diego Irarrazaval Sowle and Wainwright Elaine Mary, 121–5. London: SCM Press, 2012.

Hoenen, Peter. *Reality and Judgement According to St Thomas.* Translated by S. J. Henry and F. Tiblier. Chicago: Regnery, 1952.

Holland, Scott. *How Do Stories Save Us? An Essay on the Question with the Theological Hermeneutics of David Tracy in View.* Grand Rapids, MI: William B. Eerdmans, 2006.

Holland, Scott. 'The Poet, Theopoetics, and Theopolitics'. *Cross Currents* 64, no. 4 (2014): 496–508.

Holland, Scott. 'Theopoetics Is the Rage'. *The Conrad Grebel Review* 31, no. 2 (2013): 121–9.

Hopper, Stanley Romaine. 'The Literary Imagination and the Doing of Theology'. In *The Way of Transfiguration: Religious Imagination as Theopoiesis*, edited by Melvin Keiser and Tony Stoneburner, 207–29. Louisville: Westminster/John Knox, 1992.

Howison, Jamie. *God's Mind in That Music: Theological Explorations through the Music of John Coltrane.* Portland, OR: Wipf and Stock Publishers, 2012.

Hudson, Wayne. *Australian Religious Thought.* Clayton, VIC: Monash University Press, 2016.

Hunsinger, George. *How to Read Karl Barth: The Shape of His Theology.* New York: Oxford University Press, 1991.

Illman, Ruth and W. Alan Smith. *Theology of the Arts: Engaging Faith.* New York: Routledge, 2013.

International Theological Commission. *The Hope of Salvation for Infants Who Die without Being Baptised*, Vatican, 2007.

Irwin, Joyce L. *God Is a Question, Not an Answer: Finding Common Ground in Our Uncertainty.* Lanham: Rowman & Littlefield, 2019.

Irwin, Joyce L. *Neither Voice for Heart Alone: German Lutheran Theology of Music in the Age of the Baroque.* New York: Peter Lang, 1993.

Ito, John Paul. 'On Music, Mathematics and Theology: Pythagoras, the Mind and Human Agency'. In *Resonant Witness: Conversations between Music and Theology*, edited by Jeremy Begbie and Steven R. Guthrie, 109–34. Grand Rapids, MI: William B. Eerdmans, 2011.

Johann Roten, S. M. 'Two Halves of the Moon: Marian Anthropological Dimensions in the Common Mission of Adrienne Von Speyr and Hans Urs von Balthasar'. In *Hans Urs von Balthasar: His Life and Work*, edited by David L. Schindler, 65–86. San Francisco: Ignatius Press, 1991.

John-Steiner, Vera. *Creative Collaboration.* New York: Oxford University Press, 2000.

John, Helen J. 'Hildegard of Bingen: A New Twelfth-Century Woman Philosopher?'. *Hypatia* 7, no. 1 (1992): 115–23.

John Paul II. *The Consecrated Life: Post-Synodal Apostolic Exhortation Vita Consecrata, Consecrated Life and Its Mission in the Church and in the World*. Homebush, NSW: St. Pauls, 1996.

John Paul II. *Fides Et Ratio: Encyclical Letter of the Supreme Pontiff John Paul II, to the Bishops of the Catholic Church on the Relationship between Faith and Reason*. Strathfield, NSW: St. Pauls Publications, 1998.

John Paul II. *Letter to Women*. Vatican: Libreria Editrice Vaticana, 1995.

John Paul II. *Letter of His Holiness Pope John Paul II to Artists*. Vatican City, 1999.

John Paul II. *Mulieris Dignitatem: On the Dignity and Vocation of Women*. Vatican: Vatican Press, 1988.

John Paul II. *Pastores Dabo Vobis: Post-Synodal Exhortation on the Formation of Priests in the Circumstances of the Present Day*. Vatican City: Libreria Editrice Vaticana, 25 March 1992.

Johnson, Elizabeth A. *Ask the Beasts: Darwin and the God of Love*. London: Bloomsbury, 2014.

Johnson, Elizabeth A. *The Church Women Want: Catholic Women in Dialogue*. New York: Crossroad Pub. Co., 2002.

Johnson, Elizabeth A. *Consider Jesus: Waves of Renewal in Christology*. New York: Crossroad Publishing Company, 2017.

Johnson, Elizabeth A. *Creation and the Cross: The Mercy of God for a Planet in Peril*. Maryknoll: Orbis Books, 2018.

Johnson, Elizabeth A. 'The Marian Tradition and the Reality of Women'. *Horizons* 12, no. 1 (Spr 1985): 116–35.

Johnson, Elizabeth A. *Quest for the Living God: Mapping Frontiers in the Theology of God*. New York: Continuum, 2007.

Johnson, Elizabeth A. *She Who Is: The Mystery of God in Feminist Theological Discourse*. 25th Anniversary edn. New York: Crossroad Publishing Company, 2017.

Johnson, Elizabeth A. *The Strength of Her Witness: Jesus Christ in the Global Voices of Women*. Maryknoll, NY: Orbis Books, 2016.

Johnson, Elizabeth A. *Truly Our Sister: A Theology of Mary in the Communion of Saints*. New York and London: Continuum, 2003.

Johnson, Elizabeth A. *Women, Earth, and Creator Spirit*. New York: Paulist Press, 1993.

Kant, Immanuel. *Critique of the Power of Judgment*. Cambridge: Cambridge University Press, 2000.

Kant, Immanuel. *Religion within the Limits of Reason Alone*. New York: Harper, 1960.

Kearney, Richard. *Anatheism: Returning to God after God*. New York: Columbia University Press, 2011.

Keefe-Perry, L Callid. 'Theopoetics: Process and Perspective'. *Literature and Christianity* 58, no. 4 (2009): 579–601.

Keefe-Perry, L. Callid. *Way to Water: A Theopoetics Primer*. Eugene, OR: Cascade Books, 2014.

Keenan, Marie. *Child Sexual Abuse and the Catholic Church: Gender, Power, and Organizational Culture*. Oxford: Oxford University Press, 2012.

Keller, Catherine. 'The Flesh of God'. In *Theology That Matters: Ecology, Economy, and God*, edited by Kathleen Ray Darby, 91–108. Minneapolis: Fortress Press, 2006.

Kennedy, Philip. *Twentieth Century Theologians: A New Introduction to Modern Christian Thought*. London: I.B. Tauris & Co. Ltd., 2010.
Kepler, Johannes. *The Harmony of the World*. Translated by E. J. Aiton, A. M. Duncan and Judith Veronica Field. Philadelphia, PA: American Philosophical Society, 1997.
Kerman, Joseph. *Contemplating Music Challenges to Musicology*. Cambridge: Harvard University Press, 1985.
Kerr, Fergus. 'Adrienne Von Speyr and Hans Urs von Balthasar'. *New Blackfriars* 79, no. 923 (1998): 26–32.
Kerr, Fergus. *Twentieth-Century Catholic Theologians: From Neoscholasticism to Nuptial Mysticism*. Malden, MA: Blackwell Pub., 2007.
Kettler, Christian D. *The God Who Believes: Faith, Doubt and the Victorious Humanity of Christ*. Eugene, OR: Cascade Books, 2005.
Kierkegaard, Søren. 'The Immediate Erotic Stages or the Musical-Erotic'. In *Kierkegaard's Writing, III, Part I, Either/Or*, edited by Howard V. Hong and Edna H. Hong, 45–136. Princeton: Princeton University Press, 1987.
Kierkegaard, Søren. *Kierkegaard's Concluding Unscientific Postscript*. Translated by David F. Swenson. Princeton: Princeton University Press, 1941.
Kilby, Karen. *Balthasar: A (Very) Critical Introduction*. Grand Rapids, MI: William B. Eerdmans, 2012.
King-Lenzmeier, Anne H. *Hildegard of Bingen: An Integrated Vision*. Collegeville, MN: Liturgical Press, 2001.
King, Roberta R. 'Performing Witness: Loving Our Religious Neighbors through Musicking'. In *Arts as Witness in Multifaith Contexts*, edited by R. R. King and W. A. Dryness, 39–66. Downers Grove: IVP Academic, 2019.
Koskoff, Ellen. *Women and Music in Cross-Cultural Perspective*. Vol. 79. Illinois: University of Illinois Press, 1987.
Krabbe, Silas C. *A Beautiful Bricolage. Theopoetics as God-Talk for Our Time*. Eugene OR: Wipf and Stock, 2016.
Kropf, Richard W. *Faith, Security and Risk: The Dynamics of Spiritual Growth*. New York: Paulist Press, 1990.
Kuiken, Rebecca. 'The Living Edge of Faith: Doubt and Skepticism in the Formation of Pastor-Theologians'. In *The Power to Comprehend with All the Saints: The Formation and Practice of a Pastor-Theologian*, edited by Wallace M. Alston, Cynthia A. Jarvis, 111–30. Grand Rapids, MI: William B. Eerdmans, 2009.
Lane, Belden C. 'Writing in Spirituality as a Self-Implicating Act. Reflections on Authorial Disclosure and the Hiddenness of the Self'. In *Exploring Christian Spirituality: Essays in Honor of Sandra M. Schneiders*, edited by Bruce H. Lescher and Elizabeth Liebert, 53–69. New York: Paulist Press, 2006.
Lane, Dermot A. *The Experience of God: An Invitation to Do Theology*. New York: Paulist Press, 2003.
Langer, Susanne K. *Feeling and Form: A Theory of Art Developed from Philosophy in a New Key*. London: Routledge and Kegan Paul, 1953.
Langer, Susanne K. *Philosophy in a New Key: A Study in the Symbolism of Reason, Rite, and Art*. 3rd edn. Cambridge: Harvard University Press, 1957.
Latour, Bruno. *Science in Action: How to Follow Scientists and Engineers through Society*. Cambridge, MA: Harvard University Press, 1987.
Lawrence, Frederick G. 'Grace and Friendship. Postmodern Political Theology and God as Conversational'. *Gregorianum* 85, no. 4 (2004): 795–820.

Le Mée, Katharine W. *The Benedictine Gift to Music*. New York: Paulist Press, 2003.
Leaver, Robin A. *J. S. Bach and Scripture: Glosses from the Calov Bible Commentary*. St. Louis, MO: Concordia Publishing House, 1985.
Leaver, Robin A. 'Music and Lutheranism'. In *The Cambridge Companion to Bach*, edited by John Butt, 35–45. Cambridge: Cambridge University Press, 1997.
Leaver, Robin A. *Music as Preaching: Bach, Passions and Music in Worship*. Oxford: Latimar House, 1982.
Leibniz, Gottfried Wilhelm. *Theodicy: Essays on the Goodness of God the Freedom of Man*. Eugene, OR: Wipf and Stock, 2001.
Lerner, Gerda. *The Creation of Patriarchy*. New York: Oxford University Press, 1986.
Lescher, Bruce H. and Elizabeth Liebert, eds. *Exploring Christian Spirituality: Essays in Honor of Sandra M. Schneiders*. New York: Paulist Press, 2006.
LeVine, Mark, *Heavy Metal Islam: Rock, Resistance, and the Struggle for the Soul of Islam*. New York: Three Rivers Press, 2008.
Lewis-Williams, J. and David Pearce. 'The Southern San and the Trance Dance: A Pivotal Debate in the Interpretation of San Rock Paintings'. *Antiquity* 86, no. 333 (2012): 696–706.
Lewis, Clive Staples. *The Chronicles of Narnia*. New York: Harper Collins, 2001.
Liddy, Richard M. *Startling Strangeness: Reading Lonergan's Insight*. Lanham, MD: University Press of America, 2007.
Liddy, Richard M. *Transforming Light: Intellectual Conversion in the Early Lonergan*. Collegeville, MN: Liturgical Press, 1993.
Lim, Swee Hong. 'Forming Christians through Musicking in China'. *Religions* 8, no. 4 (2017): 1–10.
Liszt, Franz. *Les Préludes and Other Symphonic Poems*. New York: Dover, 1994.
Loewe, William P. 'Sebastian Moore, Redemptive Transformation, and the Law of the Cross'. *Downside Review* 136, no. 3 (2018): 178–85.
Loewe, William P. and Vernon J. Gregson, eds. *Jesus Crucified and Risen: Essays in Spirituality and Theology in Honor of Dom Sebastian Moore*. Collegeville, MN: Liturgical Press, 1998.
Lonergan, Bernard J. F. 'Art'. In *Collected Works of Bernard Lonergan. Vol. 10: Topics in Education*, edited by R. M. Doran and F. E. Crowe, 208–32. Toronto: University of Toronto Press, 1993.
Lonergan, Bernard J. F. 'Belief: Today's Issue'. In *A Second Collection. Papers by Bernard J. F. Lonergan S. J.*, edited by F. E. Crowe and R. M. Doran, 87–99. London: Darton, Longman and Todd, 1974.
Lonergan, Bernard J. F. 'Dimensions of Meaning'. In *Collection. Papers by Bernard Lonergan S.J.*, edited by F. E. Crowe and R. M. Doran, 252–67. New York: Herder and Herder, 1967.
Lonergan, Bernard J. F. 'Existenz and Aggiornamento'. In *Collection. Papers by Bernard Lonergan S. J.*, edited by F. E. Crowe and R. M. Doran, 240–51. New York: Herder and Herder, 1967.
Lonergan, Bernard J. F. 'The Future of Christianity'. In *A Second Collection. Papers by Bernard J. F. Lonergan S. J.*, edited by F. J. Ryan and B. J. Tyrell, 149–63. London: Darton, Longman and Todd, 1974.
Lonergan, Bernard J. F. *Grace and Freedom: Operative Grace in the Thought of St. Thomas Aquinas, Collected Works of Bernard Lonergan*, edited by

Frederick E. Crowe and Robert M. Doran. Vol. 1. Toronto: University of Toronto Press, 2000.

Lonergan, Bernard J. F. *Insight, Collected Works of Bernard Lonegan*, edited by Frederick E. Crowe and Robert M. Doran. Toronto: University of Toronto Press, 1957.

Lonergan, Bernard J. F. *Method in Theology*. New York: The Seabury Press, 1972.

Lonergan, Bernard J. F. 'Mission and the Spirit'. In *Collected Works of Bernard Lonergan. A Third Collection*, edited by Robert M. Doran and John D. Dadosky, 21–33. Lonergan Research Institute, Regis College, Toronto: University of Toronto Press, 1985.

Lonergan, Bernard J. F. 'Pope John's Intention'. In *A Third Collection. Papers by Bernard F. J. Lonergan*, edited by F. E. Crowe, 225–38. New York: Paulist Press, 1985.

Lonergan, Bernard J. F. 'Theology in Its New Context'. In *A Second Collection. Papers by Bernard J. F. Lonergan S. J.*, edited by F. J. Ryan and B. J. Tyrell, 55–68. London: Darton, Longman and Todd, 1974.

López-Cano, Ruben. 'Art Research, Music Knowledge and the Contemporary Crisis'. *Art Research Journal* 1 (2015): 69–94.

Lösel, Steffen. 'Clemency and Conversion: Theological Reflections on Mozart's La Clemenza di Tito'. *Modern Theology* 34, no. 4 (2018): 637–56.

Lundin, Roger. *Believing Again: Doubt and Faith in a Secular Age*. Grand Rapids, MI: William B. Eerdmans, 2009.

Luther, Martin. *Works*, edited by Jaroslav Jan Pelikan and Helmut T. Lehmann. Saint Louis: Concordia Pub. House, 1955.

Lynch, Danielle Anne. *God in Sound and Silence: Music as Theology*. Eugene, OR: Pickwick Publications, 2018.

Lynch, Gordon. 'The Role of Popular Music in the Construction of Alternative Spiritual Identities and Ideologies'. *Journal for the Scientific Study of Religion* 45, no. 4 (2006): 481–8.

Lynch, Gordon. *Understanding Theology and Popular Culture*. Malden, MA: Blackwell Pub., 2005.

Lynch, Gordon and Emily Badger. 'The Mainstream Post-Rave Club Scene as a Secondary Institution: A British Perspective'. *Culture and Religion* 7, no. 1 (2006): 27–40.

Mackay, Hugh. *Beyond Belief*. Sydney, NSW: Macmillan, 2016.

Macquarrie, John. *God-Talk: An Examination of the Language and Logic of Theology*. New York: Seabury Press, 1979.

Madeleva Lecturers in Spirituality, 1985–2001. *The Madaleva Manifesto: A Message of Hope and Courage*, 2000.

Madges, William and Michael J. Daley. *Vatican II: Fifty Personal Stories, Vatican 2*. Revised and Expanded edn. Maryknoll, NY: Orbis Books, 2012.

Maher, James. *The Christian Songwriter as Theologian: Giving Voice to the Converted Heart and Mind*. MCD University of Divinity, 2013.

Mahler, Margaret S. *The Psychological Birth of the Human Infant Symbiosis and Individuation*, edited by Fred Pine and Anni Bergman. London: Karnac Books, 1985.

Malone, Mary T. *Four Women Doctors of the Church. Hildegard of Bingen, Catherine of Siena, Teresa of Ávila, Thérèse of Lisieux*. Dublin: Veritas, 2015.

Manson, Jamie. 'Biblical Scholar Sr. Sandra Schneiders Celebrates Four Milestones'. *Global Sisters Report*, 25 January 2017.

Marcocchi, Massimo. 'Spirituality in the Sixteenth and Seventeenth Centuries'. In *Catholicism in Early Modern History: A Guide to Research*, edited by John W. O'Malley, 163–92. St. Louis, MO: Center for Reformation Research, 1988.

Marius, Schneider. *La Musica Primitiva*. Adelphi: Milano, 1992.

Martos, Joseph. *Doors to the Sacred: A Historical Introduction to Sacraments in the Catholic Church: Updated and Enlarged with Charts and Glossary*. Liguori, MO: Liguori Publications, 2014.

May, Melanie A. *A Body Knows: A Theopoetics of Death and Resurrection*. New York: Continuum, 1995.

McBride, Jennifer M. 'Bonhoeffer and Feminist Theologies'. In *The Oxford Handbook of Dietrich Bonhoeffer*, edited by Philip Gordon Ziegler and Michael G. Mawson, 365–84. Oxford: Oxford University Press, 2019.

McClary, Susan. *Feminine Endings: Music, Gender, and Sexuality*. Minneapolis: University of Minnesota Press, 2002.

McClary, Susan and Robert Walser. 'Theorizing the Body in African-American Music'. *Black Music Research Journal* 14, no. 1 (1994): 75–84.

McClendon, James Wm, Jr. *Biography as Theology: How Life Stories Can Remake Today's Theology*. Nashville: Abingdon Press, 1974.

McDonagh, Sean. *To Care for the Earth: A Call to a New Theology*. London: Geoffrey Chapman, 1986.

McEvoy, James Gerard. 'Theology of Childhood: An Essential Element of Christian Anthropology'. *Irish Theological Quarterly* 84, no. 2 (2019): 117–36.

McEvoy, James Gerard. 'Towards a Theology of Childhood: Children's Agency and the Reign of God'. *Theological Studies* 80, no. 3 (2019): 673–91.

McFague, Sallie. *The Body of God: An Ecological Theology*. London: SCM Press, 1993.

McFague, Sallie. *Life Abundant: Rethinking Theology and Economy for a Planet in Peril*. Minneapolis, MN: Fortress Press, 2000.

McFague, Sallie. *Models of God: Theology for an Ecological, Nuclear Age*. Minneapolis, MN: Fortress Press, 1987.

McFarland, Ian A., David A. S. Fergusson, Karen Kilby and Iain R. Torrance. *The Cambridge Dictionary of Christian Theology*. New York: Cambridge University Press, 2011.

McLeish, Kenneth. *Bloomsbury Guide to Human Thought*. London: Bloomsbury, 1993.

McGrath, Tom et al. *One Good Reason Why I'm Catholic*, 21–2. Chicago: Claretian Publications, 1994.

Mellers, Wilfrid Howard. *Bach and the Dance of God*. London: Faber, 1980.

Melling, Joseph. 'Sebastian Moore: A Life in Movements'. *Downside Review* (2018): 1–4.

Melling, Joseph. 'Sebastian Moore: Beyond Piety'. *Downside Review* 136, no. 3 (2018): 145–7.

Mercer, Joyce and Bonnie Miller-McLemore. *Conundrums in Practical Theology*. Leiden: Brill, 2016.

Messiaen, Olivier. *The Technique of My Musical Language*. Translated by John Satterfield. Paris: Alphonse Leduc, 1956.

Messiaen, Olivier and Melody Ann Baggech. 'An English Translation of Olivier Messiaen's "Traite de Rythme, de Couleur, et d'Ornithologie"'. University of Oklahoma, 1998.

Metz, Johann Baptist. *Faith in History and Society: Toward a Practical Fundamental Theology*, edited by Norman David Smith. London: Burns and Oates, 1980.
Míguez Bonino, José. *Doing Theology in a Revolutionary Situation*. Philadelphia: Fortress Press, 1975.
Miles, Margaret Ruth. *Image as Insight: Visual Understanding in Western Christianity and Secular Culture*. Boston: Beacon Press, 1985.
Moltmann, Jürgen. *The Crucified God: The Cross of Christ as the Foundation and Criticism of Christian Theology*. London: SCM Press, 1974.
Moltmann, Jürgen. *God in Creation: A New Theology of Creation and the Spirit of God*. 1st Fortress Press edn. Minneapolis, MN: Fortress Press, 1993.
Moltmann, Jürgen. *The Way of Jesus Christ: Christology in Messianic Dimensions*. London: SCM Press, 1990.
Mooney, Hilary A. *The Liberation of Consciousness: Bernard Lonergan's Theological Foundations in Dialogue with the Theological Aesthetics of Hans Urs von Balthasar*. Frankfurt: Knecht, 1992.
Moore, Sebastian. *The Contagion of Jesus: Doing Theology as If It Mattered*, edited by Stephen McCarthy. Maryknoll, NY: Orbis, 2007.
Moore, Sebastian. *The Crucified Jesus Is No Stranger*. New York: Paulist, 1977.
Moore, Sebastian. *The Fire and the Rose Are One*. London: Darton, Longman & Todd, 1980.
Moore, Sebastian. 'Four Steps Towards Making Sense of Theology'. *Downside Review* 111, no. 383 (1993): 79–100.
Moore, Sebastian. 'The Girl Next Door'. *The Irish Theological Quarterly* 62, no. 1 (1996): 49–69.
Moore, Sebastian. *God Is a New Language*. London: Darton, Longman & Todd, 1967.
Moore, Sebastian. *The Inner Loneliness*. London: Darton, Longman & Todd, 1982.
Moore, Sebastian. 'Jesus the Liberator of Desire: Reclaiming Ancient Images'. *Downside Review* 108, no. 370 (1990): 1–19.
Moore, Sebastian. *Let This Mind Be in You: The Quest for Identity through Oedipus to Christ*. Minneapolis: Winston Press, 1985.
Morris, Roy. *Declaring His Genius: Oscar Wilde in North America*. Cambridge: Belknap Press of Harvard University Press, 2013.
Muto, Susan. *Celebrating the Single Life: A Spirituality for Single Persons in Today's World*. New York: Crossroad, 1989.
Nantais, David. *Rock-a My Soul: An Invitation to Rock Your Religion*. Collegeville, MN: Liturgical Press, 2011.
Nattiez, Jean-Jacques. *Fondements D'une Semiologique de la Musique*. Paris: Unions Générale d'Editions, 1975.
Nattiez, Jean-Jacques. *Music and Discourse. Toward a Semiology of Music*. Princeton NJ: Princeton University Press, 1990.
Nattiez, Jean-Jacques. *The Battle of Chronos and Orpheus: Essays in Applied Musical Semiology*. Oxford: Oxford University Press, 2004.
Newbigin, Lesslie. *Proper Confidence: Faith, Doubt, and Certainty in Christian Discipleship*. Grand Rapids, MI: William B. Eerdmans, 1995.
Newheiser, David. *Hope in a Secular Age: Deconstruction, Negative Theology, and the Future of Faith*. Cambridge: Cambridge University Press, 2019.

Newman, John Henry. *An Essay in Aid of a Grammar of Assent, Grammar of Assent*. London: Burns & Oates, 1881.
Newman, John Henry. *The Idea of a University*. New Haven, CT: Yale University Press, 1996.
Newman, John Henry. *Newman's Apologia Pro Vita Sua*. London: H. Frowde, 1913.
Nichols, Aidan. 'Adrienne Von Speyr and the Mystery of the Atonement'. *New Blackfriars* 73, no. 865 (1992): 542–53.
Niebuhr, Richard R. *Experiential Religion*. 1st edn. New York: Harper & Row, 1972.
Nuzzi, Ronald James. *Gifts of the Spirit: Multiple Intelligences in Religious Education*. Washington, DC: National Catholic Educational Association, 1996.
O'Collins, Gerald. *Revelation: Towards a Christian Interpretation of God's Self-Revelation in Jesus Christ*. Oxford: Oxford University Press, 2016.
O'Collins, Gerald. *The Second Vatican Council: Message and Meaning*. Collegeville, MN: Liturgical Press, 2014.
O'Connor, Michael. 'The Singing of Jesus'. In *Resonant Witness: Conversations between Music and Theology*, edited by Jeremy Begbie and Steven R. Guthrie, 434–53. Grand Rapids, MI: William B. Eerdmans, 2011.
O'Donnell, John J. *Hans Urs von Balthasar*. London: Chapman, 1992.
O'Donnell, John J. *Karl Rahner*. Rome: PUG, 1986.
O'Leary, Dale. *The Gender Agenda: Redefining Equality*. Lafayette: Vital Issues Press, LA, 1997.
O'Malley, John W. *Catholic History for Today's Church: How Our Past Illuminates Our Present*. Lanham, MA: Rowman & Littlefield, 2015.
Oliver, Mary. *Truro Bear and Other Adventures: Poems and Essays*. Boston: Beacon Press, 2008.
Olson, Carl. *An Introduction to Religion and Religious Themes in Rock Music*. Lewiston, NY: Edwin Mellen Press, 2011.
Ormerod, Neil. *Introducing Contemporary Theologies: The What and the Who of Theology Today*. Alexandria, NSW: E.J. Dwyer, 1997.
Ormerod, Neil and Christiaan Jacobs-Vandegeer. *Foundational Theology: A New Approach to Catholic Fundamental Theology*. Minneapolis: Fortress Press, 2015.
Palma, Robert J. *Karl Barth's Theology of Culture: The Freedom of Culture for the Praise of God*. Eugene, OR: Wipf and Stock, 1983.
Parsons, Susan Frank. 'Accounting for Hope: Feminist Theology as Fundamental Theology'. In *Challenging Women's Orthodoxies in the Context of Faith*, edited by Susan Frank Parsons. Aldershot: Ashgate, 2000.
Pärt, Arvo. 'Da Pacem Domine'. Universal Edition, 2004.
Partridge, Christopher H. *The Lyre of Orpheus: Popular Music, the Sacred, and the Profane*. Oxford: Oxford University Press, 2014.
Partridge, Christopher H. *The Re-Enchantment of the West: Alternative Spiritualities, Sacralization, Popular Culture, and Occulture, Reenchantment of the West 1 & 2*. London and New York: T&T Clark International, 2004–2005.
Pascal, Blaise. *Pensées*. New York: Philosophical Library: Open Road Integrated Media, Inc., 2016.
Paul VI. *Apostolic Exhortation Evangelii Nuntiandi*. Vatican City, 1976.
Paul VI, *Homily, 'Artists' Mass' in the Sistine Chapel*, Thursday, 7 May 1964.

Pederson, Ann. *God, Creation, and All That Jazz: A Process of Composition and Improvisation*. St. Louis, MO: Chalice Press, 2001.

Pelikan, Jaroslav Jan. *Bach among the Theologians*. Philadelphia: Fortress Press, 1986.

Pendle, Karin. *Women & Music: A History*. Indiana: Indiana University Press, 2001.

Peter Henrici, S. J. 'A Sketch of von Balthasar's Life'. In *Hans Urs von Balthasar: His Life and Work*, edited by David L. Schindler, 7–43. San Francisco: Ignatius Press, 1991.

Peters, Ted, Joshua M. Moritz and Derek R. Nelson. *Theologians in Their Own Words*. Minneapolis: Fortress Press, 2013.

Peters, Ted and Marie Turner. *God and the Natural World: Theological Explorations in Appreciation of Denis Edwards*. Adelaide: ATF Press, 2020.

Pfeifer, Carl J. and Janann Manternach. 'The Processes of Catechesis'. In *Empowering Catechetical Leaders*, edited by Thomas H. Groome and Michael J. Corso. Washington, DC: National Catholic Educational Association, 1999.

Pickstock, Catherine. 'Quasi Una Sonata: Modernism, Postmodernism, Religion, and Music'. In *Resonant Witness: Conversations between Music and Theology*, edited by Jeremy Begbie and Steven R. Guthrie, 190–211. Grand Rapids, MI: William B. Eerdmans, 2011.

Pieper, Josef. *Only the Lover Sings: Art and Contemplation*. San Francisco: Ignatius Press, 1990.

Platinga, Richard J. 'The Integration of Music and Theology in the Vocal Composition of J. S. Bach'. In *Resonant Witness: Conversations between Music and Theology*, edited by Jeremy Begbie and Steven R. Guthrie, 215–39. Grand Rapids, MI: William B. Eerdmans, 2011.

Pope, Stephen J. *Hope & Solidarity: Jon Sobrino's Challenge to Christian Theology*. Maryknoll, NY: Orbis Books, 2008.

Prüller-Jagenteufel, Gunter. '"Restraining Power" against Evil and "Scarring Over" of Guilt: Bonhoefferian Remarks on "Penultimate" Steps toward Reconciliation'. In *Reconciliation: The Way of Healing and Growth*, edited by Janez Juhant and Bojan Žalec, 169–77. Wien-Berlin: LIT Verlag, 2012.

Quinn, Regina Ammicht. 'Dangerous Thinking Gender and Theology'. *Concilium Special Edition on Gender in Theology, Spirituality and Practice* 4 (2012): 13–25.

Rahaim, Matthew. *Musicking Bodies: Gesture and Voice in Hindustani Music*. Middletown, CN: Wesleyan Press, 2012.

Rahner, Karl. 'Experiences of a Catholic Theologian'. Translated by Declan Marmion S.M., and Gesa Thiesson. *Theological Studies* 61, no. 1 (2000): 3–15.

Rahner, Karl. 'Anonymous and Explicit Faith'. In *Theological Investigations XVI*, edited by David Morland, 52–9. London: Darton, Longman and Todd, 1979.

Rahner, Karl. 'Anonymous Christians'. In *Theological Investigations VI*. Translated by Karl-H and Boniface Kruger, 390–8. London: Darton Longman & Todd, 1969.

Rahner, Karl. *The Celebration of the Eucharist*. New York: Herder and Herder, 1968.

Rahner, Karl. 'The Christian among Unbelieving Relations'. In *Theological Investigations III*. Translated by Karl-H and Boniface Kruger, 355–72. London: Darton, Longman & Todd, 1967.

Rahner, Karl. 'Christian Living Formerly and Today'. In *Theological Investigations VII*, edited by David Bourke, 3–14. New York: Seabury, 1977.

Rahner, Karl. 'The Church and Atheism'. In *Theological Investigations XXI: Science and Christian Faith*, edited by Hugh M. Riley, 137–50. New York: Crossroad, 1982.
Rahner, Karl. 'Do Not Stifle the Spirit!'. In *Theological Investigations VII*, edited by David Bourke, 72–87. New York: Seabury, 1977.
Rahner, Karl. *Encounters with Silence*. Westminster: Newman Press, 1960.
Rahner, Karl. *Everyday Things*. London: Sheed and Ward, 1965.
Rahner, Karl. 'Faith between Rationality and Emotion'. In *Theological Investigations XVI*, edited by David Morland, 60–78. London: Darton, Longman and Todd, 1979.
Rahner, Karl. *Faith in a Wintry Season: Conversations and Interviews with Karl Rahner in the Last Years of His Life*, edited by Paul Imhof, Hubert Biallowons and Harvey D. Egan. New York: Crossroad, 1990.
Rahner, Karl. 'The Faith of the Christian and the Doctrine of the Church'. In *Theological Investigations XIV*, edited by David Bourke, 24–45. New York: Seabury, 1976.
Rahner, Karl. *Foundations of Christian Faith: An Introduction to the Idea of Christianity*, edited by William V. Dych. London: Darton Longman & Todd, 1978.
Rahner, Karl. 'Ignatius of Loyola Speaks to a Modern Jesuit'. In *Ignatius of Loyola*, edited by Helmuth Nils Loose, Rosaleen Ockenden and Paul Imhof. London: Collins, 1979.
Rahner, Karl. 'Intellectual Honesty and Christian Faith'. In *Theological Investigations VII*, edited by David Bourke, 47–71. New York: Seabury, 1977.
Rahner, Karl. 'Observations on the Problem of the Anonymous Christian'. In *Theological Investigations XIV*, edited by David Bourke, 280–94. New York: Seabury, 1976.
Rahner, Karl. 'On the Theology of Worship'. In *Theological Investigations XIX*. Translated by Edward Quinn, 141–9. London: Darton, Longman and Todd, 1984.
Rahner, Karl. *The Origin of the Church as the Second Eve from the Side of Christ the Second Adam: An Investigation of The Typological Significance of John 19:34*. Innsbruck, 1936.
Rahner, Karl. 'Poetry and the Christian'. In *Theological Investigations IV*, edited by Henry F. Tiblier, 357–67. London: Darton, Longman and Todd, 1974.
Rahner, Karl. 'Prayer for Creative Thinkers'. In *Theological Investigations VIII*. Translated by David Bourke, 1–30. London: Darton, Longman and Todd, 1971.
Rahner, Karl. 'Priest and Poet'. In *Theological Investigations III*. Translated by David Bourke, 294–316. London: Darton, Longman & Todd, 1967a.
Rahner, Karl. 'Reflections on a New Task for Fundamental Theology'. In *Theological Investigations XVI*, edited by David Morland, 156–66. London: Darton, Longman and Todd, 1979.
Rahner, Karl. 'Reflections on the Experience of Grace'. In *Theological Investigations III*. Translated by David Bourke, 86–90. London: Darton, Longman & Todd, 1967b.
Rahner, Karl. 'A Scheme for a Treatise of Dogmatic Theology'. In *Theological Investigations I: God, Christ, Mary and Grace*. Translated by David Bourke, 19–36. London: Darton, Longman & Todd, 1974.

Rahner, Karl. *Spirit in the World*. Translated by William Dych. London: Sheed & Ward, 1968.
Rahner, Karl. *Spiritual Writings*, edited by Philip Endean. Maryknoll, NY: Orbis Books, 2004.
Rahner, Karl. 'The Task of the Writer in Relation to Christian Living'. In *Theological Investigations VIII: Further Theology of the Spiritual Life*, edited by David Bourke, 112–29. London: Darton, Longman and Todd, 1971.
Rahner, Karl. *Theological Investigations I: God, Christ, Mary and Grace, God, Christ, Mary and Grace*, edited by Cornelius Ernst. London: Darton, Longman & Todd, 1974.
Rahner, Karl. 'Thoughts on the Possibility of Belief Today'. In *Theological Investigations V*, edited by Karl-H. Kruger, 3–22. London: Darton, Longman & Todd, 1975.
Rahner, Karl. *The Trinity*. Tunbridge Wells, Kent: Burns & Oates, 1970.
Rahner, Karl. 'Virginitas in Partu'. In *Theological Investigations IV*, edited by H. F. Tiblier, 134–62. London: Darton, Longman and Todd, 1974.
Rahner, Karl and Joseph Ratzinger. *Revelation and Tradition*. New York: Herder and Herder, 1966.
Rainbow Spirit Elders. *Rainbow Spirit Theology: Towards an Australian Aboriginal Theology*, edited by George Rosendale and Forum Australian Theological. 2nd edn. Hindmarsh, SA: ATF Press, 2007.
Rambo, Shelly. *Spirit and Trauma: A Theology of Remaining*. Louisville, KY: Westminster John Knox Press, 2010.
Rees, Frank D. *Wrestling with Doubt: Theological Reflections on the Journey of Faith*. Collegeville, MN: Liturgical Press, 2001.
Reynolds, Henry. 'A New Historical Landscape?'. *The Monthly*, 2006.
Ricœur, Paul. 'Naming God'. *Union Seminary Quarterly Review* 34, no. 4 (1979): 215.
Ricœur, Paul. *The Symbolism of Evil*. Boston: Beacon Press, 1969.
Ricoeur, Paul. *Essays on Biblical Interpretation*, edited by Lewis Seymour Mudge. Philadelphia: Fortress Press, 1980.
Ricœur, Paul. *Figuring the Sacred: Religion, Narrative, and Imagination*, edited by Mark I. Wallace. Minneapolis: Fortress Press, 1995.
Ricœur, Paul. *Interpretation Theory: Discourse and the Surplus of Meaning*. Fort Worth: Texas Christian University Press, 1976.
Riley, Maria. *Transforming Feminism*. Kansas City, MO: Sheed & Ward, 1989.
Rivera, Mayra. *Poetics of the Flesh*. Durham, NC: Duke University Press, 2015.
Rousselot, Pierre. *The Eyes of Faith*. Translated by S. J. Joseph Donceel. New York: Fordham University Press, 1990.
Roy, Louis. *The Three Dynamisms of Faith: Searching for Meaning, Fulfillment, and Truth*. Washington, DC: Catholic University of America Press, 2017.
Ruether, Rosemary Radford. 'Feminist Theology'. In *The New Dictionary of Theology*, edited by Mary Collins, Dermot A. Lane and Joseph A. Komonchak, 391–6. Collegeville, MN: Liturgical Press, 1987.
Ruether, Rosemary Radford. *Sexism and God-Talk: Toward a Feminist Theology. With a New Introduction*. 10th Anniversary edn. Boston, MA: Beacon Press, 1993.
Rush, Ormond. *The Eyes of Faith the Sense of the Faithful and the Church's Reception of Revelation*. Washington, DC: Catholic University of America Press, 2009.

Ryan, Eilish. *Rosemary Haughton: Witness to Hope*. Lanham, MD: Rowman & Littlefield, 1997.
Santmire, H. Paul. *The Travail of Nature: The Ambiguous Ecological Promise of Christian Theology*. Philadelphia: Fortress Press, 1985.
Sbatella, Licia. *La Mente Orchestra: Elaborazione della Risonanza e Autismo*. Milano: Vita e Pensiero, 2006.
Schaefer, Mark. *The Certainty of Uncertainty: The Way of Inescapable Doubt and Its Virtue*. Eugene OR: Wipf & Stock, 2018.
Scharen, Christian. *Broken Hallelujahs: Why Popular Music Matters to Those Seeking God*. Grand Rapids, MI: Brazos Press, 2011.
Schleiermacher, Friedrich. *The Christian Faith*, edited by H. R. MacKintosh and J. S. Stewart. Edinburgh: T&T Clark, 1976.
Schleiermacher, Friedrich. *Christian Faith: A New Translation and Critical Edition*, edited by Terrence N. Tice. Louisville, KY: Westminster John Knox Press, 2016.
Schleiermacher, Friedrich. *Christmas Eve Celebration: A Dialogue*. Translated by Terrence N. Tice. Eugene, OR: Cascade Books, 2010 (1805).
Schleiermacher, Friedrich. *Hermeneutics and Criticism and Other Writings*, edited by Andrew Bowie. Cambridge and New York: Cambridge University Press, 1998.
Schleiermacher, Friedrich. *Hermeneutics: The Handwritten Manuscripts*, edited by Heinz Kimmerle. Atlanta, Georgia: Scholars Press, 1977.
Schleiermacher, Friedrich. *On Religion: Speeches to Its Cultured Despisers*. Translated by Richard Crouter. Cambridge: Cambridge University Press, 1996.
Schlingensiepen, Ferdinand. *Dietrich Bonhoeffer, 1906–1945 Martyr, Thinker, Man of Resistance*. New York: T&T Clark, 2010.
Schlumpf, Heidi. *Elizabeth Johnson: Questing for God*. Collegeville, MN: Liturgical Press, 2016.
Schneiders, Sandra M. 'Approaches to the Study of Christian Spirituality'. In *The Blackwell Companion to Christian Spirituality*, edited by Arthur Holder, 15–33. Oxford: Blackwell Publishing Ltd, 2005.
Schneiders, Sandra M. *Beyond Patching: Faith and Feminism in the Catholic Church*. New York: Paulist Press, 2004.
Schneiders, Sandra M. 'Biblical Spirituality'. *Interpretation: A Journal of Bible and Theology* 70, no. 4 (2016): 417–30.
Schneiders, Sandra M. *Buying the Field: Catholic Religious Life in Mission to the World*. New York: Paulist Press, 2013.
Schneiders, Sandra M. 'Feminist Spirituality'. In *The New Dictionary of Catholic Spirituality*, edited by Michael Downey, 394–406. Collegeville, MN: Liturgical Press, 1993.
Schneiders, Sandra M. *Finding the Treasure: Locating Catholic Religious Life in a New Ecclesial and Cultural Context*. New York: Paulist Press, 2000.
Schneiders, Sandra M. 'The Jesus Mysticism of Teresa of Avila: Its Importance for Theology and Contemporary Spirituality'. *Berkeley Journal of Religion and Theology* 2 (2016): 43–74.
Schneiders, Sandra M. *Jesus Risen in Our Midst: Essays on the Resurrection of Jesus in the Fourth Gospel*. Collegeville, MN: Liturgical Press, 2013.
Schneiders, Sandra M. 'The Johannine Resurrection Narrative: An Exegetical and Theological Study of John 20 as a Synthesis of Johannine Spirituality'. *Pontificia Universitas Gregoriana*, 1975.

Schneiders, Sandra M. *Prophets in Their Own Country: Women Religious Bearing Witness to the Gospel in a Troubled Church*. Maryknoll, NY: Orbis Books, 2011.
Schneiders, Sandra M. *The Revelatory Text: Interpreting the New Testament as Sacred Scripture*. Collegeville, MN: Liturgical Press, 1999.
Schneiders, Sandra M. *Selling All: Commitment, Consecrated Celibacy and Community in Catholic Religious Life*. Mahwah, NJ: Paulist Press, 2001.
Schneiders, Sandra M. 'Spirituality in the Academy'. *Theological Studies* 50, no. 4 (1989): 676–97.
Schneiders, Sandra M. *Women and the Word: The Gender of God in the New Testament and the Spirituality of Women, Madeleva Lecture in Spirituality*. New York: Paulist Press, 1986.
Schoenberg, Arnold. *Style and Idea: Selected Writings of Arnold Schoenberg*, edited by Leonard Stein. Rev. paperback edn. London: Faber, 1984.
Scholl, Robert. 'The Shock of the Positive: Oliver Messiaen, St Francis, and the Redemption of Modernity'. In *Resonant Witness: Conversations between Music and Theology*, edited by Jeremy Begbie and Steven R. Guthrie, 162–89. Grand Rapids, MI: William B. Eerdmans, 2011.
Schopenhauer, Arthur. *The World as Will and Representation*. Translated by E. F. J. Payne. New York: Dover Publications, 1969.
Schumacher, Michele M. *Women in Christ: Toward a New Feminism*. Grand Rapids, MI: William B. Eerdmans, 2004.
Schüssler Fiorenza, Elisabeth. *Bread Not Stone: The Challenge of Feminist Biblical Interpretation*. Edinburgh, Scotland: Clark, 1990.
Schüssler Fiorenza, Elisabeth. *In Memory of Her: A Feminist Theological Reconstruction of Christian Origins*. New York: Crossroad, 1983.
Scruton, Roger. *Death-Devoted Heart: Sex and the Sacred in Wagner's Tristan and Isolde*. Oxford: Oxford University Press, 2003.
Segundo, Juan Luis. *Liberation of Theology*. Dublin: Gill and Macmillan, 1977.
Segundo, Juan Luis. *A Theology for Artisans of a New Humanity*. Maryknoll, NY: Orbis Books, 1973.
Sequeri, Pierangelo. *Anti-Prometeo. Il Musicale nell'Estetica Teologica di Hans Urs von Balthasar*. Milano: Glossa, 1995.
Sequeri, Pierangelo. 'Coscienza cristiana, ethos della fede e canone pubblico'. In *A Misura Di Vangelo: Fede, Dottrina, Chiesa*, edited by M. Vergottini and Associazione Teologica Italiana. Cinisello Balsamo: San Paolo, 2003.
Sequeri, Pierangelo. *Il Dio Affidabile, Biblioteca di Teologia Contemporanea*. Brescia: Queriniana, 1996.
Sequeri, Pierangelo. *Il Timore di Dio*. Milano: Vita e pensiero, 2008.
Sequeri, Pierangelo. *L'estro di Dio: Saggi di Estetica*. Milano: Glossa, 2000.
Sequeri, Pierangelo. *L'idea della Fede: Trattato di Teologia Fondamentale*. Milano: Glossa, 2002.
Sequeri, Pierangelo. *La Qualità Spirituale: Esperienza nella Fede nel Crocevia Contemporaneo*. Casale Monferrato: Piemme, 2001.
Sequeri, Pierangelo. 'Music and Resurrection'. *Toronto Journal of Theology* 29, no. 2 (2013): 417–24.
Sequeri, Pierangelo. *Musica e Mistica: Percorsi nella Storia Occidentale delle Pratiche Estetiche e Religiose*. Città del Vaticano: Libreria Editrice Vaticana, 2005.
Sequeri, Pierangelo. *Sensibili allo Spirito: Umanesimo Religioso e Ordine degli Affetti*. Milano: Glossa, 2001.

Sequeri, Pierangelo. *Senza Volgersi Indietro: Meditazioni per Tempi Forti*. Milano: Vita e pensiero, 2000.
Sequeri, Pierangelo, ed. *La Tecnica e il Senso: Oltre L'uomo?*. Milano: Glossa, 2015.
Sequeri, Pierangelo and Carlo Maria Martini. *L'oro e la paglia: Meditazioni sull'educare alla scuola della Parola di Dio*. Milano: Glossa, 1989.
Sequeri, Pierangelo and Vittorio Mathieu. *Eccetto Mozart: Una Passione Teologica*. Milano: Glossa, 2006.
Sequeri, Pierangelo, Ezio Prato and Pierluigi Lia. *Estetica e Teologia: L'indicibile Emozione del Sacro: R. Otto, A. Schönberg, M. Heidegger*. Milano: Glossa, 1993.
Sheldrake, Philip. 'Spirituality and Its Critical Methodology'. In *Exploring Christian Spirituality: Essays in Honor of Sandra M. Schneiders*, edited by Bruce H. Lescher and Elizabeth Liebert, 15–34. New York: Paulist Press, 2006.
Sicari, Antoni O.C.D. 'Hans Urs von Balthasar: Theology and Holiness'. In *Hans Urs von Balthasar: His Life and Work*, edited by David L. Schindler, 121–32. San Francisco: Ignatius Press, 1991.
Slater, Michael R. 'Theology, Metaphysics, and Realism About Truth'. *Modern Theology* 35, no. 2 (2019): 244–67.
Small, Christopher. *Music of the Common Tongue: Survival and Celebration in African American Music*. Hanover, NH: University Press of New England, 1987.
Small, Christopher. *Musicking: The Meanings of Performing and Listening*. Hanover, NH: University Press of New England, 1998.
Smith, Hazel and R. T. Dean. *Practice-Led Research, Research-Led Practice in the Creative Arts*. Edinburgh: Edinburgh University Press, 2009.
Sobrino, Jon. 'Awakening from the Sleep of Inhumanity'. *Christian Century* 108, no. 11 (1991): 364.
Sobrino, Jon. *Christ the Liberator: A View from the Victims*. Maryknoll, NY: Orbis Books, 2001.
Sobrino, Jon. *Christology at the Crossroads: A Latin American Approach*. London: SCM Press, 1978.
Sobrino, Jon. *No Salvation Outside the Poor: Prophetic-Utopian Essays*. Maryknoll, NY: Orbis Books, 2008.
Sobrino, Jon. *The Eye of the Needle. No Salvation Outside the Poor: A Utopian-Prophetic Essay*. London: Darton, Longman and Todd, 2008.
Sobrino, Jon. 'In Archbishop Romero God Passed through El Salvador'. In *Fathers of the Church in Latin America*, edited by Silvia Scatena, Jon Sobrino and Luiz Carlos Susin. London: SCM Press, 2009.
Sobrino, Jon. *Jesus the Liberator: A Historical-Theological Reading of Jesus of Nazareth*. Maryknoll, NY: Orbis Books, 1993.
Sobrino, Jon. *Jon Sobrino: Spiritual Writings*, edited by Robert Lassalle-Klein. Maryknoll, NY: Orbis, 2018.
Sobrino, Jon. *The Principle of Mercy: Taking the Crucified People from the Cross*. Maryknoll, NY: Orbis Books, 1994.
Sobrino, Jon. *Spirituality of Liberation: Toward Political Holiness*. Maryknoll, NY: Orbis Books, 1988.
Sobrino, Jon. *The True Church and the Poor*. Maryknoll, NY: Orbis Books, 1984.
Sobrino, Jon. *Witnesses to the Kingdom: The Martyrs of El Salvador and the Crucified Peoples*. Maryknoll, NY: Orbis Books, 2003.
Sobrino, Jon and Ignacio Ellacuría. *Companions of Jesus: The Jesuit Martyrs of El Salvador*. Maryknoll, NY: Orbis Books, 1990.

Sobrino, Jon, eds. *Systematic Theology: Perspectives from Liberation Theology*. London: SCM Press, 1996.
Sonnet, Jean-Pierre S. J. *Le Corps Voisé: Petite Suite Eucharistique*. Châtelineau: Le Taillis Pré, 2002.
Sonnet, Jean-Pierre S. J. *MEMBRA JESU NOSTRI: Ce que Dieu ne dit que par le corps*. Châtelineau: Le Taillis Pré, 2010.
Speelman, Willem Marie. *The Generation of Meaning in Liturgical Songs*. Kampen: Kok Pharos Publishing House, 1995.
Spencer, Jon Michael. *Blues and Evil*. Knoxville, TN: University of Tennessee Press, 1993.
Spencer, Jon Michael. 'Overview of American Popular Music in a Theological Perspective'. *Black Sacred Music: A Journal of Theomusicology* 8, no. 1 (1994): 205–17.
Spencer, Jon Michael. *Theological Music: Introduction to Theomusicology*. New York: Greenwood Press, 1991.
Spencer, Jon Michael. *Theomusicology*. Durham, NC: Duke University Press, 1994.
Speyr, Adrienne von. *The Christian State of Life*, edited by Hans Urs von Balthasar. San Francisco, CA: Ignatius Press, 1986.
St. John, Graham. *Rave Culture and Religion*. London and New York: Routledge, 2004.
Stanton, Elizabeth Cady and The Revising Committee. *The Women's Bible*, 1896–1898. https://www.sacred-texts.com/wmn/wb/.
Steiner, George. *Real Presences: Is There Anything in What We Say?*. London: Faber, 1991.
Stephenson, Bruce. *The Music of the Heavens: Kepler's Harmonic Astronomy*. Princeton: Princeton University Press, 2014.
Stevance, Sophie and Serge Lacasse. *Research-Creation in Music and the Arts: Towards a Collaborative Interdiscipline, Sempre Studies in the Psychology of Music*. London: Taylor & Francis Ltd., Routledge, 2019.
Stévance, Sophie and Serge Lacasse. 'Research-Creation in Music as a Collaborative Space'. *Media-N Journal of the New Media Caucus* 11, Issue 3 (2015).
Stoltzfus, Philip Edward. *Theology as Performance: Music, Aesthetics, and God in Western Thought*. New York: T&T Clark International, 2006.
Stone-Davis, Férdia J. *Musical Beauty: Negotiating the Boundary between Subject and Object*. Eugene, OR: Cascade Books, 2011.
Storr, Anthony. *Music and the Mind*. New York: Ballantine Books, 1997.
Strunk, W. Oliver and Leo Treitler. *Source Readings in Music History*. Rev. edn. New York: Norton, 1998.
Suk, John D. *Not Sure: A Pastor's Journey from Faith to Doubt*. Grand Rapids, MI: William B. Eerdmans, 2011.
Sutton, Matthew Lewis. 'Hans Urs von Balthasar and Adrienne Von Speyr's Ecclesial Relationship'. *New Blackfriars* 94, no. 1049 (2013): 50–63.
Tacey, David J. *The Postsecular Sacred: Jung, Soul, and Meaning in an Age of Change*. 1st edn. New York: Routledge, 2019.
Tacey, David J. *Religion as Metaphor: Beyond Literal Belief*. New Brunswick and London: Transaction Publishers, 2015.
Tacey, David J. *The Spirituality Revolution: The Emergence of Contemporary Spirituality*. Pymble, NSW: HarperCollins, 2003.
Taruskin, Richard. *Retheorizing Music*. New York: Oxford University Press.

Taylor, Charles. *A Secular Age*. Cambridge: Belknap Press of Harvard University Press, 2007.
Teresa of Avila. *The Complete Works of St Teresa of Avila*, edited by E. Allison Peers. London and New York: Burns & Oates, 2002.
Tertullian. *Apology De Spectaculis*, edited by Marcus Minucius Felix, T. R. Glover and Gerald Henry Rendall. Cambridge: Harvard University Press, 1931.
Theuring, Ashley. 'Holding Hope and Doubt: An Interreligious Theopoetic Response to Public Tragedies'. *Cross Currents* 64, issue 4 (2014): 549.
Theuring, Ashley. *Toward a Catholic Feminist Practical Theology of Hope after Domestic Violence*. Boston MA: Boston University, 2018.
Thiessen, Gesa Elisbeth and Declan Marmion. *Theology in the Making: Biography, Contexts, Methods*. Dublin, Ireland: Veritas, 2005.
Thiselton, Anthony C. *Doubt, Faith, and Certainty*. Grand Rapids, IN: William B. Eerdmans, 2017.
Tietz, Christiane. *Theologian of Resistance: The Life and Thought of Dietrich Bonhoeffer*. New York: Fortress Press, 2016.
Tillich, Paul. *Dynamics of Faith*. New York: Harper & Row, 1957.
Tillich, Paul. *The Shaking of the Foundations*. New York: C. Scribner's Sons, 1948.
Tischler, Hans. *The Earliest Motets (to Circa 1270): A Complete Comparative Edition*. New Haven: Yale University Press, 1982.
Tolle, Eckhart. *The Power of Now: A Guide to Spiritual Enlightenment*. Sydney, NSW: Hodder Headline Australia, 2004.
Tseng, Shao Kai. 'Kierkegaard and Music in Paradox? Bringing Mozart's Don Giovanni to Terms with Kierkegaard's Religious Life-View'. *Literature and Theology* 28, no. 4 (2014): 411–24.
Turner, Denys. *Faith, Reason, and the Existence of God*. Cambridge: Cambridge University Press, 2004.
Tyler, Peter and Edward Howells, eds. *Teresa of Avila: Mystical Theology and Spirituality in the Carmelite Tradition*. New York: Routledge, 2017.
Unger, Max and Willis Wager. 'From Beethoven's Workshop'. *The Musical Quarterly* 24, no. 3 (1938): 323–40.
Vahanian, Gabriel. *Theopoetics of the Word: A New Beginning of Word and World*. New York: Palgrave Macmillan, 2014.
Van Roo, William A. *Man, the Symbolizer*. Rome: Gregorian University Press, 1981.
Vattimo, Gianni, Pierangelo Sequeri and Giovanni Ruggeri. *Interrogazioni sul Cristianesimo: cosa possiamo ancora attenderci dal Vangelo?*. Roma: Edizioni lavoro, 2000.
Veeneman, Mary M. *Introducing Theological Method: A Survey of Contemporary Theologians and Approaches*. Grand Rapids, MI: Baker Academic, 2017.
Viladesau, Richard. *Theological Aesthetics: God in Imagination, Beauty, and Art*. New York: Oxford University Press, 1999.
Vorgrimler, Herbert. *Understanding Karl Rahner: An Introduction to His Life and Thought*. London: SCM Press, 1986.
Wackenroder, Wilhelm Heinrich. *Confessions and Fantasies*. University Park, PN: Penn State University Press, 1971.
Walmsley, Gerard. *Lonergan on Philosophic Pluralism: The Polymorphism of Consciousness as the Key to Philosophy*. Toronto: University of Toronto Press, 2008.
Walser, Robert. *Running with the Devil: Power, Gender, and Madness in Heavy Metal Music*. Middletown, CT: Wesleyan University Press, 1993.

Watkins, Ralph Basui. *Hip-Hop Redemption: Finding God in the Rhythm and the Rhyme*. Grand Rapids, MI: Baker Academic, 2011.

Webb, Stephen H. *The Divine Voice: Christian Proclamation and the Theology of Sound*. Grand Rapids, MI: Brazos Press, 2004.

Webb, Val. *In Defense of Doubt: An Invitation to Adventure*. St. Louis, MO: Chalice Press, 1995.

Weber, Max. 'Science as a Vocation'. In *From Max Weber Essays in Sociology*, edited by Hans Heinrich Gerth, C. Wright Mills and Bryan S. Turner, 129–56. Milton Park, Abingdon, Oxon: Routledge, 2009.

Wedemeyer-Weller, Maria von. 'Appendix: The Other Letters from Prison'. In *Letters and Papers from Prison*, edited by Eberhard Bethge, 412–19. London: SCM Press, 1971.

West, Cornel. *Race Matters, 25th Anniversary: With a New Introduction*. Beacon Press, 2017.

Westerhoff, John H. *Will Our Children Have Faith?*. Harrisburg, PA: Morehouse Pub., 2012.

Westermeyer, Paul. 'Reflections on Music and Theology'. *Theological Education* XXXI (1994): 183–9.

Wilder, Amos Niven. *Theopoetic: Theology and the Religious Imagination*. Philadelphia: Fortress, 1976.

Williams, Charles. *The Descent of the Dove: A Short History of the Holy Spirit in the Church*. New York: Oxford University Press, 1939.

Williams, H. A. *Tensions: Necessary Conflicts in Life and Love*. Springfield: Templegate, 1977.

Williams, Reggie L. *Bonhoeffer's Black Jesus: Harlem Renaissance Theology and an Ethic of Resistance*. WACO, TX: Baylor University Press, 2014.

Williams, Reggie L. 'Developing a Theologia Crucis: Dietrich Bonhoeffer in the Harlem Renaissance'. *Theology Today* 71, no. 1 (2014): 43–57.

Williams, Rowan. *Teresa of Avila*. London: Geoffrey Chapman, 1991.

Williamson, Marianne. *A Return to Love*. New York: Harper Collins Publishers, 2005.

Wolf-Devine, Celia. *Naming God: Selected Readings Representing Differing Perspectives*. New York: Crossroad Publishing Company, 2019.

Wood, W. Jay. *Epistemology: Becoming Intellectually Virtuous*. Downers Grove: InterVarsity Press, 1998.

Woodward, Kenneth L. 'Interview David W. Tracy'. *Commonweal* 146, no. 15 (2019): 54–61.

Yadlapati, Madhuri M. *Against Dogmatism: Dwelling in Faith and Doubt*. Urbana, Chicago and Springfield: University of Illinois Press, 2013.

NAME INDEX

Page numbers followed with 'n' refer to footnotes.

Adams, Tony E.   16 n.4
Allen, John L.   236 n.15
Allison, James   215
Alves, Rubem A.   34 n.74, 35 n.78
Andrews, Isolde   61 n.103
Angelini, Giuseppe   28 n.44
Anić, Rebeka Jadranka   153 n.34
Anselm   3, 3 n.5, 19, 19 n.9, 20, 77, 179, 200, 231, 267, 326, 326 n.24
Antoni Sicari, O.C.D.   178 n.29
Aquinas, Thomas   31, 45, 52, 52 nn.55–6, 77, 84, 116, 128 n.11, 129, 129 n.12, 130, 133, 191, 210, 233, 237, 246, 306, 311–12, 326, 329–32, 334, 361
Ardui, J.   86 n.77
Aristotle   46, 47, 47 n.32, 49, 50 nn.44–5, 129
Athanasius   306, 312
Audrey Assad   109–10, 110 n.56
Augustine   45, 48, 49, 50 nn.44–5, 51, 61, 70, 70 n.17, 77, 128, 168–71, 186, 186 n.64, 191, 210, 282, 282 n.13, 294, 306, 312, 326, 327, 344, 347, 360, 360 n.6
Avant-Mier, Roberto   86 n.77
Aydin, Mor Polycarpus A.   48 nn.35–6

Babbitt, Milton   88, 89 n.90
Bach, Johann Sebastian   52 n.58, 60, 65 n.1, 74, 75, 75 n.31, 76–8, 87
Balthasar, Hans Urs von   30–3, 33 n.66, 56, 61, 61 nn.105–7, 62, 62 nn.108–10, 64, 70, 71 n.18, 135, 151, 152, 170–88, 206 n.53, 235, 235 n.13, 243 nn.51–2, 344, 347, 348
Barbour, Ian   306

Barrett, Frank J.   87 n.82
Barth, Karl   27, 27 n.39, 28, 28 nn.40–1, 56, 56 n.72, 59, 59 nn.91–3, 60–1, 64, 78, 172, 173, 177, 178, 256–8, 262, 348
Bartleet, Brydie-Leigh   16 n.4
Beattie, Tina   145 n.2, 152 n.29, 180
Beaudoin, Tom   64 n.117, 86 n.74, 93, 110 n.59, 113 n.71, 117, 117 n.90
Beethoven, Ludwig van   57, 60, 63, 76, 78–9, 79 nn.48–50, 81
Begbie, Jeremy   40 n.3, 52 n.57, 57 n.74, 77 nn.42–3
Bell, John L.   111 n.65
Benedict XVI   5 n.11, 32, 32 n.62, 212, 236 n.15
Benson, Bruce Ellis   43 n.15, 46, 86 n.82
Bergson, Henri   82
Berry, Thomas Mary   303
Bethge, Eberhard   255, 257–9
Betz, John R.   103 n.30
Birch, Charles   303
Blacking, John   40 n.2
Blackwell, Albert L.   57 n.81
Blondel, Maurice   364
Bochner, Arthur P.   16 n.4
Boethius   46, 51
Boeve, Lieven   8 n.22, 11, 26 n.36
Boff, Leonardo   152 n.28, 194 n.9, 195 n.11
Bonaventure   282, 306, 310, 312
Bonhoeffer, Dietrich   56, 62–3, 63 nn.111–16, 203, 251–73, 327
Bowers, Jane M   42 n.13
Boyd, Gregory A.   28 n.43
Brahms, Johannes   58, 76
Britten, Benjamin   83

Broadhead, Bradley K.   86 n.82, 90 nn.96–7
Brock, Sebastian P.   276 n.4
Brueggemann, Walter   34 n.74
Buber, Martin   321 n.1
Buckley, Michael J.   24–5, 133 n.24
Buerkner, Paul   23 n.24
Burke, Kevin F.   199 n.28
Buzard, James   16 n.4
Bychkov, Oleg V.   33 n.66

Cage, John   83, 85
Cahill, Lisa Sowle   148 n.10, 328 n.27
Calderón, Pedro   172
Calvin, John   45, 52, 61, 74, 77, 306, 312
Câmara, Hélder   203, 265
Caputo, John   35 n.76
Carey, Patrick W.   173 n.12
Carson, Mina   42 n.13, 86 n.77
Catherine of Siena   50 n.46, 179, 274–6, 282
Chardin, Teilhard de   191, 306, 312–13
Chesterton, G. K.   224, 224 n.41, 358
Chew, Geoffrey J.   96 n.2
Chua, Daniel K. L.   47 n.30, 54 nn.62–6, 55 n.67–8, 56 n.71, 64, 79–80, 92, 92 nn.104–5
Clarke, Eric F.   97 n.10
Claudel, Paul   172
Clement of Alexandria   45, 47
Clifford, Anne M.   147 n.6, 149 n.15, 151 n.23
Clifford, Catherine E.   105 n.38
Cobb, Kelton   86 n.74
Collins, Guy   23 n.25
Coltrane, John   87, 93
Cone, James H.   86 n.76
Congar, Yves   3, 3 n.6, 11
Congregation for Institutes of Consecrated Life and Societies of Apostolic Life   157 n.51
Congregation for the Clergy   17 n.7
Congregation for the Doctrine of the Faith   152 n.27, 195 n.11, 200, 201 n.40, 375 n.67
Conway, Daniel W.   81 n.58
Conway, Eamon   243 n.52

Crowe, Frederick E.   131–2, 132 n.21, 143, 334 n.47, 364 n.13
Culbertson, Philip Leroy   85 n.73

Dadosky, John D.   30 n.55, 50 n.46, 135 n.28
Dahill, Lisa Elaine   258 n.21, 264 n.39
Dallapiccola, Luigi   85
Daly, Gabriel   303
Daly, Mary   151 n.24
Dante (or Dante Aligheri)   376
Davidson, Robert   23 n.25
Davies, Paul   305
Davies, Stephen   124 n.2, 126
Dawkins, Richard   306
Dean, R. T.   98 nn.12–13
Debussy, Claude   76, 83
De Gruchy, John W.   63 n.113
DeJonge, Michael P.   255 n.9, 257 nn.17–18
DeNora, Tia   110 n.59
Descartes, René   20–1, 21 n.12, 47, 53–4
Des Prez, Joaquin   72
Deusen, Nancy Van   50 nn.44–5
Dibben, Nicola   97 n.10
Doran, Robert M.   105–6, 105 n.41, 106 n.44, 115, 115 n.79, 117 n.89, 214–15
Dostoevsky, Fyodor   184
Dowley, Tim   50 n.47, 74 n.26, 84 nn.65–6, 111 n.61
Dramm, Sabine   255 n.9, 273
Dreyer, Elizabeth   275 n.2, 295
Dreyfus, Laurence   77 n.41
Dryness, W. A   40 n.6
Dufourmantelle, Anne   24 n.25
Dvořák, Antonín   58

Edwards, Denis   223 n.38, 227, 296–319
Egan, Harvey D.   233 n.4, 234 n.8, 249
Egan, Keith J.   274 n.1
Ellacuría, Ignazio   195 n.12, 196, 197 n.19, 198, 199, 199 nn.28–30, 202, 204
Ellis, Carolyn   16 n.4

Ellis Jr, Carl F. 90 n.96, 93
Ephrem 48, 276
Epstein, Heidi 42 n.14, 59 n.92, 64, 66 n.3, 91 n.100

Faber, Roland 35 n.76
Fell, Margaret 150, 150 n.17
Ferm, Vergilius 16 n.5
Ferraro, Benedito 152 n.28
Fillingim, David 86 n.78
Fisichella, Rino 31 n.58
Flanagan, Sabina 50 n.46
Fodor, James 33 n.66
Foley, Edward 109 n.51
Ford, David 56 n.73, 57 n.75, 177, 178 n.28, 196 n.13
Foucault, Michel 64
Fowler, James W. 28 n.42
Francis 5 n.12, 132, 144 n.1, 313–14, 341–2, 355–6
Frazão, Jose 351 n.41
Friedan, Betty 147
Fuentes, Agustin 24 n.25

Gaar, Gillian G. 86 n.77
Gadamer, Hans Georg 2 n.2, 8, 15, 15 n.1, 23 nn.21–3, 161, 161 n.67
Gaillardetz, Richard R. 201, 201 n.39, 328 nn.27–8
Galenson, David W. 96 n.3
Galilei, Galileo 298
Galilei, Vincenzo 54
Gallagher, Michael Paul 25 n.28–9, 38, 52 n.55, 128 n.10, 143, 170–1, 215 n.10, 219 n.23, 247, 269, 269 n.52, 344, 344 n.6
Gardner, Howard 6, 6 n.16, 11, 112, 112 n.66, 113
Gelinas, Robert 90 n.97, 93
Gelpi, Donald L. 106 n.41
Gershon, Walter S. 97 n.9
Gill, Theodore A. 59 n.93
Gilmour, Michael J. 85 n.73
Gilson, Etienne 364
Girard, René 215, 226
Godzieba, Anthony J. 78 n.44, 93
Goethe, Johann Wolfgang von 172
Golden, Michael 40 n.6
Gonzalez, Michelle A. 180 n.39

Gracian, Jerónimo 286
Green, Clifford J. 255 n.9, 256 n.15, 257 nn.17–18, 267 n.46, 267–9
Gregersen, Niels Henrik 305, 305 n.35
Gregson, Vernon J. 218, 218 n.21
Grenz, Stanley J. 56 n.73, 146 n.4, 192 n.4, 194 nn.8–9, 259 n.23, 262 n.32
Grey, Thomas S. 78 n.46, 79 n.50
Griffin, John Howard 365 n.15
Grimshaw, Mike 86 n.74
Groupe des Dombes 105 n.38
Guido D'Arezzo (or of Arezzo) 69, 70
Guthrie, Steven R. 40 n.3
Gutiérrez, Gustavo 193–4, 208, 236, 303

Handel, George Frideric 75
Hanning, Barbara Russano 47 n.32, 51 n.50, 74 n.23, 75 n.32, 78 n.45, 87 n.85
Hanslick, Eduard 56, 60, 60 n.98, 79, 79 n.49
Hargreaves, David J. 97 n.10
Harnack, Arnold von 256
Harrison, Carol 48 n.38, 49 n.40
Hart, David Bentley 77 n.38
Haughton, Rosemary 8 n.23, 105 n.38, 122, 274, 292, 358–82
Hawking, Stephen 305, 307, 308 n.43
Haydn, Franz Joseph 76, 78
Heaney, Maeve Louise 7 nn.18–20, 31 n.60, 102 n.28, 121 n.1
Heaps, Jonathan 153 n.34
Hecht, Jennifer Michael 22–4
Heidegger, Martin 82, 103 n.30, 233, 238, 242, 256
Henrici, Peter, S.J. 176 n.24
Hildegard of Bingen 50–2, 178, 179, 274–6
Hillman, Roger 7 n.19
Hinze, Bradford E. 78 n.44, 328 n.27
Hinze, Christine Firer 328 n.27
Hoenen, Peter 128 n.11
Holland, Scott 35 n.76, 36 n.82
Hopkins, Gerard Manly 75 n.28, 379

Hopper, Stanley Romaine 34, 34 nn.72–4
Howells, Edward 276 n.3
Howison, Jamie 87 n.84
Hozier 39, 39 n.1
Hudson, Wayne 299, 299 n.7
Hunsinger, George 61 n.103
Husserl, Edmund 82
Illman, Ruth 110 n.57

International Theological Commission 174, 212, 343
Irarrazaval, Diego 148 n.10, 328 n.27
Irenaeus 172, 306, 312
Irwin, Joyce L. 53 nn.59–60
Irwin, William 24 n.26, 36
Ito, John Paul 46 nn.28–9, 53 n.61

Jacobson, Lisa 298
Jacobs-Vandegeer, Christiaan 107
Jaspers, Karl 214
John, Helen J. 50 n.46
John B. Cobb 303
John Paul II 17 n.7, 32, 33 n.64, 103 n.32, 152, 152 n.25, 152 n.30, 173, 181, 245, 280 n.11, 298, 341
Johnson, Elizabeth A. 122, 147, 152 n.32, 201 n.39, 306, 310, 313, 320–38
John-Steiner, Vera 97 n.9
John XXIII 234

Kant, Immanuel 21, 55–6, 55 nn.69–70, 56, 79, 197 n.17, 237, 238, 243
Kasper, Walter 310
Kearney, Richard 35 n.76
Keefe-Perry, L. Callid 34 nn.69–71, 35 n.75, 35 n.79, 36
Keenan, Marie 277 n.5
Keller, Catherine 35 n.76
Kelly, Paul 299 n.6, 314, 315, 315 n.60, 318
Kennedy, Philip 256 nn.12–13, 257 n.20, 259 n.22, 264 n.41, 316 n.62
Kepler, Johannes 47, 47 n.33

Kerman, Joseph 91 n.99
Kerr, Fergus 128 n.10, 143, 181, 181 n.43, 236 n.17
Kettler, Christian D. 5 n.13, 23–4 n.25
Kierkegaard, Søren 21, 27, 56, 58–9, 61 n.104, 177, 348
Kilby, Karen 180–2
Kim, Hyun-Ah 206 n.55
King, Roberta R. 40 n.6
King-Lenzmeier, Anne H. 50 n.46
Koskoff, Ellen 42 n.13
Krabbe, Silas C. 34 n.69, 35 n.79, 36 n.84
Kropf, Richard W. 28 n.42
Kuiken, Rebecca 29 n.51
Küng, Hans 59

Labriola, Christina 206 n.55
Lacasse, Serge 98 n.13, 115 n.80
Lane, Belden C. 161 n.65
Lane, Dermot A. 146 n.4, 148 n.12, 361 n.7
Langer, Susanne K. 99 n.19, 139, 139 n.35
Lassalle-Klein, Robert Anthony 196 n.14, 199 n.28, 201 n.40
Latour, Bruno 115 n.82
Lawrence, Frederick G. 113 n.70, 117
Leaver, Robin A. 52 n.58, 76 n.34, 76 nn.36–7, 109 n.51
Leibniz, Gottfried Wilhelm 346 n.19
Le Mée, Katharine W. 69 n.14
Leoninus 70 n.16
Lerner, Gerda 147
Lescher, Bruce H. 156 n.47, 161 n.65, 384 n.3
LeVine, Mark 86 n.79
Lewis, Clive Staples 51 n.48, 364, 376, 376 n.70
Liddy, Richard M. 114 n.78, 117
Liebert, Elizabeth 156 n.47, 161 n.65, 384 n.3
Lienhard, Joseph T. 173 n.12, 179 n.35
Lim, Swee Hong 40 n.6
Liszt, Franz 76, 79 n.50

NAME INDEX

Loewe, William P.   201 n.41, 215 n.8, 218 n.21
Lonergan, Bernard J. F.   3, 6 n.14, 9 n.24, 11, 16 nn.2–3, 20, 98–118, 120, 122, 123–43, 160, 176, 214–16, 251, 266, 291, 292, 323, 334 n.47, 364, 364 n.13, 383
Lösel, Steffen   116 n.86
Lundin, Roger   23 n.25
Luther, Martin   20, 25, 52–3, 53 nn.59–60, 74–7, 216, 256, 281, 306, 312
Lynch, Danielle Anne   64, 384 n.2
Lynch, Gordon   86 n.74, 86 n.81, 93, 110 n.59
Lyte, Henry Francis   109, 110 n.56, 111

McBride, Jennifer M.   255 n.10, 264 n.38
McClary, Susan   41, 42 n.14, 90 n.95, 91 n.99, 91 n.101
McClendon, James Wm, Jr.   16 n.5
McDonagh, Sean   303, 303 n.24
MacDonald, Raymond A. R.   97 n.10
McEvoy, James Gerard   224 n.42, 300 n.10, 301 n.13
McFague, Sallie   149 n.13, 303, 306, 313
McFarland, Ian A.   210 n.1
Mackay, Hugh   299
McLeish, Kenneth   124 n.4
McMillan, James   109, 109 n.53
Macquarrie, John   3, 3 n.4, 100
Madges, William   325 n.15
Maher, Matt   109, 109 n.55
Maher MSC, James   95 n.1, 96 n.6, 111 n.63, 117
Mahler, Gustav   58
Mahler, Margaret S.   220
Malone, Mary T.   50 n.46
Marcel, Gabriel   364
Marcocchi, Massimo   276 n.3, 282 n.14
Marcy Beach, Amy   83
Maritain, Jacques   364
Marius, Schneider   67 n.7
Marmion, Declan   16 n.5, 385 n.5
Martos, Joseph   360 n.4

Mattheson, Johann   45, 45 n.26
Matthew Lewis, Sutton   174 n.15
May, Melanie A.   35 n.76
Mellers, Wilfrid Howard   76 n.34
Melling, Joseph   213 n.6, 214 n.7, 218 n.22, 227
Mendelssohn, Felix   60, 77
Merton, Thomas   364, 365
Messiaen, Olivier   84, 84 nn.68–9, 90, 90 n.98, 93, 109
Metz, Johann Baptist (or Johann-Baptist)   176, 176 n.23, 235–6, 236 n.14, 240, 240 n.34
Miell, Dorothy   97 n.10
Míguez Bonino, José   195 n.10
Miles, Margaret Ruth   112 n.67
Miller-McLemore, Bonnie   98 n.15
Moltmann, Jürgen   29, 29 n.50, 191, 196, 196 n.15, 198, 303, 303 n.26, 306, 313
Monk, William Henry   111
Monteverdi, Claudio   73, 73 n.21
Mooney, Hilary A.   135 n.28
Moore, Sebastian   209–28, 297, 303, 355, 360
Moritz, Joshua M.   16 n.5
Morrison, Toni   92–3
Mozart, Wolfgang Amadeus   57, 58, 59–61, 61 n.103, 62, 76, 78, 89, 116 n.86, 161, 347, 348
Muto, Susan   278 n.7

Nantais, David   86 n.77
Nattiez, Jean-Jacques   7 n.17, 40 n.2, 42 n.12, 97 n.7, 116 n.85, 121 n.1, 141 n.45, 164 n.72
Nelson, Derek R.   16 n.5
Newbigin, Lesslie   23 n.25
Newheiser, David   26 n.34
Newman, John Henry   4, 4 n.9, 27, 27 n.37, 30, 30 n.54, 112 n.68, 128, 142
Newton, John   110–11
Nichols, Aidan   173 n.12, 174 n.16, 189
Niebuhr, Richard   26, 26 n.33
Nietzsche, Friedrich   54, 56, 80 n.53, 80 n.55, 81, 81 n.58, 85
Nuzzi, Ronald James   7 n.16

O'Collins, Gerald   4 n.10, 114 n.77
O'Connor, Michael   44 n.21, 45 n.23, 45 n.24, 45 n.26, 48 n.34
O'Donnell, John J.   175 n.19, 182 n.46, 185 n.60, 189, 233 n.4, 239 n.28, 249
O'Leary, Dale   153 n.34
Oliver, Mary   123, 123 n.1
Olson, Carl   85 n.73
Olson, Roger E.   56 n.73, 146 n.4, 192 n.4, 194 n.8, 194 n.9, 259 n.23, 262 n.32, 263 n.34, 264 n.40
O'Malley, John   23 n.21, 276 n.3
Origen   172, 204, 232, 360 n.5
Ormerod, Neil   107, 118, 153 n.34, 215, 215 n.11, 217, 227, 323 n.9

Palestrina, Giovanni Pierluigi da   65 n.1, 75, 75 n.30
Palma, Robert J.   61 n.104
Pannenberg, Wolfhart   196, 325
Parsons, Susan Frank   152 n.29
Pärt, Arvo   7 n.19, 84, 85, 109, 109 n.52
Partridge, Christopher H.   86 n.74, 94, 110 n.59
Pascal, Blaise   339, 339 n.1
Paul VI   32–3, 33 n.63, 38, 75 n.29, 230 n.2, 274, 342, 342 n.3
Pearce, David   67 n.9
Pederson, Ann   90 n.96
Peguy, Charles   172, 364
Pelikan, Jaroslav Jan   53 n.59, 76 nn.34, 35
Penderecki, Krzystof   85
Pendle, Karin   42 n.13
Perotinus   70 n.16
Peters, Ted   16 n.5, 300 n.11, 300 n.12, 302 n.17, 306 n.37, 306 n.38, 319
Pfitzner, Hans   58
Phillip the Chancellor   49, 50 n.44, 50 n.45
Pickstock, Catherine   82 n.60, 83 nn.62, 64, 84 n.67
Pieper, Josef   47 n.31
Pitts, Stephanie   97 n.10
Platinga, Richard J.   52 n.58, 77 n.39, 77 n.40

Plato   15, 46, 47
Polkinghorne, John   306
Pope, Stephen J.   200 n.34, 201 n.41
Prüller-Jagenteufel, Gunter   251 n.1, 260 n.27, 262 n.32, 273
Pythagoras   46, 298

Rachmaninoff, Sergei   83
Rahaim, Matthew   40 n.6
Rahner, Karl   10, 10 n.25, 115, 115 n.81, 122, 172, 172 n.9, 173, 173 n.14, 176 n.23, 196, 197, 206 n.53, 209, 229–50, 290, 300, 302, 303, 306, 310, 313, 323, 323 n.8, 326, 340, 364, 384–6
Rainbow Spirit Elders   316–17
Rambo, Shelly   36 n.81
Rameau, Jean-Philippe   55, 56, 73 n.20
Rank, Otto   214
Ratzinger, Joseph   173, 195 n.11, 235, 235 n.12, 236, 235 n.15
Rees, Frank D.   5 n.13, 21 n.13, 23 n.25, 25, 25 n.31, 26 n.32, 26 n.35, 29–30
Reynolds, Henry   304 n.30
Ricoeur, Paul (or Ricœur)   8, 8 n.21, 23 n.21, 104 n.33, 161, 161 n.68, 321 n.1, 327, 332, 332 n.42, 332 n.43
Riley, Maria   147, 147 n.6
Rivera, Mayra   36 n.81, 38
Romero, Oscar   196, 197, 197 n.18
Rousseau, Jean-Jacques   55–6, 60, 73 n.20
Rousselot, Pierre   237, 237 n.21
Roy, Louis   28, 28 n.45
Ruether, Rosemary Radford   146 n.4, 147, 147 n.9, 149 n.16, 151 n.22
Rush, Ormond   181 n.44
Russolo, Luigi   83
Ryan, Eilish   361 n.8, 362 n.9, 363 n.10, 364 n.12, 364 nn.14–15, 365 nn.17–18, 366 n.22, 367 n.26, 370 nn.45–6

St. John, Graham   86 n.81
Santmire, H. Paul   303
Satie, Erik   83

Sbatella, Licia   343 n.5
Schaefer, Mark   23 n.23
Scharen, Christian   86 n.74
Schillebeeckx, Edward   204, 303, 364
Schlegel, Friedrich   78
Schleiermacher, Friedrich   21, 21 n.15, 46–58, 60, 61, 64, 74, 255
Schlingensiepen, Ferdinand   255 n.9, 256 n.14, 257 n.16
Schlumpf, Heidi   323 n.9, 324 nn.12–13, 328, 329 n.32, 330 nn.34–5
Schneiders, Sandra M.   122, 144–67, 279, 279 nn.9–10, 290, 291 nn.29–30, 295, 322 n.7, 330 n.33, 378
Schnittke, Alfred   84
Schoenberg, Arnold (or Arnold Schönberg)   82, 84, 88, 88 n.89, 94, 351
Scholl, Robert   84 n.69
Schopenhauer, Arthur   56, 58, 58 n.84, 78, 81
Schubert, Franz   60
Schumacher, Michele M.   152 n.27
Schüssler Fiorenza, Elisabeth   147, 147 n.8, 149, 149 n.14, 151, 279 n.9, 322 n.5, 364
Scruton, Roger   82 n.60
Segundo, Juan Luis   194 n.9
Sequeri, Pierangelo   28 n.44, 31 n.60, 33, 33 nn.67–8, 45–6 n.27, 49 n.42, 51 n.53, 52 n.54, 62 n.109, 66 n.2, 69 n.13, 69 n.15, 67 n.6, 71 n.18, 85, 85 nn.70–1, 186 n.64, 292, 297 n.1, 339–57, 376
Shaw, Susan M.   42 n.13, 86 n.77, 93
Sheldrake, Philip   384, 384 nn.3–4
Small, Christopher   40–2, 64, 87–90
Smith, Hazel   98 nn.12–14
Smith, W. Alan   110 n.57
Sobrino, Jon   122, 190–208, 340
Sonnet, Jean-Pierre SJ   379, 379 n.79
Speelman, Willem Marie   7 n.17, 116 n.87, 121 n.1, 206 n.55
Spencer, Jon Michael   86, 86 n.75, 91 n.102, 92 n.103, 94, 98 n.16
Speyr, Adrienne von   173, 173 nn.11–12, 174–6, 177, 177 n.27, 178, 180, 180 nn.37–8, 181, 185, 186, 188

Stanton, Elizabeth Cady   147, 150, 150 nn.18–20
Steiner, George   6, 6 n.15, 104 n.34, 346, 346 nn.20–1
Stephenson, Bruce   47 n.33
Stévance, Sophie   98 n.13, 115 n.80
Stockhausen, Karlheinz   85
Stoltzfus, Philip Edward   43 n.16, 56 n.72, 57 n.78, 58 n.83, 59 n.93, 60 n.95, 60 nn.97–9, 80, 80 n.54
Stone-Davis, Férdia J.   46 n.29, 55 n.70
Storr, Anthony   58 n.84
Stravinsky, Igor   6 n.16, 83, 84, 112 n.66
Suk, John D.   23 n.25

Tacey, David J.   299, 299 n.4
Taruskin, Richard   51 n.51
Taylor, Charles   43 n.17
Teresa of Avila   50 n.46, 178, 274–95, 378
Tertullian   253, 253 n.5
Thérèse of Lisieux   50 n.46, 177 n.27, 179, 274–6, 364
Theuring, Ashley   36 n.81
Thiessen, Gesa Elisbeth   16 n.5, 385 n.5
Thiselton, Anthony C.   5 n.13, 11, 22 n.16, 23 n.25, 29 n.48
Tick, Judith   42 n.13
Tietz, Christiane   255 n.9, 273
Tillich, Paul   27, 27 n.38, 29, 327, 332, 332 n.41
Tisa Lewis   42 n.13, 86 n.77
Tischler, Hans   49 n.43
Tolle, Eckhart   215
Tseng, Shao Kai   59 n.86
Turner, Denys   18 n.8
Tyler, Peter   276 n.3

U2   87, 87 n.83
Ustvolskaya, Galina   84

Vahanian, Gabriel   35 n.76
Van Roo, William A.   99 n.19
Vattimo, Gianni   353 n.48
Vaughan Williams, Ralph   83
Veeneman, Mary M.   146 n.4, 149 n.13, 324 n.8

Viladesau, Richard   106 n.41, 118
Vorgrimler, Herbert   233 n.4, 235 n.10, 239 n.27, 240 n.37, 249

Wackenroder, Wilhelm Heinrich   56, 58, 58 n.82
Wagner, Richard   56, 58, 60, 69, 76, 79, 79 n.50, 80–3
Wainwright, Elaine Mary   85 n.73, 148 n.10, 328 n.27
Walmsley, Gerard   115 n.80, 139 n.39
Walser, Robert   86 n.79, 90 n.95
Watkins, Ralph Basui   85, 86 n.75, 86 n.80
Webb, Stephen H.   44 n.20, 96 n.5
Webb, Val   23 n.25, 28 n.42, 29, 29 n.47
Weber, Max   54 n.64
Wedemeyer-Weller, Maria von   261 n.30, 270, 271 nn.56–7, 271 n.60
Weinberg, Steven   305
Wesley, James   74
Wesley, John   45
West, Cornel   92–3, 92 n.106

Westerhoff, John H.   29, 29 n.46
Westermeyer, Paul   96, 96 n.4
Whelan SJ, Gerard   130 n.16
Wilde, Oscar   182
Wilder, Amos Niven   34 nn.73–4, 37, 37 n.86
Williams, Charles   376
Williams, H. A.   37 n.87
Williams, J. Lewis   67 n.9
Williams, Reggie L.   256 n.15, 273
Williams, Rowan   184 n.54, 281 n.12, 283 n.15, 284 n.17, 287, 287 nn.25–6, 289 n.27, 295
Williamson, Marianne   222
Williams RSM, Kathleen   95 n.1
Wittgenstein, Ludwig   56 n.72, 64
Wolf-Devine, Celia   152 n.32
Wood, W. Jay   30 n.54

Xenophanes of Colophon   22 n.16

Yadlapati, Madhuri M.   23 n.25
Yōko Ono   86 n.77

Zubiri, Xavier   196, 199
Zwingli, Huldrych   52

SUBJECT INDEX

Abba   223, 243, 334, 336, 353, 359
aboriginal/indigenous   67, 68, 297, 299, 303–4, 313
absolute music   47, 56, 79–80, 92
activists   93
Ad gentes   304
admirabile commercium (admirable exchange)   185
aesthetic/s   30, 33, 77, 79, 116, 117, 123, 134–6, 140, 346–7, 349, 351
  in Lonergan's epistemology   138–9
  theological   19, 30–3, 37, 62, 172, 178, 182 n.48, 343, 344
    analogy of being   60, 172, 177–8
    analogy of faith   173, 178
aesthetic experience   114, 138, 140, 161, 347
aesthetic patterns   113–14, 116, 117, 128
  of human consciousness   139–40
affect/affective/affectivity   179, 345, 349–51, 359, 378
Afro-American music   40, 62, 82, 85, 87–90
Alumbrados (the Illuminated)   281
ambivalence of the sacred   353
analogy/analogical   41, 312, 327, 334, 384
analysis of faith (*analysis fidei*)   350
androcentric   323, 334–5
anonymous Christianity/Christians   235, 242–4, 247
anthropology
  anthropocentric   173, 179–81, 217, 223, 243, 261, 296, 302, 307, 350

art/s   31–3, 36, 108, 114
  defined   125–6, 139
  essential to human living and flourishing   123–5
  in human experience   139–40
  in Lonergan's epistemology   138–9
artist/artistic   97–8, 108
artistic creativity   348
artistic patterns   113–14, 116, 117, 128
  of human consciousness   139–40
ascension   7, 27
astronomy/astronomical observation   308
atheism   24, 25, 25 n.27, 133 n.24, 171, 242
atonal/dodecaphony/twelve-tone/serialism   82–4
attentive/attentiveness   8, 104, 130
Australia   125, 300, 303, 304, 314–16, 355
authenticity/authentic subjectivity   106, 106 n.46, 108, 116, 130, 131, 383
autoethnography   116, 384
avant-garde   82–5
awakening   196, 197, 199, 203
awareness   42, 44, 57, 61, 62, 99, 100, 106–10, 112, 115 n.79, 116 n.83

baptism   209, 210, 232, 260
Baroque   69, 75, 76, 78, 173
  'theory of affections'   75 n.35
base communities   193, 194

beauty/beautiful/glory 30, 30 n.56,
    31–3, 82, 169, 183–5, 188, 209
  Balthasar's approach to 176–7,
    182
  crucified 184, 187
  God 168–71, 182–3
  of human life 209–12
becoming human 266–7
being-in-love 137, 137 n.32
believing conscience 349–52, 354
believing intelligence 347
biblical hermeneutics 160–2
biblical spirituality 161
biblical text 109, 151, 156, 161
  women in 162–4
big bang 308
biodiversity 307
Black music 90
blessedness/original blessing 218–25
blues 82, 85, 86, 91–3
Body of Christ 27, 45, 102, 161,
    185, 198, 207, 211, 232,
    265, 268, 275, 280, 323,
    370, 379

Calvinist 53
canon 159
cantus firmus 63, 386
Carmelite 274, 276, 278, 286
categorical or explicit revelation 241
Catholic Inquisition 281
Catholicism 211, 256, 341, 362–3,
    365
catholicity 172, 177, 181
celibacy 274–5, 278 n.7, 292–4
  consecrated 279, 288, 378
  for the reign of God 276, 277
  sexual love and 377–8
certitude 4, 10, 17, 18, 26–8
chant 66, 68–9
charism 280, 293
chastity 276, 279, 280, 378
  celibate chastity 279, 280, 288
cheap grace 260, 261
child/childhood 209–11, 220–4, 226
Christianity/Christians 4 n.25, 44,
    57, 59, 68, 73, 89, 142, 170,
    191, 205, 229–33, 243,
    245–7, 261–3, 266, 297

Christian song-writing 95, 96, 102,
    104, 108–10, 112, 115, 141,
    386
  conversion song 110–11
Christology 57, 63, 196, 198, 215,
    217, 223, 264, 266, 267, 310,
    369
  existential Christology 217
Church
  as community 259, 261
  doctors of the 275–6, 291
  and State 145, 252 n.3, 262, 275
  teaching 211, 232, 241–6, 252
  and theology 237, 275
classical culture 132
classical music 41, 43, 66, 68, 73–6,
    78, 82, 87, 89, 91
classical theology 334
classicism/classicist 66, 90, 124, 132,
    348
cognitive uncertainty 36
colonial/neo-colonial 192
commandment 268
communion of saints 255, 275
complementarity 152, 333
concupiscence 210
condemnation 230, 232
Confessions 169, 170
consciousness/patterns of
    consciousness/ differentiations
    of consciousness 21, 67,
    100, 108, 112–15, 139–40,
    220, 349–50, 354, 361,
    367, 376
consecrated celibacy 279, 288, 378
consecrated life 278 n.7, 278–80,
    288, 293, 378, 385
contemplation 75, 142, 178, 187,
    285
context/contextual 40–1
conversion/s 105, 105–6 n.41
  intellectual 106–8, 114, 115,
    115 n.79
  moral 106–8, 111
  psychic 106–8, 110
  religious 106–8, 110–12
conversos (Jews converted to
    Catholicism) 281, 283
coproanalysis 204

SUBJECT INDEX

cosmic loneliness 217
cosmic music 46–7
cosmological/cosmic 315
cosmos 46–8, 50–1, 55, 306, 310, 348
  musical 46–7
costly grace 260
creation 45, 48–50, 54, 60–2, 297, 302, 305–7, 316
  Holy Spirit in 310–14
creative/creativity 31, 33, 43, 50, 62, 72, 89, 117, 124, 125, 348
creative thinkers 238
critical realist epistemology/critical realism 130, 136–8, 141
crucified 184, 187, 217, 310
  crucified people/God 197, 198, 200, 203, 205
culture/world view
  Baroque 69, 75, 76, 78
  Eurocentric 66
  Gothic 69, 70
  Greek 78
  Islamic 68
  Jewish 19, 44, 45
  medieval 19, 46, 49–52, 54
  modern 6, 20
  plural 62
  postmodern 6, 19, 103
  pre-modern 6, 19
  Roman 69, 78
  Semitic/anti-Semitic 81
  Sufism 68
  with theology 344–6
  Western 21, 71, 79, 91, 99, 103 n.30, 133

Darmstadt School 83, 83 n.61, 84
death 205, 230, 231, 253, 254
'death of God' movement 264
decision 137, 152
Dei Verbum 4, 5, 24, 44, 134, 155, 160, 212, 233, 235, 340, 385
dialectical theology 177, 178
discipleship 161, 256, 258–60, 262, 264, 266, 268
discursive 96, 112
distrust 219, 352, 353
doctors of the Church 275–6, 291

doctrines 31, 60, 101, 102, 104
doubt 4, 5, 10, 19, 26–30, 37
  defence of 24–6
  epistemological 26
  history of 22–4
  theology of 25

earth 297, 298
ecclesiology 173, 200, 252, 256, 261
  Church as holy and sinful 261
ecofeminist 149
ecology/ecological conversion 149, 303, 304, 313
  crisis 309
  theology 309–14
ecotheology 305
ecumenical 300, 301, 364
education 18
  philosophical and theological 113
Ego Eimi 163
elemental meaning 109, 114, 120, 139
embodied/embodiment 7, 16, 18, 27, 35, 37, 40, 49, 91, 121, 141, 148, 152 n.29, 155, 168, 238, 240, 346, 363, 373–5
  knowledge as 148–9
emotion 53, 56, 73, 75, 78, 124, 323, 349, 350, 355, 375
enlightenment 20, 55, 76–8, 80, 84
environment 309
environmental ethics 325–6
epistemology/epistemic/epistemological /cognitional 20, 25–6, 53–6, 100, 104 n.35, 108, 111, 130, 133, 200, 206, 332
eros 348, 375
Esagramma 343
eschatology 60, 155
eternity life 45, 145, 165, 186, 205, 229, 243, 266
  eternal suffering 230
ethics 258, 267–8, 309
ethnography 116
  autoethnography 16 n.4, 116, 383–7
Eurocentric 66

evangelical counsels 156, 175, 280, 378
Evangelical/Gospel feminism 157
Evangelii nuntiandi 342
evangelisation/mission 230
everyday mysticism 239, 290
evil 190, 191, 203, 209, 269, 297, 305, 325, 352, 353
evolution 305, 313

faith, public life and politics/sociopolitical 252
faith/believing/ belief/act of faith 1–2, 4, 6, 10, 18–24, 24 n.25, 25–31, 33–7, 45, 49, 57, 58, 64, 65, 72, 75–7, 82–6, 101, 102, 107, 111, 150, 160, 192–3, 230–2, 241, 242, 252–4, 252 n.4, 256, 259, 260, 265, 266, 269, 271, 340, 350
  beauty's role in 171
  and culture 355
  defence of 24–6
  defined 21
  intelligence 200
  of Jesus 29, 188, 353
  notions of 229
  obedience of 340
  as personal but not private 254
  of the poor 203
  in the public square 265–9
  role of doubt in a theology of 3–6
  shape of 26–30
  spirituality and 354
  theology of 340, 342–4, 349, 352, 354
  and worship 186–7
faith seeking understanding 3, 18, 19, 100, 200, 339–43
fallen humanity 209–12, 217–19, 221–4
falling in love 270, 292, 360, 372, 374, 376, 378
fear of God 352
feeling 53, 57, 62, 68, 92, 97, 99, 111, 169, 187, 222–3, 271, 293, 323, 336, 339, 350, 375, 377, 386

feminine genius 152
feminism/feminist/feminist awareness/ feminist scholarship/ development of feminist theology 42, 108, 146–58, 163, 171, 192, 211, 307, 325, 328, 330
feminist theologies 146–8, 151, 152, 160, 321, 326
fides qua and *fides quae* 28, 341
fides quaerens intellectum/faith seeking understanding 77
finding God in the world 306–7
First Vatican Council 18
formation and transformation 369–70
foundational figures 47–9
Foundations 7, 101–4, 101 n.27, 107, 108, 115
  accessing 109–12
  functional speciality of 215
  as a particular moment of theological method 100
Fourth Lateran Council 327, 384
freedom/freedom of consciousness 114, 126, 137, 137 n.30, 138–40, 276, 283, 288, 293
Freudian 213–14, 220
friend (of God) 280–6
friendship 230, 236, 246–8, 279, 280, 284, 286, 287, 289–91, 293
functional specialities 101–2, 128, 215
fundamental goodness/ desirableness 222

Gaudium et spes 122, 193, 245, 325, 361
gender 91, 144, 147, 148, 152–3, 153 n.34, 321, 322
  ideology 153
  justice 144 n.1
global community 307
God
  as Father 321, 336
  as Mother 334, 337
  as origin and creator 334
  as passion/passionate 371–2
  power of attraction 168–71

as 'She who is' 330–5
as trustworthy 342, 349–54
universal will of salvation 241
goodness 31
grace/experience of grace/offer of grace 200, 210, 211, 231–3, 241–4, 246, 248, 260, 261, 264
Rahner's theology of 244–6
Greek 19, 34, 73 n.19, 78, 195, 216, 334
Gregorian chants 63, 68, 69, 74
grief 253
guilt 210, 220, 224, 261, 263, 269

harmony 55, 67, 71
heaven 230, 231
heavy metal 86
hell 186, 288
'here and now' 261, 262, 266–7
heresy/heresies 232, 244, 348
hermeneutics/hermeneutical 7–8, 36, 42, 57, 96, 103, 116, 160, 164
biblical 160–2
scriptural 162
hip hop 85, 86
historical/historicity/history of thought 18–24, 44, 54, 56, 99, 160, 199, 296
history 101
of doubt 22–4
of music 54, 74, 92
of theology 43–5
of truth 19–22
Hitler 63, 254, 256–9, 263, 268
holy secularity 327
Holy Spirit 137, 156, 163, 191, 209, 224, 245, 246, 251, 275, 292, 302, 321, 340, 369
in creation 309–14
human consciousness 139–40, 220
human experience 135–40, 212–18, 366, 371
hymns 68, 111

idealism 21
identity/identity-making 95, 111
Ignatian/Jesuits 128, 141–2, 175–6, 196, 214, 235, 278, 385

image of God 25, 27, 31, 90, 119, 150, 203, 253, 325, 332, 335, 336, 342, 352, 353, 355
imagination 297, 298
improvise/improvisation 69, 75 n.33, 77, 87, 90
incarnation/incarnate 35, 45–6, 78, 100, 111, 126, 142, 160, 184, 195, 202, 224, 260, 267, 275, 290, 305, 310, 313, 321, 353, 361, 366, 371, 376
indigenous/aboriginal 297, 300, 303–5, 313–16
injustice 191, 200, 231
the Inquisition 281, 287
INSeCT. *See International Network of Societies for Catholic Theology* (INSeCT)
insight 130, 134, 135
inspired/inspiration 155, 159–63
instrumental music 44, 46, 51, 53, 55, 56, 68, 75, 78–80
integral spirituality 298
intentional consciousness. *See* intentionality analysis
intentionality analysis/intentional consciousness 104 n.35, 137
interdisciplinarity/interdisciplinary 33, 91, 97, 115
interior Castle 285
interiority 99, 103, 216, 291
International Network of Societies for Catholic Theology (INSeCT) 144 n.1, 358 n.1
interreligious 101, 135, 263, 297
intertextuality 159
intimacy 286, 289, 293
with God 290
inventio and *elaboratio* 77
Islamic 68

jazz 82, 85, 87, 90–2
Jesus (of Nazareth) 7, 29, 134, 200, 223, 267, 310, 353
Jewish 19, 44, 45
faith 45, 84
Scriptures 44
Johannine/John's Gospel 155, 163, 175, 229

Judaeo-Christian Scriptures/
    worldview 44, 67
justice 262, 263 n.32

knowledge 4, 17–19, 21–5, 30, 35,
    36, 98, 113, 114, 116, 123,
    126, 133, 135, 137, 138,
    140, 158
  as embodied 148–9
  theological 104–8

lament 354–6
language 39–40, 59, 78, 80, 97
Latina feminist theology 148
Latin American theology 194
learner/apprentice 303, 305, 313
leitmotifs 81
liberation/liberation theologies 16,
    107–8, 122, 191–6, 195 n.11,
    200, 205, 206, 303
limbus puerorum (children's
    limbo) 211
liturgy/liturgical language 48, 65, 75,
    96, 126, 364
logo-centric 80
Logos 59, 339, 348
Lonerganian 20, 99, 116, 176, 215
Lothlorien 363, 364, 366
Lumen gentium 245, 246
Lutheran 53, 210, 260

Madaleva Manifesto 153 n.33
magisterium 201, 211, 212, 244,
    329
maleness of Jesus 322
mansions 285, 287
Mariology 326, 370
Mark's Gospel 292
marriage 359–61, 371–2, 377, 379
martyrdom 253, 254
Mary 370, 376
masculinity 323, 336
meaning/meaning-making/mediation
    of meaning 3, 6–8, 15, 22,
    34, 43, 102, 107, 108, 134,
    139–40, 364
mediated immediacy 351
mediated theology 107
mendicant 278

mercy/merciful 204, 231, 342, 349,
    354, 355
  anti-mercy 204
metaphorical 160
metaphysics 103
method in theology/theological methodology 2, 60, 64, 115, 131
  defined by questions 100–8
  Haughton 366–71
  Lonergan's approach to 98–104,
    116–17
  notion of conversion in 105
  premises of 194–5
  with space for the arts 96–100
  two phases 101–2
mimetic desire 215
modern 6, 20, 170
  atheism 25 n.27, 133 n.24
  hermeneutics 57
  theology 31, 57, 117
modernity 19, 26, 66, 77, 80, 132,
    170, 210
monastic 214, 278
Moravian 57, 74
Mother Church 365
motives of credibility 341, 342
Mujerista 148
multi-modal 6–8
multiple intelligences 6–7
musical cosmos 46–7
musical figures
  influence on music 56–64, 74
  of theology performed 76–82
music-hearing 40
musicking/musickers 40–4, 48, 65,
    66, 69, 73, 75, 77, 81, 85, 87,
    90, 92, 95, 121
  Afro-American 87–90
  ecclesial 73–6, 91
  word and 69–73, 86
music-making 6, 9, 39, 40, 42, 84,
    87, 100, 102, 120, 123
musicology/musicological/new
    musicology 41, 66 n.3
  new musicology 91
music styles 47, 49, 73, 85–8, 90
  absolute music 47, 56, 79–80, 92
  Afro-American 40, 62, 82, 85,
    87–90

atonal/dodecaphony/twelve-tone/serialism 82–4
avant-garde 82–5
blues 82, 85, 86, 91–3
chant 66, 68–9
classical 41, 43, 66, 68, 82, 87, 89, 91
Darmstadt School 83, 83 n.61, 84
Gregorian chants 63, 68, 69, 74
heavy metal 86
hymns 68, 111
instrumental 44, 46, 51, 53, 55, 56, 68, 75, 78–80
jazz 82, 85, 87, 90–2
opera 58, 73–5, 78
polytonality 83
pop 85, 86
popular modernist 90
psalmody 68
punk rock 87
ragtime 85
reggae 87
rock 82, 85–7, 91
sacred 74
soul 86
symphonic 62, 79, 81, 161
tonal 82–3
vocal 44, 51, 53, 55, 68, 73, 75
Western (*see* Western music)
music theorist/theory 40, 41, 45, 47, 54, 55, 73, 79
mystical 27, 51, 60, 68, 84, 85
mystical body of Christ 275
mystic/mysticism 178, 239, 275, 276, 280, 283, 286, 290, 291, 371
myth 99

nameless 163–5
Naming God 321–3, 333
    God as Creator, Origin and Giver of life, inclusive language 320–3
    three theological principles for 327–8
narrative/story 149, 366, 369, 378
natural theology 300–2
Nazi 63, 233, 257 n.14
nonperson/nonhuman 194
non-tonal 83

'no salvation outside of the church' 204, 232, 244
notation 50, 51, 68–70, 76
Notification 201, 205
notitia Dei 351
Nouvelle Théologie 172

obedience 276, 279, 280, 288, 378
    of faith 340
objectify conversion 108
objective/subjective 97, 106
objective uncertainty 21
opera 58, 73–5, 78
operations/processes of human knowing 137
order of the affects 349, 350
original blessing 218–25
original sin/fallen humanity 209–12, 217–19, 221–4

parenting 369
Paschal mystery 184, 245, 246
passion 359, 360, 362
pastor 212, 233, 254, 257
patriarchy/Kyriarchy patriarchal 147–51, 264
Pelagianism 210, 232
performance 41–3, 56 n.72, 71, 76, 80, 83, 88, 90, 102
peritus 234
phenomenological 116, 131, 155, 156
philosophy 20, 21, 24, 30, 55, 56, 99, 103, 130, 131, 133
    of education 138
planet 296, 297, 299, 306, 308, 311
platonic/neoplatonic 47, 49, 52, 58, 170
poetry 216, 367, 372
poiesis 35
political holiness 198–9
polymorphic 29, 139
polyphilia 34
polyphony/polyphonic 49, 63, 69, 71, 74, 75
polytonality 83
poor, chaste and obedient/poverty, chastity and obedience 276, 278–80

pop 85, 86
popular music 86
postmodern 6, 19, 83, 170–1
　musical world 83–4
poverty/the poor 191–4, 198,
　　200–5, 276, 279, 280, 288,
　　378
praxis 194, 195, 198, 200, 332
　ethical 309
　and theory 200
prayer/prayer-life 174, 175, 179, 186,
　　187, 238
preaching 178, 241, 260, 263, 323
pre-modern 6, 19, 54
prima pratica 73
prophetic spirituality 363–4, 366
Protestant principle 29
psalmody 68
psychic conversion 106–8, 110
psychoanalysis 213, 216
psychology 212–18
punk rock 87
quadrivium 46, 52, 54
questions/to question 4, 5, 15, 17, 18,
　　22–4, 26–9, 31, 34, 36, 37

ragtime 85
rap 91
rational idealism 21, 58
rational/reason/reasonable 21, 22,
　　25, 34, 50, 54–7, 77, 97,
　　99 n.19, 104, 137, 332, 339,
　　341, 350
reality 190–2, 195–200, 203, 204,
　　206
receptive ecumenism 301
recognise/recognition 349–55
redemption/salvation 145, 149, 186,
　　188, 195, 203–5, 209–10,
　　215, 223, 231, 232, 241–3,
　　245, 267, 310, 353
　in the poor 205–7
Reformation 20, 45, 52–3, 73, 75
　Counter-Reform/Counter-
　　Reformation 20, 73, 75, 82
reggae 87
Reign of God 149, 252, 253, 276
relationship philosophy to theology
　　130, 133, 135

religion 57, 67, 68, 83, 100–1, 262
religionless Christianity 262
religious life and vows 278, 279,
　　288–9, 378
religious orders 278
'research-led practice,' 'practice-
　　as-research,' or 'research-
　　creation' 97
resurrection 27, 48, 109, 155,
　　159–60, 184–5, 191, 217,
　　223, 231, 276, 278, 312, 322,
　　373, 375
　of Christ 373
revelation 4–6, 104, 110, 134, 149,
　　153, 159, 160, 177, 200, 235,
　　241–3, 246
　divine revelation 4, 5
　transcendental or implicit
　　revelation 241, 242
revelatory 150, 159–61
rhythm 86, 91
rock 82, 85–7, 91
rock and roll 85
romance 358–61, 376
Romantics/Romanticism 56, 58, 76,
　　80, 81

sacred 65, 74
salvation 145, 149, 186, 188, 195,
　　198, 199, 203–5, 209–11,
　　215, 216, 223, 231, 232,
　　241–3, 245–6, 267, 310
Samaritan woman 162
science/scientific 134, 308
scriptural world view 44–6
Scripture 155, 160, 192, 194
　canon of 159
　history of feminist research
　　into 151
　women in 144–6, 150–3, 162–4
seconda pratica 73
second naïveté 7, 104, 104 n.33, 161,
　　164
Second Vatican Council/Vatican II 4,
　　5, 122, 128, 133, 134 n.25,
　　152, 154, 156, 158, 193, 211,
　　233, 234, 245, 246, 304, 324,
　　325, 340, 361, 365
secret discipline 262

secular 65, 80, 230, 239, 258, 262, 264
self-appropriation 104, 106, 108, 112–15, 128, 130, 136
self-reflexivity 104
semiotics 7, 116, 121 n.1, 206
Semitic/anti-Semitic 81
senses/sensations/s 42, 43, 46, 49, 53, 75, 76
sensus fidelium 116, 181, 212, 246
sentient intelligence 199
serialism 83, 84
sex 359–61, 371–4, 377, 379
sexism 157
sexual abuse 277
sexual intercourse 374
sexuality 277, 358–61, 370–4, 378
 and history of Christian theology 358–61
 in human life and Christian faith 361
 and marriage 360, 361
 Scripture's positive view of 360
sexual love 372–9
 and celibacy 377
sin 209–12, 217–19, 221–4, 231, 232, 260, 297, 310, 311, 325, 361, 376
 structural sin 200
socio-political oppression 202
song of songs 284
soul 86, 91
sound 67–9
space/spatial 140–1
spiritual 103, 106, 115
spiritual betrothal 282
spirituality/Christian spirituality 33, 154–6, 158–60, 175, 178, 198, 280, 288, 312, 345, 347, 354, 361, 369, 371
 biblical 161
 defined 198
 and theology 178
spirituality of sensibility/spiritual sensibility 346, 346 n.17
spiritual quality 344, 350
 of culture 33, 85
stages of meaning 99
structural poverty 194

suffering 190–1, 197–201, 203, 204, 207, 230, 231, 305, 312
 of God 312
Sufism 68
sustainability 309
symbol of God (that functions) 331–2
symbol/symbolic/symbolism 2, 7, 10, 28, 37, 51, 96, 97, 99, 113, 140, 155, 163, 327, 331–4, 352
symphonic 62
syncopation 56–64, 87
systemic oppression 147, 157

terra nullius 304
theodicy 191, 203
theologal 66, 66 n.4, 69, 89, 350
theological aesthetics 19, 30–3, 37, 62, 178, 182 n.48, 343–4
theological anthropology 180, 211, 212, 215, 322
theological education/theological formation 17, 17 n.6, 18, 36, 115, 170
theological methodology 2, 60, 64, 115, 131
 conversion in 105
 defined by questions 100–8
 Haughton 366–71
 Lonergan's approach to 98–100, 116–17
 premises of 194–5
 with space for the arts 96–100
 'a theological Pentecost' 329
Theological Specialties 101–2
theology and science 307
theology/to theologise/theologian 2, 5, 6, 15–21, 23–31, 33, 35, 36, 40, 43, 44, 46, 47, 57, 62, 64, 74, 85, 91, 98–9, 104, 107, 108, 110, 113, 115–17, 131, 140, 171, 190–2, 246, 293, 342, 360, 384
 as biographical/autobiographical and the need for introspective attention to recognise this 383–6
 of the body 151, 181

Christian philosophy and 103
Church and 237, 275
 as Church teaching 241–4
 conception of 96
 of consecrated life 278
 defined 3, 100
 discipline of 2
 ecological 310–14
 of experience 367
 of faith 18, 24, 28 n.44, 292, 340, 342–4, 349, 352, 354
  defence of doubt in 24–6
  role of doubt in 3–6
  Sequeri 349, 352, 354
  theology of grace 244–6
 feminist awareness and 146–8
 functional specialities 101–2
 of grace 244–6
 history of 43–5
 Jesus and 45
 knowledge 104–8
 liberation 192–5, 200, 206
 as a life-option 341
 of marriage 377
 modern 31, 57, 117
 as multi-modal 6–8
 musical figures to perform 76–82
 music and 2, 43–4, 49–66, 77, 90, 92
 natural 300–2
 as poetry 367
 in public square 269
 research 97
 of revelation 104
 and science 300, 302, 307
 spirituality and 178
 for twenty-first century 1–3
 Western 79–80, 99, 192, 258, 310, 343, 375
theomusicology 86
theopoet 290
theopoetics//theopoiesis 34–7, 155, 290
theory of affections 75 n.33
third space or way (*terza via*) 348
three waves or strands of feminism 146–8

tonal 82–3
Tradition/tradition 74, 85–91, 101, 104, 106, 106 n.46, 107, 108, 126, 132, 145, 192, 278, 322, 330, 367
 Catholic 145, 363, 370
 Christian 10, 147, 149, 151, 158, 223, 229, 373
 of music 44, 74, 85–91
transcendental/s 176, 182, 183
Transcendent/transcendent 8, 41, 54, 64, 76, 79, 80, 89, 91, 177, 242, 334, 336
transformation/transformational 140
transformative understanding 162
Trent 74, 75, 75 n.27
Trinity/Trinitarian 158, 181, 184, 186, 217, 224, 310, 311, 313, 321, 323, 334, 376
trust 18, 20, 24, 29, 35, 340, 349, 350
 in God 352–4
truth/truth claims 23, 123, 126, 130, 136–8, 140, 141, 161
type-story 163

uncertainty 22, 23, 26, 36
understanding 137–8
the uniqueness of each life 253–4
universal/universalist 67, 78, 81
universe in crisis 298, 307–9

values 123, 124, 137, 140
vibration 67, 68
viriditas 275
vocal music 44, 51, 53, 55, 68, 73, 75
vocation 374, 378

Wellsprings 366
Western
 anthropocentric world view 296
 Christianity 258, 296
 culture 21, 71, 79, 91, 99, 103 n.30, 133, 345, 347
 philosophy 21, 99, 199
 theology 79, 80, 99, 192, 258, 310, 343, 375

Western music 41, 50, 55, 56, 69, 87, 91
  classical 41, 73–6
  history of 45, 45 n.27, 65, 66
  origins of 69
Wisdom/Sophia (Spirit-Sophia, Jesus-Sophia and Mother-Sophia) 334, 365
witness 253, 254 n.7, 269
Womanist 148
women 275, 281, 283, 287, 288
  in biblical text 162–4
  in the Church 144–5, 152, 158, 162, 368
  in decision-making 144 n.1, 152
  experiences 147–9, 334
  inclusion of 147
  issues 144–6, 150–3
  and homelessness 369
  in Scripture 144–6, 150–3, 162
  systemic oppression 147, 157
  theology of 148
women leaders and reformers in history 280–94
Women's Bible 150
word and music 69–73, 75, 84
Word of God 6, 52, 62, 67, 69, 76, 160, 171, 187, 194, 266
world come-of-age 261
worlds of meaning 43, 99, 134, 161
worship 186, 374, 379

Young Workers Movement 301

www.ingramcontent.com/pod-product-compliance
Ingram Content Group UK Ltd.
Pitfield, Milton Keynes, MK11 3LW, UK
UKHW022307231224
452774UK00004B/52